PRECIOUS HERITAGE

PRECIOUS HERITAGE

The Status of Biodiversity in the United States

Edited by

Bruce A. Stein

Lynn S. Kutner

Jonathan S. Adams

Graphics by Nicole S. Rousmaniere

A JOINT PROJECT OF

The Nature Conservancy & Association for Biodiversity Information

OXFORD

UNIVERSITY PRESS

OXFORD

UNIVERSITY PRESS

Oxford   New York

Athens   Auckland   Bangkok   Bogotá   Buenos Aires   Calcutta
Cape Town   Chennai   Dar es Salaam   Delhi   Florence   Hong Kong   Istanbul
Karachi   Kuala   Lumpur   Madrid   Melbourne   Mexico City   Mumbai
Nairobi   Paris   São Paulo   Singapore   Taipei   Tokyo   Toronto   Warsaw

and associated companies in
Berlin   Ibadan

Published by Oxford University Press, Inc.
198 Madison Avenue, New York, New York 10016

Oxford is a registered trademark of Oxford University Press

Library of Congress Cataloging-in-Publication Data
Precious heritage : the status of biodiversity in
the United States / edited by Bruce A. Stein,
Lynn S. Kutner, Jonathan S. Adams.
p.   cm.
Includes bibliographical references.
ISBN 0-19-512519-3
1. Biological diversity conservation—United States.
I. Stein, Bruce A., 1955– .   II. Kutner, Lynn S.
III. Adams, Jonathan S.
QH76.P69   2000
333.95'16'0973—dc21   99-30213

Funding for *Precious Heritage* was provided by: The Seaver Institute, The Moriah Fund,
Mobil Foundation, The Regina Bauer Frankenberg Foundation for Animal Welfare,
the Faucett Family Trust, and Mr. Ben Hammett.

9 8 7 6 5 4 3 2

Printed in Hong Kong
on acid-free paper

CONTENTS

FOREWORD

America First. This timeworn phrase, put in the context of the natural environment, may now be given a new and beneficent meaning. In *Precious Heritage* some of the leading experts on the subject present the most comprehensive and accessible account of the state of the American biota to date. They invite us to turn inward, not by abandoning global conservation but by conserving our own fauna and flora in a manner that will set a shining example for the rest of the world.

Surely the United States is the ideal country to provide such leadership. Vast in geographical extent, it harbors the largest number of known species of any temperate country. It contains the widest spread of biome types, ranging from rain forest to Arctic tundra and from coral reefs to great lakes, of any country in the world. Few people, including even many scientists who specialize on biodiversity, have grasped the full magnitude of the American biota as summarized by the *Precious Heritage* authors. The 200,000 or so U.S. species described scientifically to date are more than 10% of all those known on Earth. Among the countries of the world, the United States leads in diversity of salamanders, crayfishes, freshwater turtles, and freshwater mollusks. It has the most species of mammals and among the richest flora of any temperate country.

Moreover, this remarkable biota is only partly explored. Hundreds of new species are still being discovered each year, especially among the more obscure invertebrates of small size. When insects, the most speciose of all groups, are thrown in, the full number of species, both those already known to science and others still unknown, might easily be doubled.

For generations Americans, thoughtlessly pursuing material advantage, have savaged their natural environment. Most of the original prairies and eastern forests are gone; rivers have been dammed and their unique plants and animals diminished in population or extinguished outright. The course of American biotic history, still accelerating downward and melancholy in aspect, is clearly summarized in *Precious Heritage*.

When conservationists and biodiversity experts gather at conferences, their talk inevitably turns to the lack of public awareness of the extinction problem. They know that a large majority of Americans do not even know the meaning of the word *biodiversity*. All agree that it is crucial to promote not only research but also grassroots education, accompanied by policy recommendations that are morally compelling. Because all politics is ultimately ethical at its base—or at least pretends to be—the decision-making processes that will save the natural environment must be grounded on moral reasoning fed into political life through education. Aldo Leopold knew this when he argued the land ethic, and Rachel Carson applied it when she appealed to the conscience of a nation.

To this end, the scientific database will be most effectively used if joined with concepts that citizens of the United States already cherish. The first is love of the land. Within the interstices of the farms and ranches that reach from sea to shining sea are the remnants of the original America, containing our flora and fauna. Environmentalists are correct in labeling them an integral part of the American land, and political leaders are advised to treat them as a sacred public trust. The ecoregions of America, on which The Nature Conservancy now wisely focuses, represent the integrative units of land where the optimum balance between developed and natural areas can be most efficiently devised.

The second concept that links science and policy—one that has been strongly promoted by The Nature Conservancy, the Association for Biodiversity Information, and authors of *Precious Heritage*—is empowerment of the fauna and flora. To the magnificent "rock and ice" parks, such as the Grand Canyon and Rocky Mountain National Park, can be added the equally magnificent biodiversity hot spots, including those whose physical vistas are unimpressive. To Americans who know natural history, and their numbers are certain to grow with each passing generation, Nevada's Ash Meadows and Florida's Lake Wales scrubland are sacred landmarks, the equivalent of Independence Hall and Gettysburg of original America.

Every native species, however humble in appearance by contemporary standards, has its place in the nation's heritage. It is a masterpiece of evolution, an ancient, multifaceted entity that still shares the land with us. Each species in turn will someday be appreciated as we now appreciate the bison and redwood; each species will be understood and protected by aficionados who will ask, "Why did we let others like it go extinct?" Future generations will know that with a relatively small amount of effort we could have saved virtually all of the biota. The natural life span of a species and its descendants is, according to group (such as mammals or flowering plants), a half million to 10 million years. Human activity has shortened the life expectancy of species by a hundred to a thousand times.

Let us suppose that about 300,000 species of plants and animals are native to the United States, and suppose that somewhat more than 300 million people will be living here by midcentury. If both reasonable assumptions are true, there will be about a thousand Americans for each species. I do not think it unreasonable to predict that with improved education and a continuing rise in concern for the environment by Americans, most of the species will have one or more persons knowledgeable about it and with a serious sense of stewardship for the third or more of the species reduced to a vulnerable state. In a country where people are so easily enraptured by rock stars, tales of the Civil War, and captive whales, it is not too much to suppose that such a level of awareness can be attained. Then the chances of saving the American fauna and flora will be greatly improved. *Precious Heritage*, with its combination of statistical analyses and fine-tuned descriptions of many of the habitats and species, represents an important step in that direction.

EDWARD O. WILSON
Museum of Comparative Zoology
Harvard University

PREFACE

Biologists are the official chroniclers of nature's wonders. Poking into corners of our natural world, field biologists have a firsthand view of the habitats and lifestyles of our plants and animals—from obscure creatures dwelling in the dark world of subterranean lakes, to spring wildflowers brightening the forest floor, to the mating rituals of sandhill cranes dancing on foggy mornings.

In the past, much of this knowledge stayed in the minds and notebooks of each individual researcher until enough insight was collected to summarize in scientific journals. Their collective wisdom can be glimpsed by the public in the displays at natural history museums; through field guides to birds, wildflowers, trees, or butterflies; or, increasingly, through nature-oriented television shows. As conservation concerns in the United States and elsewhere have grown, so has public interest in understanding the status of the nation's species and ecosystems. *Precious Heritage* is the first national look at the status of biodiversity in the United States as chronicled by the network of natural heritage programs. This ambitious undertaking synthesizes biodiversity data from all 50 states to paint a picture of the health and wealth of the biological riches of the United States.

The Association for Biodiversity Information and The Nature Conservancy sponsored the development and publication of this book for two reasons. First, there is an urgent need to better understand the status and trends of our biological diversity to inform a growing number of conservation actions. Until recently, little of the vast array of biological information from the network of natural heritage programs has been presented to a national audience. *Precious Heritage* gives a clear look at the biological diversity of the United States: what we have, what's at risk, and how it might be conserved. Second, we sought to test whether the data from the collection of independent, locally focused institutions could be combined to serve an analysis with a national perspective. While the task of compiling data across the 50 states and standardizing results proved tougher than we initially thought, the results exceeded our expectations and helped to fuel a new dream—the launch of a new institution capable of routinely aggregating and delivering biodiversity information and analyses from the separate organizations that comprise the heritage network.

Bruce Stein and his colleagues and coauthors succeeded at the Herculean task of combining information from the 50 state programs, performing quality assurance of these data, helping authors conduct innovative analyses, and then crafting accessible prose and graphics to enliven the reader's understanding and enjoyment of the many insights the book provides. Behind the team of editors and authors, however, stands a vast number of field biologists on whose work this volume is based. Indeed, *Precious Heritage* is a tribute to the work of the more than 900 employees of the Natural Heritage Network and to the thousands of biologists who have contributed their information and personal knowledge to help fill the natural heritage databases and enhance our understanding of the nation's biological diversity.

We initiated this book project five years ago. Its roots, however, began over 25 years ago, when a man with remarkable vision was faced with a tough challenge. Bob Jenkins's task was to provide sound scientific knowledge for informing the land acquisition priorities of The Nature Conservancy, then a small U.S. conservation organization. He reasoned that by documenting the location of the species and communities most at risk, conservation groups could target their actions to those places that could protect the "last of the least and the best of the rest." Jenkins and his colleagues then set about designing a biological inventory method that could collate existing knowledge, collect new data, and house all of this information in computers and on maps for easy access. Jenkins's vision and his drive to execute it led to the growth and success of a network of heritage programs across the United States and throughout much of the hemisphere. These independent programs now constitute a cornerstone of conservation efforts, annually providing biodiversity information to thousands of decision makers, conservationists, and researchers.

The publication of *Precious Heritage* is timely. Public concern for biodiversity has grown immensely over the past 25 years. Not only are many people now aware of the extinction crisis we are facing, but communities all over the country are taking positive actions to protect their local biodiversity. Membership in conservation organizations has grown dramatically; The Nature Conservancy now has over 1 million members, and local land trusts are starting across the country at the rate of one each week. In addition, the public increasingly supports local and state initiatives to provide public funds for open space and natural area protection. In November 1998, for example, bond acts for acquiring conservation lands were passed that totaled over $5 billion. In New Jersey alone, two-thirds of the voters approved a ballot initiative to spend $1 billion to preserve half of the remaining farmland and open space in the state. This growing conservation movement will do much to protect our nation's biological diversity.

Precious Heritage also marks a historic moment for the network of heritage programs. This year the Association for Biodiversity Information and The Nature Conservancy are joining their individual efforts in support of the heritage network into a single effort by creating a new, independent organization. This new organization—which will inherit the Association for Biodiversity Information's name—will provide an authoritative source for conservation-related biodiversity information from across the network of heritage programs.

Precious Heritage presents both the general reader and the specialist with surprises about the biological diversity found in the United States. We harbor natural treasures in all corners of this remarkable country. These species and ecosystems contribute to our nation's health, wealth, and happiness, and *Precious Heritage* reminds us that their fate lies in our hands. We hope you will be moved to join the growing efforts of citizens in communities throughout the country to ensure that these natural wonders will enrich the lives of our grandchildren as well.

June 1999

DEBORAH B. JENSEN
Vice President, Conservation Science
The Nature Conservancy

THOMAS F. BREDEN
Chair
Association for Biodiversity Information

ACKNOWLEDGMENTS

Precious Heritage is the culmination of much hard work and creative thinking by many people and truly represents a broad-based collaborative effort. Much of this book is based on information developed over many years by biologists working in state natural heritage data centers, and we would like to acknowledge a particular debt of gratitude to these past and present heritage staff. Their tremendous breadth of field knowledge, coupled with a commitment to carefully documenting information on species and ecosystems in their states, has enabled the authors of this volume to develop a truly national-level synthesis of U.S. biodiversity. We would also like to thank those individuals in the Conservation Science Division of The Nature Conservancy (many of whom will be joining the Association for Biodiversity Information) who have developed much of the network's global and national-level data, as well as the tools, techniques, and scientific methods that support and unite the work of the state programs. Their efforts were also indispensable to creating this overview of the nation's biological heritage.

This project benefited from the guidance and counsel of several key individuals. This book was developed and produced under Deborah Jensen's leadership as director of the Conservancy's Conservation Science Division, and we thank her for her support and guidance. Cloyce Hedge, coordinator of the Indiana Natural Heritage Data Center, provided oversight and guidance on behalf of the Association for Biodiversity Information (ABI), while Tom Breden, Kathryn Schneider, Thomas Smith, and Betty Les also provided input to the project on behalf of ABI.

A number of current and former staff members of The Nature Conservancy provided direct support to the project. Research assistance was provided by Nancy Benton, Gwendolyn Davis, Jason Dubow, Deborah Gries, Jeffrey Lerner, Eric M. Lind, David Maddox, Martha Martinez,

Kathleen Maybury, Lara Minium, Melissa Morrison, Sonal Pandya, Miriam Steiner, and Marcia Summers. Geographic information systems analyses were provided by Brooke Cholvin, Linda Evers, Stacy Hoppen, and Hal Watson. Wendy Robinson provided administrative assistance to the project in its early stages, and Robert Chipley contributed to developing the overall concept for the book. Conservancy librarian Michael Pahn graciously sought out copies of obscure references for the book's authors and editors. Gail Ross ably represented the project as our book agent and outside legal counsel, while Susan Lauscher and Paul Flint provided valuable in-house counsel.

Special acknowledgment is due to Nicole Rousmaniere, who was responsible for the formidable task of wrestling into shape the book's graphics—including maps, charts, and photographs—and who was a fourth member of the editorial team. Connie Gelb and Pat Rolston provided valuable assistance in photo research. A number of individuals kindly donated use of their photographs to help illustrate this volume, but we would like to extend particular thanks to Harold E. Malde, Alan D. St. John, and William P. Mull for the numerous wonderful images that they provided.

Peer reviews of each chapter greatly strengthened the book, and we wish to thank the following reviewers: Robert Bailey, Patrick Comer, Andrew Dobson, John Fitzpatrick, Curtis Flather, Frank Gill, Oliver Houck, Malcolm Hunter, Bob Irvin, Mark Lomolino, Thomas Loveland, David Mehlman, Nancy Morin, Peter Moyle, David Olson, Phil Pister, Dale Schweitzer, Karin Sheldon, Daniel Simberloff, Leslie Sneddon, David Stockwell, Phillip Tabas, Steven Taswell, Warren L. Wagner, David Wake, Alan Weakley, William Weeks, and David Wilcove.

Many other people contributed to this work with assistance, information, or comments on specific subjects. Although there are sure to be others that occur to us once it is too late, we thank the following: Omar Amin, Jame Amoroso, Bonnie Amos, Bruce Baldwin, James Baldwin, Denton Belk, Stephen Buchmann, Janine Caira, Kathryn Coates, Paul Chippindale, George Constantz, Robert H. Cowie, Frank Crandall, Stanley Dodson, Rodger Doyle, Niles Eldredge, Kristian Fauchald, Ben Franklin, John Gammon, Stuart Gelder, Samuel Gon, Doria Gordon, Terry Griswold, Jimmy Kagan, D. Kathman, Brian Kensley, Eugene Kozloff, Delane Kritsky, Lee Hannah, Jeffrey Hardesty, Bonnie Heidell, Sherman Hendrix, Robert Higgins, Eric Hoberg, Eric Hochberg, Glen Hoffman, Alan Holt, Duane Hope, Francis G. Howarth, William Hummon, Roy Kam, Deedee Kathman, Lewis Korniker, Terri Ann Knight, L. Korniker, E. Kozloff, Delane Kritsky, Juanita Ladyman, Gretchen Lambert, Rob Lipkin, John Logan, Chris Ludwig, Michael Mancuso, Roy McDiarmid, Jim Morefield, Bruce Mundy, Ron Myers, Gordon Nishida, Carl Nordman, Jon Norenburg, Michael O'Connell, Paul Opler, David Pawson, John Pilger, Jackie Poole, T. O. Powers, Peter H. Raven, Janet Reid, Andrew Robertson, Barry Roth, Klaus Ruetzler, Edward Ruppert, Al Scholtz, Chang-tai Shih, Susan Spackman, Richard Stemberger, Skip Sterner, David Strayer, James Thomas, Carol Todzia, Seth Tyler, George

Yatskievych, Diana Wall, Peter Warren, Kerston Wasson, Leslie Watling, Deborah White, Edward O. Wilson, Judith Winston, Robert Woolacott, James Zarruchi, and Russell Zimmer.

Mark Schwartz and Daniel Simberloff generously provided advice on the book through their participation in project workshops, and through their analyses of heritage data, which are being published elsewhere. We would like to acknowledge especially the contribution of John T. Kartesz of the North Carolina Botanical Garden, whose data, both published and unpublished, supported key portions of our analyses of U.S. plant diversity. We thank the National Center for Ecological Analysis and Synthesis of the University of California, Santa Barbara, for making computer facilities available to Ross Gerard for his contribution to chapter 6.

Much of the work in this book was first presented at the symposium held at the 1997 joint meeting of The Nature Conservancy and the Ecological Society of America in Albuquerque, New Mexico. An earlier version of chapter 8, by Wilcove et al., appeared previously in the journal *BioScience* (volume 48, number 8) and is included here with permission of the American Institute for Biological Sciences.

None of this could have happened without the financial resources needed to turn a dream into reality. We are profoundly grateful to the following financial supporters of this project: the Seaver Institute, Inc.; the Moriah Fund; the Mobil Foundation; the Regina Bauer Frankenberg Foundation for Animal Welfare; Mr. Ben Hammett; and the Faucett Family Trust.

Finally, this book would not have been possible without the vision and perseverance of Robert E. Jenkins in establishing the network of natural heritage programs. For almost two decades Jenkins provided leadership to the heritage network, and his commitment to the development of rigorous and standardized biodiversity information is largely responsible for our ability in *Precious Heritage* to present a synthetic overview of the nation's biodiversity. "Onward and upward," as he would say.

CONTRIBUTORS

Jonathan S. Adams
The Nature Conservancy

Michael Bean
Environmental Defense Fund

Mark T. Bryer
The Nature Conservancy

Stephen J. Chaplin
The Nature Conservancy

Frank W. Davis
*University of California,
  Santa Barbara*

Jason Dubow
The Nature Conservancy

Stephanie R. Flack
The Nature Conservancy

Ross A. Gerrard
*University of California,
  Santa Barbara*

Dennis H. Grossman
The Nature Conservancy

Craig R. Groves
The Nature Conservancy

Geoffrey Hammerson
The Nature Conservancy

Lynn S. Kutner
The Nature Conservancy

Elizabeth Losos
*Smithsonian Tropical Research
  Institute*

Lawrence L. Master
The Nature Conservancy

Kathleen Maybury
The Nature Conservancy

Larry E. Morse
The Nature Conservancy

Michael P. Murray
National Park Service

Ali Phillips
The Wilderness Society

Robert L. Pressey
New South Wales National Parks and Wildlife Service

David Rothstein
Northeastern University Law School

Michael Schafale
North Carolina Natural Heritage Program

J. Michael Scott
U.S. Geological Survey

Mark L. Shaffer
Defenders of Wildlife

Bruce A. Stein
The Nature Conservancy

David M. Stoms
University of California, Santa Barbara

Hal M. Watson
The Nature Conservancy

Alan S. Weakley
The Nature Conservancy

David S. Wilcove
Environmental Defense Fund

PARTICIPATING INSTITUTIONS

The Nature Conservancy
Arlington, Virginia

Association for Biodiversity
Information
Alexandria, Virginia

Alabama Natural Heritage
Program
*The Nature Conservancy,
Montgomery*

Alaska Natural Heritage Program
University of Alaska, Anchorage

Arizona Heritage Data
Management System
Game and Fish Department, Phoenix

Arkansas Natural Heritage
Commission
*Natural Heritage Commission,
Little Rock*

California Natural Diversity
Database
*Department of Fish and Game,
Sacramento*

Colorado Natural Heritage
Program
*Colorado State University,
Fort Collins*

Connecticut Natural Diversity
Database
*Department of Environmental
Protection, Hartford*

Delaware Natural Heritage
Program
*Department of Natural Resources
and Environmental Control,
Smyrna*

District of Columbia Natural
Heritage Program
*National Park Service,
Washington, D.C.*

Florida Natural Areas Inventory
*Department of Environmental
Protection, Tallahassee*

Georgia Natural Heritage
Program
*Department of Natural Resources,
Social Circle*

Hawaii Natural Heritage Program
The Nature Conservancy, Honolulu

Idaho Conservation Data Center
Department of Fish and Game, Boise

Illinois Natural Heritage Division
*Department of Natural Resources,
    Springfield*

Indiana Natural Heritage Data
    Center
*Department of Natural Resources,
    Indianapolis*

Iowa Natural Areas Inventory
*Department of Natural Resources,
    Des Moines*

Kansas Natural Heritage Program
University of Kansas, Lawrence

Kentucky Natural Heritage
    Program
*State Nature Preserves Commission,
    Frankfort*

Louisiana Natural Heritage
    Program
*Department of Wildlife and
    Fisheries, Baton Rouge*

Maine Natural Areas Program
*Department of Conservation,
    Augusta*
*Department of Inland Fisheries and
    Wildlife, Bangor*

Maryland Heritage and
    Biodiversity Conservation
    Programs
*Department of Natural Resources,
    Annapolis*

Massachusetts Natural Heritage and
    Endangered Species Program
*Division of Fisheries and Wildlife,
    Westborough*

Michigan Natural Features
    Inventory
*Department of Natural Resources,
    Lansing*

Minnesota Natural Heritage and
    Nongame Research
*Department of Natural Resources,
    St. Paul*

Mississippi Natural Heritage
    Program
*Department of Wildlife, Fisheries
    and Parks, Jackson*

Missouri Natural Heritage
    Database
*Department of Conservation,
    Jefferson City*

Montana Natural Heritage
    Program
Montana State Library, Helena

Navajo Natural Heritage Program
*Navajo Fish and Wildlife
    Department, Window Rock*

Nebraska Natural Heritage
    Program
*Game and Parks Commission,
    Lincoln*

Nevada Natural Heritage Program
*Department of Conservation and
    Natural Resources, Carson City*

New Hampshire Natural Heritage
    Inventory
*Department of Resources and
    Economic Development, Concord*

New Jersey Natural Heritage
    Program
*Office of Natural Lands
    Management, Trenton*

New Mexico Natural Heritage
Program
University of New Mexico,
Albuquerque

New York Natural Heritage
Program
Department of Environmental
Conservation, Latham

North Carolina Natural Heritage
Program
Department of Environment and
Natural Resources, Raleigh

Ohio Natural Heritage Data Base
Department of Natural Resources,
Columbus

Oklahoma Natural Heritage
Inventory
University of Oklahoma, Norman

Oregon Natural Heritage Program
The Nature Conservancy, Portland

Pennsylvania Natural Diversity
Inventory
Bureau of Forestry, Harrisburg
The Nature Conservancy,
Middletown
Western Pennsylvania Conservancy,
Pittsburgh

Rhode Island Natural Heritage
Program
Department of Environmental
Management, Providence

South Carolina Heritage Trust
Department of Natural Resources,
Columbia

South Dakota Natural Heritage
Program
Department of Game, Fish and
Parks, Pierre

Tennessee Division of Natural
Heritage
Department of Environment and
Conservation, Nashville

Tennessee Valley Authority
Regional Natural Heritage
Resource Group
Tennessee Valley Authority, Norris

Texas Conservation Data Center
The Nature Conservancy, San
Antonio

Utah Natural Heritage Program
Division of Wildlife Resources,
Salt Lake City

Vermont Nongame and Natural
Heritage Program
Fish and Wildlife Department,
Waterbury

Virginia Division of Natural
Heritage
Department of Conservation and
Recreation, Richmond

Washington Natural Heritage
Program
Department of Natural Resources,
Olympia

West Virginia Natural Heritage
Program
Division of Natural Resources, Elkins

Wisconsin Natural Heritage
Program
Department of Natural Resources,
Madison

Wyoming Natural Diversity
Database
University of Wyoming, Laramie

PRECIOUS HERITAGE

I

BIODIVERSITY
Our Precious Heritage

There are more things in Heaven and Earth, Horatio,
than are dreamt of in your philosophy.
William Shakespeare, Hamlet

Unusually heavy rains in the winter of 1969 transformed California's normally dry Owens Valley, causing an explosion of grasses and reeds along the edge of the Owens River. Lying in the eastern rain shadow of the Sierra Nevada, not far from Death Valley, the river flows south down the valley before disappearing into a dry lake bed. By summer the heavy vegetation along the river and its adjacent spring-fed marshes was sucking up moisture and releasing it into the hot, dry air. At the same time, the flow from one of these springs suddenly and mysteriously dropped, and parts of a wetland called Fish Slough began to dry up fast.

The disappearance of the small pools that make up Fish Slough would have gone unnoticed in a world not reshaped by human hands. Desert springs and marshes can be verdant one year, parched the next. Human activity, however, had made Fish Slough a vital place. The need for water to support Los Angeles and other cities has led to all manner of water projects, including dams, reservoirs, canals, and aqueducts. One of those projects, the Los Angeles Aqueduct, diverted nearly all the water from the Owens River beginning in 1913, greatly reducing the flows that once created seasonally flooded shallows along the river's edge.

Those shallow, warm waters provided ideal habitat for a unique species of fish, the Owens pupfish (*Cyprinodon radiosus*). The loss of habitat, along with the introduction of exotic species like largemouth bass, gradually eliminated the pupfish from most of its relatively limited range, until the species remained only in Fish Slough. If the marsh disappeared, so would the Owens pupfish.

Jonathan S. Adams

Bruce A. Stein

Lynn S. Kutner

The arid Owens Valley sits in the rain shadow of the Sierra Nevada (*right*, © Carr Clifton/Minden Pictures). Virtually all water flowing from the mountains into the valley is diverted to a thirsty Los Angeles, some 250 miles to the south. The shallow waters of Fish Slough (*top*, © B. Moose Peterson/WRP) are the last refuge of the Owens pupfish (*bottom*, © B. Moose Peterson/WRP). In 1969 an unexplained drop in spring flows feeding the slough almost led to the extinction of this rare desert fish.

Alerted to the potential disaster, Phil Pister, a fishery biologist working nearby with the California Department of Fish and Game, and two colleagues grabbed nets, buckets, and aerators and raced for the pond (Pister 1993). They removed the last 800 of the two-inch-long pupfish to wire mesh cages in the main channel of the slough. As his colleagues drove off, thinking the pupfish at least temporarily secure, Pister realized that the cages were in eddies out of the main current and that the water in the eddies was not carrying enough dissolved oxygen. Some of the pupfish were already floating belly-up on the surface. Pister moved the survivors to two buckets and relocated the cages. As he lugged the heavy buckets across the muddy, uneven terrain of the marsh, he realized that he held the survival of an entire vertebrate species in his hands. One false step and the Owens pupfish would be extinct.

Pister kept his balance. As a result, the recovery of the Owens pupfish continues today, though its future is far from certain.

The threats are particularly grave for the Owens pupfish and many of its relatives. Pupfish—so named for their seemingly playful habit of darting aggressively after intruders, nipping at their tails—often have extremely narrow ranges. These fish evolved from ancestors that inhabited the vast freshwater lakes that filled many areas of the Great Basin during the Ice Age. As these lakes shrank, pupfish populations became isolated, evolving into the diversity of species that now thrive in hot, isolated desert springs, salty marshes, and other extreme environments. Some live where no other fish can survive, such as in small pools just a few inches deep and in salt concentrations several times greater than seawater. Their preferred habitats make them unusually susceptible to extinction: Of the 11 pupfish species found in the United States, 10 are imperiled or vulnerable.

In 1948, researchers working with preserved specimens first identified the Owens pupfish as a distinct species. Even as biologists were formally naming the species, however, they already believed it to be extinct. In 1956, staff of the California Department of Fish and Game found the pupfish again in Fish Slough, but they were unaware of the significance of their find. It wasn't until 1964 that Pister and several of his colleagues rediscovered the species (Miller and Pister 1971). Biologists then created refuges for the pupfish, building sanctuary pools and barriers to prevent invasion by non-native fish. In 1967, the federal government added the Owens pupfish to the newly created endangered species list.

After the rediscovery of the Owens pupfish and its subsequent brush with extinction in Phil Pister's buckets, the fragility of these tiny fishes and their relatives was abundantly clear. Pister went on to help found the Desert Fishes Council, which focused attention of the plight of all Death Valley fishes, and indeed other desert fishes beyond that region. The Desert Fishes Council would play a key role in helping The Nature Conservancy acquire land not far from the Owens Valley to protect another unique pupfish, at a place in southern Nevada called Devils Hole.

Devils Hole lends its name to the most famous pupfish of all, a little blue cousin of the Owens pupfish. The Devils Hole pupfish (*Cyprinodon diabolis*) has the smallest range of any known vertebrate species, a 70-by-10-foot pool that lies at the bottom of a 30-foot-deep fissure in the side of a mountain. Some 30,000 years of isolation from any predator and any other fish species has allowed the Devils Hole pupfish to evolve into a form utterly distinct in appearance and behavior from its closest relatives. With a limited food supply—algae growing on a single sunlit ledge in the otherwise darkened pool—the population of the Devils Hole pupfish fish has never been higher than 1,000. The pupfish gained notoriety not because it is rare, however, but because the Supreme Court eventually took responsibility for its future, ruling unanimously to protect Devils Hole and its pupfish from ranching development nearby.

Remarkable enough in its own right—a strange fissure in the earth and an oasis in the desert—Devils Hole forms just one part of Ash Meadows, a unique and biologically rich ecosystem of natural springs located in the Amargosa Desert about 40 miles east of Death Valley and 90 miles northwest of Las Vegas. More than 30 springs, islands of water in a sea of

The Ash Meadows milk vetch (*Astragalus phoenix*) is one of more than 26 plants and animals found at Ash Meadows and nowhere else in the world. © Joel Sartore/National Geographic Image Collection.

A deep gash in the earth, Devils Hole is the sole habitat for the Devils Hole pupfish. This fish has the smallest range of any vertebrate species, and subsists entirely on algae that grows on the pool's single sunlit ledge. Courtesy of U.S. Fish and Wildlife Service.

aridity, create ideal places for the evolution of unique species. Some of the larger springs provide significant marsh areas for waterfowl and other migrating birds; at least 20 contain native fish; and most if not all contain endemic species of mollusks or insects. Several rare plants depend on the moist areas surrounding the springs for their survival.

Ash Meadows, now a national wildlife refuge—in an odd twist, though, Devils Hole itself is officially part of Death Valley National Park—supports a remarkable concentration of unusual species: 8 plants, 2 insects, at least 10 mollusks, 5 fishes, and 1 mammal are found in Ash Meadows and nowhere else on Earth. Only one other region in North America, the Cuatro Cienegas Basin of northeastern Mexico, supports a greater number of locally restricted organisms. Ash Meadows provides a priceless example of desert oases that are now extremely uncommon in the southwestern United States.

Like any oasis, Ash Meadows draws countless creatures seeking water in the desert. Only one, however, has the potential to use so much water that the ancient springs may run dry. Just as Los Angeles soaks up much of the Owens River, Las Vegas reaches into the enormous aquifer that lies beneath Ash Meadows, mining the fossil water left over from the Ice Age.

More than water and some peculiar species link the Owens Valley, Ash Meadows, and Las Vegas. All are part of the Mojave Desert. Though the area appears barren and remote, a remarkable diversity of living things manage to thrive here, from the distinctive Joshua tree (*Yucca brevifolia*) to the threatened desert tortoise (*Gopherus agassizii*). Given adequate fall and winter rains, a profusion of spring wildflowers can carpet the desert floor. The Mojave occupies more than 25,000 square miles of southeastern California and portions of Nevada, Arizona, and Utah, and in many ways it is transitional between the hotter Sonoran Desert to the south and

Bottom: The threatened desert tortoise plays a key role in the Mojave's ecology by digging extensive burrows. Numerous other animals take advantage of the tortoise's subterranean handiwork to escape predators or take refuge from daytime heat. © Adrienne T. Gibson/ Animals Animals.

Right: In spring the normally austere Mojave Desert can explode into a profusion of wildflowers. Fleeting beauties, each blossom on these evening primroses (*Oenothera deltoides*) lasts but a single day. © Carr Clifton/Minden Pictures.

the cooler Great Basin Desert, which extends over the intermountain region to the north. The Owens Valley itself illustrates the transition from one biotic region to another: The valley's southern reaches share vegetation with the Mojave, while the sagebrush-covered hills in the northern valley, such as around Fish Slough, more closely resemble the Great Basin. The Mojave is more than just a transition zone, however, hosting an array of unique plant species found in neither of the adjacent deserts. The Mojave also has a range of elevations not found in the other deserts, from 282 feet below sea level in Death Valley National Park—the lowest point in North America—to nearly 11,000 feet on some adjacent mountains.

The Fabric of Life: Biodiversity

From the Devils Hole pupfish to the delicate spring ecosystems at Ash Meadows to the Mojave Desert, from genes to species to ecosystems to landscapes: Each is part of the fabric of life. Each is a component of biodiversity. But what is biodiversity? Although the term is now common, many people are bewildered by it. Still others use it in an all-encompassing way to refer to any and all nature.

Biodiversity is, in essence, the full array of life on Earth. The most tangible manifestations of this concept are the species of plants, animals, and microorganisms that surround us. Yet biodiversity is more than just the number and diversity of species, as immense as that might be. It also includes the genetic material that makes up those species. And at a higher level, it includes the natural communities, ecosystems, and landscapes of which species are a part. The concept of biodiversity includes both the variety of these things and the variability found within and among them. Biodiversity also encompasses the processes—both ecological and evolutionary—that allow life on Earth to continue adapting and evolving.

While the term *biodiversity* was coined and popularized only recently (Wilson 1988), the concept is as old as the human desire to know and name

Bottom left: Reduced to fewer than 100 animals by the turn of the last century, the now abundant northern elephant seal (*Mirounga angustirostris*) lost much of its genetic variability in this brush with extinction. © G. C. Kelley/Photo Researchers.

Below: Ecological interactions among species, such as the pollination services provided by this broad-billed hummingbird (*Cynanthus latirostris*), are a key aspect of ecological diversity. © Nancy M. McCallum.

Bottom right: Landscape diversity refers to the mosaic of ecological types in a region. West Virginia's Panther Knob shows a variety of distinct natural communities, ranging from rocky outcrops and pine woodlands to dense deciduous forest. © Larry E. Morse/TNC.

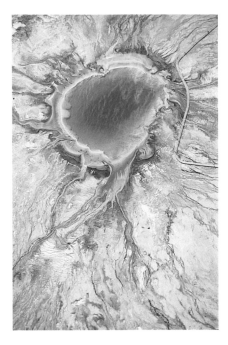

A microbe first found in hot springs at Yellowstone National Park gave rise to one of the key chemical ingredients that has enabled the biotechnology industry to thrive. © Tom Till/DRK PHOTO.

Bristlecone pines perched in the mountains above the Owens Valley are the world's oldest living trees; some date back nearly 5,000 years. © Charlie Ott.

all the creatures of the earth. Nature's daunting complexity demands some method of differentiating among its various components. Four of the principal levels of biological organization are genes, species, ecosystems, and landscapes (Noss and Cooperrider 1994, Szaro and Johnston 1996).

Genetic diversity refers to the unique combinations of genes found within and among organisms. Genes, composed of DNA sequences, are the fundamental building blocks of life. The complexes of genes found within individual organisms, and their frequencies of occurrence within a population, are the basic levels at which evolution occurs. Genetic variability is an important trait in assuring the long-term survival of most species, since it allows them to respond to unpredictable changes in their environment.

Species diversity encompasses the variety of living organisms inhabiting an area. This is most commonly gauged by the number of different types of organisms—for instance, the number of different birds or plants in a state, country, or ecosystem. While species are the most widely understood aspect of biodiversity, it is actually the individual populations that together make up a species that are the focus of on-the-ground conservation efforts.

Ecological diversity refers to the higher-level organization of different species into natural communities, and the interplay between these communities and the physical environment that forms ecosystems. Interactions are key to ecological diversity. This includes interactions among different species—predators and prey, for instance, or pollinators and flowers—as well as interaction among these species and the physical processes, such as nutrient cycling or periodic fires, that are essential to maintain ecosystem functioning.

Landscape diversity refers to the geography of different ecosystems across a large area and the connections among them. Natural communities and ecosystems change across the landscape in response to environmental gradients such as climate, soils, or altitude and form characteristic mosaics. Understanding the patterns among these natural ecosystems and how they relate to other landscape features, such as farms, cities, and roads, is key to maintaining such regional diversity.

Conservation of biodiversity requires attention to each of these levels, because all contribute to the persistence of life on Earth. More than most people realize, humans rely on wild biological resources for food and shelter. Genes from wild plants, for instance, allow plant breeders to develop disease-resistant crops or increase crop yields, passing along the benefits of biodiversity to farmers and ultimately consumers. Similarly, medicines derived from plants, animals, and especially microbes are an established part of the Western pharmacy and include such widely used medications as aspirin, penicillin, and digitalis. The emerging biotechnology industry, perhaps more than any other, depends on such wild genetic resources. Indeed, a crucial piece of the technology that enables scientists and industry to easily multiply strands of DNA—and thereby create useful commercial products—derives from the bacterium *Thermus aquaticus*, first discovered in a hot spring in Yellowstone National Park.

The value of these biodiversity goods is enormous, but even so it is just a fraction of the value of the ecosystem services on which human life depends, such as waste assimilation, climate regulation, water supply and regulation, erosion control and sediment retention, soil formation, waste treatment, and pollination. Ecosystem services, however, are largely outside the financial markets and therefore are ignored or undervalued. By one rough estimate the value of ecosystem services for the entire biosphere is $33 trillion, nearly double the global gross national product (Costanza et al. 1997).

When most people think about biodiversity, however, they think not about ecosystems and their services but rather about species. Yet scientists still don't know how many species share the planet with us. Estimates vary by an order of magnitude. A conservative guess is roughly 14 million species, only one-eighth of which have been formally named. We now recognize that the earth supports far more species than previously believed, from tremendous numbers of beetles living in the canopy of tropical trees to bacteria inhabiting rocks more than a mile beneath the earth's surface.

Individual species, like the pupfishes of the desert Southwest, form threads in the lustrous ecological tapestry of the United States. Further examination reveals a dense weave of thousands of species, many found nowhere else. Together these threads spell out superlatives: tallest, largest, oldest. Topping out at more than 360 feet in height, northern California's redwoods (*Sequoia sempervirens*) are the tallest trees in the world. Their close relatives the giant sequoias (*Sequoiadendron giganteum*) rank among the most massive living things on Earth, and bristlecone pines (*Pinus longaeva*), overlooking the Owens Valley near the summit of eastern California's White Mountains, are the world's oldest living trees, some dating back nearly 5,000 years (Schulman 1958).

The difference between two species can be visually obvious, as with the Devils Hole and Owens pupfish, or so subtle that only sophisticated molecular techniques can reveal the distinctions. Nonetheless, scientists have documented more than 200,000 species from the United States, and the true number of species living here is probably at least double this figure. By any measure, the United States is home to an exceptionally diverse flora and fauna. On a global scale the nation is particularly noteworthy for certain groups of organisms, including salamanders, coniferous plants, and freshwater fishes, turtles, mussels, snails, and crayfishes. The United States harbors nearly 16,000 species of vascular plants, about 9% of the world's total mammal species, and about 10% of known freshwater fishes worldwide.

This wealth of life owes a great deal to the nation's size and location. While covering only about 6% of the earth's total land area, the United States spans nearly a third of the globe, extending more than 120 degrees of longitude from eastern Maine to the tip of the Aleutian chain, and 50 degrees in latitude from Point Barrow above the Arctic Circle to the southern tip of Hawaii below the tropic of Cancer. Together with this expanse of terrain comes a variety of topographic features and climates, from Death Valley to Mt. McKinley. This range of climates has given rise to a wide array of ecological types, from tundra and subarctic conifer forests called taiga, to deserts, prairie, boreal forests, deciduous forests, temperate rain forests, and even tropical rain forests.

From boreal forests in Alaska (*top,* © Charlie Ott), to tropical rain forests in Hawaii (*bottom,* © Frans Lanting/ Minden Pictures), the United States encompasses a vast array of ecosystem types.

More global biomes are found in the United States than in any other country, and some are particularly well represented here. Almost a third of the earth's temperate broadleaf forest are found in the United States. © John Golden/TNC.

While still far from complete, the process of documenting the nation's ecological diversity suggests that the United States is also extraordinary from an ecological perspective. For example, of the 14 biome types world-wide that represent major ecosystem groups (Udvardy 1975), the United States contains 12, more than any other country. Three biomes—temperate broadleaf forests, temperate grasslands, and mixed mountain systems—are particularly well represented: At least 10% of their area occurs in the United States. Around the world and on a more detailed scale within the United States, ecologists have also identified relatively large areas, known as ecoregions, that in ecological terms function more or less as a unit. With 21 of 28 globally defined ecoregions (Bailey 1989), the United States is also the most diverse country in the world from an ecoregional perspective.

On a much finer ecological scale, natural heritage ecologists have identified more than 4,500 distinct vegetation communities in the United States. This figure is likely to grow as additional inventory and classification work proceeds, and we can project that on the order of 7,000 to 9,000 natural and seminatural vegetation associations ultimately will be documented from the United States.

Informing Conservation: The Natural Heritage Network

The biological discovery of America began centuries ago yet continues to this day, gradually revealing the intricacies of our natural inheritance. This knowledge has been developed by generations of biologists, working through universities, natural history museums, botanical gardens, and government agencies. Dedicated amateurs have also made important and lasting contributions to our understanding of the U.S. biota. In turn, the knowledge generated by this basic inventory serves as the backbone of our efforts to protect the nation's biological diversity.

Biological inventories, from the collection of field specimens to sophisticated satellite imaging techniques, have already yielded a tremendous amount of information on the identity, distribution, and characteristics of species and ecosystems. Even so, the true scope of the diversity of life is so overwhelming that a comprehensive inventory of species and their habitats is probably not practical in our lifetime (Raven and Wilson 1992). The vast scope of this task, and the imperative to quickly protect what is left before it disappears, challenges us to identify those biodiversity inventory needs that reflect our greatest priorities. Those responsible for making decisions about the management and use of our natural resources, including private individuals and corporations, resource managers, and policy makers, often have no choice but to rely on sketchy or sometimes contradictory biodiversity data or, perhaps worse, no data at all.

In an effort to address just these problems of insufficient and inaccessible biodiversity data, state agencies across the country together with The Nature Conservancy and the Association for Biodiversity Information have worked to create a nationwide biological inventory known as the Natural Heritage Network. The fundamental mission of the heritage network, which began with the creation of the South Carolina Heritage Program in 1974, is to gather, organize, and distribute high-quality biodiversity information. Ready access to such information is key to improving the quality of conservation decisions, as well as decisions about development activities and natural resources management.

Heritage programs help agencies and organizations set priorities for conservation by identifying those species and ecosystems that require special attention because of their rarity, endangerment, or exemplary nature. In turn, heritage biologists develop detailed information about the location and condition of these species and ecosystems and about the areas important for their survival. This information is a powerful antidote to the tendency for conservation work to be carried out on an opportunistic basis.

The rapid transformation of the American landscape has put severe limits on the opportunities for direct protection. Responsible environmental management must become a way of life in America, but all too often species and ecosystems suffer from the unintended by-product of farming, mining, forestry, or urbanization. Providing a readily accessible source of information about the location of endangered biological resources allows biodiversity concerns to be taken into account during the land use planning process as a way of improving the environmental sensitivity of such activities.

The Nature Conservancy's interest in making biodiversity information more available, both for its own use and for application more broadly, led it over the past quarter century to work with state and federal agencies to help establish heritage programs in each state. Each state program is independent and typically operated by a state agency with responsibilities for wildlife, natural areas, or natural resource management. Yet by using a standardized set of inventory and information management techniques, these state programs can pool information and expertise into a truly national effort.

Development of the heritage network's approaches to biodiversity inventory and information management were intimately tied to the conservation agenda and strategies of The Nature Conservancy. The Conservancy traces its roots back to 1917, when the Ecological Society of America, a newly formed professional scientific society, created a Committee for the Preservation of Natural Conditions. Under the leadership of Victor Shelford, the committee set about identifying those sites where conditions were still sufficiently intact to lend themselves to long-term ecological research. The book *Naturalists Guide to the Americas* (Shelford 1926) constituted a major effort on the part of the committee and was the most detailed and definitive account to that time of natural areas in the United States and elsewhere in the Western Hemisphere.

By the early 1940s, the preservation committee's advocacy for a more activist conservation role led to increasing friction with members of the Ecological Society's executive committee who were uncomfortable with the entry of a scientific society into such realms (Croker 1991). The dis-

Mianus Gorge, a remnant hemlock gulch near the New York–Connecticut border, was The Nature Conservancy's first land acquisition project and established the organization's approach to conservation through private action. © Susan Bournique.

Much of the Conservancy's land protection activities have focused on protecting those species at greatest risk of extinction. The only known occurrence of Peter's mountain mallow (*Iliamna corei*) is now a Conservancy preserve. © Maryl.

pute became increasingly polarized and acrimonious, and by 1946 the society formally abolished the preservation committee. Dismayed but not discouraged, Shelford and several of his colleagues set about creating a new organization to focus on natural areas preservation. They founded the Ecologist's Union in 1946, and one year later they changed their name to The Nature Conservancy, after a British agency that specialized in setting aside open space and wildlife preserves.

Early on the Conservancy took a direct approach to conserving natural areas: buying them. Beginning with the purchase of Mianus Gorge, a remnant hemlock ravine along the New York and Connecticut border, the small volunteer organization began to flourish and grow. By the late 1960s, the once volunteer organization had a professional staff. Land acquisition activities were also rapidly expanding and becoming the Conservancy's defining niche. Given the expense and potentially limitless scope of land acquisition as a conservation tool, the organization realized that it needed to better refine its goals for protecting natural areas. Toward that end, in 1970 the Conservancy hired its first staff scientist, a freshly minted Harvard Ph.D. named Robert Jenkins Jr. Jenkins's principal task was to help evaluate projects and properties that were being brought to the attention of the Conservancy. He did more than that, however, and helped create a more precise and sophisticated focus for Conservancy protection activities. The goal would be the preservation of what was then termed biotic diversity (Grove 1992).

Although some information was usually available about the properties under review, it was virtually impossible to put these projects into a broader biodiversity perspective. Was the proposed site ecologically unique, or was it merely an attractive parcel of open space without noteworthy biological values? The absence of consistent and accessible information made cross-site comparisons difficult or impossible. In essence, something was needed to answer the question "What's the most important site for the Conservancy to protect next?"

Preserving all biotic diversity was a tall order, though. To help focus their activities, therefore, Jenkins and his colleagues developed a coarse filter/fine filter strategy for biodiversity protection (Jenkins 1996). The philosophy behind this approach is that protecting representative examples of different ecological systems would have the effect of preserving the majority of species found in those systems. Focusing on protecting the best examples of different ecological communities would therefore provide an efficient way to protect most species.

On the other hand, such a strategy would tend to overlook those species that are rare or otherwise highly localized. They could simply slip through the sieve of this ecological coarse filter. Unfortunately, the very species that the coarse filter would tend to miss are also the organisms that, precisely because of their rarity, may be at greatest risk of extinction. Conservancy and other scientists thus developed a fine filter focusing on protection of rare species to complement the ecological coarse filter. A 1980s–era Conservancy slogan nicely summarized the coarse filter/ fine filter concept: "protecting the last of the least and the best of the rest."

The coarse filter/fine filter paradigm underlies much of the rationale for the inventory and information management strategies developed for use by the Natural Heritage Network. First, it explains why heritage methods encompass status assessment and inventory of both species and ecological communities, while most inventory efforts focus on either one or the other. Second, the coarse filter/fine filter approach highlights the pressing need for detailed locational information for those species that cannot be protected except through the fine filter—that is, the rarities. Finally, by firmly linking both coarse- and fine-filter information to on-the-ground protection efforts at specific sites, it makes clear that biological or ecological information alone is insufficient. Sites represent a common currency of land conservation, but the ability to integrate biological information with information about specific land units and uses is essential to transforming biological data into conservation-relevant information.

As the network of natural heritage data centers matured, the individual programs began to see the need for increased networkwide collaboration and cooperation. By the early 1990s a group of natural heritage program directors began focusing on the development of networkwide information products, eventually broadening the effort into the establishment of an independent nonprofit organization devoted to supporting and representing the needs and interests of natural heritage programs and conservation data centers throughout the hemisphere. Incorporated in 1994 as the Association for Biodiversity Information (ABI), the organization now plays an increasingly active role in planning for the future of the heritage inventory effort, creating the institutional framework for broader networkwide coordination, and helping to support the ongoing efforts to catalogue our nation's biological riches. Indeed, in 1999 The Nature Conservancy and the Association for Biodiversity Information formally joined forces to create a fully operational, independent institution devoted to strengthening the natural heritage effort. The scientific and technical support functions that were previously provided by the Conservancy have

The hellbender salamander (*Crypto-branchus alleganiensis*) is just one example of the biota shared between eastern North America and eastern Asia, a peculiar distribution pattern discussed in chapter 3. ©Phil A. Dotson/Photo Researchers.

Mediterranean-type vegetation is found in only five places on Earth, including California, and, as discussed in chapter 5, has given rise to some of the nation's highest levels of diversity, rarity, and endemism. © Harold E. Malde.

now been transferred over to that new institution. This book, *Precious Heritage*, is one of the first fruits of that venture.

Precious Heritage

Precious Heritage celebrates a quarter century of the natural heritage partnership and biodiversity inventory. It is the product of a collaboration between The Nature Conservancy, the Association for Biodiversity Information, and natural heritage programs in all 50 states, and it presents for the first time a national synthesis of the heritage network's effort to document the patterns of biodiversity across the United States. The following chapters offer an overview of the state of the nation's biodiversity: what exists, how it is doing, where it is found, what is threatening it, how we are doing at protecting it, and, perhaps most important, what more we *should* be doing to safeguard our precious heritage.

The discovery of life in America is far from over, and chapter 2 provides an overview of the approaches scientists use to assess biodiversity. This chapter also describes the scientific underpinnings of the methods used by heritage programs to develop and manage the information on which much of this book is based.

The United States harbors a truly exceptional flora and fauna, and chapter 3 considers national-level patterns of species diversity against a global backdrop. How did the United States come to have this rich complement of plants and animals, and why do such distributional anomalies appear linking, for instance, the southeastern United States and China?

Assessing the conservation status, or health, of species is essential to understanding the overall condition of the nation's biodiversity and to setting clear priorities for conservation. Chapter 4 considers how well the U.S. biota is doing overall, which groups of plants or animals face the greatest risk of extinction, and which species have already been lost to extinction.

Chapter 5 focuses on the state of the states, reviewing the overall geographic patterns of plant and animal species across the nation in terms of diversity, endemism, and rarity. Just as the natural geography of the 50 states varies tremendously, so too the geography of risk varies across the nation, largely reflecting ecological setting, evolutionary history, and the past and present actions of people.

In setting conservation priorities, it is important to have a finer level of resolution than states to use in identifying areas critical for protecting rare and endangered species. Chapter 6 considers the geography of imperilment at a detailed level, revealing several hot spots for imperiled species. The chapter also considers what this geography of imperilment means for the emerging scale of conservation at a national level.

Species are only part of the biodiversity story, and chapter 7 looks at the diversity, extent, and condition of ecological systems in the United States. Tracing the route of the explorers Lewis and Clark, this chapter considers ecological diversity across the United States from the coarsest scales, such as biomes and ecoregions, to fine-scale vegetation associations.

Not even the most complete data on the distribution and status of species and ecological communities in the United States can guide conservation activities without a firm understanding of the nature of the threats to our natural heritage, the subject of chapter 8. Presenting one of the first quantitative analyses of leading threats to U.S. biodiversity, this chapter confirms the primary role played by habitat destruction but offers surprises in how various other threats rank.

Addressing these threats will require a flexible and forward-looking set of conservation strategies. Chapter 9 reviews the fundamental strategies underlying most biodiversity conservation to date and suggests those that are likely to guide this vital work in the future.

The opportunities and challenges for long-term biodiversity protection relate not just to the natural distribution of species and ecosystems but also to the patterns of land ownership and management that have been laid atop them. Who owns lands important to biodiversity is the subject of chapter 10, and this question is key to addressing how we, as a nation, are doing at protecting our most sensitive biological resources.

Finally, this book raises fundamental questions about the future of biodiversity in the United States. Is there a solution to the biodiversity conservation problem, and, if so, what are its scope and scale? Chapter 11 considers what the information presented in this volume suggests about those questions and searches for answers among the increasing number of regional and ecoregional conservation planning efforts that are under way.

Saving All the Pieces

Phil Pister may have been the first person to shoulder the entire burden of responsibility for the future of a species, but, sadly, he may not be the last. We are in the midst of a global extinction crisis: The United States,

Tracing the path of the explorers Lewis and Clark, chapter 7 reviews the breadth of ecological diversity across the United States and considers the changes that have befallen these ecosystems since the time of that transcontinental journey. © Corbis/Bettmann.

Recognizing the need to move beyond traditional nature preserves to protect biodiversity, conservationists on Virginia's eastern shore are bringing together farmers, watermen, and economic development agencies. © John Hall/ TNC.

despite its prosperity and long-standing conservation ethic, is not a safe harbor from the storms that threaten to render the earth a far poorer place.

The loss of a large part of our natural heritage is unacceptable for ecological, economic, aesthetic, and moral reasons. From an ecological perspective, the variety of organisms form the cogs and wheels that drive and support all life on Earth. Though scientists do not fully understand how the pieces fit together, they now realize that the vitality of the earth rests on diverse organisms and processes that directly and indirectly regulate water, soil, and climate. Recognizing the many values of biodiversity is an important step in building support for its protection, but slowing and ultimately reversing these declines demands both that we adopt more environmentally sensitive means of using our natural resources and that we identify and protect those places critical to the survival of our species and ecosystems. Key in that process will be understanding those places well enough to know what form protection must take.

At the same time, however, we need to revisit the notion of place. Until quite recently, most conservation has focused on traditional parks and nature preserves, important in their own right but still only fragile remnants of once majestic wilderness. The Nature Conservancy, for instance, has realized that simply protecting the "last of the least and the best of the rest" is no longer sufficient. While this strategy has resulted in the protection of many wonderful and biologically significant places, a new appreciation of the importance of broad-scale ecological and evolutionary processes to conservation gives new impetus to increasing the geographic and temporal scale of our conservation efforts. We are challenged with considering not only what places are most important to protect but also what is needed to ensure the long-term survival of their species and ecological communities.

The scientific community too has taken renewed interest in the implications of scale for understanding the earth's biological diversity. By crossing disciplinary boundaries and moving out from individuals to populations, from communities to ecosystems, and from landscapes to regions, scientists have begun redrawing their maps of the natural world. Among the most powerful ideas to emerge for directing conservation efforts is that of ecologically coherent regions, or ecoregions (figure 1.1). Realms of similar climate, geology, and landforms, these regions support distinctive groupings of plants and animals. Most important, by transcending unnatural political boundaries, these ecoregions provide a powerful conservation planning tool.

The concept of ecoregions has been adopted by dozens of organizations in the United States and around the world as a way of thinking about and structuring landscape-scale conservation efforts. These regions provide the context for the Conservancy and other organizations to begin asking and answering the question "How much is enough?"

Ecoregion-based conservation highlights the biological importance of certain areas, as well as the inherent capabilities of land and water resources and the effects of management on them. Such a broad vision for conservation recognizes several things simultaneously. First, given the

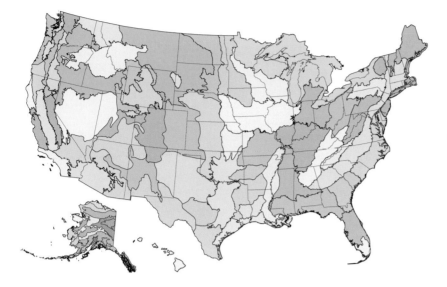

Figure 1.1. Ecoregions of the United States.

Ecologically defined regions provide a context for conservation planning that transcend political boundaries. Source: The Nature Conservancy 1999, modified from Bailey 1994.

swiftness of habitat loss, conservation efforts must be flexible enough to take urgent steps to save important areas of biodiversity. At the same time, conservationists must look beyond the immediate crises to help shape the landscape of the next century. A framework for success must also draw on the evolving fields of conservation biology and landscape ecology and yet be sensitive to the needs of policy makers, private landowners, rural communities, and all the many other stakeholders in conservation. Finally, this entire vision needs to take into account the human and financial resources of the agencies, organizations, and individuals who must transform conservation plans into effective action.

The long-term success of conservation depends in large part on making wise choices about where to invest these limited amounts of time, money, and effort. Conservation efforts in the United States historically have provided a protective umbrella for a fairly narrow set of the nation's biological wealth. These efforts often have been opportunistic, and early on they tended to focus on remote lands of limited economic value. This strategy brought numerous victories for the conservation movement, to which the many scenic "rock and ice" parks in the American West are a testament. Our broader understanding of biodiversity and the large-scale processes needed to ensure its lasting protection compel us to reach beyond this strategy, however. Many of the most biologically significant landscapes in the country are neither particularly scenic nor uninhabited.

A shift from opportunistic land protection to more carefully considered conservation planning was the driving force behind the creation of the Natural Heritage Network more than a quarter century ago. The knowledge developed as part of these and similar efforts to understand and document the nation's biological resources will form the foundation for conservation into the twenty-first century and beyond. Yet incorporating scientific information, such as that presented in this book, into conservation action remains a daunting challenge. For while the inspiration to build a conservation edifice within which we can save the full

Many existing protected areas, like North Cascades National Park, preserve wild and beautiful landscapes. Fully protecting biodiversity, however, will require a conservation focus on a far broader array of landscapes. © Gary Braasch.

Aesthetically subdued yet biologically spectacular, Florida's Lake Wales Ridge is the type of place that increasingly will need to be protected if we are to succeed in safeguarding the nation's precious natural heritage. © James Valentine.

array of our biodiversity can be informed by science, it cannot come from science alone. That inspiration will come only from a vision for the American landscape centuries from now—forged by passion, tempered with humility and compassion, and burnished with wisdom.

As he lugged his precious cargo of pupfish across Fish Slough, Phil Pister may have been thinking of the world his great-grandchildren would inherit, or he may simply have responded like a fireman to an alarm. Perhaps he accomplished the difficult task of doing both. That is the challenge we face. Our hope is that the information presented in this volume will help to illuminate the present and more clearly bring into focus a vision for the future of America's extraordinary natural heritage.

2

DISCOVERING LIFE IN AMERICA
Tools and Techniques of Biodiversity Inventory

Discovering Life in America

When John and William Bartram set off for Florida from their Philadelphia farm on a July day in 1765, a vast and largely unknown continent lay before them. Journeying in search of novel and unusual plants
for their English patrons, the virgin territories of the southeastern United
States provided fertile grounds for their biological explorations. These
pioneering naturalists, father and son, lived at a time when new scientific discoveries literally lay around each corner. On this trip alone, they
were able to collect or draw more than 200 species new to science.

    One species that slipped away from them was a "very curious" shrub
they found growing along the banks of the Altamaha River in Georgia.
Sporting beautiful white flowers accented by a central tuft of orange sta-
mens, the shrubs unfortunately yielded no ripe seeds. Only on a return
trip to Georgia some eight years later was son William able to collect seed
and bring the species into cultivation—and to the attention of the scientific world. Given the name *Franklinia alatamaha*, in honor of Bartram's
close friend and fellow Quaker Benjamin Franklin, the shrub turned out
to represent a completely new branch of the camellia family. Thanks
to its beautiful flowers and foliage, *Franklinia* quickly became a popular ornamental, and even today it is widely cultivated in gardens. But
Bartram's horticultural introduction of this unique plant was fortuitous
for another reason: The species has disappeared from its native habitat
along the Altamaha River and was last seen in the wild in 1803. Sadly,
Franklinia represents one of the first species known to vanish from the
American landscape.

    While the American frontier formally closed in 1892, the biological
discovery of America continues to this day. Not all discoveries are as spec-

Bruce A. Stein

Frank W. Davis

Franklinia alatamaha was discovered in Georgia by the early American botanists John and William Bartram. This attractive relative of the camellia was last seen in the wild in 1803. Courtesy of American Philosophical Society.

tacular as the "curious shrubs" the Bartrams had the good fortune to find, but each, in its own way, is just as important. The ongoing process of exploring our biological frontiers gradually fills in the fabric of our knowledge about the United States and its ecosystems. The knowledge generated by this basic inventory also serves as the backbone of our efforts to protect our nation's biological diversity. This chapter serves as an overview of some of the contemporary scientific tools and techniques that are being used to document and assess the nation's flora and fauna. We focus particularly on those employed by the Natural Heritage Network to transform this information into a powerful tool for biodiversity conservation.

Technology and Tradition

The impetus for John Bartram's botanical explorations was his business relationship with an English merchant, Peter Collinson, to whom he sent seeds, roots, and specimens. European naturalists and gentleman gardeners were eager to obtain new curiosities, and Bartram was well positioned to fulfill these desires. He alone was responsible for nearly doubling the number of North American plants in cultivation in Europe, and in time he was appointed King's Botanist to the colonies. Collecting and shipping methods were very primitive at the time, however. After Bartram had to abandon some particularly choice orchids, which had dried out too much for shipping to England, Collinson wrote him advising of a novel use of ancient technology. By removing the necks from large ox bladders, Bartram could fill the chamber with plants, keeping them nicely moist during his collecting forays (Berkeley and Berkeley 1982). Collinson's determination not to miss out on any more prized orchids led to Bartram's use of the equivalent of modern-day plastic bags—a staple of virtually all contemporary botanists. Thus technological advances, even in this most humble and primitive form, can significantly improve our ability to study and understand the world's biota.

Obviously, other technological innovations have had far greater impacts on our overall worldview. The invention of the optical microscope some four centuries ago was the first advance to dramatically extend our ability to observe and measure scales of biodiversity beyond the range of our senses. Today an increasingly wide set of tools is at our disposal, from molecular techniques for studying genes to satellite-borne sensors for monitoring the planetary ecosystem. But while we are now armed with an impressive array of sophisticated tools and technologies, discovering life in America is still fundamentally a human drama. Indeed, much of our basic knowledge derives from the same powers of keen observation that the Bartrams used in their explorations of the newly colonized continent.

Slogging through mud and crashing through brambles may have remained relatively unchanged, but modern-day biological explorers do have a number of advantages over their predecessors. Modern rock-climbing equipment and even construction cranes provide access to habitats such as cliff faces, caverns, and forest canopies that previously were out of reach and largely unknown. The technological accoutrements of the field biologist may now include cell phone, digital camera, global positioning system for satellite-based location and navigation, range finder for distance measurements, and laptop computer with modem links to remote computing facilities and databases. One could say that whereas in the past biologists brought field collections to the laboratory for detailed study, they are now increasingly bringing the laboratory to the field.

Novel Views of the World

Biological inventory efforts—both low- and high-tech—have yielded a tremendous amount of information on the identity, distribution, and characteristics of species and ecosystems. In turn, this has provided enormous dividends to humanity in the form of food, fiber, pharmaceuticals, and other useful products. Despite several centuries of biological exploration, however, we still remain largely ignorant about the vast majority of species and ecosystems that comprise life on Earth. Much of the inventory and exploration work to date has focused on those organisms that either are of known economic importance, are dominant elements of our human experience, or are relatively conspicuous and easy to study. For this reason, we know far more about such organisms as birds and flowers than we do about soil microorganisms.

Data gathered through traditional biological field inventories can now be combined with other environmental variables to extrapolate potential distributions and model biodiversity patterns and processes over large areas. Technologies such as satellite remote sensing and geographic information systems (GIS) have begun to have far-reaching impacts on the biodiversity inventory process. Combining data that reflect a variety of biological levels—for example, species-level field surveys and ecosystem-level satellite analysis—affords unprecedented opportunities to view biodiversity in novel ways and to more effectively plan needed inventory and conservation actions.

The orange-throated whiptail lizard (*Cnemidophorus hyperythrus*), a diminutive reptile inhabiting the coastal hills of southern California, illustrates the possibilities and limitations of integrating various types of data for conservation purposes. The orange-throated whiptail occurs from southern Baja California to southern coastal California. Across most of its range, the lizard is relatively abundant. Within California, however, the animal's situation is more precarious. Inhabiting chaparral and coastal sage ecosystems, which have largely been replaced by urban growth and agriculture, the lizard's populations have been reduced to the point where the species now is considered imperiled in California.

To help plan for the conservation of the species, researchers generated a map of predicted distribution for the lizard by combining ground survey data with digital maps of potential habitats (Hollander et al. 1994, figure 2.1a). The species' range within southern California previously was demarcated based on modern and historical field collections, indicated

The orange-throated whiptail lizard is still relatively abundant across most of its range, but in southern California its habitat has been largely replaced by urban sprawl and agriculture. © Bruce Farnsworth.

by the regional boundaries shown on figure 2.1 (Zeiner et al. 1990). Within this range, areas unsuitable for the whiptail—urban, agricultural, and grassland habitat types—were mapped (shown in gray) according to a Wildlife Habitat Relationships model (Airola 1988). The remaining area was classified as potentially suitable habitat. This representation of unsuitable versus suitable habitats was derived from a relatively coarse digital map of land use and land cover. To achieve a greater level of detail, Hollander and his colleagues further subdivided potential habitat into areas of high suitability (green) and low suitability (white) based on the statistical association between whiptail sightings in San Diego County made as part of a county-wide conservation planning effort—the red dots—and shrub cover as mapped using Landsat Thematic Mapper satellite imagery. The black dots represent whiptail locations recorded by the state's natural heritage program, known as the California Natural Diversity Database, and are based on a variety of field records from museum collections, environmental impact reports, and other sources.

Mapped vegetation is a crude proxy for the suite of habitat features that are more directly important to the lizards. Nonetheless, figure 2.1a illustrates a strong association between sightings and areas predicted to be most suitable. The sighting data, however, are far from ideal for such a mapping effort because they are not based on systematic surveys of the region for this lizard. Rather, many of these localities were documented as part of environmental impact reports and are thus concentrated near the urban fringe, where development is occurring most rapidly. Of the localities already incorporated into the heritage databases, many were

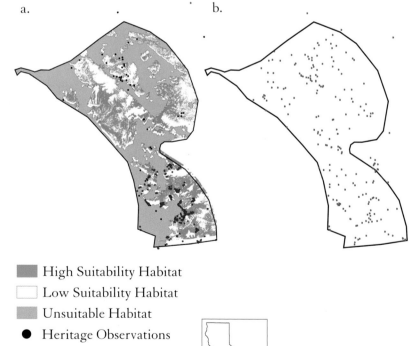

Figure 2.1. Integrating multiple data sources.

The distribution of the orange-throated whiptail illustrates the use of various sources and scales of data. (a) Predicted distributions of this lizard are based on satellite-derived maps of potential habitat, while known observations come from California's natural heritage program (black dots) and a San Diego County multiple species planning effort (red dots). (b) An updated set of occurrence records from the heritage program shows the considerable amount of new inventory data now available for this species. Sources: (a) adapted from Hollander et al. 1994; (b) CNDDB 1999.

■ High Suitability Habitat
□ Low Suitability Habitat
■ Unsuitable Habitat
● Heritage Observations
● Multiple Species Conservation Plan Observations

recorded more than 20 years ago, and the habitats in these areas subsequently have been lost. Furthermore, the point data—from museums, heritage programs, and other environmental studies—indicate only where the species was found: They are silent on the question of where biologists searched but did not find the lizard. Finally, several large areas of suitable habitat in the northwestern portion of the study area, including Camp Pendelton Marine Base, are known to harbor whiptails, but their presence is not reflected in this early 1990s survey data.

Since Hollander et al. (1994) carried out this data integration exercise, a considerable amount of inventory and conservation attention has been focused on the coastal ecosystems of southern California, greatly adding to our knowledge of species distributions in the region. An updated map of heritage records for the orange-throated whiptail (figure 2.1b), shows that numerous additional locations for the lizard have now been documented, particularly in the northern portion of its range (CNDDB 1999). Indeed, based on this newer inventory information, the lizard is considered somewhat less imperiled than previously thought.

Nevertheless, as this analysis shows, even in densely populated and relatively well studied regions, available data on the distribution of rare species and their habitats can be very limited. Integrating various sources and scales of biological and ecological data, however, can produce readily interpretable maps that help to set priorities for additional field survey and support conservation and land use planning. Indeed, the rapid declines in our natural systems make it imperative that we accelerate such efforts to document the status and distribution of our biota.

Transforming Information to Conservation

To address these problems of insufficient and inaccessible biodiversity data, state agencies across the country together with The Nature Conservancy have worked for a quarter century to create a nationwide biological inventory effort known as the Natural Heritage Network. The fundamental mission of the heritage network is to help conserve the nation's dwindling biological resources by gathering, organizing, and distributing reliable biodiversity information. Ready access to such information is key to improving the quality of conservation decisions, as well as decisions about land use and natural resources management.

Heritage programs are designed to promote biodiversity conservation in two principal ways. First, heritage programs help set these priorities for conservation by identifying those species and ecosystems that require special attention because of their rarity, endangerment, or exemplary nature. In turn, heritage biologists develop detailed information about the location and condition of these species and ecosystems and about the areas important for their survival. This information can then form the basis for proactive conservation work.

Second, heritage programs help reduce or avoid unnecessary damage to these biological resources that might result through economic de-

Natural heritage biologists focus on inventorying those species and ecological communities that are at greatest risk in order to help inform conservation activities and improve development decisions. © Lynda Richardson.

One of the rare species that is the subject of heritage inventory and monitoring efforts, the piping plover (*Charadrius melodus*) requires sandy beaches for nesting, a habitat unfortunately also in demand by millions of beachgoing humans. © Betty Cottrille.

velopment and land use activities. All too often, sensitive species and ecosystems are the victims—often unintentionally—of land development activities and natural resource extraction and management practices. Many agencies, corporations, and individuals involved in activities such as farming, mining, forestry, or construction are attempting to operate with more sensitivity to the natural environment, or are being required to do so by federal, state, and local laws. Avoiding or reducing impacts to these ecological resources requires knowledge of their existence and distribution before, rather than after, potentially damaging activities occur. By providing a readily accessible source of information about the location of endangered biological resources, heritage programs allow biodiversity concerns to be taken into account early in the land use planning process. Doing so can help decrease the conflicts with environmental regulations that corporations and other landowners may face; at the same time, it can allow agencies and citizens to review the potential impacts of proposed projects on rare and endangered species and important habitats and can help ensure compliance with established policies.

Before the creation of the Natural Heritage Network, the prevailing approach for identifying natural areas in need of protection was to draw up a list of seemingly appropriate sites and then amass information about them. Conservationists tended to choose such sites for a variety of reasons: a relative lack of disturbance, high on-site diversity, a perceived threat to the area, or geological or biological peculiarities. Certain habitats tended to be overrepresented because of their perceived "naturalness"—hemlock gullies in the Northeast, for instance. Others were well represented because of their supposed value to wildlife, such as bottomland swamps in the South. On the other hand, species and ecological communities that did not fall into these better-known and more popular habitats were often vastly underrepresented in natural area inventories. This was especially true of those things that were "unfortunate enough to be hanging on only in damaged landscapes, depauperate circumstances, or ordinary-looking places" (TNC 1982).

Robert Jenkins Jr., then science director of The Nature Conservancy, created a new approach in 1974 while working with the South Carolina Department of Wildlife and Marine Resources to create a system for identifying important natural areas in that state. Jenkins's major insight was to turn the site inventory process around. Instead of inventorying sites themselves, Jenkins and his colleagues focused the inventory on those biological features in need of conservation attention (Jenkins 1985, 1988, 1996). The collective distribution of these features would then suggest priority sites for protection. In this context, targeted features included both species and natural communities, or, to use the phrase that was coined to reflect this inclusiveness, *elements of natural diversity*. This concept of natural diversity was in many ways the functional equivalent of biological diversity, or biodiversity, a term that was not introduced and popularized until more than a decade later (Wilson 1988).

Networking the United States and Beyond

From humble beginnings in South Carolina, the geographic scope of the Natural Heritage Network has expanded considerably. Heritage inventory efforts now operate in all 50 U.S. states and elsewhere throughout much of the Western Hemisphere (figure 2.2). Most U.S. programs are part of state agencies with natural resource or fish and game responsibilities, while some are hosted by universities. The Nature Conservancy itself operates a small number. Several regional heritage programs exist in addition to the state-level programs. These include inventories focusing on lands of the Tennessee Valley Authority and the Navajo Nation, as well as several specific national parks, such as the Great Smoky Mountains. Most state heritage programs have now been in operation for between 10 and 20 years; the 50th state program, Alaska's, was established in 1989 (table 2.1). As can be appreciated by scanning the complete list of U.S. programs (see Participating Institutions), a variety of names are applied to heritage programs across the country. Although the phrase *natural heritage program* is the most common, other permutations include *conservation data center* (especially internationally), *natural features inventory*, and *natural diversity database*.

The Heritage Network goes well beyond the United States, spanning much of the Western Hemisphere. In Canada, provinces from the Pacific to the Atlantic have established Conservation Data Centers. These programs are key collaborators of their U.S. counterparts, helping to assess the overall condition of North American species and ecosystems. Data centers also operate in Latin America and the Caribbean, including more than a dozen countries as well as the Commonwealth of Puerto Rico and the U.S. Virgin Islands.

Despite the variety of names, the unifying characteristics of all these programs are their commitment to gather, organize, and distribute reliable biodiversity information and their use of a standard inventory and

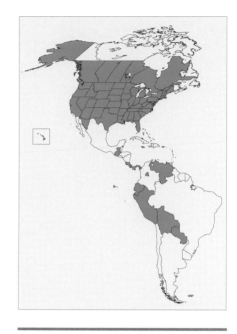

Figure 2.2. Natural Heritage Programs and Conservation Data Centers.

Heritage programs operate in all 50 states, across Canada, and in several countries in Latin America and the Caribbean. Most U.S. programs are run by state government agencies.

Heritage biologists also inventory unusual or exemplary ecological communities. This meadow along Michigan's Lake Huron is an alvar, a globally rare community that occurs on limestone bedrock on which there is little or no soil. © Harold E. Malde.

Table 2.1. Establishment dates for U.S. natural heritage programs

1974	1980	1986
South Carolina	Michigan	Delaware
Mississippi	North Dakota	Illinois
1975	1981	Georgia
Oregon	Florida	Virginia
West Virginia	Missouri	Kansas
Tennessee	Iowa	1987
1976	South Dakota	Vermont
New Mexico	1982	Nebraska
North Carolina	Pennsylvania	Hawaii
Ohio	1983	1988
1977	Connecticut	Utah
Oklahoma	Texas	Alabama
Washington	1984	1989
1978	New Hampshire	Maine
Indiana	Idaho	Alaska
Kentucky	New Jersey	
Rhode Island	Louisiana	
Wyoming	New York	
Arkansas	1985	
Massachusetts	Montana	
1979	Wisconsin	
Minnesota	Nevada	
Colorado		
California		
Arizona		
Maryland		

information management methodology. This consistency in approach allows the programs to function as a network employing the concept of local custodianship of data. Each center is responsible for developing and maintaining its own detailed information, but their standard methods and procedures allow information to be shared between state-level centers or aggregated at national and international levels. Although staffing varies among centers, heritage programs typically have a core staff that includes specialists in zoology, botany, and ecology, as well as data management and geographic systems technology. All told, about 900 scientists, information managers, and administrative support staff are associated with the network's efforts.

In addition to the locally based heritage programs, the Association for Biodiversity Information and The Nature Conservancy work to support the network as a whole. These organizations collaborate in providing training and scientific and technical assistance, carrying out research and development of the inventory methods and information management systems that support the network, and developing networkwide products, such as this book.

Development of the standard methods that enable this diverse array of institutions to operate as a network has been a truly collaborative effort. While The Nature Conservancy historically has taken the lead in developing and documenting these methods (TNC 1982), this has been accomplished with considerable input from many state and international heritage program staff members. Originally an "operating procedures group" provided a formalized process for suggesting, reviewing, and approving modifications to the methods and the associated computer systems. More recently, the Conservancy and the Association for Biodiversity Information have adopted a collaborative design process that draws representation from across the network (TNC and ABI 1999).

Mainstreaming Biodiversity Information

Over the past quarter century, public sentiment has grown immensely for protecting the environment in general, and species and ecosystems in particular. Heritage programs have become a key tool in accomplishing this goal through providing reliable information to an array of users about the condition and location of sensitive biological resources. For the most part, these users are not scientists and have neither the time nor expertise to independently piece together the relevant ecological information about a particular species, place, or project.

In 1994 the programs collectively were responding to more than 65,000 requests for information annually (Groves et al. 1995). These figures represent specific inquiries, mostly by letter, fax, or telephone, related to particular land use decisions or environmental project reviews. In the light of the Internet era and high-volume Web site "hit rates," this may not sound like such a large number, but these inquiries reflect far more than casual Web site browsing. The heritage network clearly serves as the most widely consulted source of detailed biodiversity information for land use planning and environmental management.

Interestingly, the private sector constituted the single largest user of heritage information, according to the 1994 survey, accounting for about 37% of inquiries (Groves et al. 1995). The extensive application of heritage data by corporations, consultants, and private landowners is particularly significant given the importance of private lands to biodiversity conservation, discussed later in this volume. Incentives for public or private use of biodiversity information typically derive from a supportive policy and regulatory framework (Stein 1997). Laws encouraging responsible land management, fish and wildlife conservation, and endangered species protection drive much of the use of heritage data (Cort 1996). State and provincial agencies represent about 27% of heritage users, while federal agencies constitute another 18%. County and local governments, which exert tremendous influence on local land use issues, comprise about 8% of use. Conservation and research entities account for the remaining 10% of use.

This last figure in particular demonstrates the success of the heritage enterprise in expanding its use and utility beyond conservation in the restricted sense. Heritage data has become an accepted part of the decision-making landscape, whether in helping the owner of a small land parcel, facilitating the placement of a new power line, assisting state and federal agencies with watershed management plans, or helping conservation organizations set priorities for land protection. And beyond the data itself, heritage staff offer a wealth of knowledge about their state's species and ecosystems, often including detailed understanding of their ecological requirements and management needs. Heritage programs truly help bring biodiversity considerations into the mainstream of development, land use planning, and natural resource management.

How Heritage Works

Precious Heritage celebrates the heritage network's quarter century of operation and for the first time presents a national synthesis of the network's data. To help understand the development and derivation of the information on which much of this volume is based, we briefly summarize how heritage programs conduct their inventories and manage their information.

On the most basic level, heritage programs are involved in three distinct activities: (1) *gathering information* by documenting existing knowledge and carrying out new inventory and research work; (2) *organizing, analyzing, managing, and updating this information* by using structured methods and standard database and mapping procedures; and (3) *distributing information and knowledge* by sharing data and providing users with products and services. But how are determinations made as to what data should be gathered and how it should be organized? Because heritage inventories have an applied, rather than basic, research focus, clear inventory priorities must be set that relate to the needs of the information users. Indeed, heritage programs are designed not only to set priorities for conservation but also to set priorities for the inventory and research underlying conservation efforts.

WHAT DATA? In general, heritage programs gather data designed to address a series of basic questions important to carrying out biodiversity conservation efforts. What species and ecological communities exist in the area of interest? Which are at greatest risk of extinction or are otherwise significant from a conservation perspective? What are their biological and ecological characteristics, and where precisely are these priority elements found? What is their condition at those locations, and what processes or activities are sustaining or threatening them? Where are the most important sites to protect? Who owns or manages those places deemed important to protect, and what is threatening those places? What actions are needed for the protection of those sites and the significant elements of biodiversity they contain? And how can we measure our progress toward conservation goals?

Of these questions, heritage programs focus particularly on those that relate to documenting patterns of biodiversity. Elucidating the ecological and evolutionary processes that create and sustain those patterns requires a wide variety of information, both biological and nonbiological. Further, some questions about broad-scale patterns of biodiversity are unanswerable, at least given the present state of scientific knowledge, and we must be content with measuring surrogates or making best estimates. The major types of information gathered and managed by heritage programs (table 2.2) reflect their focus on these key questions.

Table 2.2. Major information types managed by heritage programs

Elements	A unit of biodiversity, generally species or ecological communities
Element Occurrences*	An element at a specific location; generally a delineated species population or ecological community stand
Trends	Ecological or population trends
Sites*	A land unit of ecological, scientific, or conservation interest
Managed Areas*	A land unit under protective or potentially protective natural resource management
Tracts*	A cadastral (land ownership) unit and its surface boundaries, generally used for site protection planning
Sources	A source of information documenting data included in any of the above (e.g., literature citation, field notes, museum collection, photograph, satellite image, etc.)

*Indicates a geographic entity that can be mapped.

Among the pieces of biological information important for species-level work are basic taxonomy, general species distributions, the locations of priority taxa and their relative rarity or abundance, population trends, ecological relationships, and habitat requirements. Information useful for ecosystem- and natural community–level work also includes vegetation structure and composition, key environmental factors, successional status, disturbance regimes, and the spatial distribution and integrity of communities across the landscape.

Key to the functioning of heritage programs is the concept of setting priorities for information gathering and inventory. The number of possible facts and observations that can be gathered about the natural world is essentially limitless. The financial and human resources available to gather such information are not. Because biological inventories tend to be woefully underfunded, there is a premium on devising systems that are both effective in providing information that meets users' needs and efficient in gathering that information. The cornerstone of heritage inventories is the use of a ranking system to achieve these twin objectives of effectiveness and efficiency (table 2.3).

Ranking species and ecological communities according to their conservation status provides a means to apply the coarse filter/fine filter approach to conservation described in chapter 1. This ranking system also provides guidance for where heritage programs should focus their information-gathering activities. For species deemed secure, and likely to be well covered through the ecological coarse filter, only general information needs to be maintained by heritage programs. Fortunately, the more common and secure species constitute the majority of most groups of organisms. On the other hand, for those species that are by their nature rare or otherwise threatened—and thus must be protected under the fine filter—more detailed information is needed. Because of these species' very rarity, gathering comprehensive and detailed population data on them is possible, even if difficult. Gathering similarly comprehensive information on more abundant species would pose a far greater challenge.

Table 2.3. Definition of conservation status ranks

GX	Presumed extinct: Not located despite intensive searches
GH	Possibly extinct: Of historical occurrence; missing but still some hope of rediscovery
G1	Critically imperiled: Typically 5 or fewer occurrences or 1,000 or fewer individuals
G2	Imperiled: Typically 6 to 20 occurrences or 1,000 to 3,000 individuals
G3	Vulnerable: Rare; typically 21 to 100 occurrences or 3,000 to 10,000 individuals
G4	Apparently secure: Uncommon but not rare; some cause for long-term concern; usually more than 100 occurrences and 10,000 individuals
G5	Secure: Common; widespread and abundant

The definitions provided here are for general guidance only; other assessment criteria (table 4.1) are used in addition to these occurrence and abundance guidelines. This table lists basic conservation status ranks only. Modifiers used to denote uncertainty in assessments are listed in table 4.3.

The conservation status of species is assessed on the basis of various factors reflecting their extinction potential, particularly their levels of rarity, decline, and threat. This assessment and ranking process is discussed in greater detail in chapter 4. Using these rankings, a state heritage program can keep track of the entire suite of species within its jurisdiction—the rare and the common—but target intensive information-gathering and inventory efforts toward those highly ranked species that require concerted conservation attention. To complement this fine-filter species-level information, heritage programs simultaneously have worked to develop tools for applying the ecological coarse filter. This approach has focused on defining and identifying the particular ecological communities occurring within their states and, in turn, assessing the extent and status of each. The process for assessing and ranking the status of ecological communities is described in detail in chapter 7.

In gathering information, heritage procedures again emphasize efficiencies. Before any new field inventories are carried out in search of a particular target species or ecological community, all available knowledge about that element is gathered, organized, and mapped. This process relies on many different secondary sources of information, including museum collections, primary scientific literature, "gray literature," and interviews with knowledgeable biologists. In many instances, simply compiling what is already known about a species is enough to demonstrate that it is more common than previously thought and is not in immediate need of either additional inventory work or specific protection measures. When this is not the case, though, the process of exhaustively compiling existing data helps define where and when heritage biologists and their collaborators should carry out fieldwork to seek out new populations or to revisit existing populations and assess their current condition.

The swamp pink (*Helonias bullata*) depends on pristine eastern U.S. wetlands for its survival. Because only about 100 populations remain, the heritage network regards the species as vulnerable (G3). © Jeff Lepore/Photo Researchers.

HOW IS IT ORGANIZED? A distinguishing feature of the heritage effort is its close attention to the details of organizing and managing the voluminous data being gathered. From the beginning the heritage enterprise has constituted an ongoing and dynamic inventory process, not merely a time-limited project. In this regard, the emphasis is on continuity of purpose and on long-term accumulation of knowledge in the service of conservation. The heritage enterprise has also been one of the pioneers in the use of computer technologies to organize and manage biological inventory data (Morse 1993, Stein 1997). Software tools developed for use by the network codify the standards and protocols by which the network operates and have promoted the consistent application of these methods. The use of consistent information management tools has greatly facilitated the ability to compare and aggregate data across states, as has been done in the production of this volume.

The network is currently using the sixth generation of heritage computer software, known as the Biological and Conservation Data System (BCD). At its highest level the system maps out to the major types of information identified in table 2.2. Within each of these general information categories, however, may be one or more subsidiary data files covering particular information themes related to that subject. For instance, the "element" file tracks data about the identity, status, and general characteristics of particular elements of biodiversity (that is, species or ecological communities). One particular data file, the element tracking file, covers basic species or ecological community identifier information—scientific and common name, taxonomic comments, rangewide conservation status, and any legal protection status (e.g., U.S. Endangered Species Act status). Subsidiary to this file is a data file called an element ranking file, which documents the assessment of conservation status for the particular species or community. Other subsidiary files summarize general information on distribution, ecology, and life history (element characterization abstracts) and management and research needs (element stewardship abstracts).

Given the focus of heritage programs on documenting patterns of biodiversity, mapping the distribution of species, ecological communities, and land units is central to their work. A variety of mapping tools and techniques are employed to record spatial features with accuracy and precision. Undoubtedly the most important geographic feature that heritage programs map is the *element occurrence* (EO). An element occurrence depicts the geographic location for a species population or ecological community. These occurrences constitute the principal source of detailed information about the distribution of rare or imperiled species and ecological communities and are the most widely used type of information gathered and managed by heritage programs. (A detailed definition and discussion of element occurrences can be found later in this section.)

Traditionally, heritage programs mapped these occurrences on standard 7.5 minute U.S. Geological Survey topographic map sheets, a time-consuming and laborious process. With the development of powerful and relatively inexpensive geographic information systems (GIS), this spatial occurrence data is now largely managed electronically. Collectively, the heritage network manages data on nearly half a million element occurrences, virtually all of which map the location of species or ecological communities that are of conservation concern on either the global, national, or state level.

Figure 2.3a–c. Mapping the running buffalo clover.

Heritage programs map species at a variety of scales, as illustrated by these different views of running buffalo clover (bottom left, © Mark Evans/KYNHP). (a) State-level distribution and conservation status provide the coarsest level of mapping. (b) The element occurrence (EO) represents the principal and most detailed type of geographic information documented by heritage programs. Element occurrences ideally correspond to species populations, and the precisely located subpopulations shown here together comprise a single occurrence. (c) Heritage biologists also evaluate the condition or viability of the populations, reflected here in the EO ranks for all occurrences, past and present, known from West Virginia. Sources: (a) Natural Heritage Central Database; (b) and (c) West Virginia Natural Heritage Program.

a.

State Conservation Status
- ⬛ Extirpated
- ▨ Critically Imperiled
- ⬜ Imperiled

b.

c.

Condition of Population

○ Excellent	∘ Poor
○ Good	▲ Historical
∘ Marginal	× Extirpated

Managing both textual and geographic information electronically allows the heritage databases to be queried in the two major ways users wish to access the data: by elements or by place. Questions about a particular element—whether a single species, a higher taxonomic group (birds, for instance), or an ecological community—can be easily processed, as can queries that relate to a specific place (a state, county, watershed, or back-yard). Examining the distribution of species and ecosystems across the landscape is especially useful for conservation planning purposes. Meanwhile, the ability to pinpoint sensitive features at or near a particular site is of considerable utility for development planning and environmental review.

The heritage network is designed to function in a decentralized fashion, with local programs responsible for—or, in current terminology, custodians of—their own data holdings. Information about such things as basic species taxonomy, life history characteristics, and rangewide distribution are needed across the network, however, and it would be inefficient for each program to develop and manage such information independently. Further, global or rangewide assessments of species status frequently transcend the bounds of single states, and it is necessary to manage this information cen-

Table 2.4. Database summary for running buffalo clover

Scientific name:	*Trifolium stoloniferum*
Common name:	Running buffalo clover
Conservation status:	G3 (vulnerable)
Legal status:	Federally listed as endangered
Description:	A three-leaved, white-flowered clover similar in appearance to the familiar Dutch clover of suburban lawns. Blooms from mid-May through early June.
Distribution and abundance:	Formerly found from West Virginia to Kansas, the species currently is extant in limited portions of Indiana, Kentucky, Ohio, Missouri, and West Virginia. Approximately 100 occurrences are known, most of which are found in West Virginia.
Habitat:	The species most commonly grows in moist woodlands underlain by limestone or other calcareous bedrock, especially where there is a pattern of moderate periodic disturbance, such as mowing, trampling, or grazing.
Trends:	Running buffalo clover was reportedly frequent in pioneer days, benefiting from the disturbance caused by grazing bison. The species was regarded as possibly extinct until its 1983 rediscovery in West Virginia. Inventories since then have located many additional populations. Limited trend data indicate that the number of individual plants in a given population may fluctuate widely over time.
Threats:	Habitat alteration and destruction, the closing of forest canopies through succession, loss of large mammal dispersal agents, overgrazing, fungal diseases, competition from non-native invasive plant species, and alterations to the frequency and extent of disturbances.
Research and Management:	Continue inventory for additional occurrences and track threats to and dynamics of known populations. Potential management tools include maintenance of partially open canopies, use of appropriate mowing regimes to enhance flower and seed production but reduce competition, and use of light grazing and/or fire to mimic presettlement conditions.

Running buffalo clover illustrates the heritage network's management of both textual and geographic data. The above information summarizes more than 17 pages of textual data from the Natural Heritage Central Database on the distribution, status, and needs of this species. Figure 2.3 displays for this species the principal types of spatial data managed by heritage programs.

trally. The Natural Heritage Central Databases provide this hub function for the network, maintaining global- and national-level information that pertains broadly to species and ecological communities. Through a data exchange process, state programs periodically provide summaries of state-level information (for instance, state conservation status) to the central databases and receive the most current global-level information for species and communities in their jurisdiction.

The Natural Heritage Central Databases contain among the most comprehensive overviews of the distribution and status of biodiversity in the United States, and much of this book is based on information derived from these central databases. These databases contain information from and reflect the work of literally thousands of people: state heritage biologists, Conservancy staff, and independent contractors, as well as data contributors from natural history museums, botanical gardens, universities, and federal and state agencies. These central databases currently contain information on more than 50,000 plants, animals, and ecological communities.

The combination of detailed information on species and ecosystems, developed by state heritage programs, and the generalized information managed in these central databases combines in a powerful way to provide an overall perspective on the status and distribution of U.S. biodiversity. Just as the natural world is wonderfully complex, so too are the data that represent that world. Understanding this information—its sources, its strengths, and its limitations—is key to appreciating what we know about the condition of biodiversity and, just as important, what we have left to learn.

Taking the Measure of Species

While the concept of biodiversity encompasses multiple levels of biological organization, species clearly are the most widely appreciated expression of this concept. They represent the principal products of the evolutionary process, as well as the entities that vanish through the reciprocal process of extinction. Species also constitute the basic building blocks of ecosystems. Thus, even if we wish to focus attention on the conservation of higher levels of biodiversity—that is, ecological communities or ecosystems—we are inevitably drawn to a consideration of their constituent species. For these and many other reasons, the survey, classification, and inventory of species have been a central focus of the scientific and conservation communities.

Making sense of the bewildering array of life-forms is the central challenge taken on by the branch of science known as systematics. Elucidating the what and where of species is the core work of taxonomists and is an indispensable service to the rest of biology and conservation. For only through identifying and characterizing species and assigning the scientific names that become our biological lingua franca can we make sense out of the patterns of biodiversity that play out across the landscape.

The desire and need to classify and name life-forms is fundamental to the human experience and goes far beyond the Western scientific tradition. Well-developed folk taxonomies have been developed and used by native peoples around the globe, while formal classification of plants and animals dates, in the Western tradition, to at least the time of Aristotle. The age of exploration, when the American continent was first encountered by Europeans, gave a huge impetus to the endeavor by opening up vast new realms harboring strange and wondrous creatures. As accounts of these plants and animals began filtering back to the centers of learning in Europe, a small number of naturalists struggled to make sense out of this newfound diversity.

Without doubt, the most famous early taxonomist was Carolus Linnaeus, the Swedish scholar who introduced a concise form for naming plants and animals. Rather than referring to each species through a sentence-long description, the prevailing practice, Linnaeus introduced the now familiar concept of the binomial name consisting of genus and species. The first part of the name—the genus—groups an organism together with others based on shared traits, while the second part denotes the species' uniqueness from all others. Linnaeus's desire to catalogue the entire world's flora led him to send young students, whom he referred to as his apostles, to far-flung corners of the globe to retrieve specimens that could be examined and classified. Sadly, several of these students never returned, succumbing to illness and other misfortunes. Others spent years laboring in distant fields only to have their precious collections lost at sea.

One of Linnaeus's more fortunate disciples, a fellow Swede by the name of Peter Kalm, was dispatched to North America in 1748. Kalm's travels in New Jersey, in Pennsylvania, and throughout New York on the way to Canada allowed him to collect a large quantity of plants, many of which were unknown in Europe at the time. During his sojourn he sought out John Bartram in Philadelphia, relying on the American botanist for a great deal of advice and information. Kalm's return to Sweden in 1750 laden with so many novel specimens from North America also seems to have stimulated Linnaeus to finally publish his revolutionary work *Species Plantarum*, which marks the beginning of the modern taxonomic period (Reveal and Pringle 1993).

Just as Linnaeus relied on specimens made by Kalm, Bartram, and others, modern taxonomists continue to rely on reference collections. Indeed, such collections form the basis for much of our knowledge about the composition and distribution of the world's flora and fauna. Voucher specimens provide the physical verification that a species occurred in a particular location at a particular time. Specimens also serve an important nomenclatural function. Each scientific name is related to an individual specimen, known as the type. The type specimen becomes the name's physical manifestation and allows an objective comparison for determining the appropriate application of that scientific name.

Duckworth et al. (1993) estimate that the world's reference collections house about 2.5 billion specimens. Hawksworth (1995) lists a total of 2,946 plant and fungal reference collections worldwide; the 645 located in the United States together house more than 61 million specimens. He also counts 1,048 zoological reference collections worldwide, including 183 in the United States. While many museum techniques and traditions hark back to earlier centuries, contemporary natural history museums and collections are proving themselves to also be relevant to twenty-first-century needs and concerns. Cutting-edge techniques for DNA analysis of reference materials are enabling researchers to use collections

Carolus Linnaeus 15 years before publishing the landmark book that marks the beginning of the modern taxonomic period. Pictured in full Lapland garb, Linnaeus is holding a specimen of twinflower (*Linnaea borealis*), the plant that bears his name. © Courtesy of Hunt Institute, Carnegie Mellon University, Pittsburgh.

Peter Kalm, one of Linnaeus's disciples, journeyed to North America in 1748 and took back to Europe many new plants. *Kalmia*, the genus for mountain laurel, was named in his honor. © Courtesy of Hunt Institute, Carnegie Mellon University, Pittsburgh.

Natural history collections are indispensable to biodiversity inventories, revealing much about past and present distributions of species. Worldwide, collections like these at the Smithsonian Institution house some 2.5 billion specimens.
© Chip Clark/National Museum of Natural History.

to quickly expand our understanding of our natural world. The field of bioprospecting for useful pharmaceutical and other compounds (Reid et al. 1993) is also placing the museum community at the forefront of this promising area of biodiversity exploration and use. Rapid advances in computer technology are transforming museums as well, allowing them to expand beyond their physical walls by providing their catalogues and other resources on-line. Modern database management systems make it feasible to create master catalogues of taxonomic groups to organize and reconcile changing names and conflicting treatments of species (and other taxa). Such catalogues and the specimens behind them serve as basic references for biodiversity surveys (Thompson 1997).

Existing specimen collections are an indispensable component of biodiversity inventories, but they also have limitations when applied to conservation assessments. Specimens may be incorrectly labeled, either because of changing taxonomy or due to misidentification. And while older records can provide a valuable historical perspective, their geographic locations may be recorded in vague or imprecise terms. These specimen localities often require considerable effort to interpret for incorporation into conservation databases. Despite these limitations, however, specimen collections can tell us a great deal about past distributions of species and their habitats, provide evidence for species declines, and provide an essential starting point for guiding new survey efforts (Shaffer et al. 1998).

Mapping and Monitoring Species

Effective conservation requires that we know what resources exist, where they are found, and in what condition. The identity and geographical distribution of species becomes among the most important information needed for preservation efforts to succeed (Stork and Samways 1995). Ultimately, information about species derives from very local and fine-grained sampling of individuals and populations. This local sampling can then be extrapolated, or interpolated to map a species' overall distribution. This mapping can be carried out on various geographic scales, depending upon the need, from local to regional to global.

On the broadest scales, species range maps and overall distributions are used to help design field surveys, to support systematics and biogeographic studies, to study the invasion of alien species, to evaluate potential impacts of global climate change, and to site representative conservation reserve systems. Distribution mapping on the regional scale is used for these and other purposes, such as environmental impact assessment and, more recently, to devise conservation strategies for multiple, fragmented populations (Hanski and Gyllenberg 1997). On the most local scale, detailed maps of individuals and populations are important tools for ecological research, reserve design, and environmental impact assessment and mitigation or restoration, especially for rare and localized species.

Biogeographers traditionally have constructed species range maps from a set of known locations either by using a grid system or political units, such as countries or states, or by drawing a range boundary around the set of points where the species has been collected or observed (Miller 1994). The consistent cell shape and area of some grid-based mapping has special advantages for quantitative analysis and modeling of patterns of diversity. For example, the U.S. Environmental Protection Agency has designed a hexagonal grid system that provides a particularly efficient shape for covering the earth's surface (White et al. 1992). These units are of equal size regardless of their geographic coordinates. For the United States, hexagons covering roughly 160,000 acres are of a particularly useful size and shape for statistical analysis, and they form the basis for several of our analyses in chapter 6. Recent regional to national analyses of species occurrence maps have used landscapes (Caicco et al. 1995), watersheds (Davis et al. 1996), counties (Dobson et al. 1997), and hexagons (Kiester et al. 1996), to name just a few examples, many of which will be illustrated in subsequent chapters.

For most groups and for many regions of the world, survey data are not adequate to generate reliable or suitably precise species range maps. One alternative is to predict the distribution of the species based on mapped habitat variables that are thought to limit distribution on the biogeographic scale, notably climate. In this "bioclimatic modeling" approach (Lindenmayer et al. 1991, Chapman and Busby 1994), rules or statistical models are constructed based on climatic conditions where the species is known to occur, and grids of climate variables are used to extrapolate the range of the species. Such modeling, which has a long tradition in agriculture, horticulture, and forestry, has obvious potential applications in predicting not only a species' present distribution but also its possible future distributions under different global warming scenarios (e.g., Sykes et al. 1996).

Regional distribution mapping is now widely performed by applying statistical or rule-based models of species habitat preferences to digital maps of the relevant habitat factors. In the United States, the U.S. Geological Survey's Gap Analysis Program is using such a rule-based approach to predict regional distributions of relatively widespread terrestrial vertebrates by mapping suitable habitats (usually defined by general vegetation types and hydrologic features) within the known range limits of the species. The recently published *Atlas of Oregon Wildlife* (Csuti et al. 1997a) serves as a good example of the products that derive from this approach.

Yet despite the advances in modeling techniques and mapping technologies, we have the barest distribution information for most species. As the example of the orange-throated whiptail lizard shows, data are often sparse even for well-studied organisms in densely populated areas.

Beyond knowing a species' distribution, information about trends in population abundance and distribution is key to effective conservation and management. Without such trend information, it is difficult to accurately determine species' status, the causes of population fluctuations, or the effects of management activities. Nonetheless, long-term monitoring information exists for only a handful of species, attesting to the difficulty and expense of monitoring biological populations. Whatever the technique—clipping, netting, digging, sieving, sorting, coring, spotting, trapping—population monitoring is generally tedious and labor-intensive work. There are few dependable shortcuts: Each species manifests unique behavior and patterns of distribution and abundance, and survey design and sampling methods must be tailored accordingly (Sutherland 1996).

Most detailed monitoring information focuses on game species, pest species, and a few threatened and endangered species (see, for instance, LaRoe et al. 1995). Birds represent one of the few exceptions to the general dearth of trend information. Because of the great popularity of birds among professionals and amateurs alike, many relatively long-standing surveys exist for this group of animals. As a result, bird species have received considerable, and perhaps inordinate, attention as indicators of biodiversity status and trends. Examples of major programs in the United States include the Migratory Waterfowl Program, the Christmas Bird Count, and the Breeding Bird Survey. To take just one example, the Breeding Bird Survey was initiated in 1966 and has been administered by the U.S. Department of Interior's Patuxent Wildlife Research Center. The survey is conducted annually by volunteers, who record occurrence and relative abundance of all bird species at nearly 3,000 sampling routes across the United States and southern Canada.

Mapping Species Heritage-Style

A primary function of heritage programs is to fill the information void for those species that are of greatest significance from a conservation perspective. As discussed earlier, rare species are in need of specific inventory and targeting for two reasons. First, by their very nature they are not uniformly distributed across the landscape but instead tend to be quite localized. Second, their rarity confers an inherently greater risk of extinction, and consequently they become of particular interest to those devoted to "saving all the pieces."

The goal of documenting and mapping rare or otherwise at-risk species also has a practical implication. To be useful for on-the-ground conservation and environmental planning, such species must be mapped at a very precise level of detail. If the alignment of a road is at stake, a builder's permit is in jeopardy, or the boundaries of a nature preserve are being designed, one must be able to identify exactly where the sensitive resources occur. For these types of real-world applications, merely knowing the general vicinity is not enough. For the rarest of the rare, mapping on a fine scale of resolution is essential. It becomes possible to attempt not just a statistical sample of the species, but an actual census—that is, a complete enumeration of the species' populations. Of course, the potential success of such a census depends on several factors, including

Birds are one of the few groups for which good trend information is available, thanks largely to the widespread interest among professional researchers as well as amateurs. © Ben Thomas/TNC.

the life history characteristics of the organism (i.e., whether it is easy or difficult to observe or locate), the availability of knowledgeable biologists who can search for and recognize the organism, and the availability of resources to fund the inventories and process the data.

From both evolutionary and conservation perspectives, the population is clearly the most appropriate species-level unit to map. Unfortunately, populations are notoriously difficult to define and measure. Definitions of populations vary, but they tend to focus on the concept of a group of individuals more likely to interact with and breed among each other than with members of other such groups. Populations can be defined technically by using demographic or genetic measures—for instance, degree of genetic differentiation, migration, or gene flow (Nei 1972, Wright 1978). Defining and identifying populations in the field becomes even more complex in light of the very useful concept of metapopulations, discontinuous subpopulations that collectively exhibit certain population-like functions (McCullough 1996).

Detailed knowledge of the genetic and demographic makeup of populations is limited to a few intensively studied species, however, and does not provide a robust means for large-scale inventory and population mapping efforts. There are, however, operational definitions that, while not meeting the exacting standards of population geneticists and demographers, can serve as a useful first approximation for population units. Primary among them are spatial coherence and geographic separation from other such units.

The *element occurrence* (EO) is the mapping unit developed by the heritage network for documenting the distribution of species populations. Formally defined as "an area of land and/or water in which a species or natural community is, or was, present," an element occurrence ideally reflects species population units: either a distinct population, part of a population (subpopulation), or a group of populations (metapopulation) (TNC and ABI 1999). As indicated by use of the more general term *element*, the EO concept was designed to also accommodate other features of conservation interest (that is, elements of diversity), most notably ecological communities. For communities, an occurrence may represent a stand or patch, or a cluster of stands or patches. Above all, however, an element occurrence is designed to have practical value by delineating units useful for conservation action (see figure 2.3).

Applying this concept across a wide array of organisms and ecological types raises issues of consistency. An appropriate area measure for a highly mobile bird species may be quite different from that needed for a firmly rooted tree species. For this reason, element-specific definitions are essential for determining what constitutes a valid "occurrence" and is therefore appropriate to map. These definitions are embodied in *element occurrence specifications*, which are developed on a species-by-species and community-by-community basis and become part of the permanent heritage computer registry for any given species or community.

Specifications for a particular organism might include the minimum required size of population or habitat area needed to sustain or contribute to that species' survival. To help differentiate between and delineate distinct occurrences, total barriers to dispersal as well as distances sufficient to impede population movements are factored into these specifications. To a bog turtle (*Clemmys muhlenbergii*), for example, a four-lane divided highway may represent a complete barrier to movement, while dams exceeding 20 feet in height may similarly restrict the movement of salmon. Appropriate separation distances may depend on a variety of factors, such as the species' dispersal ability, home range size, and spatial and temporal patterns, but as a general guideline, one kilometer is the minimum recommended separation distance for defining two distinct occurrences.

Finally, from a conservation perspective, merely identifying and delineating a population, as difficult as that is, is only part of the story. Ideally we would also like to know about its condition. Is the population healthy and viable, or a rapidly deteriorating remnant with little hope for survival? Viability information is becoming increasingly important as conservation planning efforts become more sophisticated (e.g., Pressey et al. 1996, TNC 1996). For this reason, the quality or viability of each occurrence is assessed, albeit somewhat subjectively, in the form of an *element occurrence rank* (EO rank). In general, EO ranks are designed to represent the relative conservation value of an occurrence and are assigned on the basis of the population's size, condition, and landscape context (table 2.5).

All of the above depends on solid documentation about each particular occurrence. A computerized *element occurrence record* (EOR) stores information about any particular occurrence; it contains a number of data fields that address the population's location, extent or abundance, condition, management, ownership, and documentation sources. Documenting and crediting the source of this data is of the utmost importance. Information sources range from museum voucher specimens, photographs, and satellite or aerial imagery to field surveys and observations made by knowledgeable observers. Because some sources are more authoritative than others, documenting where the information came from and estimating the mapping precision are essential so that the information's validity and reliability can be reviewed and assessed at any time.

Because element occurrences reflect populations, these databases are not synonymous with computerized specimen records. The process of defining occurrences typically involves geo-referencing and synthesis of various information sources. Multiple voucher specimens, even those collected at different places or times, may relate only to a single species population. These specimens would therefore be treated as documenting a single occurrence and therefore as a single computer record, rather than multiple occurrences. Similarly, relevant information is also available from other primary data sources, particularly field surveys conducted as part of ecological evaluations, behavioral studies, or population dynamics investigations. This is particularly true for certain animal groups, such as birds or mammals, where for various legal, scientific, and conserva-

Table 2.5. Factors used in assessing condition of occurrences

Factor	Component	Species	Communities
Size	Area of occupancy	✓	✓
	Population abundance	✓	
	Population density	✓	
	Population fluctuation (average population and minimum population in worst foreseeable year)	✓	
Condition	Reproduction and health (evidence of regular, successful reproduction; age distribution for long-lived species; persistence of clones; vigor, evidence of disease affecting reproduction/survival)	✓	
	Development/maturity (stability, old growth)		✓
	Species composition and biological structure (richness, evenness of species distribution, presence of exotics)	✓	✓
	Ecological processes (degree of disturbance by logging, grazing; changes in hydrology or natural fire regime)	✓	✓
	Abiotic physical/chemical factors (stability of substrate, physical structure, water quality)	✓	✓
Landscape context	Landscape structure and extent (pattern, connectivity, e.g., measure of fragmentation/patchiness, measure of genetic connectivity)	✓	✓
	Condition of the surrounding landscape (i.e., development/maturity, species composition and biological structure, ecological processes, abiotic physical/chemical factors)	✓	✓

These factors are used to assess the viability of element occurrences for species and natural community. *EO ranks* are assigned to individual occurrences based on these factors, ranging from A (excellent quality) to D (poor quality). EO ranks can also indicate historical occurrences (H) or occurrences known to be extirpated (X) see figure 2.3c.

tion reasons, collecting specimens is no longer the primary method for recording presence. Nonetheless, specimens form an indispensable resource for documenting occurrences; and for many species, reference collections may constitute the entirety of our knowledge. Compiling data from existing collections, however, represents a starting point for heritage inventories, not their culmination (Stein 1993).

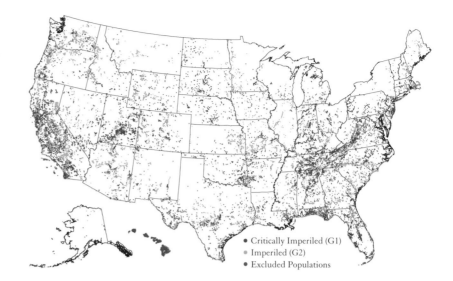

This map reflects known occurrences for critically imperiled and imperiled species, together representing 39,521 occurrences of 2,758 species. Occurrences indicated in blue do not meet key criteria and are excluded from later analyses. Note: Absence of data in any geographic area does not necessarily mean that no imperiled species are present. Data source: State Natural Heritage Data Centers 1996.

● Critically Imperiled (G1)
● Imperiled (G2)
● Excluded Populations

The Fourche Mountain salamander (*Plethodon fourchensis*) is known from only about 10 occurrences in Arkansas. Regarded as imperiled, this animal exemplifies the "rarest of the rare" that are mapped above. © Greg Sievert.

A National Perspective

For the first time, we now are in a position to create a national perspective on the distribution of the nation's rarest species by aggregating the detailed population mapping efforts of the state natural heritage programs. This national-level view represents the most comprehensive effort to date to depict the locations of endangered and imperiled species across the country. Patterns clearly begin to emerge from these maps even in their raw form, highlighting certain regions of the country that have exceptional levels of biodiversity. This basic distributional data set forms the foundation for several key analyses presented later in this volume, analyses that probe questions related to the locations of imperiled species hot spots, the design of national reserve portfolios, and the adequacy of current protection efforts (see chapters 6 and 10). Because these maps are so central to subsequent analyses, the composition of their underlying data sets is important to understand, as are their strengths and constraints.

As part of this effort, we assembled two distinct national occurrence data sets. The first focuses on the distribution of imperiled species—those ranked by the heritage network as G1 (critically imperiled) or G2 (imperiled) (figure 2.4). The second data set considers those species with formal status under the U.S. Endangered Species Act (threatened, endangered, proposed, and candidates) (figure 2.5). These national element occurrence data sets represent 1996 data provided by all U.S. state natural heritage programs as well as the Tennessee Valley Authority, Navajo Nation, and District of Columbia natural heritage programs. To create a comparable and consistent view of imperiled species across the country, this effort compiled information only on the nation's rarest species (G1 and G2), the species about which heritage programs have the most comprehensive and accurate information. Many heritage programs maintain considerable data on vulnerable species (G3), but detailed population-level data for these species is not uniformly available state to state. While important to consider for conservation purposes,

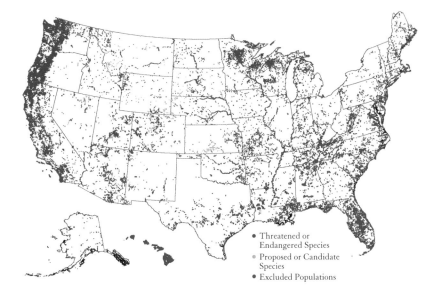

Figure 2.5. Distribution of federally
listed endangered species.

*This map reflects known occurrences of
species with formal status under the U.S.
Endangered Species Act, including 47,163
occurrences for 1,184 species and subspecies. Occurrences indicated in blue do not
meet key criteria and are excluded from
later analyses. Note: Absence of data in
any geographic area does not necessarily
mean that no endangered species are
present. Data source: State Natural
Heritage Data Centers 1996.*

- Threatened or
  Endangered Species
- Proposed or Candidate
  Species
- Excluded Populations

inclusion of these species would have introduced significant geographic
biases into the data set.

Given the considerable interest in legally protected species, we also
compiled population occurrence data for all species with legal status under
the federal Endangered Species Act, including the categories "endangered," "threatened," "proposed," and "candidate." These species also
tend to be well documented in state heritage databases.

Our particular interest is in the conservation implications of these data
sets. For this reason, these data sets were designed to portray the current,
rather than historical, distribution of U.S. species, since that is the raw
material with which contemporary conservationists have to work. To
create a data set emphasizing current, extant populations, we carried out
a careful review and screening of the more than 175,000 data records received from state natural heritage programs. This quality control and
assurance process filtered the data against several key criteria, including
taxonomic consistency, geographic precision, population persistence, and
data currency.

Taxonomic consistency. To create a nationally consistent imperiled species
data set (G1 and G2), we included full species that reflect the standard
taxonomic sources used in the Natural Heritage Central Databases. Infraspecific taxa—subspecies and varieties—were included only when
these were a part of imperiled full species. Because there is great variation in the degree to which heritage programs have inventoried subspecies and varieties, for purposes of consistency we did not include imperiled infraspecific taxa (T1 or T2) that are part of nonimperiled full
species (G3 to G5).

For the data set of federally listed species we applied a different decision rule regarding taxonomic inclusion. Under the Endangered Species
Act, full species, subspecies, varieties, and distinct population segments
can qualify for listing and, therefore, protection. To reflect the location

The above map of federally listed species
includes such animals as the Delmarva
fox squirrel (*Sciurus niger cinereus*), a
subspecies restricted to the eastern shore
of the Chesapeake Bay and considered
vulnerable by the heritage network.
Courtesy of W. H. Julian/USFWS.

of all federally protected entities, we included population occurrences for anything with status under the ESA, regardless of taxonomic level. In the case of those species where only a portion of their range is federally listed, such as grizzly bear and salmon, we included only those occurrences protected under the federal statute.

Geographic precision. The locational records for imperiled species were compiled as point locations of the centroid of each occurrence. The point data can then be used to determine the presence of the species in various geographic units, such as counties or watersheds. Such an approach partially overcomes the effects of uneven sampling, since a reasonably large sample unit can be populated for simple presence/absence with even limited inventory data. These types of spatially explicit analyses require that the underlying geographic data be sufficiently precise. We therefore included only those population occurrences that can be mapped at a precision level of one second or one minute longitude/latitude.

Population persistence. Because our goal was to map the location of extant populations, we also excluded any occurrences known or suspected to have been lost. These determinations were based on element occurrence ranks, which, as discussed above, assess population quality and viability. We excluded populations with occurrence ranks of "H" (historical and possibly extirpated) or "X" (known extirpated).

Data currency. To reflect current rather than historical distributions, we included only those populations that have been field-verified during the past quarter century. We excluded from the final data set any records based solely on observations made prior to 1970.

Applying these rigorous quality control and assurance measures to the data we compiled from the state heritage programs reduced the overall number of occurrences available for analysis but increased confidence in the resulting maps and analyses. For the map of imperiled species, the final quality-controlled data set contains 39,521 population occurrences, representing 2,758 species (1,431 critically imperiled species and 1,251 imperiled species). The final data set and map of federally listed species includes 47,163 occurrences for 1,184 species, subspecies, and populations.

These data form a key analytical tool used in this volume. While we believe they represent the best and most comprehensive information available about the distribution and status of these species as of the time of their compilation, a number of limitations must be considered in the application and interpretation of these maps and analyses.

Inventory gaps. Scientific knowledge of the biota is spotty, and heritage inventories are no exception, both within individual states and among states. These inventories are based on available information supplemented by targeted fieldwork. In most cases, however, they are not based on a comprehensive or systematic survey in even the best-known states. For this reason, heritage data, like all other biological inventory data, represents an uneven portrayal of the landscape. Some areas are more thoroughly inventoried than others. Additionally, the form in which this data is gathered indicates presence but not absence. For this reason, a blank spot on the map may either reflect the absence of significant biological features or may be the result of a lack of inventory.

By including only imperiled and federally listed species, which are generally among the best known, these inventory biases are at least reduced. For instance, Groves et al. (1995) found that 62% of heritage programs felt they had collected and processed greater than 90% of the available information for major taxonomic groups under consideration, primarily vertebrates and vascular plants.

Some of these inventory biases relate to the willingness of landowners to survey their lands. For example, various state and federal policies encourage the inventory of public lands, which often receive more attention and thorough surveys than private lands even in the same region. We also know that several regions are underrepresented because of either difficulty of access or vastness. Two such states are Alaska and Texas. In Alaska, most land is public, but the enormity of the state dwarfs on-the-ground inventory efforts. In contrast, Texas has both an active research community and a diverse flora and fauna, but most land is in private hands and is thus largely inaccessible for inventory.

Taxonomic gaps. Certain groups of organisms are well known and thoroughly studied across the country, while other taxonomic groups are poorly known or only sporadically inventoried. Vertebrates and vascular plants generally are well covered in most states, but most invertebrate groups and nonvascular plants are not.

Mapping inconsistencies. Although standard inventory and mapping conventions are employed across the network, there are inconsistencies in the way these standards are applied from program to program. This problem is more prevalent among vertebrates, which often have extensive ranges. These inconsistencies tend not to influence overall distributional patterns but can affect the total number of occurrences identified for a given species.

Data backlogs. Nearly all heritage programs have data entry backlogs, so some documented occurrences may not have been included in this data compilation.

Survey frequency. In screening this data set, we decided to exclude any occurrences not documented or reverified since 1970. Although this was done to place the emphasis on current rather than historical populations, some extant populations, and indeed entire species, undoubtedly dropped out of the data set based on this filter. Areas that have seen little inventory activity during the past quarter century but also have experienced little environmental change may be underrepresented for this reason.

Advancing Our Knowledge

Like other scientific endeavors, heritage inventories build on the efforts of many different scientists and naturalists. And while a major goal of the effort is to organize and make available existing knowledge about the status and distribution of the nation's biodiversity, heritage biologists are also committed to advancing the state of that knowledge. Through focused inventory efforts, heritage programs have in fact been quite successful at filling in details in our picture of life in America. Most of this work has involved field efforts designed to improve our understanding of the nation's rarest species: locating new populations of many species, characterizing the current condition of others, and documenting the decline or extirpation of still others. Some of the most important and tangible contributions, though, have been the many new discoveries made during the quarter century of heritage inventories. These finds include species new to science, plants or animals newly documented in a particular state, and the rediscovery of species thought to have been extinct or extirpated (Snyder 1993).

To explore the degree to which heritage programs have contributed to advancing our basic knowledge of the U.S. biota, we surveyed all state programs in 1997 to estimate the number of novel finds made directly or largely as a result of heritage activities. Forty-two states provided data, covering roughly a 10-year period.

Surveys conducted by or for heritage programs were responsible for the discovery of 43 species new to science. Florida, with 17 new taxa, and North Carolina, with 9, led the way in this category. Heritage biologists also documented more than 550 new state records over this same period: North Carolina compiled the most (77), followed by Arkansas (53) and New Jersey (52). Even more impressive are the numbers for species that were once known within a state but that were thought to have disappeared from within its boundaries (conservation status SX or SH). Heritage programs found almost 730 such plants and animals to still exist in various states; 108 of these species were relocated in the state of New Jersey alone. And finally, at least 24 species that were considered possibly or presumed globally extinct (GX or GH) have been rediscovered as part of heritage inventories.

An Ecological Approach to Surveys

While species are a major focus of conservation efforts, and thus of many biological inventory efforts, individual species exist only within an ecological context. Each plant or animal depends for its survival on complex interactions, both with other species and with the physical environment. These interactions form the backdrop against which natural selection and evolution take place. Changes in these interactions or in the physical processes maintaining a species' habitat—fire regime or flooding frequency, for instance—can cause declines in a particular organism that in turn may provoke cascading effects throughout the system.

Surveys conducted by or for heritage programs have resulted in the discovery of at least 43 U.S. species new to science. The sedge *Carex lutea* was discovered in North Carolina but is most closely related to boreal species found nearly 500 miles to the north. © Bruce A. Sorrie.

Ecological communities and ecosystems also have emergent properties. Communities provide numerous important ecosystem services (Costanza et al. 1997, Daily et al. 1997) and provide a useful framework for systematically characterizing the current condition of ecosystems and landscapes. Communities are more than just the sum of their parts, though, and are therefore suitable targets for conservation in their own right. In areas where species patterns are poorly known, ecological communities become particularly important as conservation targets. Indeed, the coarse filter/fine filter approach to conservation relies on using representative communities as a means of ensuring the protection of most biodiversity.

The use of ecological communities to accomplish conservation goals requires location and condition information about the communities, just as the success of the fine filter depends on accurate information about individual species. Simply understanding which species favor which habitats is not enough. Inventorying and assessing ecological communities, however, depends on a consistent method for recognizing and classifying the enormous variety of ecological types, and herein lies a problem: Approaches to ecological classification are far more variable than the generally agreed-upon methods for species taxonomy and classification.

Introduction of the Linnaean method for naming plants and animals helped spur the classification and inventory of species and ultimately enabled us to plan systematically for their protection. Ecologists, too, have struggled to develop common frameworks for classifying ecosystems. The absence of a universally accepted framework for ecological classification does not reflect a lack of effort. Indeed, humans have been at the task of devising a set of natural regions for the earth since at least the sixth century B.C., when the Greek philosopher Parmenides, a student of Pythagoras, divided the earth into regions called *klima* based largely on latitude.

It was not until the nineteenth century that several major advances were made in efforts to characterize and classify the earth's ecological zones. In 1805 the great German naturalist Alexander von Humboldt used his first-hand observations of Andean plant life as the basis for developing life zone concepts relating the distribution of species to their position along elevational and latitudinal gradients. A few years later a contemporary of Humboldt's, the Swiss botanist Augustin de Candolle, contributed another important insight into what would become the study of biological communities: Organisms are influenced not only by their physical environment but also by each other, through competition for resources. This burgeoning nineteenth-century interest in study of the natural world, and particularly the relationships among organisms, led the German zoologist Ernst Haeckel in 1866 to coin the term *ecology*.

Defining ecological communities, however, depends on having a clear conception of what such communities represent. After more than a century of research and debate among community ecologists, there is still no consensus on this question. To complicate matters further, different traditions for sampling and classifying communities have developed in different regions of Europe and North America (Shimwell 1971). During the early part of the twentieth century, two opposing viewpoints on the nature of plant communities were espoused by prominent American ecologists. Frederick Clements (1916) viewed plant communities as "superorganisms" that functioned and evolved together as holistic units. In the absence of disruptive influences, he regarded these assemblages as progressing toward a self-sustaining climax state controlled by climate and soil conditions. In contrast, the botanist Henry Gleason (1917) emphasized that each species responds individually to environmental conditions and gradients. Rather than evolving as a whole, he argued, plant communities represent sets of individual species that happen to coexist in the same place at the same time due to the fortuitous combination of environmental history and seed dispersal.

Even ecologists of his time viewed Clements's model as heavily teleological, and as additional work was devoted to the study of communities, broader support emerged for Gleason's individualistic view of species distributions and abundances (Barbour 1997). However, research focusing on other ecosystem properties, such as energy and nutrient flows, found that communities do have emergent properties with characteristics that can be defined and measured (Mooney et al. 1995). Whatever the relative merits of the two sides of this debate, useful and meaningful classifications of communities can be and have been developed. The subdivision of diversity into recognizable units is a fundamental and valuable tool whether or not the units have emergent properties, evolutionary characteristics, or discrete and obvious conceptual boundaries.

One approach to ecological classification builds on the realization that ecosystem patterns and processes exist within a hierarchy: Broader-scale abiotic and biotic processes constrain the kinds of patterns and processes that occur on finer scales (Rowe and Sheard 1981). For example, regional climate constrains the range of variation in soil moisture regimes that occur on a local scale as a result of interactions among topography, soil, and vegetation. Similarly, different assemblages of species are manifested on different scales of environmental control. Because species are adapted to a limited set of physical and biological conditions, the biophysical environment is likened to a set of nested filters through which species occurring in a region must pass to persist at a local site (Poff 1997). On coarse scales, regional species pools may reflect controls of regional climate and recent climatic, geologic, and evolutionary history. Within a landscape, species assemblages may be controlled by geomorphic and hydrologic processes and disturbance regime. On the finest scales, species abundance in local communities may be strongly governed by chance and competition.

Because of the difficulty in defining what precisely an ecological community is, it should not be surprising that a wide variety of ecological classification systems have been developed, each designed for—and constrained by—a specific purpose. Some consider physical factors, such as climate or soils, while others focus on ecosystem properties, distribution of animal or plant species, or structural features of vegetation. In the United States, classification and mapping efforts have encompassed variously defined entities, including potential natural vegetation types, for-

One early school of ecological thought regarded plant communities as gradually progressing to a stable, mature state, like this old-growth forest in Oregon. © Gary Braasch.

est cover types, wetlands, life zones, biotic communities, and ecoregions. Because no universally applied ecological classification system exists, however, coordinated inventory of ecological systems for use in conservation planning has been limited.

Heritage Approaches to Ecological Inventory

Since its inception, the Natural Heritage Network has recognized natural communities as an important complement to species-level inventory and conservation efforts. Just as heritage programs work to identify which species in their states are of greatest conservation concern and gather detailed information on their distribution and condition, they also work toward identifying, assessing, and inventorying their state's ecological communities.

Traditionally, each state heritage program has developed its own community classification based on the availability of existing local classifications and other information. The relative abundance and condition of these communities are then assessed using the conservation status ranking system discussed earlier (and considered in greater detail in chapter 7). For communities, these rankings tend to focus on the number of occurrences, their acreage, and whether the community type appears to be declining in condition or extent. In contrast to heritage approaches to species inventory, which tend to target the rare or threatened, community inventories focus on identifying and documenting high-quality occurrences of all natural communities, whether rare or common. This is because using communities as a coarse filter for conservation requires knowledge of the most intact and viable examples of even widespread and relatively secure community types. Second, fully functional examples of even widespread communities are becoming increasingly scarce and deserve special attention.

The locations of these communities are typically incorporated into the heritage program databases and mapped on standard U.S. Geological Survey topographic sheets or included in a geographic information system. Mapping these occurrences in a manner comparable to that used for species allows information on ecological communities to be fully integrated into the heritage databases and accessible for use in informing planning decisions and environmental reviews. Based on a combination of field reconnaissance and tools such as aerial photography, many programs gather detailed information to characterize these community occurrences. This may include information on plant species composition and cover; basic environmental variables such as slope, aspect, and elevation; and conservation-relevant characteristics, such as condition, size, landscape context, and the integrity of key ecological processes.

Although the state-level community classifications, rankings, and inventories have proven exceptionally useful for conservation planning and environmental review, differences in classifications from one state to another have impeded comparison of ecological information across state lines. For instance, one distinctive vegetation type is known in Illinois as a "dry-mesic barren," while in Minnesota this same community has been

Ecologists have increasingly recognized the dynamic nature of communities, and especially the importance of periodic disturbances, such as fires and floods, in helping to shape and maintain certain ecosystem types. © Harold E. Malde.

called an "oak woodland-brushland." These differences in nomenclature can obscure the true distribution and conservation status of a community across its entire range. One of the great strengths of the heritage inventory approach is its ability to place local inventory efforts and conservation priorities within a national and global context—something that isn't possible unless consistent units are being assessed. On a regional or national scale, use of multiple classifications may result in unnecessarily redundant protection of some ecological types and inadequate protection of many others.

The problem of inconsistent and incompatible classifications also afflicts many government agencies. Within a single agency, different geographic regions may use different classifications for their ecological inventory and mapping, limiting the ability to look at resources agency-wide. Incompatible classification and mapping approaches used by sister agencies, such as the U.S. Forest Service and the Bureau of Land Management, can also confound efforts to transcend bureaucratic boundaries and work at ecosystem scales. Thus, results of many inventory and monitoring programs, such as those conducted in national forests and parks, state forests and parks, or fish and wildlife refuges, often cannot be integrated.

A Common Currency

In response to this problem, since the early 1980s heritage programs, the Conservancy, and a wide variety of collaborators from government agencies and academia have been working toward developing standardized approaches to ecological classification for use in conservation planning and resource management. This effort developed an overall classification framework to provide the supporting structure for evaluating and linking existing classification efforts. By compiling and evaluating local and state community classifications, teams of ecologists could create "crosswalks" among them to develop regionally consistent classifications. These regional efforts were then integrated into a nationally consistent ecological classification system called the U.S. National Vegetation Classification (Grossman et al. 1998). While the classification framework is now firmly established, the actual catalogue of communities is still being refined (Anderson et al. 1998).

The primary emphasis of the national vegetation classification is to provide a uniform tool for incorporating terrestrial ecological communities into conservation planning by allowing these communities to be identified, assessed, and mapped at a level of detail fine enough to inform on-the-ground decisions. A fuller description of the development of the system can be found in Grossman et al. 1998, but some of the salient points underlying the classification are discussed here.

Vegetation-based. Ecological classifications can be based on animal species assemblages, plant assemblages, or combinations of the two, or on nonbiotic factors such as landform, soils, or climate (Brown et al. 1998).

To support the biodiversity conservation objectives described above, heritage and Conservancy ecologists determined that, at least for terrestrial systems, a classification was needed that emphasizes the biotic component of the landscape. Vegetation generally integrates the ecological processes operating on a site or landscape more measurably than any other factor or set of factors (Mueller-Dombois and Ellenberg 1974, Kimmins 1997). Vegetation is also a critical component of energy flow in ecosystems; it provides habitat for many organisms in an ecological community and often serves as a means of inferring soil and climate patterns. Finally, field-workers must be able to recognize the ecological units on the ground, and vegetation is perhaps the most easily observable and measurable component of ecological systems.

Structure and composition. To address issues of scale and accommodate the variability of inventory data from one part of the country to another, the classification system is a nested hierarchy (table 2.6). This hierarchy melds classification approaches that focus on vegetation structure with those that emphasize species composition. The highest levels of the classification framework focus on *physiognomy*, or features of vegetation structure such as height, spacing, and leaf type. These levels are based on the UNESCO (1973) world physiognomic classification of vegetation but were modified to better address wetland types (Cowardin et al. 1979). The two finest levels in the hierarchy—alliance and association—are based on *floristics*, or species composition. The classification allows the broad-scale geographic application of physiognomic characteristics to be tied to local, site-specific, floristically defined units. In combination, these hierarchical levels can satisfy a broad range of objectives in a single classification system.

Existing vegetation. The classification focuses on existing rather than potential vegetation so that inventory and conservation efforts will relate to current rather than projected conditions. This allows the system to include early successional communities as well as later successional types. Conservation of ecological diversity, processes, and functions requires maintaining a matrix of communities at these differing stages of maturity. Documenting and classifying existing vegetation also makes fewer assumptions about the often poorly understood relationships between ecological processes and vegetation dynamics. Instead, the classification is grounded in what is directly observable and measurable.

Natural vegetation. "Natural" vegetation is broadly defined to include types that occur spontaneously, without regular management, maintenance, or planting, and that generally have a strong component of native species. Although the classification framework was developed in such a way as to accommodate any vegetation types, the heritage network systematically classifies and describes only the more natural types.

The U.S. National Vegetation Classification provides a basis for iden-

Vegetation types can be characterized at different levels of the National Vegetation Classification system. A cottonwood (*Populus deltoides*) community from along New Mexico's Gila River (table 2.6) illustrates the increasingly fine detail represented by each level. © Harold E. Malde.

Table 2.6. Levels of the National Vegetation Classification

Classification level	Basis	Example
Class	Growth form and structure of vegetation	Woodland
Subclass	Growth form characteristics, e.g., leaf phenology	Deciduous woodland
Group	Leaf types, corresponding to climate	Cold-deciduous woodland
Formation	Additional physiognomic and environmental factors, including hydrology	Temporarily flooded cold-deciduous woodland
Alliance	Dominant/diagnostic species of uppermost or dominant stratum	*Populus deltoides* temporarily flooded woodland alliance
Association	Additional dominant/diagnostic species from any strata	*Populus deltoides—(Salix amygdaloides)/Salix exigua* woodland

tifying repeating vegetation types within different landscape or political units. The classification is intended to be useful for identifying specific, ecologically meaningful sites for conservation. The classification framework structure is now in place, and over 4,500 types have been identified at its finest level. Still, further development and refinement are necessary, as discussed in chapter 7. A comparable ecological classification being developed for freshwater aquatic systems focuses on a combination of physical and biotic factors (Lammert et al. 1996).

In addition to the U.S. National Vegetation Classification's use by state heritage programs and The Nature Conservancy, the framework has proven useful to various government efforts. The U.S. Geological Survey's Gap Analysis Program, for example, uses the alliance level of the classification in mapping vegetation at the state level as part of this program's effort to identify ecosystems that are underrepresented in the nation's biodiversity protection portfolio. The National Park Service is also employing the classification in mapping the vegetation of national parks and monuments across the country. Indeed, the classification's applicability for government use is broad enough that the Federal Geographic Data Committee, which oversees the development of policies and standards for producing and sharing geographic data among all federal agencies, adopted a slightly modified version as a federal standard (FGDC 1997). The minor modifications made by this committee were designed to extend the classification to cultivated types of vegetation.

Identification and classification of communities is just the start of the inventory process. The level of inventory and mapping of these communities varies considerably among state heritage programs due to regional differences in the development of the classification, level of financial and human resources available, and the underlying ecological complexity of the landscape. Some states have been able to carry out extensive inventory and mapping of their natural communities, while in other states these efforts are far less well developed. Although more than 30,000 community occurrences from across the country are computerized, these state-to-state differences mean that a comprehensive national occurrence database is not available for rare or imperiled natural communities. Nonetheless, the ecological community information that has been gathered by heritage programs can shed considerable light on national-level patterns of ecological diversity.

A Continuing Voyage of Discovery

The chapters that follow synthesize a large body of knowledge about the status and distribution of plants, animals, and ecosystems that together comprise the natural heritage of the United States. Behind the deceptively simple maps and charts lie many arduous years of fieldwork, laboratory study, and data analysis. The more than 20 years of inventory and information collection on the part of the natural heritage programs stands atop more than two centuries of concerted effort by natural scientists working across the American landscape. These scientists of earlier eras, like John and William Bartram, embarked on the same voyage of discovery that modern biologists continue to this day.

We have highlighted a few of the modern tools and techniques for inventorying species and ecological communities. But these tools still depend for their application on the human resource base: knowledgeable botanists, zoologists, and ecologists who can make sense of the nation's complex natural mosaic. We have also tried to place the Natural Heritage Network, which provides the basis for much of the information in this volume, within a broader context by describing some of the other relatively large biodiversity inventory and monitoring efforts currently under way in the United States. Several features distinguish the heritage network, though, from virtually all other biological surveys: notably, its national yet local scope, breadth of focus, and duration; its reliance on both primary field observations and other sources of field data, such as museum collections and scientific publications; and its wide variety of shared standardized information.

Given the current lack of investment in comprehensive biological surveys and the urgent need to set conservation priorities in this country and throughout the world, conservationists and planners will need to be creative in developing and integrating biological, physical, and socioeconomic data. Only by continuing this process of discovery and intelligently applying the knowledge this voyage yields will we be better able to protect our biological inheritance.

3

A REMARKABLE ARRAY

Species Diversity in the United States

The Carolina hemlock (*Tsuga caroliniana*) survives in just a few rocky streambeds along the lower slopes of the Blue Ridge Mountains. Other species of hemlock abound across the United States, but none bear a close resemblance to this particular tree. The closest relatives of the Carolina hemlock, in fact, survive in only one other forest on Earth, some 7,000 miles away in Hubei province of eastern China. The forests of eastern Asia and eastern North America are so similar that if you were suddenly transported from one to the other, you would be hard-pressed to tell them apart.

In the swift mountain streams rushing past these seemingly displaced hemlocks live a number of small, colorful fish known as darters. Darters are found only in North America and have evolved into a prolific variety of fishes. Up to 175 species inhabit U.S. waters, including the famous snail darter (*Percina tanasi*), which brought endangered species issues to the fore when it held up construction of the Tellico Dam on the Little Tennessee River.

How is it that these two organisms, hemlock and darter, one with its closest relatives on the other side of the globe and the other found nowhere else in the world, came to be living side by side? Just how many plants and animals share the piece of Earth that we know as the United States of America? Why these and not others? These are central questions for understanding the diversity of the nation's living resources.

The United States encompasses an enormous piece of geography. With more than 3.5 million square miles of land and 12,000 miles of coastline, it is the fourth largest country on Earth, surpassed only by Russia, Canada, and China. The nation spans nearly a third of the globe, extending more than 120 degrees of longitude from eastern Maine to the tip of the Aleutian chain, and 50 degrees in latitude from Point Barrow above the Arc-

Bruce A. Stein

Jonathan S. Adams

Lawrence L. Master

Larry E. Morse

Geoffrey A. Hammerson

Clinging to rocky slopes in the southern Appalachians, the Carolina hemlock's closest relative lives some 7,000 miles away in eastern China. © Harold E. Malde.

tic Circle to the southern tip of Hawaii below the tropic of Cancer. This expanse of terrain includes an exceptional variety of topographic features, from Death Valley at 282 feet below sea level to Mt. McKinley at 20,320 feet above sea level. The resulting range of climates has given rise to a wide array of ecosystems, from tundra and subarctic taiga to deserts, prairie, boreal forests, deciduous forests, temperate rain forests, and even tropical rain forests.

This ecological tapestry sustains a remarkable array of species. The coast redwood (*Sequoia sempervirens*) of northern California is the tallest tree in the world, while its relative, the giant sequoia (*Sequoiadendron giganteum*), is among the most massive living things on Earth. These behemoths, found in scattered groves along the western slope of the Sierra Nevada, can reach almost 100 feet around at their base, and individual branches can be of larger diameter than any tree found in the eastern United States. Less impressive, perhaps, but even more massive are certain aspen (*Populus tremuloides*) groves that technically are a single organism. Each trunk is connected by a common root system forming a genetically identical clone. One such grove in Utah covers 107 acres and contains about 47,000 trunks (Grant et al. 1992). Bristlecone pines (*Pinus longaeva*) are the world's oldest living trees, but the far less impressive creosote bush (*Larrea tridentata*) may be even older. Creosote, the quintessential shrub of the southwestern deserts, produces clones that form in the shape of mushroom "fairy rings," moving outward over time as the center shrubs die off. Creosote rings consisting of genetically identical shrubs have been measured at more than 25 feet across, with an estimated age of 11,700 years (Vasek 1980).

Other species are noteworthy for collective rather than individual traits. The Hawaiian honeycreepers are among the finest examples in the world of the evolutionary phenomenon known as adaptive radiation. The approximately 32 honeycreeper species evolved from a single finchlike ancestor to fill a diversity of ecological niches, including those occupied by seed-crushing parrots, insect-probing woodpeckers, and nectar-sipping hummingbirds.

The snail darter, famous for holding up construction of the Tellico Dam, is one of an extremely diverse group of fishes found nowhere else in the world. Illustration by Dolores Roberson.

While the honeycreepers represent some of America's more recently evolved species, the nation is also endowed with species that embody ancient evolutionary lineages, often colorfully if not quite accurately referred to as "living fossils." Among these are the seven U.S. species of sturgeon (*Acipenser* and *Scaphirhynchus*), armor-plated fishes that can reach an impressive 20 feet in length. These primitive creatures are related to fish that first appeared during the Devonian, or Age of Fishes, some 400 million years ago. An even more archaic creature is the horseshoe crab (*Limulus polyphemus*), a familiar yet prehistoric sight along the Atlantic and Gulf Coasts. This animal, which is not a crab at all but is more closely related to spiders and mites, is one of only four living members of a group that dates back to the Cambrian period, half a billion years ago.

Left: Reaching higher than a 35-story building, northern California's coast redwoods are the tallest trees in the world. © Gary Braasch.

Right: Aspen groves may be the most massive living organisms on Earth. In Utah, one grove in which all of the 47,000 trunks are genetically identical covers 107 acres. © Carr Clifton/Minden Pictures.

How Many Species Inhabit the United States?

Behind this deceptively simple question lies a surprisingly complex and inexact answer. As discussed in the previous chapter, the process of biological exploration and discovery is ongoing, and what we do not know still far surpasses what we do know. Our ability to consider this question for the United States is linked with what we know about the number of species worldwide. Yet the gaps in our knowledge are never more apparent than when we attempt to determine the total number of species inhabiting the earth. Estimates of the total number of living species span more than an order of magnitude—from around 3 million to more than 100 million—although a working estimate hovers around 14 million species (Hammond 1995). Of these, only about 1.5 million have received a formal Latin name.

Part of this enormous degree of uncertainty involves the very nature and variety of life itself. Living organisms range in size from giant sequoias and blue whales to microscopic bacteria. While scientists tend not to overlook trees and whales, they require specialized equipment just to observe microbes, let alone characterize and classify these organisms. And taxonomic surprises lurk even among large animals. For instance, the megamouth shark (*Megachasma pelagios*), a gigantic filter feeder inhabiting deep waters off the Hawaiian Islands, was not described scientifically until 1983.

Related in part to the ease or difficulty of observation is the amount of research that has been directed toward the study and classification of various groups of organisms. We know far more about birds than bugs. Research funding also tends to focus on those organisms perceived to be of direct value to humans. Coupled with this factor is the effect of location: Historically, most centers of taxonomic and ecological research have been located in the Northern Hemisphere, and as a result the flora and fauna in temperate zone countries tend to be more thoroughly catalogued than those of tropical nations. The relatively fewer species found in higher-latitude countries, a point to which we will return, accentuates the disparity in biotic knowledge among nations. Finally, the magnitude of the challenge simply dwarfs the number of practicing taxonomists. Thus, our knowledge of the diversity of life on Earth is skewed, first toward more conspicuous "higher" organisms, and second toward the more economically developed countries of the Northern Hemisphere.

Vertebrate animals and vascular plants are probably the best-known groups of organisms worldwide, and species numbers for these groups are fairly reliable. The world's approximately 9,700 bird species and 4,600 mammals are reasonably well known, even though the precise number of species recognized varies, reflecting healthy differences of taxonomic opinion. Other groups of vertebrates—reptiles, amphibians, and fishes—are more poorly known worldwide but are quite well catalogued in many regions, including the United States. The same is true for vascular plants—flowering plants, ferns, and gymnosperms—which include about 250,000 species around the globe. For other organisms, including many groups of invertebrate animals, algae and fungi, and especially the wide array of microorganisms, the full extent of species diversity is very poorly known, and estimates of total species numbers diverge accordingly. Ironically, these are some of the same groups of organisms that comprise much of the suspected diversity of life on Earth (figure 3.1).

Speculation about the total number of species on Earth mostly revolves around several largely uncharted realms of diversity. Measured by the number of formally described species, insects are by far the most diverse group of organisms on Earth. Researchers have long known of the incredible variety of insects, summed up most memorably more than 60 years ago by the great biologist J. B. S. Haldane. The Creator, Haldane noted pithily, "must have an inordinate fondness for beetles." Although most insect species that have been classified and named to date are from temperate zones, tropical habitats undoubtedly harbor far more insect species. Smithsonian entomologist Terry Erwin carried out a series of studies that provide a hint at the overall levels of tropical insect diversity. Employing powerful insecticides to fog individual tropical trees, Erwin and his colleagues studied the beetles that rained down from the tree canopies. Based on extrapolations from the number of different beetles found in particular tree species, Erwin (1991) suggests that as many as 30 million insect species may exist, a number that some researchers even consider too conservative.

Deep-sea environments and the soil horizon are other habitats that may yet harbor huge numbers of undiscovered species, especially microbes. Indeed, microorganisms in general are exceedingly poorly known, and the true dimensions of microbial diversity is difficult to gauge. Scandinavian researchers found at least 4,000 bacteria species in a single soil sample, and bacteria are now also known to exist in rocks up to a mile beneath the surface of the earth.

Beetles, such as this endangered American burying beetle (*Nicrophorus americanus*), display enormous variety and constitute by far the greatest number of described species. © Gary Marrone.

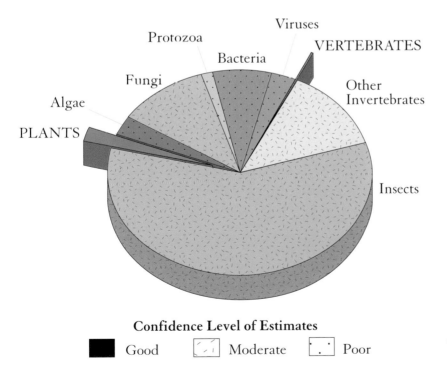

Confidence Level of Estimates
■ Good   Moderate   Poor

Figure 3.1. Estimated number of species in major groups.

Although estimates of the number of species on Earth vary enormously, a United Nations–sponsored assessment put the figure at about 14 million. Vertebrates and plants are the only groups for which scientists are reasonably confident of these estimates. Insects, however, represent by far the largest group. Source: Hammond 1995.

Potentially vast numbers of microbes complicate assessments of the globe's total species diversity. Nematodes, such as this *Pristionchus pacificus*, are perhaps the most abundant organisms on Earth. Image by Jürgen Berger and Ralf Sommer/Max Planck Institute.

Nematodes, or roundworms, are perhaps the most abundant organisms on Earth, living in ocean sediments, in freshwaters, and even in the film of water clinging to soil particles. Commenting on their ubiquitous nature, the early-twentieth-century zoologist N. A. Cobb noted that "if all matter in the universe except nematodes were swept away . . . we should find [the earth's] mountains, hills, vales, rivers, lakes and oceans represented by a thin film of nematodes." Roundworms exist not only as free-living organisms but also as parasites, illustrating another uncharted realm of diversity: symbiotic and parasitic organisms. Such organisms, which range from beneficial gut bacteria to harmful fungal infections, live only in conjunction with other species and are often highly specific in their choice of hosts. If, as some researchers suggest (May 1994), at least one microbial species is linked to each species of higher plant or animal, the number of unknown species worldwide could be vastly greater than the 14 million estimated by the United Nations Environment Programme (Hammond 1995).

The United States is fortunate that a great many scientists have focused their research on its flora and fauna, with the result that biologically it is among the better-known countries on Earth. The nineteenth century was an especially active time of biological discovery and description for many U.S. species, including most of the nation's 2,500 native vertebrates (figure 3.2). The 1850s in particular stand out as a period during which large numbers of new vertebrates in several groups were being classified and described. This peak in taxonomic activity is largely the result of work carried out or inspired by Spencer Baird, who at the time was assistant secretary of the newly created Smithsonian Institution. This era was one of tremendous discovery, especially in the West, where a number of government-sponsored expeditions were exploring areas such as the Great Salt Basin, the U.S.-Mexico border region, and various potential railroad

The search for a transcontinental railroad route sent several exploring expeditions across the West in the early 1850s, generating a bonanza of natural history specimens. Here a team is surveying the 41st parallel near Utah's Wasatch Mountains. Courtesy of National Archives.

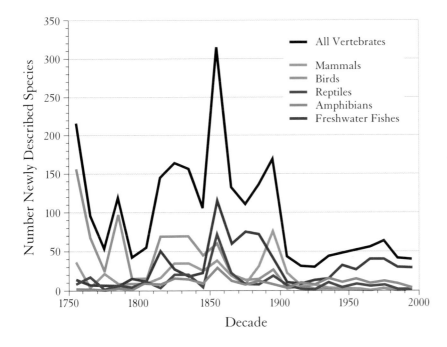

Figure 3.2. New U.S. vertebrate species.

More of the United States' 2,500 vertebrate species were described during the 1850s than any other period, largely as a result of the newly created Smithsonian Institution. New vertebrate species continue to be described, especially among fishes. Source: Natural Heritage Central Databases 1998.

routes to the Pacific Coast. The Civil War had a chilling effect on scientific activity, but descriptions of vertebrates again rose to a peak in the 1890s. This increase reflects the very active work on the nation's fishes by men such as David Starr Jordan of Stanford University, and on mammals by C. Hart Merriam. It also coincides with the 1886 establishment under Merriam's leadership of the Bureau of Biological Survey, a major federal effort charged with investigating "the geographic distribution of animals and plants."

The process of discovery and description of the U.S. flora and fauna is still ongoing, even among such well-known groups as vertebrates and vascular plants. In just the past 25 years, more than 100 species of freshwater fishes have been described, many on the basis of genetic traits revealed only through the use of modern molecular techniques. Similarly, over the last four decades the number of known amphibian and reptile species has increased by about 40%. And researchers studying flowering plants are newly describing, on average, 30 species a year from North America (Hartman and Nelson 1998).

Our tally of formally described organisms reveals that more than 200,000 species are known from the United States (table 3.1). These figures must be viewed as tentative, however, and do not include such microbial groups as bacteria, protists, or viruses. Furthermore, this estimate reflects only formally recognized species that have received a Latin name; it does not attempt to estimate the number of species that may exist but have yet to be discovered and named. Given what we know about the ratio of described species to those still unnamed, total numbers of U.S. species may range from 300,000 to 600,000 (P. Raven pers. comm.).

About 30 new North American plant species are described every year and include some major surprises. The Shasta snow-wreath (*Neviusia cliftonii*), described from California in 1992, is just the second species in a genus previously known only in the Southeast. © Barbara Ertter.

Table 3.1. Number of native species known from the United States

Common name	Phylum	Number of U.S. species	Number worldwide	Source for U.S. figures
Bacteria Kingdom		?	>4,000	
Protoctista Kingdom				
Protists: algae, protozoa, etc.	Protoctista	?	80,000	
Fungi Kingdom				
Nonlichenized fungi		>34,000	56,200	Rossman 1995; Mueller 1995
Lichens		3,800	13,500	Esslinger and Egan 1995; Eldredge and Miller 1995, 1998
Fungi subtotal		>37,800	69,700	
Plant Kingdom				
Mosses	Bryophyta	1,400	10,000	Anderson et al. 1990; Eldredge and Miller 1995, 1998
Liverworts	Hepatophyta	700	6,000	Stotler and Crandall-Stotler 1977; Eldredge and Miller 1995
Hornworts	Anthocerophyta	11	100	Stotler and Crandall-Stotler 1977
Clubmosses	Lycophyta	100	1,000	Natural Heritage Central Databases 1999
Whisk ferns	Psilophyta	2	10	"
Horsetails	Sphenophyta	10	15	"
Ferns	Filicinophyta	444	11,000	"
Cycads	Cycadophyta	1	140	"
Ginkgo	Ginkgophyta	0	1	"
Conifers	Coniferophyta	104	550	"
Mormon tea and relatives	Gnetophyta	9	70	"
Flowering plants	Anthophyta	15,320	235,000	"
Plant subtotal		18,100	265,000	
Animal Kingdom				
Trichoplaxes	Placozoa	1	1	Margulis and Schwarz 1998
Sponges	Porifera	375	6,000	K. Ruetzler pers. comm.
Hydras, jellyfish, corals, anemones	Cnidaria	1,620	9,400	Cairns et al. 1991; N. E. Eldredge pers. comm.
Comb jellies	Ctenophora	45	100	Cairns et al. 1991; Eldredge and Miller 1998
Flatworms	Platyhelminthes	6,000	20,000	S. Sterner, D. Kritsky, S. Tyler, J. Caira, S. Hendrix, G. Hoffman pers. comms.
Jaw Worms	Gnathostomulida	70	80	E. Ruppert pers. comm.
Dicyemids	Dicyemida	37	120	E. Hochberg pers. comm.
Orthonectids	Orthonectida	3	28	E. Kozloff pers. comm.
Ribbon worms	Nemertina	253	900	J. Norenburg, F. Crandall pers. comms.

(continued)

Table 3.1. (*continued*)

Common name	Phylum	Number of U.S. species	Number worldwide	Source for U.S. figures
Nematodes, roundworms	Nematoda	>5,300	20,000	D. Hope, D. Wall, T. O. Powers, E. Hoberg pers. comms.
Horsehair worms	Nematomorpha	3	240	K. Fauchald pers. comm.
Thorny-headed worms	Acanthocephala	200	1,200	O. Amin pers. comm.
Rotifers	Rotifera	700	2,000	R. Stemberger pers. comm.
Kinorhynchs	Kinorhyncha	20	130	R. Higgins pers. comm.
Priapulids	Priapulida	3	18	R. Higgins pers. comm.
Gastrotrichs	Gastrotricha	100	600	W. Hummon, D. Strayer pers. comms.
Loriciferans	Loricifera	8	11	R. Higgins pers. comm.
Entoprocts	Entoprocta	20	150	K. Wasson pers. comm.
Arachnids and relatives	Chelicerata	9,557	76,000	Schaefer and Kosztarab 1991; Eldredge and Miller 1995, 1996
Insects, centipedes, millipedes	Mandibulata	96,406	>763,200	Schaefer and Kosztarab 1991; Eldredge and Miller 1995, 1998
Crustaceans	Crustacea	9,675	45,000	J. Reid, A. Robertson, C. Shih, L. Korniker, D. Belk, L. Watling, B. Kensley, S. Dodson, J. Thomas pers. comms.; Eldredge and Miller 1995
Annelid worms	Annelida	3,360	15,000	D. Kathman, K. Coates, S. Gelder, K. Fauchald pers. comms.
Peanut worms	Sipuncula	45	320	E. Ruppert pers. comm.
Spoon worms	Echiura	30	150	J. Pilger pers. comm.
Beard worms	Pogonophora	12	120	K. Fauchald pers. comm.
Mollusks	Mollusca	7,500	50,000	Turgeon et al. 1998; Eldredge and Miller 1998
Water bears	Tardigrada	200	750	D. Kathman pers. comm.
Velvet worms	Onychophora	0	100	Margulis and Schwarz 1998
Bryozoans	Bryozoa	934	4,000	J. Winston pers. comm.
Lampshells	Brachiopoda	10	335	E. Ruppert pers. comm.
Phoronids	Phoronida	9	14	R. Zimmer pers. comm.
Arrow worms	Chaetognatha	25	115	K. Fauchald pers. comm.
Acorn worms	Hemichordata	26	90	E. Ruppert pers. comm.
Echinoderms	Echinodermata	1,110	7,000	D. Pawson pers. comm.
Tunicates	Urochordata	282	1,400	G. Lambert pers. comm.
Lancelets	Cephalochordata	3	23	L. Watling pers. comm.
Vertebrates	Craniata	>4,900	45,000	Robins et al. 1991; Eldredge and Miller 1995, 1998
Animal subtotal		>148,800	1,074,500	
Total		>204,700	ca. 1,500,000	

This table summarizes available knowledge about the number of formally described U.S. species in each phylum of plants, animals, and fungi. To the extent possible, these figures represent described native species that are accepted in current classifications and include terrestrial, freshwater, and marine species to the 200-mile U.S. territorial limits. Classification follows kingdom and phylum concepts of Margulis and Schwartz 1998. Figures for number of species worldwide generally follow Margulis and Schwartz 1998 or, for plants, Raven et al. 1999.

The Asian long-horned beetle, an alien species first noted in the United States in 1996, has already infested urban trees in New York and Illinois and could seriously damage hardwood forests across the Northeast and Midwest. Courtesy of USDA/APHIS.

Alien Species

In addition to these native species, a flood of plants, animals, and pathogens have been introduced into the United States and are spreading throughout our lands and waters. Known variously as alien, exotic, introduced, non-native, or nonindigenous, these species have been introduced—either intentionally or by accident—into areas outside their natural range. Alien species arrive in many ways. Some are the product of misguided efforts to correct other environmental problems. For instance, kudzu (*Pueraria montana*), a fast-growing vine that now blankets large areas of the Southeast, was originally imported and promoted to combat soil erosion. Others, including many non-native fish species, were introduced for sport or recreation. Many more, such as the Asian longhorned beetle (*Anoplophora glabripennis*), end up in the United States as accidental stowaways. This beetle, first noticed in New York in 1996 and now threatening urban and forest trees elsewhere in the United States, arrived from China in wood used for packing materials. With expanding global travel and trade, opportunities for such unwanted guests are only increasing.

The number of alien species that have become naturalized and are now residing in the United States is not precisely known. Perhaps 3,500 species of nonindigenous plants occur outside of cultivation (Kartesz pers. comm.), and at least 2,300 species of non-native animals inhabit the United States (OTA 1993). Non-native animals include a number of vertebrates, but invertebrates, particularly insects, make up the bulk of introduced animal species. Although this tally of exotic species may appear small compared to the number of native U.S. species, these alien invaders exert a level of ecological influence well beyond their limited numbers. Unchecked by their natural predators and diseases, many introduced species are flourishing at the expense of native U.S. species, taking over natural ecosystems and pushing many of our rarest plants and animals even farther toward extinction. As discussed in chapter 8, alien species are now the second leading threat to U.S. biodiversity.

U.S. Species in a Global Context

As the hemlock and darter illustrate, various groups of plants and animals have very different distributional patterns, resulting in quite distinctive biotas on different continents, as well as within different countries on the same continent. Impressed by such distinctions, a number of nineteenth-century scientists, among them Charles Darwin, Joseph Dalton Hooker, and Alfred Russell Wallace, attempted to characterize and explain the differences and the processes that created them. Wallace in particular, who spent much of his life traveling the world collecting natural history specimens, was struck by how the array of species shifted dramatically as he crossed ocean channels, wide rivers, or mountain ranges. In 1856, Wallace was exploring the Malay Archipelago, the group of islands that now comprise Indonesia, Malaysia, and Papua New Guinea. As he crossed from Bali, a small island just east of Java, to the slightly larger island of Lombok, Wallace noticed that the familiar Javanese birds had disappeared, even though the strait between the two islands is less than 20 miles wide. The birds on Lombok were utterly unlike anything Wallace had seen on Java or any of the islands to the west.

The peripatetic Englishman didn't know it yet, but he had crossed a boundary that would later bear his name: Wallace's line. This line, scientists later discovered, coincides with the boundaries between the shifting plates of the earth's crust. Bali lies just on the edge of the continental shelf and, during periods of lowered sea levels in the Pleistocene, was connected to mainland Asia. Lombok, however, lies just off the shelf and across a deep water trench. This line marks the biological boundary between southeast Asia and Australasia. Other such biological boundaries exist all across the globe. Some boundaries are obvious, like oceans, mountains, and deserts, while others are subtle, like gradations in rainfall or temperature. Many historical boundaries no longer exist, erased by the movement of the earth's crust. And as the curious distribution of species such as the Carolina hemlock suggests, current boundaries may not always have existed.

Most biogeographic boundaries are not as dramatic as Wallace's line. In the Western Hemisphere, for example, the separation between the *Nearctic*, the northern, temperate part of the hemisphere, and the *Neotropics* is fuzzy. Rather than an abrupt shift at the tropic of Cancer, which runs through Mexico at the southern tip of Baja California, the mix of species changes gradually across Mexico, driven largely by climate and topography. The boundaries between major regions, whether distinct and impenetrable or porous and fuzzy, highlight one of the crucial facts of biogeography: Species are not distributed evenly across the planet.

Quantifying Diversity

The uneven distribution of species has led to a search for ways to compare various regions in terms of their biological diversity. The most obvious and straightforward method of comparing regions is to count the species in them, either for a particular group of organisms, for multiple groups, or for the totality of their known species. The result is a measure of species richness—the number of species present in a given area.

Species diversity varies depending on the geographic scale on which it is studied, and several flavors of species-richness indexes may be employed to take this fact into account. The influential American ecologist Robert Whittaker (1975) suggested three separate measures corresponding to increasing spatial scales. Alpha (α) diversity refers to the number of species in some small, homogeneous area, such as a study plot or a naturally defined ecological community; beta (β) diversity is the rate of change (or turnover) in species across adjacent habitats; and gamma (γ) diversity is simply the number of species in a large geographic region.

The Furbish lousewort (*top,* © Susan Middleton and David Liittschwager) grows only in flood-scoured habitats along the St. John River (*bottom,* © Bill Silliker Jr.). Although it is locally restricted and of considerable conservation concern, this species is neither a state or national endemic because the river forms the border between Maine and New Brunswick.

Another method for assessing the biological significance of different regions is to focus on those species that are unique, or *endemic*, to an area. Endemism provides a measure of the distinctiveness of the flora and fauna. Endemism, however, is a scale-dependent concept. A species may be endemic to a single cave or mountaintop, a state, a river basin, a country, or even a continent. The term is most often used to refer to the biota of political units—states or nations—or to naturally defined regions, such as the Sierra Nevada or Great Plains.

The Furbish lousewort (*Pedicularis furbishiae*), which gained notoriety in the 1970s as one of the first major tests of the Endangered Species Act, illustrates the complexities of defining endemism. This rare plant, which grows to about three feet tall and produces clusters of yellow blossoms that look like their cousins the snapdragons, occurs only on the banks of the St. John River. Because the river forms the boundary between Maine and New Brunswick, Furbish's lousewort is not endemic to the United States or Canada, but is endemic to the St. John watershed. This odd plant, however, is of greater conservation concern than, say, the Carolina chickadee (*Poecile carolinensis*), a species that is endemic to the United States but is common throughout its relatively broad range across the southeastern part of the country. Despite this drawback, endemism does provide a measure of the unique biological diversity contained within a country, and it reflects that portion of the biota that can be safeguarded only in that country.

Yet a third approach to assessing diversity is to consider the evolutionary breadth and distinctiveness of the biota. Evolutionary distinctiveness, or taxic diversity, is also a scale-dependent concept, but in this instance the relevant scale is taxonomic rather than geographic. While the number of unique species present in an area begins to get at this issue of evolutionary distinctiveness, the level of individual species is perhaps too fine a taxonomic scale. Any endemic species may be closely related to numerous similar species. For this reason, evolutionary distinctiveness is best reflected at higher taxonomic levels, such as genus, family, or order. The presence of unique families or orders is particularly noteworthy from an evolutionary perspective.

National Patterns of Diversity

As one moves from the United States south through Mexico and on into Central and South America, not only do the species change, but they also proliferate. As diverse as the old-growth cove forests of the Great Smoky Mountains in North Carolina are, for example, the lowland tropical forests of eastern Peru pack together far more species. In the language of Whittaker's diversity measures, alpha and gamma diversity increase with decreasing latitude. To put it more simply, there are more species in the tropics than in the temperate zone.

A latitudinal gradient in diversity is about as universal as ecological patterns get, holding true for plants, bats, quadruped mammals, reptiles, amphibians, termites, and coastal fishes. It is also an ancient pattern: Fossil foraminifera show a latitudinal gradient dating back 70 million years (Rosenzweig 1995). Like all generalizations, however, even this one has exceptions. Some fungi and zooplankton show no latitudinal trend at all, while other groups, like marine algae, certain wasps, coniferous trees, bees, salamanders, waterfowl and shorebirds, and many freshwater groups are most diverse at midtemperate latitudes (Brown and Lomolino 1998).

The elevated species diversity of the tropics has long fascinated biologists. Explanations range from increased levels of solar insolation (and thus energy), to differential rates of speciation and extinction, to the simple influence of area (Pianka 1966, Rosenzweig 1995). Whatever the ultimate cause, the latitudinal gradient is a central and inescapable fact when comparing the species diversity in the United States—which lies almost entirely outside of the tropics—with other countries.

Despite its essentially temperate zone location, the United States ranks quite high in terms of its biotic diversity (table 3.2). Assessing species numbers for some of the better-studied groups of organisms provides a reasonable, if incomplete, yardstick for comparing biological richness among countries. In the following section we review some of these national patterns of species diversity and endemism for different groups of organisms. Patterns of diversity and endemism *within* the United States are addressed in chapter 5. The species diversity figures presented in the following section refer to described, native, full species only, and except where noted otherwise, the figures are derived from the Natural Heritage Central Databases (see Appendix D for major information sources to these databases).

One of the most consistent patterns in ecology is that biological diversity increases as you near the equator. Thus, the lowland tropical forests of eastern Peru contain far more species than even the richest forests in North America.
© Gary Braasch.

Table 3.2. Global significance of selected U.S. plant and animal groups

Taxonomic group	Number of U.S. species	Number of species worldwide	% of global species in U.S.	U.S. ranking worldwide
Mammals	416	4,600	9%	6
Birds	768	9,700	8%	27
Reptiles	283	6,600	4%	14
Amphibians	231	4,400	5%	12
Freshwater fishes	799	8,400	10%	7
Freshwater mussels	292	1,000	29%	1
Freshwater snails	661	4,000	17%	1
Crayfishes	322	525	61%	1
Tiger beetles	114	2,000	6%	7
Dragonflies/damselflies	456	5,800	8%	?
Butterflies/skippers	620	17,500	4%	?
Flowering plants	15,320	235,000	7%	>10
Gymnosperms	114	760	15%	2
Ferns	556	12,000	5%	>15

Several species groups have their highest levels of diversity in the United States, including freshwater mussels, freshwater snails, and crayfishes; several other taxonomic groups, such as freshwater fishes and gymnosperms, are also well represented in the United States.

Sources: U.S. figures refer to accepted, described species and are from Natural Heritage Central Databases 1999; world figures are estimates of described species and are from various sources (see table 3.1).

A look at national patterns of species diversity and endemism reveals that the United States has a number of biological features that are outstanding at a global level. Among plants, the diversity of conifers and other gymnosperms is exceptional, second only to that in China. The United States is the most diverse country in the world for salamanders and freshwater turtles. Our freshwater fish fauna is also extremely rich and represents the world's most diverse temperate fish assemblage. Invertebrates are much more poorly known, but the United States is also a world leader in numbers of freshwater mussels, freshwater snails, crayfishes, and several freshwater insect orders. The most compelling trend that emerges from this overview of overall U.S. species diversity and endemism is the truly extraordinary position of the nation's freshwater biota even at a global level.

Plants

The United States has a rich variety of plant life, ranging from tiny desert annuals to towering forest trees. Flowering plants, or *angiosperms*, are the dominant plant form on Earth and are represented in the United States by about 15,300 native species, or about 7% of the estimated world total. The incomplete knowledge of many tropical floras makes it difficult to assign a global position with certainty, but the United States probably ranks about 10th among nations for diversity of flowering plants and is one of the leading temperate zone nations. Much of the nation's plant diversity is concentrated in only a few taxonomic groups; just 10 plant families account for about one-half of all U.S. species (table 3.3). The composite family (Asteraceae), which includes such plants as asters, sunflowers, and goldenrods, is the single largest group, with about 2,225 native species. It is no wonder that student botanists quickly learn the useful epithet *DYC* ("damn yellow comp") for referring to unknown members of this prolific family. The pea (Fabaceae) and grass (Poaceae) families are also well represented in the United States: Each encompasses more than 5% of the flora.

As well endowed as the United States is in terms of flowering plants, the country's gymnosperm flora stands out at a global level. With 114 gymnosperm species, the United States is second only to China in diversity of this group. Gymnosperms include such well-known coniferous trees as pines, firs, spruce, hemlocks, cedars, and cypresses. Also included are Mormon tea (*Ephedra*), a leafless arid-land shrub, and cycads, primitive, ground-dwelling plants of which the United States has but a single species.

National-level plant endemism in the United States is still incompletely documented. About 4,000 plant species have been suggested as being endemic to North America north of Mexico (N. Morin pers. comm. in Davis et al. 1997). Although relatively few of these species would be endemic to Canada, a substantial number undoubtedly are shared between the United States and Canada. Taking a conservative approach with respect to Canada, perhaps 3,000 of these species are restricted to the U.S. portion of North America. Adding in the 1,050 vascular plant species

With more than 2,200 species, the composite family is the largest group of U.S. plants. The plethora of yellow-flowered composites, such as this giant coreopsis (*Coreopsis gigantea*) from California's Santa Cruz Island, are the bane of student botanists. © Stephen Krasemann/DRK PHOTO.

Table 3.3. Ten largest U.S. plant families

Plant family	Number of species	Percent of U.S. flora
Asteraceae (Composites)	2,225	14%
Fabaceae (Legumes)	1,108	7%
Poaceae (Grasses)	925	6%
Cyperaceae (Sedges)	796	5%
Scrophulariaceae (Figworts)	715	4%
Rosaceae (Roses)	660	4%
Brassicaceae (Mustards)	550	3%
Liliaceae (Lilies)	423	3%
Polygonaceae (Buckwheats)	360	2%
Lamiaceae (Mints)	352	2%
Total	8,114	51%

The 10 largest U.S. plant families contain more than one-half of U.S. species. Numbers reflect native species only.

Sources: Natural Heritage Central Databases 1999, adapted and revised from Kartesz 1994 and Kartesz unpublished data.

Gymnosperm diversity in the United States is second only to that of China. Coulter pine (*Pinus coulteri*), shown here with a still developing cone, produces the world's heaviest pinecones. © Stephen P. Parker/Photo Researchers.

endemic to Hawaii (W. L. Wagner pers. comm.) produces an estimate of about 4,000 plant species that can be considered U.S. national endemics, or about a quarter (25%) of the nation's native flora.

More precise endemism figures are available for ferns and gymnosperms, based largely on the recent comprehensive treatments of these groups in *Flora of North America* (FNA 1993). Two hundred ten species of ferns and fern allies (pteridophytes) are U.S. endemics, representing 38% of the native fern flora. Given the relative ease with which tiny fern spores are dispersed, this is a surprisingly large number and is due largely to the high proportion of endemic ferns in Hawaii (77%): Only 18% of mainland ferns are U.S. endemics. Among U.S. gymnosperms, 45 species, or 39% of the gymnosperm flora, are U.S. endemics. This relatively high level of endemism, coupled with the global significance of the U.S. gymnosperm flora, suggests that the United States has an important global conservation responsibility with respect to gymnosperms.

Only a single family of flowering plants, the Leitneriaceae, is strictly endemic to the United States. Corkwood (*Leitneria floridana*), the family's sole species, occurs primarily along the Gulf Coast. The plant is so evolutionarily distinctive that not only is it generally regarded as a distinct family, but also a separate taxonomic order (Leitneriales), thereby constituting the only plant order endemic to the United States. Several other plant families are nearly endemic to the United States but spill across the border into neighboring portions of Mexico or Canada. These include three southwestern plant families: the Simmondsiaceae, which includes the jojoba bean (*Simmondsia chinensis*); the Fouquieriaceae, including the desert shrub ocotillo (*Fouquieria splendens*); and the Crossosomataceae, an enigmatic family so obscure it has no common name. A fourth plant family, the Limnanthaceae, is a characteristic component of Pacific Coast vernal pools, giving rise to its common name—meadowfoam—but it ranges just slightly into Canada.

Corkwood is an evolutionarily distinctive species that is the sole representative of what generally is regarded as the United States' only strictly endemic plant family. Illustration by Yevonn Wilson-Ramsey/ courtesy Flora of North America Association.

Mammals

Among vertebrates, several U.S. groups stand out at the global level. With 416 mammal species, the United States contains about 9% of the world's total, ranking sixth among nations in mammal diversity. Among these are some of the most conspicuous and characteristic features of the American landscape. The American bison (*Bos bison*), which once formed vast herds across the Great Plains, is the largest U.S. land mammal and can weigh as much as 2,000 pounds. The nation also abounds in carnivores, including the impressive Alaskan brown bear (*Ursus arctos*), an animal that can reach a height of eight feet when standing erect. Although big or fierce mammals—moose, elk, wolverine, mountain lions, and the like—capture the public's imagination and tend to be chosen as high school mascots, the more humble rodents make up far more of the considerable diversity of mammals in the United States. Indeed, the order Rodentia, a taxonomic grouping that includes squirrels, gophers, and lemmings as well as the more familiar mice, constitute almost half (49%) of U.S. mammal species. The United States also harbors a relatively large assortment of marine mammals—whales, porpoises, and seals, among others, numbering 59 species. While approximately one-fifth of mammal species worldwide are bats (order Chiroptera), this primarily tropical and subtropical group is less well represented in the United States: With 45 species, bats only represent about 10% of U.S. mammal species.

Almost a quarter (24%) of U.S. mammals are national endemics. Among these 100 endemic mammals are such animals as the giant kangaroo rat (*Dipodomys ingens*) of California's San Joaquin Valley; the Mt. Lyell shrew (*Sorex lyelli*), found only in a small area in and around Yosemite National Park; and the black-footed ferret (*Mustela nigripes*), once nearly extinct in the wild but now reintroduced in several colonies in Montana and elsewhere.

Below: Although large mammals command the public's attention, nearly one-half of U.S. mammal species are rodents. Small mammals of the arid Southwest, like this desert pocket mouse (*Chaetodipus penicillatus*), are especially diverse. © John Cancalosi/DRK PHOTO.

Right: The tremendous speed of the pronghorn antelope, the fastest land animal in North America, likely evolved as a defense against long-extinct predators like the American cheetah. © Jim Brandenburg/Minden Pictures.

The pronghorn antelope (*Antilocapra americana*), the sole member of its family (Antilocapridae), is an evolutionarily isolated animal that is nearly endemic to the United States. Occurring mostly in the deserts and plains of the western United States, the pronghorn also ranges slightly into Canada and Mexico. The fastest land animal in North America, pronghorns are capable of sustained sprinting at more than 60 miles per hour. These speeds make the antelope about twice as fast as its swiftest predator, the coyote. The pronghorn's fleetness appears to have evolved as a defense against predators that no longer inhabit the continent, especially the American cheetah, which became extinct at the end of the Pleistocene (Byers 1997).

The mountain beaver (*Aplodontia rufa*) is another evolutionarily isolated mammal that is nearly endemic to the United States. Looking more like a tail-less muskrat than what one typically thinks of as a "beaver," this species is the sole member of the family Aplodontidae and retains the most primitive traits of any living rodent (Nowak 1991). A small and inconspicuous animal, the mountain beaver lives only in a narrow strip from southern British Columbia south along the Pacific Coast to about the San Francisco Bay region and the central Sierra Nevada. The mountain beaver also happens to be inhabited by one of the world's largest fleas (*Hystrichopsylla schefferi*), which can reach almost half an inch in length. Like its host, this flea is an evolutionary relict, suggesting a long association between these two species (Lewis and Lewis 1994).

Of the 10 mammalian orders represented in the United States, 3 have but a single U.S. species. The opossum (*Didelphis virginiana*), a distant relative of Australia's kangaroos, is the only marsupial in the United States. The nine-banded armadillo (*Dasypus novemcinctus*), of the order Xenarthra, has become a Texas icon and is inexorably expanding its range northward. The armadillo and opossum are, in fact, some of the few mammals to successfully invade North America following the so-called Great American Interchange discussed later in this chapter. The manatee (*Trichechus manatus*) is the United States' only member of the very small order Sirenia. These large, docile creatures reached the waters of southeastern North America some 50 million years ago and flourished until the climate changed during the Pleistocene.

Birds

Although delightful to watch, from a global perspective birds are not a particularly diverse group in the United States, at least in comparison with the number found in many tropical countries. About 768 bird species regularly occur in the United States, and around 720 (93%) of these species are represented by breeding populations. The United States ranks a distant 27th among nations for number of bird species, paling in comparison to countries such as Peru, which supports more than 1,700 species. With 65 bird species, or 9% of breeding birds, restricted to the United States, the nation ranks 11th in terms of endemism. This relatively high level of endemism, however, is due largely to Hawaii's 52 endemic bird

The mountain beaver, or aplodontia, is an inconspicuous animal of the Pacific Coast that retains the most primitive traits of any rodent worldwide. © Pat and Tom Leeson/Photo Researchers.

The lesser prairie chicken is one of the relatively few bird species endemic to the U.S. mainland. Restricted to the southwestern part of the Great Plains, this bird has lost much of its grassland habitat to agriculture. © John Cancalosi/DRK PHOTO.

The bristle-thigh curlew is a U.S. breeding endemic, nesting in the United States but migrating elsewhere during the winter. This species' Alaskan nesting grounds were not discovered until almost 180 years after the bird was first noted in the South Pacific. © Mitsuaki Iwago/Minden Pictures.

A drab yet evolutionarily distinctive bird, the wrentit is common in West Coast chaparral and scrub. Unrelated to any other North American bird, this species is the only U.S. representative of the predominantly Asian babbler family. © Anthony Mercieca/Photo Researchers.

species. Hawaiian endemics are dominated by the more than 30 species of honeycreepers and 6 species of honeyeaters (although about half of the former and all but two of the latter are extinct). Mainland endemics include species such as the yellow-billed magpie (*Pica nuttalli*), lesser prairie-chicken (*Tympanuchus pallidicinctus*), and Bachman's sparrow (*Aimophila aestivalis*).

Apart from strict endemics, a number of bird species are restricted to the United States during key parts of their life cycles, typically either for breeding or overwintering. For example, 20 bird species breed only within the United States but range elsewhere during the nonbreeding season. Bachman's warbler (*Vermivora bachmanii*), a bird so rare it may already be extinct, is one of these. This warbler was known to breed in canebrakes and wet woodlands in the southeastern United States, but it overwintered in Cuba. The bristle-thighed curlew (*Numenius tahitiensis*) breeds in only a limited area of western Alaska but flies south across the ocean to winter on Pacific islands, including Hawaii. Indeed, it was first discovered in 1769 on the islands of Tahiti, for which it was formally named, but its nesting grounds were not located until the 1940s, almost 180 years later. Other species exhibit the reverse pattern, breeding elsewhere but wintering only in the United States. Perhaps the most famous of these is the whooping crane (*Grus americana*), although this situation is largely a result of human-induced reduction in range. Once fairly widespread on the northern plains, hunting and agricultural conversion of the crane's main nesting areas had brought the species to the brink of extinction by the 1940s. In 1954 the nesting location of the single remaining population was discovered in the remote wilderness of central Canada's Wood Buffalo National Park. The cranes breeding at that site fly about 2,400 miles south to winter along the Texas coast.

No bird families are endemic to the United States, although the Hawaiian honeycreepers traditionally were considered a separate family. They now are widely regarded as an offshoot of the finch family (Fringillidae) and are treated as a subfamily within that group. A truly enigmatic bird is the wrentit (*Chamaea fasciata*), found mostly in West Coast chaparral. This species is unrelated to any other North American bird and has been bounced from one family to another by ornithologists. Currently it is placed among the babblers (Timaliidae) and is the only U.S. representative of this mostly Asian family. The 'elepaio (*Chasiempis sandwichensis*) is another U.S. bird with unusual affinities. The guardian spirit of Hawaiian canoe makers, this Hawaiian forest bird is the sole U.S. member of the Old World monarch flycatcher family (Monarchidae).

Several other bird families are represented in the United States by just a single species. These include the wood stork (*Mycteria americana*), the only North American stork; the plain chachalaca (*Ortalis vetula*), the only cracid that extends north as far as the United States; and the American dipper, or water ouzel (*Cinclus mexicanus*), an acrobatic little bird that frequents rushing mountain streams, where it walks underwater in search of aquatic invertebrates. The parrot family includes two U.S. species, the Carolina parakeet (*Conuropsis carolinensis*) and the thick-billed parrot

(*Rhynchopsitta pachyrhyncha*). Unfortunately, the first is extinct, and the second has been extirpated from the United States, although the species still survives precariously in the mountains of northern Mexico.

The Florida worm lizard is not a lizard at all but, instead, the only amphisbaenian reptile in the United States. This unusual group shares equivalent taxonomic standing with the much more diverse lizards and snakes. © Suzanne L. Collins and Joseph T. Collins/Photo Researchers.

Reptiles

Reptiles are reasonably diverse in the United States, although with about 280 species, or 4% of the world's total, the country ranks only 14th among nations. The United States is the world's most diverse nation for freshwater turtles, however, with 42 species representing almost a quarter (22%) of described species. Snakes and lizards are also well represented, but because these groups are so much more diverse in tropical regions, the United States does not particularly stand out. With 90 endemic reptiles, about one-third (32%) of U.S. species are restricted to this country.

At higher taxonomic levels, one reptile family, the California legless lizards (Anniellidae), is nearly endemic to the United States. Consisting of only two species, this family of burrowing, snakelike lizards is found only in California and adjacent Baja California. Other unusual U.S. reptiles include several species that are the only U.S. representatives of their groups. The Florida worm lizard (*Rhineura floridana*), a blind and earless creature, is not a lizard at all but rather the only U.S. member of the suborder Amphisbaenia. From a taxonomic perspective, amphisbaenians are on equal footing with the far more species-rich snakes and lizards, making the Florida worm lizard of exceptional evolutionary and conservation interest. Noteworthy among the true lizards is the Gila monster (*Heloderma suspectum*), the only U.S. member of the family Helodermatidae. The Gila monster and its sister species, the Mexican beaded lizard (*H. horridum*), are the only two venomous lizards in the world. The ancient crocodilian order is represented in the United States by two species, the American crocodile (*Crocodylus acutus*) and the American alligator (*Alligator mississippiensis*). Like the Carolina hemlock, the alligator's nearest relative is found in China.

One of only two venomous lizards in the world, the Gila monster is found in the Mojave and Sonora Deserts. © Kennan Ward/DRK PHOTO.

Amphibians

On the whole, amphibian diversity in the United States is not exceptional, but with regard to one particular group—salamanders—the United States is the richest country on Earth. With at least 140 described species, the United States harbors almost 40% of the world's salamanders. This is more salamanders than all tropical countries south of Mexico combined. The dominance of salamanders in the United States is further highlighted by comparing our fauna with numbers of amphibians globally. Worldwide, frogs are by far the most species-rich amphibian group, making up almost 90% of described species. In contrast, for the United States, frogs account for a mere 38% of the amphibian fauna; salamanders make up the remainder.

The lungless salamanders (Plethodontidae), with about 100 species, account for much of this diversity. The extraordinary diversification

The "tail" on this tailed frog is actually a copulatory organ, allowing this evolutionarily isolated species to perform internal fertilization, a feat unique among frogs. © Alan D. St. John.

within this group is related largely to the evolution of terrestrial breeding, which allowed many plethodontids to break away from the typical amphibian dependency on water for reproduction. Lungless salamanders have their center of diversity in the United States, but in a mysterious distributional pattern, two species occur in southern Europe and Sardinia.

With two-thirds (67%) of our species endemic, the U.S. amphibian fauna is also quite distinctive. Much of this endemism derives from the large numbers of narrowly distributed salamanders. Numerous locally restricted species have evolved in the highly dissected Appalachian mountains, such as the Shenandoah salamander (*Plethodon shenandoah*), found in just three isolated populations in Virginia. Aquatic habitats, especially in the Southeast, have also generated numerous endemic salamanders, including the black warrior waterdog (*Necturus alabamensis*), known only from the Appalachian portions of Alabama's Black Warrior River drainage. And even desert habitats have produced endemics, such as the Amargosa toad (*Bufo nelsoni*), which lives only in riparian habitats associated with the Amargosa River in Nevada.

Several U.S. amphibian families are endemic to the United States or nearly so. The tailed frog (*Ascaphus truei*) is the sole member of an evolutionarily isolated family (Ascaphidae). The "tail" is actually a large copulatory organ, enabling members of this family to perform internal fertilization, a feat unique among frogs. Inhabiting boulder-strewn mountain streams along the Pacific Coast and interior Northwest, this frog has a mostly U.S. distribution but also extends into British Columbia. Several groups of giant salamanders are largely endemic to the United States and display similar distributions. The Pacific giant salamander (*Dicamptodon ensatus*) is the largest terrestrial salamander in the world, reaching lengths of more than one foot. This species, and the three others that make up the family Dicamptodontidae, are found only in the United States, except for a small incursion into southwestern British Columbia. Also in the Pacific Northwest are the evolutionarily isolated torrent salamanders (family Rhyacotritonidae), whose four species are restricted to Washington, Oregon, and California. Two families of giant aquatic salamanders, the Amphiumidae and Sirenidae, are also largely restricted to the United States, but in these instances to the Southeast. Among the members of this latter family are the greater siren (*Siren lacertina*), an immense eel-like animal that can grow up to three feet in length. The hellbender (*Cryptobranchus alleganiensis*), a bizarre-looking inhabitant of the Appalachian and Ozark regions, is the only U.S. representative of an otherwise Asian group of giant salamanders.

The United States has the greatest diversity of salamanders of any nation. The Pacific giant salamander, a species nearly restricted to the United States, can reach more than one foot in length and is the world's largest terrestrial salamander. © Alan D. St. John.

Freshwater Fishes

Freshwater fishes exhibit an extraordinary diversity in the United States. With approximately 800 species, the United States harbors about 10% of known freshwater fishes worldwide and ranks seventh among nations, trailing only Brazil, Venezuela, Indonesia, China, the Democratic Republic of Congo, and Peru. The United States has by far the most diverse fish fauna of any temperate zone country. In contrast, only 193 fish species are known from all the countries of Europe and 188 species from Australia (Moyle and Leidy 1992). Endemism among U.S. fishes is also quite high. About 532 species, representing two-thirds (66%) of the nation's fishes, occur nowhere else.

The fish fauna of the United States is dominated by the minnow family (Cyprinidae), which is represented by some 240 U.S. species, or almost one-third (30%) of the nation's total. These minnows include numerous national endemics, especially among the dace, chubs, and shiners. The common perception of a "minnow" as any tiny fish is severely challenged by many of these species, including the Colorado pikeminnow (*Ptychocheilus lucius*), which reaches lengths of five feet. The perch family (Percidae) is also exceptionally diverse in the United States, with approximately 170 described species: All but a few of these are darters, a uniquely North American tribe. The darter genus *Etheostoma* is the single most diverse genus of U.S. fishes, and most of its approximately 125 species are national endemics.

Restricted to large rivers of the Colorado River basin, the Colorado pikeminnow can grow to an enormous size, reaching lengths of five feet. © David M. Schleser/ Photo Reseachers.

Only two fish families are entirely restricted to the United States. The cavefishes (Amblyopsidae) are a peculiar group of six species, four of which are blind and restricted to subterranean waters. Closely related to the cavefishes is a second endemic U.S. family, the pirate perch (Aphredoderidae). This family consists of just a single species (*Aphredoderus sayanus*), whose adults display the intriguing anatomical feature of having their anus located on the throat.

The United States is particularly rich in ancient fishes, some of which are U.S. endemics or nearly so. The bowfin (*Amia calva*) is the only living representative of its order (Amiiformes). Dating back to the Jurassic, the family is known from fossils in many parts of the world (Grande and Bemis 1998). The living bowfin is nearly endemic to the United States, ranging widely through the eastern part of the country but also reaching slightly into southeastern Canada. Gars (Lepisosteidae) are another group of archaic fishes centered in the United States, although two of the seven species in this family occur outside the country. The paddlefish (*Polyodon spathula*), on the other hand, is an ancient fish entirely restricted to the United States. This archaic fish has a long snout shaped like the wide end of a canoe paddle which functions as an electrosensory antenna assisting the fishes foraging in murky waters. The paddlefish family (Polyodontidae) is yet another group that displays an eastern United States–eastern Asia distribution. The only other species in this family, *Psephurus gladius*, is found in the Yangtze River system of eastern China.

The paddlefish is an ancient species entirely restricted to the United States. The extraordinary snout serves as an electrosensory antenna that apparently aids the fish in locating its planktonic food. © Norbert Wu/DRK Photo.

Insects

Insects are one of the most diverse and ecologically significant groups of U.S. organisms. Given the enormous number of insect species found within the United States—and the vast gaps in even our most basic catalogue of these creatures—briefly summarizing general patterns of insect diversity is a difficult task. At least 91,000 North American insect species

Native bees are important pollinators for both native plants and agricultural crops. This *Ptiloglossa* bee is able to extract pollen from the tubular anthers of a nightshade flower by rapidly vibrating its flight muscles, a maneuver known as buzz pollination. © Stephen L. Buchmann.

are known well enough to have received formal scientific names, while another 70,000 species or more are predicted to occur but are undescribed (Kosztarab and Schaefer 1990). In addition, at least 5,400 native insect species are known from Hawaii, adding to the overall diversity of U.S. insects (Nishida 1994). Four insect orders alone—including beetles, flies, bees, and butterflies—account for nearly 80% of these known species (table 3.4). Rather than attempt to cover the full array of insect diversity in the United States, we will touch here on just a few noteworthy groups.

The United States is extremely rich in bees, a group that plays a central economic and ecological role in pollination. As noted earlier, bees show their greatest diversity not in the tropics but rather at midlatitudes, especially in deserts and Mediterranean-type climates. A few species even range far north of the Arctic Circle. With nearly 4,000 native species of bees (Griswold pers. comm.), the United States stands out even relative to other arid regions around the world. Only the deserts of Israel and northern Mexico rival the arid southwestern United States with regard to the local diversity of bees (Buchmann and Nabhan 1996). Our native bees are, for the most part, quite different from the familiar honeybee (*Apis mellifera*), which was introduced into North America from Europe. Rather than living in large honeycomb-lined colonies, the majority of our native bees are solitary, and many burrow into the ground to nest. The great diversity of bees relates largely to the wide variety of wildflowers and other plants that are specialized for bee pollination. Some bees visit just a single type of flower—the diminutive *Perdita meconis*, for instance, restricts its pollen gathering to the very rare dwarf bearpaw poppy (*Arctomecon humilis*)—but most forage on a wider array of plants, depending on what is blooming.

Butterflies, skippers, and moths, collectively referred to as Lepidoptera, are another group that is well represented in the United States. These familiar insects are also intimately linked to the diversity of plant life. In a kind of coevolutionary "arms race," many plants have developed specific chemical defenses to ward off foraging caterpillars. Butterfly and moth larvae, in turn, have often evolved the ability to overcome these toxins, setting off another round of adaptation and counteradaptation

Table 3.4. Largest insect orders in the United States

Insect order	Examples	Number of species	Percent of insect fauna
Coleoptera	Beetles	25,030	26%
Diptera	Flies	20,627	21%
Hymenoptera	Bees, wasps, and ants	18,107	19%
Lepidoptera	Butterflies, moths, and skippers	12,261	13%
Totals		76,025	79%

Four insect orders contain most of the described insect species in the United States. More than 70,000 additional U.S. insect species may exist but are as yet unnamed.

Sources: Estimates for North America, Kosztarab and Schaefer 1990; for Hawaii, Nishida 1994.

(Ehrlich and Raven 1965). The winged adults, on the other hand, sustain themselves by visiting flowers for nectar, and in so doing they are key plant pollinators.

Lepidoptera are the best known of the four largest orders of insects in the United States, largely due to the long history of interest on the part of amateur collectors working in conjunction with professional lepidopterists. Because butterflies are among the most charismatic invertebrates, more recently a new recreational activity has developed—butterfly-watching, complete with binocular-toting participants and annual counts. About 12,300 species of lepidopterans occur in the United States, representing some 10% of described species worldwide. Regularly occurring, native species of butterflies and skippers make up only about 620 of these. The remainder are moths, many of them rather inconspicuous and falling under the term *microlepidopterans*. Butterflies and moths in the United States do include some pretty macro species, though, including the giant swallowtail (*Papilio cresphontes*), which with a wingspan of more than six inches is the nation's largest butterfly. The cecropia moth (*Hyalophora cecropia*) is even larger, with wings that occasionally reach seven inches across. Perhaps the most famous of U.S. butterflies, however, is the monarch (*Danaus plexippus*). Most monarchs migrate from their breeding grounds across North America to the mountains of central Mexico, although there are also a few small overwintering sites in coastal California and the southern United States.

The moth family Noctuidae is particularly rich in the United States. With more than 3,000 U.S. species, this is our single largest group of lepidopterans, and they are the most common moths to congregate around nighttime lights. The showy underwings (*Catocala*) stand out from most of their drab noctuid relatives, and with about 105 U.S. species, the eastern United States is their global center of diversity. Among the evolutionary peculiarities found in the United States are several rare moths in the family Micropterigidae. Rather than sipping nectar through an elongate proboscis—the typical feeding mode among butterflies and moths—this archaic group retains chewing mouthparts characteristic of primitive lepidopterans and feeds by chewing on pollen.

Hawaii has a relatively small lepidopteran fauna, but at least one genus, the endemic *Hyposmocoma*, has radiated into an impressive 355 species. More fascinating, though, are certain Hawaiian members of the moth genus *Eupithecia*, which have developed a foraging strategy unique among caterpillars: ambush predation. These inchworms sit motionless, awaiting the passage of unsuspecting flies and other insects, which they then lunge at, capture, and consume. This adaptive shift in foraging strategies has led to the development of at least 18 distinct carnivorous species, each of which uses a different plant as an ambush perch (Howarth and Mull 1992).

Hawaii is also the site of one of the most spectacular, albeit inconspicuous, insect radiations, involving fruit flies of the genus *Drosophila*. This genus, the workhorse of genetics research, is more diverse in Hawaii than anywhere else on Earth. As many as 1,000 species of fruit flies have

The cecropia moth is the largest of the United States' approximately 12,300 species of lepidoptera; its wings can span seven inches. © Janet Haas.

Monarch butterflies migrate from their breeding grounds across North America to a few small overwintering sites. The largest concentration is found high in the Sierra Madre mountains of Mexico, where masses of butterflies drape the native fir trees. © Frans Lanting/Minden Pictures.

Employing an unusual foraging strategy—ambush predation—this caterpillar of the Hawaiian moth *Eupithecia staurophragma* has captured a picture-wing fruit fly (*Drosophila heteroneura*). ©William P. Mull.

Dragonflies, such as this green darner (*Anax junius*), are superb aerial predators. Dragonfly and damselfly larvae are fully aquatic and sensitive to changes in water quality. © Janet Haas.

evolved from one or perhaps two natural colonization events (Kaneshiro et al. 1995). Of these, only about 600 have so far been named. The approximately 100 species of so-called picture-wing Drosophila have attracted the most attention, in part because of the complex courtship rituals these species have developed. This includes defense of mating territories, or *leks*, behavior that is reminiscent on a miniature scale of the dancing and booming of midwestern prairie-chickens (*Tympanuchus cupido*).

Freshwater insects in the United States are also notable on a global scale, and for three well-studied groups—caddisflies, mayflies, and stoneflies—the United States harbors more species than any other nation. Caddisflies (Trichoptera) are perhaps best known for the elaborate cases the larvae construct out of sand, pebbles, or small bits of plant material, and which are sources of fascination to children poking about the sides of pools or streams. The United States harbors about 1,400 caddisfly species, or roughly 13% of the total described worldwide. Mayflies (Ephemeroptera) are well known to anglers, and most artificial fishing "flies" are modeled after one or another of these species. The aquatic larvae give way to flighted adults, which have an exceedingly ephemeral life span: After emergence the adults do not eat, and they typically live just a single day—only long enough to mate. The approximately 590 U.S. species represent almost one-third (30%) of known mayfly species. Stoneflies (Plecoptera) are another well-studied aquatic insect group for which the United States is a global leader. Stonefly nymphs depend on cool, clean water for their development and therefore are useful indicators of the health of streams and rivers. With about 610 species, the United States is home to 40% of the world's known stonefly species.

Dragonflies are superbly adapted aerial predators that contribute iridescent splashes of color to streamside habitats. Their larvae are fully aquatic and, like stoneflies, sensitive to the health of the nation's rivers, streams, ponds, and wetlands. Dragonflies and damselflies (Odonata) represent one of the most ancient insect groups, having first appeared more than 300 million years ago during the Carboniferous period. Their basic body plan, which allows both forward and backward flight, has changed little over time, although no living species can rival the two-and-a-half-foot wingspan of the fossil species *Meganeuropsis permiana*. The approximately 450 species of dragonflies and damselflies found in the United States make up approximately 8% of described odonates worldwide.

Other Invertebrates

Among other U.S. invertebrates, three groups stand out at the world level: freshwater and terrestrial mollusks, freshwater crayfishes, and cave obligate species. With nearly 300 species of freshwater mussels, the United States harbors almost one-third (29%) of known species and is by far the most diverse nation on Earth for this group. By comparison, Europe has only 10 known mussel species, Africa 56, India 54, and China 38 (Bogan 1993). Much of this mussel diversity is concentrated in the southeastern United States. The United States also harbors the largest number of crayfishes, with 322 species, representing an extraordinary 61% of the world's known total. Of these species, 96% are restricted to the United States, giving crayfishes one of the highest levels of national endemism for any group of organisms.

Snails—of both land and water—also exhibit globally outstanding diversity in the United States. For freshwater snails, the United States again is the most species-rich nation on Earth: Its approximately 660 species represent around 17% of the world's described species. Terrestrial snails are another group of organisms that has radiated extensively in the Hawaiian Islands. More than 750 native tree snail species are, or were, found in the Hawaiian Islands, most of them in just a few genera, such as *Achatinella*, *Partulina*, and *Amastra*. Terrestrial snails are also quite diverse on the mainland, where some 990 species occur (B. Roth pers. comm.). Many of the mainland species also inhabit what might be characterized as islands—in this case, habitat islands. Isolated western mountain peaks often have highly localized snail species. In the Midwest, certain snail species are even Ice Age relics, persisting in small patches of unusually cool and moist habitat known as *algific slopes*.

The United States is also home to an extraordinary diversity of subterranean invertebrates. These animals are found only in caves and other underground habitats and are adapted for life in complete darkness. Nearly 1,000 such species have been discovered and described within the United States, including both terrestrial organisms, known as *troglobites*, and animals of subterranean aquatic habitats, or *stygobites*. Most of these invertebrates are flatworms, arachnids, insects, crustaceans, annelid worms, or mollusks. These obligate cave-dwellers are characterized by extreme rarity and endemism, and many species are known from just a single location. Geographically they are concentrated in karst landscapes, where rock, especially limestone, is dissolved by chemical action to form caves and other subterranean cavities and passages. Given the difficulty of surveying underground habitats, and the small number of scientists working on the taxonomy of these animals, most subterranean species probably are yet to be found. Indeed, as many as 6,000 obligate cave-dwelling species may exist in the United States (Culver and Holsinger 1992).

Understanding Diversity Patterns: The Area Effect

Lists of species, whether U.S. endemics or not, by themselves say little about why these species occur where they do. For generations, data on species distribution lay scattered about like the species themselves, without comprehensive theories to tie them all together. The meaning of these disparate data have been clarified greatly over the past few decades, thanks largely to several scientific advances, including the rigorous application of mathematics to ecology and the confirmation and widespread acceptance of plate tectonics theory.

The United States has by far the most diverse collection of freshwater mussels of any nation; its nearly 300 species account for almost one-third of the earth's total. © Lynda Richardson.

Jewels of the forest, more than 750 native tree snails evolved in the Hawaiian Islands. The brightly striped *Achatinella sowerbyana* exists in just a few valleys high in the mountains of Oahu. ©William P. Mull.

The observations of many earlier naturalists held the seeds of what later researchers would flesh out with mathematics. In 1772, for example, Johann Reinhold Forster, a Prussian naturalist on James Cook's second voyage, observed: "Islands only produce a greater or lesser number of species, as their circumference is more or less extensive." Forster had recognized a perfectly intuitive yet profound pattern that would become the fulcrum for much modern biogeography and eventually conservation biology: Smaller areas contain fewer species than larger ones. The Swedish botanist Olof Arrhenius formalized this observation in the 1920s, but it was not until the work of Frank Preston, an optical engineer who dabbled—but to great effect—in ecology, that the species-area relationship was refined into its present mathematical formulation.

In two important papers published in the early 1960s, Preston provided a mathematically elegant description of the pervasive species-area pattern observed in nature. At about the same time, two other scientists puzzled over an explanation for that pattern. Robert MacArthur of Princeton and E. O. Wilson of Harvard argued that the explanation for the species-area relationship on islands was the result of an equilibrium: a balance between the two competing forces of extinction and immigration. As some species on an island became extinct, others colonized the island from elsewhere. Their theory postulated that each island has an equilibrium point between extinction and immigration, determined largely by size and degree of isolation. Large islands, for example, have sizable populations of species that are less likely to go extinct than small populations. New immigrants are also more likely to find their way to larger islands than to small ones. On the other hand, more remote islands will tend to receive fewer colonists but will still experience similar rates of extinctions. They should thus tend to support fewer species than a more accessible island of similar size.

MacArthur and Wilson (1967) offered the most complete version of their ideas in *The Theory of Island Biogeography*, which became one of the most influential ecological treatises ever written. Despite the book's title, the authors had developed a theory applicable not only to islands but to virtually any isolated habitat, a point they stress early on in the book. Equilibrium theory can apply to mountaintops, caves, tide pools, lakes, areas of tundra within taiga, and areas of taiga within tundra. Their book, together with MacArthur's (1972) later volume titled *Geographical Ecology*, inspired innovative experimental ecology, the results of which sometimes supported the theory and sometimes did not (Rosenzweig 1995). Island biogeography led to some of the most important advances in conservation science, particularly the idea that conservationists should pay close attention to the scale of their efforts and the landscape context within which they are working.

Why does the United States harbor so many species? Size clearly is a factor. Covering more than 3.5 million square miles, the United States is an enormous country. But perhaps even more important than overall size in determining the diversity of species is the nation's diversity of habitats. Diversity tends to increase when a greater variety of habitats is

The study of island biogeography has led to some of the most important conceptual advances in conservation science. © Harold E. Malde.

present, and on average, larger areas have more habitats than smaller ones. The United States has an exceptionally diverse set of climatic, topographic, and geologic features, leading to a remarkable diversity of ecological types, as will be discussed in detail in chapter 7.

Origins of the U.S. Biota

Diverse and disparate species inhabit the United States, from hellbenders, pronghorns, dippers, and darters to cycads, sunflowers, sycamores, and sequoias. How did such a melange of species come to inhabit the United States? Each plant or animal, whether the vestige of an ancient lineage or a relative newcomer, has its own evolutionary story. But while evolutionary histories are highly individual, certain distributional patterns appear repeatedly, implying shared, even if not identical, histories. For instance, how is it that the Carolina hemlock, American alligator, hellbender, and paddlefish—all inhabitants of the eastern United States—each have their only close relatives in eastern Asia? Other species, such as the ubiquitous creosote bush (*Larrea tridentata*) of the southwestern deserts and the nine-banded armadillo of Texas and neighboring states, have their affinities with species in the arid regions of southern South America. These biogeographical puzzles both perplex and delight biologists searching to understand the origins and relationships of the U.S. biota.

Explanations for how species came to be distributed are legion. Linnaeus, a devout Christian, believed all species had spread from Mt. Ararat, the legendary landing point of Noah's ark. Linnaeus did not explain why different areas have different species, or how species could have crossed inhospitable habitats, so one of his contemporaries, Comte de Buffon, offered an alternative. Buffon postulated a large northern landmass from which species could have migrated as climatic conditions changed. Both Linnaeus and Buffon assumed a single origin for all species, largely because they believed species to be immutable. This view was, of course, an outgrowth of their religious convictions.

The idea of a single origin for all species may now seem naïve or even quaint, but determining the birthplace of species or taxa remains enormously difficult despite the advances of evolutionary biology. How do we explain, for example, species like the Carolina hemlock or creosote bush and their far-off relatives? These are called *disjunct* species, cases in which two or more closely related taxa live today in widely separated regions and are absent from areas in between. Many scientists, including prominent thinkers like Charles Lyell, regarded as the father of geology, argued that disjunct species spread across the globe on vast but now submerged land bridges and ancient continents, including one that supposedly covered the entire South Atlantic Ocean.

Charles Darwin opposed such ideas. One of Darwin's most important contributions to the modern understanding of the origin of species was the idea of long-distance dispersal, and he lamented that the "extensionists,"

The American alligator illustrates the remarkable biotic connection between eastern Asia and eastern North America. China is home to the world's only other alligator species. Courtesy of Dick Bailey/ USFWS.

like Lyell, created land bridges "as easy as a cook does pancakes." We now recognize that disjunct species may reflect several types of historical events. Species can disperse across geographical barriers, such as mountain ranges or oceans, as, for instance, when a migrating bird gets blown off course during a storm. These physical barriers may also arise over time, splitting a widely distributed species into two or more isolated populations, or changing climate may reduce suitable habitat so that disjunctions represent the surviving remnants of once more widespread species. Species, and indeed entire biotas, can even be fragmented and carried to distant regions on the shifting crust of the earth.

Drifting Continents and the Science of Plate Tectonics

No scientific advance has revolutionized our understanding of the distribution of plants and animals more than the theory of plate tectonics, or "continental drift." Just as Darwin and Wallace showed that species were not immutable, so too would geologists prove that the continents themselves have changed dramatically over time. Although suggestions of drifting continents date back to the writings of the Flemish geographer Abraham Ortelius in the sixteenth century, a German meteorologist named Alfred L. Wegener is widely credited with developing the theory of continental drift, which he first proposed in 1912. Wegener drew on evidence from numerous fields, including the distribution of living and fossil species, to make his case. The theory, weakened by numerous factual errors, faced intense opposition, and colleagues scorned Wegener himself. Convincing evidence for the theory, and the science now called plate tectonics, would not emerge for another five decades. The revolution in deciphering plate tectonics occurred during the 1960s, based largely on data obtained through paleomagnetic mapping of the ocean floors. As the physical evidence mounted, plate tectonics became the unifying theory for understanding earth science and helped elucidate many of the most intractable biogeographic riddles.

The shifting boundaries among the continents played a major role in shaping life in North America. We summarize several of the key geological events in table 3.5, while figure 3.3 depicts the relative positions of the North American continent at different times in the earth's history. To simplify a complex series of events, about 250 million years ago, at the end of the Paleozoic era, the various continental landmasses merged together. The resulting supercontinent, known as Pangea, stretched from pole to pole. During this period, many life forms began developing adaptations for colonizing dry habitats in addition to the lowland, swampy habitats that were available in earlier times. By 180 million years ago, in the Jurassic, Pangea began breaking apart; the northern lands are known as *Laurasia* and the southern ones *Gondwanaland*. In the north, Asia separated from a still-combined North America and Europe. Africa, meanwhile, had become severed from Europe but was still connected to North America via South America. At this time, conifers, gingkos, ferns, and cycads dominated the plant world. Reptiles, meanwhile, had undergone tremendous radiation: Dinosaurs, along with swimming and flying reptiles, were the dominant land animals.

By about 160 million years ago, the precursors of North and South America split apart, effectively separating the Northern and Southern biotas. At roughly 100 million years ago, in the mid-Cretaceous, sea levels worldwide rose to a maximum: Water covered about one-third of the earth's present land area. Among the areas submerged by this "Cretaceous flood" was a large swath down the middle of North America, from the Arctic Ocean to the Gulf of Mexico. This so-called *epeiric* sea effectively split the continent, separating western North America from eastern North America and Europe.

Flowering plants, which first appear in the fossil record about 145 million years ago in the latest Jurassic (Sun et al. 1998), went through an explosive diversification during the mid- to late Cretaceous. Evolving in concert with insect pollinators, flowering plants came to dominate terrestrial vegetation by the end of this era. Most modern groups of vertebrates were also present at this time, including frogs, salamanders, turtles, lizards, snakes, and both placental and marsupial mammals.

By the end of the Cretaceous, the midcontinental sea had begun to recede, and the exposed land reconnected the eastern and western parts

Table 3.5. Key geological events shaping life in North America

Geological period	Age (approx.)	Event
Early Permian	290 Ma	Final Appalachian uplift begins
Late Permian	255 Ma	Consolidation of all continents into supercontinent of Pangea
Jurassic	180 Ma	Asia and Euroamerica split; North America's connection with Africa severed
Mid-Cretaceous	100 Ma	Shallow sea separates western North America from eastern North America and Europe
Late Cretaceous	75 Ma	Land connection with Asia established across Bering Strait; midcontinental sea recedes
Paleocene	66 Ma	Rocky Mountains uplift begins
Mid-Eocene	40 Ma	Southerly North Atlantic land connection interrupted
Early Oligocene	30 Ma	Northerly route across North Atlantic disappears
Miocene	20 Ma	Western cordillera begins uplift
Late Miocene	10–5 Ma	Central American archipelago provides possibility of stepping-stone dispersal
Pliocene	3.5 Ma	Central American land bridge formed, leading to Great American Interchange
Pleistocene	2 Ma	Ice Age begins
Pleistocene	18,000 years	Last glacial maximum

A number of geological events have had considerable influences on the development and evolution of life in North America. These include mountain-building episodes and connections with other continents, which facilitated or impeded movement of flora and fauna. Ma = million of years ago.

Sources: Brown and Lomolino 1998; Dott and Prothero 1994; Graham 1993, 1999; McKenna 1983.

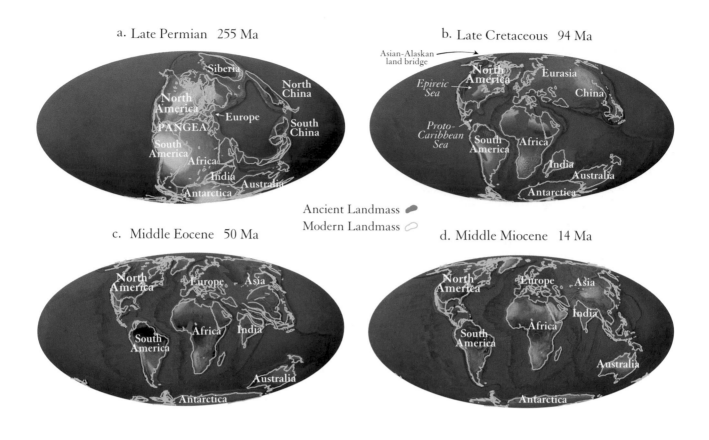

a. Late Permian 255 Ma

Siberia
North China
North America
PANGEA
Europe
South China
South America
Africa
India
Australia
Antarctica

b. Late Cretaceous 94 Ma

Asian-Alaskan land bridge
North America
Eurasia
China
Epireic Sea
Proto-Caribbean Sea
South America
Africa
India
Australia
Antarctica

Ancient Landmass
Modern Landmass

c. Middle Eocene 50 Ma

North America
Europe
Asia
South America
Africa
India
Australia
Antarctica

d. Middle Miocene 14 Ma

North America
Europe
Asia
India
South America
Africa
Australia
Antarctica

Figure 3.3a–d. North America's shifting tectonic position.

This series of reconstructions shows the past position of North America relative to other continents. (a) During the late Permian, all continents were united into the single supercontinent of Pangea. (b) By the Cretaceous, the continents had mostly split apart, and western and eastern North America were separated by a shallow continental sea. (c) By the middle Eocene, North America had pulled away from Europe yet was still connected to Asia. (d) In the Miocene, the world had assumed a modern configuration, although the gap between North and South America did not close until just 3.5 million years ago. Map source: PALEOMAP Paleogeographic Atlas, Scotese 1997.

of the continent. North America also became connected directly to Asia through the emergence of the Bering land bridge, starting about 75 million years ago. The effectiveness of this land bridge as a dispersal pathway initially was limited, however, by its far northern position (McKenna 1983). Meanwhile, North America and Europe appear to have been connected across the North Atlantic at lower latitudes and more moderate climates. Two land bridge routes crossing the North Atlantic appear to have existed—the Thulean in the south and the DeGeer to the north, both of which linked up with Greenland (Tiffney 1985). Mild temperatures and the occurrence of subtropical climates at relatively high latitudes during the early Eocene promoted an intensive exchange of biota between these two continents (Webb 1985). The North Atlantic land bridges had largely disappeared by the beginning of the Oligocene, but by this time the Bering land bridge had moved into a more southerly position and had become an increasingly important conduit for faunal exchanges between North America and Asia. By Miocene times, about 14 million years ago, the continents assumed essentially the configuration they have today.

Formation of a land bridge between North and South America was an especially important event for the biogeography of both continents. The tectonic history of the Central American region is, however, extraordinarily complex and still not well understood. Since the separation of North and South America about 160 million years ago, no connection had existed between these two continents, but about 10 million years ago, in the late Miocene, an island archipelago appears to have provided possibilities for stepping-stone dispersal between North and South America (Briggs 1994). Fusion into a complete land bridge, however, did not take place until the late Pliocene, a mere 3.5 million years ago.

Perhaps the most important geological event affecting the current distribution of plants and animals on the North American continent was the Pleistocene ice ages, which commenced about 2 million years ago. In North America at least four major glacial advances occurred, with the final, or Wisconsin, reaching its maximum extent some 18,000 years ago. The end of the Ice Age and the beginning of the present epoch—called the Holocene or "recent"—occurred between 7,000 and 8,000 years ago. Because of the importance of the Ice Age in determining the regional distribution of plants and animals within the United States, chapter 5, which addresses state-level patterns of biodiversity, presents a more detailed discussion of this event.

An Eastern Asia Connection

How does this welter of geological periods and shifting plates help us understand such things as the long-distance disjunction between the Carolina hemlock and its sister species in Hubei, China, or the similar disjunctions among paddlefish, alligators, and hellbenders? Linnaeus first noted a biotic connection between eastern Asia and eastern North America in 1750. The subject remained largely unexplored, however, until the great American botanist Asa Gray began a fruitful correspondence with Charles Darwin in 1855 (Boufford and Spongberg 1983).

Of particular interest to both Gray and Darwin was the emerging pattern indicating that the generic and specific affinities between the eastern North American and eastern Asian floras were greater than those between the eastern and western American floras. From his post at Harvard, Gray had the opportunity to study specimens gathered in Japan during a military exploring expedition. Gray's careful analysis of these collections formed the basis for his classic 1859 paper detailing the strong botanical relationships between eastern Asia and eastern North America and represented an early attempt at an analytical approach to biogeography. The broadleaf deciduous forests in these two regions, in particular, are strikingly similar, and more than 100 plant genera now are reported to have eastern Asian–eastern North American distributions (Hsü 1983). Prominent among them are primitive flowering plants descended from some of the early angiosperms that appeared in the late Cretaceous. These include members of the magnolia family, as well as such archaic genera as star-anise (*Illicium*) and star vine (*Schisandra*).

A notable example of a disjunct species pair in the magnolia family is tulip poplar, a genus containing but two species. One, *Liriodendron tulipifera*, is a dominant tree in eastern North American broadleaf forests, while the other, *L. chinense*, is found in similar forests of China. These patterns don't occur only in trees: A number of similar disjunctions are

The broadleaf deciduous forests of eastern North America and eastern Asia are strikingly similar, sharing more than 100 plant genera. © Laura Mansberg Cotterman/NCNHP.

Among the plant genera disjunct between eastern North America and eastern Asia are the tulip poplar (*Liriodendron*) (*above,* © Gary Braasch), with one U.S. and one Chinese species, and ginseng (*Panax*) (*below,* © Fred Whitehead/Earth Scenes), whose root is highly prized in traditional Chinese medicine.

found among herbs. Ginseng, the source of a highly prized medicinal, is an understory herb with two closely related but disjunct species on both continents, American ginseng (*Panax quinquefolius*) and Chinese ginseng (*P. ginseng*). Similar patterns occur in numerous other herbs, such as mayapple (*Podophyllum*) and jack-in-the-pulpit (*Arisaema*).

The most obvious explanation for the similarities between eastern Asia and eastern North America is that the species took the shortest route and migrated over the land bridge that once connected Russia and Alaska. This may not have been the case, however. Many of the ancient plant families represented by these disjunctions were components of a widespread Northern Hemisphere flora that extended across Asia, Europe, and North America during the middle part of the Tertiary. At the time many of these species were dispersing, the North Pacific land bridge would have been in a far northerly position, with fairly harsh climatic conditions. Instead, these plants may have crossed to North America via the North Atlantic connection, which was in a much more favorable climatic position than the more direct Bering route. Indeed, Europe's fossil tree flora is as diverse as that of Asia, and far more so than that of North America (Latham and Ricklefs 1993). The current disjunction pattern appears to have emerged through the extinction of a widespread Tertiary flora in different parts of its range. Western North America seems to have lost much of its deciduous forest elements during a drying trend that began in the Pliocene (Graham 1999). Europe's broadleaf forests, on the other hand, were decimated during the Pleistocene because the east-west barriers posed by the Alps and the Mediterranean Basin provided no southerly migration route for escaping the advancing glaciers. With the forests of western North America and Europe severely altered, while those in eastern Asia and eastern North America remain as relics of a much earlier time.

Origin of a Uniquely American Fish

If these U.S. plants and animals represent relicts of a more widespread biota, how then did such uniquely American creatures as the darters come to inhabit streams coursing through the same deciduous forests? The darters are without doubt among the most successful examples of evolutionary radiation of any group of American fishes. The nearly 170 species of darters, many of which are brilliantly colored and among our most attractive fishes, are members of the perch family. Within that family, they constitute a distinct evolutionary pathway, taxonomically recognized as a tribe that is restricted to North America. The perch family as a whole appears to have originated in Europe, dispersing into North America via the North Atlantic land route sometime between the end of the Cretaceous and the beginning of the Eocene (Briggs 1986). With the interruption of that land bridge sometime in the Eocene, these original colonists subsequently evolved in isolation from their Old World ancestors.

Development of novel ecological and physiological responses to the North American environment allowed these fishes to undergo an explosive radiation. Key to their success was specialization for living in shallow, often turbulent habitats where they can hide along the bottom under rocks and logs. The dynamic nature of many of their stream habitats, coursing through the ancient Appalachian and Ozark terrains, also promoted speciation. Periods of isolation in headwater regions allowed genetic divergence among populations, while the geological process of stream capture provided occasional mixing of the locally diverged fish stocks.

Some 50 million years after the arrival of the ancestral darters, two additional perch genera reached North America. The new colonists presumably came to North America from the opposite direction, across the Bering land bridge from Siberia. In comparison to the extraordinary numbers of darter species that evolved in North America, these more recent arrivals are represented by just three U.S. species—the walleye (*Stizostedion vitreum*, one of the United States' most popular sports fishes), sauger (*S. canadense*), and yellow perch (*Perca flavescens*). By the time they joined the darters on this continent, the evolutionary trajectories of these two groups of colonists had long been set, with the result that the latter are most closely related to Old World fish, while the amazingly diversified darters have no near relatives outside North America.

The rainbow darter (*Etheostoma caeruleum*) is one of nearly 170 species of darters, the most successful examples of evolutionary diversification of any group of American fishes. © Mac Albin.

The Great American Interchange

Because direct connection between North and South America was broken about 160 million years ago, before the evolution and spread of many modern groups of plants and animals, biotic exchanges with Europe and Asia played the dominant role in the development of the North American flora and fauna. The emergence of a Central American land bridge about 3.5 million years ago, and the subsequent reconnection of North and South America, set in motion a vast experiment that profoundly altered the mix of species on both continents. This exchange, known as the Great American Interchange, was far from even. South America, which for more than 100 million years had been isolated from other continents, had developed a highly unusual fauna that was in many ways comparable to the other great island landmasses of Australia and Madagascar. This "splendid isolation," as G. Gaylord Simpson (1980) described it, gave rise to a rich mammalian fauna, including many forms of marsupials and at least one monotreme, a relative of Australia's duck-billed platypus (*Ornithorhynchus anatinus*).

The disparity in the exchange between North and South America is most evident when one looks at the derivation of mammal species on each continent. About half of all contemporary South American mammals are of North American ancestry, while only a tenth of North American species trace their origins to South America (Brown and Lomolino 1998). In addition to some of the more typically North American animals that crossed into South America—such as cats, bears, and deer—several other North American groups are now more characteristic of South America than of their North American homeland. These include tapirs, peccar-

Guanaco, wild relatives of the domesticated llama, are a quintessential South American mammal, yet their camel-like relatives actually originated in North America. © Bruce A. Stein/TNC.

ies, and camels. The camels, in particular, which originated in North America but disappeared here about 10,000 years ago, gave rise to a quintessential South American animal group: the domesticated llama and its wild relatives the alpaca, vicuña, and guanaco.

Some of the southern animals that did reach North America were spectacular creatures, such as giant ground sloths the size of bears and anteaters the size of hippos. Most of these were casualties of the end-of-Pleistocene die-off that eliminated so many large animals from the American landscape. Only three mammals of South American origin occur in the United States today: the opossum (*Didelphis virginiana*), the nine-banded armadillo (*Dasypus novemcinctus*), and the porcupine (*Erethizon dorsatum*).

The Great American Interchange is not yet over: Both armadillos and opossums are still expanding their ranges northward. Although armadillos are known from the United States as Pleistocene fossils, the first contemporary U.S. records were from Texas in 1849 (Taulman and Robbins 1996). Readily adaptable to living around humans, the nine-banded armadillo has been expanding its range at an average rate of four to six miles per year. This robust creature now reaches as far north as Kansas, Missouri, and Illinois, and as far east as South Carolina, and climatic factors appear suitable for them as far north as New York. Similarly, at the time of European colonization the opossum did not occur north of Pennsylvania. Aided by its ability to adapt human alterations of the landscape, they reached Ontario, Canada, by 1858 and New England during the early 1900s (Nowak 1991).

The standard explanation for this lopsided exchange between the continents is that the northern species, forged in the evolutionary furnaces of the largely interconnected northern continents, outcompeted their more insular southern counterparts. The story is more complex, however, and involves differences in the degree to which the two faunas were able to persist and further evolve. While a similar number of northern and southern mammalian genera appear to have moved across the land bridge, once in South America the northern genera differentiated considerably, more than doubling in number (Webb and Marshall 1982). In contrast, southern-derived genera in North America did not go through a comparable evolutionary diversification and instead dwindled to fewer than half the number that initially dispersed north.

Although mammals provide the best fossil record and the most dramatic story from the Great American Interchange, they were obviously not the only organisms involved. Unfortunately, groups such as reptiles, birds, and bats leave fewer fossils than most terrestrial mammals, and the traces that remain are more difficult to interpret. Reptiles, birds, and bats are better than land mammals at crossing water to colonize new areas—birds and bats by flying, reptiles by floating on logs or other debris—so there had probably been a greater degree of exchange in these organisms between North and South America using the island archipelago for stepping-stone dispersal prior to the emergence of the land bridge. A number of these groups show a more balanced exchange, or even a predominance of successful southern invasions. Many neotropical migratory birds, such as wood warblers, vireos,

Armadillos are one of the few South American mammal groups that have successfully invaded North America. The nine-banded armadillo is still expanding its range north at about four to six miles per year. © E. R. Degginger/Animals Animals.

and tanagers, are South American in origin (Brown and Lomolino 1998). Pigeons, owls, woodpeckers, and jays, on the other hand, probably colonized South America from the north (Vuilleumier 1985). Among reptiles, the two largest families of New World lizards, iguanas (Iguanidae) and whiptails (Teiidae), have dispersed north from South America, as have most snakes (Brown and Lomolino 1998).

Plants, too, were better able to overcome the water barrier between North and South America, and considerable exchanges may have occurred by Eocene times (Raven and Axelrod 1974). Nonetheless, most of the South American plant groups that moved north are restricted largely to the more tropical regions of North America, including Mexico; relatively few currently reach as far north as the United States (Gentry 1982). Not surprisingly, most North American plant groups that moved into South America are concentrated in the higher-elevation montane regions, where conditions are similar to those in their temperate areas of origin.

A fascinating distributional pattern, termed *amphitropical*, is that of plants found only in North America and southern South America, but not in the intervening tropical regions (Raven 1963). The creosote bush (*Larrea tridentata*) of our southwestern deserts is so closely related to shrubs in Argentina (*L. divaricata*) that it is considered by some to be the same species. In an unusual twist, creosote has actually left a genetic trail tracing its northward dispersal. Creosote plants in South America, where the genus apparently originated, contain 13 pairs of chromosomes. The shrub appears to have moved north via long-distance dispersal, perhaps using pockets of arid vegetation in the Pliocene or Pleistocene Andes as stepping stones. But however it ultimately landed in the Chihuahuan Desert of northern Mexico, plants there also contain the original complement of 13 chromosomes. As the species continued its northward march, this seemingly immutable plant made some remarkable genetic transformations: Those that reached the Sonoran Desert have double the number, 26, while those in the Mojave Desert, farther north, have a triple complement, or 39 chromosomes (Hunziker et al. 1977).

Now the dominant shrub across vast areas of our southwestern deserts, creosote bush dispersed north from Argentina, leaving in its wake a trail of chromosomal changes as evidence of the journey. © Charlie Ott.

Evolution on an Island Hot Spot

Biogeographers once fiercely debated the relative importance of long-distance dispersal in the distribution of organisms; some even went so far as to reject its importance in the global distribution of plants and animals. The latter view—termed *vicariance*—argues that species disjunctions emerge when physical barriers arise and separate species that were once more widely distributed. Conversely, entire biotas may be transported across oceans on continental plates, as occurred when the Indian subcontinent broke away from Africa some 100 million years ago and rafted across the ocean to slam into Asia (creating the Himalayan Mountains in the process). Our modern geological understanding of the origins of the Hawaiian Islands definitively ends the debate over the importance of long-distance dispersal, however. Given that the archipelago has never been connected to any other landmass, its entire terrestrial biota has de-

The island of Hawaii, the youngest in the Hawaiian archipelago, is still growing as lava from the Kilauea volcano flows into the ocean, creating new land. © Michael Wilhelm/ENP Images.

rived from long-distance dispersal events. Indeed, Hawaii serves as the premier example of such colonization and subsequent evolution (Carlquist 1974).

Plate tectonics opened the door to an entirely new explanation of the origin of the Hawaiian archipelago. Now the unifying theory for volcanic islands around the world, this interpretation suggests that the islands are being created as an oceanic plate moves across a fixed hot spot located beneath the earth's crust. In the case of the Hawaiian archipelago, this hot spot has apparently been active for more than 75 million years, periodically perforating the oceanic plate and forming a volcanic island (Carson and Clague 1995). The hot spot has produced an island arc almost 2,200 miles long, although most of the islands have long since eroded to either low atolls or underwater sea mounts (figure 3.4). Despite the great antiquity of the hot spot and overall island chain, the high islands that currently make up the Hawaiian archipelago are quite recent in origin. Kauai, the oldest of the high islands, was formed only about 5.1 million years ago. The island of Hawaii, the youngest, dates from 400,000 years ago to the present, and active volcanoes continue to add to its land area (Carson and Clague 1995).

The Hawaiian Islands are the most isolated significant landmass on Earth, and any terrestrial organism must cross at least 2,500 miles of open ocean to colonize the archipelago. Colonists that arrive on the islands through such sweepstakes dispersal tend to have certain traits that enable them to survive the long trip, such as small, light seeds, or the ability to tolerate seawater. They tend not to reflect the full array of continental life-forms, creating a biota that is out of harmony, or *disharmonic*, relative to their source areas. Indeed, no amphibians or land reptiles were able to reach the islands, and just a single land mammal, the hoary bat (*Lasiurus*

Figure 3.4. Hawaii-Emperor volcanic chain.

Movement of the Pacific plate over a geological hot spot located beneath the earth's crust has produced an island arc almost 2,200 miles long, indicated here by the outline of two-kilometer depth contours. Most of the islands have long since eroded to form either low atolls or underwater sea mounts. Source: Modified from Clague and Dalrymple 1987.

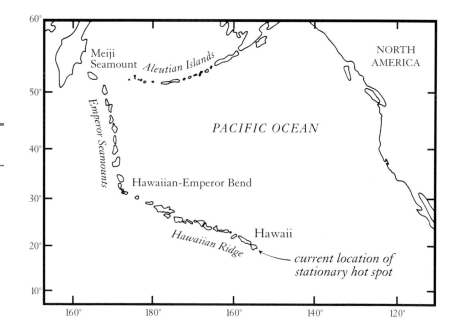

cinereus semotus), occurs there naturally. On the other hand, certain groups of plants and animals have a higher representation than is typical, an effect enhanced by the potential for postcolonization evolution and speciation. For instance, an eighth of Hawaii's native flowering plants are in the lobelia family (Campanulaceae), a group that in most continental regions represents a relatively small part of the overall flora.

Although few plants and animals successfully made the voyage to the remote archipelago, those that did arrive had a wide array of unoccupied ecological niches available to them, resulting in a number of spectacular evolutionary radiations. For flowering plants, about 290 original colonists apparently evolved into the present-day flora of approximately 1,023 native species (Sakai et al. 1995a, 1995b). A mere 15 original colonists may account for all 53 species of endemic Hawaiian land birds (Berger 1981). Even more striking is the fact that nearly 1,000 species of *Drosophila* fruit flies have evolved on the islands from one colonization or, at most, two.

The island chain's extreme isolation, great climatic and topographic diversity, and rich volcanic soils have given rise to some of the most extraordinary levels of endemism on Earth, including 43% of its vertebrates and 87% of its vascular plants. Considering all terrestrial and marine plants and animals, more than 8,800 endemic Hawaiian species are known, representing about half of the native biota (Eldredge and Miller 1998). Endemism in particular groups can range even higher: Hawaiian insects reach the astonishing level of 97% endemism.

Despite the archipelago's greater proximity to North America, most plants that have colonized the Hawaiian Islands appear to be of Malesian affinity (Wagner et al. 1990). This may partially be due to the movements of the jet stream, which blows from the west to the east, accelerating over Indo-Malaysia and decelerating over Hawaii (Carlquist 1980). North America has contributed some notable features to the Hawaiian flora, however, including the dramatic silversword (*Argyroxiphium sandwicense*) and its relatives. These plants, members of the sunflower family, apparently evolved from a single tarweed species that arrived in Hawaii from California, probably on the order of 5 million years ago (Baldwin and Sanderson 1998). This ancestral tarweed must have crossed vast stretches of open ocean, perhaps stuck to a wayward bird. It has since evolved into a complex of 3 genera and 28 species, some of which, like the silversword, are among the most recognizable natural symbols of the Hawaiian Islands.

North America has made a strong contribution to the Hawaiian avifauna, most notably in the honeycreepers. These species represent the most spectacular evolutionary radiation among Hawaiian birds and apparently derived from a North American finch ancestor. Traditionally, all honeycreepers have been considered to derive from a single colonist, but molecular evidence suggests that one, the Maui creeper (*Paroreomyza montana*), may have evolved from a second colonization event (Tarr and Fleischer 1995). Other North America–derived birds include the Hawaiian thrushes and the Hawaiian hawk. Asian or southeast Asian affinities are indicated for several other Hawaiian birds, including the honeyeaters, Old World warblers, and monarchid flycatchers.

One of the most spectacular evolutionary radiations in Hawaii involves plants in the lobelia family, including this *Lobelia kauaensis*. Many of the Hawaiian lobelioids have assumed a treelike habit, a feature unusual in this typically herbaceous plant group. © Warren L. Wagner.

Nearly 1,000 species of *Drosophila* fruit flies have evolved in Hawaii from one or, at most, two colonizations. Picture-wings, such as *D. digressa*, exhibit unusual territorial mating behaviors. © William P. Mull.

Most of the colorful and varied Hawaiian tree snails appear related to groups found in the western Pacific, and they probably dispersed to Hawaii from that region (Carlquist 1980). Among the freshwater organisms, many probably arrived by sea, later adapting to freshwater conditions, while most winged insects, such as moths, beetles, and wasps, probably blew in on the breezes. More precisely pinning down the origins of many of Hawaii's insect groups is problematic: While the largest numbers belong to north temperate groups, many could have come from either Asia or North America (Howarth and Mull 1992).

Summary of U.S. Diversity

With more than 200,000 species, the United States is home to an exceptionally diverse flora and fauna, thanks to its large size, its long geological history, its varied climate and topography, and the resulting diversity of ecological types. On a global scale, the country is particularly noteworthy for certain groups of organisms, including salamanders, coniferous plants, and freshwater turtles, fishes, mussels, snails, and crayfishes. This varied U.S. biota derives from a number of sources. Because there were connections to Europe or Asia through much of the geological past, many species were exchanged with those two continents, and some evolved into uniquely North American forms. Reconnection with South America occurred very late in the geological past and contributed still other species to the North American continent, although at least for mammals, most of this exchange flowed from north to south. Hawaii, in contrast, has never been connected to another landmass, and any terrestrial species there necessarily had to disperse over thousands of miles of open ocean. Upon reaching the Hawaiian archipelago, many of these species went through evolutionary radiations that have produced one of the most interesting and unique biotas in the world.

The Haleakala silversword (*left,* ©Warren L. Wagner) is one of the most spectacular natural symbols of the Hawaiian Islands. All three genera and 30 species in the silversword alliance apparently evolved from a single tarweed colonist, related to California's *Madia elegans* (*right*, © Harold E. Malde).

4

VANISHING ASSETS
Conservation Status of U.S. Species

"The air was literally filled with pigeons; the light of noonday was obscured as by an eclipse." So observed John James Audubon, the eminent naturalist and bird artist, of a mass migration of passenger pigeons (*Ectopistes migratorius*) passing through Kentucky in 1813. For three days the pigeons poured out of the Northeast in search of forests bearing nuts and acorns. By Audubon's estimate, the flock that passed overhead contained more than *1 billion* birds, a number consistent with calculations made by other ornithologists. As the pigeons approached their roost, Audubon noted that the noise they made "reminded me of a hard gale at sea passing through the rigging of a close-reefed vessel." Indeed, they were so numerous that by some accounts every other bird on the North American continent was probably a passenger pigeon at the time of European colonization (Schorger 1955). Yet despite this extraordinary abundance, barely 100 years later the last passenger pigeon, a female bird named Martha, died in the Cincinnati Zoo.

The vast flocks of passenger pigeons moved around eastern North America, feeding mostly on the fruits of forest trees such as beechnuts and acorns. Two factors conspired to seal their fate. Because of their huge numbers, the birds were easy to hunt, especially at their roosting sites. Hunters were ingenious in developing increasingly efficient ways to slaughter the birds. Armed with sticks, guns, nets, or sulfur fires, hunters swept through the enormous roosting colonies, carting away what they could carry and feeding the remaining carcasses to their pigs. One of these methods, in which a decoy pigeon with its eyes sewn shut was attached to a perch, or stool, gave rise to the term *stool pigeon*. As the railroads expanded west, enormous numbers could be sent to major urban markets like New York, where pigeons became the cheapest meat available. They were so cheap and abundant that live birds were used as targets in shooting galleries.

Lawrence L. Master

Bruce A. Stein

Lynn S. Kutner

Geoffrey A. Hammerson

Once the most abundant bird on the North American continent, the passenger pigeon was exterminated in less than a hundred years in the face of relentless hunting and the spreading destruction of its forest habitat. © Corbis/Bettmann.

At the same time that this frontal assault on the pigeons was under way, human settlers were expanding into the interior of the country, clearing large areas of the forests on which the flocks depended for food. As the forests receded and the birds suffered huge losses from hunting, the great flocks became a thing of the past. For reasons not entirely understood, fragmentation of these flocks had a profound influence on the reproduction of these intensely social birds. Even though large numbers still existed, in essence the species had entered the downward spiral of a negative feedback loop. The fewer the birds, the less likely the survival of those who remained. By the 1880s the flocks were dwindling rapidly throughout their range, and in 1914 Martha dropped dead off her perch in Cincinnati.

The demise of the Ash Meadows poolfish (*Empetrichthys merriami*) stands in sharp contrast to the passenger pigeon. Always rare, this diminutive fish lived in just five isolated desert springs in the Ash Meadows region of Nevada near Death Valley. First discovered in 1891, the fish was not seen again until 1930. During the late 1930s and early 1940s, concerted inventory efforts yielded very few specimens, and researchers collected the last known individual in September 1948 (Miller et al. 1989). The fish slipped into oblivion sometime between 1948 and 1953, when other researchers unsuccessfully attempted to find the species. What was the principal cause for the disappearance of this rare and very localized fish? During the 1930s two voracious predators, bullfrogs (*Rana catesbeiana*) and crayfish (*Procambarus clarkii*), first appeared in the springs harboring the Ash Meadows poolfish. Not naturally found in these delicate ecosystems, these two introduced species apparently ate the poolfish into extinction, perhaps aided by general deterioration of some of the fish's spring habitats (Miller et al. 1989).

Each extinction is a unique event. Some species, like the passenger pigeon, have declined from amazing abundance through human actions. Others, like the Ash Meadows poolfish, were always very rare and susceptible to environmental perturbations, both human and natural. No matter what the starting point or the specific causes, the results are the same—the permanent loss of that species' genetic heritage.

To effectively conserve our biological inheritance and guard against additional extinctions, we must have an indication of how U.S. plants and animals are faring. Assessing a species' conservation status is similar to conducting a medical examination. Ideally, we would like to know about the current health of the species. How abundant, widely distributed, and secure is the organism? What is its prognosis over the mid- and long term? Are there threats or other risk factors looming on the horizon that have the capacity to strike down even an apparently healthy species? The following section describes the scientific techniques used by the Natural Heritage Network for assessing the conservation status—or health—of species. Using these species-by-species evaluations, we can then address the question of how the U.S. biota is doing overall, and which groups of plants or animals are at greatest risk of extinction. Finally, we consider those species that have already succumbed and joined the passenger pigeon and the Ash Meadows poolfish.

Assessing Conservation Status

Which species and communities are thriving, and which are at the brink of extinction? These are crucial questions for targeting conservation toward those species and ecosystems in greatest need. To answer these questions, the Natural Heritage Network has developed a consistent method for evaluating the health and condition of both species and ecological communities. This assessment leads to the designation of a conservation status rank, an estimation of relative imperilment. This provides an approximation of a species' risk of extinction (Master 1991, Stein et al. 1995b). Other systems also have been developed for assessing status and identifying species in danger of extinction. The U.S. Endangered Species Act, for instance, defines legal categories of endangerment, while at an international level the IUCN Species Survival Commission has developed threat categories for its red lists. In this section we focus on the heritage assessment system which is the most comprehensively applied approach in the United States. Later in this chapter, we compare the heritage approach and its assessments with these other approaches.

Although there are numerous possible causes of extinction, they can be grouped into two major types: those that are systematic pressures, directionally pushing a species toward extinction, and those that are random (Quammen 1996). Systematic pressures can include such human activities as hunting, water diversions, or habitat destruction or can be the result of environmental shifts like climate change or the evolution or introduction of a new competitor or predator to the species. Random, or stochastic, pressures are often less obvious, but it is becoming increasingly clear that random events play a major role in the life of species and in the functioning of ecosystems. Shaffer (1981, 1987) identified four classes of random events that can contribute to an increased probability of extinction: (1) environmental uncertainty—for instance, variations in weather (as distinct from long-term climatic trends), in food supply, or in the populations of predators, competitors, parasites, and disease organisms; (2) catastrophe, such as floods, fires, or drought; (3) demographic stochasticity, or fluctuation in births and deaths in a population, and the consequent variation in numbers and sexes of individuals; and (4) genetic stochasticity, including such processes as genetic drift and inbreeding depression.

Conservation status assessments are an attempt to determine the relative susceptibility of a species to extinction. Ideally, then, they should take into account the various factors described above, which can play contributing and interacting roles in the decline and ultimate demise of a species. The assessment process developed and used by the heritage network considers several key factors that relate to both deterministic and stochastic threats to a species' survival (table 4.1). These criteria combine information about the intrinsic vulnerability of the species and external threats that may be operating on it.

Rare species are particularly vulnerable to both human-induced threats and natural fluctuations and hazards. As Rosenzweig (1995) notes, "The several widely accepted theories of extinction are grounded in the assump-

Even if they are seemingly buffered from human threats, geographically localized species may still be susceptible to extinction from random accidents or catastrophic natural events, such as hurricanes, fires, droughts, or volcanic eruptions. © Gerry Ellis.

Table 4.1. Criteria used in assessing conservation status

Occurrences	Number of distinct populations or subpopulations
Condition	Viability of extant populations
Population size	Number of extant individuals (census population size)
Area of occupancy	Total area of occupied habitat across range
Range	Extent of overall geographic range
Trends	Short-and long-term increase or decrease in population numbers, area of occupancy, or condition of occurrences
Threats	Known or suspected current threats, or likely future threats
Fragility	Inherent susceptibility to threats due to intrinsic biological factors
Protected occurrences	Number of adequately protected populations

tion that rarity matters." But while rarity is a key predictor of extinction potential, it is complex and thus hard to characterize. For this reason, four of the criteria specifically focus on assessing different aspects of rarity: the number of different populations or occurrences of the species; the total population size, or abundance, as measured by the number of individuals; the breadth of the species' geographic range; and the extent of occupied habitat. While the number of extant populations is one of the key assessment criteria, viability of these populations is also an important factor. This is especially true for species whose populations are greatly reduced in number or extent. Viability is a function of population size, condition (e.g., reproductive output, intact biological and ecological processes), and landscape context (e.g., genetic connectivity). For example, the white wartyback mussel (*Plethobasus cicatricosus*) has disappeared from virtually all of its former range in the Ohio River system but is still found in at least one location in Tennessee. Unfortunately, the fish on which the mussel's larvae depend as an intermediate host has been extirpated from that system, unable to survive in the deeper, colder waters produced by a series of dams. Thus, while the white wartyback mussel is still extant as a species, with no intermediate hosts to aid in its breeding, no viable populations are left. Although we do not know when the last of these long-lived creatures will die, as a species it is already functionally extinct—a member of the living dead (Stein and Flack 1997).

As the passing of the passenger pigeon makes clear, however, rarity alone is not adequate to assess a species' risk of extinction. Population trends, especially declines, are also important to consider. Information on population trends—whether a species' numbers are increasing, stable, or declining—and trends in occupancy, total range, and population condition are key factors in status assessments when such information is available. Extinction, after all, is simply the ultimate decline in population numbers.

Threats to a species, human and natural, are key predictors of future decline and are thus important to determine both as part of the assessment process and as a way to identify appropriate conservation measures for those species that are in trouble. An additional factor is the inherent fragility of a species—that is, whether due to its biology it is particularly sensitive to perturbations or intrusions of its physical or biological environment.

Pushed to the brink of extinction by changes to its river habitat, the last of the white wartyback mussels have joined the ranks of the living dead. © Kevin S. Cummings/Illinois Natural History Survey.

Heritage Conservation Status Ranks

Global conservation status ranks are based on a one-to-five scale (table 4.2), ranging from critically imperiled (G1) to widespread, abundant, and demonstrably secure (G5). An example of a critically imperiled, or G1, species is the whooping crane (*Grus americana*), a species so reduced in its numbers that in 1995 only about 200 existed, of which more than half were in captivity (USFWS 1995). White-tailed deer (*Odocoileus virginianus*), a very common eastern U.S. mammal whose soaring numbers in the absence of its natural predators are contributing to the deterioration of natural forests, is an example of the type of species ranked as G5. Species known to be extinct (GX), or missing and possibly extinct (GH), are recorded independently. The passenger pigeon is consigned to the GX ranking because there is no question about the continued existence of the species. On the other hand, a considerable number of species have not been seen in many years, yet biologists cannot say with certainty that the species is extinct. Such "missing" species, like Bachman's warbler (*Vermivora bachmanii*), are assigned the more conservative rank of possibly extinct, or GH (the *H* stands for "historical").

The term *species at risk* as used in this volume generally refers to those species classified as vulnerable or more rare (G3 to GX). Collectively, these species represent those plants and animals that have elevated risks of extinction and are therefore of greatest conservation concern. We should note, however, that widespread and abundant species (ranked G4 and G5) that are experiencing dramatic population declines may also be of particular concern to conservationists, although they are not here included in the definition of species at risk.

While species are generally regarded as the most basic taxonomic unit for conservation, subspecies and varieties, known as *infraspecific taxa*, represent distinctive geographic, morphological, and genetic variants. These infraspecific taxa may be at risk of extinction even while the overall species to which they belong is abundant and secure. The conservation status assessment procedure is designed to allow an independent assessment

The whooping crane is an example of the extreme rarity and vulnerability of species accorded the conservation status of G1, or *critically imperiled*. Typically such species are found in fewer than five locations on Earth. © Ray Richardson/ Animals Animals.

Although the last confirmed sighting of the Bachman's warbler was in 1962, biologists are not yet convinced it is extinct. Such missing species are ranked *possibly extinct* (GH) rather than placed in the more definitive *presumed extinct* (GX) category. © J. H. Dick/VIREO.

Table 4.2. Definition of conservation status ranks

GX	Presumed extinct: Not located despite intensive searches
GH	Possibly extinct: Of historical occurrence; missing but still some hope of rediscovery
G1	Critically imperiled: Typically 5 or fewer occurrences or 1,000 or fewer individuals
G2	Imperiled: Typically 6 to 20 occurrences or 1,000 to 3,000 individuals
G3	Vulnerable: Rare; typically 21 to 100 occurrences or 3,000 to 10,000 individuals
G4	Apparently secure: Uncommon but not rare; some cause for long-term concern; usually more than 100 occurrences and 10,000 individuals
G5	Secure: Common; widespread and abundant

The definitions provided here are for general guidance only; other assessment criteria (table 4.1) are used in addition to these occurrence and abundance guidelines. This table lists basic conservation status ranks only. Modifiers used to denote uncertainty in assessments are listed in table 4.3.

of these subspecies and varieties apart from the full species. The status of infraspecific taxa is indicated by combining a "T" rank (for "trinomial") with the global status ("G" rank) of the full species. For example, the Florida panther (*Felis concolor coryi*) is an endangered subspecies of the mountain lion, a wide-ranging species found throughout much of the Western Hemisphere. As a species, *Felis concolor* is abundant and secure and is therefore ranked G5; the subspecies *F. c. coryi*, however, is regarded as critically imperiled. Thus, the Florida panther subspecies of mountain lion receives a global conservation status rank of G5T1.

Standards for assessing the status of infraspecific taxa and assigning T ranks follow the same principles outlined above. It is important to recognize that a T rank cannot imply that the subspecies or variety is more secure than the species' basic global rank. To put it another way, the overall assessment of a species must reflect the condition of its component subspecies or varieties. Thus, a G2T4 rank would be a logical impossibility, since if a subspecies is abundant enough to be regarded as T4 (apparently secure), then the overall species would also be considered secure enough to warrant ranking as at least a G4.

Conservation priorities must be established on a variety of geographic and political scales. Therefore, the conservation status assessments developed by the heritage network are designed to assess a species' status not only across its entire distribution (i.e., at the global or rangewide level) but also at national and state levels. A similar one-to-five numeric scale is used to assess and describe imperilment and vulnerability on national and subnational (e.g., state or province) scales, resulting in N and S ranks, respectively. For example, at a rangewide level, the Mexican sabal palm (*Sabal mexicana*) is considered to be common and secure throughout its primarily Mexican range and is therefore ranked G5. Its status within the United States, where it is known as the Texas palmetto, is a different story.

Top left: Restricted to a small range in California's San Joaquin Valley and threatened by agricultural development and urbanization, the blunt-nosed leopard lizard (*Gambelia sila*) is an example of a species regarded as *imperiled* (G2). © B. Moose Peterson/WRP.

Bottom left: Having suffered dramatic reductions in numbers, yet still abundant across the plains region, the black-tailed prairie dog (*Cynomys ludovicianus*) is only considered *apparently secure* (G4). Continued declines may push the species into the *vulnerable* (G3) category. © Jeremy Woodhouse/DRK PHOTO.

Right: Prized by gardeners, the beautiful Gray's lily (*Lilium grayi*) is restricted to a small area of the southern Appalachians. With just a few populations, and subject to threats ranging from bulb collecting to changes in its habitat, the species is considered *vulnerable* (G3). © Paul Somers.

Reaching just into Texas, the palm is extremely rare in that state and therefore for the United States as a whole. For this reason it receives a U.S. national rank of N1, as well as a Texas state rank of S1.

From a conservation perspective, there is considerable difference between a common species' rarity along the periphery of its range and a species that is nowhere common and everywhere rare or otherwise at risk. Nonetheless, peripheral populations of even common species may harbor interesting and unusual genetic resources (Millar and Libby 1991). In part this may occur because these populations are isolated from the main range of the species and thus may be on an independent evolutionary trajectory. Additionally, the peripheral populations may be responding to environmental conditions quite different from those that influence populations at the center of the species' range. Loss of rare peripheral populations of common species may thus represent more of an erosion of the genetic level of biodiversity than would at first be apparent to someone looking simply at the species level. Assessing the global, national, and state status separately allows us to take such considerations into account and to base conservation priorities on a clear understanding of the relative levels of risk at different geographic scales.

Conservation status assessments must be continually reviewed, refined, and updated. During 1996 alone, natural heritage and Conservancy scientists reappraised and updated the status of almost 5,000 species. In making and documenting conservation status determinations, natural heritage biologists rely on the best available information, including such sources as natural history museum collections, scientific literature and previously published reports, and other documented sightings and surveys by knowledgeable biologists. To augment this existing knowledge, heritage biologists conduct extensive field inventories and population censuses, especially targeting those species which are thought to be imperiled or for which few data exist. Most year-to-year changes in status assessments tend to reflect this improved scientific understanding of the actual condition of the species or community.

The ability to assign status ranks accurately depends largely on the amount of information available about a species. For this reason, it is important to be able to document the level of confidence or uncertainty in any particular assessment. Two tools for this job are in place. First, a computerized ranking form (the Element Global Rank record) is filled out during the assessment process; this form documents the information and criteria on which the final assessment is based. Second, an array of ranks and modifiers are used that immediately flag uncertainty (table 4.3). These notations allow heritage biologists to make at least preliminary assessments based on available, even if incomplete, information.

If a species has not yet been assessed, a default rank value of "?" (e.g., G?) draws attention to this fact and to the need for a first approximation assessment. In the event that a species cannot be assessed in even a preliminary way, due to either complete absence of data or serious taxonomic issues, a rank of "U" (e.g., GU) denotes that the species is currently unrankable. On the other hand, if some information is available

Conservation status can be assessed separately for full species and for subspecies or varieties. Mountain lions, for instance, are regarded as *secure* (G5) rangewide, although the Florida panther subspecies is ranked as *critically imperiled* (G5T1). © Tom and Pat Leeson/Photo Researchers.

The Mexican sabal palm is widespread and abundant in Mexico, yet extremely rare in the United States. It is therefore regarded as *secure* globally (G5) but is given a U.S. national rank of *critically imperiled* (N1). © Harold E. Malde.

Table 4.3. Modifiers to basic conservation status ranks

G?	Not yet ranked
G_?	Preliminary assessment (e.g., G3?)
G_G_	Rank ranges reflecting upper and lower bounds of confidence: insufficient information to rank more precisely (e.g., G2G4)
G_Q	Questionable taxonomic status (e.g., G1Q)
GU	Unrankable with current information

These modifiers allow heritage biologists to indicate a level of uncertainty associated with a ranking or to denote other unusual circumstances affecting a species' status rank

but it is insufficient for assigning a precise rank, one may make a preliminary assessment by describing the upper and lower bounds of uncertainty. For instance, a species that, based on the little information available, might fall into either the imperiled (G2) or vulnerable (G3) categories would receive a rank of G2G3. These "rank ranges" can then be revisited and refined as additional information is developed or otherwise becomes available. If there is a higher degree of certainty, but for some reason questions still remain about the status rank, a question mark can be used to modify the rank (e.g., G3?), again drawing attention to the need for additional resolution. For purposes of the following analyses, imprecise ranks have been "rounded off."

Finally, there is the problem of assessing species of questionable taxonomic status. Opinion about what constitutes distinct and recognizable species can differ dramatically among taxonomists, with the result that even some species names in wide use may reflect questionable biological entities. Heritage biologists may assess the status of these taxa and assign a rank, but that rank is qualified with the notation "Q" (e.g., G2Q) for "taxonomically questionable." The taxonomic concerns leading to this designation are documented in the accompanying ranking form. This Q designation signals *caveat emptor*, notifying users of taxonomic uncertainties or discrepancies but leaving the decision whether to heed or ignore it in their hands.

State of the Nation's Species

What, then, do these conservation status assessments say about the overall condition of the U.S. flora and fauna? Given the paucity of information available about most of the nation's more than 200,000 species, we must recognize that any attempt to characterize the status of the biota overall will necessarily be incomplete. Nonetheless, over the past 20 years natural heritage programs together with The Nature Conservancy have assessed the status of more than 30,000 U.S. species and subspecies. These assessments are comprehensive for 14 of the best-known plant and animal groups. That is, the conservation status has been evaluated for each and every species in these groups. These 14 groups, which include all vertebrates and vascular plants, represent about 20,900 species. While there are large gaps in our understanding of status, the assessments available begin to paint an overall picture of the condition of wildlife in America. And that picture is not particularly good.

Overall, a surprisingly high one-third of the native U.S. flora and fauna is considered to be of conservation concern (figure 4.1). The proportion of species at risk varies greatly from one group of plants and animals to another, from a high of 69% to a low of 14% (figure 4.2.). These figures reflect species ranked as either extinct, imperiled, or vulnerable (categories GX to G3), and for consistency among groups, they include only full species (no subspecies, varieties, or distinct populations are included).

Freshwater-dependent animals, such as mussels, crayfishes, stoneflies, amphibians, and fish, are clearly the most vulnerable groups as measured by proportion at risk. Freshwater mussels, with an astonishing 69% of their species in trouble, lead all other species groups. This includes more than 1 in 10 mussel species that have become extinct or are missing. In contrast, several vertebrate groups appear to be on relatively secure footing, at least at the full species level measured here. This includes the two groups of animals that typically receive the majority of public conservation attention (and conservation funding): Of all groups, birds are best off, with about 14% of their species at risk, followed closely by mammals, at about 16%.

Number of species tells quite a different story. While on a proportional basis freshwater species appear to be at greatest risk, based on the number of species actually involved, flowering plants dominate by a huge margin (figure 4.3, table 4.4). With more than 15,300 native U.S. species, the one-third (33%) of flowering plants at risk translates to a sobering 5,090 species. This number of at-risk species is more than an order of magnitude larger than that of any other group. By number of species, freshwater fishes rank a distant second, with 300 species at risk. Groups containing fewer than 100 species at risk include dragonflies, mammals, reptiles, conifers, and tiger beetles.

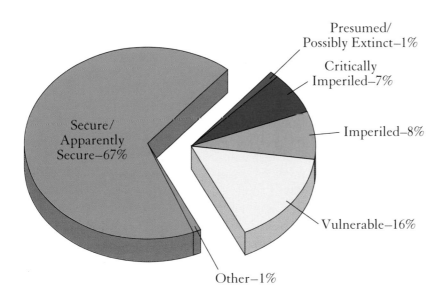

Figure 4.1. Proportion of U.S. species at risk.

Based on an assessment of 20,892 species, one-third of the native U.S. flora and fauna appears to be of conservation concern.

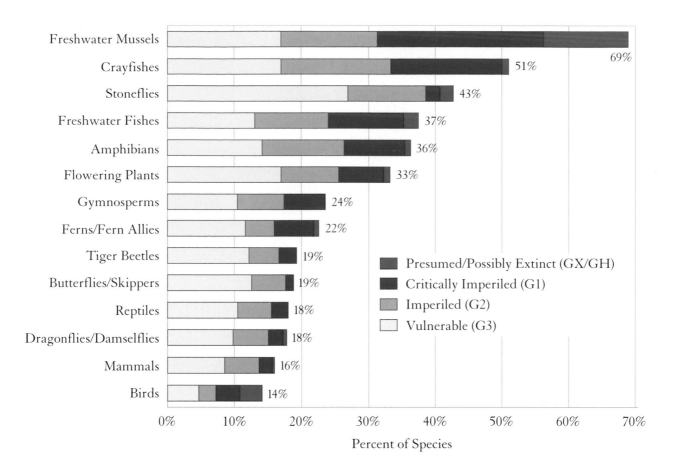

Figure 4.2. Proportion of species at risk by plant and animal group.

Those groups relying on freshwater habitats—mussels, crayfishes, stoneflies, amphibians, and fishes—exhibit the highest levels of risk.

Given the large number of flowering plants, representing nearly three-quarters of the total number of species assessed, is it possible that the overall proportion of species at risk (figure 4.1) reflects little more than the ratio of flowering plants at risk? To examine this possibility, we excluded flowering plants and recalculated the overall proportion at risk. Even without this major group, the overall at-risk figure is 29%, lower but not dramatically different than the inclusive figure of one-third. Although plants represent the largest number of species of conservation concern among those groups analyzed here, it is important to note that many invertebrate groups, particularly insects and other arthropods, are poorly known and therefore are not included in these assessments. These organisms likely will dominate the list when more complete data are available. However, even as additional groups are assessed and included, these general trends in status should remain reasonably accurate, based as they are on a substantial and diverse sample of the biota.

Status of U.S. Endemics

Many of the species included in the above figures are also found outside the United States, ranging either south into Mexico, the Caribbean, and beyond, or north through Canada. While the United States has a global responsibility for helping to ensure the survival of these organisms, because of their transnational distribution the U.S. does not bear sole re-

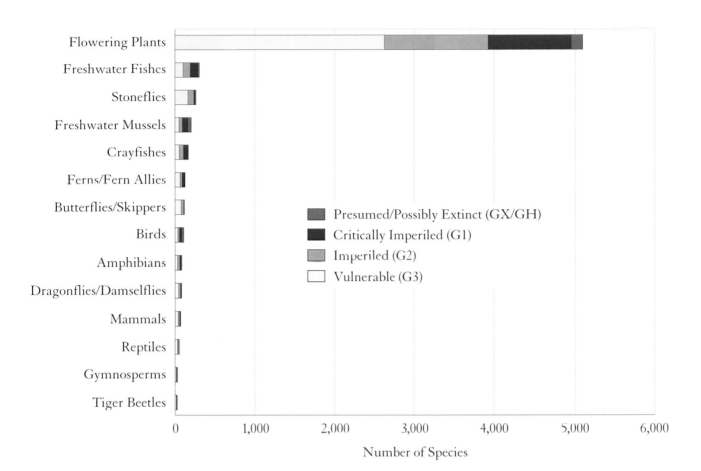

Number of Species

sponsibility for their protection. Not so for those plants and animals that are restricted to the United States. These species are necessarily of special concern. We are the exclusive heirs and guardians of these species and therefore have sole responsibility for them.

How, then, does the conservation status of these U.S. endemics differ from the status of the biota as a whole? Not surprisingly, this seemingly simple question turns out to be quite complex. *Endemic* can be defined in several ways, depending on the goal. Because our purpose here is to use the concept as a conservation assessment tool, we consider as "endemics" those species that are essentially restricted to the bounds of the 50 states, disregarding minor border incursions and records of accidental wanderings beyond these bounds. We also include as "breeding endemics" the 20 bird species that range beyond U.S. borders but breed only within the United States. For example, the golden-cheeked warbler (*Dendroica chrysoparia*) breeds only on the Edwards Plateau of Central Texas, but it overwinters in Central America. From a conservation perspective the United States bears unique responsibility for preservation of these birds through our sole control of their breeding grounds.

For the 875 vertebrate species endemic to the lower 48 states, almost half (47%) are of conservation concern, compared to just a quarter (24%) for all 2,497 U.S. vertebrate species. Because of the disjunct natures of Hawaii and Alaska, it is also illuminating to consider the status of endemics in these

Figure 4.3. Numbers of species at risk.

Flowering plants have by far the greatest number of at-risk species, contrasting sharply with analyses based on proportion (figure 4.2).

Table 4.4. Species report card: Conservation status of U.S. plants and animals

	Presumed extinct (GX)	Possibly extinct (GH)	Critically imperiled (G1)	Imperiled (G2)	Vulnerable (G3)	Apparently secure (G4)	Secure (G5)	Other	Total
Vertebrate animals									
Mammals	1	0	8	21	36	96	253	1	416
Birds	22	3	27	20	36	87	572	1	768
Reptiles	0	0	7	14	30	45	186	1	283
Amphibians	1	1	21	28	33	42	104	1	231
Freshwater Fishes	16	1	91	87	105	147	351	1	799
Vertebrate totals	40	5	154	170	240	417	1,466	5	2,497
Invertebrate animals									
Butterflies/skippers	0	0	8	31	78	101	388	14	620
Crayfishes	1	2	54	53	55	87	69	1	322
Freshwater mussels	17	20	73	42	50	44	42	4	292
Dragonflies/damselflies	0	2	10	24	45	91	268	16	456
Stoneflies	1	11	13	71	164	168	178	0	606
Tiger beetles	0	0	3	5	14	19	62	11	114
Invertebrate totals	19	35	161	226	406	510	1,007	46	2,410
Vascular plants									
Ferns/fern allies	0	4	32	24	65	168	242	21	556
Gymnosperms	0	0	7	8	12	27	60	0	114
Flowering plants	11	126	1,031	1,309	2,615	4,469	5,618	141	15,320
Vascular plant totals	11	130	1,070	1,341	2,692	4,664	5,920	162	15,990
Totals	70	170	1,385	1,737	3,338	5,591	8,393	213	20,897

This table presents the conservation status for 14 groups of plants and animals for which comprehensive status assessments are available. These numbers represent species that are native to and regularly occur in the United States and include described, currently accepted, full species only. Data source: Natural Heritage Central Databases 1999. Botanical data compiled and edited by Larry E. Morse with the assistance of Nancy B. Benton, Martha Martinez, Gwendolyn Thunhorst, and Debbie Gries; adapted and revised from Kartesz 1994 and Kartesz unpublished data. Zoological data compiled by Lawrence L. Master, Geoffrey Hammerson, Melissa Morrison, Dale F. Schweitzer, Miriam Steiner, and Lara Minium.

two outliers. Among Hawaii's 40 extant endemic vertebrates, a whopping nine-tenths (90%) are of conservation concern. Alaska, with 8 endemics, has far fewer species, but even there almost half are at risk.

Other Approaches to Assessing Status

The conservation status assessments conducted by Conservancy and heritage biologists are among the most comprehensive and widely used in the United States. Several other approaches to assessing status also exist, however. These include the endangerment categories used by the U.S. government in implementing the Endangered Species Act, systems developed by specialized societies or initiatives, and the international efforts of the World Conservation Union (IUCN). We now turn to how these various systems for determining the relative security or risk of species relate to the findings of the heritage conservation status assessments.

U.S. Endangered Species Act

Enacted in 1973 in the flush of popular support for the environment, the Endangered Species Act (ESA) is the nation's broadest and most powerful law for providing protection of endangered species and their habitats. A key aspect of the act's implementation is the need to determine the status of plants and animals at risk of extinction and compile a list of species in need of federal protection. The ESA recognizes two principal status categories, "endangered" and "threatened." As defined in the act, *endangered* refers to species that are "in danger of extinction within the foreseeable future throughout all or a significant portion of its range," while *threatened* refers to "those animals and plants likely to become endangered within the foreseeable future throughout all or a significant portion of their ranges" (USFWS 1988). As part of the listing process, two additional categories exist, "candidate" and "proposed" species. *Candidate* species are those for which the implementing agency, either the U.S. Fish and Wildlife Service or the National Marine Fisheries Service, has sufficient information about vulnerability and threats to support listing. *Proposed* species are those for which listing rules have been published in the *Federal Register* but formal listing still awaits administrative action.

Within the context of the ESA, the terms *endangered* and *threatened* have both biological and legal meanings. From a legal perspective, these terms are reserved for those species formally listed under the act. Biologically, however, species may be "endangered" or "threatened" regardless of their legal status. The dual meaning of these terms complicates discussions about endangered species, and for that reason heritage conservation status ranks avoid this terminology. For clarity, in this book we use the terms *endangered* or *threatened* only to refer to those species formally listed under the ESA. Listed endangered and threatened species are referred to collectively as "federally listed" species; when proposed and candidate species are included as well, we employ the more general phrase *species with federal status*.

The Endangered Species Act itself sets out the basic criteria to be used in making status determinations and listing decisions. The act specifies that the following factors be considered in determining whether any particular species is endangered or threatened: (1) the present or threatened destruction, modification, or curtailment of its habitat or range; (2) overutilization for commercial, recreational, scientific, or educational purposes; (3) disease or predation; (4) the inadequacy of existing regulatory mechanisms; or (5) other natural or man-made factors affecting its continued existence. In practice, application of these criteria is somewhat subjective. With no objective standards against which decisions for listing species are made (Easter-Pilcher 1996), considerable ambiguity exists in determining the thresholds for listing as endangered versus threatened (Murphy 1992, Rohlf 1991).

The golden-cheeked warbler is a U.S. breeding endemic, nesting only on the Edwards Plateau of Texas. Almost half of vertebrates endemic to the lower 48 states are of conservation concern. Courtesy of Steve Maslowski/USFWS.

Listings under the Endangered Species Act included 1,048 U.S. species as of April 1998, with 831 in the endangered category and 217 in the threatened category. Another 109 were proposed for listing, and 164 were on the candidate list. For consistency with the geographic coverage of this volume, these figures exclude any U.S. species occurring only in Puerto Rico, the U.S. Virgin Islands, or U.S. protectorates and territories in the Pacific.

While more than a thousand listed species represent a significant number, these figures provide a very imperfect overall measure of the condition of U.S. species. First, the ESA defines the term *species* to include "any subspecies of fish or wildlife or plants, and any distinct population segment of any species or vertebrate fish or wildlife which interbreeds when mature." Thus, the above figures combine various taxonomic levels, from full species to subspecies and varieties, to particular populations or fish runs. For salmonid fish, for instance, the key concept employed is the "evolutionarily significant unit" (ESU), which defines unique genetic stocks worthy of protection. Note also that the population provision applies only to vertebrate animals, not to plants or invertebrate animals. Of the plants and animals federally listed as threatened or endangered, three-quarters (75%) are species, nearly a quarter (22%) are subspecies or varieties, and just 3% are vertebrate populations.

Second, these figures are not a comprehensive assessment of the endangerment status of U.S. species. They reflect the number of plants and animals legally recognized as threatened or endangered, not the total number biologically recognized as such. The process for formally listing species under the ESA is time-consuming and expensive, and the rate of species listings has varied greatly over the act's 25-year history (figure 4.4). The rate of listings has been sensitive to changes in the law, budget constraints, bureaucratic processes, and policy changes (Langner and Flather 1994).

About 100 species, including the Owens pupfish described in chapter 1, had been designated as threatened or endangered under earlier legislation passed in 1966, and these formed the foundation for the subsequent Endangered Species Act list. The period from 1974 through 1978 was characterized by a gradually increasing number of listings, including—in August 1977—the list's first plants. A decrease in the rate of listings occurred from 1979 through 1983, largely due to changes in the listing process introduced through 1978 amendments to the act. Listings once again picked up in 1984, continuing until a year-long moratorium in 1995 was imposed by new leadership in the U.S. Congress. Since listings resumed, they have continued at a rate of between 5% and 8% a year.

The increase in the number of vertebrate and invertebrate listings has grown steadily but gradually over time. As can be seen in figure 4.4, however, since the mid-1980s the shape of the overall listing curve is strongly influenced by the relatively large numbers of plants that have been added to the list. In part this is due to settlement of lawsuits against the U.S. Fish and Wildlife Service that required the agency to step up the listing of plants, particularly in Hawaii and California.

Early listings under the Endangered Species Act tended to focus on charismatic animals. Vertebrates receive one additional benefit: Distinct populations, such as grizzly bears (*Ursus arctos horribilis*) in the lower 48 states, are eligible for listing. © Stephen Krasemann/DRK PHOTO.

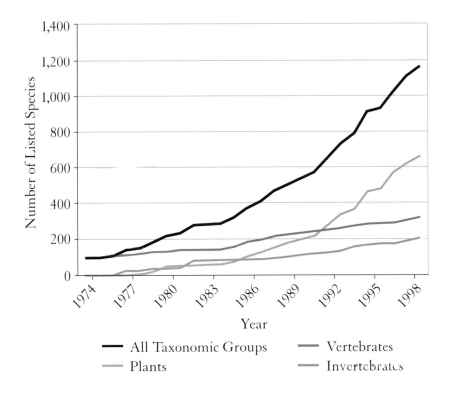

Figure 4.4. Endangered Species Act listings.

The increased rate of listings since the mid-1980s largely reflects the addition of numerous plants.

Another key change occurred following the 1995 moratorium: a redefinition of what are regarded as candidates for listing. Prior to that time, three different candidate lists were maintained by the U.S. Fish and Wildlife Service. The Category 1 candidate list contained species for which sufficient information was available to support a listing determination. Category 3 included those species considered unsuitable for listing, either because they were extinct, because they were no longer regarded as valid taxonomic units, or because they were found to be more abundant and widespread or less subject to threats than previously believed. The Category 2 list, which with more than 4,000 species was the largest of the three, contained species that had yet to be properly evaluated. Because of the manner in which species could be nominated for inclusion on this candidate list, in practice Category 2 candidates became an amalgamation of species with legitimate status issues and species that were unlikely to merit federal protection. The result was a large list that was scientifically indefensible, yet widely viewed, especially by opponents of the act, as awaiting listing. Even though these candidate species were not formally protected under the ESA, many federal agencies and others took a prudent approach and extended consideration and protective measures toward them. In 1995, however, the Fish and Wildlife Service changed its approach to candidate species, creating a single list containing only those species for which sufficient information exists to indicate that listing is merited. This new candidate list is in essence the equivalent of the old Category 1 candidates. Redefining candidate species had the effect of sharply decreasing the overall number of species with federal status.

Figure 4.5. Comparison between
federal status and heritage ranks.

*Significant discrepancies are apparent for
many species groups when heritage status
assessments are compared with status
under the Endangered Species Act. Note:
For comparability, federal categories
include full species only.*

Over the past decade there has also been an increased emphasis on listing of plants and invertebrate animals. Early in the act's implementation, most attention was focused on vertebrates. In 1973, when the act won easy congressional approval, most supporters had in mind such charismatic vertebrates as bald eagles and grizzly bears. Even with the considerable number of plant and invertebrate additions to the federal endangered species list, Metrick and Weitzman (1996) report a significant tendency for listed species to be both large and "higher organisms" or closer to humans in evolutionary terms.

A comparison of species with federal status and those considered imperiled (G1 or G2) or historical (GH) according to heritage conservation status ranks supports this observation (figure 4.5). Looking only at the species level, correspondence between the two systems is quite good for birds and mammals (birds, 6.8% ESA versus 6.5% heritage; mammals,

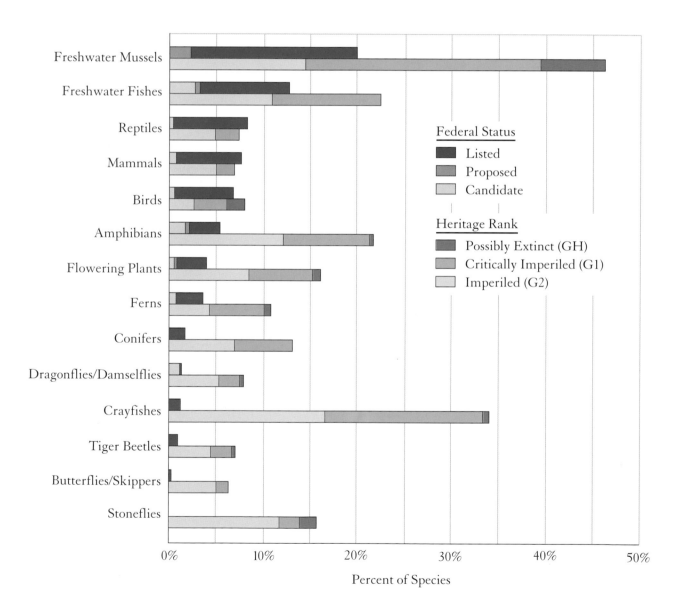

7.7% ESA versus 7.0% heritage). Reptiles are even slightly overrepresented by ESA listings (8.3% versus 7.4%). On the other hand, for most groups there is a large discrepancy in species regarded by heritage rank as biologically at risk and the proportion afforded protection under the ESA. This is not to say that all G1 and G2 species require federal listing, or that no G3 or G4 species may be appropriate for federal protection. However, these comparisons provide a general perspective on where listings coincide with and differ from the biological assessments of the heritage network. Overall, it appears that the Endangered Species Act does a much better job protecting imperiled mammals, birds, and reptiles than it does other organisms.

Another way to look at correspondence between the two status assessment systems is to evaluate the different federal endangerment categories according to the heritage conservation status ranks assigned to their constituent species (figure 4.6). Examining the status of all federally listed taxa, the heritage network ranks 92% as imperiled or historical (G1, G2, or GH) (figure 4.6). Only 6% of listed species fall into the vulnerable category (G3), and fewer than 2% belong in the more secure categories of G4 and G5. Those few species that are regarded by the heritage network as "secure or apparently secure" (G4 or G5) are, for the most part, wide-ranging vertebrate species in which only certain population segments are federally listed. While few in number, these also tend to be high-profile species, such as the gray wolf, bald eagle, wood stork, chinook salmon, brown pelican, and woodland caribou.

Given the small populations that characterize most G1 and G2 species, this comparison between heritage status ranks and ESA listings support Wilcove et al.'s (1993) finding that most federally listed species have very small population numbers by the time they are listed. Analyzing listings made between 1985 and 1991, these researchers found that for vertebrates the median population size at the time of listing was only 1,075 individuals. Invertebrates and plants had even smaller populations, with 999 and 120 individuals, respectively.

From the definitions of *endangered* and *threatened* provided in the Endangered Species Act, one would predict that species listed as endangered should receive higher heritage ranks than those listed as threatened. Indeed, this is the case (figure 4.7). Among all species listed in the endangered category, the heritage network ranks 74% as critically imperiled (G1) and only 16% as imperiled (G2). This ratio reverses for species listed in the threatened category: The proportion regarded as critically imperiled (G1) drops to 36%, and those considered imperiled (G2) rises to 47%. Although previous authors (e.g., Murphy 1992, Rohlf 1991) have questioned how distinctions between endangered and threatened are applied in listing decisions, these figures support the notion that listings do tend to reflect differences in biological status.

The relative status of listed species also varies according to taxonomic groups. Vertebrates have a higher proportion of listed taxa included in the more secure status categories than plants or invertebrates do (figure 4.8). Whereas 5% of listed vertebrates are ranked either G4 or G5, no listed

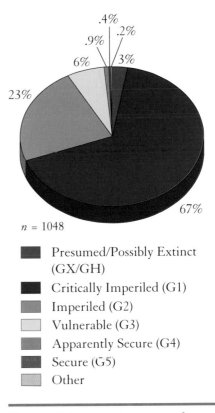

.4%
.2%
.9%
6%
3%
23%
67%

$n = 1048$

▪ Presumed/Possibly Extinct (GX/GH)
▪ Critically Imperiled (G1)
▪ Imperiled (G2)
▪ Vulnerable (G3)
▪ Apparently Secure (G4)
▪ Secure (G5)
▪ Other

Figure 4.6. Conservation status of federally listed species.

The vast majority of federally listed threatened and endangered species are regarded by the heritage network as imperiled (G1 or G2). Note: Because federally listed species include full species as well as subspecies, varieties, and populations, this analysis combines assessments of full species (G ranks) and infraspecific taxa (T ranks).

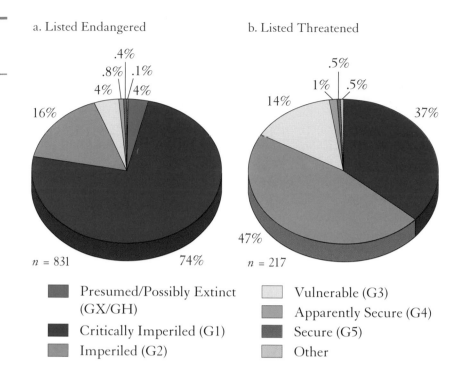

Figure 4.7a–b. Comparison of status between federal endangered and threatened categories.

Species classified as endangered exhibit a higher degree of rarity, as measured by heritage status ranks, than those listed as threatened.

a. Listed Endangered

.4%
.8% .1%
4% 4%
16%
n = 831   74%

b. Listed Threatened

.5%
1% .5%
14%
37%
47%
n = 217

Presumed/Possibly Extinct (GX/GH)
Critically Imperiled (G1)
Imperiled (G2)
Vulnerable (G3)
Apparently Secure (G4)
Secure (G5)
Other

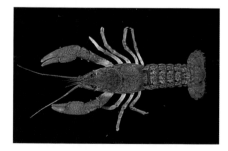

Many invertebrate groups are underrepresented on the endangered species list relative to their heritage status. The critically imperiled *Cambarus pristinus* exists in just a single Tennessee creek yet, like most other crayfishes, receives no federal protection. © Kevin S. Cummings and Christopher A. Taylor/Illinois Natural History Survey.

plants or invertebrates fall into these status categories. Furthermore, 13% of listed vertebrates are regarded as vulnerable (G3), compared to only 5% of plants and less than 1% of invertebrates. These differences are largely due to the greater mobility of many vertebrates and the ability to designate distinct populations for listing. These figures are also consistent with Wilcove et al.'s (1993) findings that the population numbers and status of listed vertebrates is more variable, and often more secure, than those for most listed invertebrates and plants.

American Fisheries Society

In contrast to listings under the Endangered Species Act, status assessments conducted by the American Fisheries Society (AFS) for several species groups correspond closely with heritage conservation status ranks. The AFS's Endangered Species Committee has assessed the status of several groups of freshwater species using four categories: endangered (in danger of extinction throughout all or a portion of its range); threatened (likely to become endangered throughout all or a portion of its range); special concern (may become endangered or threatened by relatively minor disturbances to its habitat and deserves careful monitoring of its abundance and distribution); and currently stable (distribution is widespread and stable; species is not in need of immediate conservation management actions). These categories are roughly similar to heritage conservation

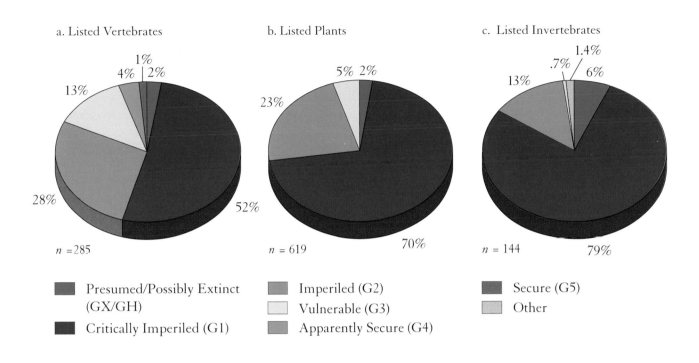

a. Listed Vertebrates

1%
4% | 2%
13%

28%

52%

n = 285

b. Listed Plants

5% 2%
23%

70%

n = 619

c. Listed Invertebrates

1.4%
.7% / 6%
13%

79%

n = 144

■ Presumed/Possibly Extinct (GX/GH)

■ Critically Imperiled (G1)

■ Imperiled (G2)

□ Vulnerable (G3)

■ Apparently Secure (G4)

■ Secure (G5)

□ Other

status ranks of critically imperiled (G1), imperiled (G2), vulnerable (G3), and apparently secure/secure (G4 and G5), respectively. Applying these AFS categories, Williams et al. (1993) reported that 72% of mussels were of conservation concern, compared with 69% considered at risk according to heritage rankings. The figures for crayfishes were also similar, with Taylor et al. (1996) noting 48% to be of conservation concern, versus 51% according to our data. An AFS assessment of freshwater fishes (J. E. Williams et al. 1989), although not strictly comparable, lists 180 U.S. species of freshwater fishes, or about one-third of the total species, as of conservation concern. These figures are similar to the approximately 38% of U.S. freshwater fishes ranked by the heritage network as imperiled or vulnerable.

IUCN Species Survival Commission

Outside North America, the most widely used system for assessing the status of species is that of the Species Survival Commission (SSC) of the World Conservation Union (IUCN). Beginning in the early 1960s, IUCN introduced the concept of red lists and red data books to identify the threatened species in a given country or region. Over time the SSC has grown into a worldwide volunteer network of more than 7,000 scientists and conservationists. These volunteers are organized into "specialist groups," each of which focuses on monitoring and assessing the status of various groups of animals and plants and developing conservation action plans for the groups.

The IUCN threat assessments historically consisted of three major categories—endangered, vulnerable, and rare. Unfortunately, there was

Figure 4.8a–c. Status comparisons among federally listed species in different taxonomic groups.

Invertebrates and plants, in general, must be extremely rare before they receive federal protection; only among vertebrates do significant numbers of species receive lesser heritage status ranks.

Most plants tend to be extremely rare by the time of their federal listing. Only about 10 populations of the endangered blowout penstemon (*Penstemon haydenii*) remain. Restricted to the Sandhills of Nebraska, this habitat specialist grows in sand craters excavated by the wind's action. © Craig C. Freeman.

little consistency in the way that these categories were applied from one country to another and among different specialist groups, and the criteria used were quite subjective (Mace and Lande 1991). In an effort to create a more scientifically defensible and objective system for assessing status, in 1994 IUCN adopted a new set of threat categories and criteria for their application (IUCN 1994). These categories attempt to quantify the likely persistence of species over time. Similar to heritage conservation status ranks, species are evaluated based on several criteria, including trends in population, area of occupancy, range size, or habitat quality; range size; area of occupancy; population size; and number of populations. The IUCN system particularly emphasizes trends or anticipated trends in population numbers as a basis for predicting persistence over time, and thus threat category.

IUCN issued the latest version of the red list for animals in 1996 (IUCN 1996), and released the first worldwide red list for plants in 1998 (Walter and Gillett 1998). The *1996 IUCN Red List of Threatened Animals* was the first to use these new threat categories; Conservancy and heritage information was extensively used in the reevaluation and assessment of U.S. species for that work. The *1997 IUCN Red List of Threatened Plants* (Walter and Gillett 1998) makes use of the older IUCN threat categories, since reevaluation of the more than 30,000 species included in that work was not possible within the publication timetable. The threat assessments for North American and Hawaiian plants in that red list, however, are directly based on the Conservancy and heritage conservation status ranks for these species.

In comparing IUCN assessments of U.S. vertebrate species with heritage ranks for the same taxa, one finds that in general the IUCN evaluations tend to be more conservative (figure 4.9). This appears to be due partly to the greater emphasis on trend information, which is in short supply for many species, perhaps accounting for the many species that IUCN places in its "data deficient" category. The IUCN categories also appear to place greater emphasis on projected threats, used as a surrogate for projecting future trends, and less emphasis on population numbers and range size as indicators of vulnerability.

Extinctions in America

Extinction is the ultimate consequence of imperilment. Once the last individual of a species has died, the fate is the same whether it originally was abundant and widespread, like the passenger pigeon, or naturally rare and restricted, like the Ash Meadows poolfish. Unfortunately, extinction is a fate that has afflicted an increasing number of U.S. species over the past 200 years, and one that threatens to eliminate many more.

Over geologic time, extinction is a natural event as species give rise— or give way—to other species. Through Earth's history, however, this process has been counterbalanced by the evolution of new species of plants and animals. The interplay between these two processes over millions of

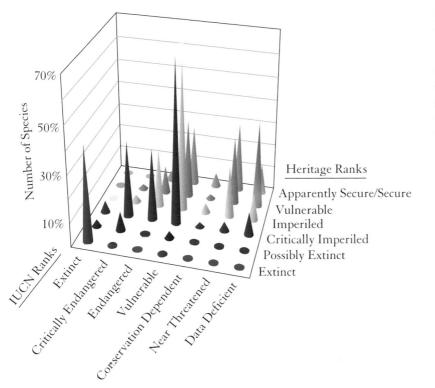

70%

50%

Number of Species

30%

10%

IUCN Ranks

Extinct
Critically Endangered
Endangered
Vulnerable
Conservation Dependent
Near Threatened
Data Deficient

Heritage Ranks

Apparently Secure/Secure
Vulnerable
Imperiled
Critically Imperiled
Possibly Extinct
Extinct

Figure 4.9. Comparison of IUCN and heritage status assessments.

IUCN evaluations tend to be more conservative than heritage assessments, partly due to a greater emphasis on trend information, which is in short supply for most U.S. species.

years has been responsible for increasing the overall diversity of life on Earth, including the array of biological resources on which humans depend. But today's spate of human induced extinctions is anything but natural. The pace of extinction now far exceeds anything seen in the fossil record since at least the end of the Cretaceous period, at which time the impact of an enormous meteor profoundly disrupted life throughout the planet. Unlike at the end of the Cretaceous, however, the current extinction spasm is due not to extraterrestrial causes but to impacts that we ourselves have inflicted on the earth.

Estimates of the current rate of extinctions are conservatively estimated to be 100 to 1,000 times greater than background levels (Lawton and May 1995, Hanski et al. 1995), and evolution of new species are unlikely to see a similar increase in rate to offset these losses. Indeed, the same forces that are driving so many species toward extinction are also disrupting the natural processes that over evolutionary time—usually on the order of thousands to millions of years—could lead to the emergence of new species.

Documenting extinctions presents a difficult challenge. Whereas the *existence* of a species can be documented directly and unambiguously— sightings, specimens, or telltale signs—the *absence* of a species often must be inferred from circumstantial evidence. In documenting extinctions, we are dealing with negative information—looking for what isn't rather than what is. Most general estimates of levels and rates of extinctions worldwide therefore derive not from species-by-species documentation but rather from estimates and inferences made using basic ecological principles. Prominent among these are the relationship between area and species number (discussed in chapter 3) and the implications that reductions in habitat would have on the number of species that habitat can support (Simberloff 1986, Reid 1992, Pimm et al. 1995a).

In reviewing extinctions in the United States, here we summarize our information about those species we currently know or suspect to be extinct, rather than attempting to estimate the total number of extinctions. We further restrict our discussion to full taxonomic species; we do not consider the numerous subspecies, varieties, and distinct populations that are known to have vanished. As described earlier, heritage conservation status ranks provide a consistent way of evaluating the condition of species, and special care is given to distinguishing those plants and animals that are, or may be, extinct. Because of the inherent difficulties of documenting extinctions, we are very conservative in our approach. A species is not classified as "presumed extinct" (GX) unless exhaustive searches of all suitable habitat have been carried out and there is no more cause for hope. The more cautious category of "possibly extinct," or "historical" (GH), is used for species that have not been sighted in many years or whose only recorded occurrences are known to be destroyed—species that warrant further searches before being given up for gone.

A total of 539 U.S. species are recorded in the Natural Heritage Central Databases as extinct or missing (table 4.5). Of these, 100 meet the stricter criteria of presumed extinct, with another 439 falling into the possibly extinct category. These extinctions span the gamut of organisms, including vertebrates such as the great auk (*Pinguinus impennis*) and West Indian monk seal (*Monachus tropicalis*), plants like the Santa Catalina monkeyflower (*Mimulus traskiae*) and falls-of-the-Ohio scurf-pea (*Orbexilum stipulatum*), and invertebrates such as the Wabash riffle-shell (*Epioblasma sampsonii*) and the Colorado burrowing mayfly (*Ephemera compar*). The complete listing of these extinct or missing plants and animals is presented in Appendix A, together with the states in which they formerly occurred and, where known, the year last recorded. If extinct subspecies and varieties were included, this list would grow considerably.

Snails have been particularly hard hit by extinctions. With 26 species presumed extinct and another 106 species missing and possibly extinct, gastropods lead all other groups in this unenviable category. The largest numbers of snail extinctions are clustered in two areas, Hawaii and the southeastern United States. In Hawaii these extinctions have involved several genera of tree snails, whereas extinct snails in the southeastern United States are mostly freshwater species.

Among vertebrates, birds have been most severely affected by extinctions, with 22 species of birds presumed extinct and another 3 missing. Although several bird species have disappeared from the mainland United States—passenger pigeon, Carolina parakeet (*Conuropsis carolinensis*), Labrador duck (*Camptorhynchus labradorius*), and great auk—most extinct U.S. birds are Hawaiian. Indeed, the 19 Hawaiian birds listed here

A total of 100 U.S. species are, like the great auk, presumed extinct. Last seen in 1844, this large flightless bird formerly occurred in the North Atlantic but was killed in massive numbers for eggs, feathers, meat, and fuel oil. © George Bernard/Animals Animals.

Table 4.5. U.S. species extinctions by taxonomic group

	Presumed extinct (GX)	Possibly extinct (GH)	Total (GX & GH)
Vertebrate animals			
Mammals	1	0	1
Birds	22	3	25
Reptiles	0	0	0
Amphibians	1	1	2
Freshwater fishes	16	1	17
Vertebrate total	40	5	45
Invertebrate animals			
Freshwater mussels	17	20	37
Snails	26	106	132
Crustaceans	1	5	6
Insects	4	162	166
Other invertebrates	1	5	6
Invertebrate total	49	298	347
Vascular plants			
Ferns/fern allies	0	4	4
Gymnosperms	0	0	0
Flowering plants	11	126	137
Vascular plant total	11	130	141
Nonvascular plants			
Fungi	0	2	2
Nonvascular plants	0	4	4
Nonvascular plant total	0	6	6
Total	100	439	539

Of the 100 U.S. species that with certainty are considered extinct (GX), snails have suffered the largest number of losses, followed by birds. Among the 439 species that are "missing" and may be extinct (GH), insects and flowering plants have been affected most. Appendix A lists the name, former distribution, and year last observed for all presumed and possibly extinct U.S. species.

Source: Natural Heritage Central Databases 1999.

underestimate the full extent of bird losses in Hawaii, since we include only those species known to have been extant at the time of first European contact. There is now considerable fossil evidence that a large number of birds succumbed following the initial Polynesian colonization of the archipelago (Olson and James 1982). At least 60 Hawaiian bird species are known only from fossils, and still others may have vanished without a trace (Pimm et al. 1995a, Steadman 1995).

Large numbers of plants are also extinct or missing from the U.S. landscape. Because plants can persist as seeds for long periods of time, or can grow inconspicuously in remote regions, our figures for plant extinctions are very conservative. Only 11 species have received sufficient scrutiny to justify a ranking as presumed extinct, whereas another 130 are regarded

Rediscovered on a remote mountain peak in Montana, the land snail *Discus brunsoni* was the beneficiary of a small grants program designed to relocate missing species. © Paul Hendricks/MTNHP.

as missing and assigned to the less certain category of possibly extinct. These latter include such species as *Thismia americana*, a tiny, translucent plant discovered in 1912 near Chicago and seen for the last time in 1913. The mystery of thismia's disappearance only deepens when considering the bizarre disjunction that this tiny plant represents—it is the only North American member of the tropical plant family Burmanniaceae, and its nearest relatives exist in rain forest thousands of miles to the south. The prairie on which this anomalous plant was found is now an industrial site. Nonetheless, midwestern botanists have not yet given up on the species and conduct regular thismia hunts across the region in hopes of refinding this highly unusual yet probably extinct flower.

In recent years, considerable effort has been directed toward attempting to relocate such missing species. These targeted inventories have brought both good news and bad news. In 1997 and 1998 a small grants program developed by the Conservancy with support from Canon USA, enabled researchers to search for possibly extinct (GH) species across the United States. Of 104 targeted species, 16 were rediscovered, including 5 snails, 4 plants, 3 insects, and 2 freshwater mussels. This indicates that in certain circumstances the lack of recent records may merely reflect the low level of field inventory directed toward some of these lesser known and taxonomically difficult groups. On the other hand, 85% of the targeted species were not relocated despite intensive searches, indicating that many if not most species considered "missing in action" may indeed no longer exist. Although most of the species that were not refound during these searches have been retained in the missing status category (GH), based on these searches at least one—the stonefly *Alloperla roberti*—has now been reassigned to the ranks of the presumed extinct.

Where the Wild Things Aren't

Virtually every state has been affected by species extinctions, although these losses have not occurred uniformly across the nation. States with large numbers of extinct or missing species tend to have either high overall numbers of species (many of which may be very localized), an inherently fragile flora or fauna, or intense human alteration of the landscape. Extinctions in the United States have been especially prominent in the Pacific islands and sweep across the continent in a southerly arc from the Pacific Coast to the Southeast (figure 4.10). Based on all 539 presumed and possibly extinct U.S. species recorded in the Natural Heritage Central Databases, figure 4.10 charts the number of species lost from each state in the nation. This map reflects the historic distribution of globally extinct species—that is, species that have disappeared completely, not just species that have been lost from one state but still exist in another.

Hawaii tops the list, with 249 extinct species (29 presumed and 220 possibly extinct), reaffirming its position as the extinction capital of the United States. The number of extinctions is all the more extraordinary given the relatively small overall number of native species that occur in

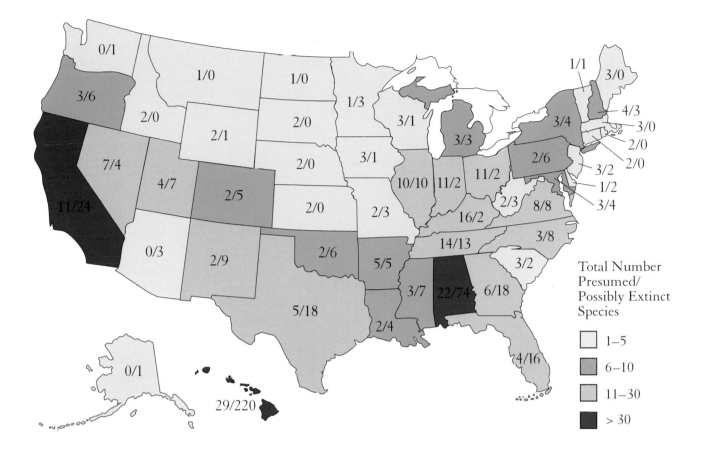

Figure 4.10. Extinctions in America.

The number of presumed and possibly extinct species lost from each state. Based on all 100 presumed extinct (GX) and 439 missing (GH) species, this map reflects species that have disappeared across their range—not just species that have been lost from one state but still exist in another.

Hawaii (see chapter 5). Because of the archipelago's isolation, most of its species are unique to Hawaii. The absence of continental predators and competitors also makes these native Hawaiian species especially susceptible to the kinds of outside disturbances introduced first by the Polynesian immigration and later by European colonists.

On the mainland, Alabama tops the list of extinction-prone states, with 96 species gone (22 presumed and 74 possibly extinct). Alabama is home to an exceptionally rich freshwater fauna, thanks to an ancient and complex geological terrain and more than 235,000 miles of waterways spanning three major river basins. Also, the state was never scoured by Pleistocene glaciers, so the flora and fauna were able to continue diversifying even during this period of major climatic and geological perturbations. Unfortunately, many of these rivers and streams, which successfully weathered the vicissitudes of the ice ages, have now been dammed and otherwise severely altered, leading to high levels of extinction, especially among freshwater mussels and snails.

California ranks third in the nation, with 35 extinctions (11 presumed and 24 possibly extinct). The state's turbulent geological history has produced a multitude of habitats, which in turn have given rise to a suite of often highly localized plant and animal species. The intensive alteration of the state's lands and waters for agriculture, urbanization, and other uses has had a severe impact on many of the wild landscapes that support these

Above: Surprisingly, Alabama has lost more species than any other mainland state, largely because of the effect of dams and other water developments on its rich aquatic fauna. © James Godwin/ALNHP.

Right: With nearly 250 species missing or extinct, Hawaii has lost by far the most species of any state. © Harold E. Malde.

unusual species. At the other end of the spectrum are several states, including Alaska, Montana, North Dakota, and Washington, that have been little affected by species extinctions.

These extinction figures start to hint at the disparity in biological diversity among states, as well as the varying levels of impacts that different regions and states have suffered. Extinction is perhaps the crudest measure of the health of a state's biodiversity, however. What is needed instead are perspectives on the diversity and health of states that allow us to intelligently respond to the conservation challenges ahead, rather than lament that which we already have lost. Such measures are the subject of the next chapter, which addresses the state of the states.

5

STATE OF THE STATES

*Geographic Patterns of Diversity,
Rarity, and Endemism*

The natural geography of the 50 states varies tremendously, supporting
an equally varied suite of wild species—from flocks of tropical birds in
southern Florida to caribou migrations across the Alaskan tundra. The
geography of risk, too, varies across the nation, reflecting the interaction
between natural and human history. Similarly, present-day land and water
uses will largely determine the future diversity and condition of the flora
and fauna. We can learn much, though, from looking at the current condition of a state's biota, since this both reflects the past and helps illuminate the future.

A state's ecological complexion and the evolutionary history of its biota
are the primary determinants of its biological diversity. These environmental factors have encouraged spectacular diversification in many regions: for instance, the freshwater fish fauna in the Southeast, the magnificent conifers along the Pacific cordillera, and the small mammal assemblages of the arid Southwest. Conversely, geological events such as the
expansion and contraction of the ice sheets have left other areas of the
country with a more modest array of species.

States, however, are artificial constructs laid out on the landscape's
natural ecological patterns. While some state lines follow natural
boundaries, such as shorelines or major rivers, most cut across the land
with no sensitivity to natural features or topography. Nonetheless, urban
and rural dwellers alike identify with the major ecological regions
within which they live, and this is often the source of considerable pride.
Montana is "big sky country," referring to the vast open plains that
sweep up against the eastern phalanx of the Rocky Mountains.
California's moniker "the golden state" now refers more to its tawny
hills of summer—unfortunately at present composed mostly of alien
species—than to the nuggets first found at Sutter's Creek. Maryland,

Bruce A. Stein

Lynn S. Kutner

Geoffrey A. Hammerson

Lawrence L. Master

Larry E. Morse

home of the Chesapeake Bay, offers the tasty blue crab (*Callinectes sapidus*) as its unofficial invertebrate mascot. The list could go on, evidenced by the growing number of states that offer vanity license plates celebrating their natural environment.

Natural features have always played a dominant role in determining patterns of settlement and land use. It is no accident that many of the major cities along the eastern seaboard are located at the fall line between the coastal plain and the Appalachian Piedmont. Sailing ships could travel inland only as far as this point, explaining the location of such cities as Philadelphia, Washington, D.C., and Richmond, Virginia. Other population centers grew up around natural harbors, such as San Francisco, New York, and Boston. Most other major cities, too, grew up along rivers or other bodies of water.

Use, or abuse, of natural resources has also been the primary driver of the country's settlement patterns. The earliest European explorers of the continent's interior were trappers and traders in search of fur-bearing mammals. Later settlers penetrated and colonized various parts of the country to exploit agricultural soils, timber, forage, minerals, or energy resources. Even today, in an information-based service economy where fewer and fewer jobs are tied to resource-dependent industries, natural features still guide human migration and colonization patterns. The current population influx into interior western states, several of which are among the fastest-growing in the nation, is based on the desire of many people to live close to natural resource–based recreational opportunities.

While people inherently relate to their ecological surroundings, their primary sense of identity is with their state of residence. So, too, our knowledge of the distribution and condition of plants and animals is largely organized around state boundaries. Recording distributions by state has the advantage that these boundaries are universally recognized,

The 50 states harbor a spectacular array of wildlife across their varied climates, from caribou migrations in Alaska (*right*, © Michio Hoshino/Minden Pictures) to flocks of roseate spoonbills in the Florida Everglades (*below*, © Tim Fitzharris/ Minden Pictures).

easily discernible, and quite stable. From a pragmatic perspective, states are also the framework within which most political, administrative, and conservation activities take place. A considerable downside is the enormous variation in size among states. With Rhode Island the smallest, at 1,231 square miles, and Alaska the largest, encompassing 615,230 square miles, states vary in size by more than two orders of magnitude. Western states in particular tended to be laid out with straight rules, their boxy frames encompassing vast areas.

This chapter focuses on state-level patterns of species diversity, endemism, and rarity. We start by considering the widest array of species by aggregating information across all taxonomic groups for which we have comprehensive distributional information at a state level. This allows us to highlight overall geographic patterns that cross taxonomic groupings and to discuss key factors influencing the distribution of plant and animal species across the United States. Because different groups of plants and animals have their own distinctive evolutionary histories, tell their own biogeographic stories, and have their own conservation needs, we next examine these groups individually. These assessments first consider vascular plants as a whole and then review overall patterns for vertebrate animals. Finally, we discuss patterns evident within each individual group of vertebrates: mammals, birds, reptiles, amphibians, and freshwater fishes.

State-based assessments allow us to consider the broadest array of species, both rare and common, and to frame general biogeographic patterns. Ideally, however, we would prefer to consider species distributions unconstrained by artificial political boundaries. The next chapter (chapter 6) takes our assessment to that next level, at least for those species regarded as the "rarest of the rare." And in chapter 7, ecological systems themselves are the focus of attention, providing a complementary perspective on the distribution of biodiversity across the United States.

Assessing the State of the States

From a conservation perspective, three measures provide particularly useful characterizations of the state of the states—species diversity, endemism, and patterns of rarity. The number of species, or "species richness," is the most common means of measuring diversity. Such analyses are limited, however, by the number of plant and animal groups for which good data are available. The Natural Heritage Central Databases are a rich source of state-level distributional information for vertebrates and vascular plants, as well as selected groups of aquatic invertebrates, such as crayfish and freshwater mussels. These data sets offer the opportunity to portray the overall native species diversity found in each state, as well as to consider the state-by-state distributions and biogeographic patterns exhibited by each individual group of organisms. The distributional information in the Natural Heritage Central Databases derives, in turn, from a wide variety of sources, including database records from state

State endemics are not necessarily rare species. The California newt (*Taricha torosa*), for instance, is abundant even though it is restricted to that state. Continued loss of habitat could change its outlook, however. © Joe McDonald/ Corbis.

Growing on just a single hilltop above a dry lake in eastern Oregon, the rare *Stephanomeria malheurensis* is a recently evolved species that has never occurred beyond its present location. © Leslie D. Gottlieb.

natural heritage programs, published literature, museum records, and field observations (see Appendix D for principal taxonomic sources used in these databases). This chapter graphically summarizes patterns of diversity, endemism, and rarity in a series of maps; the data on which these maps are based is presented in tabular format in Appendix B.

Endemism is a measure of biological uniqueness. How many of the species that occur within a given geographic area, such as a state, are found there and nowhere else? While endemism is a concept that can be applied at virtually any geographic level, state and nation are two of its most common applications. The mere fact that a species is endemic does not—or should not—in itself confer special conservation significance to that species. Given a large enough state—say, Texas—the entire range of even fairly common and widespread species may fall entirely within that state. Narrowly distributed species are often restricted to a single state, and these endemics can be of considerable conservation interest. A species with a very limited distribution may or may not be endemic to a single state, though. The Columbia torrent salamander (*Rhyacotriton kezeri*), for instance, lives in just a small area around the mouth of the Columbia River but occurs in both Oregon and Washington. Nonetheless, the level of endemism serves as a rough marker for the distinctiveness of a state's biota and indicates which species must be the focus of conservation action within that state if they are to be protected anywhere.

Over the past few decades, considerable progress has been made in developing methods for reconstructing evolutionary trees and establishing the time of origin, or divergence, for many species. Although a continuum exists between those species that are recently evolved and those that originated in the geologically distant past, in considering narrowly endemic species a useful distinction relates to evolutionary age. Those species that are very localized because they evolved relatively recently have been termed *neoendemics*, while more ancient species, which were formerly more widespread but are now relictual and restricted in range, are referred to as *paleoendemics* (Stebbins and Major 1965). Neoendemic species often reflect episodes of rapid speciation. The Malheur wire lettuce (*Stephanomeria malheurensis*), a spindly herb found on just a single desert hilltop in eastern Oregon, appears to have recently originated as a new species (Gottlieb 1973). This rare plant has apparently never ranged beyond its hilltop perch. The California condor (*Gymnogyps californianus*), on the other hand, exemplifies a species that occurred far more widely during earlier geologic times but in historic times has been restricted to a much narrower range. Because they represent ancient evolutionary lineages, many conservation biologists believe that such paleoendemics are of particular conservation interest.

Rarity offers insight into the condition and fragility of a state's flora and fauna and indicates the relative magnitude of the conservation challenge. As discussed in chapter 4, rarity may stem from natural or human factors. These factors often reinforce one another, and teasing apart the relative contributions can sometimes be difficult.

The Florida torreya (*Torreya taxifolia*), another paleoendemic species, illustrates the complexity of this interaction. The genus *Torreya* ranged widely across the Northern Hemisphere during the Tertiary and is part of the shared flora of North America and eastern Asia referred to in chapter 3. One species, California nutmeg (*T. californica*), survived in the western United States, and another survived in the East. In recent times the eastern species (*T. taxifolia*) grew naturally in only about a dozen ravines along the Apalachicola River in Florida and adjacent Georgia. The unusual topography and soils of these ravines keep them cooler and moister than the surrounding landscape, preserving a remnant of the more temperate flora that existed in the region during the ice ages. Flooding by a major dam has destroyed most of this rare plant's habitat in Georgia. Unfortunately, a fungal blight that prevents the tree's reproduction is attacking its few remaining populations. The natural and human pressures acting together on this species conspire to make it one of the most threatened trees in the United States.

The Florida torreya, now found only along the Apalachicola River, occurred far more widely in earlier geological times. Its natural rarity has been compounded by construction of dams and the attack of a fungal blight. © Larry E. Morse/TNC.

States vary tremendously not only in their biological diversity and ecological features but also in the history and intensity of land uses. In general, the combination of a rich biota and intensive land use does not bode well for a state's plants and animals. Well-intentioned laws notwithstanding, in showdowns between wild species and human desires, the wild species generally lose. Viewed as a whole, though, patterns of species diversity, endemism, and rarity provide a useful overview of the natural state of the states.

Overall State Patterns

To assess the overall patterns of diversity, endemism, and rarity among states, we start with the broadest set of species for which we have comprehensive state distribution information (figures 5.1a, b, and c). Combining native species of vascular plants, vertebrates, and two invertebrate groups, mussels and crayfish, creates an aggregate data set representing 19,101 species. The following discussions of *overall* patterns refer only to regularly occurring native species in these plant and animal groups. Obviously, a great many other species of invertebrates, nonvascular plants, algae, fungi, and microorganisms also are found in these states, but currently we do not have the comprehensive information on these groups that would enable us to include them in this analysis of overall state-level diversity patterns.

Patterns of overall species richness vary considerably across the United States (figure 5.1a). The most diverse states generally stretch coast to coast across the southern portion of the country. California and Texas, both with more than 5,500 species, lead the nation in number of native species, while three other states—Arizona, New Mexico, and Georgia—harbor more than 4,000 species. Although not in the top tier, Alabama and Florida, two other species-rich southeastern states, both support more than 3,800 species. At the other end of the spectrum, Rhode Island, Alaska, North Dakota, and Hawaii have the fewest.

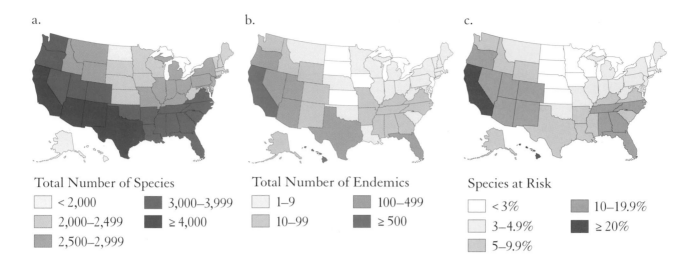

a.

b.

c.

Total Number of Species

☐ < 2,000   ■ 3,000–3,999

☐ 2,000–2,499   ■ ≥ 4,000

☐ 2,500–2,999

Total Number of Endemics

☐ 1–9   ■ 100–499

☐ 10–99   ■ ≥ 500

Species at Risk

☐ < 3%   ■ 10–19.9%

☐ 3–4.9%   ■ ≥ 20%

☐ 5–9.9%

Figures 5.1a–c. Overall state patterns of diversity, endemism, and rarity.

Combining state distribution information for all native vascular plants, vertebrates, mussels, and crayfish (19,279 species in total) provides an indication of overall state biodiversity patterns.

California leads the nation in overall species richness, number of state endemics, and rare species. The state's biological significance is largely due to a combination of its size, diversity of habitats, and relative isolation from the rest of the continent. © Carr Clifton/ Minden Pictures.

Endemism also highlights the biological significance of the state of California (figure 5.1b). California harbors almost 1,500 state endemics among the groups of species considered, representing about a quarter (26%) of its biota. Although Hawaii ranks last among states in the total number of native species, about 1,100 of these are restricted to the archipelago, so it is second only to California in number of endemics. Considered as a proportion of its biota, though, Hawaii's 82% level of endemism among these organisms dwarfs that of any other state. Texas has the third highest number of endemics in the nation, with 301 species restricted to the Lone Star State.

Rarity patterns largely correspond to overall diversity, and California again leads the nation, with more than 1,800 rare species, or almost one-third (32%) of its total (figure 5.1c). The most significant differences between patterns of rarity and diversity, however, relate to two of the states with the fewest species. Hawaii's more than 800 rare species translate into fully 60% of its total, by far the largest proportion of any state. Alaska, too, shifts considerably in significance: With 8% of its species at risk, Alaska ranks high among states based on proportion of rare species, compared with its near-last ranking for total species diversity. In general, however, states with the highest diversity are also those with the highest levels of rarity. Among the most diverse states—those with 3,000 species or more—levels of rarity typically exceed 10%.

The wide variations in species numbers among states relate primarily to differences in size, geographic location, and environmental complexity. When it comes to species numbers, size matters. As discussed in chapter 3, the species-area relationship is a well-established ecological principle: All things being equal, larger areas tend to support more different species. The influence of size can be seen in the map of state-level species richness. California, the most diverse state in the country, ranks number three in area, with about 159,000 square miles. The second most diverse state, Texas, is also the second largest state, at more than 267,000 square miles. Arizona and New Mexico, the two other states in the top tier of diversity, rank sixth and fifth for area, respectively. What about the nation's largest state, Alaska, then, or its fourth largest, Montana? These two states illustrate that "all things" are, of course, not equal, as we shall see below.

The diversity map also reflects another general biogeographic principle discussed earlier: that the number of species tends to increase as one moves closer to the equator. Many hypotheses seek to account for this observation, but in general warmer, more equable climates tend to be conducive to the development and persistence of greater numbers of species. The most species-rich states in the nation all occupy the southern border of the continental United States. These states also benefit from the presence of numerous species more typical of Mexico or the Caribbean that reach their northern limits just inside our southern borders. For this reason, southeastern Arizona, southern Texas, and South Florida are justly renowned among birders. In southeastern Arizona, for example, a number of Mexican and Central American birds, such as the white-eared hummingbird (*Hylocharis leucotis*), berylline hummingbird (*Amazilia beryllina*), and elegant trogon (*Trogon elegans*), either are regular summer visitors or breed in the canyons of this region's isolated mountain massifs. Similarly, species widespread in the Caribbean reach into the Florida Keys and South Florida, greatly enriching that state's flora and fauna. The rare American crocodile (*Crocodylus acutus*) as well as the common tropical tree *Cordia sebestena*, both occur throughout the Caribbean Basin but range only as far north as extreme southern Florida.

Alaska illustrates the interplay between area and geographic location. Accounting for about 16% of the United States' land area, Alaska should be an enormously diverse state based on size alone. But even the tiny District of Columbia surpasses Alaska in number of species. Indeed, only North Dakota and Hawaii trail Alaska in species richness. Alaska's proximity to other northern lands, such as boreal Canada and Siberia, provides a conduit for sharing species with these other regions. The harsh climatic conditions of the boreal forests and arctic tundra, however, are not especially conducive to the evolution and persistence of numerous species. Rather, most northern species are fairly widespread, creating a shared circumboreal flora and fauna consisting of relatively few species. What Alaska lacks in number of different species, though, it makes up for in the quantity of those it does possess, such as its vast seabird colonies, enormous caribou herds, and healthy predator populations.

Hawaii is our southernmost and only entirely subtropical state. Nonetheless, at least for the groups assessed here, it has by far the fewest species, an apparent contradiction to the general rule that species numbers increase as latitude decreases. While Hawaii is one of the smaller states, size alone doesn't explain this situation. Several other states, including Rhode Island, have many more species. The answer relates not to Hawaii's latitude but rather to its distance from other landmasses. The product of midoceanic volcanic activity, the Hawaiian Islands are the most remote archipelago in the world, which as discussed in chapter 3 accounts for its relatively depauperate but highly endemic biota.

States along the southern U.S. border are enriched by a number of species characteristic of Mexico or the Caribbean. The elegant trogon, a resident of Mexico and Central America, also breeds in the sycamore-lined canyons of southern Arizona's mountains. © Sid and Shirley Rucker/DRK PHOTO.

Factors Accounting for Regional Patterns

For overall patterns of diversity, western states show higher levels of species richness than those in the East, a feature related to their generally larger size and their greater environmental complexity. Geologically, topographically, and climatically diverse, the western United States is a crazy quilt of environments—from frigid peaks to scorching deserts, and from foggy, dripping coasts to parched plateaus. Two major mountain chains traverse the area, the Rocky Mountains to the east and Sierra Nevada and Cascades Mountains to the west. Between these two chains lies the Basin and Range region, an area punctuated by numerous isolated mountain ranges separated by valleys, while along the Pacific Ocean rise the coastal ranges. In geologic terms the western mountain ranges are still relatively young. In the tug-of-war between mountain building and erosion, the western mountains still have the upper hand. Consequently, the geology of the region is raw and exposed, and sharp topographic gradients are common. The most extreme gradient is found in eastern California, where in the space of a mere 80 miles elevations descend from 14,494 feet at the summit of Mount Whitney, which looms above the Owens Valley, to 282 feet below sea level at Bad Water in Death Valley. Viewing the landforms of the United States as if from space (figure 5.2), the extraordinarily complicated and dissected topography of the western one-third of the country is immediately apparent.

Figure 5.2. Landforms of the United States.

Portrayal of the nation's land surface as if viewed from space reveals the extraordinarily complicated and dissected topography of the western one-third of the country, which has contributed to the extensive diversification of plants and animals in that region. Source: U.S. Geological Survey.

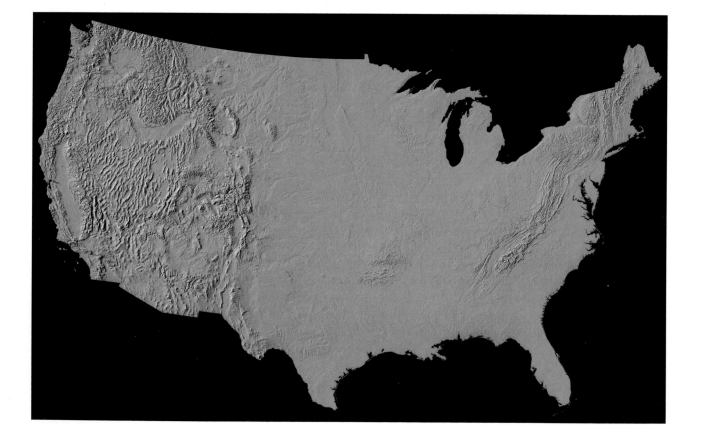

Climate is a primary factor controlling the distribution of plants and animals, and topographic diversity has a powerful effect on local climatic patterns. In the eastern and northern United States the movement of major air masses—principally the cold arctic airstream from the north and the warm tropical airstream from the south—governs the overall climate, creating relatively large climatic zones with gradual transitions among zones (Brouillet and Whetstone 1993). In the western United States a third air mass, the Pacific airstream, complicates the climatic situation as it interacts with the various mountain ranges to create highly regionalized weather patterns. These steep climatic gradients create a multitude of distinct and geographically discrete habitats. This high turnover in habitat types promotes the high turnover in species, which contributes to the region's overall diversity.

PLEISTOCENE GLACIATION Past climatic events also have played major roles in determining the present distribution and diversity patterns of the nation's flora and fauna. In particular, the repeated glaciations that occurred throughout the Pleistocene, starting about 2 million years ago, created widespread fluctuations in temperature and precipitation. The physical presence of ice on about half of North America, and the resulting shifts in climate, displaced the biota from large areas of the continent. In the northern and eastern United States the repeated glacial advances and retreats were the major factor influencing the distribution of plants and animals. The last ice age, known as the Wisconsin, is responsible for many of the current state-level distributional patterns that we see in the United States. Reaching its maximum about 18,000 years ago, the glacial advance covered large areas of the Upper Midwest and Northeast, with lobes reaching as far south as central Iowa and central Illinois (figure 5.3). In addition to those areas covered with ice, a zone of permafrost apparently extended from 50 to 120 miles along the front of the glaciers, and discontinuous permafrost extended south along the high Appalachian summits as far south as the Great Smoky Mountains (Péwé 1983).

The north-south-trending Appalachian range allowed the latitudinal displacement of significant parts of the flora and fauna during cycles of glacial advance and retreat. Several regions appear to have provided refuge for species that were able to migrate southward during the glacial advances. These apparently included the southern Appalachians, the Ozark highlands, and the region around the mouth of the Mississippi. However, the deciduous forests that now characterize the Appalachians appear to have been completely displaced from their slopes during the height of the ice advance, and most deciduous species must have survived the last ice age in the Mississippi region (Davis 1983). Other species, particularly Appalachian habitat specialists, may have persisted in small gorges or other sites along the edges of the Appalachians.

Cool and moist conditions similar to those found during the glacial periods still exist in some of these regions, allowing a number of northern species to maintain relictual outposts far to the south of their normal ranges and enrich the biota of those states. Some of these relict habitats

Ice

Ice-Free Area

Figure 5.3. Ice Age glacial maximum.

The last glacial period of the Pleistocene, known as the Wisconsin, reached its maximum about 18,000 years ago and is responsible for many of the current distributional patterns in the United States. Source: Modified from Brouillet and Whetstone 1993.

The northern flying squirrel is characteristic of more northern climes but holds to a tenuous existence at high elevations in the southern Appalachians. © Stephen Dalton/Photo Reseachers.

The typically boreal twinflower grows at an unusually low elevation at West Virginia's Ice Mountain, thanks to ground-level microclimates cooled by the mountain's unusual ice core. © Charlie Ott.

are found along the summits and high bogs of Appalachian peaks, where northern species such as balsam fir (*Abies balsamea*), cranberry (*Vaccinium macrocarpon*), northern flying squirrel (*Glaucomys sabrinus*), and water shrew (*Sorex palustris*) continue to persist. Occasionally these relicts have become so isolated that they have diverged into separate species. For example, isolated populations of balsam fir extend south as far as West Virginia; still farther south, patches of Fraser fir (*Abies fraseri*) appear in the high elevations of some of the southern Appalachian peaks. Fraser fir apparently represents an evolutionary derivative from relict southern populations of balsam fir. Other even more specialized habitats occur at lower elevations. In the winter, ice forms deep within the talus crevices of West Virginia's Ice Mountain (Core 1968). During the summer, cool air oozes out of this so-called algific slope, creating tiny ground-level microclimates suitable for sustaining such typically northern species as dwarf dogwood (*Cornus canadensis*) and twinflower (*Linnaea borealis*).

The Pleistocene glaciers scraped land bare and moved large quantities of material to new locations. These surface deposits created new landscape features, such as the terminal moraines that form Cape Cod and Long Island. Leaving scoured surfaces in some places, and deep deposits of glacial till in others, the receding ice exposed a blank canvas onto which the remnants of the displaced biota could once again colonize. Colonization did not happen uniformly; rather, some species migrated north into the newly available habitats more quickly than others (Pielou 1991). For example, based on analysis of pollen cores, the northward migration of four prominent tree species that currently have overlapping distributions—maple, chestnut, eastern white pine, and eastern hemlock—began from different points and proceeded at quite different paces. White pine (*Pinus strobus*) and hemlock (*Tsuga canadensis*) survived the glaciers in the eastern foothills of the Appalachians and the adjacent coastal plain, while the two hardwood tree species apparently found refuge far to the south, near the mouth of the Mississippi River. Their average rates of advance northward varied from a fairly rapid 300 to 350 meters per year for the pine and 200 to 250 meters per year for the hemlock to 200 meters per year for maple (*Acer* spp.) and only 100 meters per year for the heavy-seeded chestnut (*Castanea dentata*) (Davis 1981). Because of its slow pace of advance, chestnut was actually a relatively recent arrival in the Northeast, having reached Connecticut, for instance, only about 2,000 years ago.

The upper midwestern and northeastern states in general have relatively low levels of species diversity and rarity. Although this is partly because harsher northern climates support a less diversified biota, it is also significant that virtually all of the plants and animals inhabiting the area covered by the Wisconsin glaciers have migrated there since the end of the last glaciation, about 10,000 years ago. Thus, virtually the entire biota of the affected states is geologically recent. Most states in the Midwest have relatively little topographic diversity, and climatic zones generally grade subtly from one area to another. As a result, there has been relatively little environmental basis for local differentiation among species in these regions. Rarity and endemism in the region is also low.

In contrast to such places as Florida and Hawaii, where most rare species are highly localized, in the Midwest rare species tend to be widespread but spotty in their distribution. This often relates as much to large-scale human conversion of their habitats as to conditions of natural rarity. Mead's milkweed (*Asclepias meadii*), for instance, historically ranged throughout much of the tallgrass prairie but now is restricted to only about 100 sites in Illinois, Iowa, Kansas, and Missouri. The decline and current rarity of this imperiled species is due primarily to the extensive destruction of the virgin tallgrass prairie that made up its principal habitat. Kirtland's warbler (*Dendroica kirtlandii*), one of America's rarest birds, is a notable exception to this rule: It is restricted in its breeding to young jack pines in a single small area in north-central Michigan.

Even in those regions farther from the ice shield, the cyclic changes in climate were a major factor in the diversification and distribution of plants and animals. Whereas in the eastern United States the dominant ice age shifts in vegetation and other biota occurred mostly along latitudinal gradients—that is, vegetation shifted south during glacial periods and north during the interglacials—in the western United States, major shifts occurred along elevational gradients. Indeed, glaciers covered much of the western mountain ranges; their scouring action created such dramatic landscapes as California's Yosemite Valley. Vegetation zones shifted downward during the cooler, wetter glacial periods and upward during the warmer, drier interglacials (Raven and Axelrod 1978). The resulting expansion and contraction of ranges led to the isolation of individual populations, creating conditions well suited to rapid speciation. On the other side of the country, in Florida, the lowering of sea level associated with glacial periods had the effect of nearly doubling the peninsula's exposed land surface, greatly expanding the area of xeric habitats (Webb 1990).

During the late Pleistocene, immense lakes formed in the Great Basin, filling many of the basins characteristic of the region. As these virtual inland seas began drying and shrinking, fish populations became isolated in smaller lakes and springs, leading to evolutionary differentiation in such organisms as pupfishes (Cyprinodontidae) and trout (Salmonidae). So while the direct influence of the Pleistocene glaciers was most profound in the eastern United States and helps explain relatively low levels of diversity, in other parts of the country these fluctuations were responsible for increasing species diversity because they resulted in conditions promoting speciation.

Surprisingly, much of Alaska was not covered with ice during the Pleistocene glaciations. Ice-free refuges apparently existed over a great deal of central Alaska and along the Pacific Coast of Alaska and western Canada. Hultén (1937) first deduced the ice-free nature of central Alaska, based largely on a careful study of plant endemism. He hypothesized that the relatively high frequency of limited-range plants was the result of a Pleistocene refuge in the Beringian region. Other lines of evidence subsequently supported this theory. This refuge is one reason why endemism and rarity levels are higher in Alaska than one might expect for such a northern land.

Most rare species in the Midwest tend to be widespread but spotty in their distribution, often as a result of large-scale habitat conversion. Mead's milkweed formerly ranged throughout the tallgrass prairie but is now restricted to about 100 sites. © Susan Middleton and David Liittschwager.

Nevada's Pyramid Lake is a remnant of the once vast lakes that formed during the Pleistocene and filled large parts of the Great Basin. The drying of these lakes sparked the evolution of numerous distinctive trout and pupfishes. © Harold E. Malde.

Largely restricted to rocky slopes of volcanic-derived rhyolite, the funeral milk vetch (*Astragalus funereus*) is found at just a few sites near Death Valley. © Susan A. Cochrane.

Just one of the bizarre creatures that have adapted to life underground in regions of karst topography, the Texas blind cave salamander lacks pigmentation and functional eyes yet retains its larval gills into adulthood. © Paul Freed/Animals Animals.

SOILS AND SUBSTRATE   Yet another factor contributing to overall species diversity is the complexity of underlying bedrock and the range of soil types that different bedrocks create. Soils with unusual chemical or physical properties often support highly characteristic species adapted to life in fringe environments. The complex and exposed geology in the western United States created prime conditions not only for the commercial extraction of a large number of minerals but also for the development of plant species associated with unusual soil types. These so-called *edaphic endemics* subsist on classes of soil that often are unsuitable for other species. Many have restricted distributions and are quite rare. Among the best-known examples of this phenomenon is the general class of rocks known as ultramafics, and specifically the rock called serpentine for its scaly sheen. Soils derived from these rocks have high concentrations of magnesium, nickel, chromium, and other heavy metals and are toxic to most vegetation. Despite the high concentrations of metals and low levels of nutrients plants normally require, some widespread species tolerate these soils, while others are largely or entirely serpentine-restricted. Since fewer species can grow on serpentine soils, those that can gain a competitive advantage.

Ultramafic soils tend to be found in areas that have been tectonically active, and they occur particularly along the edges of continental plates. In the United States they occur extensively in California and southern Oregon and crop up sporadically in the eastern United States from New York and Vermont south to Alabama. In California alone, 215 species and varieties of plant are restricted to or closely associated with serpentine soils (Kruckeberg 1984). These include tree species such as Sargent's cypress (*Cupressus sargentii*) and shrubs such as Jepson's ceanothus (*Ceanothus jepsonii*), both of which form dense stands on serpentine hillsides in northern California. Many species of annual herbs, too, are restricted to serpentine soils, especially in the mustard genus *Streptanthus* and the flax genus *Hesperolinon*, and it is likely that the patchy distribution of these soils has promoted the high levels of diversification in both of these genera. Other chemically unusual soil types that support distinctive plant assemblages include highly calcareous soils, gypsum soils, acidic sands, and young volcanic soils.

The relationship between geological substrate and animal distribution is usually less direct, although substrate can be very important, especially for small organisms or those that burrow. An example of such substrate specialization is the fringe-toed lizards (*Uma*) of California and Arizona. The three species of fringe-toed lizards are entirely restricted to aeolian (wind-blown) sand dunes; one, the critically imperiled Coachella Valley fringe-toed lizard (*U. inornata*), is confined to but a single dune system.

The distribution of aquatic and subterranean animal species is strongly influenced by underlying geology and topography. River and stream geomorphology and drainage system evolution are primary determinates of the fishes and aquatic invertebrates that occur in any particular river reach. Karst terrains, characterized by highly soluble limestone bedrock, contain numerous springs and underground caverns that support rich subterranean faunas. These geologic and hydrologic features are often quite isolated from one another, creating ideal circumstances for the development of unique and highly restricted species. And while most obligate subterranean organisms are insects and other invertebrates, a number of fish and amphibian species are also characteristic of these habitats, enriching the vertebrate fauna of several southeastern and midwestern states. Many of these vertebrates show bizarre adaptations to life underground, such as the Texas blind cave salamander (*Eurycea rathbuni*), a creature restricted to water-filled caverns in the Edwards Aquifer.

Patterns of Plant Diversity

Plant life in the United States is impressive even viewed from a global perspective. The nation's large size, broad latitudinal and longitudinal spread, past and present connections with other landmasses, and great environmental heterogeneity have combined to produce a rich and diverse flora. Among the more noteworthy features of the country's flora are the exceptional diversity of coniferous trees found along the Pacific cordillera, the rich and ancient flora covering the southern Appalachians, the Mediterranean-climate flora of California, the highly endemic flora of Hawaii, and the many unusual insectivorous plants that inhabit our southeastern bogs and wetlands.

Plant diversity is greatest among states in the western United States—and particularly the Southwest—with a secondary center in the Southeast (figure 5.4a). California is remarkable in supporting nearly 5,000 native species—the most in the nation and more than twice the national average. The next most diverse state, Texas, has considerably fewer species (about 4,400), despite its larger size. All states in the top tier for plant diversity—those with 3,000 species or more—are found in the Southwest

Figure 5.4a–c. Plant diversity, endemism, and rarity.

(a) Vascular plant species diversity is highest along the Pacific Coast and in the Southwest, while (b) endemism and (c) rarity are especially high in California and Hawaii. Sources: (a) Natural Heritage Central Databases 1999, adapted and revised from Kartesz 1994 and Kartesz unpublished data; (b) updated from Gentry 1986; and (c) Natural Heritage Central Databases 1999.

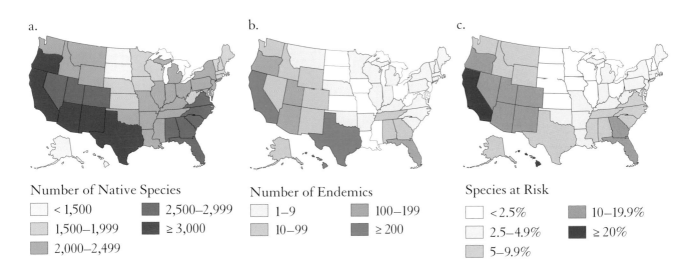

a.

b.

c.

Number of Native Species
- ☐ < 1,500
- ☐ 1,500–1,999
- ☐ 2,000–2,499
- ■ 2,500–2,999
- ■ ≥ 3,000

Number of Endemics
- ☐ 1–9
- ☐ 10–99
- ☐ 100–199
- ■ ≥ 200

Species at Risk
- ☐ <2.5%
- ☐ 2.5–4.9%
- ☐ 5–9.9%
- ☐ 10–19.9%
- ■ ≥ 20%

or along the Pacific Coast. The next tier of states, containing more than 2,500 species, is dominated by southeastern states, led by Georgia and Florida.

Another way to look at plant diversity is to consider higher taxonomic levels, such as the plant family. Families are distinguished by more fundamental characteristics than are species, and they represent more profound evolutionary differences. Thorne (1993) charted the number of flowering plant families found by state, showing that those states with the greatest familial diversity are the most southerly and tropical areas (figure 5.5). Florida and Texas have the greatest diversity of families(187 and 177 respectively), due in part to the influence of the diverse tropical and subtropical floras emanating northward from Mexico and Central and South America. Several other southern states are enriched by a number of archaic plant families shared with Southeast Asia but found nowhere else in the United States (see chapter 3). A contrast is provided by California, which is so rich in species but at the family level is not particularly diversified: With 140 families it contains about the same number as New Jersey.

Plant Endemism

Accurate figures for state-level plant endemism are more difficult to come by than overall species-richness figures (figure 5.4b, Appendix B). We compiled figures from a variety of sources, including recent floras, state heritage program botanists, and other knowledgeable researchers. Where no other recent figures were available, we relied on estimates presented by Gentry (1986). With 1,416 endemic vascular plants, representing nearly 30% of the native flora (Hickman 1993), California has by far the largest number of endemic plants in the nation. As a percentage of the native flora, however, Hawaii's 1,048 endemic vascular plants show an extraordinary level of distinctiveness, with about 87% endemism (W. L. Wagner pers. comm.). Texas, with 251 endemic species (B. Amos pers. comm.), has the third largest number, although its 6% endemism rate is a distant third to that of California and Hawaii. Florida, the only eastern state with substantial numbers of endemics, has about 155 state-restricted species (Wunderlin 1998), representing about 5% of its flora. The only other states with endemism levels greater than 1% are western; most eastern and midwestern states have few or no state endemics.

Hawaii's insular nature, which led to the in situ evolution of much of its biota, is responsible for its high levels of species endemism. Hawaii also has exceptional plant endemism at higher taxonomic levels. While none of its relatively few families are endemic, the 33 endemic Hawaiian genera represent a generic endemism level of 15%, the highest in the world (Wagner et al. 1999).

In many ways California is also an island—an ecological island distinct from the rest of the continent. Much of the state is climatically favored, tempered by the cool Pacific Ocean and largely characterized by mild wet winters and warm dry summers. Coupled with this equable climate is an

Figure 5.5. Diversity of plant families by state.

The highest diversity of plant families occurs in the Southeast, due in part to the presence of tropical floral elements and ancient relicts. Source: Thorne 1993.

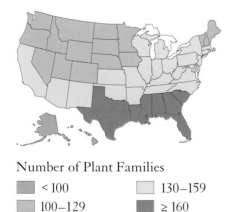

Number of Plant Families

■ < 100   □ 130–159
▨ 100–129 ■ ≥ 160

extremely complex physical environment, a product in part of the earth-shaking tectonic activity for which the state is justly famous. That part of the state to the west of the Sierra crest, known to botanists as the California Floristic Province, is particularly rich in plant species, many of them highly localized. While endemism for the state as a whole is around 30%, for this floristic province alone the figure rises to nearly 50%, among the highest levels of continental endemism in the world (Stebbins and Major 1965, Raven and Axelrod 1978).

Hawaii's plants exhibit the highest level of generic endemism in the world. Endemic Hawaiian genera include *Kokia*, a hibiscus relative, represented here by *K. kauaiensis*. © Gary Braasch.

Texas's enormous size and breadth of major climates, soils, and vegetation types contribute to the numerous endemics found in the state. The Texas hill country, in particular, is a region of enchanting beauty and high plant endemism. This distinctive vegetation region is almost wholly restricted to Texas, so the many plants unique to the Edwards Plateau also tend to be endemic to the state.

Florida's peninsular geography, southern position, distinctive geology, and long geological history together account for the presence of numerous species not shared with any of its neighboring states. Many of Florida's endemics are concentrated in the Lake Wales Ridge, a sandy region that has been continuously above water since the Tertiary, in some ways creating an island in time. The semi-arid habitat preserved on these sandy soils disappeared from adjacent states during and after the Pleistocene, contributing to the distinctiveness of Florida's plant life. Underlying geology is a factor that has been important in the development of endemics in the Miami Ridge rocklands of South Florida. The Florida Panhandle is another center of endemism in the state, partly due to the presence of shaded, moist habitats that have allowed a number of relict species to survive there, including the Florida yew (*Taxus floridana*) and Florida torreya.

Considering endemism only at the state level, however, obscures some key patterns in the distribution of limited-range plant species. Apart from Hawaii, California, Texas, and Florida, several other areas stand out in terms of regional plant endemism. Both the Appalachian region and the southern coastal plain have high levels of endemism (Takhtajan 1986, Thorne 1993), but because each of these areas covers parts of several states, there are few state-level endemics. The southern Appalachians harbor an exceptionally rich flora in their broadleaf forests, including many species that represent quite ancient plant groups. A number of narrowly restricted endemics in this region are associated with rock outcrops of various types, including the shale barrens of the mid-Appalachian region and the ancient granitic outcrops of the Georgia Piedmont. In total, about 90 plant species are endemic to eastern rock outcrops. These outcrop endemics do not appear to have a high fidelity for any particular rock type. Instead, they seem to be responding to the high light levels afforded by the barrens and glades rather than to particular chemical characteristics of the rocks themselves (Baskin and Baskin 1988).

With its springtime hillsides clothed in bluebonnets and paintbrush, the Texas hill country is a region of stunning beauty and high regional plant endemism. ©Tim Fitzharris/Minden Pictures.

The coastal plain, a topographically undifferentiated region wrapping around from the Atlantic to the Gulf of Mexico, is especially interesting in having a number of archaic plant elements, an unusual circumstance

About 90 plant species are endemic to eastern rock outcrops and barrens. Among the most interesting of these habitats are ancient granitic outcrops in Georgia's Piedmont region. © Harold E. Malde.

given that it may have been underwater repeatedly during the Pleistocene (Thorne 1993). Examples of these ancient genera include *Franklinia*, a camellia relative now extinct in the wild; *Leitneria*, the sole representative of the only plant family endemic to the United States; *Illicium*, a primitive flowering plant related to the star-anise of the Old World; and *Taxodium*, the bald cypress that provides the region with so much atmosphere. Presumably these plants survived along the borders of the coastal plain or in the adjacent Appalachians and recolonized once the waters receded.

Another fascinating group of plants characteristic of the Appalachian Mountains and the southern coastal plain are the insectivorous plants that inhabit many bogs and wet savannas. Among these is the famous Venus-flytrap (*Dionaea muscipula*), which has fascinated naturalists since the time of Linnaeus. Pitcher plants of the genus *Sarracenia* are also largely restricted to the southern Appalachians and coastal plain and represent another very old group of plants. With a bizarre distributional pattern, the only other two representatives in the pitcher plant family are northern California's cobra plant (*Darlingtonia*) and the genus *Heliamphora*, which grows atop the "lost world" tepuis of the geologically ancient Guayana Shield of Venezuela.

The intermountain West is another region with relatively high regional endemism. The combination of isolated mountain ranges and numerous unusual soil types has led to the development of a profusion of highly localized species. Most endemics in this region are relatively recently evolved species in large genera such as locoweed (*Astragalus*), rockcress (*Arabis*), wild buckwheat (*Eriogonum*), and spring-parsley (*Cymopterus*). Kartesz and Farstad (1999) found that the Colorado Plateau Shrublands ecoregion, with 290 unique species, harbored more endemics than any other ecoregion they examined; they counted another 151 endemics for the Great Basin Shrub Steppe ecoregion. As part of an effort to document centers of plant diversity and endemism worldwide, Davis et al. (1997) highlighted several other areas in the United States. These include the Klamath-Siskiyou region of California and Oregon, the Apachian/Madrean region of southern Arizona and New Mexico, and the Olympic Mountains of Washington.

Plant Rarity

Patterns of rarity in plants generally coincide with overall patterns of diversity and endemism (figure 5.4c). That is, rarity is most pronounced in the southwestern and western states, with secondary centers in the Southeast. As with endemism, Hawaii and California dominate in terms of absolute numbers (737 and 1,699 at-risk species, respectively) and as a proportion of native flora at risk (61% and 35%, respectively). The distinction between endemism and rarity is well illustrated, however, by more closely examining the second-tier states. While Florida has about as many endemic species as Utah and Arizona, both of these southwestern states surpass Florida in the number of rare plant species, as well as the propor-

The Venus-flytrap is perhaps the most famous of the insectivorous plants characteristic of the southern coastal plain. Found in the wild at only about 100 sites in the Carolinas, the species is under severe threat from overcollecting. © Harold E. Malde.

tion of their flora that these represent. The glaciated Midwest and Northeast have relatively low levels of rarity, as do most of the Great Plains states.

Hawaii's extremely dissected topography has led to the highly localized distribution of many plants, which are then vulnerable to human disturbance. Indeed, most of the native lowland vegetation is completely gone, having first been degraded when the Polynesians colonized the archipelago between approximately 1,500 and 2,000 years ago (Kirch 1982). In more recent times the extensive residential, agricultural, and tourist developments that now ring most of the islands have taken a significant toll on the remaining lowland species. As a result, less than 40% of the land surface of Hawaii is covered with native-dominated vegetation, most of which is confined to areas of higher elevation (Jacobi and Atkinson 1995).

Insular biotas often tend to be particularly susceptible to invasions by species introduced from continental areas (Carlquist 1974). A by-product of the isolation and relaxed competitive environment that promotes such wonderful examples of species radiations on islands also tends to leave those species at a disadvantage in dealing with introduced plants and animals. Physical defenses, such as thorns, tend to be lacking, as are the complex chemical elixirs that many plants produce to stave off hungry vertebrate and invertebrate browsers. As an indication of the degree to which alien species have changed Hawaii's overall flora, more than half (51%) the flowering plants known from Hawaii are not native (Wagner et al. 1999).

California's rich and varied flora also has both high levels of natural rarity, combined with some of the most intense development pressures anywhere in the nation. Large-scale agriculture has converted virtually all of the vast Central Valley, home to many restricted-range vernal pool species. Meanwhile, residential development centered in southern California, the San Francisco Bay region, and increasingly the foothills of the Sierra Nevada has taken a toll on other restricted-range California plants. The state's climate is also ideal for the establishment and spread of many invasive weedy species, which are further displacing the native flora. About 17% of plant species currently growing wild in the state are of nonnative origins (Hickman 1993).

Florida is the only eastern state with greater than 15% of its flora at risk, which also corresponds to its relatively high level of state endemism. In addition to supporting many species that are intrinsically rare and restricted in range or habitat, Florida has experienced some of the most intensive land conversion in the country. The state's central ridge, in particular, is the site of massive conversion for citrus groves, while southern Florida has seen major residential and agricultural development.

Patterns of Vertebrate Diversity

During the summer of 1848 Louis Agassiz, a Swiss-born zoologist recently appointed as a Harvard professor, was traveling along the shores of Lake

Florida is the only eastern state with greater than 15% of its flora at risk, due to a combination of numerous locally restricted species and widespread habitat conversion, such as has occurred in the Florida Keys. © Mark Robertson/TNC.

Superior conducting one of the first natural history field seminars in the country's history. Agassiz had established his reputation as a geologist and paleontologist in Europe, making a name for himself particularly in the study of glaciers and fossil fishes. His insights into the glacial origins of the Great Lakes would, in fact, be honored by the naming of Lake Agassiz, North America's largest Ice Age lake. Collecting fish for his budding museum back at Harvard, Agassiz caught a gar (*Lepisosteus*) and was surprised to recognize in this living creature a fossil that he had described back in Europe (Elman 1977). This discovery, along with others, prompted him to embark on one of the most ambitious attempts yet to document the natural history of the United States and catalogue its rich vertebrate species, which led to the founding of Harvard's Museum of Comparative Zoology in 1860.

Although a great geologist, zoologist, and teacher, Agassiz held strong creationist views and was a vocal opponent of Darwin's newly proposed theory of evolution (Mayr 1982). Ironically, his careful work documenting North America's vertebrate fauna provided a great deal of evidence for the very evolutionary processes he denied. Even more important than his own work, though, was Agassiz's role in inspiring students such as David Starr Jordan, who went on to become the world's foremost ichthyologist, the first president of Stanford University, and a leading evolutionist. The work of scientists such as Agassiz and Jordan laid much of the foundation for our current understanding of the enormous diversity and wealth of vertebrate life.

This variety is certainly on display in the United States, where vertebrate wildlife spectacles include migrating whales, huge flocks of migrating sandhill cranes, brown bears feasting on spawning salmon, herds of bison roaming the Great Plains, and waves of warblers passing through eastern forests and cities. But for each such spectacle, many more reclusive creatures remain largely unseen. Among them are the spring peepers that add music to warm evenings, the salamanders that lurk beneath the leaf litter, or colorful darters settled along the bottom of a mountain stream.

Overall vertebrate species richness is highest in the southeastern United States, with Texas, Alabama, Georgia, North Carolina, and California the five leading states (figure 5.6a, b, c).[1] Texas, with 1,038 species, has by far the most vertebrates of any state, almost a quarter more than Alabama, the next most diverse. Texas dominates vertebrate richness by virtue of its enormous size and its location spanning the moist southeastern coastal plain, the arid southwestern deserts, the lower reaches of the Great Plains, and the

1. For purposes of our analyses we include in state-level distributions only species that regularly occur (or occurred) in a state—that is, are resident year-round, breed or overwinter, or regularly pass through on migration. The following distribution maps and figures are based on state-level status ranks developed by state natural heritage programs. While every effort is made to treat these distributions consistently from state to state, some inconsistencies may occur, particularly for marine mammals and seabirds. Appendix B summarizes in tabular form the data on which these maps are derived.

extreme upper reaches (in the Rio Grande Valley) of subtropical Mexico. This expansive geographic and ecological breadth has resulted in high levels of bird, reptile, mammal, and amphibian diversity and moderate levels of fish diversity. The high level of vertebrate diversity in the Southeast is related strongly to the distribution of fishes and amphibians, two groups well represented in these warm, wet, unglaciated environments. Freshwater fishes alone constitute about one-third of all U.S. vertebrate species and therefore have a considerable influence on overall diversity figures. A secondary region of vertebrate diversity is the Southwest, where California, New Mexico, and Arizona figure prominently. In contrast to the situation in the Southeast, these western states are highly diverse for mammals and birds, whereas reptiles are well represented in both regions.

State-level endemism in vertebrates is most strongly displayed in three states: California, with 62 endemic species; Hawaii, with 57; and Texas, with 36 (figure 5.6b). On a proportional basis, however, Hawaii once again stands out. With only 141 regularly occurring native vertebrate species, the fewest of any state, Hawaii's endemics represent 40% of its vertebrate fauna. When marine mammals and nonbreeding birds are excluded, Hawaii's vertebrate endemism rises to 64%. Secondary centers of vertebrate endemism are found in the West (Nevada and Oregon) and Southeast (Alabama, Tennessee, and Florida). Interestingly, Alaska also has eight endemic vertebrates despite its relatively low overall vertebrate diversity.

Patterns of rarity in vertebrates are generally consistent with what one would expect based on the diversity and endemism levels described above (figure 5.6c). Hawaii again shows extremely high rates of rarity, exceeding 50% of its vertebrate fauna. The next tier, with levels of rarity in the 10% to 20% range, is led by California and includes Tennessee, Georgia, and Alabama.

Many of the factors discussed earlier regarding overall patterns of diversity and patterns in the diversification of plants apply equally to interpreting vertebrate patterns. These include the latitudinal gradients that accentuate diversity in southern states, area effects that tend to increase diversity in larger states, and the influence of environmental heterogeneity, which creates more opportunities for speciation and more distinct habitats for different species to occupy. A number of mammals, birds, and reptiles are found in marine habitats, and thus, not even considering marine fishes, proximity to the ocean has an influence on vertebrate patterns of diversity and rarity.

Different groups of vertebrates are influenced by and respond to these features in distinct ways. Because "vertebrates" encompass an enormous variety of life-forms and body sizes, generalizations about them as a group are of limited utility. Vertebrate species range from extraordinarily vagile species—in the case of some birds and whales, annually migrating thousands of miles—to species of salamanders that may never in their lifetime wander the length of a football field. Other species, such as salmon, may disperse during their adult stages but return to their natal stream when it is time to breed. Isolating mechanisms that lead to speciation may be re-

Large charismatic vertebrates, like the American bison (*top*, © Frank Oberle), tend to capture the public's attention, but most of the nation's vertebrates—and animal biomass—is made up of small, reclusive creatures such as this ornate chorus frog (*Pseudacris ornata*) (*bottom*, © Suzanne L. Collins and Joseph T. Collins/Photo Researchers)

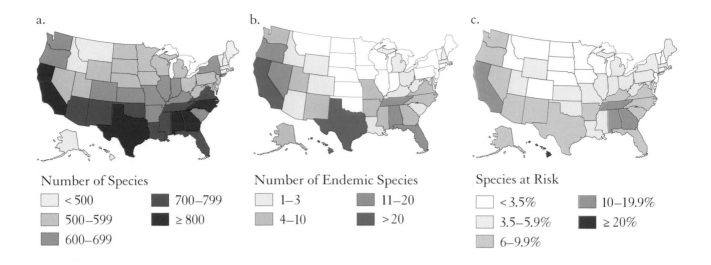

a.

Number of Species

☐ < 500	■ 700–799
☐ 500–599	■ ≥ 800
☐ 600–699	

b.

Number of Endemic Species

☐ 1–3	■ 11–20
☐ 4–10	■ > 20

c.

Species at Risk

☐ < 3.5%	■ 10–19.9%
☐ 3.5–5.9%	■ ≥ 20%
☐ 6–9.9%	

Figure 5.6a–c. Vertebrate diversity, endemism, and rarity.

(a) Factors affecting patterns of species diversity include latitudinal gradients that accentuate diversity in southern states; area effects that tend to increase diversity in larger states; the influence of environmental heterogeneity, and the lingering effect of Pleistocene glaciation. (b) Texas, California, and Hawaii stand out in terms of endemism, (c) while for rarity, Hawaii leads all other states in the proportion of its vertebrate species at risk.

lated to geographic complexity, such as the isolated southwestern mountain peaks known as sky islands, or may be due to behavioral traits that prevent interbreeding among co-occurring populations.

Vertebrates on the whole are an ancient group, but most of the environments that their modern representatives occupy are geologically quite recent. It is precisely this interplay between ancient lineages and recent landscapes that produces some of the most interesting biogeographical puzzles. We will now review some of the more interesting patterns observed among the various major groups of vertebrates.

Mammals

The concept of charismatic megafauna was essentially defined around mammals. Species such as grizzly bear, American bison, gray wolf, mountain lion, and bighorn sheep are photogenic representatives of America's biodiversity, and to many people such species are synonymous with wildlife. Many of these examples are big, fierce predators, and that, too, defines *wildness* for many people, even to the extent that some organizations have proposed the creation of continental-scale reserve networks around such species (Noss 1992). Large mammals, though, represent only a small fraction of the mammalian diversity found in the United States. Most mammal species are far less glamorous. The masked shrew (*Sorex cinereus*) may be the country's most common mammal, but this tiny, burrowing species is completely unfamiliar to the average person. The decidedly unglamorous order Rodentia makes up about half of the nation's mammalian fauna. Not that these rodents are uninteresting. Flying squirrels (*Glaucomys*) glide from tree to tree in northern and eastern forests on flaps of skin stretching from their forelegs to their hind legs. Kangaroo rats (*Dipodomys*), found in the Southwest, are exquisitely adapted for desert life and perform the metabolic feat of never needing to drink water. Springing along on their well-developed hind legs, these rodents can jump a distance that, for people, would be the equivalent of leaping from home plate to the pitcher's mound on a baseball diamond.

Although mammals are important components of virtually all terrestrial ecosystems across the United States, mammalian diversity and endemism exhibits a decidedly western and southwestern pattern. Most western states have more than 100 mammal species; otherwise only North Carolina and Oklahoma top that threshold (figure 5.7a). The desert regions in particular—from the Sonoran and Chihuahuan Deserts along the Mexican border to the Mojave and Great Basin Deserts farther north—have diverse rodent assemblages. The hoarding behavior of one group of rodents, woodrats of the genus *Neotoma*, has produced some of the most compelling records of past climates in these deserts. Fossilized woodrat middens record with considerable accuracy vegetation growing near these rodents' nests as long ago as 40,000 years (Betancourt et al. 1990). Southwestern states are also particularly rich in bat species; the largest numbers occur in Texas and Arizona.

Marine mammals are another significant component of the biota for many coastal states. At least 59 species of marine mammals inhabit U.S. waters, including 43 cetaceans (whales, dolphins, and porpoises) and 13 seals, as well as walrus (*Odobenus rosmarus*), West Indian manatee (*Trichechus manatus*), and sea otter (*Enhydra lutris*). Defining *regularly occurring* for species that spend their lives underwater and often far from shore is difficult, and many marine mammals are known in a given state only from occasional strandings. For example, although 20 marine mammals have been recorded from Texas waters, only 5 are known to occur regularly. In contrast to the relatively depauperate marine mammal fauna of the Gulf of Mexico, 16 to 20 species of marine mammals regularly visit most Atlantic coastal states. The waters of the eastern Pacific are richer still, reaching a peak in Alaska, which is visited by 33 marine mammal species.

Superbly adapted for life in the arid Southwest, kangaroo rats never need to drink water, deriving all the moisture they need from their diet of seeds. The banner-tailed kangaroo rat (*Dipodomys spectabilis*) extends from Arizona to western Texas. © Joe McDonald/Animals Animals.

Figure 5.7a–c. Mammal diversity and rarity.

(a) Mammal diversity is highest in the Southwest, reflecting the many species of small mammals populating the arid West. (b) Rarity, in contrast, appears to be highest in coastal states, but this is largely a reflection of several rare yet wide-ranging marine mammals. (c) Considering rarity only for land mammals elevates the significance of certain interior states.

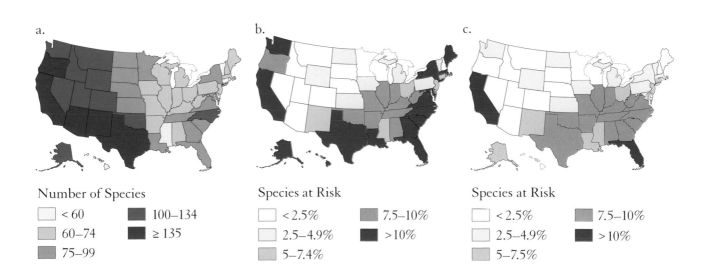

a.

Number of Species

< 60	100–134
60–74	≥ 135
75–99	

b.

Species at Risk

< 2.5%	7.5–10%
2.5–4.9%	>10%
5–7.4%	

c.

Species at Risk

< 2.5%	7.5–10%
2.5–4.9%	>10%
5–7.5%	

Alaska harbors the richest marine
mammal fauna of any state; 33 species,
including the walrus, live in or regularly
visit its waters. © Jo Overholt.

State-level endemism among U.S. mammals is not high, and only a
handful of states have even a single endemic mammal (table 5.1). California leads the nation, with 18 endemic mammal species. Most of these
are rodents, including 6 kangaroo rats. A notable exception is the island
gray fox (*Urocyon littoralis*), which is restricted to the Channel Islands
off the coast of southern California. The only other states with multiple
endemics are Alaska and Oregon.

Patterns of mammalian rarity stand in apparent contrast to those for
species richness and endemism (figure 5.7b). While the latter reflect the
influence of limited-range species in the arid West, mammalian rarity, at
least when viewed as a percentage of total fauna, appears to be highest in
coastal states. This is due in part to several rare yet wide-ranging marine
mammals, such as the right whale (*Eubalaena glacialis*) and the sei whale
(*Balaenoptera borealis*). All five rare mammals noted for Rhode Island, for
example, are whales. It is noteworthy, though, that the only documented
mammalian extinction in the United States is a marine mammal, the West
Indian monk seal (*Monachus tropicalis*), which historically reached its
northernmost distribution in the waters of the Florida Keys.

Considering rarity patterns only for land mammals (that is, nonma-
rine species) provides a very different perspective (figure 5.7c). Not surprisingly, interior states are more prominently represented, while several
coastal states move down in importance. Three states that shift dramatically when marine species are factored out are Washington, Rhode Island,
and Hawaii.

The considerable mobility of many mammals means that in contrast
to rare species in many other groups, a number of vulnerable mammals
are—or were—quite widely distributed. This is particularly true in the
eastern United States, where many states share a few of these wide-
ranging, or formerly wide-ranging, mammals at risk. The red wolf, for
example, formerly ranged from Texas to the Atlantic Ocean yet now exists
only in a few places where it has been reintroduced to the wild. Several
rare yet fairly widespread bats are found across a number of midwestern
and eastern states, including the Indiana, gray, and eastern small-footed
bats (*Myotis sodalis, M. grisescens,* and *M. leibii*).

Birds

In the days of John J. Audubon, the famous pioneer naturalist and bird
artist, the most important aid to field study was a shotgun. Lacking the
portable optical equipment that now enables us to view distant objects
clearly, scientists of his day needed to have specimens in hand in order to
carefully examine the birds. Audubon's great contribution to bird illustration, in fact, was to break away from painting his subjects in the stiff,
lifeless pose of a mounted specimen and to depict them as they behave in
nature. Such observations became far easier and available to large numbers of nonspecialists with the advent of two things: high-quality, inexpensive binoculars, and, perhaps just as important, the concept of the field
guide. The latter, pioneered in the 1930s by Roger Tory Peterson, pro-

Table 5.1. State-endemic mammals

State	Scientific name	Common name	Conservation status
Alaska	*Dicrostonyx exsul*	St. Lawrence Island collared lemming	G4
	Dicrostonyx nelsoni	Nelson's collared lemming	G4
	Dicrostonyx rubricatus	Bering collared lemming	G4
	Dicrostonyx unalascensis	Unalaska collared lemming	G3
	Lepus othus	Alaska hare	G4?Q
	Sorex hydrodromus	Pribilof island shrew	G2
	Sorex yukonicus	Alaska tiny shrew	GU
California	*Ammospermophilus nelsoni*	Nelson's antelope squirrel	G2G3
	Arborimus pomo	California red tree vole	G3
	Dipodomys agilis	agile kangaroo rat	G2G3
	Dipodomys heermanni	Heermann's kangaroo rat	G3G4
	Dipodomys ingens	giant kangaroo rat	G2
	Dipodomys nitratoides	Fresno kangaroo rat	G3
	Dipodomys stephensi	Stephens' kangaroo rat	G2
	Dipodomys venustus	narrow-faced kangaroo rat	G4
	Perognathus alticous	white-eared pocket mouse	G1G2
	Perognathus inornatus	San Joaquin pocket mouse	G4
	Perognathus xanthonotus	yellow-eared pocket mouse	G2G3Q
	Reithrodontomys raviventris	salt-marsh harvest mouse	G1G2
	Sorex lyelli	Mt. Lyell shrew	G2G4Q
	Spermophilus mohavensis	Mohave ground squirrel	G2G3
	Tamias alpinus	alpine chipmunk	G4
	Tamias ochrogenys	yellow-cheeked chipmunk	G3G4
	Tamias sonomae	Sonoma chipmunk	G4G5
	Urocyon littoralis	Island gray fox	G2
Florida	*Podomys floridanus*	Florida mouse	G3
Hawaii	*Monachus schauinslandi*	Hawaiian monk seal	G2
Idaho	*Spermophilus brunneus*	Idaho ground squirrel	G2
Massachusetts	*Microtus breweri*	beach vole	G1Q
New Mexico	*Sorex neomexicanus*	New Mexico shrew	G2
Nevada	*Tamias palmeri*	Palmer's chipmunk	G2
Oregon	*Sorex bairdi*	Baird's shrew	G4
	Sorex pacificus	Pacific shrew	G3G4
	Thomomys bulbivorus	camas pocket gopher	G4
Texas	*Geomys texensis*	llano pocket gopher	G2Q
Utah	*Cynomys parvidens*	Utah prairie dog	G1
Washington	*Marmota olympus*	Olympic marmot	G3
Wyoming	*Thomomys clusius*	Wyoming pocket gopher	G2

California has by far the largest number of single state endemic mammal species, followed by Alaska and Oregon. For interpretation of conservation status ranks, see tables 4.2 and 4.3.

vided an easy means for field identification of birds (and later other groups of animals and plants) and opened up the world of bird observation to a whole new, and continuously growing, set of people.

Part of the ancient human fascination with birds is that they are without doubt the most conspicuous members of the animal world. They lend color, song, and interest to walks through virtually every imaginable habitat, from the seashore to the woods, and from deep wilderness to city parks. Birds are also the most intensively studied part of our entire biota. The considerable professional and amateur interest in birds means that there is more information about the distribution, status, trends, and life histories of birds than about any other species group. The United States has been a particular center of ornithological activity, with the result that our avifauna is extraordinarily well documented. Among the most important efforts in documenting the distribution and status of the United States' birdlife are the North American Breeding Bird Survey, coordinated by the U.S. Geological Survey's Biological Resources Division, and the Christmas Bird Count, coordinated by the National Audubon Society. Both of these efforts depend largely on the time and expertise of amateur birders and are excellent examples of the contribution that individuals can make to advancing the understanding of our native biota.

Texas has by far the most bird species of any state (figure 5.8a). With 472 regularly occurring birds, this state hosts almost two-thirds of the nation's bird species. Texas's remarkable diversity is due to its size, ecological diversity, and central placement along our southern border. Many eastern birds, such as the prothonotary warbler (*Protonotaria citrea*), reach their westernmost distribution in the state, while western birds, like the phainopepla (*Phainopepla nitens*), find their eastern limits there. In addition, the ranges of a number of tropical birds extend north into the United States just as far as Texas. Two of the three U.S. species of kingfishers— ringed kingfisher (*Ceryle torquata*) and green kingfisher (*Chloroceryle americana*)—are tropical species that reach no farther than our southernmost states. Three other states also have more than 400 regularly occur-

Figure 5.8a–b. Bird diversity and rarity.

(a) Although total bird diversity is highest in southwestern states, northern states are also relatively species-rich due to the ability of birds to breed at higher latitudes and migrate south to overwinter. (b) State rarity levels typically are quite low, with the exception of Hawaii, where almost half (49%) of native birds are at risk.

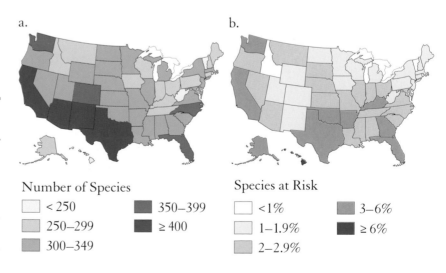

a.

b.

Number of Species

☐ < 250 ■ 350–399
☐ 250–299 ■ ≥ 400
■ 300–349

Species at Risk

☐ <1% ■ 3–6%
☐ 1–1.9% ■ ≥ 6%
■ 2–2.9%

ring birds: New Mexico, Arizona, and California. Each of these states also benefits from a position along the southwestern border with Mexico and is enriched by a number of Mexican and Central American species.

While southwestern states have the highest numbers of bird species, perhaps the most interesting feature of U.S. bird diversity patterns is the relatively small degree of variation in species numbers among states. While northern states consistently rank low in diversity for most groups of plants and animals, with 317 bird species North Dakota has diversity levels comparable to typically more species-rich western or southern states, such as Nevada or Georgia. Considering only breeding species, the typical latitudinal gradient in species richness is further confounded. Maps of breeding species richness derived from the North American Breeding Bird Survey show their highest numbers in the extreme northern part of the United States and southern Canada (figure 5.9). Similarly, in a continental-scale analysis of bird species richness, Currie (1991) found a pronounced midlatitude peak in diversity at 44°N, about the latitude of Eugene, Oregon, or Portland, Maine. Wintering bird diversity, in contrast, conforms to typical trends in latitudinal diversity, with a smooth transition between higher diversity in the South and lower richness in the North (figure 5.10).

What accounts for the relative richness of northern states in birds, unlike most other vertebrate groups? Flight is the key to success for birds as a group and as individuals (notwithstanding the occasional evolution of flightlessness). This ability has allowed the adoption of long-distance seasonal migration as a major life history strategy. Migration, in turn, is without doubt the most important factor influencing the distribution and abundance of North American birds. Of the 707 bird species that regularly occur in the continental United States, 507 (71%) are long-distance migrants.

Temperate regions are characterized by strong seasonality, experiencing major fluctuations in light and temperature. During the winter months, plant photosynthesis largely shuts down in northern climes. Animals have three major strategies: go dormant for the winter and live off body reserves, as in the case of hibernating bears; remain active and feed on foodstuffs that persist through the winter, as in the case of seed-eating chickadees; or move to warmer more biologically active regions. As the spring moves across northern lands, a tremendous flush of biological activity takes place. Plants leaf out and insects emerge in enormous quantities. Food resources in the warmer, more tropical regions where many migrants overwinter tend not to go through such drastic seasonal fluctuations. Competition for food resources can be intense in these southern regions, with year-round residents vying with any visitors for resources. The spring and summer pulse of readily available, high-quality energy resources in northern regions is what makes migration worthwhile for so many bird species. This food, particularly the protein-rich insects available, provides an especially productive environment in which to breed and rear chicks. Of course, the advantages of gaining access to this rich food resource are countered by the rigors of the migration itself.

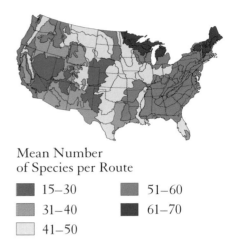

Mean Number
of Species per Route

▮ 15–30	▮ 51–60
▮ 31–40	▮ 61–70
▢ 41–50	

Figure 5.9 Breeding bird diversity.

The highest number of breeding bird species occur in the extreme northern parts of the United States, as indicated by the number of species observed on standard routes of the North American Breeding Bird Survey. Source: Robbins et al. 1986.

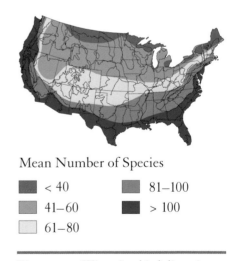

Mean Number of Species

▮ < 40	▮ 81–100
▮ 41–60	▮ > 100
▢ 61–80	

Figure 5.10. Wintering bird diversity.

In contrast to breeding birds, diversity of wintering birds—as measured by the National Audubon Society's Christmas Bird Count—shows a uniform north-to-south decline in diversity. Source: Robbins et al. 1986.

Our rarest songbird, the Kirtland's warbler, is a U.S. breeding endemic, nesting only in a small region of northern Michigan but migrating to the Bahamas for the winter. © Ron Austing/Photo Researchers.

On balance, the advantages of migration must outweigh the costs. For instance, of 233 species of birds that breed in Michigan (Brewer et al. 1991), fewer than 17 are completely nonmigratory there. Several distinct migratory patterns are evident in North American birds. Some species, particularly waterfowl, move south within the United States, congregating in regions with more moderate winter climates. The Central Valley of California and the Chesapeake Bay of Maryland and Virginia are two areas that are heavily used by wintering ducks and geese. Other species, such as the endangered whooping crane (*Grus americana*), spend the winter along the Gulf Coast.

Many songbird species, especially from the eastern United States, move south of our borders. These are termed *neotropical* migrants, in reference to their overwintering in the New World tropics (the Old World tropics, or *paleotropics*, refers to the tropical regions of Africa and Asia). The major wintering areas for most such neotropical migrants are in Mexico and Central America. Others move to Caribbean islands, and a few move south as far as South America, including some of our most widespread forest-dwelling birds, such as the red-eyed vireo (*Vireo olivaceus*), veery (*Catharus fuscescens*), and cerulean warbler (*Dendroica cerulea*).

Some U.S. migrants, particularly certain raptors and shorebirds, cover remarkable distances. The American golden-plover (*Pluvialis dominica*), for example, breeds in the tundra of Alaska and winters on the pampas of Argentina. Taking a circular route, in the fall it flies east to Labrador and then south directly over the Atlantic Ocean to Brazil, returning north in spring via Central America and the Mississippi Valley. These birds cover more than 7,500 miles each way.

Using modern technology, it is even possible to follow the migratory movements of individual birds. Researchers fitted an osprey (*Pandion haliaetus*) that nested at The Nature Conservancy's Mashomack Preserve on eastern Long Island, New York, with a satellite telemetry device and tracked the bird to and from its wintering ground in the Pantanal region of southwestern Brazil (M. Martell unpubl. data). The record for long-distance migration, however, is probably that of the arctic tern (*Sterna paradisaea*), which leaves its nesting sites in Alaska and spends a "second summer" in Antarctica—a round-trip of as much as 25,000 miles (Elphick 1995).

A few specific places have taken on overwhelming significance in the migrations of certain species. Red knots (*Calidris canutus*) annually move back and forth between their high arctic breeding areas and southern South America. A critical stage in their northern migration is a May stop at the Delaware Bay, timed to coincide with the mass breeding of horseshoe crabs. The horseshoe crab eggs provide a high-energy resource that allows the knots to undertake the final stage of their journey. Up to 80% of the North American population of red knots pass through the Delaware Bay during spring migration. Another key migratory stopover is the Platte River of Nebraska, where sandhill cranes (*Grus canadensis*) spend about a month during early spring, foraging before their trip back to northern breeding grounds. Historically the Platte River was "a mile wide and an inch deep," enabling the cranes to forage in the wet prairies alongside the river during the day and roost at night standing in the shallow waters, unperturbed by four-legged predators. The Platte's flow has been significantly altered; it no longer provides such an expanse of shallow water. Nonetheless, approximately half a million cranes still congregate and forage along the shores and in the adjacent farm fields, creating the largest crane concentration in the world and one of the most spectacular wildlife sights in North America.

State-level endemism is extremely low for U.S. bird species, with the notable exception of Hawaii. In the continental United States only three birds are restricted to a single state. California contains two of these state-endemic birds. The yellow-billed magpie (*Pica nuttalli*) closely resembles the widespread black-billed magpie (*P. pica*) but biologically is quite distinctive and replaces the latter species west of the Sierra Nevada. The island scrub jay (*Aphelocoma insularis*), a close relative of the widespread western scrub jay (*A. californica*), is restricted to Santa Cruz Island off the coast of southern California. This species only recently was formally recognized as fully distinct at the species level, based on morphological and genetic evidence. California is also the only mainland U.S. region recognized as an Endemic Bird Area in a worldwide review carried out by Birdlife International (Stattersfield et al. 1998). These authors highlight five additional species that, while not strictly endemic to the state, all have restricted ranges: Allen's hummingbird (*Selasphorus sasin*), Nuttall's woodpecker (*Picoides nuttallii*), California thrasher (*Toxostoma redivivum*), tricolored blackbird (*Agelaius tricolor*), and Lawrence's goldfinch (*Carduelis lawrencei*).

The only other state-level endemic is the Florida scrub jay, *Aphelocoma coerulescens*, another bird recently elevated from subspecies to full species status. Found only in the rapidly disappearing scrub habitat of central Florida, this bird represents a fascinating disjunction, since its closest relatives are in central Texas. Together with other more typically southwestern species such as the burrowing owl (*Athene cunicularia*) and crested caracara (*Caracara plancus*), the Florida scrub jay is part of a semi-arid fauna that stretched across the Gulf coastal plain from Texas to Florida during much of the Quaternary. Increasingly wet climatic conditions along the Gulf Coast during the middle part of the Pleistocene appear to have isolated the Florida scrub jay population, leading to its evolutionary divergence (Webb 1990). Perhaps in response to the reduction of its arid habitat, this scrub jay species has evolved a number of peculiar behavioral traits, including delayed breeding, group living, and cooperation among family members in defending territory and caring for young (Woolfenden and Fitzpatrick 1984).

Four other U.S. bird species qualify for classification as state-level *breeding* endemics. That is, these species breed in just a single state, even though they range beyond that state outside the breeding season. Two such species occur in Alaska: the bristle-thighed curlew (*Numenius tahitiensis*) and McKay's bunting (*Plectrophenax hyperboreus*). The bristle-thighed curlew is known to breed in only two locations on the Seward Peninsula and numbers only about 7,000 individuals, while McKay's bunting breeds mainly on Hall and St. Matthew Islands in the Bering Sea.

About half a million sandhill cranes congregate along Nebraska's Platte River during their spring migration, creating one of the most breathtaking wildlife spectacles in North America. © Harold E. Malde.

The Kirtland's warbler (*Dendroica kirtlandii*), with only about 600 breeding pairs left, is among our rarest U.S. songbirds and breeds only in a small region of jack pine savanna in northern Michigan. These warblers are known to overwinter only in the Bahamas archipelago. The fourth species restricted in its breeding to a single state is the golden-cheeked warbler (*Dendroica chrysoparia*). This bird breeds only in juniper woodlands on the Edwards Plateau of central Texas and winters in Central America.

In contrast to the low levels of state endemism on the U.S. mainland, Hawaii's birdlife is one of the most extraordinary examples of endemism in the world. When Captain Cook first visited the Hawaiian Islands in 1778, at least 115 native bird species regularly occurred in the archipelago. Of these, 52 are endemic, representing just under one-half (45%) of Hawaii's avifauna (table 5.2). Considering only the state's 70 species of breeding birds, endemism levels rise to three-quarters (75%), while among just the 49 land birds the endemism rate climbs further, to 96%. Researchers studying fossil bird bones have identified another 60 endemic land bird species that existed prior to Cook's arrival but became extinct following the colonization of the islands by Polynesian peoples (Steadman 1995).

Among birdwatchers the term *rarities* often connotes birds that are accidental or vagrant in an area and therefore are infrequently seen. We use the term here in a way consistent with elsewhere in this chapter—that is, to refer to regularly occurring species that have a conservation status of extinct, imperiled, or vulnerable. Hawaii again ranks first for rare birds, containing almost half of the nation's bird rarities (figure 5.8b). With 56 rare species, almost one-half (49%) of Hawaii's total native bird species are considered at risk. Looking at just endemic Hawaiian birds, the numbers are even more striking. Over a third (35%) of Hawaii's endemic species are already extinct (GX). A sobering 92% of Hawaii's endemic birds are either extinct, imperiled, or vulnerable.

State rarity levels on the mainland typically are quite low; most states have fewer than 10 rare species, representing 3% or less of their avifauna. Alaska is an exception to this rule: With 16 species of rare birds, this northern state trails only Hawaii in both number and proportion (6%) of rare species. Most of Alaska's rare species are waterbirds, such as the spectacled eider (*Somateria fischeri*), Steller's eider (*Polysticta stelleri*), and red-legged kittiwake (*Rissa brevirostris*). In an interesting biological link between the above two states, a population of the rare bristle-thighed curlew migrates south and spends the winter on Laysan Island in the Hawaiian chain.

The United States' vast coastline hosts many species of seabirds, some of which only forage in U.S. waters and do not breed on U.S. land. These seabirds add to the totals for coastal states yet complicate the job of assessing patterns of avian species diversity and rarity. Removing seabirds that do not breed in the United States (mostly tube noses and alcids) from our analysis results in the three Pacific Coast states of California, Washington, and Oregon shifting down somewhat in both number and proportion of rare species.

In addition to overall rarity patterns, population trends are important to consider, even for those species that are not yet rare. A considerable body

The Hawaiian honeycreepers are among the finest examples of adaptive radiation. With their amazing variety of beaks, each of which is suited to a particular foraging strategy, these birds evolved from a single finchlike ancestor. © H. Douglas Pratt.

Table 5.2. Endemic Hawaiian birds

Family	Common name	Scientific name	Conservation status
Accipitridae	Hawaiian hawk	*Buteo solitarius*	G2
Anatidae	Laysan duck	*Anas laysanensis*	G1
	Hawaiian duck	*Anas wyvilliana*	G1
	Hawaiian goose	*Branta sandvicensis*	G1
Corvidae	Hawaiian crow	*Corvus hawaiiensis*	G1
Fringillidae	Kona grosbeak	*Chloridops kona*	GX
	ula-ai-hawane	*Ciridops anna*	GX
	black mamo	*Drepanis funerea*	GX
	Hawaii mamo	*Drepanis pacifica*	GX
	Lanai hookbill	*Dysmorodrepanis munroi*	GX
	greater akialoa	*Hemignathus ellisianus*	GX
	Oahu amakihi	*Hemignathus flavus*	G3
	Kauai amakihi	*Hemignathus kauaiensis*	G3
	nukupu'u	*Hemignathus lucidus*	G1
	akiapolaau	*Hemignathus munroi*	G1
	lesser akialoa	*Hemignathus obscurus*	GX
	anianiau	*Hemignathus parvus*	G3G4
	greater 'amakihi	*Hemignathus sagittirostris*	GX
	Hawaii amakihi	*Hemignathus virens*	G3
	'apapane	*Himatione sanguinea*	G3
	palila	*Loxioides bailleui*	G1
	'akekee	*Loxops caeruleirostris*	G2
	'akepa	*Loxops coccineus*	G2
	po'ouli	*Melamprosops phaeosoma*	G1
	akikiki	*Oreomystis bairdi*	G1
	Hawaii creeper	*Oreomystis mana*	G2
	akohekohe	*Palmeria dolei*	G2
	kakawahie	*Paroreomyza flammea*	GH
	Oahu alauahio	*Paroreomyza maculata*	G1
	Maui alauahio	*Paroreomyza montana*	G4
	Maui parrotbill	*Pseudonestor xanthophrys*	G1
	'o'u	*Psittirostra psittacea*	G1
	lesser koa-finch	*Rhodacanthis flaviceps*	GX
	greater koa-finch	*Rhodacanthis palmeri*	GX
	Laysan finch	*Telespiza cantans*	G1
	nihoa finch	*Telespiza ultima*	G1
	'i'iwi	*Vestiaria coccinea*	G4
Meliphagidae	kioea	*Chaetoptila angustipluma*	GX
	Oahu o'o'	*Moho apicalis*	GX
	Bishop's o'o'	*Moho bishopi*	GX
	Kauai o'o'	*Moho braccatus*	GX
	Hawaii o'o'	*Moho nobilis*	GX
Monarchidae	'elepaio	*Chasiempis sandwichensis*	G4
Rallidae	alae keokeo	*Fulica alai*	G2
	Laysan rail	*Porzana palmeri*	GX
	Hawaiian rail	*Porzana sandwichensis*	GX
Silviidae	millerbird	*Acrocephalus familiaris*	G1
Turdidae	olomao	*Myadestes lanaiensis*	G1
	kamao	*Myadestes myadestinus*	G1
	omao	*Myadestes obscurus*	G4
	puaiohi	*Myadestes palmeri*	G1
	amaui	*Myadestes woahensis*	GX

Of the at least 52 bird species that are endemic to the Hawaiian Islands, more than one-third are already extinct (GX) or missing (GH). Another 60 species appear to have become extinct following the Polynesian colonization of the islands and before first Western contact. For interpretation of conservation status ranks, see tables 4.2 and 4.3.

of knowledge about bird trends now exists, thanks largely to the massive efforts carried out as part of the North American Breeding Bird Survey. Among the most interesting findings to come out of this long-term data set is that grassland and shrubland birds are experiencing the most consistent and widespread declines of any group of species (Peterjohn et al. 1995). Declines appear most prevalent in the eastern United States, but they are also occurring in the Great Plains, which is the heart of the breeding range for many of these grassland species. Many woodland birds, in contrast, appear to be increasing in numbers, although there are regions where this is not the case, such as the southern Appalachians, and the Pacific Coast from Oregon to central California.

Reported declines in populations of neotropical migrants have generated considerable interest, and this issue has stimulated a major multinational and multi-institutional conservation effort, Partners in Flight. The trend data, however, are somewhat inconsistent, with both declines and increases evident, depending on which species are assessed, what geographic areas are considered, and over which time periods trends are calculated. In a seminal paper on the subject, Robbins et al. (1989) concluded that most neotropical migrant bird species that breed in forests of the eastern United States declined in abundance between 1978 and 1987, following a period of relatively stable or increasing populations. Summarizing more recent evidence, however, Robinson (1997) argued that, when viewed as a whole and averaged over large geographical areas, neotropical migrant populations have remained generally stable, particularly in the western United States. Certain species, however, are declining at especially fast rates, such as the wood thrush (*Hylocichla mustelina*), a species that overwinters in Mexico and Central America, and the cerulean warbler, a bird that travels farther south into the tropical Andes.

Birds have suffered a disproportionate number of extinctions relative to other vertebrate groups. As mentioned previously, fossils reveal that at least 60 species of Hawaiian land birds became extinct even before the European "discovery" of Hawaii. Since that time, another 18 Hawaiian species have disappeared, and 1 more is missing and may be extinct (for complete listing, see Appendix A). On the mainland, 4 U.S. species have become extinct, all from the eastern United States. The great auk (*Pinguinus impennis*) and Labrador duck (*Camptorhynchus labradorius*) were both North Atlantic seabirds that formerly occurred along the coast of several northeastern states. The passenger pigeon (*Ectopistes migratorius*) and Carolina parakeet (*Conuropsis carolinensis*) both were extremely abundant species that occurred across much of the eastern United States. In contrast, Bachman's warbler (*Vermivora bachmanii*) had always been uncommon in its predominantly southeastern breeding range. Even though this warbler has not been seen since the 1960s, ornithologists still hold out hope that the species still survives. The status of another former southeastern resident, the ivory-billed woodpecker (*Campephilus principalis*), is also unclear at present. The bird was last sighted in the United States in the mid-1940s (in Louisiana), but as late as the 1980s it was known to persist in old-growth pine forests of eastern Cuba. Based on extensive and

Declining populations of such neotropical migrants as the wood thrush have sparked great concern about the fate of these birds on both their North American breeding grounds and their Latin American wintering sites. © G. Bailey/ VIREO.

fruitless surveys of the bird's Cuban habitat, some researchers had given up hope for the species (Lammertink 1995). New reports from a different part of the island, however, suggests that the bird may still survive.

Reptiles

Reptiles include some of the most characteristic creatures of the U.S. landscape, from the voracious alligator snapping turtle (*Macroclemys temminckii*)—which can grow more than a yard long and weigh over 300 pounds—to the chuckwalla (*Sauromalus ater*), a vegetarian relative of the iguana that nibbles on desert flowers. Reptiles are an ancient group, having originated more than 300 million years ago toward the close of the Paleozoic era, and were the first vertebrates completely adapted to life on dry land. Many of our contemporary species represent ancient evolutionary lineages.

Texas far surpasses all other states in terms of reptile diversity (figure 5.11a). With 149 species, Texas has half again as many reptile species as Arizona, the next most species-rich state. In general, diversity in reptiles is highest in the southern states, in both West and East, and declines to the north. No reptiles make it as far north as Alaska. Looking at continent-wide patterns, both Kiester (1971) and Currie (1991) found that reptile diversity has a remarkably regular north-south gradient. No terrestrial reptiles have colonized Hawaii without the assistance of humans: All six of that state's native reptiles are marine.

The exceptional reptile diversity in Texas is due both to the state's large size and to its strategic location at the crossroads of several distinct reptilian faunas. Among snakes, for instance, more than one-third (36%) of Texas's species are essentially eastern, reaching their westernmost distribution in the state (Gehlbach 1984). Another quarter (23%) are western, with Texas defining their eastern limits. The state's fauna is also enriched by Great Plains species that extend south into the state, as well as tropical species that range northward from Mexico into the state's Tamaulipan region.

Diversity patterns differ markedly among the various groups of reptiles. Turtles have their greatest concentration of species in the eastern United States, and especially in the Southeast. The Gulf coastal plain is an area of particular diversification for several genera of freshwater turtles, such as the map turtles (*Graptemys*). Lizards, which are well suited to life in arid regions, show their greatest diversity in the Southwest, although some individual genera, such as the skinks (*Eumeces*), are more diverse in the moister East. Snakes are quite diverse in both the eastern and western United States, although the types of snakes that have diversified most in the two regions differ. All 10 species of water snakes (*Nerodia*)—which as the name implies spend their lives in and around rivers, streams, and lakes—are found only from Texas eastward. In contrast, only 4 of 13 rattlesnake species (*Crotalus* and *Sistrurus*) have eastern distributions. Topography also seems to be involved in defining the density of reptile species. In contrast to the pattern in mammals and amphibians, Kiester (1971)

The chuckwalla, a pudgy relative of the iguana, frequents rocky outcrops in the southwestern deserts. © Charlie Ott.

Figure 5.11a–b. Reptile diversity
and rarity.

*(a) Texas towers above all other
states for reptile diversity. (b) Rarity
patterns, however, are complicated
by several widespread yet rare species
of sea turtles; their presence in
certain coastal states with otherwise
low reptile diversity distorts state
rarity percentages.*

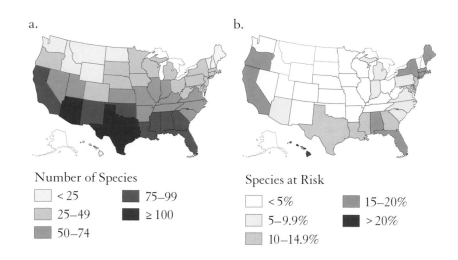

a.

b.

Number of Species

☐ < 25   ■ 75–99

☐ 25–49   ■ ≥ 100

☐ 50–74

Species at Risk

☐ < 5%   ☐ 15–20%

☐ 5–9.9% ■ > 20%

☐ 10–14.9%

found that reptiles are most diverse in lower-elevation regions lacking
much topographic relief—for instance, the Mississippi Valley and the
eastern coastal plain.

Endemism in reptiles is concentrated in three states: Texas has six endemic species, while California and Florida both have five. Among other
states, only Alabama, Mississippi, and Colorado have even a single endemic reptile. Florida's long geological history and xeric climate has given
rise to some fascinating endemics. The sand skink (*Neoseps reynoldsi*) is
an enigmatic lizard restricted to scrub habitats on Florida's central ridge.
This species is the sole member of a genus endemic to Florida and is in
the evolutionary process of losing its limbs as it becomes further adapted
for its burrowing lifestyle. The Florida worm lizard (*Rhineura floridana*),
another burrower, is the United States' only member of the suborder
Amphisbaenia. This species has a somewhat wider distributional range
than the sand skink and, based on a recent report, may even occur beyond the state's boundaries in Georgia.

Among California's endemics, the Coachella Valley fringe-toed lizard
(*Uma inornata*) is an example of extraordinary adaptation to a specialized
environment. Fringe-toed lizards occupy desert sand dunes and have
developed elongated scales, or fringes, on their hind feet to provide traction as they race across the windblown sands. Other adaptations include
a shovel-shaped head to help in diving beneath the sand, and ear and
nostril modifications to keep sand out of these orifices.

While the popular image of Texas is one of wide-open dry rangeland,
all six of its endemic reptiles are essentially aquatic. Indeed, the 12 species of freshwater map turtles (*Graptemys*) best exemplify the southeastern reptilian radiation. Two of these, the Texas and Cagle's map turtles
(*G. versa* and *G. caglei*), are endemic to Texas and found in separate river
systems. Several other rivers draining into the Gulf of Mexico also have their
own unique map turtles. The yellow-blotched map turtle (*G. flavimaculata*),

found only in the Pascagoula River system, is a Mississippi state endemic. Other species of map turtle are endemic to the Apalachicola in Florida and adjacent Georgia, the Pearl in Mississippi and Louisiana, and Mobile Bay in Alabama.

At a regional level, one of the more interesting reptiles is the sharp-tailed snake (*Contia tenuis*), a serpent that feeds exclusively on slugs. This species is nearly endemic to the United States and, until recently, was regarded as the only member of its genus. Occurring in the coast ranges and Sierra Nevada of California and into the moist forests of the Pacific Northwest, the species just crosses over the border into British Columbia. The snake's name refers to the terminal spine on its tail, which it thrusts into the ground in an effort to gain leverage as it attempts to subdue its slimy prey. While the Midwest is not known for restricted-range species, several snakes are midwestern regional endemics. These include Butler's garter snake (*Thamnophis butleri*), the shorthead garter snake (*T. brachystoma*), and Kirtland's snake (*Clonophis kirtlandii*), each of which is found in just a few states.

Rarity patterns among U.S. reptiles (figure 5.11b) are complicated by the widespread coastal distribution of sea turtles, all six of which are considered rare. For example, one-fifth (20%) of Massachusetts reptiles are regarded as rare when sea turtles are included, but the state's level of rarity drops to just 4% when only terrestrial or freshwater species are considered. The contrast in Hawaii is even more stark: All six of its native reptiles are marine, and five are sea turtles (the sixth is a sea snake).

While reptile species suffer many of the same problems as other groups of animals, such as conversion of necessary habitat, many also face active human persecution based on deeply held hostility toward snakes. To many people any snake is potentially venomous and should be killed. This attitude takes a toll not only on rattlers and cottonmouths but also on many other snakes that are actually helping control other animals that people typically consider "vermin." Reptiles hold a particular fascination among collectors, and the pet trade is a significant threat to many of our more interesting or attractive species. The bog turtle (*Clemmys muhlenbergii*) commands high prices among reptile fanciers, and commercial collectors have completely extirpated a number of populations of this rare animal. Casual collectors, even children, can also take a toll. Countless horned lizards (*Phrynosoma* spp.) have perished in makeshift shoe-box terrariums.

Roads pose a special hazard to reptiles. Because reptiles are exothermic, or cold-blooded, they are often attracted to the warmth of asphalt in the cool of the evening. In the southwestern deserts, this behavior provides herpetologists with one of their best sampling strategies: cruising slowly looking for snakes or lizards lying atop the roadbed. Unfortunately, most cars are neither cruising slowly nor so careful not to drive over these creatures. The combination of roads and reptiles produces many flattened snakes and crushed turtles. Because many reptile species are long-lived and slow in reproducing, road mortality can play a major role in the declines of local populations.

Map turtles exemplify the reptilian radiation that has taken place along the Gulf Coast. The ringed map turtle (*Graptemys oculifera*) is found only in the Pearl River system of Louisiana and Mississippi. © Greg Sievert.

A member of the Pacific Northwest's distinctive herpetofauna, the sharp-tailed snake feeds exclusively on slugs, thrusting its spine-tipped tail into the ground to gain traction while capturing its glutinous prey. © Suzanne L. Collins/Photo Researchers.

Amphibians

Amphibians were the first group of animals to emerge from the early seas, some 360 million years ago during the Carboniferous period. Dominating the earth's young terrestrial ecosystems during this period, they were later overtaken by reptiles, and then mammals, vertebrate groups better adapted to the rigors of dry land. Nonetheless, amphibians occupy a major, if often unnoticed, role in contemporary ecosystems. In some habitats, such as the deciduous forests of the Appalachians, amphibians constitute the most abundant vertebrates. Because many of these animals are small, secretive, or nocturnal, they represent much of the United States' "hidden" vertebrate biodiversity.

Amphibian species diversity shows a strong southeastern pattern (figure 5.12a), with North Carolina harboring the most species (79), followed closely by Georgia (77) and Virginia (72). While both salamanders and frogs have their greatest concentrations in the Southeast, these two groups differ in their areas of diversification. Salamanders are most diverse in the Appalachian region, and this is particularly true of the large numbers of plethodontid salamanders that have evolved in this ancient mountain range. Frogs and toads, on the other hand, are most diverse along the southeastern coastal plain, showing an east-west speciation pattern similar to turtles and snakes (Blair 1958). The Pacific Northwest has only moderate numbers of amphibian species, but at higher taxonomic levels it exhibits quite a diverse fauna. Three amphibian families are found in the United States only in this region: the evolutionarily unique tailed frog (Ascaphidae); the giant salamanders (Dicamptodontidae); and the torrent salamanders (Rhyacotritonidae), diminutive animals that, as the name implies, live in and adjacent to cold mountain streams. Amphibian diversity declines rather sharply in the northern part of the country as well as in the Rocky Mountain and Great Basin states, although seven species extend as far north as Alaska. The vast stretch of saltwater separating Hawaii from any other landmasses was apparently too much of a barrier for amphibian dispersal: No native amphibians occur in the island group.

Wet conditions are especially conducive for amphibians, explaining much about their distribution across the United States. Amphibian eggs lack the shells that protect reptile and bird eggs from desiccation, and amphibians therefore require water or moist microsites for breeding. These requirements can be met in many creative ways, though, allowing amphibians to successfully live in even some of the driest desert regions. Amphibians are ectothermic, or "cold-blooded," so warmer climes allow them to maintain higher activity levels through more of the year. In a review of overall patterns of amphibian diversity, Kiester (1971) found that the distribution of U.S. amphibians is correlated both with annual rainfall and with mountainous regions. Salamanders, and to a lesser degree frogs, seem to be more cold-tolerant than most reptile species, a factor that may explain their greater diversity in mountain environments. Some frogs can even freeze and thaw without damage, as long as temperatures do

Amphibians have developed a variety of strategies to survive in arid regions. During dry periods the Great Basin spadefoot toad (*Spea intermontana*) burrows into the ground, emerging only at the sound of rain or thunder. © Alan D. St. John.

a.

b.

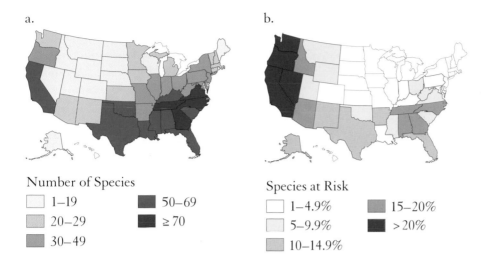

Number of Species
- ☐ 1–19
- ☐ 20–29
- ☐ 30–49
- ☐ 50–69
- ☐ ≥ 70

Species at Risk
- ☐ 1–4.9%
- ☐ 5–9.9%
- ☐ 10–14.9%
- ☐ 15–20%
- ☐ >20%

Figure 5.12a–b. Amphibian diversity and rarity.

(a) Amphibian diversity is most pronounced in the southeastern United States, where a combination of generally wet conditions and ancient landscapes have contributed to diversification. (b) Rarity shows a contrasting pattern, with the more arid West exhibiting the highest levels of amphibian rarity.

not drop below about –10°C. Species such as the wood frog (*Rana sylvatica*) and the spring peeper (*Pseudacris crucifer*) produce "antifreeze" that helps them weather the subzero temperatures (Storey 1986).

State-level endemism in amphibians is concentrated in California, with 17 endemic species, and in Texas, which has 11 endemics. The California endemics include both abundant species, such as the California newt (*Taricha torosa*), and very rare and localized species like the limestone salamander (*Hydromantes brunus*), known only along one segment of the Merced River below Yosemite National Park. A narrowly endemic slender salamander, *Batrachoseps gabrieli*, was recently discovered in the relatively well studied San Gabriel Mountains above Los Angeles (Wake 1996), suggesting that even more locally restricted amphibians are yet to be found in the state.

The Edwards Plateau in Texas is particularly rich in restricted-range amphibians and has given rise to some of the most unusual species in North America. Several of this region's brook salamanders (*Eurycea*) retain juvenile characteristics even as adults, a condition referred to as *neoteny* or *paedomorphosis*. Larval salamanders generally have frilly external gills that disappear as the animals mature. In several of these Edwards Plateau endemics, the gills persist throughout the salamander's life. Examples include the recently described Barton Springs salamander (*Eurycea sosorum*), found only at a complex of springs within the city of Austin. One of these springs feeds a popular city-run natural bathing pool, presenting unique conservation challenges (Bury et al. 1995). Even more bizarre is the Texas blind salamander (*E. rathbuni*), which lives underground in water-filled caverns of the Balcones escarpment. In addition to retaining external gills, this ghostly species lacks pigment and has only vestigial eye remnants beneath its skin. A larger relative, the Blanco blind salamander (*E. robusta*), is known from just a single specimen from under the Blanco River and is perhaps the rarest of North American salamanders.

The Edwards Plateau of Texas is particularly rich in rare and unusual amphibians, including the recently discovered Barton Springs salamander, a species that lives only in a natural spring used as a municipal swimming pool. © Paul Freed/Animals Animals.

Widespread declines among amphibians, including the California red-legged frog (*Rana aurora draytoni*), hero of Mark Twain's famous story "The Jumping Frog of Calaveras County," may be a harbinger of broader environmental health problems. © B. Moose Peterson/ WRP.

Certain areas rich in local endemics do not stand out based on state-level distributions, because state boundaries run through natural regions. The most important of these areas of regional amphibian endemism include the Appalachian uplands, the interior highlands of Arkansas and Oklahoma, and the sky islands of New Mexico and Arizona.

Amphibian rarity contrasts strongly with diversity patterns (figure 5.12b). Western states dominate in terms of rarity; this partly reflects their lower overall amphibian diversity but also highlights the difficult conditions for aquatic and wetland species in the arid West. More than a quarter of amphibian species are rare in California, Oregon, Nevada, and Washington.

These figures on rarity are based largely on number and size of populations for individual species and known or suspected threats. Over the past two decades a great deal of evidence has been accumulating that even some widespread amphibians are suffering long-term and often inexplicable declines. Although many of these observations have been anecdotal, the increased scrutiny now being focused on this issue confirms that at least some of these declines are real (Blaustein et al. 1994b, Pounds et al. 1997). Also of concern are large numbers of frog deformities being observed in states such as Minnesota. Because frogs have permeable skin and are in close contact with water during key parts of their life cycles, they can function as useful biological indicators for environmental contaminants. As a result, both the declines and the deformities in amphibians may indicate cause for concern about human health and safety.

While many amphibian declines can be linked to such clearly discernible causes as habitat loss or predation by introduced species, the cause for declines in otherwise "pristine" areas remains a mystery. Several hypotheses have been advanced to explain these mysterious declines. Explanations range from the influence of climate change (Pounds et al. 1999), and the effect of increased ultraviolet radiation due to depletion of the ozone layer (Blaustein et al. 1994a), to the presence of man-made contaminants that might mimic natural hormones and disrupt amphibian growth and development (Hayes and Noriega 1997). A fungal disease has also been discovered that attacks the skin of certain amphibians, interfering with their respiration (Berger et al. 1998). Although a scientific consensus is developing that global amphibian declines are real, as yet there is no satisfactory general explanation for the phenomenon. Indeed, the underlying reasons for these declines probably vary from place to place and to some degree work in combination with one another.

Only one U.S. amphibian, the Las Vegas leopard frog (*Rana fisheri*), is known to be extinct, and at least one other, a salamander from Mississippi (*Plethodon ainsworthi*), has not been seen since 1964 and is missing. Another amphibian, the Tarahumara frog (*Rana tarahumarae*), has apparently been extirpated in the United States, although it is still extant in northern Mexico (Hale et al. 1995).

Freshwater Fishes

As American ichthyologists like Louis Agassiz and David Starr Jordan began thorough studies of the nation's freshwater fishes, it became apparent that North America was extraordinary in the variety and number of species, especially compared to Europe. A single U.S. river—Tennessee's Duck—contains more species of fish than all of Europe. In large part this exceptional richness is due to the north-to-south flow of the Mississippi River, which allowed most fish species to disperse southward ahead of the glacial advances during the Pleistocene. Just as Europe's trees had the misfortune of an east-west mountain range obstructing their southward migration, most of Europe's major rivers flow north. Glaciers formed not only in the mountainous headwaters but also in the northern regions near their mouths, and with few exceptions, these rivers could not provide convenient escape routes for fish caught by the increasingly frigid conditions (Kuehne and Barbour 1983).

Freshwater fish diversity shows a strongly southeastern pattern (figure 5.13a). Tennessee and Alabama both harbor more than 280 species, followed closely by Georgia's nearly 270. Indeed, with the exception of Missouri, all states supporting more than 200 species lie east of the Mississippi River. Diversity drops off sharply as one moves west. In general, western states have only about a quarter the diversity of eastern states; none has more than 70 species, and many have fewer than 50.

Diversity patterns largely reflect the dominant role that the Mississippi River has played in the evolution of the nation's fish fauna. The Mississippi Basin covers about one-third of the continental U.S. land area and is one of the world's major rivers, exceeded in length only by the Nile and the Amazon. During the Pleistocene the Mississippi River fauna apparently remained relatively free of extinctions because of its large size, its stability, and its lack of barriers to southern refuges. During postglacial periods, it also provided an important dispersal pathway back into those regions that had been covered in ice. Indeed, the massive pluvial lake

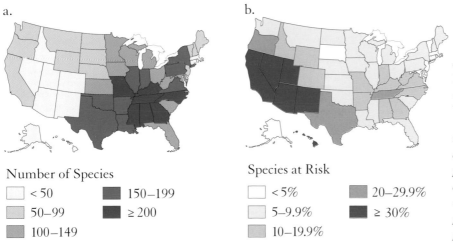

a.

b.

Number of Species

☐ < 50   ■ 150–199
■ 50–99   ■ ≥ 200
■ 100–149

Species at Risk

☐ <5%   ■ 20–29.9%
☐ 5–9.9%   ■ ≥ 30%
■ 10–19.9%

Figure 5.13a–b. Freshwater fish diversity and rarity.

(a) Freshwater fishes exhibit extraordinary levels of diversity in the Southeast due to a combination of a diverse physical geography, favorable climate, and long but dynamic history. (b) Strongly contrasting with diversity patterns, rarity among fish is most pronounced in the West.

Madtoms, a type of small catfish, are the nocturnal equivalent of darters and exemplify the Southeast's extraordinary fish diversity. The yellow-fin madtom (*Noturus flavipinnis*) is one of the rarest, occurring in just a small part of the upper Tennessee River basin. © Kate Spencer.

named in honor of Louis Agassiz connected at various times to the Mississippi drainage and served as the hub for fish species recolonizing the glaciated northern lands (Pielou 1991). Most of the Mississippi Basin's diversity is not concentrated in the main stem of the river but rather is in its tributaries, especially those that penetrate the Appalachian highlands and the Ozark Mountains.

In contrast, the arid West has far fewer rivers, streams, and lakes available for freshwater organisms. The relatively small and much more climatically unstable basins in the interior West did not fare as well during the ice ages, no doubt leading to higher extinction levels during this geological period. The postglacial swelling of the pluvial lakes in the Great Basin, and their subsequent shrinking, did lead to the diversification of at least one unusual group of fishes, the pupfish (*Cyprinodon*), which includes the Owens and Devils Hole pupfishes, discussed in chapter 1. Salmonids, salmon and trout, are abundant in the West, including both those that inhabit only inland waterways and those that are anadromous and migrate into the ocean for feeding before returning to their stream of birth to spawn. What the Pacific Northwest lacks in overall fish diversity is made up in the enormous quantities of salmon that, at least formerly, passed through the Columbia River basin.

Endemism is particularly high in several western states: In California and Nevada, more than a quarter (29%) of fish species are endemic, followed by Oregon (15%) and Utah (10%). Several southeastern states, including Tennessee and Alabama, have relatively large numbers of endemics, but because of their overall fish diversity, as a percent endemism levels are not exceptionally high. About half of all states, mostly in the Upper Midwest and Northeast, have no endemic fish species at all, including some surprises, such as the Appalachian state of West Virginia.

Again, state boundaries tend to blur some areas of regional endemism. The Tennessee-Cumberland drainage is by far the nation's richest and includes more endemics than any other North American basin (Jenkins et al. 1972). McAllister et al. (1986) identified several other regions that are high in endemics, including the northern California and southern Oregon area, the Atlantic Coastal Plain, the Ozark and Ouachita Mountains, and the Rio Grande–Rio Pecos area.

Rarity patterns conform rather closely to those seen for endemism. That is, those relatively few fish species found in western states tend to be at greater risk than the larger numbers of species in the East (figure 5.13b). Some of the southwestern states have extraordinarily high levels of rarity. While the two-thirds of Hawaii's fish that are rare can be readily explained by the few fish present, Arizona, Utah, and Nevada all have more than 60% at risk. New Mexico and California are not far behind: 51% and 44% of their fish species, respectively, are rare. These are by far the highest rates of state-level rarity for any group of vertebrates, and they demonstrate the very precarious condition of aquatic fauna in the western United States, especially the Colorado River basin. Numerically, Tennessee, Alabama, and Georgia have the greatest number of species at risk, which reflects both the extremely diverse fish faunas in these states and the extensive alteration of many of their riverine habitats. Nearly a quarter (22%) of Tennessee's species are at risk—a particularly sobering figure in light of the state's immense fish diversity.

The various reasons for the perilous condition of U.S. freshwater fishes are discussed in greater detail elsewhere (see chapters 6 and 8), but several broad conclusions can be reached. First, there is a great deal of natural rarity in certain regions. The highly dissected topography of the Appalachian highlands, the isolation of western basins and desert springs, and climate-induced changes in stream drainage patterns all have contributed to the development of naturally localized fish species. The extensive rearrangement of the nation's rivers and waterways—including construction of dams and diversion of water—has eliminated large areas of habitat formerly occupied by many species. Silt flowing into rivers from agriculture, logging, and construction degrades even seemingly intact aquatic habitats, making them unsuitable for many fish species that require clear water and clean bottoms for breeding and feeding. The introduction of invasive exotics and overfishing have also played major roles in the reduction of various species.

The decline of salmon stocks has been particularly dramatic in the Pacific Northwest. At the full species level, most of the anadromous salmon are not rare in the traditional sense of the word, but the large number of local extirpations and the tremendous population declines in many stream systems are cause for serious conservation concern. Many individual fish stocks, representing genetically distinctive populations, are rare and threatened. At least 214 salmon and steelhead stocks in 7 different species are at risk of extinction, and another 106 populations have already disappeared (Nehlsen et al. 1991). In the Pacific Northwest an insidious combination of hydroelectric dam construction, intensive fishing pressures, and poor land management practices have reduced these salmon and trout populations to a mere vestige of their former astounding numbers.

At least 16 full species of freshwater fishes have already suffered the ultimate decline and now are considered extinct. Another species has not been sighted in some time and may also be gone. Most of these extinct species were western and had very restricted distributions. The Utah Lake sculpin (*Cottus echinatus*), the Las Vegas dace (*Rhinichthys deaconi*) of Nevada, the Miller Lake lamprey (*Lampetra minima*) of Oregon, and the thicktail chub (*Gila crassicauda*) of California all had very limited ranges, making them highly susceptible to the impact of human activities. Other extinct fish, such as the Great Lakes' deepwater cisco (*Coregonus johannae*), ranged more widely. This species was found in Michigan, Wisconsin, Illinois, and Indiana before succumbing to overfishing, predation by sea lamprey, and hybridization with other ciscos. The harelip sucker (*Moxostoma lacerum*), last seen in 1893, was found even more widely, ranging across the Ohio River basin states of Ohio, Indiana, Tennessee, Kentucky, Alabama, Georgia, and Virginia. Siltation resulting from the massive agricultural conversion of the region appears to have destroyed this fish's warm-water river habitats, leading to its turn-of-the-century extinction.

Salmon runs have declined dramatically in the Pacific Northwest over the past several decades. As many as 15 million salmon once spawned in the Columbia River basin, while only a few hundred thousand now return to the region's waterways. © Charlie Ott.

6

THE GEOGRAPHY
OF IMPERILMENT

Targeting Conservation toward
Critical Biodiversity Areas

The Lake Wales Ridge stretches out along Florida's central spine, pointing southward like an arrow toward Lake Okeechobee and the Everglades beyond. The "river of grass," as the Everglades are known, attracts visitors from around the world to experience this unique ecosystem and view its immense wildlife concentrations. Compared to its famous neighbor to the south, the Lake Wales Ridge is virtually unknown to the public. From a biological perspective, though, these low, scrub-covered sand hills are of perhaps greater interest than the immense wetlands of the Everglades, because the ancient sand dunes that form this ridge are home to some of the most distinctive and highly localized species in the world. Yet most of the scrub vegetation that supports these species has been destroyed, replaced by agriculture and housing developments: Only about 15% of this unique habitat remains (Menges 1997).

Among the rarest of the ridge's inhabitants is the Lake Placid scrub mint (*Dicerandra frutescens*), known from just a handful of localities. This mint produces chemicals that have a powerful deterrent effect on insects and that could provide the key to developing new forms of insect repellents useful to people (Eisner et al. 1990). Although these chemicals protect the mint from being devoured by insects, the plant has little protection against the development pressures that threaten it. Another resident of the ridge is the yellow scrub balm (*Dicerandra christmanii*), a closely related mint that has an even more restricted distribution. Both of these plants are regarded as critically imperiled (G1), and both are listed by the federal government as endangered.

Sharing the Lake Wales Ridge with these rare plants is the Florida scrub jay (*Aphelocoma coerulescens*), a bird that is mostly restricted to the scrub along Florida's central ridge but occurs in scattered locations along Florida's Gulf and Atlantic Coasts as well. Florida scrub jays have the

Stephen J. Chaplin

Ross A. Gerrard

Hal M. Watson

Lawrence L. Master

Stephanie R. Flack

Composed of a series of ancient dunes originating some 2 million years ago, Florida's Lake Wales Ridge is home to a host of highly distinctive and locally restricted species, making it an important target for conservation. © Harold E. Malde.

Among the rarest inhabitants of the Lake Wales Ridge is the Lake Placid scrub mint, a federally listed plant with potentially useful chemical properties. © Thomas Eisner/Cornell University.

unusual characteristic of living in family groups. To survive in a particular location, these birds need a large enough area of suitable habitat to support a number of these family groupings. This species is regarded as vulnerable (G3) and listed as threatened under the Endangered Species Act.

Understanding the geography of species at risk is key to planning for their protection and to designing an effective preserve system. Most reserve planning for the Lake Wales Ridge, for instance, has focused on the needs of the scrub jay (Fitzpatrick et al. 1991), with an implicit assumption that other rare species will be protected under the sheltering umbrella of this relatively high-profile species. Although the scrub jay has a highly restricted distribution on a global scale, more options are available for its protection than for the few populations of the Lake Placid scrub mint, or the even fewer localities for the yellow scrub balm. Identifying sites for conservation requires balancing the needs and distributions of multiple species, some highly localized and others more broadly distributed. This balancing act is a central challenge in designing systems of nature reserves. How can we maximize the amount of biodiversity protection that can be accomplished given the limited resources available to do the job?

Protecting biodiversity is an expensive business. Buying land, developing management plans, reaching out to stakeholders, and providing long-term stewardship generally require more resources than are available. Consequently, a primary goal in conservation planning is to maximize the efficiency of a network of reserves by designing each individual reserve in a way that meets multiple conservation goals. Overall, this strategy suggests that we should attempt to protect the maximum number of conservation targets—species or ecological communities of concern—in as small an area as possible consistent with their needs for long-term survival.

Achieving efficiency in choosing nature reserve sites has largely been approached in two ways. The first approach centers around identifying concentrations of species, often described as biodiversity hot spots. The underlying assumption with this hot spots approach is that greater efficiency can be achieved by focusing protection efforts in places where the largest number of species coexist and, consequently, where multiple conservation goals can be met simultaneously. The primary drawback to relying on species-richness hot spots to define protection areas is that they may do a poor job representing the full array of biodiversity in a region. Focusing only on those areas of highest diversity may protect some species many times over while missing other species entirely (Williams et al. 1996).

A second approach to designing reserve systems focuses on identifying a set of complementary areas that capture all conservation targets in the fewest number of reserves or the smallest possible area. Starting with the most diverse area, this approach typically identifies additional areas in a stepwise fashion, giving priority to any species not included during earlier steps in the design. As additional reserves are added to the system, they are devoted to expanding coverage to previously unprotected species (Kirkpatrick 1983). More recently, optimization models that use powerful quantitative methods to pick a full set of reserves simultaneously have been applied. Such models can ensure complete species coverage in the smallest possible area (Toregas et al. 1971). The downside of choosing minimum sets of reserves is that the protection areas may be widely dispersed and isolated. Nonetheless, such minimum set analyses can set lower bounds on the magnitude of effort needed to achieve complete coverage.

The targets of these conservation planning efforts can vary depending on the purpose of the plan and the interest of the individuals and organizations involved in the process. Previous targeting efforts have focused on groups such as vertebrates (Scott et al. 1987, Kiester et al. 1996), species with unique evolutionary lineages (Crozier 1997), and federally listed endangered species (Dobson et al. 1997). As The Nature Conservancy begins to identify portfolios of conservation sites within each of the nation's ecoregions (TNC 1996, 1997), targets for protection include imperiled and vulnerable species, rare and unusual ecological communities, and high-quality representatives of all other ecological communities.

Assessing the distribution of species at risk by looking only at their presence within individual states, as we have done in chapter 5, is useful for broadly identifying the magnitude of the conservation challenge in different regions. To accomplish on-the-ground conservation, it is necessary to have a much finer level of knowledge about the distribution of these species. We now consider the detailed distribution of imperiled species on scales fine enough to influence specific conservation actions. This chapter provides a first-ever national analysis of the distribution of those species nearest extinction, based on number and size of populations and their trends. We then identify a minimum set of areas across the country that collectively could encompass each of these imperiled species. We also turn our attention to the needs and distribution of aquatic species, which as a group are the most vulnerable organisms in the United States (see chapter 4), and identify a set of critical watersheds for protecting the nation's aquatic biodiversity.

Most conservation planning on the Lake Wales Ridge has focused on the needs of the Florida scrub jay, a threatened species with a broader distribution and more options for conservation than many of region's very localized plant species. © J. H. Robinson/Photo Researchers.

Traditional Views of Endangered Species

Efforts to identify endangered species hot spots in the United States traditionally have focused on those species legally protected under the Endangered Species Act. Even for these threatened and endangered species, however, detailed distributional information has not been widely available. Although the U.S. Fish and Wildlife Service and National Marine Fisheries Service, the two agencies with responsibility for implementing the act, gather detailed information during the endangered species listing process, there is no coordinated federal effort to maintain and update locational information for these species. For this reason, most national-level efforts to map the distribution of endangered species and identify hot spots of imperilment are based on county-level data pieced together from various sources (e.g., Flather et al. 1994, 1998; Dobson et al. 1997).

Because of the significance of federally listed species for conservation planning and land use issues, state natural heritage programs are involved in gathering precisely located collection and observation information on the distribution of these species. These occurrence records provide a new and more comprehensive view of the distribution of federally listed species. Figure 6.1 displays the distribution of 958 federally listed species, represented by almost 43,000 population occurrences. Even from a casual examination of this map, it is clear that endangered species are not distributed evenly across the United States. Certain areas stand out even at this level, particularly Hawaii, the Pacific Northwest, coastal California, and portions of Florida.

As discussed in chapter 2, the patterns emerging from this map reflect two different phenomena, one biological and one human. Biological patterns relate primarily to interactions of the physical environment, evolutionary history, and human land uses and depict a geography of endangerment. The degree to which this map accurately reflects the situation on the ground, though, relates to a second phenomenon: the uneven level of our scientific knowledge and, specifically, the widely varying degree to which different areas and taxonomic groups have been intensively inventoried.

Identifying concentrations of endangered species with raw element occurrence data has a major constraint: The same species may be repre-

Figure 6.1. Distribution of federally listed threatened and endangered species.

Population occurrences offer a striking view of the distribution of federally listed species. This map represents 42,892 occurrences of 958 species and subspecies. Note: Only post-1970 occurrences are shown. Absence of data in any particular geographic area cannot be interpreted to mean that no endangered species are present. Data source: State Natural Heritage Data Centers 1996.

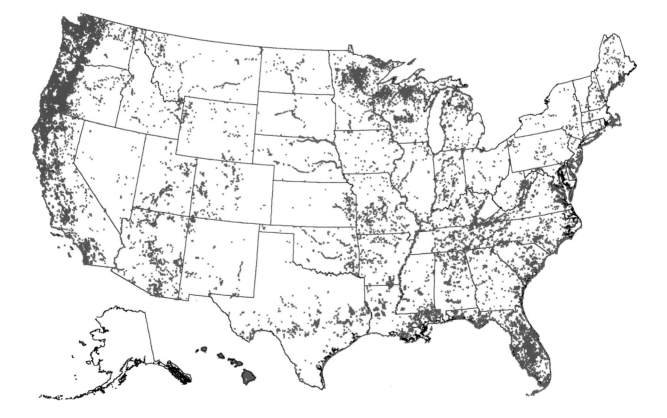

sented by multiple records in close proximity. While individual populations should be represented by just a single occurrence record, depending on how the standard heritage methods are applied at the local level some records may reflect populations or subpopulations in close proximity. Multiple inventory records for the same species may thus exaggerate certain population clusters. To overcome the effects of uneven sampling—both oversampling and undersampling—a better representation of endangered species diversity is provided by determining the number of *different* species occurring in a given sample unit. Even limited inventory directed at individual species can usually document the presence of a species within large sampling units. The strength of point location data is that it can be used for analysis on many different scales—including but not limited to counties, watersheds, and ecoregions—depending on the purpose of the analysis.

The detailed occurrence-level data, for example, can be used to identify the number of different threatened and endangered species by county (figure 6.2). This produces a traditional view of endangered species distributions that may differ in details but is substantially similar to maps developed by previous researchers (Flather et al. 1994, 1998; Dobson et al. 1997). The vast difference in sizes among counties introduces a regional bias and complicates interpretation, however. The problem is especially acute in the western United States, where counties can be enormous. San Bernardino County in California, for example, is almost 40 times the size of most eastern counties. Teasing apart the influence of size and biological richness is

Figure 6.2. County distribution of federally listed species.

Depicting the number of different threatened and endangered species in each county presents a traditional view of U.S. endangered species distributions. The vast difference in size among counties, however, complicates interpretation.

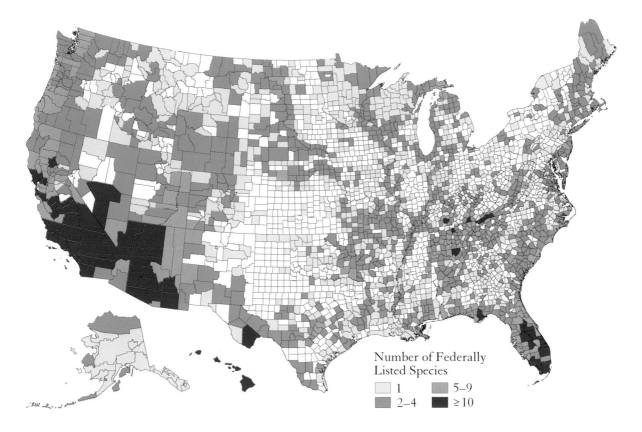

Number of Federally
Listed Species

1   5–9
2–4   ≥10

complicated because larger counties will tend to encompass more different species due to size alone, although certain of these large counties also happen to harbor exceptional numbers of endangered species. Flather et al. (1998) attempted to account for this disparity by separately analyzing and comparing "large" and "small" counties. Nonetheless, such traditional county-level analyses will always be problematic, producing results that are, at best, difficult to interpret, or, at worst, misleading.

A more accurate picture of the distribution of federally listed threatened and endangered species can be obtained by portraying the number of different species found within each cell of an equal-area grid (figure 6.3). A useful grid for this purpose is provided by the hexagons developed for the Environmental Protection Agency's Environmental Monitoring and Assessment Program (EMAP). These hexagons are part of a hierarchical system that completely covers the surface of the world (White et al. 1992). Each unit is of equal size, regardless of latitude or geographic location, and covers about 160,000 acres (648.7 square kilometers). This translates to somewhat less than half the size of an average county in the northeastern United States. Within the political boundaries of the 50 U.S. states, 15,413 of these hexagons cover the terrestrial landmass.

Contrasting the distribution of federally listed species by hexagons (figure 6.3) starkly illustrates overemphasis on large southwestern counties inherent in the county-level depiction (figure 6.2). An examination

Figure 6.3. Federally listed species by equal-area hexagons.

Mapping endangered and threatened species on a uniform grid more clearly depicts areas with concentrations of different species. Distributions are based on occurrence data from figure 6.1.

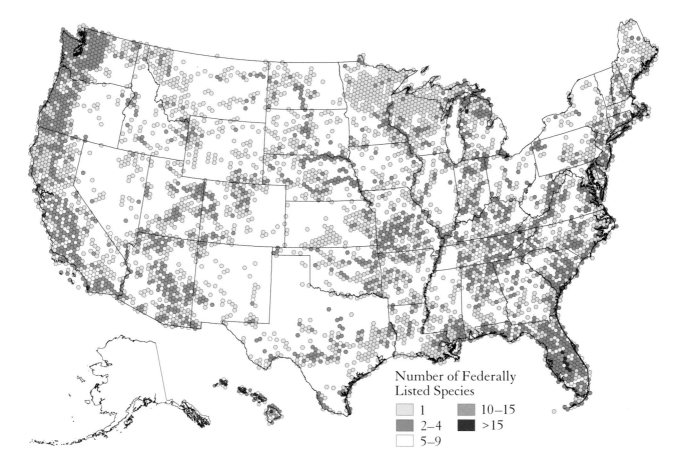

Number of Federally Listed Species

1	10–15
2–4	>15
5–9	

of the data also shows that the dense concentrations of federally listed endangered species populations in the Pacific Northwest (figure 6.1) consist of relatively few different species, such as the northern spotted owl (*Strix occidentalis caurina*). Similarly, most of the endangered species populations spread across upper Minnesota and Wisconsin represent a single species, the bald eagle (*Haliaeetus leucocephalus*).

A New Look at Imperiled Species

A problem with assessing biodiversity hot spots based on the distribution of federally listed endangered species is that these plants and animals represent a relatively small portion of the U.S. species considered to be at risk. As suggested by Ehrenfeld et al. (1997), a more accurate indication of such areas would be provided by the fuller array of species identified by the heritage network as imperiled or vulnerable. The availability of detailed occurrence information for nearly 2,800 imperiled species (conservation status G1 and G2) allows us to take such a new look at the geography of imperilment.

The difference in basing geographic analyses on federally listed species versus imperiled species is well illustrated by considering the overlap between the two groups. Of the federally listed endangered species included in figure 6.1, 91% are categorized as imperiled by the heritage network, while the remaining 9% are regarded as either vulnerable (G3) or secure (G4 or G5). The relatively few species in these latter categories, however, represent more than half (55%) of all occurrences documented in figure 6.1. A few relatively widespread federally listed species have such large numbers of occurrences that they tend to disproportionately influence geographic analyses of federally listed species. The extreme example is the bald eagle. Accounting for more than 6,900 records in this national aggregation, the bald eagle represents about 18% of all endangered and threatened species occurrence records documented here for the continental United States. Indeed, the bald eagle is now abundant enough that the federal government has announced its intention to remove the bird from the endangered species list.

Figure 6.4 displays the distribution of 2,758 imperiled species across the United States, as documented by almost 40,000 detailed occurrences (table 6.1). Again, this map reflects both the biological distribution of these organisms and the gaps in our inventory knowledge as of the time that the data were assembled. Even in their raw form, these imperiled species distributions highlight certain key areas. Hawaii stands out for the exceptionally high density of occurrences scattered among its islands. Indeed, with almost 5,000 discrete population occurrences, this state has the highest density of imperiled species in the country. Other areas with high population occurrence densities include the Panhandle and central ridge of Florida, coastal southern California, the southern Appalachians, and the Edwards Plateau in Texas. In contrast, the entire state of Alaska has only 44 imperiled species occurrence records in this data set, reflecting

The dense concentrations of federally listed species occurrences in the Pacific Northwest consist of relatively few species, such as the northern spotted owl. These species, however, have received considerable attention and survey work. © Gary Braasch.

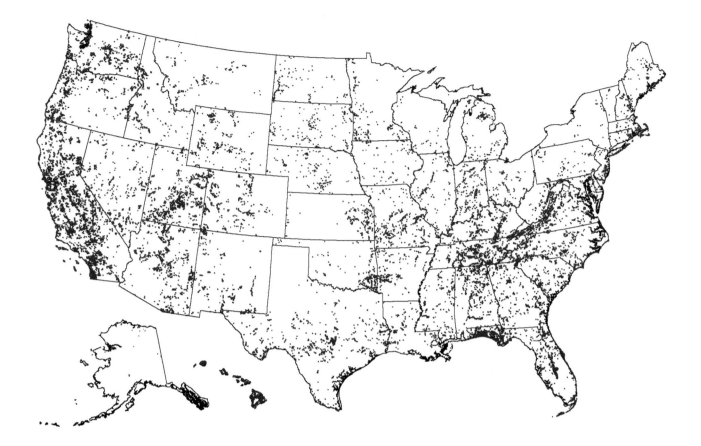

Figure 6.4. Distribution of imperiled
species.

*The detailed distribution of imperiled
species provides a new perspective on the
geography of risk in the United States.
This map includes 2,758 imperiled species,
documented by 39,521 detailed population-level occurrences. Note: Only post-
1970 occurrences are shown. The absence
of data in any particular geographic area
does not necessarily mean that no
imperiled species are present. Data source:
State Natural Heritage Data Centers
1996.*

both the relatively few globally imperiled species there and the relative
lack of computerized inventory information for the state.

As discussed above, identifying hot spots of imperilment with raw
population occurrence data will overemphasize areas that have been particularly well inventoried and where multiple populations of the same
species are recorded. Using a geographic information system (GIS), this
precise locational information can be analyzed to determine the number
of different species in any particular area. Calculating the number of different species in such mappable units as ecoregions, watersheds, or equal-
area grids helps to overcome inconsistencies in inventory intensity and
provide a truer picture of the geography of imperilment.

Ecoregional Distribution
of Imperiled Species

Ecoregions are large geographically defined areas that integrate various
environmental conditions, such as climate and geology, and that support
distinctive groupings of species and ecological communities. Reflecting
natural geographic units, ecoregions are in many ways superior to political boundaries, such as states, for conservation planning purposes (see
chapter 7 for further discussion of ecoregions). The Nature Conservancy

Table 6.1. Summary of imperiled species occurrences by taxonomic group

	Number of imperiled species (G1-G2)	Number of element occurrences	Number of hexagons occupied	Percent of hexagons occupied	Mean Number of hexagons per species	Percent of species in single hexagon
Plants	1,841	23,479	3,145	20	3.9	29
Mollusks	309	5,373	773	5	5.5	44
Arthropods	324	1,944	631	4	2.7	55
Fish	158	2,957	803	5	6.6	20
Reptiles and amphibians	64	1,655	427	3	7.3	30
Birds	32	2,653	340	2	15.8	22
Mammals	19	1,441	502	3	26.8	11
Other	11	19	14	<1	1.1	82
Totals	2,758	39,521	4,836	31.4%	4.5	33

This table summarizes the imperiled species data set that is depicted on figure 6.4 and that forms the basis for additional geographic analyses. Columns referring to hexagons relate to analyses based on equal-area grid (figures 6.6 through 6.12).

has adopted an ecoregion-based approach for setting priorities and protecting biological diversity (TNC 1996), as have a number of federal agencies and other conservation organizations. The Conservancy has adopted and modified for its use an ecoregional classification originally developed by the U.S. Forest Service (Bailey 1995, 1998b) and recognizes 63 ecoregions across the contiguous states.

Analyzing the imperiled species occurrences presented above by ecoregion, five mainland ecoregions stand out in terms of their diversity of imperiled species, each harboring in excess of 150 such species (figure 6.5a). At a national level this ecoregional analysis highlights the biological significance of the Appalachians, coastal California, and the Great Basin. The Cumberlands and Southern Ridge and Valley ecoregion supports the greatest number of imperiled species (186), while the Central Appalachian Forest to its north also has an impressive 154 imperiled species. Both of these ecoregions support similarly large numbers of imperiled aquatic organisms, but the more southerly ecoregion contains more than twice as many plant species of concern. Surprisingly, the Great Basin ecoregion ranks second in diversity, with 169 imperiled species. Although no single area in this region has exceptionally high concentrations of imperiled species, the numerous restricted-range plants in this vast region combine with a relatively rich vertebrate fauna to elevate it to this position. California's South and Central Coast ecoregions, with 158 and 155 imperiled species respectively, are also dominated by rare plants.

Another way to look at the relative significance of ecoregions for imperiled species is to examine the number of these species that are endemic, or restricted, to a single ecoregion (figure 6.5b). By this measure, three mainland areas are particularly noteworthy—the California South Coast ecoregion, with 138 ecoregional endemics; the Great Basin, with 113; and the California Central Coast, with 108. A second tier of ecoregions with high numbers of imperiled endemics is found mostly in the southeastern and southwestern United States. Only three ecoregions have no unique

Figure 6.5a–b. Distribution of
imperiled species by ecoregion.

(a) *The Appalachians, the Great Basin,
and coastal California stand out in this
assessment of imperiled species according
to Nature Conservancy–defined
ecoregions of the lower 48 states.*
(b) *Focusing on those imperiled species
that are restricted to a single ecoregion
further highlights the significance of
coastal California and the Great Basin.*

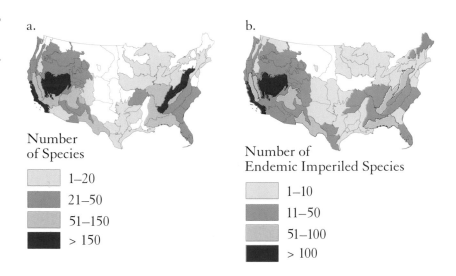

a.

Number
of Species

▢ 1–20

▨ 21–50

▨ 51–150

◼ > 150

b.

Number of
Endemic Imperiled Species

▢ 1–10

▨ 11–50

▨ 51–100

◼ > 100

imperiled species: the Northern and Central Tallgrass Prairie ecoregions
and Northern Great Plains Steppe.

A Hexagonal View of Imperiled Species

Although ecoregional analyses represent a more natural approach to
mapping distribution than counties or states, they are still plagued by
problems of consistency in size. Consider, for instance, the difference in
size between the massive Great Basin ecoregion, which ranks second in
imperiled species numbers, and the much smaller California South Coast
ecoregion, which ranks third. And while ecoregions are useful as planning units, a much finer scale of resolution is necessary to determine specific areas that should be targets for conservation within them. The hexagon grid, introduced above, provides a sampling unit of uniform size that
is large enough to help smooth the uneven nature of data collected in a
nonsystematic fashion, yet small enough to reflect biological patterns and
assist with conservation planning on a continental scale.

By calculating the number of different imperiled species contained
within each hexagon, a striking picture emerges of hot spots of imperiled species richness across the United States (figure 6.6). Perhaps most
significantly, only about one-third (31%) of the hexagons harbor even a
single imperiled species. To put it another way, more than two-thirds of
all hexagons covering the United States have no imperiled species at all.
And of the hexagons that do contain imperiled species, about half (51%)
contain just a single species.

Globally imperiled species are just what their name implies: rare and
uncommon even within those hexagons where they are found. The amount
of land on which imperiled species occur *within* these hexagons varies considerably. Presence in a hexagon should not be taken to indicate that the
entire area of the hexagon is populated by the imperiled species, and therefore these figures do not imply that this is the proportion of U.S. land

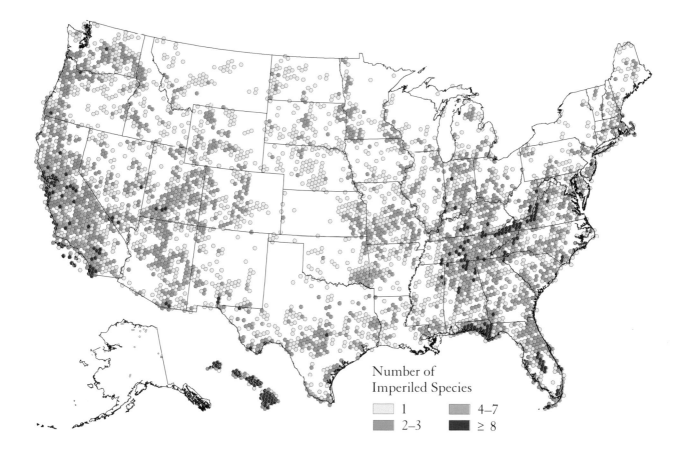

Number of
Imperiled Species

⬜ 1	▨ 4–7
▨ 2–3	⬛ ≥ 8

actually occupied by imperiled species. In Hawaii, where all of the hexagons contain at least one imperiled species, most land in nearly all hexagons is not—or at least is no longer—suitable habitat for these species.
Imperiled species are often limited in their distribution to remnant natural
areas, since most land already has been converted to intensive human uses.
For this reason, the amount of land these hexagons represent is generally
an overestimate of the area actually occupied by these species.

This hexagon hot spots map distills and brings into better focus the patterns suggested by earlier analyses. Concentrations of imperiled species are
particularly prominent in four major regions: Hawaii, California, the southern Appalachians, and Florida (figure 6.6). Hawaii has extraordinarily high
concentrations of imperiled species and contains the top 13 hexagons in
terms of number of imperiled species. The hottest of these hexagons is located on the island of Kauai and centered on the Alakai Swamp, one of the
wettest places on Earth. Here a record 128 different imperiled species are
found within a single hexagon. Of these, 115 are rare plants, although with
8 bird species this region retains one of the most intact examples of Hawaii's
unique and imperiled avifauna as well.

The highest concentration of imperiled species on the mainland is a
hexagon centering on the Clinch and Powell Rivers in southwestern Virginia that contains 27 imperiled species. Large numbers of imperiled
species in a single hexagon often represent the convergence of several

Figure 6.6. Imperiled species by equal-
area hexagons.

*A striking picture of imperiled species
distribution emerges by mapping the
number of different species by equal-area
hexagons. This map is based on occurrence
data depicted in figure 6.4.*

An area centered on the Alakai Swamp on the island of Kauai supports 128 imperiled species, the most of any hexagon analyzed. One of the rainiest places on Earth, the Alakai receives more than 500 inches of rain per year. © Gary Braasch.

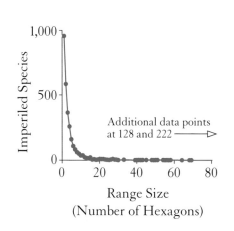

Figure 6.7. Imperiled species range sizes.

This graph plots the frequency of imperiled species range sizes, as measured by the number of hexagons a species occupies. Most are quite restricted; the mean range size is only 4.5 hexagons, and one-third of these species are restricted to a single hexagon.

different habitat types, each supporting different species. In the Clinch and Powell hexagon, for example, 8 of these species are associated with caves and 19 with rivers and streams. Of the latter, 18 species are freshwater mussels, giving this region the distinction of having the greatest number of imperiled species in the country for this highly threatened group of organisms.

In notable contrast, the Great Plains, the northern Rocky Mountains, the agricultural Midwest, and New England all tend to lack large numbers of imperiled species. A relative lack of topographical diversity and a history of Pleistocene glaciation are likely explanations for the low numbers of geographically restricted species in these areas (see chapter 5). Because geographically restricted species are the most likely to become imperiled when under stress, it is not surprising that areas with few limited-range species also contain few imperiled species.

Range Sizes among Imperiled Species

Breadth of distribution is a key factor in assessing the conservation status of species (chapter 4). Narrowly restricted species tend to be more vulnerable to local perturbations, whether natural or human-induced, while species with wider ranges are often better buffered from such threats. The number of hexagons in which an individual species occurs provides a useful standardized measure of range size. Calculating the mean number of hexagons occupied by each species in a given taxonomic group can therefore provide an index of the range size for the group as a whole (table 6.1).

The mean range size for all imperiled species is only 4.5 hexagons. Most of these species occur in only one or two hexagons, and fully one-third (33%) are restricted to a single hexagon. Plotting the number of species against range size, one can see an exponential decrease in the number of species occupying larger numbers of hexagons (figure 6.7). Few occupy more than

20 hexagons, a finding consistent with the criteria used for assessing a species' conservation status as imperiled or critically imperiled.

Average range sizes vary considerably among different taxonomic groups, however, reflecting the underlying biology of the constituent species. Arthropods and plants have the most restricted ranges: Imperiled arthropods occupy on average 2.7 hexagons per species, while plants average 3.9 hexagons. As might be expected, birds and mammals exhibit considerably larger range sizes, averaging 15.8 and 26.8 hexagons per species, respectively. These figures help to quantify the perception that in general imperiled species tend to have highly restricted range sizes but that groups with greater mobility, such as birds and mammals, have wider average ranges.

The most expansive range of any imperiled species—222 hexagons—belongs to the Indiana bat (*Myotis sodalis*) (figure 6.8). In the winter this bat has quite a restricted distribution: Most of its population hibernates in just a few large caves in Indiana, Illinois, Missouri, and Kentucky. During the rest of the year the species ranges widely, frequenting riparian areas throughout the Midwest to feed on airborne insects. The Indiana bat has experienced considerable declines in population numbers due to destruction or disturbance of wintering sites and elimination of summer habitat. Despite the bat's remarkably wide range, its classification as imperiled (G2) is warranted based on the limited number of overwintering sites (hibernacula), the species' precipitous population declines, and its continued vulnerability.

Hot Spots of Rarity and Richness

Identifying biodiversity hot spots has become an important tool for conservation planners. Most attempts to identify hot spots tend to focus on areas with the greatest total diversity of species, or the greatest number of species at risk (Williams et al. 1996). Such diversity hot spots are generally defined as representing some arbitrarily defined upper percentile of sampling units (Prendergast et al. 1993). In figure 6.6, hot spots may be characterized as those hexagons with eight or more imperiled species (depicted in red), which correspond to the upper 5% of occupied cells. The wide variance in range sizes described above, however, illuminates a major problem with identifying hot spots only by using the total number of species, imperiled or otherwise. Species that are distributed widely and

Figure 6.8. Distribution of the Indiana bat.

The most expansive range of any imperiled species—222 hexagons—belongs to the Indiana bat. Despite this wide range, the species warrants its classification as imperiled (G2) based on steep population declines and a very limited number of overwintering sites (far left, © Merlin D. Tuttle, Bat Conservation International/Photo Researchers).

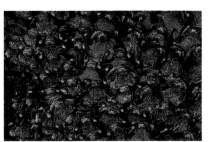

found in many different hexagons have a disproportionate impact in creating areas of high diversity. Clusters of high-diversity hexagons may simply represent the same set of species found together repeatedly in adjacent hexagons.

To overcome this problem, we take another approach to identifying hot spots, one that relies not only on the overall richness of a hexagon but also on the relative rarity of its species. Rarity in this context refers to species with restricted distributions. This "rarity-weighted richness" approach tends to favor the identification of hot spot clusters that represent concentrations of limited-range species, as well as high turnover of species between adjacent cells (Csuti et al. 1997b). The logic behind this method is that a hexagon assumes increased conservation significance if a number of species occur only in that cell, since protection of these unique species cannot be accomplished elsewhere. At least with regard to those species, the hexagon is "irreplaceable" from a conservation perspective. On the other hand, if a hexagon contains a high diversity of species, all of which can be found in other hexagons as well, that cell would not be irreplaceable to the protection of those species (although it might still be extremely important in their conservation). Employing this concept of irreplaceability, two hexagons with the same number of imperiled species may differ considerably in their conservation significance.

The rarity-weighted richness index (RWRI) provides a structured manner for identifying such hot spots (Williams et al. 1996, Csuti et al. 1997b). Each species is assigned a score—or weight—based on the inverse of the number of hexagons in which it occurs. For instance, if a species is found in only a single hexagon, that species receives the maximum possible score of 1/1, or 1.0. The score for a species that occurs in 20 hexagons would be 1/20, or 0.05. The individual scores for all species in a hexagon are then summed to yield a rarity-weighted index for the cell. This can be expressed mathematically as:

$$\mathrm{RWRI} = \sum_{i=1}^{n} \frac{1}{h_i}$$

where h_i = the number of hexagons that species i occupies, and n = the number of species found within a hexagon. In the case of a hexagon containing two species, one of which is restricted to that hexagon and the other occurs in 19 other cells, the RWRI for the hexagon would equal 1.05. This score may be thought of as the hexagon's index of irreplaceability.

By calculating this index for each of the almost 5,000 hexagons in the United States that contain imperiled species, we were able to create a continuous surface map of rarity-weighted richness across the country. This surface can be visualized through isoclines that clearly depict hot spots of rarity and richness (figure 6.9). Based on this rarity-weighted richness approach, six biodiversity hot spots emerge as the most significant in the United States (RWRI values >2.25 x 10^{-3} per km^2). These areas are: Hawaii as a whole, two different areas in California, the Death Valley region of Nevada, the Panhandle of Florida, and the southern Appalachians. A pictorial overview of each of these six hot spots follows this chapter on page 187.

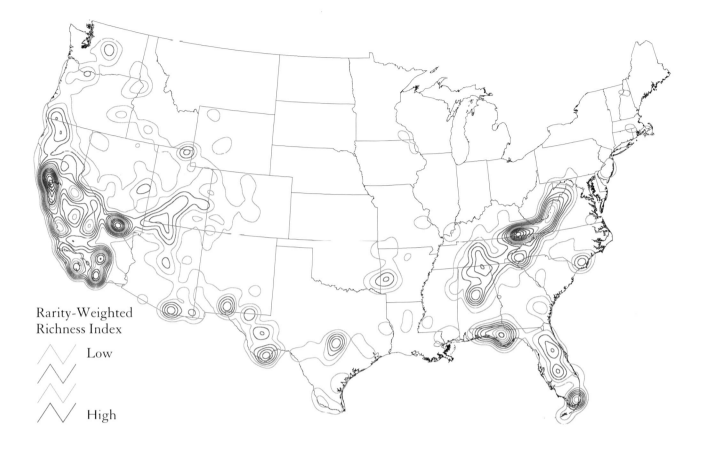

Rarity-Weighted
Richness Index

⋀ Low

⋀⋀

⋀⋀⋀ High

This analysis also highlights a number of other regions that rank highly based on this combination of richness and rarity. These include South Florida, home to many locally restricted plant species; central Alabama, a little-recognized center of freshwater biodiversity; the Big Bend region of Texas; the southern Channel Islands and central coast of California; and the Sierra Nevada Mountains. These second-tier hot spots of imperiled biodiversity may be of great interest because the identity and significance of several of them is less well known. A third tier of hot spots is also discernible and includes the Klamath-Siskiyou areas of California and Oregon; the Colorado Plateau of southern Utah and northern Arizona; the Edwards Plateau of Texas; the sky islands of Arizona and New Mexico; the central ridge of Florida, where we began this chapter; the Blue Ridge escarpment gorges of southwestern North Carolina; and the limestone region of northern Alabama and south-central Tennessee.

Minimum Areas Needed to Protect Imperiled Species

Maximizing the efficiency of reserve systems in protecting biodiversity requires that we have a way to evaluate the contribution each site makes to the overall protection goal. One particularly powerful approach to examining this issue is to consider the minimum area that would be re-

Figure 6.9. Hot spots of rarity and richness.

Employing a "rarity-weighted richness index" (see text) produces a map that highlights regions in the lower 48 states with large numbers of limited-range species. The highest peaks represent hot spots of rarity and richness, and include two regions in California, the Death Valley region, the Panhandle of Florida, and an area centered in the southern Appalachians. The Hawaiian Islands, although not shown here, are by far the region with the greatest concentration of restricted range species.

quired to protect all conservation targets—in this case, almost 2,800 imperiled species. Advances in high-performance computing over the past two decades now make it possible to solve such a large and complex coverage problem and identify a minimum set. Most important, an analysis of the minimum area required to encompass all imperiled species offers insight into the magnitude of the land protection effort needed, as well as an indication of priority areas where conservation activities can yield high returns.

The hexagons used in the previous hot spots analysis are a useful scale for conducting such a national-level minimum set analysis. We should emphasize, however, that these hexagons are a statistical framework and are not intended to define actual conservation units. They point to the general areas of significance, but actual conservation efforts must be designed around the needs of the individual species and ecosystems to be protected. Furthermore, simply because a species is recorded in a particular hexagon does not mean that a viable population of the species exists there. The population in that hexagon may be of low quality and unlikely to persist or may represent just a portion of the area required by species with wide-ranging individuals.

There are a number of possible ways to pick a minimum set of areas that capture each conservation target at least once (Csuti et al. 1997b). We used several different mathematical approaches and found that the true minimum is 932 hexagons (figure 6.10).[1] This is the equivalent of about 6% of

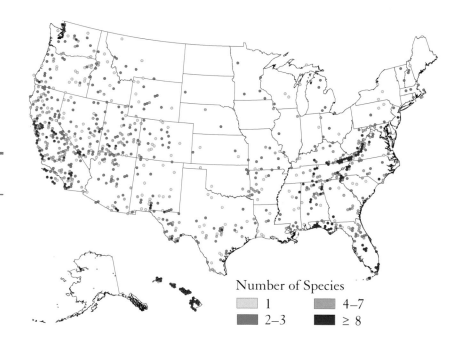

Figure 6.10. Minimum set for covering all imperiled species.

All 2,758 imperiled species can be covered at least once in a minimum of 932 hexagons, representing about 6% of the U.S. land area. Assuring the survival of these species, however, often will require protection in multiple locations, not just the single hexagon represented in this minimum set analysis.

Number of Species
1 4–7
2–3 ≥ 8

1. The 932-hexagon solution was derived using the set covering location problem (SCLP) of Toregas et al. (1971), a method in which the computer examines all hexagons simultaneously to identify a guaranteed optimal solution. The more simplistic and widely used stepwise "greedy heuristic" algorithm yielded a slightly larger solution set of 945 hexagons.

the U.S. land area to cover at least one example of each of 2,758 imperiled species. While 932 hexagons is the minimum number that can cover all these species, the particular set of hexagons portrayed in figure 6.10 is not unique; it is just one of many alternative 932–cell solutions. Most alternative sets differ in only minor ways, swapping adjacent or nearby cells containing the same species. We chose this particular representation because through use of another model, we know that it also maximizes the number of species that are covered twice (discussed below).

Although there are many alternate sets of 932 hexagons, they differ in detail, not in overall pattern. All permutations identify hexagons scattered across the country, although the upper Great Plains, the Midwest, and New England are sparsely represented. Clusters of adjacent hexagons still appear in Hawaii, the southern Appalachians, the San Francisco Bay Area, and southern California. These clusters suggest that there are substantial differences in the imperiled species among adjacent hexagons in these hot spots, indicating that in addition to high species richness, these regions have high geographic turnover in their species assemblages.

As is evident from the hues of the various hexagons in this minimum set map (figure 6.10), not all hexagons contribute equally. Some contain multiple imperiled species, while others include just a single species. This disparity highlights the trade-off between the amount of land targeted for protection and the number of species protected. By calculating a species accumulation curve, we can quantify this trade-off and identify the number of species that can be covered by fewer than the full 932 hexagons (figure 6.11). The accumulation curve shows a steep initial increase as hexagons with numerous imperiled species are selected first. The initial 10 hexagons cover 449 species, the next 10 incorporate an additional 173 species, and the third set of 10 incorporates only another 119. By 190 hexagons, each additional cell adds on average only 3 additional species, which drops to 2 additional species at 290 hexagons. Finally, after 480

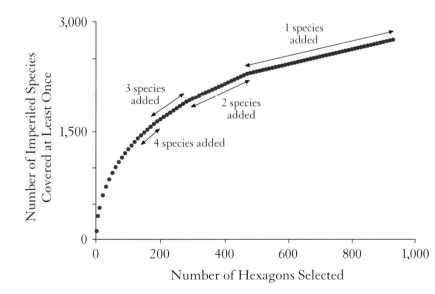

Figure 6.11. Species accumulation curve for minimum set analyses.

This graph shows the maximum number of species that can be covered by any given number of hexagons. The arrows span the range of hexagons where the inclusion of one more hexagon will result in the addition of the indicated number of species. This curve was generated using the maximal covering location problem (MCLP) mathematical model (Church and ReVelle 1974).

hexagons are selected, each additional cell contributes just 1 species. At this point, it takes 450 additional hexagons to include the remaining 450 imperiled species.

This accumulation curve shows that 80% of imperiled species can be represented at least once in 480 hexagons, or about 3% of the U.S. landmass. To encompass the remaining 20% of species, we must double the area selected to about 6% of the United States. In instances where most species are widely distributed, accumulation curves can be very steep, and total coverage can be attained with a relatively small number of sites (Gerrard et al. 1997). In contrast, the imperiled species that we are dealing with here are, for the most part, narrowly distributed, and there is less opportunity to protect the bulk of these species in just a few sites.

Dobson et al. (1997) carried out a county-level hot spots analysis to explore similar questions regarding concentrations of endangered species and the scale of land area needed for their protection. Assessing the county distribution of threatened and endangered species, these researchers determined that counties totaling 500,000 square miles, or 14% of the U.S. land area, would be necessary to encompass all federally listed species. They also identified a smaller number of hot spot counties that collectively contain 50% of listed species in each taxonomic group.

A comparison of this county-based study with our hexagon-based approach reveals some interesting differences. First, our hexagon-based analysis identifies a much smaller land area (6% vs. 14%) needed to encompass a much larger number of species (924 listed species vs. 2,758 imperiled species). This difference is largely due to the finer scale of hexagons, which are about half the size of typical eastern counties but many times smaller than typical western counties. Second, the hot spots identified by Dobson et al. (1997) are concentrated in the western United States, in number and especially in combined area. Our hexagon-based approach identifies a much more widely distributed set of areas across the country and shows a more even distribution between the eastern and western United States. In part this may be due to numerous eastern aquatic species that are imperiled but not formally listed under the Endangered Species Act. In addition, the stepwise selection protocol used by Dobson et al. (1997) to identify hot spots would preferentially select large counties first, since due to size alone these will tend to have the greatest number of endangered species. Nonetheless, the counties they identify as covering 50% of listed species include at least minimal representation in the major richness and rarity hot spots we identified earlier (figure 6.9). These relatively few counties miss several secondary hot spot regions, however, including the Big Bend area of Texas, southern Utah, the sky islands of southern Arizona, and the Siskiyou region of northern California and southern Oregon.

Differences among Taxonomic Groups

Identifying the minimum area needed for protecting species in different taxonomic groups can shed light on the question of how well one group can serve as a surrogate for others in conservation planning. For example, if a reserve system were set up to protect all imperiled bird species, how well would that system also protect imperiled mammals or arthropods? Analyses of each taxonomic group show that only 11 hexagons can cover all imperiled bird species at least once—the fewest needed for any taxonomic group—while the large number of plants require the most, 634 hexagons (table 6.2). As might be expected, the groups requiring the largest number of hexagons coincidentally covered the greatest proportion of other groups (table 6.2). For example, the 634 hexagons needed to cover all imperiled plants also cover from 22% of arthropod species to 94% of birds.

More Than the Minimum: Protecting Multiple Occurrences

A fundamental principle of both financial investing and conservation is diversification. The previous analyses have established an important baseline by focusing on the minimum number of areas needed to protect at least one example of each imperiled species. From a conservation biology perspective, however, a single protected example is not sufficient to guarantee the survival of a species. Rather, multiple protected examples are desirable to guard against catastrophic loss of any population or any particular part of the reserve network. Furthermore, multiple examples of each species help maintain the genetic diversity that will enable species to retain their ability to evolve in the face of changing environmental conditions.

To assess the implications for building redundancy into a national preserve portfolio, we make the simplifying assumption that protecting multiple occurrences of a species requires that species' inclusion in mul-

Table 6.2. Minimum set analyses for different taxonomic groups

Optimum solution sets	Plants	Arthropods	Mollusks	Fishes	Herptiles	Birds	Mammals	Other taxa
Number of species	1,841	324	309	158	64	32	19	11
Minimum solution— number of hexagons	634	206	139	100	49	11	17	10
Percent of total hexagons	4.1%	1.3%	0.9%	0.6%	0.3%	0.1%	0.1%	0.1%
Species per hexagon	2.9	1.6	2.2	1.6	1.3	2.9	1.1	1.1
Coincident coverage analysis								
Plants	1.00	0.20	0.23	0.12	0.05	0.12	0.02	0.00
Arthropods	0.22	1.00	0.12	0.04	0.05	0.01	0.01	0.05
Mollusks	0.50	0.29	1.00	0.23	0.04	0.09	0.00	0.04
Fish	0.39	0.23	0.41	1.00	0.06	0.01	0.01	0.03
Herptiles	0.47	0.34	0.20	0.20	1.00	0.02	0.02	0.00
Birds	0.94	0.38	0.63	0.31	0.16	1.00	0.09	0.00
Mammals	0.68	0.32	0.21	0.16	0.16	0.05	1.00	0.05
Other taxa	0.00	0.36	0.09	0.18	0.09	0.00	0.00	1.00
All other combinations	0.39	0.22	0.23	0.13	0.05	0.09	0.01	0.02

This table presents minimum set solutions for different taxonomic groups. To cover all 1,841 imperiled plant species, for instance, requires 634 hexagons, accounting for 4.1% of the total number of hexagons. The bottom portion of the table quantifies the degree to which minimum sets for one taxonomic group coincidentally cover species in other taxonomic groups.

Figure 6.12. Area implications of extending coverage to multiple hexagons.

This graph shows the relationship between extending coverage of imperiled species to more than one hexagon, and the minimum number of hexagons needed to provide such coverage. The green line (right axis) indicates the percentage of imperiled species that occur in multiple hexagons, while the blue line (left axis) plots the percentage of total hexagons that would be required to provide that level of coverage.

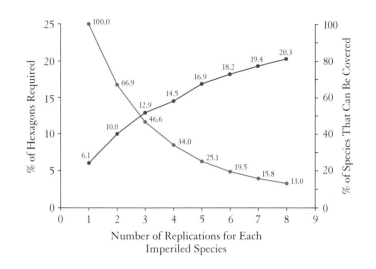

tiple hexagons. This allows us to project, albeit in a simplified way, how the scale of land protection changes as we go beyond the minimum and factor in the protection of multiple species occurrences (figure 6.12). We note, however, that hexagons are merely statistical units and that multiple populations need not be protected only in different hexagons. These units represent reasonably large areas—160,000 acres—and multiple occurrences of a species can occur, and be protected, within a single hexagon.

To choose a set of hexagons that maximizes redundancy in coverage, we used a computer model first developed for siting fire stations and other facilities, known as the backup coverage problem (BACOP1) (Hogan and ReVelle 1986). Analyzing the various permutations of 932 hexagons that can cover all imperiled species at least once, one configuration emerged in which more than a third (36%) were also covered twice.[2] This is the version shown in figure 6.11 and used as the basis for the various minimum set analyses discussed above. Providing double coverage wherever possible, while still requiring at least single coverage for each species, requires a minimum of 1,545 hexagons. Unfortunately, the opportunities for representing species multiple times are seriously constrained by the restricted distribution of many of these species. Since most species are known from only a few hexagons, progressively fewer can be represented at higher levels of replication. Only about half (47%) of these imperiled species occur in three or more hexagons, and just an eighth (13%) are found in as many as eight. As one attempts to maximize coverage for three or more multiples, the amount of land needed increases to a certain extent. Covering species at least three times where possible requires 1,992 hexagons; four times increases this to 2,239 and eight times to 3,130 hexagons.

Expressed in terms of the land area these hexagons represent, covering each imperiled species at least once would require about 6% of the

2. The multicovering problem model (MCP) (Toregas 1971) was used jointly with BACOP1 for this purpose. The MCP model is useful for quickly identifying minimum sets, while BACOP1 is best suited for choosing among minimum sets to select the one with the most redundant coverage.

U.S. land area (figure 6.12). Extending double coverage to the species that can benefit from this approach takes about 10% of the landmass. Covering species eight times, though, only doubles this figure to 20% of the U.S. land area. In interpreting these figures, it is important to bear in mind that these percentages represent the total land area within these hexagons: In most instances, imperiled species habitat represents only some fraction of this land area.

Rivers of Life: Hot Spots for Aquatic Biodiversity

The decline of salmon populations in the Pacific Northwest and New England is the focus of great public attention, investment, and debate. Few people recognize, however, what an astonishing abundance of other life-forms also inhabits our nation's streams, rivers, and lakes. Mostly hidden from view, these creatures go largely unnoticed and unappreciated. Colorful and whimsical names hint at the diversity and beauty living beneath these waters: Wabash pigtoe mussel, dromedary pearly mussel, white catspaw mussel, warpaint shiner, and frecklebelly madtom.

Worthy of these epithets, many freshwater species display complex and intriguing lifestyles that have evolved as adaptations to their watery world. Consider the orange-nacre mucket (*Lampsilis perovalis*). As adults, these mussels are unable to move a significant distance. How, then, can they colonize new habitat, especially upstream areas?

The orange-nacre mucket employs a sophisticated ruse to get help from passing fishes in moving its young around. The female mussel creates a fishing lure, using her offspring as bait (Hartfield and Butler 1995). The larval offspring are packaged at the end of a jellylike tube, which can stretch up to eight feet. Dancing in the current of rocky riffles, the end of this tube bears a striking resemblance to a minnow. When a fish takes the bait, the tube shatters and releases the larvae—called glochidia into the stream. A few are able to attach themselves to the gills of the duped fish, where they absorb nutrients from the host and continue their development. After a week or two the mussel larvae drop off their mobile incubator, settling to a new home on the stream bottom.

Found only in rivers and creeks in the Mobile River basin of Alabama, populations of orange-nacre mucket have declined precipitously. The species is classified by the heritage network as imperiled (G2) and is federally listed as threatened. The orange-nacre mucket's reproductive strategy illustrates the complex interactions and interdependencies within freshwater ecosystems. Mussel and fish are linked, and both require suitable conditions for survival: the right water flow, clarity, temperature, oxygen levels, and substrate. Unfortunately, the odds are now against a young mussel settling into such suitable habitat.

Despite these intricate dependencies—or perhaps because of them— an astounding array of mussels, fishes, and other organisms has evolved to populate the nation's freshwaters. Indeed, as emphasized in chapter 3,

In a sophisticated ruse, the orange-nacre mucket extends a minnow-like "lure" to attract potential fish hosts for its larvae. © Sam Beibers.

the United States stands out as a global center of freshwater biodiversity. Aquatic life in the United States stands out in another way as well: Species that depend on freshwater ecosystems are, as a whole, faring the worst of any group of U.S. organisms. As discussed in chapter 4, fully two-thirds (67%) of freshwater mussels are vulnerable to extinction or are already extinct, 51% of crayfish are imperiled or vulnerable, and 37% of freshwater fish are at risk. Startling as these findings are, they are consistent with other recent assessments of the deteriorating condition of freshwater species and ecosystems in the United States (Wilcove and Bean 1994, Warren and Burr 1994, Williams et al. 1992).

In much the same way that we have looked at the overall distribution of imperiled species to identify hot spots of diversity and key areas for conservation, we now turn our attention to identifying critical watersheds for the protection of freshwater species at risk.[3] To do so, we examine in detail the distribution of freshwater fishes and freshwater mussels, the two aquatic groups with the most complete inventory record. In contrast to the analyses presented earlier, which consider only species categorized as imperiled (G1 or G2), for this assessment of freshwater biodiversity we also include species classified as vulnerable (G3). Together these imperiled and vulnerable species constitute the full suite of fish and mussel species considered to be at risk. The following analyses are based on precise location data collected by state natural heritage programs for 307 vulnerable or imperiled fish species and 158 mussel species.[4] The heritage-derived locational data were supplemented with information from the scientific literature and experts knowledgeable about different species to compile the most complete distributional information possible. Alaska was excluded from the analysis because it has no freshwater fish or mussel species currently considered to be at risk. Hawaii was also excluded because of its distance from North America, although its islands are home to four vulnerable freshwater fishes, each of which occurs on five islands.

A Watershed Approach to Hot Spots

Freshwater species distributions are governed largely by hydrology, especially watershed boundaries, and the local geologic and climatic forces that shape the landscape. Reflecting hydrologic factors, the contiguous United States can be divided into 48 large freshwater regions, each of which consists of a large river basin or multiple river basins.[5] Each of these freshwater regions supports significantly different aquatic assemblages. On a much finer scale the nation can be divided into 2,111 small watersheds, which are

3. An earlier version of this section was published as the report *Rivers of Life: Critical Watersheds for Protecting Freshwater Biodiversity* (Master et al. 1998).

4. In this analysis we consider full species only and do not include at-risk subspecies or fish stocks.

5. The U.S. Forest Service classifies freshwater ecological units in a seven-level hierarchy: subzones, regions, subregions, river basins, subbasins, watersheds, and subwatersheds (Maxwell et al. 1995). Here we use the more generic term *region* to refer to their "subregion."

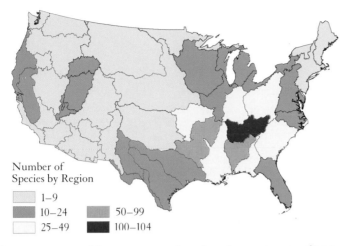

Number of
Species by Region

1–9
10–24
25–49
50–99
100–104

Figure 6.13. Regional concentrations of aquatic biodiversity.

Based on the number of at-risk fish and mussel species, the Tennessee-Cumberland and Mobile River basins in the Southeast have extraordinarily diverse assemblages of freshwater animal species.

of a size more amenable to conservation planning and action.[6] Using a geographic information system we assigned each species both to freshwater regions and to small watersheds. Experts in all states then reviewed the data to refine the small-watershed distributions for these species.

Although at-risk freshwater species are distributed throughout the United States, two particular hydrologic regions dominate, containing 35% of all vulnerable and imperiled fish and mussel species (figure 6.13): the Tennessee–Cumberland River basins (including Tennessee and parts of six other states) and the Mobile River basin (including Alabama, parts of Georgia and Mississippi, and a bit of Tennessee). Of these at-risk species, 70% (113) occur nowhere else in the world; they are endemic to one of these two regions. These basins are also rich in other freshwater species, including snails and turtles (Lydeard and Mayden 1995). The Interior Highlands region—located in Arkansas, southern Missouri, southwestern Oklahoma, and northeastern Texas—is another regional center of diversity, and with 54 species, it has the next-highest count of fish and mussel species at risk.

Of the more than 2,000 small-watershed areas found across the continental United States, about 1,300 (61%) support one or more fish or mussel species at risk. In turn, 87 of these stand out as hot spots, harboring 10 or more vulnerable or imperiled species (figure 6.14). These hot spots of aquatic diversity are largely concentrated in the Southeast. Four river basins alone—the Tennessee, Ohio, Cumberland, and Mobile—contain 18 of the top 20 watersheds. The upper Clinch River on the Virginia-Tennessee border surpasses all other watersheds in the country, with 48 imperiled and vulnerable fish and mussel species, including 21 that are federally listed as endangered or threatened. In the analysis of all imperiled species presented earlier (figure 6.6), this is the same area that emerged as the single most diverse hexagon in the continental United States.

The extraordinary diversity of southeastern rivers results from the coincidence of a diverse physical geography, a favorable climate, and a long but dynamic history. The numerous streams of the southeastern

6. These small watersheds are the equivalent of the U.S. Geological Survey's eight-digit Hydrologic Cataloguing Unit, which is roughly the equivalent of the U.S. Forest Service's "subbasin."

Figure 6.14. Hot spots for fishes and mussels.

Watersheds with 10 or more at-risk fish and mussel species are concentrated in the Southeast, reflecting the exceptional diversity of rivers and streams in this region. Data source: State Natural Heritage Data Centers 1996.

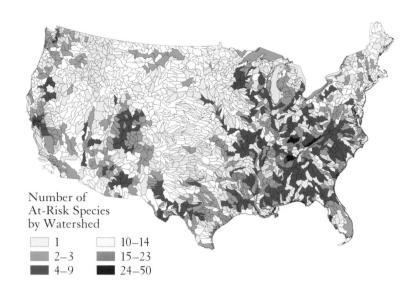

Number of
At-Risk Species
by Watershed

☐ 1   ☐ 10–14
▨ 2–3   ▨ 15–23
▨ 4–9   ■ 24–50

United States flow across geologically and topographically diverse landforms. This varied landscape was also spared the repeated advances of continental ice sheets during the Pleistocene, allowing the aquatic fauna to persist and evolve over time. Patterns of evolution were, however, affected by the changes in climate, stream drainage patterns, and coastline position that accompanied the repeated glacial advances and retreats in the North. These cyclic changes isolated many populations, enabling them to diverge genetically and evolve into new species.

For hot spots to be useful in defining conservation priorities, they must be defined at an appropriate scale. For many aquatic species the small watershed units used in this analysis is such a scale. In certain circumstances, however, conservation activities may be effectively employed on a larger scale (for example, in several adjacent watersheds) or a smaller scale (such as in a small headwater stream or a single spring within the watershed), depending on the nature of the threats and the species of concern. Looking beyond small-watershed boundaries is also essential when vulnerable streamlife regularly moves between drainages, as do sturgeons, squawfishes, and anadromous fishes like salmon and shad. On the other hand, viable populations of at-risk fish and mussel species may be found only in a small portion of the watershed, not its entire area. Additionally, threats to the continued existence of at-risk species may be manageable only in a small area of the subbasin. Some threats may require attention upstream, such as the effects of large dams and water diversions. Surprisingly, other threats may require abatement downstream—for instance, dams blocking fish passage, or channelization and gravel extraction that can cause destructive upstream-progressing river channel erosion.

An Aquatic Conservation Portfolio

While the watershed hot spots highlighted in the previous section harbor the greatest diversity of vulnerable and imperiled species, some at-

Figure 6.15. Critical watersheds for conserving aquatic biodiversity.

Protecting and restoring 327 watersheds—15% of the nation's total—would conserve populations of all at-risk freshwater fish and mussel species in the United States.

risk fish and mussels exist only outside these areas. Conservation strategies based solely on hot spots would leave these species out in the cold. An extension of this hot spots approach is thus needed that identifies a suite of watersheds that could efficiently and comprehensively protect these imperiled species. The following analysis of critical watersheds for conservation based on fish and mussel species at risk suggests that a relatively small number of watershed areas—15% of the total—could conserve much of the nation's rich aquatic diversity (figure 6.15).

Rather than focus on the minimum number of watersheds that would capture one example of each target mussel and fish species, in this analysis we chose to use a process that incorporated knowledge about threats, viability, and population quality. We also set two additional goals to improve the overall conservation effectiveness of the portfolio. First, we included each species in at least two of the priority watersheds to increase the chances for long-term survival. Second, we made certain that at least one watershed was included in each of the 63 ecoregions covered by the analysis to broaden the genetic and ecological representation of the portfolio.

Using the approach for identifying hot spots of richness and rarity described above for hexagons, we calculated a rarity-weighted richness index (RWRI) for each of the approximately 1,300 small watersheds containing at-risk fish or mussel species. To assemble the portfolio, we selected the watershed within each ecoregion that exhibited the highest RWRI. Additional watersheds were then added that represented areas of either exceptional rarity and richness or that contributed species not already covered by other selected watersheds.[7] The watershed portfolio

7. All watersheds with an RWRI value of 1.5 or greater were included, as were watersheds with 14 or more aquatic species at risk. Watersheds that contain at least 2 vulnerable or imperiled species and that are already the focus of freshwater conservation efforts were then added into the portfolio, as were those needed to ensure that all 465 fish and mussel species were captured at least twice (with the exception of species restricted to a single subbasin).

Alabama's Cahaba River is the state's longest essentially free-flowing river and supports more fish species than any similar-size river in North America. © Beth Maynor Young.

was reviewed by conservationists and other scientists to eliminate those known to have either nonviable populations of the target species or insurmountable threats.

The resulting 327 small watersheds constitute 15% of the small-watershed areas in the lower 48 states (figure 6.15). This set of watersheds is not a definitive list for protecting all freshwater biodiversity, but it does provide a starting point. Although the analysis is based on the best currently available scientific information, it represents only the species groups for which reasonably complete information is available. Such analyses should be repeated in the future as more is learned about other freshwater groups (such as crayfishes, snails, and aquatic insects), subspecies or stocks (such as salmon or cutthroats), and newly recognized species.

In some parts of the country, information may be available that will point to additional watersheds that are critical to the survival of imperiled streamlife other than fish and mussel species. For example, the Wood Pawtucket watershed in Rhode Island has no fish or mussel species at risk but is home to eight species of imperiled and vulnerable dragonflies and damselflies. Similarly, Eagle Lake in California has no fish or mussel species at risk but is home to genetically distinct populations of rainbow trout (*Oncorhynchus mykiss*) and tui chub (*Gila bicolor*), as well as a number of endemic snail species.

The Scale of the Conservation Challenge

The foregoing analyses help us gain perspective on the scale of the conservation challenge ahead of us. As the United States enters the next century, we are confronted with a growing number of declining and imperiled species. It is important to note, though, that most of the country has relatively few of these species at risk: In our analysis of the distribution

The threatened blue shiner (*Cyprinella caerulea*) was last seen in the Cahaba River in 1971, although conservationists are considering a plan to reintroduce this fish to the watershed. © Malcolm Pierson.

of imperiled species by hexagon, only a third of all hexagons contain even a single imperiled species. Certain regions, however, have especially high numbers, presenting both opportunities and challenges. Concentrations of rare and imperiled species in such hot spots as Hawaii, California, and the Appalachians mean that efficiencies in biodiversity protection can be achieved by designing preserves around multiple species and carrying out other actions designed to stop the decline of these plants and animals. The challenge, though, is that conservation activities required to stop and reverse these trends can be expensive and can compete with other societal needs for resources. To make efficient use of the resources available for biodiversity conservation—time, land, and money—we will need to have the type of detailed geographically based information presented above and to focus our attention on places where the largest number of imperiled species can be protected simultaneously.

The scale of the task ahead is suggested by what would be required to protect at least one example of each of the nearly 2,800 imperiled species. Our hexagon analysis indicates that this minimal representation would encompass only about 6% of the United States. In some ways, however, this figure represents an overestimate, since hexagons are a statistical unit, and imperiled species are typically restricted in their distribution even within these general areas. Rare species usually are just that: hard to find even where there are concentrations of them. Many plants, invertebrates, and even sedentary vertebrates can probably maintain viable populations in an area smaller than the 160,000 acres represented by each hexagon. In other important ways, though, the 6% figure represents an underestimate, since some species will require much larger areas than are encompassed by these hexagon units.

Ensuring the long-term survival of imperiled species typically will require that we go beyond the minimum and protect more than a single population of each species. There will need to be adequate replication in any reserve network to counter the effects of catastrophic events, allow for genetic change and evolution, and increase the chances of dispersal and colonization. Expanding coverage of each imperiled species to two hexagons increases the total area needed to 10% of the United States. Covering those species that can be included up to eight times only increases this figure to 20%. A similar analysis looking at aquatic organisms finds that just 15% of the nation's small watersheds could protect all at-risk fish and mussel species at least twice.

While these estimates are based on the best information available at this time, we must also remember that with more inventory work, additional locations of these species will be found. Meanwhile, as human activities proceed, additional species will require active protection. Nonetheless, these analyses provide an encouraging first estimate and baseline for looking at the overall scale of the conservation challenge facing us.

As important as imperiled species are, they comprise only a small portion of the total biodiversity of the United States. The goal in conservation planning must be the long-term maintenance of all native species and, indeed, biodiversity at all levels. Conservation planning based on

Thanks to reintroduction efforts, 9 of the 12 native fish species that historically occurred in the upper portion of Arizona's Verde River can still be found in the river's main stem and its tributaries. © Harold E. Malde.

ecoregional boundaries can be an important tool for accomplishing this goal. Toward that end, The Nature Conservancy (1997) has undertaken the task of identifying a portfolio of sites within each ecoregion that collectively could maintain the full suite of native species. Part of this job will be to design sites that are of sufficient size and configuration to maintain the imperiled species, the still-common species, and the ecological processes that sustain both.

An important complement to focusing only on species, rare or otherwise, is to use a coarse-filter approach to conservation, using ecological levels of diversity—the subject of the next chapter (chapter 7). Protection of a representative sample of each ecological community in an area is perhaps the best strategy for protecting the full array of biodiversity, including those species in poorly known taxonomic groups. Such ecological approaches to conservation, however, complement rather than replace species-level conservation. Indeed, the very species that are most likely to be missed by this coarse filter will be those that are rarest and at greatest risk of extinction. These rarities include not only the imperiled species that are the focus of the above hexagon analyses but also vulnerable species, locally rare species, and species that are still abundant but declining. Such species will need to be addressed on a species-by-species basis, even if their protection solution involves ecosystem-scale conservation strategies (Weeks 1997). Whichever approaches are employed, however, detailed knowledge of the geography of imperilment will be a vital part of the conservation solution.

A Portfolio of the Nation's Hot Spots

Life does not lie evenly across the landscape. For a variety of reasons—evolution, geography, climate, or historical accident, to name a few—some places harbor more species than others. The earth's hot spots of diversity serve as beacons for conservation, evoking not only scientific curiosity but also awe for nature's intricate beauty and a powerful sense of the urgent need to protect these places and the species they harbor.

Conservation scientists have developed a variety of ways to identify biological hot spots. Measuring the total number of species, or the number of species at risk, in a given area are two of the most widely employed approaches. As described earlier in this chapter, however, these straightforward measures may not provide adequate guidance for conservation. An alternative that takes into account both the richness and the relative rarity of species highlights six biodiversity hot spots in the United States (figure 6.9). The following profiles of these biological jewels summarize the number and type of imperiled species for each hot spot—derived from our rarity and richness analysis—along with important habitats, and key threats these regions face.

Home to more than 50 imperiled species, the Florida Panhandle is one of the United States' leading biodiversity hot spots. Many of these rare plants and animals depend on longleaf pine forests, a vanishing habitat. © James Valentine.

San Francisco Bay Area

Death Valley Region

Coastal and Interior Southern California

Hawaii

Southern Appalachians

Florida Panhandle

HAWAII

Above: West Maui ridges and valleys.
© Stephen Krasemann/DRK PHOTO.

Below right: Green turtle (*Chelonia mydas*). © Andrew Wood/Photo Researchers.

HOT SPOT SUMMARY

Imperiled Species:
  Mostly plants, birds, and invertebrates

Important Habitats:
  Tropical wet forest, tropical dry forest

Biodiversity:
  Among the highest levels of endemism in the world

Key Threats:
  Habitat conversion, alien species

The most isolated archipelago of high islands in the world, Hawaii lies some 500 miles from its nearest neighbor, the tiny, low-lying Johnston atoll, and over 2,000 miles from the nearest continents and other high islands of the Pacific. Yet plants and animals found their way to the islands, as tiny spores and seeds carried by the wind; floating seeds or tiny occupants on logs washing ashore; or seeds, insects, spiders, and even land snails nestled in the feathers of ocean travelers like the golden plover and wandering tattler.

Hawaii is the far northern outpost of the fauna and flora that constitute the Indo-Pacific marine biogeographic province. Though politically part of the United States, Hawaii's marine life more closely resembles the Indian Ocean coast of Africa, nearly 11,000 miles away. Terrestrial species are a different story. Many of Hawaii's plants trace their ancestry to Southeast Asia and Indonesia, while flying insects and birds arrived from both Asia and the Americas. Hawaii has only one native land mammal, a bat, and no native land reptiles or amphibians. The waters around the islands, however, support the endemic Hawaiian monk seal and a wealth of other marine life, including humpback whales and five species of sea turtles.

Although the majority of Hawaii's approximately 9,000 endemic species are invertebrates, the forest birds are perhaps the most remarkable part of the archipelago's biodiversity. Like the Galapagos finches made famous by Charles Darwin, the Hawaiian finches—or honeycreepers, as they are also known—offer a spectacular example of the phenomenon called adaptive radiation. The ancestors of these modern finches may have reached the islands as long as 15 million years ago. They found numerous ecological niches to exploit and evolved into dozens of different spe-

Top left: A daisy relative, *Hesperomannia arbuscula.* © John Obata/HINHP.

Above: An Oahu tree snail (*Achatinella apexfulva*). © William P. Mull.

Below: High elevation rainforest. © Stephen Krasemann/DRK PHOTO.

cies, some with beaks resembling woodpeckers, and others those of parrots or warblers. Still others, such as the remarkable 'akiapola' au (*Hemignathus munroi*), with its long, curved upper bill and short, stout, lower bill, are unlike any other bird on Earth.

Hawaii's isolation ended with the arrival of the Polynesians between 200 and 500 A.D. The Polynesian colonists cleared lowland forests and converted coastal wetlands to fishponds and wet valley floors to irrigated fields. They also brought domesticated animals, such as dogs, pigs, and jungle fowl, as well as uninvited guests, like rats. Fossils provide a clue to the subsequent ecological upheaval: At least 60 bird species disappeared following the arrival of the Polynesians.

A second period of ecological devastation began with the arrival of Captain Cook in 1778. By the middle of the nineteenth century, European colonists had cleared most of the lowland forests for firewood, the sandalwood trade, or agriculture, particularly sugarcane. Virtually all the lowland forests have now been destroyed. Overall, about two-thirds of Hawaii's original forest cover is now gone, and only high-elevation habitats are still relatively intact. Even these are threatened by the scourge of alien species.

Westerners introduced an increasing number of invasive aliens to the islands, including cats, Indian mongoose, and European pigs, a far more ecologically destructive breed than the smaller pigs originally brought by the Polynesians. Introduction of diseases such as avian pox and malaria, together with their mosquito vectors, has had a particularly devastating impact on the island's unique birdlife. Largely as a result of habitat destruction and alien species, Hawaii has the dubious distinction of containing about one-third of the United States' roster of federally listed endangered species. At least 479 Hawaiian species are imperiled, and the archipelago may already have lost another 249 to extinction, by far the most in the nation.

SOUTHERN APPALACHIANS

Above: Jordan's salamander (*Plethodon jordani*). © Suzanne L. Collins and Joseph T. Collins/Photo Researchers.

Below right: Cumberland Knob, North Carolina. © Carr Clifton/Minden Pictures.

Roughly 425 million years ago, portions of the earth's crust slammed together, and a long process of mountain building began. As the geological ages passed, vast supercontinents came together and broke apart, eventually forming what we now call the Appalachians. This ancient mountain chain runs from Newfoundland to Alabama, and save for erosion it has changed relatively little for the past 200 million years.

The ages of geological stability, coupled with a variety of soils, landforms, climate, and geology, have fostered enormous biological diversity in the Appalachians, particularly toward the southern end of the chain, where glaciers never covered the land. During the Pleistocene glaciations, the Appalachians acted as a drier and warmer refuge for a number of more northerly species and communities. Some of the cold-adapted species and communities, such as cranberry bogs, remained after the retreat of the glaciers. The southern Appalachians thus mix some characteristically northern species with southern counterparts.

Individual watersheds and peaks in the Appalachian chain, isolated for millions of years and boasting benign environmental conditions, provided a perfect setting for the evolution of unique species of plants, invertebrates, salamanders, crayfishes, freshwater mussels, and fishes. At the same time, water seeping through sedimentary portions of the mountains gradually ate away at their limestone heart, creating what geologists call karst topography, marked by extensive systems of caves. These cav-

HOT SPOT SUMMARY

Imperiled Species:
Freshwater mussels, fishes, cave invertebrates, plants, and amphibians

Important Habitats:
Rivers and streams, caves, shale barrens, and cove forests

Biodiversity:
Rich freshwater fauna, world center of salamander diversity

Key Threats:
Dams, water pollution, mining, poor agricultural and logging practices

erns gave rise to a diverse set of specialized cave invertebrates, many of them extremely localized and sporting bizarre adaptations for life in the dark. Other rare habitat types, such as shale barrens and glades, fostered an array of specially adapted plant species.

The southern Appalachians form a center of richness and rarity in the United States. One area of roughly 13,000 square miles centered in western Virginia contains 144 imperiled species, many of which rely on the region's rivers and streams. The southern Appalachians are legendary for their diversity of freshwater organisms such as fishes and mussels. One river basin alone, Tennessee's Duck, harbors more species of fishes than are found in all of Europe.

Southern Appalachian forests represent the last American stronghold of a forest type once widespread in the northern hemisphere. Strangely, the only other relict of these ancient forests to have escaped the ravages of time and climate changes is thousands of miles away, in eastern China. The "sister forests" of the Appalachians and eastern Asia share a large number of taxa. Many genera and some species, including hickory, trillium, tulip tree, ginseng, dogwoods, hellbender salamanders, copperheads, and paddlefish, have their closest relatives on opposite ends of the earth. Perhaps the most remarkable of all the animal groups found in the southern Appalachians, however, are the salamanders. These forests represent the center of the earth's salamander diversity. Not only are there numerous species, but salamanders also are incredibly abundant here, often accounting for the most vertebrate biomass in a given patch of forest.

These rich deciduous forests have been profoundly altered over the past few centuries. The stately American chestnut once dominated low-elevation forests in the Appalachians, but a fungus accidentally introduced from China in the 1890s virtually eliminated the chestnut by the middle of the twentieth century. The loss of the chestnut led to the proliferation of other hardwood species, such as oak, hickory, locust, and birch. At higher elevations, red spruce and the endemic Fraser fir form coniferous communities, adding to the landscape diversity of the region. Tragically, Fraser fir is now also succumbing to an exotic pest: the tiny, aphidlike, balsam woolly adelgid.

Left: Mammoth Cave, Kentucky. © David Muench.

Right: Little River, Great Smoky Mountains. © Larry Ulrich/DRK PHOTO.

Appalachian elktoe (*Alasmidonta raveneliana*). Courtesy of Richard Biggins/USFWS.

SAN FRANCISCO BAY AREA

Above: Antioch Dunes evening-primrose (*Oenothera deltoides* ssp. *howellii*). © N. H. (Dan) Cheatham/DRK PHOTO.

Below right: Point Reyes headland. © David Muench.

Sophisticated San Francisco consistently ranks at or near the top of lists of the most livable cities in America, and millions of tourists visit the city by the bay each year. San Francisco's dramatic natural setting by the spectacular Golden Gate, the Pacific Ocean, and the bay itself provides the backdrop for a rich and vibrant city life.

But San Francisco can boast of far more than a wealth of urban pleasures. The San Francisco Bay–Delta Estuary, the largest estuarine system on the western coast of North and South America, is an ecological treasure of twisted tributaries, sloughs, and islands. The estuary, composed of the waters of San Francisco, San Pablo, and Suisun Bays, and California's two largest rivers, the Sacramento and the San Joaquin, supports more than 130 fish species, including four separate Chinook salmon runs. This enormous system drains nearly 40% of California's land, provides drinking water to 20 million Californians, and irrigates 4.5 million acres of farmland and ranches growing nearly half of the nation's produce.

The San Francisco Bay Area is one of the most highly developed areas in the country, and a variety of interests—economic, ecological, urban, and agricultural—now compete for the region's natural resources. The system thus faces enormous stresses, and while conservationists and government agencies have made numerous efforts to address these problems, the issues are complex and interrelated, and many remain unresolved.

The combination of biological richness and intense development pressures in the Bay Area creates one of the highest concentrations of imper-

HOT SPOT SUMMARY

Imperiled Species:
Mostly plants and vernal pool invertebrates

Important Habitats:
Vernal pools, salt marshes, serpentine outcrops, and coastal mountains

Biological Diversity:
The Bay-Delta is the largest estuary on the West Coast

Key Threats:
Development pressures, alien species, and water diversions

iled species in the United States. Of the 135 imperiled species found within a roughly 13,000–square-mile area, 113 are plants. This remarkable concentration of imperiled plants is the result of a habitat mosaic produced by the interaction of highly localized climates and an extremely complex geology. The region's active tectonic history has produced many unusual soil types that in turn support plants with restricted distributions. Serpentine, a mineral so named because of its greenish color and slick surface, has high concentrations of minerals that are toxic to most plants, and outcrops occur throughout the San Francisco region. The few plant species that thrive in these inhospitable soils rarely exist anywhere else. California's serpentine may be the richest of all temperate serpentine floras.

Coastal prairie scrub, mixed hardwoods, and oak woodlands are found along the rolling hills and mountains that descend to the Pacific Ocean, while redwood forests abound in coastal areas subject to dense summer fogs. Vast salt marshes once lined San Francisco Bay, although only about 8,000 of the original 345,000 acres of tidal marsh remain. The remaining salt marshes, together with the brackish and freshwater wetlands of the Bay-Delta, furnish important resting and feeding places for birds and waterfowl migrating along the Pacific Flyway.

Top left: Vernal pool, Jepson Prairie. © Barbara Hopper.

Top right: Salt-marsh harvest mouse (*Reithrodontomys raviventris*). © B. Moose Peterson/WRP.

Above: California clapper rail (*Rallus longirostris obsoletus*). © B. Moose Peterson/WRP.

COASTAL AND INTERIOR SOUTHERN CALIFORNIA

Above: El Segundo blue butterfly (*Euphilotes battoides allyni*). © B. Moose Peterson/WRP.

Below right: Torrey pine. © Jan Butchofsky-Houser/Corbis.

An acre of top-of-the line, ready-to-build beachfront property in Orange County, California, can sell for $4 million. Even raw land on the shore in southern California can sell for $1 million per acre. Despite these astronomical prices, the pleasures of California's warm, dry summers and the cool, wet winters still draw buyers. Between 1990 and 2005, population growth is projected to exceed 40% in San Diego, San Bernardino, and Riverside Counties.

Southern California's climate resembles that of the Mediterranean, another spot long attractive to human settlement. Only three other places—coastal Chile, the tip of South Africa, and southwestern Australia—have similar conditions. These five regions support plant communities known as Mediterranean shrublands, among the world's richest and most endangered plant communities. Mediterranean-type vegetation covers just a fraction of the earth's surface, but these regions have among the highest levels of plant endemism anywhere.

The southern California climate that helps create a booming economy also fosters a wealth of natural habitats, making the region one of the richest in the United States for biological diversity. San Diego County, in particular, is also something of an ecological crossroads. Northern species like big-leaf maple (*Acer macrophyllum*) survive here but not any farther south, and the county is the northern limit of such southern species as Shaw's agave (*Agave shawii*) and other species typical of Baja

HOT SPOT SUMMARY

Imperiled Species:
Mainly plants, desert fishes, and dune invertebrates

Important Habitats:
Coastal sage scrub, vernal pools, pavement plains, perennial grasslands

Biodiversity:
Mediterranean shrublands supporting high plant, bee, and butterfly diversity

Key Threats:
Development pressures, alien species, altered fire regime

California. Two small areas in southern California, one along the coast and the other inland in the San Bernardino Mountains, together covering roughly 7,600 square miles, contain 81 imperiled species, 72 of which are plants.

Among the most diverse and endangered of southern California's habitats is coastal sage scrub, which occurs in coastal terraces and foothills from sea level to 3,000 feet. The thirst for beachfront and oceanview property, however, poses a great threat to this unique ecosystem: More than 85% of coastal sage scrub has already been lost.

Among the most remarkable of southern California's rare species dominates the high bluffs overlooking the ocean just north of San Diego. The Torrey pine (*Pinus torreyana*) is the rarest pine in the United States and occurs only in Torrey Pine State Reserve and offshore in a small population on Santa Rosa Island. The trees are relicts of a once far larger population dating from the mid-Tertiary, some 50 million years ago, when the climate was cooler and wetter than it is today. Torrey pines now exist only in those tiny areas where persistent fog approximates the conditions of geological ages past.

Other important ecological communities occur not far inland. Shallow depressions in the basalt-capped mesas of the Santa Rosa Plateau, for example, fill with water to form vernal pools. These seasonal pools support a fascinating set of wildflowers that begin life as fully aquatic plants and become increasingly terrestrial as the ponds dry. Farther inland, the San Bernardino Mountains harbor a variety of ecological islands with specialized conditions that harbor many locally restricted species. In scattered places on the Mojave Desert side of the mountains, closely packed reddish pieces of rock—Saragossa quartzite—litter the ground, resembling pavement. Ancient and stable, these treeless pavement plains are located on remnants of a dry lake bed that may be more than a million years old. Numerous endemic species like the ash gray Indian paintbrush (*Castilleja cinerea*) and Bear Valley sandwort (*Arenaria ursina*) are adapted to these harsh conditions. The scattered remnants of this habitat, threatened by rapid resort development, contain among the highest densities of rare plant species in the United States.

Above left: Oak woodland, Santa Rosa Plateau. © Harold E. Malde.

Above: Stephens' kangaroo rat (*Dipodomys stephensi*). © B. Moose Peterson/WRP.

Below: Coastal chaparral, Laguna Beach. © Harold E. Malde.

Bottom: Baldwin Lake pavement plains. © Tim Krantz.

FLORIDA PANHANDLE

Above: Ponce de Leon Springs.
© James Valentine.

Below right: Manatee (*Trichechus manatus*). © Patrick M. Rose/Save the Manatee Club.

HOT SPOT SUMMARY

Imperiled Species:
  Mainly plants, freshwater fishes and mussels, amphibians, and reptiles

Important Habitats:
  Longleaf pine woodland, ravine forests, rivers, and coastal bays

Biodiversity:
  Exceptional array of reptiles and amphibians, many restricted to single river basins

Key Threats:
  Dams, development pressures, altered fire regimes, intensive silviculture

ncient Caribbean legend told of a river that could restore a person's youth. A less ancient but no less fanciful legend has it that Juan Ponce de Leon set out to find that river. The ambitious and ruthless Spaniard actually had no interest in any such fountain—he sought more worldly goods, such as wealth and power—but a creative historian wove the tale, and Ponce de Leon will wear it always. The only elements of reality amid these various myths are Florida's natural springs themselves, magical places tucked into the shadows of magnolias or live oaks. The springs, while not the fountains of legend, form a distinctive part of Florida's natural history and biological diversity.

Springs reflect Florida's distinctive geology. Soluble limestone lies beneath the peninsula, and in places carbonic acid (formed when rainwater picks up carbon dioxide from the atmosphere and soil) has carved out caves and sinkholes, creating drains into which water flows to form subterranean streams. Some rivers in Florida drop off the surface and reappear miles away as bubbling springs. Overall, Florida contains more than 300 large artesian springs.

The deepest of all these springs, Wakulla Springs, emerges at a depth of 200 feet and feeds the St. Marks River in the Florida Panhandle. This region of Florida is one of the country's most important areas of biological diversity: One 3,100-square-mile area in the Panhandle contains 53 imperiled species. In addition to the springs, the Panhandle includes a striking variety of habitats, including steep bluffs and ravines, hardwood forests, seepage slopes, pitcher plant bogs, caves, cypress swamps, pine flatwoods and savannas, floodplain forests, coastal sand dunes, and

sandhills, all of which harbor rare species. The Panhandle's white sand beaches and numerous bays also provide nesting habitat for large numbers of leatherback and green turtles and important staging areas for songbirds and shorebirds migrating across the Gulf of Mexico.

The Panhandle's hardwood forests—known in Florida as "hammocks" —contain among the largest number of tree species per unit area of any forests in the United States. Of particular note are the temperate forest hammocks of the Apalachicola bluffs, which contain two endemic tree species, the Florida torreya (*Torreya taxifolia*) and the Florida yew (*Taxus floridana*). These forests may be true relicts, ancient communities that predate the last ice age. Some of these forests remained above sea level during the Pleistocene and thus served as a refuge for temperate species that migrated southward.

Two plant communities, sandhills and flatwoods, dominate the Panhandle. The open, rolling, longleaf pine savannas of the sandhills caught the imagination of early explorers and settlers, but humans would have to contend with the two natural processes that help shape the Panhandle's vegetation: hurricanes and fire. The Florida Panhandle is the most hurricane-prone shoreline in North America, and wildfires once swept across the region every two to five years. With the spread of tree plantations, agriculture, and housing development, however, fire suppression efforts eliminated most of the natural burns that once revitalized the pine forests. Lack of natural fire, together with extensive conversion of these forests to other uses, has eliminated more than 98% of longleaf pine forests from the southeastern coastal plain.

Top left: Florida bog frog (*Rana okaloosae*). © Suzanne L. Collins and Joseph T. Collins/Photo Researchers.

Top right: Apalachicola bluffs. © Harold E. Malde.

Below: Whitetop pitcher plant (*Sarracenia leucophylla*). © Maresa Pryor.

DEATH VALLEY REGION

Above: Jackrabbit Spring, Ash Meadows. Courtesy of U.S. Fish and Wildlife Service.

Below left: Devils Hole pupfish. Courtesy of U.S. Fish and Wildlife Service.

Below right: White bearpaw poppy (*Arctomecon merriamii*). © Terri Ann Knight/TNC.

HOT SPOT SUMMARY

Imperiled Species:
   Mostly fishes, aquatic snails, and plants

Important Habitats:
   Deserts springs and riparian areas, desert mountains

Biodiversity:
   Among highest local endemism in the continental United States

Key Threats:
   Groundwater extraction, overgrazing, off-road vehicles, and alien species

The very thought of an oasis seems to bring relief, as if the word itself could slake a deep thirst. *Oasis*, the Greek transliteration of an Egyptian word that originally meant "a pot full of water used for cooking," conjures up exotic images of camels and caravans laden with dates and spices, but oases occur in every desert, and in every desert they are remarkable and important places. North American deserts are no exception.

Some of the most distinctive of all the oases in the United States can be found in the northern Mojave Desert near Death Valley, straddling the border between California and Nevada. Ash Meadows, a group of more than 30 springs and seeps located about 40 miles east of Death Valley and 90 miles northwest of Las Vegas, has the highest local endemism of any area in the continental United States, including 10 or more mollusks, 8 plants, 5 fishes, 2 insects, and 1 mammal. Only one other region in North America, the Cuatro Cienegas Basin of northeastern Mexico, supports a greater diversity of endemic organisms. An area of roughly 4,600 square miles centering on Ash Meadows contains 52 imperiled species.

The Mojave was not always as dry as it is today. During the Pleistocene, the changes in global climate that caused ice to cover the northern lands brought tremendous rains to usually arid parts of the continent. The rains created a network of interconnecting lakes and river systems that covered low-lying areas of the Death Valley region and much of the Southwest. An enormous pluvial lake, called Lake Ash Meadows, slowly dried, leaving behind desert and small, isolated springs, fed by groundwater forced to the surface by faults deep in the earth.

A few species found sanctuary in these isolated springs and pools. The most famous resident by far is a little blue fish called the Devils Hole pupfish (*Cyprinodon diabolis*). This pupfish has the smallest range of any known vertebrate species, a 70-by-10-foot pool that lies at the bottom of a 30-foot-deep fissure in the side of a mountain. Devils Hole was one of the first springs to be isolated as the ice age lake dried up, and some 30,000 years of complete isolation from any predator and any other fish species

has allowed the Devils Hole pupfish to evolve into a form utterly distinct from its closest relatives. The pupfish gained notoriety not because it is unique and rare—the population of the fish has never been large, probably no more than 1,000—but because responsibility for its future eventually fell to the Supreme Court.

In 1952, the federal government made Devils Hole a part of Death Valley National Monument (now National Park), even though the eastern border of Death Valley lies far to the west, on the other side of the California-Nevada border. In 1968, the owners of a ranch near Devils Hole began pumping groundwater from the aquifer for irrigation, posing an immediate threat to the pupfish. The government filed suit to stop the pumping, and in 1976 a unanimous Supreme Court ruled in favor of the fish and limited the amount of groundwater that ranchers could remove from the aquifer.

Above: Eureka Dunes grass (*Swallenia alexandrae*). © Bruce A. Stein/TNC.

Left: Mesquite Flat, Death Valley. © Carr Clifton/Minden Pictures.

7

MORE THAN THE SUM OF THE PARTS
Diversity and Status of Ecological Systems

On July 5, 1803, Captain Meriwether Lewis of the First Infantry left Washington, D.C., and headed west. His destination was St. Louis, Missouri, where he was to take command, with his good friend William Clark, of the aptly named Corps of Discovery. President Thomas Jefferson had long dreamed of exploring the West, and on the day before Lewis set out from the capital, Jefferson doubled the size of the country, purchasing 820,000 square miles from France for 3 cents an acre.

Jefferson planned the expedition partly to expand commerce in the young nation—he sought the "Northwest Passage," a water route from coast to coast—but, just as important, to further scientific understanding. Lewis shared with his commander in chief a deep curiosity about the natural world, and the expedition set out with a presidential charge to discover the flora and fauna of the United States. Jefferson, as talented a scientist as has ever held the office of president, introduced Lewis to the leading natural scientists of the day, and they trained him to collect samples of plants and animals. Jefferson instructed the two commanders to record everything they could about the countryside—"the soil and face of the country, its growth and vegetable productions . . . the animals of the country . . . the remains and accounts of any which may be deemed rare or extinct," he said. And so they did, plainly but accurately.

Jefferson's personal library, one of the largest collections in the country and later the nucleus of the Library of Congress, included copies of works by Linnaeus and John Bartram, along with many other scientific texts. Meriwether Lewis served as Jefferson's private secretary for two years before leading the expedition west, and Jefferson undoubtedly introduced his protégé to those works. The Corps of Discovery, like the Bartrams and Peter Kalm, played an important role in the ongoing effort to document the natural heritage of the United States.

Mark T. Bryer

Kathleen Maybury

Jonathan S. Adams

Dennis H. Grossman

Collected by Meriwether Lewis in what is now Idaho, *Clarkia pulchella* was named in honor of his fellow explorer. Lewis himself is commemorated by the plant genus *Lewisia*. Courtesy of Hunt Institute, Carnegie Mellon University, Pittsburgh.

Lewis and Clark found a rich and diverse country with many of its most characteristic species still unknown to Western science, including the grizzly bear (*Ursus arctos horribilis*), badger (*Taxidea taxus*), mule deer (*Odocoileus hemionus*), pronghorn antelope (*Antilocapra americana*), western gray squirrel (*Sciurus griseus*), and horned lizard (*Phrynosoma* spp.). West of the Rockies, they were the first to document 33 new land mammals, 30 land birds, and 26 aquatic birds (Cutright 1969). They also collected numerous plants, many of them new to science. The genera *Lewisia* and *Clarkia*, plants first discovered on the expedition, were later named in their honor. They also saw an incredible variety of landscapes and habitats, from the thick deciduous forests of the Appalachians to the open grasslands of the Great Plains, the coniferous forests of Rockies, and the dense rain forests of the Pacific Northwest. Lewis and Clark recorded everything they saw, providing the first account of the diversity of a nation that did not yet stretch from coast to coast.

Despite their diligence and skills, a simple transect across the continent could only touch on a fraction of the ecological diversity that exists in what is now the United States. Expansion of U.S. sovereignty to the southwestern territories in 1848 incorporated the enormously diverse desert regions into the nation's ecological fabric. The purchase of Alaska in 1867 and the annexation of Hawaii in 1898 added still more varied ecosystems, ranging from tundra to tropical forest. Though the process of documenting and characterizing the nation's ecosystems still continues, one thing is already clear: The United States is one of the most ecologically diverse countries in the world. Just as the United States has a host of species that are best represented here or found nowhere else, a number of U.S. ecological systems are also noteworthy on a global scale, including the eastern broadleaf forests, the southeastern pinelands, the midwestern prairies, and California's Mediterranean-type vegetation.

Unfortunately, millions of acres of the nation's natural ecosystems have been degraded or destroyed. This vast alteration of the landscape began before Lewis and Clark crossed the continent, but the pace of

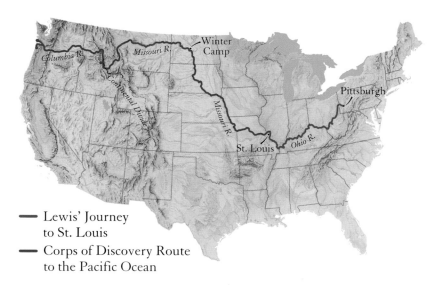

— Lewis' Journey
  to St. Louis
— Corps of Discovery Route
  to the Pacific Ocean

ecosystem conversion has quickened considerably since. Especially hard hit have been ecosystems in areas desirable for human endeavors—agriculture, forestry, ranching, or urbanization. Tallgrass prairies, for example, formerly covered more than 167 million acres of the Midwest. The prairie's deep loam soils proved ideal for growing grains and other crops, and less than 4% of this ecosystem still remains intact (Sampson and Knopf 1994). Similarly, agriculture, tree farming, and fire suppression have reduced the dominant forest type throughout the southeastern coastal plain—longleaf pine (*Pinus palustris*)—by as much as 98% (Noss 1988). Wetlands have fared poorly in the arid West, primarily from draining for agriculture but also from livestock grazing, mining, urban development, and invasion by exotic plants. With almost 100 million acres of wetlands destroyed, the lower 48 states now have only about half of their precolonization acreage (Dahl 1990).

Much of this book has focused on the diversity, distribution, and conservation of species in the United States, partly because these organisms represent the most readily identifiable elements of our natural inheritance, and partly because a wealth of information now exists about those species that are at greatest risk and therefore are in need of concerted conservation attention. But conservation must occur within the context of the ecosystems on which these species depend. It is no accident that habitat destruction is the leading cause of species endangerment, as detailed in the next chapter. The limitations of species-by-species approaches to conservation have become painfully apparent over the past few decades (Noss et al. 1997).

While species-level conservation will remain an essential protection strategy, ecosystem-scale conservation is increasingly viewed as an important complement. The Nature Conservancy has long employed a coarse filter/fine filter approach to conservation that recognizes the complementary nature between ecosystem-scale and species-scale efforts. Treating ecological communities—unique assemblages of plants and animals—as targets of conservation efforts provides a means for extending protection efforts to the full array of species, known and unknown, charismatic and obscure. Ecosystems, however, are more than the sum of their parts. Taken as a whole, an ecosystem reflects the complex interactions and mutual dependencies of the biological inhabitants and physical processes within it. For this reason, ecological communities are also worthy of being targeted for conservation in their own right.

Protecting the full range of U.S. biological diversity requires that we have a sound understanding of what ecological systems exist, where they are found, and how they are faring. This chapter reviews our current understanding of the ecological diversity within the United States and the condition of our nation's ecological resources.

The rich soils of the Midwest have been so thoroughly converted to agriculture that most unplowed prairie remnants are now found along railroad rights-of-way or in old cemeteries. © Stephen Krasemann/DRK PHOTO.

Partitioning a Continuous Landscape

Lewis and Clark explored the United States with their five senses, some simple equipment, and native intelligence. Their modern counterparts explore with an impressive body of ecological theory; a sophisticated set of tools, including satellites and computers; and an urgent conservation mission. Yet the essential goal remains the same: to learn how life lies upon the land, shaping it and being shaped by it.

For Meriwether Lewis to get from Washington to St. Louis in 1803 required first traveling on horseback to Pittsburgh, then sailing down the Ohio, and then paddling up the Mississippi. Jefferson, Lewis, and the Corps of Discovery set their gaze on the uncharted territory beyond the Mississippi, but even the well-traveled roads leading from the capital provided ample opportunities for an inquiring naturalist like Lewis. Soon after passing through the rich farmlands of the Piedmont of Jefferson's native Virginia, Lewis crossed the Appalachian Mountains, a region still thickly clothed in forest. Descending to the plateaus and rolling hills of western Pennsylvania he found—amid the ever expanding farms— deciduous forests full of American chestnut, sugar maple, buckeye, beech, and oak.

Ecologists call these mixed mesophytic forests, and they are among the most biologically diverse temperate regions on Earth. There may be 30 species of trees at a single site, and the forests abound in songbirds, salamanders, and other wildlife (see chapters 3 and 5). These lower-elevation forests, with their sugar maples and beeches, are distinct from the oak forests of the Appalachians; the species and ecosystem processes are reasonably consistent within each forest type but are distinct from one another. Classification, the process of identifying and documenting these distinctions, lies at the heart of nearly every effort to understand the natural world. Any attempt to grasp the diversity of the United States, to say nothing of an entire continent or the earth as a whole, demands such a systematic approach. Casual observers, naturalists, and scientists have long tried to understand the natural world by dividing it into smaller pieces. This natural impulse reflects that most human of activities, the need to organize and simplify by searching for patterns.

The modern scientific expression of this urge traces its roots to the German geographer Alexander von Humboldt, who began his explorations of South America shortly before Lewis and Clark set off for the American West. Studying the distribution of plant life in the Andes, Humboldt noted how vegetation responded to climate by forming characteristic zones that varied by altitude and latitude. An American ornithologist, C. Hart Merriam, built on that concept and identified seven principal life zones in North America (Merriam 1894). Natural history museums across the country adopted Merriam's life zone approach, creating dioramas that would introduce thousands of people to these basic concepts of ecology.

More than a century later, ecological classification still presents both practical and theoretical problems. For ecologists that focus on vegetation, one of the most fundamental and persistent of these problems has been the question of whether recurring assemblages of species can be said to exist at all. Some vegetation ecologists have considered assemblages of species to be almost like a single organism, responding to the environ-

The "Edge of Appalachia" region of southeastern Ohio was still thickly forested at the time that Lewis passed through en route to meeting his men in St. Louis. © Ian Adams.

ment as a group (Clements 1916, Daubenmire 1966). In contrast, the continuum concept, promoted by Gleason (1926), Curtis (1959), Whittaker (1956, 1962), and others, asserts that distinct assemblages do not exist. Instead, this theory suggests that each species has an independent response to the environment, with the result that species assemblages change more or less gradually across environmental and geographical gradients, with no clear demarcation lines. Most vegetation ecologists, however, fall somewhere between these two positions, believing that while species respond individually to their environments, those species found in a given area are also influenced by interactions with each other and with their environment in such a way that certain combinations of species tend to recur in certain environments (Austin and Smith 1989; Wilson 1991, 1994). In other words, relative discontinuities in the continuum allow us to partition a continuous landscape into reasonably discrete ecological units.

Isolated mountains in the Southwest, known as sky islands, show characteristic altitudinal shifts in climate and vegetation that C. Hart Merriam embodied in his life zone concept. © Harold E. Malde.

Diversity on a Global Scale

Debates about ecological continuums and the reality of species assemblages would no doubt have baffled Lewis and Clark. Lewis, however, was an unusually capable naturalist for his day, and his methods were more consistent with scientists of the twentieth century than with those of his own (Cutright 1969). The journey of the Corps of Discovery, while not a systematic attempt at ecological classification, nevertheless fits in the centuries-long evolution of scientific techniques for understanding the natural world. The expedition used the best information and tools available—Lewis's library on the trip included the first textbook on botany in the United States—and both he and Clark carried on the tradition of naturalists like the Bartrams. Approaches such as Merriam's life zones and the continuum concept, however, would have to await the development of the ecological sciences, a century after Lewis and Clark paddled up the Missouri.

Biogeographers armed with a deeper ecological understanding have developed numerous classifications that describe the ecological diversity of the earth. All such classifications must address the fundamental challenge of encompassing immense areas and complex ecological interactions. Consequently, a variety of researchers (e.g., Holdridge et al. 1971; Udvardy 1975; Walter 1985; Bailey 1989, 1998a; Schultz 1995) have tackled the daunting yet alluring task of classifying the broad patterns of ecological diversity into ecological regions. Classification philosophies and methods vary considerably depending on the specific use for which the classification is designed and the information available. On a global scale, most focus on one or just a handful of factors, such as climate, physiography (that is, structure of land), or the distribution of selected groups of plants or animals. Some classification methods base their maps on projections of the biological influence of climatic variables (e.g., Holdridge et al. 1971, Bailey 1989), while others use remote-sensing imagery to map actual landscape features (e.g., Defries et al. 1995, Loveland and Belward 1997).

One global-level classification designed specifically to assist in biodiversity conservation planning is Miklos Udvardy's (1975) map of the world's biogeographical provinces. Developed for the World Conservation Union (IUCN), this classification and map was designed to provide a tool to evaluate how well existing protected areas represented each of the earth's major biotic regions and to suggest where additional protected areas were needed to fill gaps. Combining information on the distribution of major ecosystem types and faunal and floral distributions, Udvardy recognized 193 unique biogeographical provinces. Each biogeographic province is categorized as part of one of 14 biome types (figure 7.1). These biomes represent major ecosystem groups—for instance, temperate grasslands or tropical humid forests—and generally follow the major vegetation formations developed by UNESCO (1973).

Biomes provide the coarsest measure of ecological diversity in various regions and countries. By this measure the United States is the most ecologically diverse country on Earth: It contains 12 of 14 biomes (table 7.1), although it covers only 6% of the earth's land area. Two biomes are particularly well represented in the United States. Temperate broadleaf forests, which cover only about 6% of the earth's land surface, have almost one-third (31%) of their extent in the United States. Temperate grasslands,

Figure 7.1. Biomes of the world.

Each of the earth's 14 biome types represents a major ecosystem group. Source: Udvardy 1975.

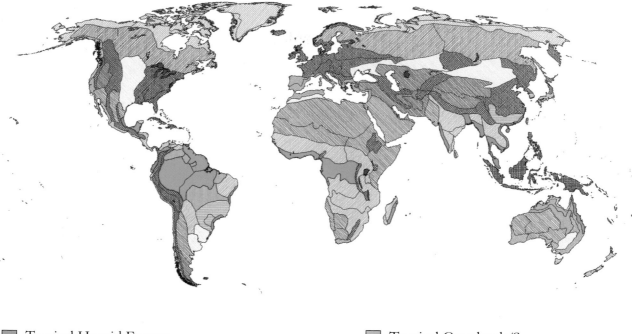

Tropical Humid Forests
Subtropical/Temperate Rain Forests/Woodlands
Temperate Needleleaf Forests/Woodlands
Tropical Dry Forests/Woodlands
Temperate Broadleaf Forests
Evergreen Sclerophyllous Forests
Warm Deserts/Semideserts

Tropical Grasslands/Savannas
Temperate Grasslands
Mixed Island Systems
Tundra Communities
Mixed Mountain Systems
Cold-Winter Deserts
Lake Systems

Table 7.1. Global ecological diversity

Country	Number of biomes	Number of ecoregions	Percent of global area
Former USSR	7	17	15%
Canada	7	11	7%
China	8	16	6%
United States	12	21	6%
Brazil	7	7	6%
Australia	7	11	5%
World total	14	28	100%

Among the six largest nations on Earth, the United States contains the greatest diversity of higher-level ecological systems as measured both by biomes (Udvardy 1975) and by division-level ecoregions (Bailey 1989).

comprising 7% of global land area, are represented in the United States by one-fifth (20%) of their distribution. Four other biomes—mixed mountain systems, subtropical and temperate rain forests, cold deserts and semideserts, and temperate needleleaf forests—each have more than 5% of their worldwide extent within the United States.

Other global analyses focus on specific types of ecological systems and can provide further insight as to which ecological types are best represented in the United States. In assessing the world's freshwater wetlands, for example, Aselmann and Crutzen (1989) found that the United States holds about 10% of the world's freshwater wetlands. This includes about 1% of bogs worldwide, 22% of fens, 7% of swamps, 15% of marshes, and 12% of floodplains.

Ecoregions: Transcending Political Boundaries

Global classifications like Udvardy's provide useful insights into the broad distribution of biodiversity. They are enormously valuable in terms of demonstrating the richness of the earth, a difficult task made even harder by the temptation, reinforced by the popular media, to equate biological diversity with tropical rain forests.

Broad views of the landscape, however, provide only a coarse picture of diversity. Lewis and Clark, for example, though they traveled through a complex and diverse landscape, passed through just six of Udvardy's biogeographic provinces, and only two from when they left St. Louis to where the Missouri ends, not far from modern-day Bozeman, Montana. Udvardy's classification system, since it covers the entire globe, cannot capture fine but nonetheless important distinctions, as between the forests of the Appalachian highlands and those lower-elevation forests just to the west.

Captain Lewis may not have noticed the subtle transition as he traveled from one familiar eastern forest to another, but the Corps of Discov-

At the time Lewis and Clark crossed the Missouri River valley, tallgrass prairies covered more than 167 million acres and supported vast quantities of wildlife. Less than 4% of this ecosystem remains intact. © Harold E. Malde.

ery began to see dramatic new landscapes soon after they started the trip up the Mississippi. A few weeks after leaving what is now Kansas City, Lewis and Clark walked to the top of a bluff and "observed the most butifull prospect imaginable." The explorers were gazing at the Missouri Valley in the heart of the central tallgrass prairie, once among the largest and most diverse prairies on Earth. The carpet of grasses they found so beautiful in spring would reach six feet in height by late summer. The Missouri Valley supported a rich diversity of life, and Lewis and Clark saw bison, deer, elk, and other animals covering the grasslands in numbers they could scarcely believe.

Despite its enormous size and variety of habitats, the central tallgrass prairie functions more or less as a unit—the ecological communities and dynamics within it are largely similar and are distinct from neighboring areas. The central tallgrass prairie can be defined and delineated as an ecological region, or ecoregion. Ecoregions are ecosystems of regional extent, smaller than Udvardy's provinces but distinct from their neighbors in terms of environmental conditions and groupings of species and ecological communities.

The distinction between one ecoregion and another can be subtle or obvious; Captain Lewis did not need to call on his scientific training to see the distinction between the northern Great Plains and the Rocky Mountains. Delineating consistent ecoregional units, however, as with other classification efforts, requires close attention to details and clear criteria for differentiating one region from another.

Among the best developed and most widely adopted efforts to characterize ecoregions worldwide is that of Robert Bailey (1989, 1995, 1998a, 1998b) of the U.S. Forest Service. To address issues of scale, Bailey's system is hierarchical, distinguishing four ecological levels—domain, division, province, section—at increasingly fine levels of detail. This classification and map use large-scale climate—or macroclimate—as the principal factor for identifying continental-scale ecosystem regions, since macroclimates are among the most significant factors affecting the distribution of life on Earth. Domains, and within them divisions, are based on the broad ecological climate zones. Climate subzones form the basis for subdividing divisions into provinces, which correspond to major plant formations. Mountain provinces are those that exhibit altitudinal zonation and the climatic regime of the adjacent lowlands. They are distinguished according to the character of the zonation by listing the altitudinal zones present. Because landforms exert the major control over the climate at finer scales, landform is used as a basis for identifying subprovinces, called sections.

Bailey's ecoregions provide another standardized measure for evaluating global-level ecological diversity. The 28 division-level ecoregions Bailey (1989) recognizes worldwide represent a finer level of resolution than Udvardy's biomes. The United States encompasses 21 of these ecoregions, again emerging as the most ecologically diverse country on Earth (table 7.1). Several of these ecoregions have an especially high level of representation in the United States, which can be quantified through a geographic information system analysis (table 7.2). The Appalachian highlands, for instance, comprise more than half (54%) of the world's limited supply of "hot humid continental mountains." Covering less than 1% of the earth's land but containing numerous plants and animals that are the last living examples of once widespread organisms—so-called living fossils—hot, humid mountains are found only in the United States, Japan, North Korea, and China. Similarly, approximately 1% of the earth's land is classified as "temperate steppe mountains," and the United States' portion of the Rocky Mountains encompass almost two-fifths (38%) of this ecoregion.

Several global ecoregions are especially well represented in the United States, including temperate steppe mountains, an ecoregion exemplified by the Rocky Mountain front range in Montana. © Harold E. Malde.

Ecoregions provide a tool that ecologists can use to pull together the full spectrum of biological diversity in an area and to transcend political boundaries often unrelated to natural boundaries. This makes ecoregions extremely useful for characterizing ecological diversity on a national scale and for planning conservation efforts on a regional scale. Rather than organize on-the-ground conservation work on the basis of state boundaries, as has usually been the case, ecoregion-based planning allows conservationists to gain a broader, more holistic perspective. Ecoregions provide a sufficiently large unit of analysis for capturing representative examples of all conservation targets, both species and ecological communities, in sufficient numbers and extent to ensure their long-term survival. These relatively large land areas are big enough to encompass processes and multiple occurrences of conservation targets, but small enough to serve as a basis for planning and carrying out conservation activities.

Another widely used ecoregional classification has been developed by James Omernik (1987, 1995a, 1995b) of the U.S. Environmental Protection Agency. He has devised a system that integrates a variety of environmental factors, including potential natural vegetation, physiogeography, land use, and soils. Because he uses a combination of characteristics, the factors that delineate ecoregions are given greater or lesser weight from one part of the country to another. Omernik (1987) recognizes 76 ecoregions across the conterminous United States.

The Global 200, a system developed by World Wildlife Fund (WWF), builds on Omernik and other analyses to provide a global-level view of ecoregions and to highlight those ecoregions worldwide that are particu-

Table 7.2. Global ecoregions well represented in the United States

Ecoregion	U.S. example	Global extent	U.S. portion
Hot humid continental mountains	Appalachian Highlands	<1%	54%
Temperate steppe mountains	Rocky Mountains	1%	38%
Subtropical humid	Southeastern Coastal Plain	2%	35%
Hot humid continental	New England Lowlands	1%	34%
Humid marine mountains	Cascade Mountains	2%	31%
Temperate steppe	Shortgrass Prairie	3%	25%

Six ecoregions have at least a quarter of their worldwide distribution within the United States. Extent of division-level ecoregion is estimated from Bailey 1989.

larly significant and should be priorities for conservation action (Olson and Dinerstein 1998). This analysis, innovative in considering terrestrial, freshwater, and marine systems together, identifies 237 ecoregions world-wide that represent the most outstanding examples of the earth's major habitat types, based on judgments of species richness and endemism, unique higher taxa, unusual ecological or evolutionary phenomena, and rarity of major habitat types. The United States is well represented on this list, encompassing all but 3 of WWF's 19 globally defined major habitat types; of their 237 ecoregions, 27 occur within our borders (14 terrestrial, 7 freshwater, and 6 marine). U.S. ecoregions in the Global 200 include the Klamath-Siskiyou coniferous forests, Hawaiian dry forests, Colorado River, and Bering and Beaufort Seas.

Several efforts have attempted to describe the ecoregions of the United States (e.g., Bailey 1995, 1998b; Omernik 1987, 1995b; McNab and Avers 1994; Maxwell et al. 1995; TNC 1997; Ricketts et al. 1999). Bailey has mapped domains and divisions at the global level, and provinces for North America. Bailey (1998b) identifies 46 provinces in the United States. Of these, 10 are found in Alaska, 1 in Hawaii, and the remainder across the lower 48 states (figure 7.2). As an extension of Bailey's system, the U.S. Forest Service formed an Ecological Classification and Mapping Task Team (ECOMAP) to develop a consistent approach to ecosystem classification and mapping on even finer geographic scales. The ECOMAP team has completed mapping sections across the United States (McNab and Avers 1994).

The Nature Conservancy also has used Bailey's ecoregional approach, together with the ECOMAP framework, as the basis for identifying ecoregions similar in scale to Bailey's provinces across the United States (TNC 1997) in order to facilitate conservation planning. Based on input from Conservancy and heritage ecologists, several of Bailey's eco-regional boundary lines were modified or new ones added to create

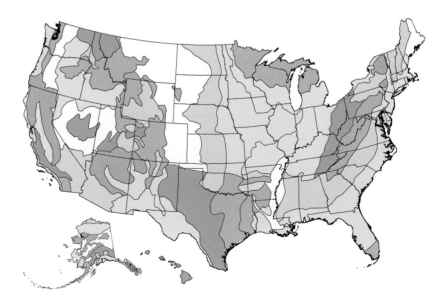

Figure 7.2. Bailey's ecoregions of the United States.

Of 47 ecoregions in the United States defined by Bailey (1984, 1998b), 10 are found in Alaska, 1 in Hawaii, and the remainder across the lower 48 states.

more homogeneous units in terms of representative vegetation cover, physiography and ecological processes. For example, Bailey's Outer Coastal Plain Mixed Forest province, which encompasses the entire Atlantic and Gulf coastal plain and much of Florida, was divided into seven distinct ecoregions based on latitudinal and longitudinal discontinuities in regional vegetation. The Conservancy's map recognizes 63 ecoregions across the conterminous United States, 10 in Alaska, and one in Hawaii (figure 7.3).

Studies such as these highlight the exceptional ecological richness of the United States, and ecoregions in particular provide an appropriate unit for conservation planning. Conservation, however, also requires a finer-scale understanding of ecological communities. Armed with such an understanding, ecologists can attempt to reconstruct the landscapes of the United States as Lewis and Clark saw them and can also begin to envision what those landscapes may look like a century from now.

A Map of Potential Diversity

Lewis, Clark, and their men spent the winter of 1804–1805 on the northern Great Plains in what is now North Dakota. When the weather broke, the Corps of Discovery again pushed west, crossing the Continental Divide and then hacking their way across the Bitterroot Range, still one of the most inaccessible regions of the country. The Corps eventually reached the Clearwater River, and for the first time since Lewis reached the confluence of the Ohio and the Mississippi two years earlier, the expedition paddled with the current rather than fighting against it. When they reached the Columbia River, though they had no way of knowing it at the time, Lewis and Clark were floating down one of the most remarkable rivers in North America.

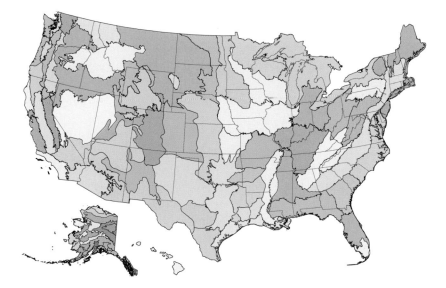

Figure 7.3. The Nature Conservancy's ecoregions of the United States.

A modification of Bailey's classification, the Conservancy's (1999) ecoregional map recognizes 63 ecoregions across the conterminous United States, 10 in Alaska, and 1 in Hawaii.

The enormously powerful Columbia River has been almost completely transformed. The Bonneville and other dams have largely turned the river into a series of long pools and have devastated the basin's formerly immense salmon runs. © Gary Braasch

The almost complete conversion of such natural ecosystems as the Palouse grasslands creates a serious challenge to understanding what the pre-European diversity of ecological types might have been. © Gary Braasch.

The explorers witnessed an enormously powerful river, with a flow 7 times greater that of the longer Colorado, and 200 times greater than the still-longer Rio Grande. The river collects water from a 250,000–square-mile plateau, an area bigger than France, and the Columbia River system once sustained one of the largest salmon runs in the world. The hand of man has tamed few rivers the way it has tamed the Columbia, however. The Columbia is one of the most dammed rivers in the world, providing hydropower to an entire region.

The dams provide the most obvious symbol of the transformation of the Columbia River, but the changes go far deeper. When the Corps of Discovery first entered the plateau in the fall of 1806, they crossed a tree-less area of plump hills called the Palouse grassland. Not until the Corps crossed the area again on their return trip the following spring did Lewis and Clark realize that while the Palouse lies in the rain shadow of the Cascades, the spring rains would nonetheless support farming (Dietrich 1995). The Palouse would eventually become one of the nation's most productive wheatlands. Conversion to agriculture has destroyed nearly all of the Palouse grasslands (Grossman et al. 1994).

Dramatic alterations to natural ecosystems like the Columbia River and Palouse grasslands that have occurred since European colonization of North America present a difficult problem for assessing the variety and extent of the nation's ecological resources. What was the pre-European diversity of ecological systems, and what baseline can we use to assess changes over time in this diversity?

In the early 1960s a botanist and geographer at the University of Kansas named A. W. Küchler attempted to provide such a baseline by portraying the major vegetation formations of North America (Küchler 1964). Küchler determined and mapped potential natural vegetation (PNV), which represents the projected mature or stable end points of vegetation development over time. Sometimes called late seral vegetation (a sere is a stage in community succession), or climax vegetation, PNV is projected to occur and persist on a site in the absence of disturbance, whether human-caused or natural. Küchler characterized potential natural vegetation types using a combination of physiognomy (life-form characteristics, e.g., tree, shrub, grass) and dominant genera. In this classification, for example, the dominance of oaks distinguishes the Appalachian highland forests from the lower-elevation mixed mesophytic forests, in which such species as sugar maple, buckeye, beech, and tulip tree share dominance.

Küchler (1964, 1985) described and mapped 106 potential vegetation types for the conterminous United States (figure 7.4, Appendix C). These types are not evenly distributed across the United States, in either size or location: More than half (56%) of the total area of the conterminous United States is covered by just 15 types. The most extensive vegetation type is oak-hickory-pine forest, found mostly in the Southeast, which covers more than 8% of the land area, followed by the neighboring oak-hickory forest, covering an additional 7%. Sagebrush steppe, a very different vegetation type occurring in the Southwest, is third in area,

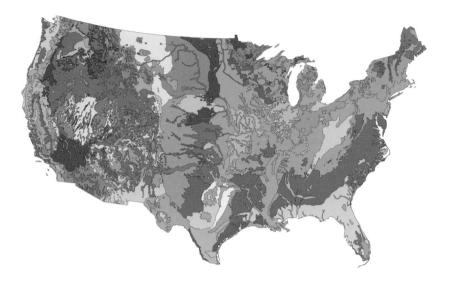

Figure 7.4. Potential natural vegetation.

The 106 potential natural vegetation types mapped by Kuchler (1985) across the conterminous United States are defined as the vegetation projected to occur and persist on a site in the absence of disturbance.

extending over 5% of the landscape. In contrast, 74 vegetation types each cover less than 1% of the total area. These include such types as Nebraska sandhills prairie, California oakwoods, and Great Lakes spruce-fir forest. Several types were estimated to cover no more than a tenth of a percent of the land area, such as redwood forest, mesquite bosques, and southeastern spruce-fir forests. As a group, grasslands are particularly well represented, with 25 different vegetation types covering about a quarter (24%) of the lower 48 states (table 7.3). Needleleaf forests, although they cover just under a sixth (15%) of the area, have slightly more types of vegetation (26).

Küchler's approach is not without drawbacks, however. His map describes vegetation types on a relatively coarse scale (about 1:3 million), excluding vegetation types not mappable on that scale. In addition, focusing on mature or climax vegetation as a baseline for "naturalness" ignores early seral communities, even those created by natural disturbances. Such an approach omits a number of important vegetation types. Extensive natural stands of trembling aspen (*Populus tremuloides*) in the

Table 7.3. Potential natural vegetation types summarized by formation

Vegetation formation	Number of potential natural vegetation types	Percent of U.S. area
Grassland	25	24%
Mixed forests	15	20%
Needleleaf forests	26	15%
Broadleaf forests	10	15%
Shrub/grassland	7	9%
Shrub	11	8%
Grassland/forest	12	8%

A summary by major vegetation formations of the number and extent of potential natural vegetation types as defined by Küchler (1985).

western United States, for example, are not mapped because they arise following wildfires and are eventually replaced by evergreens. Therefore, they are considered an early rather than a late seral vegetation type. In the southeastern coastal plain, the predominant broad-scale regional vegetation type—longleaf pine (*Pinus palustris*)—also is not portrayed, presumably because it was considered to be the result of fires and would eventually be replaced by hardwood-dominated forests.

The omission of early- to midseral vegetation is one of the most serious constraints in using these maps for conservation purposes. We are only now beginning to appreciate the vital effects of disturbance in maintaining vegetation mosaics on a landscape scale (Pickett et al. 1997). Rather than viewing areas affected by fire, flooding, or windthrows as setbacks in their inevitable and inexorable progression toward a mature state, we now understand that ecological communities exist in time as well as space. Many communities have developed in response to just such natural disturbances and depend on them for persistence over time, even if not in exactly the same place.

Riparian communities in the Southwest, for example, depend on periodic scouring by floods. Otherwise, upland plants tend to invade and eventually replace these important communities, which provide critical wildlife habitat in the region. These riparian communities are transient in both time and space on the landscape but are permanent parts of the overall ecological tapestry.

From a conservation perspective, using the concept of potential natural vegetation to describe the ecological diversity of the United States has other strengths and weaknesses as well. Mapping potential vegetation synthesizes our knowledge into a predictive model of what likely could occur on a given land area, including each major successional stage that could occur there in route to a mature state. In most places where we lack detailed historical information, this model provides us with some insight into what types of natural vegetation may have existed on a particular site, thus providing clues as to what systems we could attempt to restore and where. Potential natural vegetation can be misleading, however, if we try to use it to determine what "should" exist on a given site without considering the natural disturbance regimes.

Still, Küchler's map remains the most comprehensive and detailed effort describing the potential natural vegetation of the United States, and his maps (1964, 1975, 1985) form the foundation of most subsequent efforts to describe ecological regions as a tool for making conservation and management decisions (Klopatek et al. 1979, Crumpacker et al. 1988, Martin et al. 1993). Numerous other researchers, though, have been involved in describing and mapping broad vegetation patterns across the United States, addressing both potential and existing vegetation (e.g., Vankat 1979, Eyre 1980, Barbour and Billings 1988, Barbour and Christensen 1993). Both Vankat (1979) and Barbour and Billings (1988) focus on major vegetation formations of North America (table 7.4), providing a wealth of information about the composition, structure, distribution, function, and successional processes of various broadly defined veg-

Table 7.4. Major vegetation formations of North America

The major vegetation formations occurring in North America as defined by Vankat (1979), and representative examples of each.

Tundra
   Alpine
   Arctic
   Boreal

Coniferous forest
   Appalachian Mountains
   Rocky Mountains
   Sierra Nevada and Cascade Mountains
   Northwest Coast

Deciduous forest
   Hemlock–white pine–northern hardwoods
   Maple-basswood
   Beech-maple
   Mixed mesophytic
   Oak-chestnut
   Oak-hickory
   Southern mixed hardwoods

Grassland
   Tall grass
   Mixed grass
   Short grass
   Desert grassland
   Palouse prairie
   California grassland

Desert
   Great Basin Desert
   Mojave Desert
   Sonoran Desert
   Chihuahuan Desert

Temperate shrubland, woodland, and savanna
   Rocky Mountain region
   Scrub oak–mountain mahogany shrubland
   California region
   Grassland–deciduous forest boundary region

Tropical
   South Florida lowland subtropical forest

etation communities. Neither of these comprehensive treatments applies a consistent classification; instead, both discuss generalized vegetation categories. Nonetheless, these summaries provide an excellent overview and introduction to the bewildering complexity of ecological types in North America.

A Finer Scale of Diversity: The National Vegetation Classification

The full ecological richness and complexity of the United States can be obscure even to careful observers like Lewis and Clark. The vast prairies of central North America and the huge bison herds they supported, for example, dominated the Corps of Discovery's journey from the time they left St. Louis until they reached the Rockies. At first glance, the two commanders saw a homogeneous sea of prairie. On closer inspection, however, the landscape revealed a much more complex and dynamic ecology. Cottonwood and willow forests hugging the floodplains of the Missouri River and its tributaries provided the Corps with firewood and material for canoes. Upland oak forests and woodlands provided shelter for many of the small vertebrates they captured and sent back for further scientific study. Wetland areas dominated by sedges and cattails nursed the fish that sustained the travelers during parts of their journey.

Ecoregional classifications, and even broad vegetation types like Küchler's PNV, necessarily simplify landscapes like these as a way of highlighting major patterns. Useful as these classifications are, to protect the full array of ecological resources we must have a finer-grained understanding of their diversity, distribution, and status. The concept of ecological communities can provide a sufficiently fine-scale resolution of the landscape. Communities can be defined as assemblages of species that co-occur in defined areas at certain times and that have the potential to interact with one another (Whittaker 1962, McPeek and Miller 1996). Ecological communities constitute unique sets of natural interactions among species, provide numerous important ecosystem functions (Costanza et al. 1997, Daily et al. 1997), and create part of the context for species evolution.

Until recently, however, there has been no accepted national standard for ecological community classification. In the past, identification of fine-scale natural communities proceeded by way of local efforts using independently developed classifications. This piecemeal approach has helped identify important sites within many states, but using such fine-scale efforts at a national level to guide conservation would result in unnecessarily redundant protection of a few communities and inadequate protection of many others. The lack of a common classification for natural communities also means that conservation scientists and planners cannot integrate or compare the results of many inventory and monitoring programs, such as those conducted in national forests and parks, state forests and parks, or fish and wildlife refuges.

In response to this need, The Nature Conservancy, together with the network of natural heritage programs, undertook the development of a consistent yet flexible ecological community classification system (Grossman et al. 1998, Anderson et al. 1998). Known as the U.S. National Vegetation Classification (USNVC), the system can be used to classify all types of vegetated communities, from wetland systems to arid deserts, and from old-growth forests to fire-maintained grasslands. Developing this classification system represents a major collaborative effort, not only between the Conservancy and heritage network but also among a wide array of federal agencies—such as the U.S. Geological Survey's Biological Resources Division, the U.S. Fish and Wildlife Service, the U.S. Forest Service, and the National Park Service—as well as professional societies, including the Ecological Society of America, and individual researchers around the country. The Federal Geographic Data Committee, an interagency body responsible for coordinating federal government–wide approaches to developing and using spatial information, also collaborated in the development of the classification and has adopted it as a federal standard.

A team of Conservancy and state heritage ecologists used this system to develop an initial catalogue of ecological communities for the United States (Anderson et al. 1998); this effort represents the first time that the nation's terrestrial vegetation has been classified using a single system on a scale fine enough for making site-specific conservation decisions. A parallel effort is under way to develop a freshwater classification system appropriate for aquatic conservation that focuses on aquatic fauna and geomorphology (Lammert et al. 1996, Higgins et al. 1998).

The association concept distinguishes between stands of jack pine on moist substrates, which grow together with balsam fir, as shown here, and those on dry sandplains in the same region where the pine occurs with an understory of bearberry. © Don Faber-Langendoen/ TNC.

The Association Concept

The finest units in the U.S. National Vegetation Classification are called associations. Each association represents a plant assemblage that always exhibits similar total species composition and vegetation structure and that occurs repeatedly across the landscape, wherever certain habitat conditions exist. The association concept encompasses both the dominant species (those that cover the greatest area) and diagnostic species (those found consistently in some vegetation types but not in others), regardless of whether they are large trees or diminutive herbaceous plants. This means that the association concept can reflect greater ecological specificity than a classification based solely on the dominant "cover" species (those dominant in the upper stratum of the vegetation). Such dominant cover species are often widespread and may occur with many different species over large, heterogeneous landscapes (Mueller-Dombois and Ellenberg 1974, Kimmins 1997). For example, in northern Minnesota and adjacent parts of Canada, jack pine (*Pinus banksiana*), a generalist species, occurs with an understory of balsam fir (*Abies balsamea*) on moist bedrock substrates. On dry sandplains, however, jack pine grows with an understory of bearberry (*Arctostaphylos uva-ursi*) shrubs (Sims et al. 1989). These two distinct plant associations are responding to profoundly different environmental conditions and represent distinct ecological units despite sharing the same overstory species.

Despite their relatively high degree of ecological specificity, associations—with few exceptions—repeat across the landscape. Individual occurrences of the same or different associations, however, may range greatly in size. For example, some western grasslands occur naturally in patches of tens of thousands of acres. In contrast, southeastern "beech gaps," characterized by stunted, gnarled beech trees, often occur in sharply bounded mountaintop stands of only a few acres.

The association concept is intended to be fine enough to be useful in identifying specific, ecologically meaningful sites for conservation, but broad enough to be connected to landscape scale processes and patterns. For this reason the Conservancy chose the association as the fundamental unit for characterizing and conserving the ecological diversity of the United States.

Diversity and Distribution of Ecological Communities

The United States harbors a tremendous diversity of ecological communities. The U.S. National Vegetation Classification recognizes more than 4,500 vegetation associations from across the country (table 7.5). This fig-

Table 7.5. Diversity of U.S. vegetation types

Vegetation classification level	Number of types	Example
Class	7	Forest
Subclass	22	Evergreen forest
Group	62	Needleleaf evergreen forest
Formation	231	Conical-crowned needleleaf evergreen forest
Alliance	1,642	*Tsuga canadensis* forest alliance
Association	4,515	*Tsuga canadensis/Rhododendronm maximum—Leucothoe fontanesiana* forest

The number of natural vegetation types recognized at each level of the U.S. National Vegetation Classification. A particular eastern hemlock (*Tsuga canadensis*) community illustrates the increasingly fine detail represented by each level.

ure is likely to grow as additional inventory and classification work proceeds, and we can project that on the order of 7,000 to 9,000 natural and seminatural vegetation associations ultimately will be documented from the United States. At the next higher level of the classification, the system recognizes over 1,600 vegetation alliances, a number that will probably increase only slightly with additional information and analysis.

Forest types make up one-third (33%) of the currently recognized vegetation associations, the largest number of any structural class (table 7.6). Evergreen forests in particular account for the largest number of forested communities, comprising just under half of all forests and 16% of all community types. With their ability to use the sun's energy anytime temperatures are warm enough, evergreen trees are able to take advantage of the short growing seasons found in boreal and montane habitats. The low surface area of needleleaf evergreens restricts transpiration, allowing these trees to thrive in places where growing seasons are dry or where soils frequently freeze in winter. Thus, evergreen forests occur in all parts of the United States, from the Sitka spruce and western hemlock communities of the Pacific Northwest rain forests, and pinyon forests in the desert Southwest, to alpine forests dominated by red spruce and balsam fir in New England's White Mountains, and live oak–dominated tropical and subtropical hammocks in South Florida's Everglades and elsewhere in the South.

Herbaceous vegetation types, such as grasslands, are the next-largest structural class, constituting about a quarter (27%) of associations. These vegetation types often occupy environments where a lack of precipitation, extremes in temperature, soil conditions, or fires, floods, tidal influences, or other disturbances prevent the permanent establishment of woody plants. Examples of these herbaceous communities include big bluestem–dominated prairies in the Midwest, coastal salt marshes along the Gulf of Mexico, and alpine meadows in the Rocky Mountains.

Table 7.6. Structure and growth form of U.S. vegetation associations

Class Subclass	Number of associations	% of all associations
Forest	1,505	33
Evergreen forest	740	
Deciduous forest	572	
Mixed evergreen-deciduous forest	193	
Woodland	813	18
Evergreen woodland	582	
Deciduous woodland	175	
Mixed evergreen-deciduous woodland	56	
Shrubland	738	16
Evergreen shrubland	386	
Deciduous shrubland	334	
Mixed evergreen-deciduous shrubland	18	
Dwarf-shrubland	129	3
Evergreen dwarf-shrubland	105	
Deciduous dwarf-shrubland	24	
Herbaceous	1,225	27
Perennial graminoid vegetation	964	
Perennial forb vegetation	170	
Hydromorphic rooted vegetation	76	
Annual graminoid or forb vegetation	15	
Nonvascular	12	<1
Bryophyte vegetation	4	
Lichen vegetation	6	
Algal vegetation	2	
Sparse Vegetation	93	2
Consolidated rock sparse vegetation	42	
Boulder, gravel, cobble, or talus sparse vegetation	15	
Unconsolidated material sparse vegetation	36	
Total	4,515	100

Source: Natural Heritage Central Databases 1997.

Ecological communities are distributed unevenly across the country (figure 7.5a). Although the still-incomplete inventory of ecological communities complicates assessing geographic patterns of diversity, current information shows that the areas of highest community diversity are mostly in the western United States and secondarily in the Southeast. In addition to the sheer size of the western states, steep gradients in environmental conditions influence the number of communities encountered there. The lack of glaciation and other recent catastrophic disturbances in the southeastern United States has given rise to diverse species and soil types. North Carolina, for example, stands out because of the state's diverse natural regions and climates, but also because it has among the most thoroughly classified and inventoried vegetation associations of any state in the nation.

Assessing the number of communities by ecoregion provides a slightly different perspective on the distribution of ecological diversity, as well as the level of completeness of the classification (figure 7.5b). Using Bailey's (1995) ecoregional provinces, we determined the number of currently recognized vegetation associations occurring in each ecoregion. This portrayal highlights several regions, including: a band stretching from the Pacific Northwest across to and down the Rocky Mountains, and the southeastern coastal plain. Again, these patterns reflect both ecological diversity and completeness of inventory. Furthermore, as with states, ecoregions display a wide variation in size, further complicating the task of ranking ecoregions in terms of diversity. For instance, the southeastern coastal plain, as defined by Bailey (1995), encompasses almost 174,000 square miles, compared to a mere 10,300 square miles covered by California's coastal chaparral.

Identification of all terrestrial community types is far from complete, especially at the finest levels of this hierarchical system. Nonetheless, this initial effort provides a major advance in our ability to characterize the ecological diversity across the United States and forms an important baseline for assessing the distribution and status of our ecological resources. Continued inventory will undoubtedly result in the recognition of additional associations and refinements, especially in geographic areas and for vegetation types not yet well classified. These include most of Alaska, the Great Basin, parts of the southeastern United States, and many sparsely vegetated types and most nonvascular-dominated vegetation types.

An Example of Diversity in the Grasslands: Scotts Bluff National Monument

The national vegetation classification allows scientists to assess ecosystems in a standardized way on a much finer scale than before. Such an assessment can produce some surprising results. Ecologists, for example, often describe the area east of the Rockies and west of the Mississippi as just

Figure 7.5a–b. Diversity of ecological communities.

Although the classification and inventory of vegetation associations are incomplete, current information indicates that states with the highest community diversity are mostly in the West and Southeast.

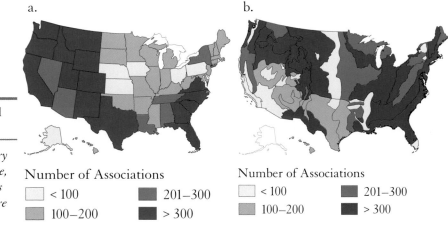

a.

b.

Number of Associations
□ < 100   ■ 201–300
■ 100–200   ■ > 300

Number of Associations
□ < 100   ■ 201–300
■ 100–200   ■ > 300

three different types of grasslands—shortgrass, mixed-grass, and tallgrass prairies. But as travelers such as Lewis and Clark experienced, there are many more than just three ecosystems, and not all of them are prairies. The national vegetation classification currently recognizes over 500 ecological communities in this region alone, only about half of which are composed primarily of herbaceous vegetation like grasses. Each of these 500 communities occurs as a result of a particular combination of soil, geology, hydrology, climate, and historical effects that give rise to different assemblages of living organisms. In turn, each community provides unique habitat and ecosystem benefits that support the diversity of life across the region.

The vegetation of Scotts Bluff National Monument illustrates the fine-scale patterns of diversity within this grassland region. The Nature Conservancy, the Nebraska Natural Heritage Program, the United States Geological Survey, and the National Park Service have mapped the vegetation of this national monument, located in western Nebraska, as part of a nationwide effort to document and map the vegetation of the National Park System (TNC and ESRI 1994). In an area of only about 3,000 acres, 20 different ecological communities were documented and mapped (figure 7.6), typifying the considerable ecological diversity present even

A prominent landmark for pioneers traveling the Oregon Trail, Nebraska's Scotts Bluff is now a national monument. The monument's ecological communities were mapped (see figure 7.6) using the U.S. National Vegatation Classification. Courtesy of National Park Service.

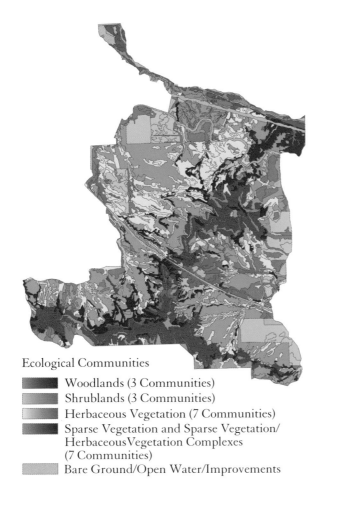

Ecological Communities

▮ Woodlands (3 Communities)
▮ Shrublands (3 Communities)
▮ Herbaceous Vegetation (7 Communities)
▮ Sparse Vegetation and Sparse Vegetation/ HerbaceousVegetation Complexes (7 Communities)
▮ Bare Ground/Open Water/Improvements

Figure 7.6. Vegetation of Scotts Bluff National Monument.

Twenty distinct ecological communities occur in this area of just 3,000 acres, demonstrating the considerable ecological diversity that may be present even in regions such as Nebraska with low species richness. Source: Courtesy USGS-NPS Mapping Program.

The temperate rain forests of the Pacific Northwest are among the most impressive on Earth, with trees reaching enormous sizes and ancient ages. Old-growth in this region, however, has been reduced to a small fraction of its former extent. © Gary Braasch.

in regions not generally associated with high species richness. This ecological diversity makes conservation more challenging, since we must protect a great many more places than we have so far if we are to protect the diversity of the entire country. As if that were not challenging enough, the threats to biological diversity continue to grow, reshaping the American landscape nearly every day.

The Changing Face of America

Of all the ecosystems that Lewis and Clark traversed in their journey west, the most remarkable may have been the last. On November 12, 1805, while camped along the mouth of the Columbia River just short of their final destination, Clark found trees that were 7 to 8 feet in diameter and 200 feet tall. Thick stands of conifers, some growing on downed and moss-covered trees, blanketed the low hills. Clark had reached the coastal rain forests of the Pacific Northwest, one of the most impressive forests on Earth.

The temperate rain forests that extend from the Gulf of Alaska to northern California exhibit some of the greatest biomass accumulation and highest productivity of any forests on Earth, temperate or tropical (Franklin 1988). These maritime forests are the product of the long life spans of the dominant species—Douglas fir (*Pseudotsuga menziesii*), for example, has a potential life span of 1,200 years (Franklin and Waring 1980)—and the infrequency of major fires and other disturbances. Together these factors have produced a forest where trees are capable of reaching enormous sizes and ancient ages.

The winter rains that characterize this region made life miserable for Lewis and Clark and their men. They nevertheless explored the forest and its wonders. Lewis discovered and described in great detail a number of trees and other plants that were unknown to science until then, including the Sitka spruce (*Picea sitchensis*), one of the dominant trees of this ecosystem. They measured one particularly grand example of the tree at 14 feet in diameter. Of the various animals that Lewis studied, 11 mammals, 11 birds, and 2 fishes were described as species new to science. These remarkable ancient forests, however, are virtually a thing of the past: The Pacific Northwest as a whole has lost up to 25 million acres—90%—of its ancient forests (Noss and Peters 1995).

A Temperate Dilemma

The fate of the Pacific Northwest coniferous forests has not been unusual. Natural ecosystems across the United States have been severely altered or destroyed. Although tropical rain forests are justifiably the focus of great conservation concern, harboring as they do a disproportionate amount of the earth's biodiversity, the world's temperate regions have sustained much greater historical disturbance of the natural habitats they contain. Hannah et al. (1994) found that humans have disturbed or eliminated natural habitat from nearly three-quarters of the earth's habitable land surface (figure 7.7). In assessing these disturbance patterns based on biome types (as characterized by Udvardy 1975), these researchers also found that temperate biomes on average are much more disturbed than are tropical biomes, while boreal and arctic biomes are least disturbed (Hannah et al. 1995). Not surprisingly, those climates most hospitable to humans have been hardest hit. Of the 13 major terrestrial biome types, 4 of the 5 most disturbed biomes are temperate: temperate broadleaf forests, evergreen sclerophyllous forests, temperate grasslands, and mixed mountain systems (figure 7.8).

The temperate broadleaf forest biome, covering eastern North America, parts of Europe, and parts of eastern Asia, is the most disturbed biome of all: Just 6% remains undisturbed worldwide (Hannah et al. 1995). The percentage of evergreen sclerophyllous forest—a hard-leafed vegetation type found around the Mediterranean Sea and in the Mediterranean climates of California, Chile, South Africa, and southwestern Australia—that remains undisturbed is only slightly higher (6.4%). Given that this biome covers only 4% of the global land area, it has the least amount of undisturbed area of any vegetation type. Only a little over a quarter (28%) of the world's temperate grasslands remain in a natural state, and much of that may be in the form of isolated remnants surrounded by agriculture.

With most of its land area in the temperate zone, the United States has had a long history of intensive human land use and consequent habitat loss. In the century between 1780 and 1880, the population of the United States rose from under 3 million to more than 50 million. The population boom led to an enormous demand for cropland and timber, and along with the demands of the Civil War and increasing industrialization, these pressures became the driving force behind the reshaping of the our eastern landscape (Cronon 1983, Whitney 1994). By 1900 most virgin forests in the eastern United States were gone (Davis 1996).

Despite this almost complete transformation, the forests that now blanket much of New England and the mid-Atlantic states bear some resem-

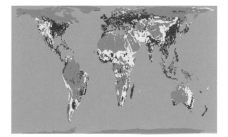

■ Disturbed
☐ Partially Disturbed
▨ Undisturbed

Figure 7.7. Disturbance of natural habitat worldwide.

Humans have disturbed or eliminated natural habitat from nearly three-quarters of the earth's habitable land surface. Source: Hannah et al. 1994.

Figure 7.8. Disturbance by biome.

Temperate biomes (dark green) have generally suffered greater levels of disturbance than have tropical biomes, while boreal and arctic biomes are least disturbed. Source: Hannah et al. 1995.

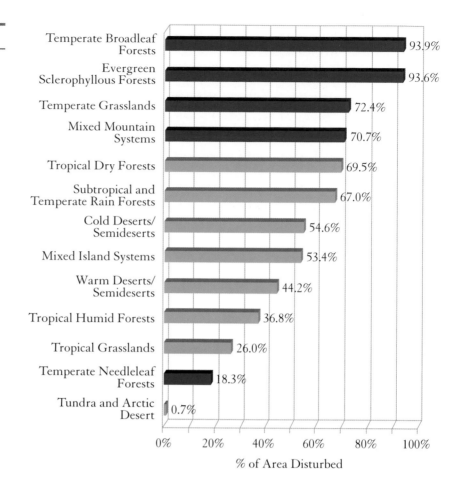

Biome	%
Temperate Broadleaf Forests	93.9%
Evergreen Sclerophyllous Forests	93.6%
Temperate Grasslands	72.4%
Mixed Mountain Systems	70.7%
Tropical Dry Forests	69.5%
Subtropical and Temperate Rain Forests	67.0%
Cold Deserts/ Semideserts	54.6%
Mixed Island Systems	53.4%
Warm Deserts/ Semideserts	44.2%
Tropical Humid Forests	36.8%
Tropical Grasslands	26.0%
Temperate Needleleaf Forests	18.3%
Tundra and Arctic Desert	0.7%

% of Area Disturbed

blance to those that Lewis passed through en route to his rendezvous with Clark. Broadleaf forests have returned to large parts of the East, albeit in the form of second-growth stands. A key event behind the remarkable reforestation of the East was the Louisiana Purchase, the same act that set the stage for the Corps of Discovery's journey. With new land available, huge numbers of eastern farmers and loggers pushed westward. The loggers moved out of absolute necessity—essentially no mature forests remained in the East—while the farmers sought the more fertile, less rocky soils of the midwestern grasslands.

The forests that have regrown in the eastern United States are a hopeful sign, and one that speaks to the resiliency and restoration potential of some ecosystems given sufficient time. The return of these forests was aided by the fact that, despite the almost complete loss of virgin forest, at any one time no more than about half the area was without tree cover (Pimm et al. 1995b). Depending on the size and condition of the particular tract, these second-growth forests may provide some of the ecological equivalents of the original forests. Regardless of their size and age, however, these forests are fundamentally different than the old-growth forests that existed in the nation's early days. They often lack the structural features that are characteristic of old-growth forests, such as large, standing dead trees called snags, which provide habitat for wildlife, and a multi-age, multilevel canopy. In addition, second-growth forests may be less species-rich: Stands as old as 85 years have been found to have only half the number of herbaceous species as stands of old-growth (Duffy and Meier 1992). Another significant difference between today's eastern forests and those of Lewis and Clark's era is the virtual absence of one of the eastern forest's keystone species, the American chestnut (*Castanea dentata*).

American chestnut was once among the most abundant trees in the eastern United States and together with oak constituted the dominant forest type through much of the Appalachians (Greller 1988). A wide variety of wildlife depended on its large, nutritious nuts for food, and people prized its wood and nuts as well. Beginning in 1904, an introduced Asian fungal blight, *Endothia parasitica*, began attacking the species; within 50 years the American chestnut had virtually disappeared as a canopy tree in eastern forests. At present the species survives only as stump-sprouts or understory saplings, which typically are afflicted by the blight before they can reach maturity. The loss of the chestnut makes it unlikely that eastern forests will ever regain the composition, structure, and set of evolutionary interactions they once supported.

Reconstructing the Past and Assessing the Present

The story of the American chestnut and the eastern forests illustrates the difficulty of assessing changes in biological diversity over time. The forests may appear functional, but they obviously contain a different mix of species than they did just a century ago. Are these forest still "natural"? Making such determinations is problematic in part because of the lack of good historical data: Unlike Lewis and Clark, most of the earliest colonists and explorers did not record much detail about the habitats and the natural history of the regions through which they were passing. The challenge becomes even greater when human influences are far more pervasive and ancient than the introduction of a pathogen like the fungus that eliminated the chestnut. Given the long history of Amerindians in North America, and the much shorter history of Polynesians in Hawaii, teasing apart "natural" conditions from the influences of indigenous peoples in ecosystems is difficult. In the Palouse and other regions, for example, Native Americans routinely used fire to create habitat for game animals, to flush the game during hunts, and to rejuvenate desirable grasses and forbs.

Considerable debate surrounds the degree to which these and similar practices changed the ecological complexion of the landscape or simply reinforced the effects of naturally set fires (Agee 1990). Many ecologists, however, consider pre-European settlement vegetation to be the appropriate baseline for naturalness in North America. The historical distribution of a community type, a key factor in determining extent of decline, is generally measured from the time of European settlement.

Assessments of a community type in the context of a pre-European settlement landscape challenges us to understand site-vegetation relation-

Once among the most abundant trees in the eastern United States, American chestnut was virtually wiped out by a Chinese fungal blight. The elimination of these trees radically altered the composition and structure of eastern hardwood forests. Courtesy of Forest History Society, Durham, N.C.

ships, including natural disturbance regimes, and Native American land management practices. Recorded observations of early explorers and settlers, and studies of witness-tree data—trees that surveyors marked to help settlers locate surveying posts that indicated legal property boundaries (e.g., Abrams and Ruffner 1995)—as well as fire scars on stumps and cross sections (e.g., Taylor 1993, Brown and Swetnam 1994), Native American impacts (e.g, Dorney 1981), and even accumulations of plant matter in gopher mounds (Cox 1986) have been brought to bear. Comer et al. (1998) used General Land Office surveys to reconstruct the vegetation of Michigan circa 1800 (figure 7.9). Although designed for purposes other than vegetation mapping, these surveys provide a wealth of historical information, and the effort to reconstruct Michigan's past vegetation is among the most detailed of its kind. These researchers explicitly take into account the varied activities of Native Americans in Michigan, including clearing fields for crops, fishing, hunting, and collecting wild rice.

Reconstructing the landscapes of a century ago would be simply a historical exercise without techniques to assess what remains of the varied habitats that once covered the United States. Status assessments of natural vegetation involve an assessment of quantity (how much is left?) as well as quality (how intact and well functioning is what remains?). Satellite imaging devices represent a powerful tool for examining the first of these questions. On a continental scale, satellite imagery from the Advanced Very High Resolution Radiometer (AVHRR) provides a current and comprehensive picture of national land-cover and vegetation patterns. This remote sensing device is used primarily for weather applications and provides daily coverage at the fairly coarse resolution of one square kilometer. Interpretation of these data by U.S. Geological Survey

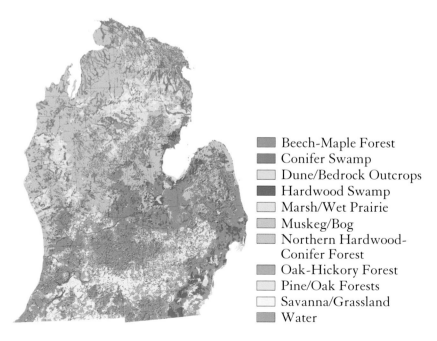

Figure 7.9. Historical vegetation of Michigan.

Few historical baselines exist for reconstructing past vegetation. This vegetation map of Michigan's Lower Peninsula, circa 1800, is based on information contained in General Land Office survey records. Source: Comer et al. 1995.

Beech-Maple Forest
Conifer Swamp
Dune/Bedrock Outcrops
Hardwood Swamp
Marsh/Wet Prairie
Muskeg/Bog
Northern Hardwood-Conifer Forest
Oak-Hickory Forest
Pine/Oak Forests
Savanna/Grassland
Water

researchers produces a striking picture of the existing land cover and vegetation of the conterminous United States (figure 7.10).

This land cover map shows that in the lower 48 states about 38% of the land is forested, 29% is rangeland or grassland, and 23% is agricultural land (Loveland et al. 1991, Loveland and Hutcheson 1995). Another 1% of the land area appears to be urbanized (Danko 1992). Because of the coarse scale of the underlying data, this land-cover map cannot distinguish among certain key vegetation features—for example, vegetation structure, seral stages, exotic versus native species, and natural forest versus tree plantations. Nevertheless, it provides an important tool for detecting changes over time in the large-scale vegetation patterns of the United States.

Küchler's (1985) map of potential natural vegetation (figure 7.4) offers an avenue for investigating changes over time in U.S. vegetation and consequent habitat loss. One approach to assessing change over time compared 1990 AVHRR satellite data to Küchler's PNV map and determined that about 61% of the conterminous United States has the same general vegetation patterns, with similar physiognomic characteristics to those predicted by Küchler (Loveland and Hutcheson 1995). Their analysis also confirms a high degree of alteration in the central and eastern grasslands and Florida's sand pine scrub. Loveland and Hutcheson's assessment, however, is not able to distinguish between natural and altered vegetation: An even-age tree plantation is mapped as forest, even though the plantation and the natural forest have little ecological similarity. The authors recognize the need for closer ecological examination of vegeta-

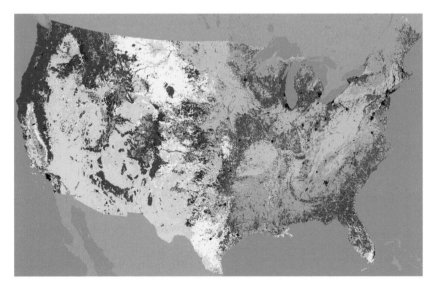

Figure 7.10. Land cover of the United States.

Existing land cover of the lower 48 states based on interpretation of coarse-resolution satellite imagery (AVHRR). This analysis finds that about 38% of the land is forested, 29% is rangeland or grassland, and 23% is agricultural. Source: Loveland and Hutcheson 1995.

■ Urban
▨ Cropland
▨ Cropland/Woodland Mosaic
■ Cropland/Grassland Mosaic
▨ Needleleaf Forest

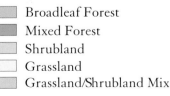

▨ Broadleaf Forest
▨ Mixed Forest
▨ Shrubland
▢ Grassland
▨ Grassland/Shrubland Mix

tion change due to the limits of AVHRR data, and they acknowledge that their estimate of 61% does not explain the quality and finer-scale patterns of vegetation. O'Neill et al. (1997) also compared Küchler's map to the 1990 data and found that in the Atlantic and Gulf Coasts, the Midwest, and the Central Valley of California, more than half of the natural vegetation has been lost, while the mountainous areas have largely retained natural vegetation.

Klopatek et al. (1979) used older data than either Loveland and Hutcheson or O'Neill et al. but conducted a finer-scale analysis in an effort to determine whether existing vegetation was natural or altered. They used 1967 county-level land use data to assess the amount of each of the 106 potential natural vegetation types that had been converted from a natural state. The result was a county-by-county gauge of the extent to which human uses had preempted natural vegetation. Their interpretation of natural vegetation included all successional types that could lead to Küchler PNV types, unless that successional type was known to occur in a particular place because of human forces.

Klopatek and his colleagues estimated that just over 65% of the conterminous United States remained in natural vegetation and that human-induced changes had reduced the area of 23 of the 106 vegetation types by more than one-half (figure 7.11a). These 23 vegetation types once occupied up to one-half of the entire conterminous United States, but by the late 1970s they covered less than 7% of the total land area. These researchers identified four vegetation types, in particular, that had lost 85% or more of their original area: tule marshes in California, Nevada, and Utah; elm-ash forest in Ohio, Indiana, and Michigan; bluestem prairie in the Midwest; and sand pine scrub in Florida.

We assessed changes in natural vegetation through a similar analysis of potential natural vegetation types using 1992 AVHRR satellite-derived land cover data for comparison (figure 7.11b). In our analysis we followed the methodology of Klopatek et al. by considering early- and midsuccessional vegetation as natural if the disturbance that created it was believed to have been natural. For example, we considered trembling aspen stands in the West, which are naturally maintained by fire and other disturbance, to be natural even though they did not match a particular Küchler PNV type. Conversely, we considered vegetation non-natural if we determined that it was present because of a non-natural disturbance. Mesquite shrublands, for example, dominate much of the Southwest primarily because of overgrazing by non-native livestock (National Research Council 1994).

While data differences in this study and Klopatek's confound direct comparisons between specific vegetation types, the overall decrease in most types over this 25–year period is compelling (figure 7.11). We found that only 42% of the United States remained in natural vegetation, compared with 65% described by Klopatek et al. (1979).

Our analysis identified 52 Küchler vegetation types that have lost more than one-half their original area, compared to 23 in Klopatek's study. Geographically, Klopatek identified most of the Upper Midwest, as well

a.   b.

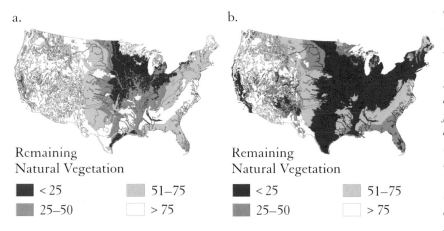

Remaining   Remaining
Natural Vegetation   Natural Vegetation

■ < 25   ▨ 51–75   ■ < 25   ▨ 51–75
▨ 25–50   □ > 75   ▨ 25–50   □ > 75

Figure 7.11a–b. Changes in natural
vegetation.

*(a) An analysis by Klopatek et al. (1979)
that compared 1967 county-level land use
data with potential natural vegetation,
found that human uses had preempted
about 35% of the nation's natural
vegetation. (b) Our analysis comparing
land cover based on 1992 satellite
(AVHRR) imagery with potential natural
vegetation indicates that 58% of the
conterminous United States no longer
supports natural vegetation.*

as smaller areas in South Florida, coastal Texas, and the Central Valley
of California, as having lost more than 50% of their natural vegetation.
Our analysis indicates that similar reductions of 50% or more now affect
nearly the entire Midwest from North Dakota to Texas; all of Florida;
coastal California; most of the deep South; and much of New York and
southern New England. In both analyses, areas with the largest amount
of remaining natural vegetation were located in areas that are sparsely
populated and poorly suited for agriculture or other types of development,
such as portions of the intermountain West, Pacific Northwest, and desert
Southwest.

Declining Ecosystems

Perhaps the most comprehensive review of ecosystem declines in the
United States was conducted by Noss et al. (1995). These researchers attempted to determine to what extent natural ecosystems have been reduced in area or degraded in quality by human activities. They asked local
and regional experts—many of them state heritage ecologists—about the
condition of the lands they knew best and combined information from
these experts with that gleaned from the literature into a compilation
of estimated declines in U.S. ecosystems. These researchers took the
most inclusive view possible on ecosystem definitions and considered
systems spanning the range of geographic and ecological scales—from
regional landscapes to fine-grained plant associations. Because of this
wide variation and lack of consistency among the different units assessed, it is difficult to synthesize the overall results of that study. Taken
together, however, these reports present a sobering litany of loss in nearly
every state.

Based on loss of area and degradation, these researchers identified 27
"critically endangered" ecosystem types that they estimate have lost more
than 98% of their extent since European settlement (table 7.7). These
include plant communities and habitats from across the country, such
as eastern deciduous old-growth, oak savanna in the Midwest, pine
rocklands in South Florida, canebrakes in the Southeast, native grasslands
in California, and Palouse prairie in the Pacific Northwest. An "endan-

Table 7.7. Vanishing U.S. ecosystems

Ecosystem types—plant communities and habitats—that according to Noss et al. (1995) have declined by 98% or more in the United States since European settlement

Old-growth and other virgin stands in the eastern deciduous forest biome

Spruce-fir (*Picea rubens–Abies fraseri*) forest in the southern Appalachians

Red pine (*Pinus resinosa*) and white pine (*Pinus strobus*) forests (mature and old-growth) in Michigan

Longleaf pine (*Pinus palustris*) forests and savannas in the southeastern coastal plain

Slash pine (*Pinus elliottii*) rockland habitat in South Florida

Loblolly pine–shortleaf pine (*Pinus taeda–Pinus echinata*) hardwood forests in the West Gulf Coastal Plain

Arundinaria gigantea canebrakes in the Southeast

Tallgrass prairie east of the Missouri River and on mesic sites across range

Bluegrass savanna-woodland and prairies in Kentucky

Black Belt prairies in Alabama and Mississippi and in the Jackson Prairie in Mississippi

Ungrazed dry prairie in Florida

Oak savanna in the Midwest

Wet and mesic coastal prairies in Louisiana

Lakeplain wet prairie in Michigan

Sedge meadows in Wisconsin

Hempstead Plains grasslands on Long Island, New York

Lake sand beaches in Vermont

Serpentine barrens, maritime heathland, and pitch pine (*Pinus rigida*)–heath barrens in New York

Prairies (all types) and oak savannas in the Willamette Valley and in the foothills of the Coast Range, Oregon

Palouse prairie (Idaho, Oregon, and Washington and in similar communities in Montana)

Native grasslands (all types) in California

Alkali sink scrub in southern California

Coastal strand in southern California

Ungrazed sagebrush steppe in the Intermountain West

Basin big sagebrush (*Artenisia tridentata*) in the Snake River Plain of Idaho

Atlantic white cedar (*Chamaecyparis thyoides*) stands in the Great Dismal Swamp of Virginia and in North Carolina and possibly across the entire range

Streams in the Mississippi Alluvial Plain

gered" category, defined as having declined from 85% to 98%, includes another 42 ecosystem types, while 13 are regarded as "threatened," with declines of 70% to 84%.

Summarizing these patterns, Noss and Peters (1995) listed 21 U.S. ecosystems they consider to be most endangered. In addition to decline in area since European settlement, the researchers used present area (rarity), imminence of threats, and number of federally listed threatened and endangered species to make this assessment. These ecosystems encompass a broad range of ecological types and landscape units, from broad habitat classes, like cave and karst systems, which are distributed across the country, to such geographically restricted and specific types as Hawaiian dry forest.

Ecosystem status can also be evaluated on the basis of entire ecoregions, as World Wildlife Fund has done (Ricketts et al. 1999). These researchers examined the ecoregions of the United States and Canada based on biological distinctiveness and conservation status. They found geographic patterns of habitat loss similar to the previous studies in the areas most changed by human influences, and "truly staggering" losses of large representative examples of intact habitat. Only seven ecoregions in the conterminous states have more than 40% of their habitat intact, and one-third of the ecoregions across North America have few or no large blocks of natural habitat remaining. The mixed forests east of the Mississippi and the grasslands/savanna/shrub ecoregions, in particular, lack large blocks of intact habitat, posing a considerable conservation challenge for such species as migratory songbirds (Ricketts et al. 1999).

The WWF study also examined future threats, defined as habitat conversion, habitat degradation, wildlife exploitation, and invasive species, in assessing conservation status. Perhaps the most alarming information is that when these threats are added to the habitat assessments, the analysis found that out of 76 ecoregions in the conterminous states, only 6 in the Southwest and 3 others (Western Great Lakes Forest, Nebraska Sandhills Mixed Grasslands, and Cascade Mountains Leeward Forests) were *not* considered to be in critical, endangered, or vulnerable condition. Only the remote, sparsely inhabited boreal forests/taiga and tundra habitat types in Alaska still contain relatively intact ecoregions (Ricketts et al. 1999).

Midwest oak savanna is one of the nation's ecosystem types that has declined by more than 98%. © Jason Lindsey.

Wetland Loss

The loss of one general ecosystem type, wetlands, has received a great deal of public and regulatory attention in recent decades. This attention derives largely from the critical ecological services that wetlands provide to humans, such as flood control and pollutant filtration, and their role as fish and wildlife habitats. Prior to the 1970s, official government programs encouraged wetland drainage and conversion to uses such as agriculture. The Swampland Acts, for instance, granted 65 million acres of wetlands to states for conversion between 1849 and 1860 (Pavelis 1987). From 1940 to 1977 the federal government provided assistance in draining some 57 million acres of wetlands for farming (USDA 1997).

Policies actively promoting wetland conversion, together with a general indifference to wetland protection, were extraordinarily effective at reducing the amount of wetland habitats found across the country. In the 200 years since 1780, the United States lost almost a third (30%) of its wetlands (Dahl 1990). This figure, however, includes the vast and mostly unspoiled wetlands of Alaska. More than one-half (53%) of wetlands have been lost just in the conterminous United States.

The greatest loss of wetland acreage has been in the states along the southeastern coastal plain, along the lower reaches of the Mississippi, and in the upper Midwest (figure 7.12a). Florida has lost the most wetlands of any state: More than 9 million acres have been converted, totaling 46% of the state's original wetland area (Dahl 1990). A cluster of midwestern states, along with California, show the greatest declines in their wetland acreage (figure 7.12b). California leads the nation in percentage of wetland converted, having lost 91% of its original 5 million acres of wetlands (Dahl 1990).

Encompassing the vast Mississippi delta, Louisiana has a higher proportion of wetlands than any state other than Florida. Almost half of Louisiana's original wetlands, however, have already been lost. © David Woodfall/ DRK PHOTO.

Figure 7.12a–b. Wetland losses by state.

The United States lost almost a third (30%) of its wetlands over the past 200 years, including more than one-half (53%) in the conterminous United States alone. Source: Dahl 1990.

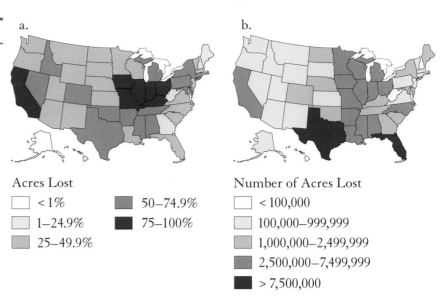

a.

b.

Acres Lost

☐ < 1%   ▨ 50–74.9%
▨ 1–24.9%   ■ 75–100%
▨ 25–49.9%

Number of Acres Lost

☐ < 100,000
▨ 100,000–999,999
▨ 1,000,000–2,499,999
▨ 2,500,000–7,499,999
■ > 7,500,000

Public policies for protecting remaining wetlands, and the controversy surrounding these regulations, has led to intense interest in the definition and delineation of these ecosystems (NRC 1995). Remarkably, however, our nationwide inventory of wetlands remains imprecise and fragmented, in part due to the charged political atmosphere that accompanies such studies. Nonetheless, the relative wealth of data on wetlands, compared to other even less easily defined and largely unregulated ecosystems, creates the impression that wetlands have declined more severely than the rest of the landscape. The Everglades, for example, serve as an icon for environmental degradation. Across Florida, however, most endangered communities occur on the dry uplands (Noss et al. 1995) because that is where people prefer to live. Indeed, many ecologists consider that nationwide tillable and buildable upland ecosystems, especially near population centers, have declined far more than most wetlands. The decline of wetlands, however, provides a revealing case study of how the human desire to exploit particular resources determines broad patterns of alteration of the natural landscape.

Conservation Status of U.S. Ecological Communities

Knowing the status of an ecological type as a whole, such as wetlands, provides a broad perspective on conservation challenges, but is not specific enough to focus detailed conservation actions. For example, across the United States some wetland communities are abundant and secure, like black spruce bogs in the northern forests, while others, such as vernal pools in California, teeter on the brink of elimination. Protecting those ecological communities that are at the greatest risk of disappearing thus requires a finer scale appreciation of ecological patterns.

A primary motivation for developing the U.S. National Vegetation Classification was to provide a consistent and rigorous way to assess the rangewide conservation status of relatively finely defined ecological communities for use in conservation planning. By identifying the relative rarity and imperilment of each community across its full range of occurrence, conservation efforts can be targeted toward those at greatest risk. In addition, by documenting the status of more widespread and still secure ecological communities, conservationists can identify and protect the best examples of these communities before they decline into a critical state.

To provide a means for incorporating ecological information into overall biodiversity conservation decisions, the Natural Heritage Network has developed a method for assessing the conservation status of ecological communities that is parallel to, and complements, the status assessments conducted for species (see chapter 4). Just as with species, conservation status ranks for communities are based on a one-to-five scale, with one regarded as critically imperiled and five as widespread and secure (table 7.8). Communities have quite different characteristics from species, though, and the factors used to assess their status have been adapted to reflect these differences.

Conservation status ranks are based on a number of relative endangerment factors. The two primary factors used in assessing the conservation status for communities are the total number of occurrences, or stands, and the total acreage over which the community is found. Additional ranking factors include the condition or viability of stands, known or potential threats, degree of decline from historic extent, degree of al-

Table 7.8. Conservation status definitions for communities

GX	ELIMINATED throughout its range, with no restoration potential due to extinction of dominant or characteristic species
GH	PRESUMED ELIMNATED (HISTORICAL) throughout its range, with no or virtually no likelihood that it will be rediscovered, but with the potential for restoration (e.g., *Castanea dentata* forest)
G1	CRITICALLY IMPERILED. Generally 5 or fewer occurrences and/or very few remaining acres or very vulnerable to elimination throughout its range due to other factor(s)
G2	IMPERILED. Generally 6–20 occurrences and/or few remaining acres or very vulnerable to elimination throughout its range due to other factor(s)
G3	VULNERABLE. Generally 21–100 occurrences. Either very rare and local throughout its range or found locally, even abundantly, within a restricted range or vulnerable to elimination throughout its range due to specific factors
G4	APPARENTLY SECURE. Uncommon, but not rare (although it may be quite rare in parts of its range, especially at the periphery). Apparently not vulnerable in most of its range
G5	SECURE. Common, widespread, and abundant (though it may be quite rare in parts of its range, especially at the periphery). Not vulnerable in most of its range

Note: *G* refers to global (rangewide) status. National (*N*) and subnational (*S*) ranks can also be assessed.

teration of the supporting natural processes, and the environmental specificity exhibited by the type.

Conservation ranks are customarily assigned by heritage regional ecologists along with various state heritage ecologists. As with species, a rank can be assigned to each community type on three geographic scales: global (the rangewide rank, preceded by a *G*); national (*N*), and state (*S*), though most communities thus far have received only global assessments.

Patterns of Ecological Rarity and Imperilment

Conservation status assessments are now available for most of the more than 4,500 associations currently recognized. These assessments represent a substantial accumulation of knowledge about the patterns imperilment among the nation's vegetation communities. More than half of the recognized ecological communities are of conservation concern, with 31% critically imperiled or imperiled, and another 26% considered vulnerable (figure 7.13, table 7.9). The primary focus of classification and ranking efforts to date has been on communities of high conservation significance, so although 18% of associations have not been ranked, or are unrankable with current information, completion of these assessments should not profoundly alter this picture. Relatively few of these currently unranked communities are expected to fall into the imperiled categories.

As yet, no association is considered "extinct" (GX), but a few are regarded as "historical" (GH). Like the American chestnut–dominated forests that once covered much of the East, these are communities that were once a part of the national landscape but that now occur nowhere in the United States or elsewhere in the world. Because the component species—

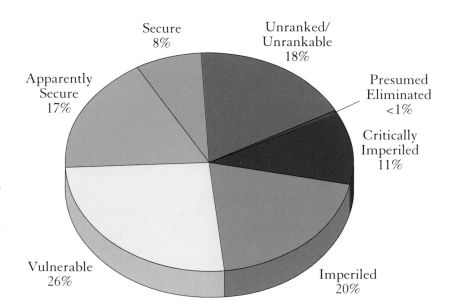

Figure 7.13. Proportion of ecological communities at risk.

More than half of nationally recognized ecological communities are of conservation concern, with status ranks of either critically imperiled, imperiled, or vulnerable.

a.   b.

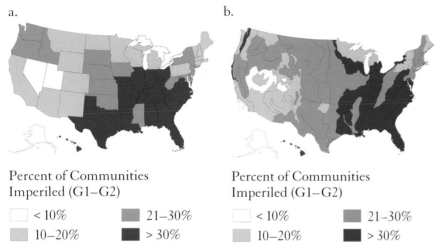

Figure 7.14a–b. Distribution of
imperiled ecological communities.

Percent of Communities   Percent of Communities
Imperiled (G1–G2)   Imperiled (G1–G2)

☐ < 10%   ▨ 21–30%   ☐ < 10%   ▨ 21–30%
▨ 10–20%   ■ > 30%   ▨ 10–20%   ■ > 30%

(a) More than 30% of ecological
communities in many midwestern and
southeastern states are regarded as
imperiled or critically imperiled.
(b) Ecoregions across much of the
Midwest and Southeast also show
high levels of community imperilment.

like the American chestnut—are not biologically extinct, however, they
may still be recoverable, at least in theory.

Figure 7.14 illustrates the percentage of all currently defined associations occurring in each state and in each U.S. Forest Service ecoregion
that are imperiled (G1 or G2). An astounding 30% or more of the natural communities in areas such as Hawaii, Oregon's Willamette Valley, and
vast portions of the Midwest and Southeast are in danger of vanishing
from our national landscape.

Seeing the Forest and the Trees

The United States is exceptionally rich in its diversity of global ecological types, many of which are better represented here than anywhere
else in the world. Of the 14 global biomes identified by Udvardy (1975),
12 occur in the United States—more than in any other country. Of these,
the temperate broadleaf forests, temperate grasslands, and mixed mountain systems all have more than a tenth of their global coverage in the
United States. Similarly, several global ecoregion types are particularly
well represented in the United States. On much finer scales, we have
documented more than 4,500 vegetation associations for the United States,
demonstrating the extraordinary level of ecological diversity contained
within the nation's bounds.

The level of responsibility for protecting these global resources matches
the significant proportion of their occurrence in the United States. This
responsibility is not to be taken lightly. Most of the United States' natural systems have been severely altered or degraded since European settlement. About one-fifth of the world's temperate grasslands, for example—
more than in any other single country—were once located within the
present-day borders of the United States. Today, these natural grasslands
have been reduced to tiny fragments. Overall, just 42% of the contiguous
United States remains in natural vegetation.

Table 7.9. Imperiled associations by structural class

Class Subclass	Number of associations	Number of imperiled (G1, G2) associations	Percent of imperiled associations
Forest	1,505	393	26
Evergreen forest	740	179	24
Deciduous forest	572	157	27
Mixed evergreen-deciduous forest	193	57	30
Woodland	813	317	39
Evergreen woodland	582	198	34
Deciduous woodland	175	88	50
Mixed evergreen-deciduous woodland	56	31	55
Shrubland	738	181	25
Evergreen shrubland	386	94	24
Deciduous shrubland	334	74	22
Mixed evergreen-deciduous shrubland	18	13	72
Dwarf-shrubland	129	37	29
Evergreen dwarf-shrubland	105	30	29
Deciduous dwarf-shrubland	24	7	29
Herbaceous	1,225	437	36
Perennial graminoid vegetation	964	375	39
Perennial forb vegetation	170	46	27
Hydromorphic rooted vegetation	76	8	11
Annual graminoid or forb vegetation	15	8	53
Nonvascular	12	5	42
Bryophyte vegetation	4	2	50
Lichen vegetation	6	3	33
Algal vegetation	2	0	0
Sparse vegetation	93	18	19
Consolidated rock sparse vegetation	42	9	21
Boulder, gravel, cobble, or talus sparse vegetation	15	0	0
Unconsolidated material sparse vegetation	36	9	25
Total	4,515	1,388	31

The conservation of our remaining ecological systems is a high priority, not only for their role in providing habitat for species that we value and for the ecological services on which we depend but also as components and expressions of biodiversity in their own right. Effective conservation of ecological systems must be based on a broad understanding of their diversity and patterns across the landscape on coarse as well as fine scales. Developing a sound understanding of the geographic patterning of these communities, the processes that maintain them, and the stresses that threaten them is critical for developing suitable conservation strategies. To assist in this task, a considerable amount of detailed information is now available on the distribution, trends, ecological relations, and conservation status of U.S. ecological systems (Anderson et al. 1998, Grossman et al. 1998).

The Conservancy, together with its natural heritage partners, are working to ensure the effective protection of our biological resources on an ecoregional basis. Ecoregions provide an appropriate scale and perhaps the best context for understanding multiple systems interconnected by similar ecological process, climate, and geologic history. The Conservancy's strategy for conservation on an ecoregional scale is to identify a portfolio of conservation sites that would be sufficient to protect every natural community and native species over the long term. The specific inclusion of ecological communities in such a conservation goal challenges us to identify the most appropriate means for incorporating ecological information into conservation planning and activities. The classification of U.S. vegetation types and the assessment of their conservation status provide a fundamental baseline for incorporating ecological information into conservation decisions. Protecting the full suite of ecological communities will depend on both identifying and preserving those that are rarest—whether naturally or through human action—as well as those that are still relatively widespread and intact. Indeed, these latter offer some of the best prospects for maintaining large, functioning landscapes.

An example of this approach is the conservation plan for the Northern Appalachian/Boreal Forest, an ecoregion that covers most of Maine and parts of Vermont, New Hampshire, and northeastern New York. To use ecological communities as conservation targets in this ecoregion, planners focused particularly on the size of patches these communities typically form. Communities vary greatly in their extent of occurrence and ecological specificity. Some, such as red spruce–balsam fir forests or maple-beech-birch northern hardwood forests, cover huge areas of varying topography, geology, and hydrology. These matrix communities can extend over as much as 1 million contiguous acres. Occurring in large patches, but not nearly so vast as the matrix types, are communities like red maple–black ash swamps or rich northern hardwood forests. These large patch communities may cover up to a thousand acres, but a single dominant ecological process—drainage or fire, for instance—usually bounds the community. At the other extreme, small patch communities, such as the rare slender sedge fen, occur only where a number of local conditions come together in a precise way. These small patch communities are inextricably linked to the landscapes in which they occur (TNC 1998b).

In the northern Appalachians, matrix communities blanket close to three-quarters of the remaining natural landscape but account for a mere 5% of all vegetation associations. Traditionally, conservationists would not have focused on such still-abundant and widespread communities. These communities are essential, however, to maintain the biological integrity and fundamental structure of the region. To encompass the full

To encompass the full array of biodiversity, conservation efforts in places like the northern Appalachians must consider both the matrix communities, which can occur over vast areas, as well as smaller patch communities, such as this bog. © Harold E. Malde.

array of biodiversity, both abundant and imperiled, the ecoregional conservation strategy for the northern Appalachians focused on identifying a network of sites which contained expansive areas of intact matrix forest but within which were embedded old-growth and smaller patch communities. Explicit criteria for identifying which community occurrences were of greatest significance relied on factors such as size, current condition, and landscape context—whether the surrounding area is intact, farmed, or intensely developed. This combination of scale, size, condition, and context represents one unified approach to the assessing ecological community viability and applying ecological classification and status assessments for conservation purposes.

8

LEADING THREATS TO BIODIVERSITY
What's Imperiling U.S. Species

David S. Wilcove

David Rothstein

Jason Dubow

Ali Phillips

Elizabeth Losos

On April 28, 1987, a biologist hiking through the remote Alakai swamp on the island of Kauai paused to listen to the sweet, flutelike song of a distant bird.[1] He recognized the song as belonging to a Kauai 'o'o (*Moho braccatus*), a sleek chocolate-brown bird native to these woods. He was surely aware of the significance of this particular song, for during the past four years this particular 'o'o, the very last of its kind, had been the object of much attention among scientists and conservationists. But he could not have known that he was about to become the last person ever to hear it. The next time biologists visited the Alakai swamp, the 'o'o was gone, and yet another American species had moved from the realm of the living to the realm of the dead.

The causes of the Kauai 'o'o's extinction are reasonably clear, although the precise role each factor played in the species' demise is debatable. Much of the bird's forested habitat was destroyed for agriculture, leaving only a relatively few safe havens on steep slopes or in wet, inaccessible places. Most of these places, in turn, were eventually overrun with alien species, including feral pigs that destroyed the native vegetation, as well as plants and song-birds transported to Hawaii from around the world. The introduction of mosquitoes to Hawaii, which occurred in 1826 when the crew of a sailing ship dumped the mosquito larvae–infested dregs from their water barrels, created additional problems for Hawaii's beleaguered birds. The mosquitoes became a vector for the spread of avian malaria and avian pox, diseases that were probably carried by the introduced birds. The native avifauna, presumably including the 'o'o, lacked resistance to these diseases, and many species quickly succumbed. Soon, only the forests at higher elevations, where cold temperatures kept the mosquitoes at bay, offered a disease-free environment for the native birds. Eventually, however, the mosqui-

---

1. A version of this chapter was published previously in *BioScience* (Wilcove et al. 1998) and includes tests for statistical significance.

Mosquitoes have infected Hawaii's native birds with a variety of diseases, contributing to the decline and extinction of numerous species. Ship crews dumping the dregs of water barrels accidentally introduced mosquitoes to the islands in 1826. © Chris Johns/National Geographic Society Image Collection.

Massive slaughter of American bison in the nineteenth century drove the species to the brink of extinction. Overexploitation is just one of the threats to biodiversity referred to by E. O. Wilson as the "mindless horsemen of the environmental apocalypse." Courtesy of Burton Historical Collection, Detroit Public Library.

toes reached even these forests, including the Alakai swamp, abetted by feral pig wallows, which created pools of stagnant water ideal for breeding mosquitoes. Thus a combination of factors, including habitat destruction, alien species, and diseases, contributed to the demise of the Kauai 'o'o.

Horsemen of the Environmental Apocalypse

As the loss of the Kauai 'o'o demonstrates, the accelerating pace at which species in the United States—and around the world—are declining is anything but natural. Biologists are nearly unanimous in their belief that humanity is responsible for a large-scale assault on the earth's biological diversity. The ways in which we are launching this attack reflect the magnitude and scale of human enterprise. Everything from highway construction to cattle ranching to leaky bait buckets has been implicated in the demise or endangerment of particular species. The "mindless horsemen of the environmental apocalypse," as E. O. Wilson (1992) terms the leading threats to biodiversity, include habitat destruction, introduction of alien species, overexploitation, and diseases carried by alien species. To this deadly quartet we may add yet a fifth horseman, pollution, although some might consider it a form of habitat destruction.

Surprisingly, there have been relatively few analyses of the extent to which each of these factors—much less the more specific deeds encompassed by them—is responsible for endangering species. In general, scientists agree that habitat destruction is currently the primary lethal agent (Ehrlich 1988, Wilson 1992), followed by the spread of alien species (Wilson 1992). Apart from several notable exceptions—including studies of North American fishes by J. E. Williams et al. (1989), endangered plants and animals in the United States by Flather et al. (1994, 1998), aquatic organisms by Richter et al. (1997), and imperiled birds by Collar et al. (1994)—few quantitative studies of threats to species have been conducted. More such studies are needed to provide conservationists, land stewards, and decision makers with a better understanding of the relationships between specific human activities and the loss of biodiversity.

In this chapter, we quantify the extent to which various human activities are imperiling plant and animal species in the United States. Our analysis has two parts: a coarse-scale examination of the numbers and types of U.S. species imperiled by the major categories of threats, and a fine-scale analysis of the types of habitat destruction affecting U.S. plants and animals protected under the federal Endangered Species Act (ESA). We also speculate on how these threats have changed over time and are likely to change in the future, and we conclude with a brief discussion of the implications of our findings for the long-term protection of imperiled species in the United States.

An Overview of Threats to Imperiled Species

To obtain an overview of the leading threats to biodiversity in the United States, we assessed nearly 2,500 imperiled and federally listed species to determine which were affected by the five broad threat categories described above—habitat destruction, alien species, overharvest, pollution (including siltation), and disease (caused either by alien or native pathogens). For vertebrate and invertebrate animals, we included in our analysis all full species with conservation status ranks of possibly extinct (GH), critically imperiled (G1), or imperiled (G2). Because of the large number of imperiled U.S. plants, we included only those full species with status ranks of possibly extinct (GH) or critically imperiled (G1). Additionally, we included all species, subspecies, and populations listed under the ESA as threatened, endangered, or officially proposed for listing as of January 1996. A total of 2,490 species, subspecies, and populations fit these criteria.

Detailed and reliable information on threats to individual species is often difficult to obtain. We consulted a number of different sources. For federally listed species, our primary reference was the *Federal Register*, which publishes detailed listing notices for all species designated as threatened or endangered under the ESA. For imperiled plants and animals without federal status, the Natural Heritage Central Databases served as our primary source of information. Other sources included a survey of biologists conducted by Richter et al. (1997) for aquatic species, and interviews with specialists in particular species groups and geographical regions. We included only known threats; we excluded potential or hypothetical ones. We did not attempt to distinguish between ongoing and historical threats, partly because such information is usually lacking and partly because the distinction itself is problematic in the case of habitat destruction. Nor did we try to distinguish between major and minor threats to each species, because such information is not consistently available. In those few cases where it was impossible to assign a particular human activity to one of the major threat categories, it was excluded from our coarse-scale analysis.

In total, we were able to obtain information on threats for 1,880 imperiled and listed species, or three-quarters (75%) of the plants and animals that met our criteria for inclusion in this study. The availability of threats information varied by taxonomic group, however—from a high of 97% for mammal and bird species to a low of 54% for dragonflies and damselflies; for plants, the largest single group included in our analysis, threats information was available for 71% of the species we reviewed.

There are some important limitations to the data we used. The attribution of a specific threat to a species is usually based on the judgment of an expert source, such as a U.S. Fish and Wildlife Service employee who prepares a listing notice, or a state natural heritage program biologist who monitors imperiled species in a given region. Their evaluation of threats facing that species may not be based on experimental evidence or quantitative data. Indeed, such data often do not exist. With respect to species listed under the ESA, Easter-Pilcher (1996) has shown that many listing notices lack important biological information, including data on past and possible future impacts of habitat destruction, pesticides, and alien species. Depending on the species in question, the absence of information may reflect a lack of data, an oversight, or a determination that a particular threat is not harming the species.

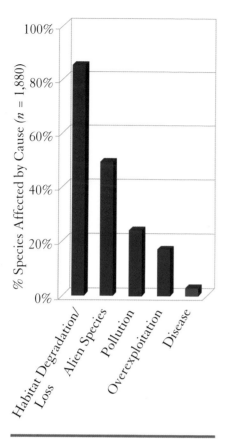

Figure 8.1. Major threats to biodiversity.

Habitat loss is the greatest threat to imperiled and federally listed species, followed by alien species. See also table 8.1.

Ranking the Threats

Habitat destruction and degradation, not surprisingly, emerge as the most pervasive threat to U.S. biodiversity, contributing to the endangerment of 85% of the species we analyzed (figure 8.1). Competition with or predation by alien species is the second-ranked threat overall, affecting nearly half (49%) of imperiled species. About one-quarter of imperiled species (24%) are affected by pollution, less than a fifth (17%) by overexploitation, and 3% by disease.

Different groups of species vary in their vulnerability to these broad-based threats (table 8.1). Habitat degradation and loss remain the top-ranked threat for all species groups in terms of the number and proportion of species they affect. Alien species, however, affect a significantly higher proportion of imperiled plants (57%) than animals (39%). Certain animal groups, most notably birds and fishes, also appear to be as broadly affected by alien species as plants are. For all aquatic groups—amphibians, fishes, freshwater mussels, and crayfishes—pollution ranks ahead of alien species and is second only to habitat loss as a cause of endangerment. Our finding that a large number of aquatic species are threatened by pollution may reflect our including siltation in the definition of pollution.

Significantly higher proportions of Hawaiian birds and plants are threatened by alien species than are birds and plants on the mainland (figure 8.2). This finding is consistent with numerous other studies suggesting that island ecosystems are especially vulnerable to harm by alien species (Culliney 1988, Simberloff 1995). Similarly, a much higher pro-

Habitat destruction is by a wide margin the most pervasive threat to U.S. biodiversity. © Gary Braasch.

Table 8.1. Percentages of imperiled or federally listed species affected by major threat categories

	Number of species	Habitat degradation/loss	Alien species	Pollution	Overexploitation	Disease
All species	1,880	85	49	24	17	3
Vertebrates	494	92	47	46	27	11
Invertebrates	331	87	27	45	23	0
Plants	1,055	81	57	7	10	1
Mammals	85	89	27	19	45	8
Birds	98	90	69	22	33	37
Reptiles	38	97	37	53	66	8
Amphibians	60	87	27	45	17	5
Fish	213	94	53	66	13	1
Freshwater mussels	102	97	17	90	15	0
Crayfish	67	52	4	28	0	0
Tiger beetles	6	100	0	0	33	0
Butterflies and skippers	33	97	36	24	30	0
Other invertebrates	104	94	52	19	46	0

Note: Categories are nonexclusive and therefore do not sum to 100.

portion of Hawaiian birds than continental birds is threatened by disease. By contrast, nearly the same proportion of Hawaiian and continental plants is affected by disease.

A Closer Look at Habitat Destruction

Given the primacy of habitat loss and degradation as a threat to biodiversity, a deeper understanding of this threat is necessary to help inform conservation efforts. For assessing the relative importance of different forms of habitat loss and degradation, we defined 11 major categories: (1) *agriculture*, including agricultural practices, land conversion and water diversion for agriculture, pesticides and fertilizers; (2) *livestock grazing*, including range management activities; (3) *mining, oil, gas and geothermal exploration and development*, including roads constructed for and pollutants generated by these activities; (4) *logging*, including impacts of logging roads and forest management practices; (5) *infrastructure development*, including navigational dredging, and construction and maintenance of roads and bridges; (6) *military activities*; (7) *outdoor recreation*, including swimming, hiking, skiing, camping, and off-road vehicles; (8) *water development*, including diversion for agriculture, livestock, residential use, industry, and irrigation; dams, reservoirs, impoundments, and other barriers to water flow; flood control; drainage projects, aquaculture; navigational access and maintenance; (9) *pollutants*, including siltation and mining pollutants; (10) *land conversion* for urban and commercial development; and (11) *disruption of fire regimes*, including fire suppression.

Figure 8.2. Threats in Hawaii versus the continental United States.

A significantly higher proportion of (a) birds and (b) plants in Hawaii than on the mainland are threatened by alien species. Similarly, disease affects a much higher proportion of birds in Hawaii than on the mainland.

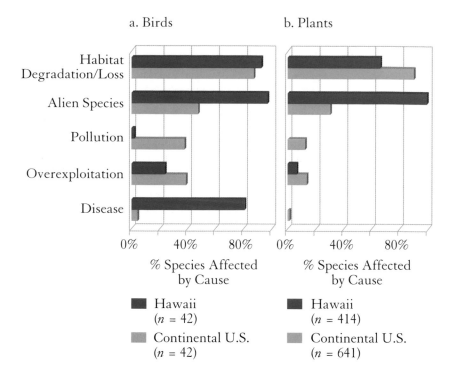

To assess the relative contribution of each of these threats to the loss of biodiversity, we tabulated the number of endangered species affected by each threat category. In this fine-scale analysis we focused exclusively on species, subspecies, and populations listed or proposed for listing under the Endangered Species Act (as of January 1996) because more detailed information is usually available for them than for imperiled but unlisted species. We included federally listed species from all 50 states plus Puerto Rico, the U.S. Virgin Islands, and the Pacific Trust Territories. A total of 1,207 species, subspecies, and populations were included in this fine-scale analysis of habitat destruction and degradation.[2] As in the coarse-scale analysis, we did not distinguish between current and historical threats or between major and minor threats. In many instances, the apparent threat to a species was actually spawned by another threat; wherever possible, we attributed threats to their ultimate cause, based on information in the *Federal Register* listing notices. For example, logging operations near a stream can lead to siltation, which is harmful to certain rare fishes and mussels. Thus, logging rather than siltation would have been scored as the threat to those fishes and mussels.

Again, we note some caveats with respect to the data in this analysis. Species added to the endangered species list prior to 1980 (238 species) tended to have fewer threats delineated in the listing notices than species listed in later years. Although there may be a biological basis for this dif-

2. The entire Hawaiian snail genus *Achatinella* is listed as endangered, with all 18 surviving species (of about 41 total) lumped together in the formal listing notice. In this analysis, therefore, we included the entire genus as one "species."

ference, we strongly suspect that it reflects the less controversial nature of endangered species protection at that time. Before 1980, the U.S. Fish and Wildlife Service was under less pressure to produce detailed justifications for its listing decisions. Also, as noted in our coarse-scale analysis, assessments of threats to individual species are often based on the subjective opinions of knowledgeable individuals rather than experimental evidence or quantitative data.

Ranking the Types of Habitat Loss

The most overt and widespread forms of habitat alteration are, as might be expected, the leading threats to endangered species as measured by the number of species they affect (figure 8.3, table 8.2). Agriculture affects the greatest number of listed species (38%), followed by commercial development (35%). Water development ranks third, affecting 30% of endangered species. Not surprisingly, the impacts of water development are felt most acutely by aquatic species. Indeed, 91% of endangered fish and 99% of endangered mussels are affected by water development. Dams and other impoundments alone affect about 17% of listed species.

Outdoor recreation ranks fourth, harming a surprisingly large number of endangered species (27%) and affecting a significantly higher proportion of plants than animals (33% versus 17%). Within the category of outdoor recreation, the use of off-road vehicles is implicated in the demise of approximately 13% of endangered species.

Among the major categories of habitat alteration, agriculture affects the greatest number of federally listed species. Courtesy of USDA/Natural Resources Conservation Service.

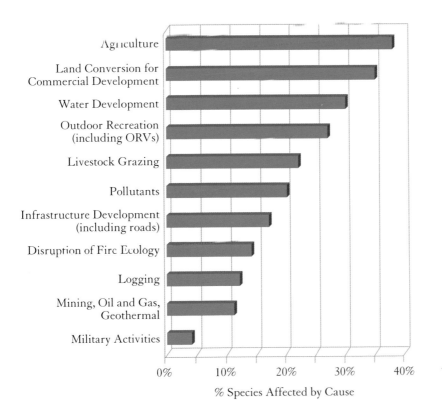

% Species Affected by Cause

Figure 8.3. Importance of various forms of habitat degradation.

Agriculture, commercial development, and water development ranked as the most frequent causes of habitat degradation affecting federally listed endangered and threatened species. See also table 8.2.

Table 8.2. Percentages of federal endangered, threatened, and proposed species harmed by various types of habitat destruction and degradation

Cause	Overall (n=1,207)	Vertebrates (n=329)	Invertebrates (n=155)	Plants (n=723)	Mammals (n=67)	Birds (n=91)	Reptiles (n=39)	Amphibians (n=16)	Fish (n=116)	Insects (n=39)	Arachnids (n=4)	Crustaceans (n=20)	Mollusks (n=23)	Mussels (n=69)
Agriculture	38	40	57	33	25	42	33	63	45	56	75	55	35	64
Land conversion for commercial development	35	30	42	36	31	33	56	44	16	67	75	65	13	29
Water development	30	47	66	15	10	22	28	63	91	21	0	70	48	99
Outdoor recreation (including ORVs)	27	16	19	33	18	15	31	25	9	41	0	30	26	4
Livestock grazing	22	17	10	33	19	20	8	19	16	15	0	30	9	1
Pollutants	20	27	66	7	5	10	21	25	55	26	75	55	48	97
Infrastructure development (including roads)	17	16	12	20	9	8	28	38	17	23	25	10	9	6
Disruption of fire regimes	14	5	6	20	7	8	5	6	0	18	25	0	4	0
Logging	12	16	25	7	12	18	13	19	19	5	25	5	13	46
Mining, oil and gas, geothermal	11	12	31	11	2	3	13	13	23	10	0	0	17	58
Military activities	4	2	1	5	2	3	5	0	0	0	0	5	4	0

Livestock grazing threatens about 22% of endangered species, ranking fifth among causes of habitat degradation. Again, this land use activity is particularly harmful to plants, affecting 33% of listed plant species, a figure significantly higher than the 14% of listed animals harmed by grazing. Pollutants affect about 20% of species, followed by infrastructure development (17%). Within the category of infrastructure development, roads alone affect 15% of species, confirming their reputation as a leading threat to biodiversity (Noss and Cooperrider 1994).

Alteration of ecosystem processes is increasingly being recognized as a significant threat to biodiversity. Disruption of fire regimes, for example, affects 14% of listed species. About half of these species are threatened by fire suppression, and the others are vulnerable to controlled or uncontrolled fires.

Logging and mining have contributed to the decline of 12% and 11%, respectively, of the endangered species we considered. Both of these activities are especially serious threats to freshwater mussels, probably because they result in increased amounts of silt and, in the case of mining, toxic pollutants in rivers. Finally, military activities, such as training maneuvers and bombing practice, affect about 4% of listed species.

Comparisons with Other Studies

Flather et al. (1994) catalogued the threats to U.S. endangered species based on information from the *Federal Register*, the U.S. Fish and Wildlife Service's *Endangered Species Technical Bulletin*, recovery plans for individual species, federal agency reports, and consultations with Fish and Wildlife Service biologists and state natural heritage program scientists. Their analysis covered 667 species, subspecies, and populations protected by the Endangered Species Act as of August 1992. Although the manner in which they categorized threats was not identical to our approach, the major findings from the two studies can still be compared. Flather et al. also identified habitat loss and alien species as the two most widespread threats to endangered species, affecting more than 95% and 35% of listed species, respectively. Comparable figures from this study are 85% for habitat destruction and 49% for alien species. The smaller percentage of species affected by exotics in the earlier study probably reflects the large number of Hawaiian plant species that were included in our study but were not on the endangered species list at the time Flather et al. conducted theirs.

Two studies have focused on threats to aquatic species. J. E. Williams et al. (1989) catalogued threats to 364 species and subspecies of imperiled fish from Canada, the United States, and Mexico; Richter et al. (1997) surveyed aquatic biologists to identify the threats to 135 imperiled freshwater fishes, crayfishes, dragonflies and damselflies, mussels, and amphibians in the United States. Narrowing the scope of Williams et al. to imperiled U.S. and Canadian fishes (254 species), we can compare their results with our own. The findings of the two studies are similar: These researchers identified habitat destruction and degradation as the most widespread threat to imperiled fish, affecting 96% of the species (versus 94% in our study; table 8.1). Next in significance was an amalgamated category of hybridization, alien species, predation, and competition, which affected 39% of the fish species (compared to our tally of 53% for alien species, which probably covers most of the same threats). Finally, overharvest and disease affected 4% and 2% of the species, respectively, in their study (versus 13% and 1% in ours).

Richter et al. (1997) concluded that the three leading threats to aquatic species nationwide were agricultural nonpoint pollution (e.g., siltation and nutrient inputs), alien species, and altered hydrologic regimes due to dams and impoundments. This is consistent with our own findings from the fine-scale analysis of habitat degradation, which identified pollution and impoundments (including dams) as significant threats to fishes and mussels (table 8.2). Our coarse-scale threats analysis, which included a larger pool of imperiled species than the fine-scale analysis, also highlighted the importance of alien species as a threat to U.S. fishes. Richter et al. (1997) point out that there are important geographic differences in the nature of the threats facing aquatic species. Aquatic species in the eastern United States are experiencing particular harm from agricultural nonpoint pollution; in the West the dominant threat is alien species, followed by habitat degradation and altered hydrologic regimes. These researchers attribute the distinction to differences in land use patterns between the two regions and to differing ecological sensitivities of eastern versus western species.

Using information from the U.S. Fish and Wildlife Service recovery plans, Schemske et al. (1994) identified the primary cause of endangerment for each of 98 U.S. plant species protected under the ESA. These authors did not distinguish between historical and contemporary threats, and they listed only one (i.e., the primary) threat per species, although they acknowledged that most species experience more than one threat. The top six threats in their study (in terms of frequency of appearance) were development (affecting 20% of the species); grazing (10%); collecting (10%); water control (8%); oil, gas, and mining (8%); and trampling (8%). By contrast, our coarse-filter analysis identified habitat destruction and alien species as the two most widespread threats to imperiled plants, affecting 81% and 57% of species, respectively. Moreover, in our fine-scale analysis of habitat destruction, the top five threats to plants protected under the ESA were land conversion (i.e., development; 36%), agriculture (33%), grazing (33%), outdoor recreation (33%), and disruption of fire ecology (20%).

The consistently higher percentages for all threats in our study compared to Schemske et al. undoubtedly stem from our practice of tallying multiple threats per species. Perhaps the most noticeable difference between the two studies is the importance attributed to alien species as a threat to rare plants. Schemske et al. considered alien species the primary threat to only 6% of the plants they studied, whereas we found that 57% of imperiled plants were affected by alien species. Their lower percentage stems in part from the small number of Hawaiian plants that were listed as endangered or threatened at the time of their study. Our results indicate that alien species are a frequent threat to continental plants as well (figure 8.2), although not necessarily the primary threat, which may account for the remainder of the difference.

Birds are perhaps the only major group for which a global analysis of threats has been performed. Collar et al. (1994) identified the primary threat to each of the 1,111 species they regarded as threatened. Because they evaluated threatened birds worldwide, focused on primary threats only, and categorized threats differently than we did, their results are not directly comparable to ours. Nonetheless, it is worth noting that both studies identified habitat loss as the most widespread threat. In Collar et al.'s study, the next most important threats, in order of decreasing frequency, were small range or population, overhunting, and alien species. In our study the next most important threats for U.S. birds were alien species, diseases, overhunting, and, finally, pollution. The higher rankings accorded alien species and diseases in our analysis are probably due to the Hawaiian avifauna, which constitutes a large fraction of endangered birds in the United States and is profoundly affected by those two threats. In our study we did not classify small range per se as a threat.

Finally, Stein and Flack (1996) assessed the impact of alien species on federally listed threatened and endangered species. They determined that of 958 U.S. species on the endangered species list as of September 1996, 43% had been threatened, at least in part, by alien species. Our slightly higher figure of 49% probably reflects the larger number of imperiled species included in our analysis, including many imperiled but not yet listed Hawaiian plants.

Changes in Threats over Time

As human activities and customs change over time, so too do the types and degree of threats to biodiversity. During the eighteenth and nineteenth centuries, unregulated market hunting for meat, eggs, pelts, and feathers took a major toll on many wild bird and mammal populations, endangering some and leading to the extinction of others, such as the great auk (*Pinguinus impennis*). The shift away from reliance on game food, combined with passage and enforcement of wildlife management and protection laws, has reduced the importance of overexploitation as a threat to imperiled species. Overcollecting does remain a serious threat to some rare plants, reptiles, and invertebrate animals. Because our study does not distinguish between historical and contemporary threats, however, it is not well suited to tracking these changes over time. For example, the relatively large percentage (17%) of species we document as being affected by overexploitation includes a variety of animals that were once hunted but are now reasonably well protected from this threat. These include such high-profile endangered species as the whooping crane (*Grus americana*) and California condor (*Gymnogyps californianus*). Similarly, pesticide

Since DDT was banned in the United States, peregrine falcons have been making a strong comeback. This pesticide is still used in some countries where peregrines migrate, putting these birds at continued risk of reproductive failure. © Janet Haas.

Alien species are the second greatest threat to imperiled species overall, and their impact is worsening. The deceptively beautiful purple loosestrife chokes wetlands, rendering them inhospitable to native plants and wildlife. © Stephen G. Maka/DRK PHOTO.

pollution is listed as the primary threat to the bald eagle (*Haliaeetus leucocephalus*) and North American populations of the peregrine falcon (*Falco peregrinus*), even though the principal pollutant harming both species—DDT—has been banned in the United States since 1972. (DDT continues to be used in other countries where peregrines spend the winter, however.) Thus our study may overestimate the number of animals that are currently harmed by overexploitation and pollutants.

Alien Nation

The problem of invasive alien species, on the other hand, is clearly worsening. There are no accurate figures on the total number of alien species now established in the United States, although the Office of Technology Assessment (OTA) (1993) has estimated at least 4,500, a number the agency acknowledges is probably an underestimate. What is indisputable, however, is that the cumulative number of alien species in this country has skyrocketed since the late eighteenth century (Sailer 1978, OTA 1993); this pattern holds for all types of species, from plants to insects to vertebrates. Given that the cumulative number of alien species is increasing steadily, one may confidently predict that alien species will pose an ever increasing threat to our native flora and fauna.

A somewhat more complicated question is whether the rate of alien introductions has increased over time, which would indicate a rapidly worsening situation for imperiled species. The data from published studies are ambiguous on this point. Reviewing the numbers of alien terrestrial vertebrates, fish, mollusks, and plant pathogens added to the United States per decade over the past 50 years, the OTA (1993) found no consistent increase for any of the groups. The greatest numbers of terrestrial vertebrates and fish were added during the 1950s and 1960s, while the 1970s saw the greatest increase in the numbers of mollusks and plant pathogens. On the other hand, a detailed study of alien species invasions of San Francisco Bay shows that there have been more introductions in recent years than in earlier periods (Cohen and Carlton 1995).

Many factors influence the rate at which alien species are introduced into the United States, so the lack of a consistent increase in that rate should not be surprising. Species can be brought into the country and released intentionally, or their release can occur as an unintentional by-product of cultivation, commerce, tourism, or travel. Each new development in the field of transportation creates new opportunities for the transport of alien species, from the first sailing ships to reach U.S. shores, to the building of the nation's road and highway system, to the advent of jet airplanes. As transportation technology changes, so do the opportunities for alien stowaways.

Empty cargo ships arriving in the United States used to carry dry ballast in the form of rocks and soil, which was then off-loaded around wharves to provide cargo space. Numerous insects and plants were accidentally introduced to the United States in this dry ballast, including such problem species as fire ants (*Solenopsis invicta* and *S. richteri*) and purple loosestrife (*Lythrum salicaria*). Today, ships use water for ballast instead of dry material, thus ending the spread of alien species via dry ballast. However, the release of ballast water into U.S. waterways has been implicated in the introduction of at least eight alien species since 1980, including the zebra mussel (*Dreissena polymorpha*), which has rapidly become one of the principal threats to the nation's imperiled freshwater fauna. Finally, the public's growing infatuation with ornamental plants, tropical fish, and tropical birds has led to numerous unintentional releases of alien species, including over 300 plants in California alone (McClintock 1985).

Population Growth

As the human population of the United States continues to grow, an increase is likely in the frequency of biodiversity threats associated with urbanization, such as infrastructure development, water development, and land conversion. Comparable increases in the proportion of species affected by agriculture are also a possibility. There is, in fact, good reason to suspect that a growing human population in the United States will disproportionately affect the nation's imperiled species. The analyses of imperiled species distributions presented in chapter 6, along with other studies such as Dobson et al. (1997) and Flather et al. (1998) indicate that many of the imperiled species in the United States are clustered in a relatively small number of areas. Comparing imperiled species hot spots (figures 6.7, 6.11) with a projection of population density in the year 2025 (figure 8.4) reveals several regions likely to experience increasing conflicts between development and endangered species protection. Hawaii, Cali-

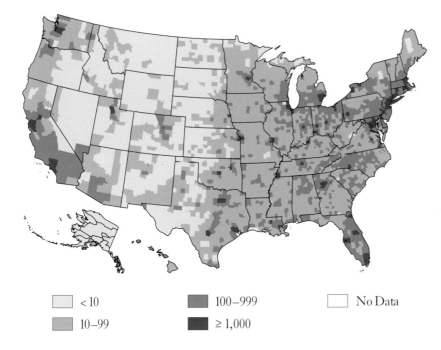

Figure 8.4. Projected U.S. population in 2025.

Estimated county population per square mile in 2025 based on 1995 U.S. Bureau of the Census projections of state populations. © Rodger Doyle 1998.

< 10	100–999	No Data
10–99	≥ 1,000	

fornia, and Florida are especially important areas for endangered species, and human populations in all three states are projected to increase well beyond the national average. Whereas the population of the United States as a whole is expected to grow by 14% between 1995 and 2010, the populations of Hawaii, California, and Florida are projected to increase by 27%, 27%, and 22%, respectively (U.S. Bureau of the Census 1995).

Climate Change

Climate change, while not regarded as a current threat to any of the species we assessed, is almost certain to become one in the foreseeable future due to increasing concentrations of greenhouse gases from fossil fuel use, land use changes, and agriculture. Climate models developed by the Intergovernmental Panel on Climate Change predict a 0.9–3.5°C increase in global mean temperature over the course of the next century (Houghton et al. 1995). Attendant to that increase will be a rise in sea levels of 15–95 centimeters and significant changes in the frequencies of severe floods and droughts.

These climate changes are likely to affect a broad array of imperiled species. The Nature Conservancy, for example, estimated that 7–11% of North America's vascular plant species would no longer encounter a suitable climatic regime ("climate envelope") within their present ranges in the event of a 3°C increase in temperature(Morse et al. 1993). Due to their small ranges and weak dispersal abilities, imperiled plants would be disproportionately affected. Morse et al. estimate that 10–18% of rare plants (i.e., species with a conservation status of G1, G2, or G3) could be excluded from their climate envelope due to climate change.

Likewise, Britten et al. (1994) noted that relictual populations of the critically endangered Uncompahgre fritillary butterfly (*Boloria acrocnema*), living atop a few peaks in the San Juan Mountains of southwestern Colorado, were extremely vulnerable to unusual weather events. They further hypothesized that a regional warming trend, as might occur due to global climate change, could eliminate all of the butterfly's habitat, essentially pushing it off the mountains and into extinction. Indirect support for this hypothesis comes from a study of another butterfly, the Edith's checkerspot (*Euphydryas editha*). Parmesan (1996) censused populations of this butterfly throughout its known range—Baja California, the western United States, and western Canada—and found significant latitudinal and altitudinal differences in the proportion of populations in suitable habitat that had become extinct. Populations in Mexico were four times more likely to have vanished than those in Canada, a north-south gradient in survival that is consistent with the predicted impacts of global warming on species' ranges.

An Accumulating Management Debt

The major findings of this chapter confirm what most conservation biologists have long suspected: Habitat loss is the single greatest threat to

Climatic warming due to global climate change would create particular problems for montane species such as the Uncompahgre fritillary, a butterfly that occurs only in isolated alpine areas atop Colorado's San Juan Mountains.
© John Cancalosi/DRK PHOTO.

biodiversity, followed by the spread of alien species. However, the discovery that nearly half of the imperiled species in our country are threatened by invasive aliens—coupled with the growing numbers of alien species—suggests that this particular threat may be far more serious than many people have heretofore recognized. The impact of alien species is most acute in the Hawaiian Islands, as demonstrated by the fact that virtually all of the archipelago's imperiled plants and birds are threatened by alien species, compared to 30% and 48%, respectively, for imperiled mainland plants and birds (figure 8.2).

Pollution, including siltation, ranks well below alien species as a threat to imperiled species in general, but among aquatic organisms, it nearly equals or exceeds alien species. As Richter et al. (1997) point out, the pollutants affecting the largest numbers of aquatic species are agricultural pollutants, such as silt and nutrients, that enter lakes and rivers as runoff from farming operations. These nonpoint source pollutants have proved to be exceedingly difficult to regulate and control (Young and Congdon 1994).

Finally, our analysis of biodiversity threats underscores the serious management challenges that conservationists face in their efforts to save imperiled species. A high proportion of imperiled species is threatened either by fire suppression within their fire-maintained habitats or by the spread of invasive alien species. Both types of threats must be addressed through hands-on management of the habitat, such as pulling up invasive plants and trapping alien animals or using prescribed fire to regenerate early successional habitats. Although the Endangered Species Act prohibits actions that directly harm listed animals and, to a lesser extent, listed plants, it does not require landowners to take affirmative actions to maintain or restore habitats for listed species. Thus, a landowner is not obliged to control alien species, undertake a program of prescribed burning, or do any of the other things that may be absolutely necessary for the long-term survival of a majority of our endangered species. In fact, it may be possible for a landowner to rid himself of an endangered species "problem" by literally doing nothing and waiting until the habitat is no longer suitable for the species in question.

Even those landowners who care deeply about endangered species and wish to protect those on their property face a daunting burden. The cost of undertaking these management actions can be considerable and, at present, is usually not tax-deductible. With a growing list of species in need of attention and less money to spend per species (Wilcove et al. 1996), the U.S. Fish and Wildlife Service cannot hope to cover the necessary management costs for most of the plants and animals it aspires to protect. Nor can it count on the goodwill of landowners to contribute their own money or labor for actions that they are not obligated to perform and that ultimately may result in restrictions on the use of their property. As a nation, therefore, we are incurring a growing "management debt" associated with our efforts to protect imperiled species (Wilcove and Chen 1998). Addressing this problem will require that the regulatory controls of the Endangered Species Act and other wildlife protection laws be

Merely prohibiting actions that directly harm endangered species is not enough to protect many of these plants and animals. Active management, such as use of prescribed burns, will be necessary to maintain or restore habitat. © Harold E. Malde.

supplemented with a wide array of incentives to reward landowners who wish to manage their property to benefit endangered species.

Halting the threats to biodiversity will require a combination of strategies and approaches that are appropriate for both the public estate and private lands (chapter 9). Only with a clear understanding of the nature of the threats facing imperiled species can we intelligently design conservation programs that are capable of preventing the imminent loss of a large fraction of the nation's natural heritage.

9

STRATEGIES FOR
BIODIVERSITY PROTECTION

After a half century of ditching, diking, and draining the swamplands   *Michael J. Bean*
of southern Florida, a major effort to undo some of the ecological dam-
age of those activities is now under way. In what is perhaps the largest
ecological restoration effort of its kind anywhere, the federal and state
governments are buying up large parcels of private land, changing dramatically the timing and quantity of freshwater flows to the huge "river
of grass" that comprises the Florida Everglades, and even restoring the
meanders and backwaters to the same Kissimmee River that an earlier
generation of engineers "improved" by straightening and channelizing
so as to eliminate its meanders and backwaters. Hundreds of millions of
public dollars will be spent in this effort. If it succeeds, the steady degradation of one of the most biologically diverse and distinctive environments
of the United States will be halted, and its recovery will have begun. The
wood stork (Mycteria americana), snail kite (*Rostrhamus sociabilis
plumbeus*), and Florida panther (*Felis concolor coryi*) are among the endangered species that this effort may ultimately benefit.

Several hundred miles to the north, in the sandhills of North Carolina, a more modest but no less noteworthy conservation effort is under
way. There, private owners of woodlots, horse farms, resorts, and even
residential property are actively managing their longleaf pines to encourage the presence on their own land of another endangered species, the
red-cockaded woodpecker (*Picoides borealis*). After a quarter century in
which many private landowners came to fear the presence of endangered
species on their land, sandhills landowners are now inviting them. The
state and federal governments are spending few public dollars in this
effort, and its scale is much smaller than that of the Everglades restoration. What drives the novel effort in North Carolina is a creative and flexible use of the provisions of the Endangered Species Act to encourage the

The Florida Everglades are the focus of one of the most ambitious and costly ecological restoration efforts ever. This unprecedented effort is intended to restore the flow of water needed to sustain this extraordinary ecosystem and its "river of grass." © Maresa Pryor.

The wood stork, which uses its touch-sensitive bill to catch fish and other small animals, is one of the endangered species that will benefit from efforts to restore the Everglades. © Gary Braasch.

sort of positive land stewardship that many landowners are willing to embrace.

As the Florida and North Carolina examples illustrate, the challenge of effectively conserving the natural biological diversity of the nation requires the use of a flexible and diverse array of strategies. At present, numerous federal and state laws, as well as still more numerous federal, state, local, and nongovernmental programs, focus at least in part on the conservation of biological diversity. This section does not attempt to catalog or examine exhaustively all of these laws and programs. Rather, it seeks to discern and explore the principal conservation strategies underlying most of these efforts.

This chapter draws a necessary but somewhat arbitrary distinction between strategies aimed at conserving biodiversity and strategies aimed at securing other, often overlapping, environmental goals. Laws and programs aimed at reducing air and water pollution, controlling the use or disposal of hazardous chemicals, planning transportation networks, revitalizing urban areas, or reducing suburban sprawl can and do have a profound effect on the nation's biological diversity. Similarly important is the National Environmental Policy Act and the numerous state laws modeled after it that require governmental decision makers to examine and disclose the expected environmental impacts of the decisions they make, including impacts on biological diversity. This chapter, however, focuses on those strategies that more specifically address biodiversity conservation issues.

While the conservation of biological diversity is a national concern, the task cannot be left to the federal government alone. For that matter, it cannot be left to government alone. Rather, all levels of government—federal, state, and local—and nongovernmental organizations must be engaged if the goal of conservation is to be achieved. The strategies appropriate to each will vary, but without the active involvement of all, the continued loss of our natural heritage is inevitable.

Although there are a great many different laws and programs that pertain to conservation, they utilize four basic strategies. The most fundamental of these is ownership of land and water. If one seeks maximum influence over the fate of the plants and animals at a given site, the solution is fairly obvious: Buy it. The strategy of acquiring land for conservation is long established and one that both governmental and nongovernmental interests can employ. For a variety of reasons, however, acquisition alone is unlikely to be a sufficient conservation strategy. A second strategy, one that is available only to government, is to regulate the use of land and water so as to further the goal of conservation. As will be described later, however, regulation has its limits, both legal and practical. Largely because of those limits, a third strategy seeks to further conservation by influencing land and water use through nonregulatory means.

Each of these three strategies addresses the conservation of biological diversity somewhat indirectly by controlling or influencing the ownership and use of land or water. A fourth strategy seeks to further the conservation of biological diversity more directly by regulating the use of wild plants and animals. Together, these four strategies comprise the tool kit available for conserving the nation's biological wealth. The sections that follow examine each of these tools in more detail and illustrate the diversity of approaches available in the use of each tool.

Owning Land and Water

Ownership of land, water, or any other form of property carries with it a significant right of control over the use of that property. Thus, conservation interests—both governmental and nongovernmental—have long used land ownership as a principal means of furthering conservation goals (NRC 1993).

As the United States expanded westward, it acquired huge areas from foreign governments and Indian tribes. Although much of this "public domain" land was subsequently sold or given to railroads, homesteaders, miners, and others, by the late nineteenth century the policy of wholesale disposal of public domain lands began to change in favor of retaining certain areas with unique values. The National Forest System has its origins in a series of forest reservations during this era. The National Park System has an even older genealogy, dating to the designation of Yellowstone as the world's first national park in 1872. The National Wildlife Refuge System got its start in 1903 when President Theodore Roosevelt set aside Florida's Pelican Island for wildlife conservation purposes.

Today, the U.S. federal government owns more than 650 million acres of the nation's land, about one-quarter of the total land area; excluding Alaska, the federal government owns about 400 million, or one-fifth of the total. For largely historical reasons, most federal land is concentrated in 17 western states. Four major federal land systems comprise the bulk of this acreage: the Bureau of Land Management's National Resource Land System (264 million acres); the U.S. Forest Service's National Forest System (191 million acres); the U.S. Fish and Wildlife Service's National Wildlife Refuge System (92 million acres); and the National Park Service's National Park System (83 million acres). The conservation of biological diversity is a paramount objective for only one of these four federal land systems—the National Wildlife Refuge System. Even there, the government's purpose in acquiring and managing specific areas has often been not the conservation of biological diversity per se but, rather, the conservation of some particular wildlife resource, such as waterfowl or, more recently, selected endangered species. National wildlife refuges are often managed to favor some particular desired suite of species. By contrast, the National Park System is generally characterized by a hands-off, let-nature-take-its-course management philosophy. The park system, though it contains many areas of exceptional wildlife abundance and diversity, consists principally of areas with outstanding scenic, recreational, or historical values (TNC 1977).

The remaining two federal land systems, the national forests and the National Resource Lands, are subject to a system of "multiple-use" man-

Through use of a creative and flexible provision in the Endangered Species Act, private landowners in North Carolina's sandhills (*below*, © William Campbell/ DRK PHOTO) are beginning to manage their forests in a way that invites, rather than discourages, endangered red-cockaded woodpeckers (*above*, © C. C. Lockwood/Animals Animals).

National wildlife refuges, such as Bombay Hook, are the only federal lands where biodiversity conservation is a primary objective. Refuges traditionally have focused on waterfowl production or single-species management rather than broader biodiversity conservation goals. © Jeff Lepore.

agement in which wildlife conservation is one of many potential uses, including grazing, logging, mining, recreation, and other commodity and noncommodity uses. Many of the lands in these last two federal land systems have unique values for biological diversity, but the mandate to manage these lands according to multiple-use principles has often given rise to intense conflicts between those promoting competing uses.

Most states also own significant areas variously designated as state parks, wildlife management areas, state forests, or state natural resource areas. While the purposes of such areas vary widely, the conservation of biological diversity is often at least one of the purposes for many state-owned areas. Local governments also own a variety of lands, including local parks and recreation areas, many of which contribute importantly to the conservation of biological diversity locally and sometimes nationally. Together, state and local governments own about 108 million acres of land in the United States outside Alaska, or about a fourth of the area owned by the federal government.

Among the purposes for which federal, state, and local governments have acquired land, the conservation of biological diversity is a relatively recent priority. As a result, there is often a rather poor overlap between the areas with the highest biological diversity and the areas where land is publicly owned and managed for conservation purposes. Assessing the extent of that overlap has been one of the primary purposes of the Gap Analysis Program of the Interior Department (Scott et al. 1996). If one could redistribute the acreage currently in public ownership so as to maximize its potential for conserving biological diversity, the resulting map of public lands would likely look quite different from the map of such lands today. For a host of reasons, however, that is unlikely to occur (Dobson et al. 1997). The alternative is to add to the existing land base by acquiring areas of exceptional conservation value.

Expanding the existing public land base faces a host of difficulties, not the least of which are the high cost of land and the limited public budget available for its acquisition. At the federal level, since 1964 the principal source of funding for acquisition of conservation and recreation land has been the Land and Water Conservation Fund. Each year an amount—currently $900 million—is credited to the fund from outer continental shelf oil and gas leasing revenues and various other federal receipts. Congress then determines how much money from the fund to spend for further land acquisition (figure 9.1). Congress has rarely decided to spend all the money available in the fund in a given year; thus, a "paper balance" has been steadily growing in the fund and now totals more than $11 billion. From time to time, conservation interests have mounted campaigns to free up much of this accumulated balance for further land acquisition, but so far they have not achieved any notable success. Indeed, annual appropriations from the Land and Water Conservation Fund have recently declined, in absolute terms and even more dramatically in constant dollar terms.

A separate and older federal fund for land acquisition is the Migratory Bird Conservation Fund. Revenues in this fund are derived from the

Although wildlife conservation is one of many potential uses on BLM multiple-use lands, competing uses like grazing often take precedence. © Rod Planck/Photo Researchers.

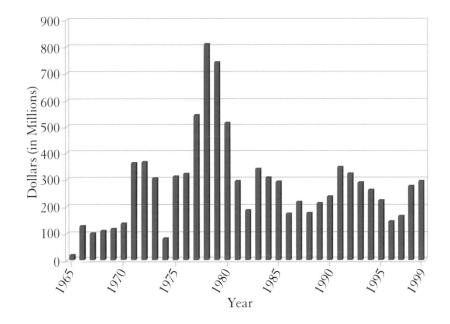

900
800
700
600
500
400
300
200
100
0

Dollars (in Millions)

1965   1970   1975   1980   1985   1990   1995   1999

Year

Figure 9.1. Federal appropriations for conservation land acquisition.

Although about $900 million is credited annually to the Land and Water Conservation Fund, typically just a fraction of that amount is actually appropriated and available for acquisition purposes. Source: U.S. Department of Interior 1999.

sale of "duck stamps," which are required of all who hunt migratory waterfowl, and more recently from special congressional appropriations. Lands acquired with money from the Migratory Bird Conservation Fund are included within the National Wildlife Refuge System and are selected on the basis of their potential contribution to waterfowl conservation goals.

The Migratory Bird Conservation Fund was one of several enduring conservation initiatives that began during the presidency of Franklin D. Roosevelt. Another was the Pittman-Robertson Act, which imposed a special federal excise tax on hunting equipment and provided for the transfer of revenues from that tax to state fish and wildlife agencies for the support of state-level conservation programs. As a result of the Pittman-Robertson Act and similar later legislation imposing an excise tax on fishing equipment, more than $300 million is made available annually to the states to support conservation programs aimed at game species. In many states, these shared federal tax revenues, together with receipts from the sale of hunting and fishing licenses, make up most of the budget of the state fish and wildlife agencies.

Shared federal excise tax revenues are an important source of funding for conservation land acquisition at the state level. Other sources are quite varied. Florida has dedicated a portion of its real estate transfer tax to fund a 10-year, $300 million per year conservation land acquisition program called Preservation 2000. Thus, Florida has enjoyed the distinction of spending more in some recent years for conservation land acquisition than the federal government has done in all 50 states combined. Other states have financed major land acquisition programs through special bond issues, including major new bond issues recently approved by the voters in California, New York, and New Jersey.

Another recent federal program aimed at promoting the acquisition and conservation of wetlands was created by the North American Wet-

Strategies for Biodiversity Protection   259

Joint management agreements are one of the newer conservation tools being used by The Nature Conservancy. Along North Carolina's lower Roanoke River, the Conservancy and a timber corporation have agreed to jointly make key timber management decisions affecting ecologically important bottomland hardwood forests. © Ken Taylor.

lands Conservation Act of 1989. It seeks to promote public-private conservation partnerships aimed at furthering the goals of a North American Waterfowl Management Plan. Wetlands conservation projects under this program may be carried out in the United States, Canada, or Mexico.

Public land acquisition for conservation purposes is significantly supplemented by acquisition efforts by private conservation organizations. The Nature Conservancy, the Trust for Public Lands, and Ducks Unlimited are among the national organizations that acquire lands for conservation purposes, either holding and managing it themselves, or ultimately transferring it to public agencies. The Nature Conservancy alone has protected over 10 million acres of land in the United States, sometimes acquiring a parcel of land outright, or, increasingly in recent years, through lease or management arrangements (figure 9.2). At the state and local levels, a host of land trusts have recently been created to preserve open space, farmland, historical sites, and other amenities. While land protected by local land trusts sometimes has significant ecological value, the conservation of biological diversity is seldom a primary purpose of local land trusts. As of 1998, more than 1,200 land trusts operated at the local, state, and regional levels. Collectively, these trusts have protected 4.7 million acres of land through acquisition, easements, and other means (figure 9.3).

Conservation Easements

Despite the creativity of financing evident particularly at the state and local levels, and despite the growing role played by private conservation organizations, ultimately the amount of money available for acquiring

Figure 9.2. Selected Nature Conservancy land protection activities.

Cumulative growth in acres protected by The Nature Conservancy through four land protection strategies: ownership, conservation easements, conservation leases, and management agreements.

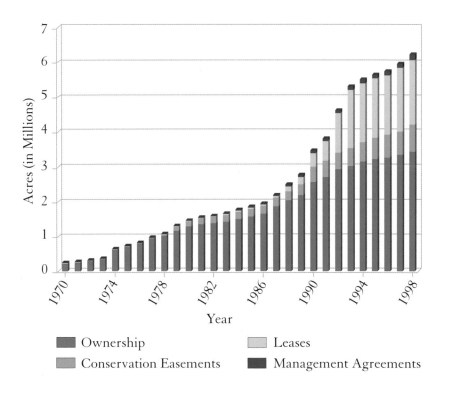

conservation land is limited. Those limits force conservation planners to consider not only what lands are most important to acquire but also whether those lands' conservation values can be protected by acquiring only a "partial interest" in them.

The law of property is a flexible and dynamic instrument. One does not simply own or not own a parcel of land. Rather, it is possible to divide a piece of land conceptually into multiple constituent elements and to have each of those elements owned by different owners. Rental arrangements are a familiar example; the landlord retains ownership of the property, while the tenant acquires a temporary right to occupy and use it. There are many other, less familiar types. For example, surface occupancy rights can be separated from the subsurface mineral rights, future interests can be separated from present interests, or development rights can be transferred or extinguished while the right to use a parcel of land for other purposes is retained.

Conservation easements form a key property interest. Typically, a conservation easement is donated or, more rarely, sold by a landowner to a governmental agency or a nonprofit conservation organization. By conveying a conservation easement, a landowner typically either gives up a right to use his or her property for a particular purpose—for example, development—or agrees to manage the property in a particular way—by selective harvest rather than clear-cutting of timber, for instance. Conservation easements can be in perpetuity or for fixed periods. They also "run with the land," meaning that they restrict the ways in which both present and future owners may use the land.

Conservation easements are a popular protection tool largely because of tax incentives that can provide substantial benefit to landowners making such donations. Indeed, such donations are a major factor fueling the growth of the land trust movement. Owning an easement is also a way for conservation organizations to help protect land yet avoid many of the management costs that inevitably follow from land acquisition. Thus, limited conservation dollars can be stretched over more acres through the acquisition of easements than through the purchase of land. This cost advantage, however, may not be as great as it first appears. Conservation easements are often carefully tailored to meet both the landowner's objectives and the conservation objectives of the agency or organization acquiring the easement. For this reason the costs of case-by-case negotiation and appraisal can be higher than the transaction costs associated with buying land outright. In addition, the agency or organization acquiring the easement must monitor compliance with its terms and, in the event of a breach, must be prepared to enforce it. These costs can also be significant and may become more so in the future, as lands subject to conservation easements are transferred from the owners who originally conveyed the easements to new owners who may be less happy to strictly comply with the easements.

Other considerations also have a bearing on the relative advantages of land versus easement ownership. When land is acquired by governmental or private conservation interests, it generally comes off local tax rolls,

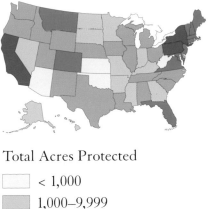

Total Acres Protected

	< 1,000
	1,000–9,999
	10,000–49,999
	50,000–299,999
	> 300,000

Figure 9.3. Land trust protection activity

As of 1998, more than 1,200 land trusts operated at the local, state, and regional levels, and collectively have protected 4.7 million acres of land through acquistion, easements, and other means. Figures do not include lands protected by national organizations. Source: Land Trust Alliance 1998.

Conservation easements can provide permanent land protection from development in exchange for tax benefits to the owner. This easement helps protect Idaho's Silver Creek Valley and allows a fourth-generation rancher to maintain his land as a working ranch. © Harold E. Malde.

Acres Enrolled

☐	0
☐	1–999
☐	1,000–4,999
☐	5,000–9,999
■	≥ 10,000

Figure 9.4. Enrollment in Wetlands Reserve Program.

Created in 1990, the Wetlands Reserve Program enrolled more than 315,000 acres from 1992 to 1996; applications were received for more than 1 million acres. Source: Wiebe et al. 1996.

a fact that sometimes generates local opposition or resentment. Land subject to a conservation easement, on the other hand, remains on local property rolls. To the extent that land subject to an easement remains in active agricultural or timber production, impacts on the local economy can also be avoided. On the other hand, the flexibility to adapt to changed circumstances and to alter management in response to those changes is greatest if one owns land outright. By contrast, changed circumstances can completely negate an easement's purpose. For example, an easement designed to protect the habitat of a rare species may be rendered useless if future research shows that the species' survival depends on somewhat different management measures than those to which the easement commits the landowner. Finally, because conservation easements are still a fairly new tool, it is unclear whether they will have enduring benefits for conservation, or whether legal challenges and the expense of monitoring and enforcement will show them to be a poor substitute for outright ownership.

Despite these uncertainties, the political balance at the federal level seems to have tilted decidedly in favor of easement rather than fee acquisition. At the same time that federal dollars for conservation acquisition have been declining, major new easement acquisition programs have been brought on-line. For example, the Wetlands Reserve Program, created in 1990, seeks to purchase conservation easements on a million acres of wetlands to be restored on former farmland (figure 9.4). The less ambitious Forest Legacy Program, also authorized in 1990, seeks to prevent the conversion of forested land to nonforest use through the purchase of conservation easements (figure 9.5). The 1996 Farm Bill authorized the new Farmland Protection Program to help protect farmland from conversion to nonfarm uses. This program makes federal funding available to supplement state funds for purchase of development rights on agricultural lands.

None of these three easement acquisition programs will necessarily contribute significantly to the conservation of biological diversity. Both farmland and forest land can be managed in ways that contribute little to biological diversity, or are even detrimental to it, and even wetlands restoration may not offer many benefits to some of our most unusual and imperiled biological resources. But by forestalling development and maintaining a "working landscape" where suburban sprawl might otherwise exist, these easement programs at least keep open the opportunity for later, more focused action that could more directly benefit species and their habitats.

Regulating Land and Water Use

If the acquisition of land or interests in land were the only tool available for conservation, much biological diversity would likely still be lost as a result of activities on land not in governmental or private conservation ownership. Indeed, such activities can even result in losses of biological diversity on land in conservation ownership. This can occur if the conversion of surrounding land creates an island of natural habitat trapped in a sea of incompatible land use. It can also occur if off site activities cut off or alter essential resources or ecological processes—for instance, the water flows into Everglades National Park, or the source of wind-blown sand needed to maintain the Coachella Valley's unusual sand dunes habitats.

Recent advances in our understanding of conservation biology, and especially the dynamics of species populations and ecological processes, make clear the importance of the overall landscape context in which conservation lands exist. Furthermore, protecting the nation's biodiversity will require the use by wildlife of lands outside these formally protected lands, highlighting the need for tools that can effectively influence how land not in conservation ownership is used.

One of the tools available to governmental agencies at all levels—federal, state, and local—is the use of regulatory powers to further conservation goals. This is a legitimate and appropriate governmental function for a variety of reasons, among them the fact that wildlife resources have always been considered public trust resources. Thus, in the United States, there is no private ownership of wildlife—that is, wild animals living in a noncaptive environment. In general, wildlife is a resource belonging to the people as a whole, not to the owners of land on which it may exist. Historically, at least, the "wildlife" that constituted a public trust resource was often understood to refer to those relatively few vertebrate species valued for hunting, fishing, or commerce. Over time, however, it has come to refer to an ever broader array of animal species, encompassing both vertebrates and invertebrates. Plants, on the other hand, are generally regarded as part of the land itself, and thus the property of the landowner. To protect the public interest in wildlife, therefore, the government can regulate practices counter to that interest. To say that the government can do this, however, is not to say that there are no practical

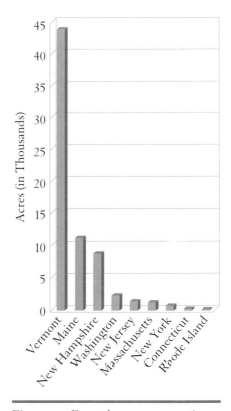

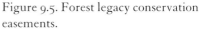

Figure 9.5. Forest legacy conservation easements.

The Forest Legacy Program was authorized in 1990 and seeks to prevent the conversion of forested land to nonforest use through the purchase of conservation easements. Source: U.S. Forest Service 1999.

and legal constraints on how far the government can go. Indeed, the tension created by those constraints is a frequent source of controversy.

Historically, the principal means by which the government used its regulatory power to conserve biological resources was through the control of hunting, fishing, and other activities directed at the collecting, capture, or killing of particular species. More broadly, many regulatory efforts aimed at a different purpose—for example, open space preservation, which coincidentally furthered the goal of biological conservation.

Governmental authority over land and water use has a long history in the United States. While zoning restrictions may reduce the value of any given parcel of land, they have generally been upheld against compensation claims because zoning restrictions offer both benefits and burdens to property owners. Generally, compensation is available only when all economic use of the property has been removed.

Local governments have long had primary responsibility for zoning and other restrictions on land use. Until quite recently, the conservation of biological diversity rarely played a role in local zoning decisions. However, low-density zoning, agricultural use zoning, open space set-asides, tree replanting requirements, and other common elements of local zoning decisions can clearly further biological conservation goals. Moreover, in a few places conservation itself has recently become a goal of local zoning efforts, though usually as a response to federal or state regulatory programs.

State governments historically have had relatively minor roles in land use planning decisions. However, state roles in planning for development in the coastal zone have increased in response to enactment of the federal Coastal Zone Management Act, which offered financial assistance and other inducements to stimulate better planning in the coastal zone. A few states have recently enacted "growth management" laws that recognize that certain local development activities can have impacts of more than local significance, including impacts on environmental resources.

Perhaps the state land use roles most directly relevant to biological conservation are state forest practices acts and state wetlands regulation programs. The former regulate a variety of forest management practices, including tree harvest within specified distances of streams, the size of clear-cuts, and reforestation efforts. The latter typically require state approval for development activities that affect wetlands.

The Clean Water Act and the Endangered Species Act (ESA) are the two principal laws that have increasingly involved the federal government in land use regulation that historically was a local prerogative. The Clean Water Act requires a permit from the U.S. Army Corps of Engineers to discharge "fill" into waters of the United States, including wetlands. Through judicial interpretation and regulatory action, the reach of the act has been substantially expanded, from an initially narrow focus on navigable waters and wetlands adjacent to them, to a more scientifically defensible broadened focus on aquatic systems without regard to traditional notions of "navigability." The cost of a more scientifically defensible focus, however, has been frequent political and legal clashes between landowner interests seeking unfettered use of their land and governmental and conservation interests seeking to protect environmental resources.

Similar conflict has also accompanied the imposition of restraints on land use to protect rare species under the Endangered Species Act. That 1973 law prohibits the "harming" of endangered animal species, a prohibition that the U.S. Fish and Wildlife Service has interpreted broadly to encompass certain forms of habitat destruction. Prohibitions under the Clean Water Act and the Endangered Species Act, however, are not absolute: Both allow otherwise prohibited activities under certain circumstances. A rarely used mechanism under the ESA allows a Cabinet-level committee, informally dubbed the "God Squad," to waive requirements of the act for essential federal activities. This was the mechanism invoked in proceeding with construction of the Tellico Dam in Tennessee despite the projected harm to the snail darter (*Percina tanasi*), which at that time was known only from the dam site.

Habitat Conservation Plans

A more common mechanism for authorizing exceptions to the harm provision under the Endangered Species Act is the use of habitat conservation plans. Habitat conservation plans were first authorized by the Endangered Species Act in 1982, but few such plans were developed and approved during the ensuing decade. In recent years, however, the number of approved plans has grown rapidly. Habitat conservation planning can be fairly simple, straightforward, and unexciting: one landowner proposing a single project and, in return for regulatory approval, agreeing to mitigate for project impacts on or near the project site. But habitat conservation planning can also be a creative mechanism through which local governments exercise their traditionally broad zoning authorities in order to reach the nontraditional goal of conserving biological diversity. This is the aim of a form of habitat conservation planning now under way in California and known there as "natural communities conservation planning."

Rather than reviewing development proposals on a project-by-project basis, this form of habitat conservation planning offers a means of more comprehensive planning that looks across a broader landscape and seeks to optimize opportunities for integrating the conservation of biological diversity with other land uses. It also provides a means of addressing threats to species that may not be addressed by the Endangered Species Act's harm prohibition. One good illustration is the problem of invasive alien species. Simply halting planned development projects in the habitat of imperiled species may be of little long-term value if that habitat is being changed as a result of the presence of exotic species. In such cases, halting a development project may only be a Pyrrhic victory in the course of a lost war. Through habitat conservation planning, securing a portion of the habitat and the means of effectively controlling exotic species may be a far preferable outcome both to conservation interests and to development interests.

An early habitat conservation plan resulted in the establishment of the Coachella Valley Preserve, designed to protect the endangered Coachella Valley fringe-toed lizard. This plan had to consider not only the dunes on which the lizard lives but also the sand source in distant canyons. © Harold E. Malde.

The nation's first habitat conservation plan, for the endangered mission blue butterfly (*Icaricia icarioides missionensis*) on San Bruno Mountain south of San Francisco, had exactly this justification. Housing development posed an imminent threat to the butterfly's habitat, but the butterfly would have been in serious peril even without the development because of the decline of native perennial lupines, its larval food plants, in the face of encroaching exotic weeds.

Another of the early habitat conservation plans, for the Coachella Valley fringe-toed lizard (*Uma inornata*) in California, offers yet another example of how such plans can address conservation threats that otherwise are beyond the reach of the Endangered Species Act. This endangered lizard lives on sand dunes along the valley floor that persist because they receive a continual influx of wind-blown sands originating in distant mountain canyons to the west. It might have been possible to prevent the development of the lands currently covered by the lizard's sand dune habitat, but without habitat conservation planning, it is doubtful that the source of the sand, and therefore the sand dunes, would have been protected into the future. The link between incremental development in the area of the sand sources, and the loss of lizards in the dunes, would have been too imprecise and the time lapse too great for this problem to have been addressed under the traditional prohibitions of the Endangered Species Act.

Habitat conservation plans have often engendered strong criticism despite these potential benefits. Much of that criticism focuses on the inadequacy of scientific information to make the sorts of long-term decisions about what areas can be developed and what areas must be protected that habitat conservation plans often entail (Hood 1998, Bean et al. 1991). This criticism focuses particularly on use of the "no surprises" clause, in which landowners are exempted from additional regulations related to changed circumstances after the plan is approved. This has the effect of locking in long-term development rights and management approaches for large areas even as scientists are still learning what these species and habitats need for their survival. Such arrangements may ultimately lead to unintended and unsatisfactory results. On the other hand, so too may incremental, small-scale development that does not warrant regulation under the Endangered Species Act or that engenders piecemeal or ad hoc mitigation requirements that accomplish little conservation over the long term.

Another recent innovation in the use of regulatory authority to promote the conservation of biological diversity goes by the name of "safe harbor" agreements. Whatever their purpose, regulatory programs often have unintended consequences, and the Endangered Species Act is no exception. Because the potential restrictions on land use stemming from the presence of endangered species are so great, some landowners have determined that they are better off avoiding land management practices that could result in endangered species occupying their properties. Thus, forest landowners in both the Southeast and the Northwest cut trees before they reach a sufficient age that they might serve as habitat for endangered species dependent on older-growth characteristics. Farmers in the Central Valley of California plow fallow land to ensure that endangered species do not occupy it between plantings. Still other landowners forego habitat restoration activities because of concern that restored habitats, if occupied by endangered species, will be subject to land use restrictions the landowners would prefer to avoid. Safe harbor agreements offer a means of overcoming these fears on the part of landowners and enlisting their help in conservation efforts through the simple mechanism of promising the landowner that, in return for beneficial management measures, the government will not impose added regulatory restrictions on the landowner, even if endangered species respond favorably to the management measures by occupying the land in question. In effect, the landowner is given a "safe harbor" from added regulatory restrictions in return for voluntary actions that benefit imperiled species. Encouraging early results from safe harbor agreements for the red-cockaded woodpecker in the sandhills region of North Carolina and for the Attwater's prairie chicken (*Tympanuchus cupido attwateri*) in coastal Texas suggest that in at least some cases it may be possible to improve upon the status quo by loosening the regulatory screws on landowners rather than tightening them.

Mitigation Banking

Mitigation banking is another regulatory innovation. In essence, mitigation banking is a means of carrying out mitigation activities, typically wetlands restoration, enhancement, or creation, in advance of any particular planned development activity, and then using "credits" from the successfully established "mitigation bank" as allowable mitigation for subsequent development activities. Thus far, its use has been limited largely to wetlands mitigation contexts, though it seems likely to have increased application in endangered species mitigation contexts as well.

Off-site mitigation banking is an increasingly popular approach to compensating for wetlands loss. The 11,500–acre Disney Wilderness Preserve is being protected and restored as mitigation for current and future expansion of Disney World in Orlando. © Harold E. Malde.

The advantages touted for mitigation banking include the ability to carry out larger-scale mitigation projects that have a higher likelihood of succeeding than if this work were done in a piecemeal, project-by-project fashion, and the greater certainty of success in mitigation when done in advance through banking than if done contemporaneously with project implementation. One of the major concerns with mitigation banking is that it will shift attention away from avoiding or minimizing wetland losses and instead encourage compensation for such losses through "technological fixes" such as the restoration, enhancement, or creation of wetlands elsewhere. Implicit in this concern is the belief that existing wetlands are likely to be more enduring or of higher quality than those achieved by restoring, creating, or enhancing wetlands.

Complications to Employing Regulatory Approaches

Recent innovations in regulatory approaches have been prompted by the recognition that traditional regulation has not always worked so well. As with other conservation strategies, there are significant practical, legal, and political limitations to the use of regulatory authority to conserve biological diversity. On the practical side, regulatory programs entail significant costs, both to the agencies charged with administering and enforcing them and to the landowners regulated by them. If the goals of regulatory programs are clearly understood and widely embraced, and the means of achieving those goals are regarded as fair and reasonable, the challenge of enforcing those programs is manageable. To the extent that those conditions are not met, however, the task of administering and enforcing such programs becomes significantly more complicated. Regulated interests find creative ways to do the bare minimum required or to comply with the letter of the law while acting contrary to its purpose and spirit. For example, some landowners comply with the Endangered Species Act by ensuring that they never create the conditions that might attract endangered species to their land (Wilcove et al. 1996).

Alongside these practical limitations are legal ones. The Fifth Amendment to the United States Constitution provides that private property may not be taken for a public purpose without "just compensation." Regulations at some point can trigger a legal obligation to compensate a property owner for the "taking" of his or her property. The line that separates reasonable regulation from regulation that goes too far and constitutes a taking of private property is anything but clear and has been the subject of numerous opinions from the United States Supreme Court. The Court has never articulated a simple formula, such as some percentage reduction in property value, as the bright line test to be applied in such cases. Rather, the Court has repeatedly emphasized that each case involves weighing many different factors, including not only the extent of the impact on the value of the affected property but also the nature of the regulation, the reasonableness of the landowner's expectations, when the property was acquired in relation to the date of the regulation, and other factors.

Few governmental regulations of private land use have been found to constitute a "taking" worthy of compensation. Nevertheless, many people believe that the burden of federal regulations is not distributed fairly, and the political backlash that has resulted can constrain regulatory efforts as much as practical or legal considerations. In recent years, the legislatures in many states and the U.S. Congress have considered a variety of proposals to require compensation even when the Constitution does not require it. Though most of these efforts thus far have fallen short of enactment, they remain a constant reminder that the political limits to regulatory powers may lie short of the legal limits.

Influencing Land and Water Use through Nonregulatory Means

Land acquisition and regulation are not the only strategies for conserving biological diversity. Desirable on-the-ground results can sometimes be achieved indirectly by influencing voluntary behavior. Thus, nonregulatory strategies represent a third way of furthering the goal of conserving biological diversity, one that both governmental and nongovernmental interests can employ (Fischer 1994, The Keystone Center 1995).

Tax Incentives

Tax incentives offer one means of indirectly influencing land use. As land values rise in areas facing development pressure, the disparity grows between the value of farm or forest land assessed at its "highest and best use" value—typically its development value—and its value as it is actually being used. Since local property taxes typically are based on highest and best use values, farmers and forest land owners often find themselves squeezed by rising property taxes. The rising property tax burden becomes yet another factor pushing them toward selling or developing their land.

To counter these pressures, in 1956 Maryland became the first state to enact "preferential assessment" legislation. Today, all 50 states have similar legislation, which typically allows farm or forest land to be assessed at its actual use value rather than its higher development value. Landowners who opt for such preferential assessments typically commit to retain the land in the preferred use for a specified number of years and will incur a substantial penalty if they fail to do so. In effect, preferential property tax assessment schemes represent rental by the government of privately held development rights. Though such preferential assessment laws may forestall the conversion of farm and forest land to development for a period, the tax benefits generally have not been sufficient to offset development pressure. In 1977 Maryland became the first state to enact a program of actually purchasing development rights from farmers, a tacit acknowledgment that its pioneering preferential assessment legislation had been insufficient to prevent the loss of the state's farmland.

A similar tax provision at the federal level values farmland at its actual use rather than its "highest and best" use for federal estate tax purposes. Heirs must agree to manage the land as a family farm for a specified period of years. Other federal tax provisions encourage the donation of conservation easements to qualified conservation organizations. The value of such easements can be deducted from income in the year of the donation, and the value of property subject to a conservation easement is reduced by the value of that easement for federal estate tax valuation purposes. Qualifying conservation easements must be permanent but may be for a variety of conservation purposes, including the protection of wildlife habitat.

In addition to incentives providing real property tax relief, there are other tax incentives that can encourage property owners to improve management of their land or that can encourage donations of conservation easements or gifts of conservation land. Some states have even enacted tax benefits to encourage specific conservation management activities.

Cost-Share Programs

In addition to various tax incentive measures, conservation of biological diversity can be advanced through a variety of cost-share programs, particularly in agriculture, in which state or federal governments agree to cover a portion the cost of specified land management practices that benefit the environment. The Wetlands Reserve Program, for example, in addition to authorizing the acquisition of easements over restored wetlands, also provides federal funds to assist in restoring those wetlands. The Forest Stewardship Incentives Program provides cost-share assistance to nonindustrial forest land owners to help in implementing forest management plans, one purpose of which may be wildlife conservation. Other such cost-share efforts include the U.S. Department of Agriculture's Wildlife Habitat Improvement Program and the U.S. Fish and Wildlife Service's Partners for Fish and Wildlife Program.

Dwarfing all of these is the Conservation Reserve Program. This technically is not a cost-share program but, rather, a program in which farmers enroll land for at least a decade and receive an annual rental payment for planting trees or grass. Established in 1985, the Conservation Reserve Program enrolled more than 36 million acres of farmland (figure 9.6). Originally targeted at highly erodible farmland, located principally in the Great Plains, the program has steadily broadened its focus to encompass other lands with environmental significance. The conservation of biological diversity has never been a stated goal of the program, but significant biodiversity benefits have resulted from it. Although participating landowners do not convey an easement to the government, they do convey a type of rental interest in land enrolled in the program. Thus, the Conservation Reserve Program could be considered a cross between a land acquisition program and a nonregulatory incentives program. However

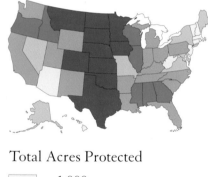

Total Acres Protected

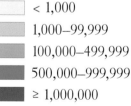

< 1,000

1,000–99,999

100,000–499,999

500,000–999,999

≥ 1,000,000

Figure 9.6. Enrollment in Conservation Reserve Program.

More than 36 million acres of farmland, located principally in the Great Plains, have been enrolled in this program. Since its inception in 1985, the program has steadily broadened its focus on erosion to encompass other lands with environmental significance. Source: Osborn et al. 1995.

regarded, it clearly shows the power of economic incentives to alter private landowner behavior.

Still another nonregulatory strategy involves bestowing recognition on landowners whose management of environmentally sensitive lands is exemplary. For nongovernmental organizations, this is a common practice intended to thank and reward, in a nonfinancial way, those individuals who demonstrate by example how private landowner objectives can be met at the same time that the public interest in environmental protection is furthered. Precisely quantifying the benefits of such recognition programs is impossible, but the benefits are nevertheless real.

Regulating the Use of Wild Plants and Animals

We have thus far emphasized tools for influencing land use because the single greatest threat to biological diversity is the alteration of habitat. Few species are seriously threatened at present by hunting, trapping, or commercial exploitation. This has not always been the case, and to a substantial degree, the current situation exists because such activities have long been extensively regulated, particularly by the states. Absent that regulation, these threats would undoubtedly be much more serious for many species.

Authority over hunting, fishing, and similar practices is shared by the state and federal governments, although the federal government generally has deferred to the states in such matters. Notable exceptions to this include migratory birds, marine mammals, and endangered species. In each of these cases, Congress has determined that state regulation was inadequate to accomplish the national conservation goal. In the case of migratory birds, federal action followed the negotiation of an international treaty with Canada that recognized the shared nature of the migratory bird resource and that without international coordi-

Trade in orchids, even those that are not particularly rare, like this showy lady's-slipper (*Cypripedium reginae*), is regulated under the Convention on International Trade in Endangered Species. © John J. Bishop.

nation either country could destroy the value of the resource. The Marine Mammal Protection and Endangered Species Acts were prompted in part by the recognition that state wildlife conservation efforts traditionally had focused on only a few species of recreational or commercial interest. Without federal initiative a wider spectrum of species, including nongame animals, invertebrates, and plants, would continue to be at risk (Bean and Rowland 1998). Most states have subsequently enacted their own endangered species laws, which supplement the federal prohibitions on hunting and fishing but often do not address the threat of incompatible land use.

International commerce in rare species of plants and animals is regulated through the Convention on International Trade in Endangered Species of Wild Fauna and Flora (CITES), of which more than 130 nations are parties. Trade in the rarest species for primarily commercial purposes is barred. For those less imminently imperiled, trade is permitted, but only under a system of strict regulation.

Unwelcome Invaders

The movement of plants and animals in commerce sometimes has conservation implications beyond the threat of overexploitation. When living organisms escape or are released into new environments, they sometimes become successfully established and wreak ecological havoc on the natural communities into which they were introduced. Indeed, as noted in chapter 8, nonindigenous species represent the second most common cause of endangerment in the United States. The release of nonindigenous organisms is sometimes deliberate but is more often accidental or unintended. The pathways for such introductions are myriad. They include ballast water in oceangoing vessels, which take on water in one area and discharge it in another, releasing countless non-native organisms in the process; nursery stock carrying pests and other organisms in the soil surrounding the roots or on or in the plant itself; aquaculture facilities from which nonindigenous species escape as a result of storms, facility failures, or other reasons; and imported logs, fruits, vegetables, fish, and shellfish from throughout the world.

Strategies for dealing with the threat are only now emerging and focus on preventing new introductions, detecting and eradicating new infestations as early as possible, and controlling and managing any well-established invasions. In the United States, deliberate importation of known harmful species has long been prohibited. This "prohibited list" approach, however, is ineffective, since the potential for injury is often discovered only after a species has become established and begun causing damage. A more sensible approach would be to consider any foreign species potentially harmful unless otherwise indicated. In this regard, an "approved list" identifying those species known or suspected to be ecologically benign would be a better basis for making importation decisions.

Recent legislation regulating ballast water discharges promises to reduce the threats from this source. This action came only after the extraordinary ecological and economic damage caused by the unwitting introduction of the zebra mussel through this means, and the legislation still applies only to certain waterways. Quarantine requirements for imported live animals and strict phytosanitary requirements for imported fruits, vegetables, and other foodstuffs can reduce threats as well, but the ever increasing globalization of trade and movement of peoples makes virtually inevitable the risk that injurious organisms will escape detection.

The threat to biological diversity from nonindigenous organisms is not simply from "foreign" species becoming established in the United States. The intentional or unintentional introduction of species native to one part of the country into another can have ecological consequences no less dramatic. The introduction of native game fish into naturally fishless alpine lakes in the West has severely disrupted the natural communities of those lakes, as have similar introductions into many western rivers. No federal law regulates this practice, although many states now require an evaluation of potential environmental consequences before allowing deliberate introduction of nonindigenous species into natural environments.

Ballast water from freighters has been a particularly important vector for transporting alien species, and efforts are under way to regulate their discharge into U.S. waterways. © Holt Confer/DRK PHOTO.

Strategies for Conservation: A Synthesis

Conservation of biological diversity cannot be accomplished by any of the above strategies alone. Nor can effective conservation be achieved by government alone, or by any individual level of government. Each strategy has its practical, financial, and legal limits. Each level of government has its own sphere of authority and limitations. Each private conservation organization has its particular strengths and weaknesses. Understanding and being sensitive to these is a necessity if an effective coordination of these various strategies is to be achieved.

It is also important to keep in mind that though public support of conservation goals has remained strong, differing times require different emphases in the choice of strategies. At the beginning of the twentieth century, overharvest of birds and other species for their feathers, their meat, or their fur was a dominant conservation concern. As the century draws to a close, that threat has receded in importance for most species (although it remains a concern for many ocean fish stocks). The tools for dealing with yesterday's threats are not likely to be well suited for handling tomorrow's challenges. In addition, in the last half century, many shifts in national mood have occurred with respect to the relative roles of state and federal governments, the need for stringent regulation of private activity, the importance of competing social goals for limited public spending, and other factors. Smart conservation recognizes that each of these shifts presents not just challenges but also opportunities. The availability of a diverse array of conservation strategies, and the ability to shift emphasis from one to another as the prevailing sentiments dictate, will make possible a sustained effort at conserving the nation's biological diversity.

10

OWNING UP TO OUR RESPONSIBILITIES
Who Owns Lands Important for Biodiversity?

Standing watch over San Francisco Bay, Ring Mountain lies just a short stretch north of the Golden Gate Bridge. The mountain rises from the Tiburon Peninsula, lined with exclusive residential communities and one of San Francisco's most desirable suburbs. The slopes of Ring Mountain are exclusive in another sense as well: Here lives the world's sole population of the Tiburon mariposa lily (*Calochortus tiburonensis*). Found in the open grasslands near the summit of the mountain, this attractive flower grows only on an unusual rock type known as serpentine for its slick, scalelike, blue-green appearance. A product of California's restless geology, these rock formations also support several other rare plant species, including the Tiburon paintbrush (*Castilleja affinis* ssp. *neglecta*) and Tiburon jewelflower (*Streptanthus niger*). While serpentine occurs elsewhere in California and beyond, the Tiburon mariposa lily does not.

The view from atop Ring Mountain, a spectacular vista of water, mountains, and skyscrapers, would fetch top dollar for residential development. Bulldozers may well have overrun this unique piece of real estate if The Nature Conservancy had not purchased and managed it as a nature preserve. In buying the land on Ring Mountain, the Conservancy also bought the earth's entire population of the Tiburon mariposa lily. This created a weighty responsibility, but it also freed the organization to take any action necessary to ensure the survival of this flower and Ring Mountain's other rare species. Ownership offers the most direct and absolute way to offer conservation to those plants and animals inhabiting a piece of land. On the other hand, land ownership also conveys rights that allow management of property in ways not nearly so beneficial to our native species.

Of the four basic strategies for biodiversity conservation discussed in the previous chapter, three relate directly to land: owning and managing

Craig R. Groves

Lynn S. Kutner

David M. Stoms

Michael P. Murray

J. Michael Scott

Michael Schafale

Alan S. Weakley

Robert L. Pressey

The serpentine slopes of Ring Mountain (*below*, © Lynn Lozier/TNC), just across the bay from San Francisco, are home to several rare plant species, including the Tiburon mariposa lily (*above*, © Steve McCormick/TNC), found nowhere else on Earth.

land; regulating land use; and influencing land use through nonregulatory means. If we are to understand not only the current condition of species and ecosystems in the United States but also the opportunities and challenges for their long-term protection, we must also understand how the underlying natural patterns relate to the patterns of land ownership and management that have been laid atop them.

The influence of land ownership and management, good or bad, cannot be overstated. Quite simply, landowners have the ability to conserve these biological resources or degrade and, in some cases, destroy them. This is as true for public land managers as it is for private owners, and for corporations or agencies that control vast acreages as for owners of small woodlots.

The outlook for imperiled species, however, differs for those that occur on private lands versus those that occur on the public estate. And there are different opportunities available for species that inhabit lands managed primarily for their natural values rather than for extractive uses. There are even different legal issues that pertain to plants versus animals: Most higher animals are regarded as property of the state, even when they are found on private lands, while plants "convey" with property title.

This chapter examines the best available data on who owns the land on which imperiled species occur. These data affirm that all major landowners have important roles to play in the conservation of imperiled species, though some have greater responsibility than others. That conclusion carries important consequences for how and where we must work, but it should not obscure a significant and troubling gap in our information: We simply do not know the ownership status for land on which many of these imperiled species occur. Successful conservation will depend, in part, on determining and tracking land ownership much more closely.

A system of protected areas or reserves remains the cornerstone of conservation (WRI et al. 1992). As the analysis in this chapter will show, however, the existing reserve network covers only a small fraction of the species at risk in the United States. Conservationists and ecologists increasingly recognize that improving the effectiveness of reserves means selecting and designing them so that they incorporate not just species and populations but communities and ecosystems (Scott et al. 1993).

Ecological communities can serve as surrogates for species in setting conservation priorities (Csuti and Kiester 1996). Furthermore, a systematic effort to protect communities or ecosystem types could prevent many species from becoming extinct (Scott and Wilcove 1998). Although a national classification of these communities exists (Anderson et al. 1998), there is no national-level data on their distribution that is comparable to the detailed species distributional data used in this assessment. At least in some regions, however, we have enough data on communities to help make conservation decisions. In addition, we often have better information on the land ownership of these communities and the degree to which these lands are being legally protected than we do for species. The second half of this chapter explores three different approaches for how information on the distribution of ecological communities and land ownership can be used to target conservation efforts on a scale above the species and, concurrently, to determine how well ecological communities are represented within the existing network of conservation lands.

Species Distributions and Land Ownership

The options available for managing and conserving species depend on knowing with specificity which plants and animals occur on different lands. Two crucial questions are: To what degree are imperiled and endangered species found on public lands, and how are we doing at protecting them? Conversely, how many species are found exclusively on private lands?

Despite the clear importance of answering these questions, relatively little information currently exists relating the distribution of imperiled species to land ownership patterns. Two previous studies, one by the U.S. Natural Heritage Programs (Natural Heritage Data Center Network 1993; Stein et al. 1995a) and the other by the U.S. Government Accounting Office (USGAO 1995), examined the significance of federal lands for maintaining federally listed endangered species. The two studies came to similar conclusions, although they used substantially different methods. The heritage study found that only about half of federally listed species occurred at all on federal lands, while the GAO report calculated that between one-third and one-half of federally listed species did not occur on federal lands.

Our analysis builds on the 1993 heritage study and updates it in several important respects. In addition to examining the distribution of species with federal status, we also assess the distribution of those species classified as imperiled (G1 or G2) by the heritage network. We also examine species distribution patterns not only for federal lands but also for other major landowner types throughout the United States. This includes land owned or managed by local or state government, private property owners, Native American tribes, and conservation nonprofits like The Nature Conservancy.

Heritage data are well positioned to answer questions about land ownership and conservation. While natural heritage inventory efforts focus on documenting the locations for species and ecological communities at greatest risk, heritage programs also record a variety of ancillary data about each documented location. One of the principal pieces of nonbiological information relates to ownership or management of the area on which the species or ecosystem occurs. Except in the case of public agencies, this information normally characterizes the general type of landowner (i.e., federal, state, or local agencies; corporations; private nonprofits; or unspecified private) rather than naming specific landowners. State heritage programs store this information, together with a variety of other data, in their databases, which collectively form the basis for the national database on imperiled and endangered species presented in this volume. Because landowner type typically is recorded, this aggregated national data set of more than 175,000 occurrence records—which generally reflect species populations or ecological communities—provides an excellent opportunity to address national-level questions regarding the ownership and management of lands on which imperiled and endangered species reside. After screening for quality control (see chapter 2), the nationally aggregated data yielded data sets of 39,521 population occurrences for imperiled species and 47,163 populations for species with federal status (endangered, threatened, proposed, and candidate species).

Determining land ownership can sometimes be difficult, and not all heritage programs routinely record land ownership information. The problem is especially acute for aquatic organisms, but for these organisms, determining ownership in the strict sense is probably less significant for influencing conservation than identifying the parties that have responsibility for the quality and flow of water. For these reasons, specific land ownership types cannot be attributed to a number of occurrence records in this national data set. Many heritage programs also tend to conduct more inventories of public lands than private lands, introducing another potential complication. Nonetheless, these population-level data represent the most comprehensive information currently available about the detailed distribution of these imperiled and endangered species, and one of the only sources of information about the ownership and management status of these populations (see chapter 2 for further details and limitations of these data).

Land ownership patterns form a complex mosaic across the United States; consequently, where federally listed and imperiled species are found, they cut across this mosaic (figures 10.1 and 10.2). Some of these patterns are evident even from a casual perusal of these maps. For instance, federal lands are a dominant component of the western U.S. landscape, strikingly illustrated by the many populations on federal ownership shown as blue dots. Other regions with concentrations of imperiled or federally listed species on federal lands include the Florida Panhandle and central Appalachian Mountains. Imperiled and federally listed species on private lands are found in greatest concentrations in the Great Plains, the Midwest, the Southeast, and portions of California.

Significance of Public Lands for Species Conservation

The U.S. government owns roughly 400 million acres of land, not including federal holdings in Alaska. Most of this land is concentrated in the West: The federal government owns nearly half of the land in the 11 westernmost states, and more than 80% of Nevada. In contrast, federal lands account for roughly 10% of the 6 southeastern states and just 5% of the 6 New England states, although New York, at 0.4%, has smallest proportion of federal land.

Based on an analysis of the data presented in figure 10.1, federal lands support at least one example of about three-fifths (59%) of federally listed

Landowner Types
- ● Federal
- ● State
- ● Private
- ● Unknown

species, and a similar percentage of imperiled species (figure 10.3).[1] State lands, which account for just over 90 million acres excluding Alaska, harbor at least one example of 43% of imperiled species and 58% of federally listed species. In some states, such as Florida, state agencies are carrying out aggressive natural area conservation programs. These figures indicate that these efforts may be having success in protecting critical biodiversity, and not just scenic areas. At the same time, significant numbers of imperiled or listed species occur on state lands that are unprotected yet could probably be managed in a way that would benefit these species.

Due to numerous federal laws and policies aimed at conserving natural resources, federal land management agencies can play a special role in the conservation of imperiled and endangered species. When we look in detail at the distribution of these species and their populations on the federal estate (figure 10.4), we find that Department of Defense lands contain the most federally listed species of any agency, with at least one example of about one-fifth (21%) of all federally listed species. This find-

Figure 10.1. Land ownership for federally listed species.

Occurrences of species with federal status (endangered, threatened, proposed, and candidates) are displayed according to the major landowner types on which they are found. Source: State Natural Heritage Data Centers 1996.

1. Analysis of the current data set provides a somewhat higher figure for federally listed species than the 50% calculated as part of our earlier study (Natural Heritage Data Center Network 1993, Stein et al. 1995a). The heritage network has carried out a significant amount of federal lands inventory work since the time of the previous study, and that study included only the 728 species that were listed as endangered or threatened as of March 1993. The current analysis considers a larger pool of species with federal status: 1,184 species, constituting endangered, threatened, proposed, and candidates listed as of 1996.

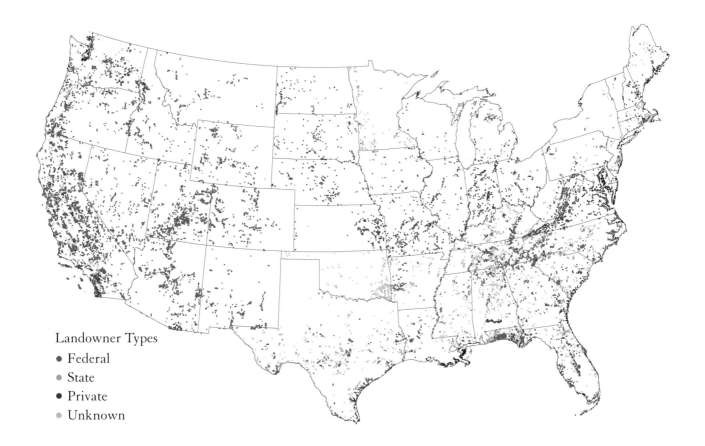

Landowner Types
- ● Federal
- ● State
- ● Private
- ● Unknown

Figure 10.2. Land ownership for
imperiled species.

*Occurrences of imperiled species (G1–G2)
are displayed according to the major
landowner types on which they are found.
Source: State Natural Heritage Data
Centers 1996.*

ing is particularly striking, given that these lands represent just 3% of the
federal estate. Many military bases turn out to be strategically placed, not
just from a military standpoint but also from a biological perspective.
Often found in coastal areas with fast-growing human populations, many
of the Department of Defense land holdings, such as southern California's
Camp Pendelton Marine Base, are becoming islands of natural habitat
in rapidly urbanizing regions.

The greatest number of imperiled species are found on U.S. Forest
Service lands (26%). Lands of the U.S. Fish and Wildlife Service, which
as an agency has mandate responsibility for the Endangered Species Act,
provide shelter for the fewest federally listed and imperiled species. This
seemingly incongruous result is apparently a reflection of the agency's
historical focus on acquiring refuges that provide opportunities for hunting, particularly waterfowl hunting, rather for protecting endangered
species (NRC 1993). Our findings in these analyses are consistent with
an earlier study (Flather et al. 1994) that used a different data set but
reached similar conclusions.

A FOCUS ON POPULATIONS While species may be the target of conservation efforts, populations are the operative unit for conservation action.
Analyzing ownership patterns for the population occurrences displayed
on figures 10.1 and 10.2, one discovers that about one-third of   popula-

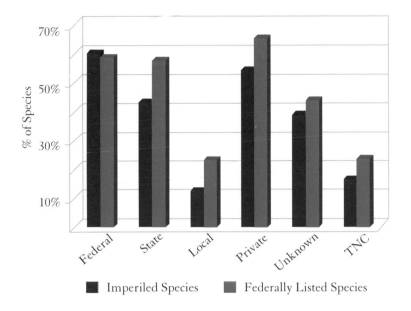

Figure 10.3. Percent of species represented on major landowner types.

The greatest number of federally listed species occur on private lands, while the most imperiled species are found on federal lands. Note: A species is recorded for a particular jurisdiction if it occurs at least once on that ownership type.

tions for both federally listed and imperiled species are found on the federal lands (figure 10.5). Although this percentage is roughly equivalent to the percentage of U.S. land under federal ownership (30%), excluding Alaska—which represents a huge expanse of the federal estate yet has relatively few imperiled or federally listed species—the federal government manages less than one-fifth of the land area. The disparity between the proportion of imperiled and endangered species populations found on federal lands and what these lands represent as a percentage of the overall landscape emphasizes the disproportionate importance that federal lands have for maintaining imperiled and endangered species.

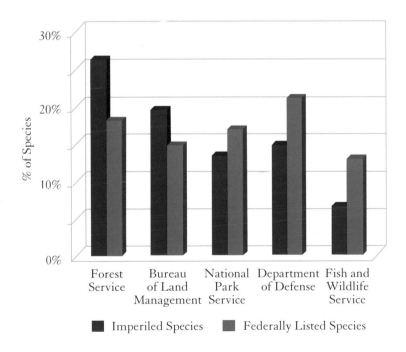

Figure 10.4. Number of species on federal lands.

Among the major federal agencies, Department of Defense lands appear to contain the largest number of federally listed species, while U.S. Forest Service lands harbor the most imperiled species.

Figure 10.5. Percent of species populations on major landowner types.

The largest number of populations for both federally listed and imperiled species occur on federal lands. Percentages add up to more than 100% because some occurrences span multiple landowners.

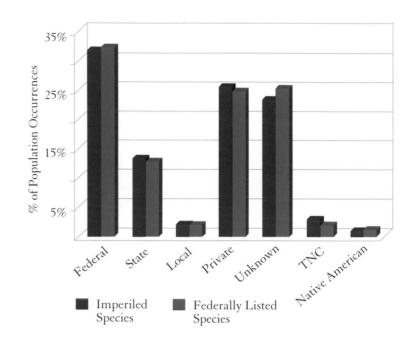

% of Population Occurrences

■ Imperiled Species   ■ Federally Listed Species

Forest Service lands are exceedingly important in protecting biodiversity, supporting the greatest number of imperiled species and by far the largest number of populations for both imperiled and endangered species populations.
© Larry E. Morse/TNC.

The most striking feature apparent from the ownership map for federally listed species (figure 10.2) is the dense concentration of populations stretching throughout the Pacific Northwest, including northern California, Washington, and Oregon, which are mostly on federal properties. The numerous occurrences recorded from this region are attributable primarily to a single species, the northern spotted owl (*Strix occidentalis caurina*). Indeed, more than one-third of the more than 45,000 mapped populations for federally listed species belong to just three species—spotted owl, red-cockaded woodpecker (*Picoides borealis*), and bald eagle (*Haliaeetus leucocephalus*)—each of which has been the focus of intensive conservation, regulatory, and inventory attention. Excluding these three species from the analysis does not, however, significantly change our results: Without the three birds, the proportion of federally listed species found on federal lands drops slightly, to just under one-third, while the proportion found on private lands increases slightly. Federal and private lands remain the two most important ownership types for listed species regardless of whether the analysis considers the spotted owl, red-cockaded woodpecker, and bald eagle.

Among federal agencies, U.S. Forest Service lands harbor by far the greatest number of imperiled and endangered species populations, including more than two-fifths of the populations documented for imperiled species and more than half of populations for federally listed species (figure 10.6). Relative to the amount of federal land found within their jurisdictions (indicated in figure 10.6 as green cylinders), both the Department of Defense and the Forest Service manage disproportionate numbers of imperiled and endangered species populations. Lands of both the Bureau of Land Management (BLM) and the U.S. Fish and Wildlife Service appear to be underrepresenting endangered species populations

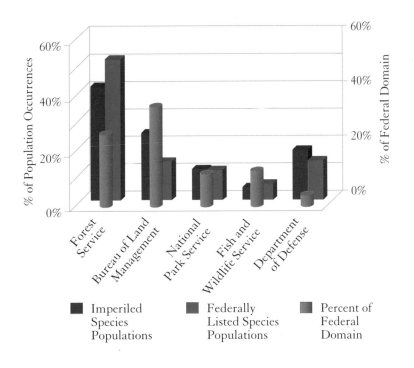

Figure 10.6. Percent of populations among federal agencies.

Comparing the proportion of imperiled and federally listed species populations occurring on lands of different agencies with the percentage of the overall federal estate under their domain (green cylinders) emphasizes both the disproportionate role that defense lands play for imperiled and endangered species and the underrepresentation of Fish and Wildlife Service lands.

relative to their total jurisdictions. This situation for BLM is probably due to the vast nature of its western landholdings, many of which are intensively used and poorly inventoried. For the Fish and Wildlife Service, which harbors a mere 6% of federally listed species populations, this underrepresentation is probably more of an indication of refuge acquisition priorities, which historically have not tended to focus on endangered species protection.

The Role of Private Lands

The role of private lands in biodiversity management is receiving increasing attention from lawmakers, agency officials, conservationists, and landowners themselves. The U.S. Department of Agriculture (1997) estimates that 60% of land in the United States (roughly 1.4 billion acres) is privately owned; if Alaska is excluded, this figure rises to about 70%. Determining the significance of private lands to our nation's imperiled biodiversity is an essential step in designing an appropriate role for these lands in long-term conservation efforts.

Private lands harbor at least one population of more than half of all imperiled species and two-thirds of federally listed species (figure 10.3). From a population perspective (figure 10.5), private lands account for about one-quarter of the documented populations of both imperiled and endangered species, a figure that is probably an underestimate given the relatively large number of occurrences for which we have no ownership information ("unknown" category on figure 10.5). Although our information on specific types of private landowners is limited, figure 10.7 shows in greater detail how these species are distributed among individual, cor-

Department of Defense lands, such as the Goldwater Air Force Range, turn out to be strategic from a biological as well as military perspective. Courtesy of U.S. Air Force.

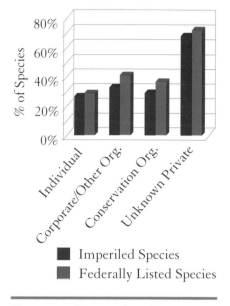

Figure 10.7. Percent of species on different private lands.

For those species known to occur on private lands, this chart assesses the type of private lands on which they are found. The Nature Conservancy is included in "conservation organizations."

porate, and conservation owners. We should note, however, that the largest number of both imperiled and endangered species are found on private lands for which we have no information on owner type.

The significant numbers of imperiled and endangered species inhabiting private lands provide an indication of the great importance of privately owned lands for conservation in the United States. For this reason a variety of strategies designed to encourage conservation on private lands are being actively pursued; they include tools such as habitat conservation plans and tax incentives (Bean and Wilcove 1997, Kaiser 1997, Mann and Plummer 1997). Corporate lands in particular harbor a large number of these species, and although there are many instances of poor corporate land management, these lands also offer future opportunities. In a competitive business world, consumers are increasingly looking for differences among companies. As a result, responsible environmental management is becoming a marketable commodity, evidenced by the growth in "green certification" programs. Given this market incentive and the scale of their operations, many large corporations could afford to take positive actions to protect sensitive biological resources on their properties.

The relatively large number of species found on private conservation lands also offers encouragement for the future and demonstrates that systematic land protection activities have had a noticeable effect on biodiversity protection. The Nature Conservancy, for instance, manages about 1.5 million acres, or less than 0.1% of the U.S. land area. While the organization is by far the nation's largest private land trust, compared to most federal agencies it is a small landholder. Conservancy lands are notable for containing at least one population of about 15% of all imperiled species and over 20% of federally listed species (figure 10.3). These figures place the Conservancy well ahead of both the National Park Service and the U.S. Fish and Wildlife Service—which both have land holdings nearly a hundred times larger—in the number of imperiled and fed-

Conservancy lands, such as Pine Butte Preserve, encompass about 15% of imperiled species and 20% of federally listed species, more than either the National Park Service or U.S. Fish and Wildlife Service, each of which has land holdings nearly a hundred times larger. © Harold E. Malde.

erally listed species found on land under its jurisdiction. Such results are strong validation of the systematic approach the Conservancy has used in its land protection efforts, focusing acquisition priorities in large part on heritage-derived information.

Restricted Distributions, Special Responsibilities

Many species are distributed across multiple land ownership types, and opportunities for their conservation—as well as potential threats—broaden with the variety of landowners. For some species, however, co-incidence of geography, evolutionary history, and land titles has resulted in distributions restricted to but a single land ownership type. As with the Tiburon lily, which is found entirely on private lands, some landholders own most or all of the world's population of a species and thus have special responsibilities. To assess the degree to which these special responsibilities fall to various landowner types, we calculated the number of imperiled and federally listed species that are largely restricted to a single landowner type, as measured by the individual species having more than 90% of its populations on that land type (figure 10.8).

Almost a quarter (23%) of imperiled species and an eighth (12%) of federally listed species are restricted largely to federal properties. Fewer imperiled and federally listed species (about 10% for each) are confined mostly to private lands, with fewer still restricted to state lands. These results are in general agreement with previous reports by Wilcove et al. (1996) and Bean and Wilcove (1997), who noted, based on information from a 1995 GAO report, that less than a tenth of the species protected by the Endangered Species Act occur exclusively on federal land.

The Peaks of Otter salamander (*Plethodon hubrichti*) is an example of an imperiled species virtually restricted to federal lands—in this case, the U.S. Forest Service's Jefferson National Forest and the Blue Ridge Parkway, administered by the National Park Service. This reclusive sala-

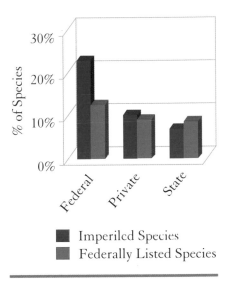

Figure 10.8. Species restricted to single ownership types.

This chart graphs the percentage of imperiled and listed species for which more than 90% of the populations are found on a specific land ownership types. Almost a quarter of imperiled species are largely restricted to federal lands.

The imperiled Peaks of Otter salamander is virtually restricted to federal lands, giving federal agencies special responsibilities for its protection. © Lynda Richardson.

mander lives only atop several high peaks along the Blue Ridge Mountains of Virginia, where it inhabits mature hardwood forests, usually on cool north-facing slopes.

Bell's twinpod (*Physaria bellii*) illustrates an imperiled plant species found predominantly on private lands. Ranging across three counties along the Front Range foothills of Colorado, this mustard relative is known from about 25 sites, where it grows only on specific shale and limestone formations. Apart from two populations found on City of Boulder open space land, all other known populations are on private lands, where they face such threats as suburban expansion, road construction, and invasion by noxious weeds.

How Adequate Are Existing Nature Reserves?

Looking at land ownership provides some understanding of the potential for conservation of imperiled and endangered species but does not shed light on the actual protection afforded these species. To address questions about the adequacy of conservation for vulnerable species, we must turn our attention to the management of these lands. Ideally, such an assessment would compare the distribution of imperiled and federally listed species to the coverage of lands managed in such a way as to offer conservation for these biological resources, lands often called nature reserves, protected areas, or conservation lands (table 10.1). In prac-

Table 10.1. Land management categories

Intended management	GAP status	Definition	Examples
Biodiversity areas	1	Permanent protection from conversion of natural land cover; managed primarily for biodiversity maintenance with natural processes and disturbances allowed to proceed	Most research natural areas, national parks and monuments, and Nature Conservancy preserves; some wilderness areas
Natural areas	2	Protection from conversion of natural land cover; managed generally for natural values but some uses may degrade biodiversity	Most national wildlife refuges, wilderness areas, and areas of critical environmental concern; some state parks
Multiple use	3	Some protection from permanent conversion of natural land cover; subject to extractive uses. Often confers protection to federally listed species	Undesignated public lands of the U.S. Forest Service and Bureau of Land Management
Intensive use	4	Little or no legal protection from permanent conversion; managed primarily or exclusively for intensive human use. Also includes lands not assignable to other categories for lack of information	Most private lands (except those with conservation easements), Department of Defense lands, and undesignated state lands

These land management categories are based on those used by the Department of the Interior's Gap Analysis Program. Source: Modified from Scott et al. 1993.

Only a small percentage of imperiled and federally listed species occur on lands affording the highest levels of biodiversity protection (Status 1 or 2), such as the Superstition Wilderness, a designated wilderness area in Arizona. © Larry Ulrich/DRK PHOTO.

tice, such a national-level assessment of gaps in the portfolio of lands managed for conservation purposes is exceedingly difficult to carry out because of the lack of consistent, detailed information about the location and management of these conservation sites.

A managed area database developed at the University of California, Santa Barbara, provides at least a first approximation of the location and management status of protected lands in the United States (McGhie et al. 1996). Analyzing our species distribution information with respect to this managed area database provides at least a rough first estimation of the degree to which lands under varying management practices will offer long-term protection to species of conservation concern. We used two estimation techniques for assessing the percentage of imperiled and endangered species populations found within protected areas, leading to a range of values within each protection category (table 10.2).

Only a small percentage of imperiled and federally listed species populations are located on lands affording the highest levels of biodiversity protection. The most protective areas (Status 1) encompass only a small fraction of the populations, from 3% to 5%, while somewhat less protected

Table 10.2. Species populations on conservation lands

Management status	All species	Plants	Vertebrates
Biodiversity areas (Status 1)	3–5%	2–4%	3–5%
Natural areas (Status 2)	1–4%	2–5%	1–3%
Multiple-use lands (Status 3)	21–29%	18–30%	14–35%

This table represents the percentage of imperiled and federally listed species populations that are known to occur on lands under different management status. Ranges in percentages reflect different estimation techniques employed.

Most species of concern occur either on multiple-use (Status 3) lands or on land available for intensive use (Status 4). Species occurring on multiple-use lands, such as this national forest, may be managed in a way that is not particularly conducive to their protection. © Gary Braasch.

areas (Status 2) contain another 1% to 4% of these populations. Thus, nationwide, those parts of the landscape affording the highest degree of biodiversity protection harbor less than a tenth of known imperiled and endangered species populations. In contrast, as many as three-quarters of imperiled and endangered species populations are located on lands open to intensive uses (Status 4) that offer little or no legal protection from habitat disturbance and destruction.

Several caveats apply to these results. Most important, the national-level managed area database used in this analysis does not include significant amounts of BLM lands. In addition, this managed area database has a coarse resolution of 1:2 million. Its minimum mapping area of approximately 250 acres does not include many small biodiversity and natural areas and almost certainly underestimates populations located on small reserves. In North Carolina, for example, where we have more detailed information, nearly a third of federal lands classified as biodiversity areas or natural areas (Status 1 or 2 lands) are smaller than this 250-acre minimum mapping unit. Yet these small sites appear to contain at least a fifth of the populations for imperiled and federally listed species in the state. Despite these shortcomings, these results strongly suggest that lands with a legal mandate for being managed primarily for biodiversity or natural values encompass only a small percentage of the nation's populations of imperiled and federally listed species.

Ecological Communities and Land Ownership Patterns

Ecological communities offer one of the most powerful ways to plan for the protection of biodiversity as a whole, rather than just single species. But to use the coarse-filter approach effectively, we must pay attention not only to rare communities but also to the common ones, which together harbor so much of the nation's overall plant, animal, and microbial life. Accordingly, conservationists are directing a great deal of effort toward finding appropriate and cost-effective approaches for assessing the status and distribution of ecological communities—both common and rare—and evaluating the adequacy of their protection within the existing network of conservation lands (Anderson et al. 1999). Only by identifying gaps in our current conservation portfolio will we be able to make informed choices about how and where to invest additional resources in natural community conservation efforts.

How well are ecological communities incorporated into the current portfolio of conservation lands? A number of recent studies, primarily associated with the Gap Analysis Program, have attempted to address this question (Davis et al. 1995, Caicco et al. 1995, Stoms et al. 1998). A relatively consistent result has emerged from these studies: About two-fifths of community types existing within any given state or region appear to have less than 10% of their total land cover represented in the existing network of conservation lands. Even though these studies have been conducted on different scales and with varying definitions of adequate protection, the results nevertheless suggest that a large proportion of ecological communities currently are inadequately protected. The consistency of these findings strongly supports the suggestion that a systematic effort to better incorporate ecological communities within conservation lands should be a high national priority (Scott and Wilcove 1998, Soulé and Sanjayan 1998).

Such efforts, though possible, must overcome uneven and inconsistent information about communities. Species provide a ready unit of analysis, and a reasonably stable classification system has been in use for centuries. In addition, we now have a national-level database on the distribution of our nation's most vulnerable species. The same does not hold true for ecological communities. While there is now a national classification of vegetation communities (see chapter 7), a national-level database on the detailed locations of even the most vulnerable of these communities does not yet exist. Further, classification of aquatic communities and identification of gaps in their conservation is in its infancy on a national scale. As a result, previous efforts to assess the status of communities or ecosystems on a national level (e.g., Noss et al. 1995) have had to use highly variable data in terms of quality and quantity and have relied heavily on literature reviews and expert opinion.

The amount of ecological community data available varies considerably across the United States. In some parts of the Northeast and Southeast, we have comprehensive information on the distribution, conservation status, and ecological quality of communities at such fine-scale levels in the national vegetation classification as the plant association (see chapter 7). In other regions, including much of the West, the geographic scale and ecological complexity of the landscape have made it difficult for ecologists to develop comparable fine-scale information. Instead, most data are available only at coarser levels in the national vegetation classification, and mapping is often based on remote sensing imagery rather than ground surveys. This variability in available information compels us to consider a variety of approaches for evaluating how well ecological communities are incorporated into the current portfolio of conservation lands.

We consider three regional examples that focus on different approaches for addressing this question. First, the use of fine-scale ecological data is exemplified by our analysis of two ecoregions in the southeastern United States, the Southern Blue Ridge and the Mid-Atlantic Coastal Plain. A second example, using coarse-filter data with a gap analysis approach, focuses on the Columbia Plateau ecoregion of the interior Northwest. A third approach, considering the variability of vegetation types across their entire range, analyzes two widely distributed western vegetation types characterized by their dominant tree species: ponderosa pine (*Pinus ponderosa*) and white fir (*Abies concolor*).

In all three examples, we combine information on the distribution of ecological communities on a variety of scales with information on the land ownership, land management, and, in some cases, quality of these com-

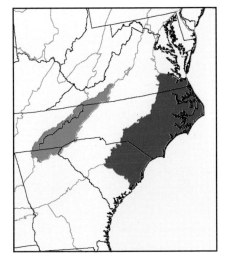

■ Southern Blue Ridge
■ Mid-Atlantic Coastal Plain

The Southern Blue Ridge is a rugged, mountainous region thickly clothed with hardwood forests. Much of the land is in public ownership. © Harold E. Malde.

munities, to assess which community types are underrepresented or completely missing from the existing network of conservation lands. This approach provides us with the information necessary to set priorities for communities that are poorly represented or entirely lacking on conservation lands.

Fine-Scale Community Analysis: Two Southeastern Ecoregions

The Southern Blue Ridge and Mid-Atlantic Coastal Plain ecoregions offer a study in contrasts. The Southern Blue Ridge constitutes the eastern edge of the Appalachian chain, a mountainous region characterized by oak, spruce-fir, and northern hardwood forests (McNab and Avers 1994). The federal government, primarily the U.S. Forest Service, manages almost two-thirds (60%) of this ecoregion. The Mid-Atlantic Coastal Plain is a low-elevation alluvial plain in which remaining natural vegetation consists mostly of pine forest and savanna, mixed forests, swamp forest, and wetland shrublands. In contrast to the Blue Ridge, less than one-tenth of the coastal plain is under federal control.

The North Carolina Natural Heritage Program has classified and selectively inventoried the ecological communities in the North Carolina portion of these two ecoregions using a combination of aerial photography and field inventories (Schafale and Weakley 1990). Forty-five different communities occur in the Southern Blue Ridge and 70 communities in the Mid-Atlantic Coastal Plain. These communities are roughly the equivalent of the *association*, the finest level of the national vegetation classification.

Figure 10.9. Ownership of southeastern ecological communities.

Proportion of communities in the North Carolina portion of the Southern Blue Ridge and Atlantic Coastal Plain ecoregions represented at least twice on major land ownership types.

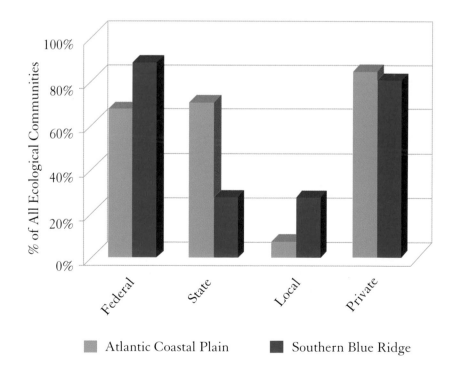

The Mid-Atlantic Coastal Plain is a flat, low-elevation region with abundant wetlands, pine forests, and wet savannas. Most of the land in this ecoregion is in private ownership. © Harold E. Malde.

Most ecological communities in both the Blue Ridge and the Atlantic Coastal Plain are represented on public lands, either at the local, state, or federal level. In the Southern Blue Ridge, 88% of the communities are found at least twice on federal lands, and 80% have at least two occurrences on private land (figure 10.9). Coastal plain communities, in comparison, are not as well represented on federal lands but are better represented on state lands. Private lands, including private conservation lands, harbor high percentages of ecological communities in both regions. Few communities are restricted to a single major landowner type, even in a region with a high degree of federal land ownership such as the Southern Blue Ridge. These results indicate that the relative distribution of communities among land ownership types will differ from place to place. Efforts to incorporate representation of all community types—both rare and common ones—in a network of reserves will necessarily require the collaborative efforts of a diverse group of public and private landowners.

To examine the degree to which ecological communities in these two regions are represented in areas managed primarily for their biodiversity values, we assigned a land management category (table 10.1) to all known examples of communities in these two ecoregions (as recorded in the databases of the North Carolina Heritage Program). In both regions, communities are well represented on lands managed primarily for biodiversity conservation or natural values (Status 1 or 2 lands): Two-thirds or more of all communities have at least three occurrences on such lands. Only six communities in the Southern Blue Ridge do not occur on biodiversity or natural area lands, while seven communities in the Mid-Atlantic Coastal Plain ecoregion are completely unrepresented on conservation or natural area lands (table 10.3). Overall, about one-third of all known occurrences of communities in the Blue Ridge are found on biodiversity or natural area lands, whereas about a quarter of community occurrences in the coastal plain are found on such lands.

Table 10.3. Southeastern communities not represented on conservation lands

Southern Blue Ridge ecoregion	Mid-Atlantic Coastal Plain ecoregion
Floodplain pool	Low-elevation seep
Low-elevation seep	Wet marl forest
Nonriverine wet hardwood forest	Chestnut oak forest
Montane red cedar–hardwood woodland	Little River seepage bank
Dry mesic oak-hickory forest	Piedmont longleaf pine forest
Mesic pine flatwoods	Calcareous coastal fringe forest
	Little River bluff

Presence alone, however, is an imprecise measure. Ideally we would like to know the quality of the community stands to gauge the long-term integrity and persistence of the occurrence. To address this question, natural heritage programs assess the quality of each occurrence based on several factors, including size, condition of biotic and abiotic factors, and landscape context (table 2.5). In these two ecoregions, about four-fifths of the communities had at least one high-quality (A- or B-ranked) occurrence represented on lands managed for biodiversity or natural area values.

The inclusion in conservation lands of high-quality examples of most ecological communities in these two ecoregions provides a solid foundation for building a network of reserves to sustain these communities and ecosystems. Long-term conservation will require multiple high-quality examples of each type within suitable conservation areas. However, even existing conservation lands may not necessarily be secure and will require long-term management for biodiversity.

This analysis demonstrates the power of applying detailed community-level inventory and conservation assessment information to the problem of setting ecoregional conservation priorities. The experience in these ecoregions, however, may not be replicable in most other places, given the large quantity of data needed to classify vegetation on this fine scale. How, then, can ecological communities inform conservation planning in areas lacking such detailed information?

Coarse-Scale Community Analysis: The Columbia Plateau

Planning efforts in the Columbia Plateau ecoregion employed a different ecological community-based approach to identifying conservation priorities. Encompassing a vast arid region stretching across portions of Washington, Oregon, Idaho, Nevada, California, Utah, and Wyoming, the Columbia Plateau is characterized by sagebrush steppe vegetation. As the name implies, this vegetation is dominated by sagebrush (*Artemisia* spp.) and shadscale (*Atriplex confertifolia*) interspersed with short bunchgrasses. Extensive areas of big sagebrush (*Artemisia tridentata*), low sagebrush (*A. arbuscula*), and agriculture dominate the region's land cover (figure 10.10).

To set priorities for representation of all ecological communities in the Columbia Plateau within conservation sites, we used a gap analysis

The Columbia Plateau is a vast, arid, inland region largely characterized by sagebrush steppe vegetation. © Harold E. Malde.

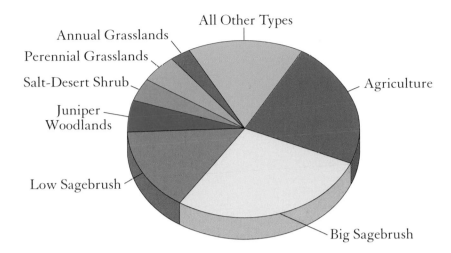

Figure 10.10. Land cover in the Columbia Plateau.

About two-fifths of the Columbia Plateau is covered by sagebrush, while agriculture accounts for a quarter of the region's land cover.

approach (Scott et al. 1993) to determine which vegetation types are missing or underrepresented within existing conservation lands. Gap analysis, while subject to several limitations,[2] provides a rapid baseline assessment of the distribution and management of biodiversity elements at a given point in time. To do so, it attempts to characterize the variability of dominant vegetation types and terrestrial vertebrates across large geographic regions using moderately low-resolution map information.

For our analysis of the Columbia Plateau ecoregion, we use an ecological community level roughly equivalent to the *alliance* of the national vegetation classification (see chapter 2). This represents a coarser level in the vegetation classification than applied in the Southern Blue Ridge and Mid-Atlantic Coastal Plain example. Alliances are defined by diagnostic species, which as a rule dominate the uppermost strata of the vegetation, making them amenable to mapping from satellite imagery. For example, the ponderosa pine alliance is characterized by its dominant tree. Vegetation data from gap analysis programs were derived from state land-cover maps compiled primarily from satellite imagery (1990 Landsat Thematic Mapper or Multispectral Scanner). As described in more detail elsewhere (Stoms et al. 1998), we used a geographic information system to intersect maps of land management and ownership with maps depicting the distribution of land-cover types and to generate figures and

2. There are three major limitations: First, some vegetation communities, such as riparian habitats, frequently occur in patches smaller than the 250-acre (100-hectare) minimum unit of GAP's current mapping phase. Consequently, they may be underestimated or entirely omitted in regional analyses. Their omission highlights the need for complementary assessments of vegetation communities on finer scales to more completely characterize the ecological diversity in a region (Grossman et al. 1994). Second, gap analysis provides little or no information on current ecological conditions or past trends. These "point in time" land-cover maps do not document either the loss of original vegetation or ongoing impacts from grazing or other activities that may change the quality of the cover type but not its classification. Third, gap analysis categorizes land management status by designations that reflect what land managers are legally allowed or obligated to do rather than what they actually do, which is more difficult to ascertain.

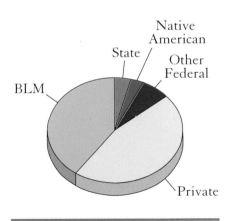

Figure 10.11. Land ownership in the Columbia Plateau.

Over half of lands in the Columbia Plateau are under public management.

Figure 10.12. Land management status
in the Columbia Plateau.

*Only 4% of the ecoregion is managed as
biodiversity or natural area lands, which
offer the most biodiversity protection. For
definitions, see table 10.1.*

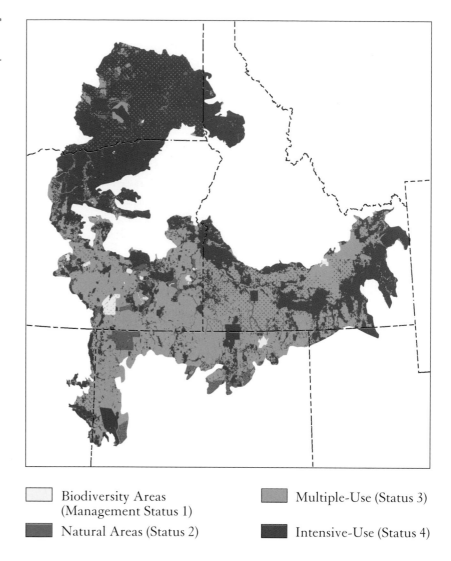

☐ Biodiversity Areas
(Management Status 1)

■ Natural Areas (Status 2)

▨ Multiple-Use (Status 3)

■ Intensive-Use (Status 4)

tables summarizing the percent of each vegetation type in various land
management categories.

Over half of the land in the Columbia Plateau ecoregion is publicly
owned (figure 10.11), yet current land designations allow extractive resource uses on almost the entire region. Multiple-use lands account for
43% of the region, while intensive-use lands represent another 53% (figure 10.12). Just 1% of the region's landscape is designated for biodiversity
management (Status 1), with an additional 3% managed as natural areas.
The Bureau of Land Management, U.S. Fish and Wildlife Service, Department of Energy, and various state agencies manage the majority of
this protected land.

We mapped 47 ecological communities for the region, including three
cultural land-use types. Half of these communities have limited cover-
ages in the region, with mapped distributions of less than 1,000 square
kilometers (386 square miles) each, or a third of a percent of the region's
area. By overlaying a land-cover map of the region with information

on the management status, we could estimate the degree of protection afforded each community. This analysis reveals that most (about 80%) ecological communities have less than a tenth of their distribution represented in those lands under the greatest degree of protection and management for biodiversity (Status 1 and 2 lands) (Stoms et al. 1998).

No widespread communities in the Columbia Plateau ecoregion appear to be well represented in lands managed for biodiversity or natural area values—that is, with greater than a tenth of their overall distribution in such management. The few ecological types that are reasonably well represented in protected lands tend to be small isolated patches, such as marshes and sand dune systems, some of which have been the focus of conservation activities. On the other hand, the only communities completely absent from any protection within the Columbia Plateau ecoregion are certain forest and woodland types, alpine tundra, and meadows, and all of these are more characteristic of neighboring montane ecoregions, where most are well protected (Caicco et al. 1995).

Aside from the small area of alpine tundra, no ecological communities occur entirely on public or private land, although some types are predominantly on one or the other as a result of historic land settlement patterns. About 90% of the remaining moist perennial grassland (*Festuca* spp.) is found primarily on private lands but has been substantially modified by introduced annual grasses. Maintaining adequate representation of this bunchgrass type will require a combination of conservation and active management. In contrast, 82% of juniper woodland (*Juniperus osteosperma* and *J. scopulorum* alliances) are publicly owned. However, given that juniper woodlands are expanding into sagebrush steppe, reassessing fire suppression strategies is a more pressing management concern than increasing representation of these woodlands in designated conservation lands or natural areas.

Rangewide Assessment of Western Vegetation Types

Communities are not homogeneous across their range, and conservation planners increasingly recognize the value of protecting representative samples from across their entire distribution (Noss and Cooperrider 1994, TNC 1997). Few researchers or practitioners, however, have focused on setting and testing explicit goals for the amount of each community to conserve or on where these conservation units should be located. Building upon the coarse-level analysis of the Columbia Plateau example, we combined vegetation cover data from several western states to examine the distribution and degree of existing protection for ecological communities dominated by ponderosa pine and by white fir.

Our approach assumes that adequately capturing genetic variation and species composition differences means conserving examples across the community's environmental gradient. In these rangewide analyses, we attempt to take into account variability on both regional and continental scales by using a combination of elevation and latitude/longitude. Con-

Ponderosa pines, named for their ponderous size, are one of the most widespread and characteristic western pines. Efforts to protect ponderosa communities must take into account the variation in their composition across the species' extensive range. © Gary Braasch.

sidering these factors in conserving a community across its distribution may help ensure long-term viability and evolutionary potential in the face of human impacts such as global climate change (Hunter et al. 1988). We used land-cover maps prepared by gap analysis projects in California, Oregon, Washington, Idaho, Montana, Wyoming, Nevada, Utah, Arizona, and New Mexico (maps for Colorado and the Dakotas were incomplete at the time of this analysis). Each cover type is defined by the species that dominate the uppermost level of the canopy. Methods used to map the vegetation are described elsewhere (Caicco et al. 1995).

We divided the distribution of each cover type into a three-dimensional sample according to the broad environmental parameters of latitude, longitude, and elevation. The distribution of each vegetation type was divided into quartiles of latitude and longitude, creating a grid of four-by-four cells. Each cell in the resulting 16–cell grid was further subdivided by elevational classes. Elevation was used to arbitrarily divide each cell into six equal classes, with each class ranging between 1,000 and 2,000 meters in width, depending on the cover type. We then overlaid the distribution of the cover type with the distribution of managed areas classified as biodiversity areas or natural areas (table 10.1). At sites where the cover type and management areas coincided, we considered the cover type to be represented in conservation areas. Since there are no generally accepted target thresholds for the amount of an ecological community that should be conserved, we repeated our analyses using three different minimum target levels for the communities found within each cell: 12%, 25%, and 50%.

REPRESENTATION IN CONSERVATION AREAS Overall, about 6% of lands dominated by ponderosa pine are contained within biodiversity or natural area lands, with moderate levels of protection in the southwestern portion of its range but low levels to the east (figure 10.13). Using the most conservative target level for protection (12%), about one-third of elevational classes met the target goal for representation. Proportionally fewer elevation classes met their goal as the target levels were increased to 25% and 50%. White fir cover types exhibited an overall coverage of 18% in conservation lands, a higher level of protection than seen in ponderosa communities (figure 10.14). Similarly, white fir showed higher numbers of elevational classes meeting target goals than did ponderosa pine. The difference in conservation coverage between these two community types is largely a function of environmental preference. White fir communities generally occur at higher elevations than ponderosa pine–dominated communities. Their better representation on conservation lands corresponds to the traditional allocation of protected areas to higher-elevation areas less suitable for resource extraction and development.

While these results reflect the unit of analysis—16 geographic cells by six elevational classes—changing the resolution by altering the numbers of elevational classes or latitude/longitude cells results in roughly the same outcome. Moreover, the two-dimensional (latitude/longitude) mapping results alone provide important insights into the patterns of ecological community inclusion in conservation areas.

a.

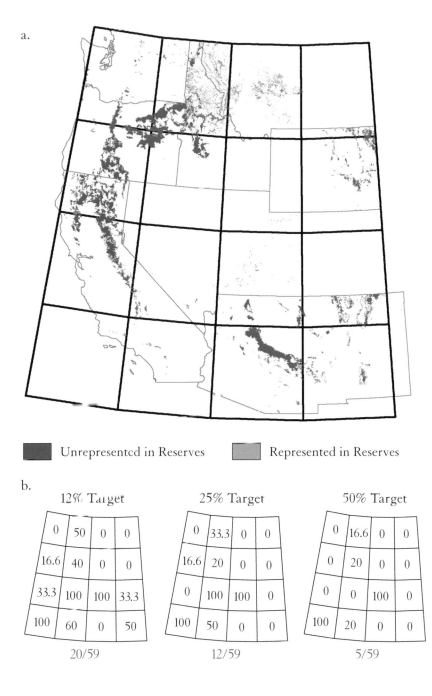

Figure 10.13a–b. Conservation coverage of ponderosa pine.

(a) Overall, about 6% of ponderosa pine communities occur on protected lands.
(b) Percent of elevational classes meeting various conservation targets are represented by the figures within each latitude-longitude cell (see text).

◼ Unrepresented in Reserves   ▢ Represented in Reserves

b.

12% Target			
0	50	0	0
16.6	40	0	0
33.3	100	100	33.3
100	60	0	50

20/59

25% Target			
0	33.3	0	0
16.6	20	0	0
0	100	100	0
100	50	0	0

12/59

50% Target			
0	16.6	0	0
0	20	0	0
0	0	100	0
100	20	0	0

5/59

Our findings reveal that existing biodiversity and natural area lands are not adequately incorporating the full spectrum of potential ecological and compositional differences across the range of these communities. Natural heritage ecologists, for example, have identified 40 different vegetation associations that together make up the ponderosa pine alliance across its range (Anderson et al. 1998). Concentrating conservation efforts for ponderosa pine vegetation in just one portion of that type's expansive range would miss many of these finer-scale community types and the plant and animal species associated with them.

Figure 10.14a–b. Conservation coverage of white fir.

(a) About 18% of white fir communities are found on protected lands. (b) Percent of elevational classes meeting various conservation targets are represented by the numbers within each latitude-longitude cell (see text).

a.

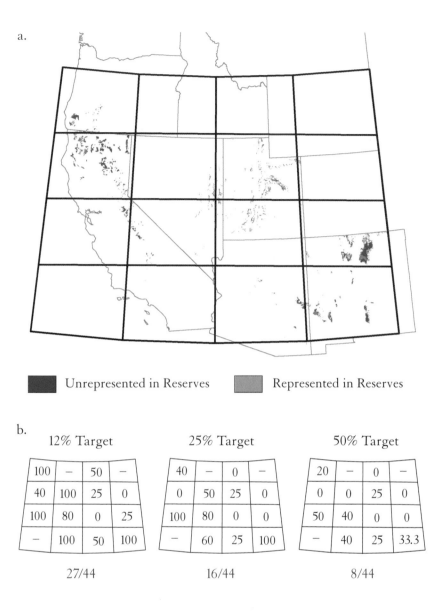

■ Unrepresented in Reserves   ▨ Represented in Reserves

b.

12% Target			
100	–	50	–
40	100	25	0
100	80	0	25
–	100	50	100

27/44

25% Target			
40	–	0	–
0	50	25	0
100	80	0	0
–	60	25	100

16/44

50% Target			
20	–	0	–
0	0	25	0
50	40	0	0
–	40	25	33.3

8/44

White fir generally occurs at higher elevations than ponderosa pine, and white fir communities are consequently better represented on conservation lands. © Gary Braasch.

We suggest that decisions regarding conservation representation of ecological communities should focus on their entire distributions. Such a focus is critical to the successful implementation of the coarse-filter conservation approach (discussed in chapter 1) and will often necessitate cross-ecoregional conservation efforts. At a minimum, this approach requires application of a consistent vegetation classification across states and ecoregions. This rangewide focus is best accomplished by using established land-cover maps in concert with geographic information system analyses, to incorporate important environmental parameters that may drive differences within vegetation cover types. Expert knowledge of the environmental and biological variability within a given ecological community is also a necessary supplement to efforts to identify and select those areas across a community's range that should be incorporated into conservation lands or reserves.

Ecological Communities as a Conservation Planning Tool

Together these three regional examples provide a generalized approach to the conservation of ecological communities, an approach that does not depend on the scale of information available and illustrates the different levels of information available in different regions. These analyses and examples suggest four clear lessons for the future if we are to plan systematically for conserving communities and ecosystems. First, many reserves occur over relatively small areas, sometimes as small as tens or hundreds of acres. Broad-scale analyses will miss smaller conservation lands and occurrences of communities, but high cost may prevent the creation of a national information base of conservation lands at a sufficient scale to capture all such reserves. Thus, a more appropriate scale at which to conduct these analyses is likely an ecoregion or state rather than the nation as a whole.

Second, we need a more operational classification of land ownership and management. The Department of Interior's Gap Analysis Program has defined four categories of land management status based primarily on the legal protection afforded certain types of lands (table 10.1). What is lacking, though, is a classification that incorporates both legal protection and the type of management actually taking place at a particular area. A national consensus on such a classification could go a long way toward helping measure how well we are capturing vulnerable species and representative communities and ecosystems within portfolios of conservation lands or reserves.

Third, we lack information on what species and communities of conservation concern occur in many existing conservation lands and natural areas. For example, no one has yet systematically surveyed either The Nature Conservancy's system of preserves or the U.S. Fish and Wildlife Service's National Refuge System on even a coarse scale to determine which ecological communities are represented within these lands. Efficient use of scarce conservation dollars depends on knowing which elements of biodiversity already come under the umbrella of a reserve network.

Finally, if we are to measure our success at representing communities within conservation lands and to use resources to fill the highest-priority gaps in the reserve network, we must move toward consistently using the same unit of measure for communities. Assessing representation on scales ranging from plant associations to alliances and above across different states or ecoregions makes it exceedingly difficult to determine which ecological communities are most threatened and most in need of better representation within a network of conservation lands.

Several other important findings emerge from these three examples of coupling ecological communities information with land ownership and management to assess the adequacy of coverage by current conservation lands. In the two ecoregions examined in the southeastern United States, we found that efforts to represent communities in a network of reserves are off to a good start. In contrast, the situation in the Columbia Plateau in the interior Northwest is just the opposite: Representation of communities on conservation lands is woefully inadequate. Our rangewide analyses of two tree-dominated cover types—a first coarse-level estimate of how well we are accomplishing the laudable goals of conserving ecological communities across their range of distribution and environmental gradients—demonstrate that we have a considerable distance yet to go. What progress we make will also have a substantial impact on how well the coarse-filter side of our conservation strategy actually works.

As Scott and Wilcove (1998) suggest, ensuring that ecological communities are adequately represented in the network of conservation lands will be a formidable challenge. There are technical hurdles that must be overcome related to the scale at which we collect and manage information on ecological communities and conservation lands, the manner in which we classify land management and protection, and our incomplete biological assessment of current conservation lands. Yet more imposing than these technical shortcomings are the social, economic, and political realities of expanding the portfolio of conservation lands so that representatives of all habitats and ecosystems are adequately protected. Overcoming such constraints will require that private and public stakeholders and decision makers agree to embrace and expand on the concept of a national system of protected areas for the conservation of biological diversity, a system that would conserve both imperiled species and the variety of communities and ecosystems that sustain them.

11

SAFEGUARDING OUR PRECIOUS HERITAGE

Nestled amid the Appalachian Mountains of southwestern Virginia and northeastern Tennessee lies the Clinch Valley, the nation's leading hot spot for imperiled aquatic organisms. The Clinch River is the only undammed headwater of the Tennessee River basin, which in turn is the nation's most biologically diverse drainage system. The surface waters of the Clinch run rich indeed: They are home to at least 29 rare mussels and 19 rare fish. Underground, the region's limestone bedrock is honeycombed by more than a thousand caves and uncounted underground springs and streams. This little-known world is filled with a menagerie of rare beetles, isopods, and other subterranean insects. These underground realms have yielded more than 30 species new to science in just the past few years.

The Clinch Valley is largely rural and sparsely populated. Most residents make their living directly from the land, either mining coal, harvesting timber, grazing cattle, or planting crops. These rural lifestyles have maintained much of the region in a relatively natural state, and more than two-thirds of the Clinch Valley remains forested. The forested hills mask a history of ecologically unsound land use practices, however, that have degraded the legendary quality of the region's waterways. Virtually anything released in the valley flows downhill into the streams and rivers. Among the greatest threats to the valley's extraordinary aquatic life are heavy metals leaching from abandoned coal mines, sediment eroding from cutover slopes, and nutrients released by streamside-grazing cattle. These and other threats have already taken a toll on the region's extraordinary biological richness. Where once there were 60 kinds of freshwater mussels, only about 40 remain.

Coastal southern California, in contrast, is one of the most densely populated regions in the nation. It, too, is a hot spot for imperiled spe-

Mark L. Shaffer

Bruce A. Stein

The Clinch Valley in southwestern Virginia and northeastern Tennessee is the nation's leading hot spot for imperiled aquatic organisms. © Jon Golden/TNC.

cies. Its dry Mediterranean climate and varied topography have favored the evolution of a host of unique plants and animals. Altogether, some 86 imperiled species are found along the coast and in the mountains of this nationally significant center of biodiversity. Certain areas stand out even by California standards as having a truly extraordinary diversity of rare species. The Otay Mountain area, near San Diego, for instance, lends its name to a host of locally restricted species, including the Otay Mesa mint (*Pogogyne nudiuscula*), Otay manzanita (*Arctostaphylos otayensis*), Otay tarweed (*Hemizonia conjugens*), and Otay Mountain lotus (*Lotus crassifolius* var. *otayensis*).

Coastal southern California differs dramatically from the Appalachian valley of the Clinch River. One is among the poorest regions in the country, the other one of the wealthiest. While traditional land uses in the Clinch revolve around extracting a living from the land, the high-tech economy of southern California depends almost entirely on imports of raw materials—particularly water. Fertile fields once planted to oranges, avocados, and strawberries now sprout housing developments. But while the flat agricultural lands are some of the easiest to develop, the scenic hills overlooking the Pacific Ocean are among the most desirable. An acre of prime ocean-view land can be worth as much as $4 million. Unfortunately, even as increasing numbers of people are seeking homes here, these hills are also the last refuge for a number of increasingly rare or imperiled species.

Coastal sage scrub, an austere yet aromatic mixture of shrubs, is one habitat that has been particularly devastated by southern California's human population explosion. Once it blanketed millions of acres in the southern part of the state, but now coastal sage scrub is found on only about 400,000 acres. The demise of these shrublands has precipitated a decline in those species that rely on them for their survival, most famously the California gnatcatcher (*Polioptila californica*). Federal listing of this diminutive bird as a threatened species provided a catalyst for developers, conservationists, and government officials to tackle the region's toughest conservation issue: how to allocate scarce lands needed for the survival of wildlife in the face of relentless development pressures.

Conservation must ultimately take place at specific sites and be carried out by local communities. Each place represents a unique mix of ecological and human values, and effective conservation efforts must take both into account (Weeks 1997). What works in rural southwestern Virginia may be entirely inappropriate for the urbanizing hills of coastal California, and vice versa. On the other hand, while conservation action typically occurs at the local level, biodiversity conservation is not just a local enterprise. It is precisely because conservation has regional, national, and even global dimensions that this book takes a broad view of the status of biodiversity across the United States. Only with such a perspective can we effectively and efficiently set priorities for local action that support larger-scale conservation goals.

This book has mostly focused on the past and the present. This chapter is about the future. What will be the state of the nation's wildlife as we approach the next millennium, a thousand years from now? What

The Clinch River once supported 60 kinds of freshwater mussels, but pollution and sedimentation have taken a heavy toll: only about 40 mussel species remain. © Jon Golden/TNC.

does the preceding assessment of the current status of species and ecosystems suggest about solving the biodiversity conservation crisis in a way that will allow us to reach that distant future with a landscape that is still biologically and ecologically intact? Can we envision a solution that, while recognizing the primacy of local action, is national in scope? If so, what is the scale of that solution? This chapter attempts to address those questions based on what we have learned through the preceding chapters and from the American conservation experience to date. The approaches we suggest, like conservation itself, are not science, but judgments based on science. They are not an experimentally verified surefire formula for the conservation of biodiversity, for there is no such formula. Rather, they represent a weaving together of what we have learned, what we know, and what we suspect into an approach to safeguarding the rich biological diversity of the United States.

Reprise: State of the Nation's Biodiversity

The Appalachian Mountains and coastal California are but two of the nation's ecological treasures. As *Precious Heritage* documents, from a biological perspective the United States is an extraordinary place even on a global scale. Spanning a wide array of ecosystem types, from arctic tundra to tropical forest to blistering hot desert, the nation supports an enormous diversity of plant, animal, and microbial species. Although precise species counts are impossible given how little scientists still know about many groups of organisms, more than 200,000 species have been formally documented from the United States. And among those plants and animals about which we do have good information, several are better represented in the United States than in any other nation on Earth. No other country equals the United States in its diversity of salamanders, freshwater mussels, or freshwater turtles, for instance, and our freshwater fishes and coniferous trees are also impressive on a global scale. The United States is also particularly well endowed with such globally significant large-scale ecosystems as temperate broadleaf forests and prairies, and it harbors one of only five examples worldwide of Mediterranean-climate vegetation. The flora and fauna of the Hawaiian Islands exhibit some of the highest levels of endemism of any region on Earth, adding considerably to the biological significance of the United States.

Many of our natural ecosystems, however, have been despoiled over the past few hundred years. Consequently, the species that depend on those ecosystems have declined. Although naturally rare species are particularly vulnerable to environmental disturbances, even species with seemingly inexhaustible populations—such as the passenger pigeon or Carolina parakeet—can succumb to human depredations and disturbance. Indeed, more than 500 native species already are extinct or missing. Overall, about a third of the U.S. species that we examined in detail are of conservation concern and can be regarded as having an elevated risk of extinction. The levels of risk vary considerably for different

Federal listing of the California gnatcatcher, which depends on coastal sage scrub, provided a catalyst for a regional effort designed to allocate scarce lands for biodiversity conservation.
© Bruce Farnsworth.

A sea of red-tiled roofs is rapidly overtaking southern California's remaining coastal sage scrub and related natural habitats, driving an array of species in this biological hot spot closer to extinction.
© C. C. Lockwood/Earth Scenes.

More than 200,000 species inhabit the United States; of these species, our freshwater organisms are especially impressive on a global scale. Aquatic species, such as this shasta crayfish (*Pacifastacus fortis*), are in particular peril. © B. Moose Peterson/WRP.

More than 500 U.S. species are already extinct or missing, including the colorful Carolina parakeet. The huge flocks of these parakeets were shot out of the skies by the late 1800s, although the last individual did not die until 1914. © The Academy of Natural Sciences, Philadelphia/Corbis.

groups of organisms, however. While such conspicuous groups as birds and mammals appear to be doing relatively well, those animals dependent on freshwater habitats are especially vulnerable. Almost three-quarters of freshwater mussels—a group for which the United States is a world leader—are vulnerable, imperiled, or already extinct, and the figures for other aquatic organisms, such as amphibians, fishes, and crayfishes, are also alarmingly high. Plants, which make up a considerable amount of the diversity of terrestrial habitats, also exhibit high levels of rarity and risk: About one-third are of conservation concern.

The natural ecosystems on which these species depend have been disturbed by human activities across the country. Outright habitat conversion for the production of food, fuel, and fiber and the construction of housing and other infrastructure has consumed vast areas. Our assessment of remaining natural vegetation, based on coarse-resolution satellite imagery, suggests that only about two-fifths of the conterminous United States remains in natural cover. Even this is likely an overestimate of intact natural habitat.

Other forms of ecosystem degradation are more subtle than the replacement of a forest with a shopping mall or a prairie with a wheat field. Disruption of natural fire regimes has transformed or diminished many ecological communities, such as the longleaf pine forests that formerly covered much of the southeastern coastal plain. Similarly, the extensive replumbing of the nation's waterways to generate power, supply drinking water and irrigation, and provide flood control has disrupted natural flow regimes, profoundly altering the functioning and composition of the nation's aquatic ecosystems. The spread of alien species is also wreaking havoc in both terrestrial and aquatic systems and is now the second leading threat to biodiversity, trailing only habitat destruction. The ecological and economic impacts of these invasive foreign species are escalating rapidly, and preventing additional introductions and controlling existing invasions will be a major challenge to society over the coming decades.

The nation's biodiversity is, of course, not uniformly distributed. Regions differ both in their biological richness and in the levels of current and potential future threats. In general, states with the highest levels of species diversity occur along the southern edge of the United States, from California across to Florida. Looking at the geography of risk—that is, the proportion of a state's flora and fauna considered vulnerable or imperiled—many of these same states stand out. Hawaii, however, towers above all other states in the level of risk to its native biota. Because Hawaii's magnificent flora and fauna evolved in isolation, its species are unusually susceptible to human perturbations. Sadly, more extinctions have occurred on this small island chain than anywhere else in the United States.

Most rare species are localized or, if distributed more broadly, are restricted to few populations or occur at low densities. Even where they occur, they often are difficult to find and easy to overlook. The rarest of the rare, however, are precisely the species that are most susceptible both to human activities and to natural perturbations. Unless specifically targeted for protection, these are the most likely to fall through our conservation safety nets. To incorporate them into conservation efforts, though, we must have a sound understanding of their ecological requirements and geographic distribution. We can now broadly decipher the geography of imperilment, thanks to the wealth of detailed data gathered on the distribution of imperiled species over the past quarter century by state natural heritage programs. Building on the work of field biologists from universities, natural history museums, botanical gardens, and other governmental agencies, this detailed population-level heritage information presents a powerful picture of species imperilment across America.

Habitat destruction is the leading threat to the nation's biodiversity, and only about two-fifths of the nation retains its natural vegetation. © Gary Braasch

Certain regions harbor exceptional concentrations of imperiled species, a product of their ecological attributes, geological history, and the scale of human alteration to the landscape. Hot spots of rarity and richness for imperiled species occur in such places as the Hawaiian Islands, the southern Appalachians, central and southern California, the Death Valley region, and the Florida Panhandle (figure 11.1). The flip side of this tendency for rare and imperiled species to be concentrated in some areas is that many regions have few or no such species. In analyzing the known distribution of nearly 2,800 imperiled species (chapter 6), we found that more than two-thirds of the United States lacked any imperiled species. Indeed, fully one third of these species are not known to occur in more than one of the 160,000 acre sampling grids used in that analysis.

Although over time the nation's portfolio of protected areas has incorporated many national treasures, biodiversity typically has not been a primary factor determining which lands are protected by public agencies. As a result, our protected lands do a far better job of preserving scenic landscapes than they do of safeguarding imperiled species and unique ecosystems. We are a nation with many rock and ice parks but with relatively few that—like Ash Meadows National Wildlife Refuge and its complement of rare desert fishes, snails, and plants—focus on protecting the less glamorous but in many ways most needy of our biological inheritance. Only a small percentage of the nation's imperiled and federally listed species populations are located on lands that afford the highest levels of biodiversity protection. Based on our analyses of species distributions and land ownership patterns (chapter 10), lands that provide the best protection, such as national parks, wilderness areas, wildlife refuges, or private nature preserves, safeguard fewer than one-tenth of imperiled species populations. Most populations of imperiled species occur either on multiple-use lands or on lands subject to intensive uses that offer little or no legal protection.

Even as efforts can be made to improve the degree to which biodiversity is safeguarded on the public estate, the importance of private lands to protecting our imperiled species and ecosystems is becoming increasingly evident. For example, among species legally protected under the federal Endangered Species Act, we found that about two-fifths are not known to occur anywhere on federal lands, so protection of these species must occur on nonfederal lands—state, tribal, and private. Yet the tools that we have in hand to encourage the conservation of biodiversity on private lands still

Figure 11.1. Hot spots for imperiled
species.

*While certain regions harbor exceptional
concentrations of imperiled species, many
others have few or no such species; more
than two-thirds of the United States lacks
any known imperiled species. Biodiversity
conservation efforts will need to account
for this uneven distribution of imperiled
species across the landscape.*

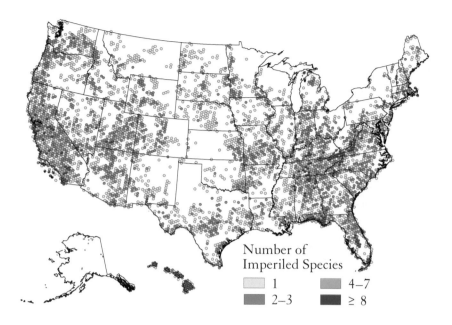

Number of
Imperiled Species

1   4–7
2–3   ≥ 8

rely primarily on regulation rather than on providing incentives for the
maintenance of functional ecosystems and healthy species populations.

Comparing the location of biodiversity hot spots (figure 11.1) with the
density of human population (figure 11.2) makes it clear that conservation in the future increasingly will require balancing human needs and
aspirations with the ecological requirements of these species and the ecosystems on which they depend. How will we succeed in doing so? And
with finite resources—biological, financial, and human—what is success
likely to look like?

What Successful Conservation Means

Biodiversity is a vastly complex resource, difficult to atomize into free-
standing units whose worth or value can be assessed independently. Considerable ink has been spilled arguing whether or not any individual species is inherently worth saving, either because it is essential to ecosystem
integrity or because it is indispensable to human existence. The Endangered Species Act is itself a formal testament to American society's concern that the variety of living things is something worth sustaining. Given
that commitment, and the foregoing assessment of the perilous condition
of much of our biodiversity heritage, is a solution possible? If so, what
will it take to achieve that solution?

We have already seen that significant numbers of species and natural
communities are at elevated risk of extinction and that most of these are
in that condition owing to habitat destruction or alteration. Habitat loss
and alteration are themselves fueled by the growing demands of human
society, the changing ways in which we choose to use our lands and waters, and by alien species, which generally are introduced deliberately or

Figure 11.2. Night lights of the United States.

Comparing the location of biodiversity hot spots (figure 11.1) with the density of human population, as revealed by the nighttime satellite view of the United States, makes it clear that future conservation will involve balancing human needs and the ecological requirements of the species and the ecosystems on which we depend. Source: National Oceanic and Atmospheric Administration.

accidentally by humans. For many species, population size and/or number depend on the amount of habitat available. The more habitat there is, the more or larger populations there are. A well-known principle of conservation biology is that the chances of extinction for a species depend, at least in part, on population size and number (Soule 1987). The smaller or fewer populations a species has, the greater the likelihood the species can become extinct simply by chance alone. As the human population grows and more and more land area is converted from natural habitat to human uses, populations of those wild species that depend on natural habitats will necessarily become fewer and smaller.

The biodiversity crisis is, in essence, about room. Many species and communities are simply running out of the room they need to survive. And with them will go the incredible wealth of the species' genetic information and the ecological connections that represent the wiring for functional, sustainable ecosystems. Arresting this downward spiral and successfully conserving biodiversity means leaving room in the national landscape for some of everything—all native species and all natural communities—and enough room for each to last. Successful biodiversity conservation comes down to this: *Save some of everything, save enough to last.*

This simple admonition belies the complexity of determining the adequate representation of species and communities throughout their historical ranges, or the difficulties of determining the spatial requirements for long term survival. Nevertheless, some simple principles can help inform conservation efforts. These principles can be termed *representation, resiliency,* and *redundancy.*

Some of Everything: Representation

Noah's ark is a common, but too simple, metaphor for biodiversity conservation. Biodiversity is composed of species, the genes they contain, the communities and ecosystems they form, and the processes that connect them. Consequently, successful biodiversity conservation means saving more than the species themselves. It means saving the ecological and evolutionary patterns and processes that not only maintain but also generate those entities we call species. Because every species' genetic makeup is shaped, through natural selection, by the environments it has experienced, successful conservation also means saving populations of each species in the array of different environments in which it occurs.

Take pumas (*Felis concolor*) as an example. Their historical distribution stretched from Canada to Tierra del Fuego—the widest natural distribution of any mammal in the Western Hemisphere, with the exception of humans. Across this broad range they inhabited a variety of environments from temperate to tropical, interacting with, and helping shape, many different species, from mule deer (*Odocoileus hemionus*) in the coniferous forests of the Rocky Mountains to guanaco (*Lama guanicoe*) in the mountain grasslands of the southern Andes. We can "save the puma" by maintaining them only in Canada and letting them disappear elsewhere. But this will not fully accomplish biodiversity conservation. For that, we need healthy populations of pumas in most or all of their environments. So do the mule deer and guanaco.

Similarly, on a broad scale, some ecological systems occupy vast areas of the United States. Just as a species' genetic composition can change from one environment to another, so assemblages of species within a coarsely defined ecological system can vary from one place to another along an environmental gradient. An example is the tallgrass prairie ecoregion discussed in chapter 7. Although named for its most prominent vegetation feature, this region actually encompasses numerous ecological communities, including oak woodlands and floodplain forests in addition to many discrete grassland types. Many of these communities are restricted to the Great Plains and play important ecological roles in the overall system. Clearly, protecting only "tallgrass prairie" remnants will not result in truly representative conservation of this ecoregion's diversity. Nor will preserving tiny fragments of prairie encompass the large-scale ecological processes that are so important in maintaining these systems. Again, we will be challenged to recognize our conservation targets in a way that captures the full spectrum of such natural variation across the landscape, and on a geographic scale that can truly encompass this ecological diversity and its attendant processes. The principle of representation—saving some of everything—will require identifying conservation targets not simply as species and communities but as the complexes of populations, communities, and environmental settings that are the true weave of biodiversity.

Enough to Last: Resiliency and Redundancy

In August 1998, a driver transporting chemicals used for manufacturing Styrofoam took a wrong turn. En route from Georgia to Connecticut, the driver somehow left the highways that are approved for the transport of his hazardous materials and ended up navigating the winding roads of

Mountain lions inhabit a wide range of habitats, from Canada to Tierra del Fuego. Successfully conserving this cat will require that populations be maintained through all or much of that environmental range. © Tom and Pat Leeson/Photo Researchers.

the Clinch Valley. Driving too quickly around one sharp turn, the tanker tipped on its side, discharging about 1,250 gallons of highly toxic liquid into the Clinch River. The Clinch ran a snowy white color, shutting down the water filtration plant at Richlands, Virginia, and killing off most aquatic organisms along a seven-mile stretch of river (Hylton 1998). Unfortunately, this reach of the Clinch harbored three federally listed freshwater mussels, including one of the only two populations on Earth for the tan riffleshell (*Epioblasma florentina walkeri*). That tan riffleshell population was completely destroyed, wiping out half the world's supply of this mussel in one freak accident. The only other population of this critically imperiled mussel, located in a nearby creek, was narrowly spared the lethal effects of the toxic effluent. Although this single population of the tan riffleshell still survives, the organism is now even closer to the brink of extinction. Literally, all of its eggs are in a single watery basket.

Complex machines, such as jet airplanes or spacecraft, are engineered with backups for their critical systems so that failure of a single component will not lead to catastrophic failure. These system redundancies provide the margin of safety needed to make such things as flight and space travel safe for humans. So, too, biological systems need *redundancy* in the engineering sense of having essential backups in place to guard against complete system failure. And just as each component in a jet or spacecraft is engineered to be as resilient to failure as possible, *resiliency* is also essential for the long-term survival of a species.

The issue of viability is key to understanding how resiliency and redundancy inform the scope and scale of a solution to the biodiversity problem. Viability, in the conservation context, is a simple concept to understand but difficult to quantify or predict. A species or its component populations are viable if they continue to exist. They are not viable if they go extinct. A variety of factors can determine the outcome: long-term climate change, arrival of a new competitor or predator, evolution of a new parasite or disease, or a misread map.

Virtually any factor that can bring a species to extinction can operate in one of two different ways, either as a systematic pressure or as a random perturbation. Take climate, for example. A long-term, rangewide shift in climate may make the environment so unsuitable for a particular species that its reproduction does not keep pace with mortality and the overall population size begins to decline. If that species fails to adapt to the change through natural selection, it will eventually become extinct no matter how large its populations are or how many it has. Such a long-term climate shift can be thought of as a systematic pressure on the species.

On the other hand, even in times of stable climate, no two years are exactly alike. There is almost always annual variation in temperature and rainfall. These annual variations, if severe or prolonged, may also cause a species to decline. Whether or not the species survives depends on the balance between its initial population size, the degree to which the random environmental factors depress population growth, and the duration of the unfavorable conditions. A large population of long-lived individuals might be able to endure a 5- to 10-year drought, but a small popula-

A toxic spill in August 1998 killed most aquatic organisms along a seven-mile stretch of the Clinch River (*above*, © Jon Golden/TNC), including one of only two populations of the tan riffleshell mussel (*below*, © Richard Biggins/ USFWS).

tion might not. This type of year-to-year random variation in weather, in the absence of any long-term directional change in climate, is an example of a random perturbation.

Clearly, any species subjected to a continuing, systematic pressure sufficient to produce a population decline is not viable. If that pressure cannot be relieved, the species will become extinct. On the other hand, a species with a population growth rate that, on average, is positive, may or may not be viable. Its long-term survival depends on the number and size of its populations in relation to the types and amounts of random perturbations they are likely to experience.

The relationship between habitat area and a species' population size and persistence has been demonstrated for an array of species on a variety of scales (Meffe and Carroll 1997). For example, Newmark (1995) documented a strong negative relationship between the size of 14 western North American national parks and the number of local mammal extinctions from those parks in the years since their establishment. Similarly, the importance of multiple populations for a species' persistence has been demonstrated for such disparate organisms as checkerspot butterflies (*Euphydryas editha*, Murphy 1990) and Furbish lousewort (*Pedicularis furbushiae*, Menges 1990).

Determining the viability of a species or its populations is a challenging task. For the vast majority of species, including most of those in need of conservation, we lack the level of detailed knowledge necessary to quantify how viability will respond to changes in population size and number. We do know that, all else being equal, the chances of maintaining a species at a site will increase as the size of the site increases. Further, we know that, all else being equal, the chances of maintaining a species overall will increase as the number of sites at which it is maintained increases. We can think of the size of sites as a measure of *resiliency*, and the number of sites as a measure of *redundancy*.

Saving enough to last will require designing conservation sites that are large enough to support populations of the target species and that are resilient to the types of random perturbations inherent in the natural world. As the tan riffleshell mussel reminds us, no single population is immune to the chance of catastrophic extinction—from causes as diverse as hurricanes and toxic spills. Saving enough to last will therefore also require protecting enough sites to provide the backup redundancy necessary as a hedge against the failure of any individual population.

The Emerging Scale of Habitat Need

Conservation in America historically has focused on a narrow range within the full spectrum of biodiversity. Early efforts in wildlife management and natural area conservation targeted either particularly charismatic species, or outstanding examples of natural features. Regulating hunting and fishing were important initial steps in the conservation movement but affected relatively few species. Our first protected areas, such as Yellowstone and Yosemite, were designated as much for, and delimited as much by, their geological features as by an understanding of their ecological value.

Even our most ambitious biodiversity conservation law, the Endangered Species Act, takes an incremental, species-by-species approach to conservation. A species must be judged to be in danger of extinction throughout all or a significant portion of its range, or of becoming in danger of such extinction, to qualify for protection efforts. Even then, the efforts to protect such species are often narrowly focused on that species without broader consideration of the natural system of which it is part. The net result has been a steady accumulation of species listed as endangered or threatened, a proliferation of species-specific recovery plans, and a growing backlog of unmet demand for conservation action.

The recent proliferation of multispecies habitat conservation plans, in which natural groupings of species are treated together, is a step in the right direction in many cases. Even habitat conservation plans, however, hinge on some species' becoming so rare as to qualify as threatened or endangered. This often means waiting until few options remain for successful conservation, either because there are too few populations left or because the ones left are too small to be resilient. There is no indication that continued reliance on this approach, alone, will halt the accelerating erosion of biodiversity. Putting an end to the ever growing list of endangered and threatened species, and the growing backlog of unmet conservation needs, will require new, more comprehensive approaches to the problem.

One alternative approach would be to use the kind of information presented in this book, along with the principles discussed above, to design a system of lands and waters capable of protecting the full range of biodiversity. Such a national portfolio would encompass multiple (*redundant*), *resilient* populations and natural communities that *represent* the full range of environmental and ecological settings in which those species and communities normally occur. If such a system of lands and waters could be identified and then managed to maintain the elements of biodiversity they currently support, we might have a comprehensive solution to the biodiversity conservation issue, at least for that part due to habitat loss.

Are such designs possible? If so, what would they look like? How big would they be? What issues and challenges do they raise for the conservation community and our broader society?

Encompassing Imperiled Species

In chapter 6 we considered how much land area would be required to encompass each of nearly 2,800 imperiled species in the United States. Based on detailed species population data from each U.S. natural heritage program, we mapped the known distribution of these imperiled species using a uniform grid in which each hexagonal cell covers about 160,000 acres. Because many imperiled species are concentrated in certain regions, we found that protecting habitat in cells covering just 6% of the United States could capture at least one example of each imperiled species. Even this is probably an overestimate of the total land area re-

What might a national portfolio of protected lands look like that encompasses the concepts of redundancy, resiliency, and representation? © Frank Oberle.

quired, since these cells are statistical units rather than naturally defined areas, and imperiled species typically are restricted in their distribution even within these general areas.

This 6% solution may meet the simplest representation goal by covering each species at least once, but what about the redundancy in coverage necessary to improve the species' chances for survival and guard against catastrophic extinction of any single population? Although multiple populations of a given species may occur within a single hexagon, let's assume that each cell encompasses but a single population of any species. Our ability to provide replication is limited by the distributions of the organisms themselves: Only two-thirds are found in two or more hexagons, just a quarter are found in five hexagons or more, and a mere 13% of these species are distributed in as many as eight (figure 6.12). Extending double coverage to those species that occur in two or more hexagons increases the land area needed to 10%. Further extending coverage to include up to eight hexagons per species increases this figure to about 20% of the land area.

Admittedly, this analysis provides only a crude initial estimate of the scale of habitat need for imperiled species. We know that the inventory effort on which the analysis is based is still incomplete. Furthermore, this includes only imperiled species, which are the rarest of the rare and geographically among the most restricted plants and animals. This analysis also doesn't take into account many other declining or threatened species, some of which are wide-ranging and require habitat that extends well beyond a single hexagon. Nonetheless, it offers one of the first quantitative efforts to address the emerging scale of habitat need by looking at the issues of representation and redundancy at a national level.

Ensuring Viability: Closing the Gaps in Florida

At least one major effort to design a comprehensive habitat system for protecting biodiversity has gone beyond representation and taken into account the principles of resilience and redundancy. In 1994, the Florida Game and Freshwater Fish Commission published a report entitled *Closing the Gaps in Florida's Wildlife Habitat Conservation System* (Cox et al. 1994). This pioneering work sought to determine what set of lands in the state would, if kept in their current condition, provide adequate habitat for the state's declining wildlife species and rare plant and animal communities. Although the plan was not able to address the specific needs of all the thousands of species found in Florida, it employed a well-reasoned list of focal species selected either for their value in indicating the presence of specific habitats and natural communities or because, like the Florida panther, the species needed large amounts of habitat.

The plan also set out explicit criteria for evaluating viability. Adequate conservation, under this plan, was defined as providing enough habitat for at least 10 populations of at least 200 individuals for each focal species. Distributed correctly, such multiple, large populations could address the principles of redundancy, resiliency, and representation. The planning effort also took the sensible approach of first determining whether the viability criteria for each focal species could be met on existing conservation lands, most of which are already in public ownership.

At the time of the study, existing conservation areas covered just under 7 million acres, or about a fifth of the state (shown in blue on figure 11.3). These lands were sufficient in size to meet the conservation needs of 14 of the 44 focal species; that is, the above viability criteria for these species could be satisfied somewhere on existing public and private conservation lands. Meeting the needs of the remaining species would require conservation of additional lands. The report identified another 4.8 million acres of mostly private lands, which the authors designated as Strategic Habitat Conservation Areas (shown as red on figure 11.3). These additional lands represent about an eighth of the state. If the report's recommendations were implemented fully, approximately one-third of the land area in Florida would fall into some type of conservation land use.

The results of this study contain good news and bad. First, the good news. The fact that such a planning effort was possible is itself remarkable. The study bears witness to our growing level of knowledge of the distribution and status of many of the elements of biodiversity, made possible, in part, by the network of state natural heritage programs—the Florida Natural Areas Inventory, in this case—and to our growing understanding of the factors that affect the long-term viability of populations and species. Second, to the extent that the design principles employed prove to be functional, a comprehensive solution to the biodiversity habitat conservation problem appears to be possible. Third, implementing that solution will not affect most of the land in the state.

Now the bad news. Although this solution to the habitat conservation issue in Florida would not affect most of the land in the state, it does involve a large amount of land, a good portion of which is privately owned. The estimated purchase price for the privately held Strategic Habitat Conservation Areas identified in the plan was $5.7 billion at 1994 market prices. To place this figure in context, consider that through its Preservation 2000 Program—probably the most ambitious state habitat ac-

The Florida plan for creating a habitat conservation system considered the viability requirements of a carefully selected set of focal species, like this gopher tortoise (*Gopherus polyphemus*) (*top,* © Stephen Krasemann/DRK PHOTO), and the degree to which existing conservation areas, such as Big Cypress National Preserve (*bottom,* © Carr Clifton/Minden Pictures), could satisfy these needs.

Existing Conservation Areas

Strategic Habitat Conservation Areas

Figure 11.3. Closing the gaps in Florida.

This map shows those habitat areas in Florida that should be conserved if key components of the state's biological diversity are to be maintained. Existing conservation areas are shown in blue, while additional lands needed are indicated in red. Together, these account for about one-third of the state. Source: Cox et al. 1994.

quisition effort in the nation—the state of Florida has spent $3.2 billion during the 1990s to acquire important natural areas. During this same period the federal government's expenditure to acquire habitat and natural areas nationwide was only about $250 million annually, a figure less than what this one state alone is spending. On the other hand, the January 1998 proposed annual budget for the state of Florida amounted to $45 billion, and a single B-2 stealth bomber costs $2 billion.

A Geography of Hope: Designing Ecoregional Portfolios

The Nature Conservancy's effort to design portfolios of conservation sites within each of the nation's ecoregions (see figure 1.1) represents a similarly comprehensive approach for assessing the scale of habitat needs. Now a cornerstone of the Conservancy's efforts, ecoregion-based conservation grew out of the organization's realization that successfully conserving ecological communities and imperiled species will require working on increasingly broader scales and across state boundaries (TNC 1996). This approach also recognizes the inherent conservation value of the biodiversity contained within each ecoregion, and not just in areas that stand out as imperiled species hot spots. Although the Conservancy is designing these portfolios on the scale of ecoregions, the collective portfolio, when completed, will represent a truly national conservation blueprint.

Chapter 10 discusses one of the first such ecoregional planning effort, focusing on the interior Northwest's Columbia Plateau. Plans are complete or under way in numerous other regions, ranging from the Central Shortgrass Prairie and the Northern Appalachians to the East Gulf Coastal Plain. Within each of these ecoregions, the objective is to identify portfolios of conservation sites that together could provide for the long-term survival of each of the region's viable native species and natural communities. Although each ecoregion is unique, planners are using a consistent process to set planning goals (TNC 1997). Conservation targets typically include vulnerable species and communities—including species that may still be abundant but are of special concern due to declines or other factors—and the full range of ecological communities, both common and rare. Identifying a wide spectrum of conservation targets allows planning teams to address the principle of representation discussed earlier. Explicit conservation goals for each target focus on the number of populations or occurrences that would be needed to maintain the viability of these species and communities. Together, these conservation targets and goals incorporate the concepts of representation, resiliency, and redundancy into the process. The resulting portfolio of conservation sites would represent a "geography of hope" (TNC 1997).

While many of these ecoregional planning efforts are still under way, we already are learning some important lessons about the scale of land conservation that will be necessary to achieve these ambitious conservation goals. In the Central Shortgrass Prairie—a sparsely populated ecoregion

The Pawnee Buttes in the western high plains of northern Colorado are included in one of the conservation sites identified in the Central Shortgrass Prairie ecoregional plan. © Harold E. Malde.

that occurs mostly in Colorado but extends into Kansas, Nebraska, New Mexico, Texas, and Wyoming—the planning team analyzed the protection needs of about 200 species and natural communities (TNC 1998a). These researchers identified a set of proposed conservation sites that encompass just under a quarter (22.5%) of the region's area (figure 11.4). Of these portfolio lands, 15% are already in public ownership. If managed for the protection of their biodiversity, this portfolio of sites would protect about two-thirds of the species and communities identified as conservation targets. Only about a quarter of the targets, however, are represented in these sites in numbers sufficient to achieve the viability goals the planners set for themselves, an indication that the opportunity to build fully resilient conservation systems with adequate redundancy is fast slipping away.

Most other completed ecoregional plans call for the conservation of similar ratios of land, ranging from about 15% to 25% of the ecoregion's area. The Columbia Plateau plan, for instance, identified a portfolio of sites encompassing 21% of the region. Although about 60% of these portfolio lands are in public ownership, even here private lands will play a critical role in meeting biodiversity conservation goals.

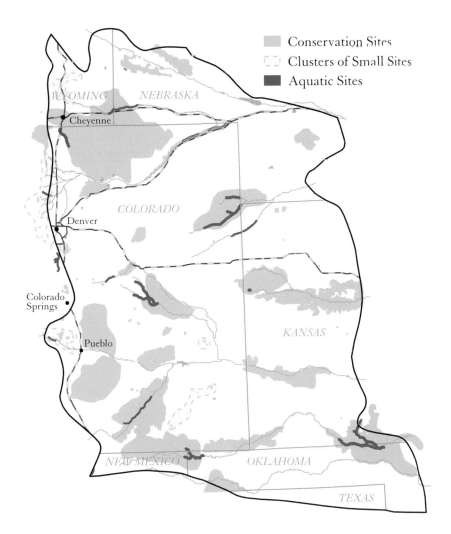

Figure 11.4. A conservation portfolio for the Central Shortgrass Prairie ecoregion.

Conservation planners have identified a set of proposed conservation sites that encompass just under a quarter of the region's area. If managed for conservation, this portfolio of sites would protect about two-thirds of the region's key species and communities. Source: TNC 1998a.

Standing in sharp contrast is the highly fragmented landscape of the Northern Tallgrass Prairie, an ecoregion spanning North and South Dakota, Minnesota, Iowa, and Manitoba. During the ice ages, glacial Lake Agassiz covered much of this region, leaving behind the flat terrain of the Red River Valley and the surrounding gentle rolling plains. This area has been subjected to intensive agricultural conversion, and at present only about 4% of the region remains in any form of natural vegetation. Because of the relatively few areas remaining in natural habitat, the conservation portfolio identified for this ecoregion encompasses only 3% of the land area, almost all of which is located in just a handful of large-scale landscapes. The Northern Tallgrass Prairie provides a dramatic illustration of how our existing options for biodiversity conservation can be severely constrained. It also points to the role that restoration may need to play as part of the long-term strategies for conserving and restoring biodiversity in highly altered regions.

Community Conservation in California

Like the Northern Tallgrass Prairie, southern California is another area where biodiversity conservation choices have already been severely constrained, in this case primarily by rampant urbanization. This hot spot of imperiled species is the location of another regional planning approach to allocating scarce land for conservation.

Known as the Natural Community Conservation Planning (NCCP) program, a broad coalition of conservationists, government agencies, and the business community have come together to try and determine what will be needed over the long haul to preserve the unique ecological communities and species that inhabit this rugged yet populous region. Each of these parties has a powerful incentive to work toward an overall solution to the problem. As natural habitats have declined, so too have the species dependent on them, leading to increasing numbers of endangered species listings by the federal and state governments. Although listing of the California gnatcatcher as threatened was just one such decision, its reliance on coastal sage scrub affected development and land use decisions throughout the region, creating political pressure to resolve the issue. Developers were frustrated by time-consuming delays and the uncertainty of outcome—the by-product of regulating on a species-by-species and parcel-by-parcel basis. The conservation community, for its part, recognized that the largely uncoordinated process of environmental review and development meant that regionally habitat would continue to be lost, as would any hope of creating meaningful and long-lasting conservation areas out of the region's remaining natural habitat.

In 1991, the state of California created the NCCP as a way of developing conservation strategies and guidelines for the entire region in an atmosphere of collaboration rather than confrontation. The process was designed to avoid the type of bitter and costly environmental battles then raging in the Pacific Northwest over the listing of the spotted owl. A scientific panel worked to create a vision for establishing a reserve network that could protect the full array of ecosystems in the region. While the coastal sage scrub would be a focal community, the plan would extend to all other natural communities as well. Basic principles included keeping blocks of habitat contiguous, linking habitat preserves through corridors where possible, and buffering habitat from encroaching development (CDFG 1993).

In central Orange County a plan has now been approved that sets aside more than 37,000 acres for preservation. Meanwhile, the City of San Diego to the south has approved plans for a 164,000-acre preserve system. While the Orange County plan mostly involves public lands and relatively few large landowners, the San Diego effort encompasses numerous smaller land parcels and landowners. The eventual purchase of about 27,000 acres of private lands for the San Diego preserve system is estimated to cost between $300 million and $400 million. Although science has strongly informed the preserve selection process, the NCCP necessarily operates within the political environment as well, and the process has made important strides in bringing together previously warring factions. Whether these lands will be sufficient to safeguard the region's declining wildlife over the long term is still a matter of scientific debate. Nonetheless, these preserves offer some hope for the host of imperiled species that were steadily losing ground to a sea of red-tile-roof housing developments.

As part of California's Natural Community Conservation Planning effort, Orange County has approved a plan that sets aside more than 37,000 acres for preservation of the region's dwindling wildlife resources. © Harold E. Malde.

Beyond Acquisition

The message from these regional planning efforts—from Florida's attempt to close its gaps to The Nature Conservancy's effort to create ecoregional conservation blueprints—makes one thing abundantly clear. Approaching biodiversity conservation through land acquisition alone would be an extremely costly venture, probably in the range of hundreds of billions of dollars. This represents an undertaking akin to building the Interstate Highway System or similar major public works program. But as the authors of the Florida report point out, the real issue is not acquisition but management. Much of the land identified in their Strategic Habitat Conservation Areas is in low-intensity land uses, such as forestry or rangeland. These lands, if maintained and appropriately managed, could sustain the elements of biodiversity that are still present. In this sense, the conservation challenge is not to change the ownership of these lands but to find positive incentives to encourage current and future owners to maintain conservation-compatible land uses.

As a nation we are accumulating a substantial management debt that no amount of land acquisition will solve. Certain threats to our native biodiversity—the spread of alien species, disruption of natural fire regimes, or alteration of hydrological flows—can so transform affected ecological systems as to render them unsuitable for sustaining native species. Paying off this management debt will increasingly be the focus of conservation efforts. Indeed, in the future conservation will be less about preserving pristine settings—these are already few and far between—and more about improved management of seminatural lands and restoring degraded landscapes.

Land that could be managed in a conservation-compatible manner make up a surprisingly large amount of the nation's landscape. Just over half (55%) the land in the United States is thought to be in seminatural condition, that is, neither intensively used nor carefully preserved (Weeks 1997). In contrast, probably only about 3% of the landscape is strictly protected as parks or nature preserves (Noss and Cooperrider 1994). Clearly, these seminatural lands will take on considerable importance if we are to achieve the levels of land protection—one-sixth to one-quarter of the landscape—indicated by the various studies discussed earlier. Biodiversity conservation in the future will increasingly rely on such seminatural lands, not only as buffers around and corridors among protected areas, but also as biodiversity reservoirs in their own right.

Our accumulating management debt applies equally to public lands and private, although as a society we are in a better position to address the problem on the public estate. Fortunately, many government agencies are beginning to recognize the problem and take steps to manage their lands with an eye toward preserving the natural biodiversity values. The Department of Defense, for instance, is an unlikely ally in the fight to protect our natural heritage. As our chapter 10 analyses demonstrate, with bases located in a number of biologically significant regions, relative to their surface area defense lands are inhabited by a disproportionately large number of endangered and imperiled species. The various branches of the armed services generally have taken seriously their role and responsibility to maintain these species. Some installations, such as Eglin Air Force Base in the heart of northern Florida's imperiled species hot spot, have been especially vigorous in managing their lands in a way that maintains biodiversity (Leslie et al. 1996)

Improved management of public lands, however, is unlikely to be sufficient by itself, given what we know about the frequency with which imperiled species occur on private lands and the effect that management of private lands can have on such public resources as rivers and streams. We urgently need incentive-based approaches to working with private landowners. In the Clinch Valley, for example, conservationists are experimenting with a variety of techniques to encourage landowners to employ land management practices that will benefit the region's extraordinary aquatic biota. These incentives focus on reducing the sediments and other contaminants from their lands due to incompatible land use practices. Farmers are being encouraged, and receiving financial incentives, to fence off sensitive riparian areas from grazing cattle. In 1998 conservationists began establishing an innovative forest bank for the valley that would allow landholders to enroll forested acreage and receive a long-term financial benefit from the harvest of timber, yet have the forest bank as a whole managed according to ecologically sound forestry principles.

Truly turning around the problem of protecting endangered species on private lands will require a fundamental shift in how they are perceived by private landowners. Endangered species are now often perceived by landowners as a net liability, something that may interfere with economic uses of the property. What is needed are incentives that can turn the presence of these species into an economic asset. Although locally based incentive programs, such as those under way in the Clinch, are encouraging, a national-level commitment to providing incentives for the protection of endangered species and biodiversity habitat on private lands will be essential.

Into the New Millennium

Much of this chapter has focused on issues of scale, especially the geographic scale needed for habitat protection. Entering the new millennium, however, compels us to consider scale of a different sort: time. Thousand-year increments—millennia—represent virtually an eternity in human time. Yet we are now confronted by choices that will reverberate not only for decades but for centuries and, indeed, millennia. These choices will largely determine what wild species will survive into a third millennium, and what the condition of the earth's ecological support systems will be. Given that humans themselves depend on the natural services provided by functioning ecosystems, these choices will also be crucial for human well-being and existence.

While a thousand years may seem a long time from a human perspective, this still is too short a period to consider. On a geological and evolutionary timescale, a thousand years is barely perceptible. The origin and evolution of life in what is now the United States has ancient roots, as reviewed in chapter 3. The uplift of the Appalachian Mountains, for instance, began almost 300 million years ago, and amphibians had emerged from the early seas at least 60 million years earlier. Continental plates have shifted positions through the ages, but North America essentially took up its current position by about 14 million years ago.

The history of life on Earth has been one of increasing diversity and complexity. This largely has been a result of two competing forces operating over the vastness of evolutionary time: *speciation*, the evolution of new species, and *extinction*, the demise or transformation of previously existing species. The diversification of life on Earth has not been without interruptions; five mass extinction events have occurred, the most drastic about 250 million years ago, marking the end of the Permian period. The most recent, and famous, is the mass extinction that happened some 65 million years ago at the end of the Cretaceous period, apparently as a result of an asteroid smashing into the earth in the vicinity of the present-day Yucatan Peninsula. After each of these extinction events the earth has rebounded in diversity, although accompanied by major shifts in the constellation of living organisms. The Cretaceous extinction, for instance, brought the age of dinosaurs to a close and ushered in the age of mammals, leading ultimately to humans. Humans, in turn, are responsible for the current surge in extinctions, which many biologists consider the beginning of a sixth period of mass extinctions.

Given the earth's track record for rebounding from the previous five extinction events, and the fact that extinction is a "natural" process, why should we be overly concerned with the biological losses confronting us now? This brings us back to the issue of temporal scale. In the evolutionary interplay between extinction and speciation, we have greatly accelerated the extinction side of the equation. Extinctions can now be measured in the very human span of years and decades (see Appendix A). Any counterbalancing evolution, however, will tend not to occur on a timescale relevant to human existence. Instead, emergence of new species typically occurs over tens of thousands or millions of years. Furthermore, the very activities pushing so many species toward extinction in the first place are also impoverishing the genetic reservoirs that ordinarily might serve as the raw materials for future evolution.

But though the asteroid that is headed toward us this time is, figuratively speaking, of our own making, we also have the power to avoid it. To have a chance for success, though, the conservation choreography will have to occur on the very human timescale of the next few decades. Doing so will also require knowledge and commitment to action.

Knowledge will be key to tackling this monumental task: What species and ecosystems exist, where they are found, what is their condition, and what are their needs? *Precious Heritage* is a celebration of one effort—the Natural Heritage Network—to gather and make accessible just this sort of knowledge to inform and improve land use and conservation decisions. Meeting the massive conservation challenges ahead of us, however, will require that we substantially increase our basic knowledge about the natural world, both what exists and how it functions. This task must necessarily involve the entire research and inventory infrastructure—universities, museums, agencies, and individuals—that contributes to the ongoing discovery of life in America.

Yet knowledge is just the first step and must be transformed into action. This conservation action must take place before our options have evaporated and been converted to strip malls, housing developments, and wood chips. The Clinch Valley offers an example of a biologically diverse region which presents significant conservation challenges but in which numerous options are still available. Coastal southern California provides a stark illustration of the high costs—biological and financial—once conservation options are severely constrained.

As we learn more about how natural ecosystems work, we are drawn inevitably to thinking on broader scales, both geographically and temporally. To be successful, though, we must take that grand vision and translate it into action at particular places inhabited by real people. Ultimately all conservation is local. The long-term success of biodiversity conservation efforts will hinge on local communities' embracing the need for healthy ecosystems and flourishing wildlife populations. It will also depend on an enlightened economics that has learned to value not just individual species but the very fabric of biodiversity.

Safeguarding the nation's precious natural heritage will be a central challenge as we enter the new millennium. © Jim Brandenburg/Minden Pictures.

One of the great contributions of the Natural Heritage Network has been its ability to link local biodiversity concerns with national and global priorities. That attribute challenges us to think on these broader scales even as we ground our conservation actions in particular ecosystems and local communities. As the new millennium dawns, we are greeted by a set of choices that will be critical for the future of life in America, not just into the next decades but into yet another millennium. Many of these choices may be difficult—scientifically, politically, socially, or financially. Solving the biodiversity crisis and protecting the nation's extraordinary biological heritage will force us to reach beyond today's efforts, but is an imperative that we cannot let slip through our grasp.

Appendix A

EXTINCT AND MISSING SPECIES
OF THE UNITED STATES

The following appendix lists those species presumed to be extinct (List 1), species missing and possibly extinct (List 2), and species extinct or missing in the wild but still extant in cultivation or captivity (List 3). Information provided includes common and scientific names, former distribution within the United States, and, where known, date last observed in the wild. Source: Natural Heritage Central Databases 1999.

List 1: Species presumed to be extinct (status GX)

Taxonomic group	Scientific name	Common name	U.S. distribution	Date last observed
Vascular plants				
Asteraceae	*Cirsium praetcriens*	Palo Alto thistle	CA	1901
Boraginaceae	*Plagiobothrys lamprocarpus*	a popcornflower	OR	1921
Cyperaceae	*Carex aboriginum*	Indian Valley sedge	ID	1899
Fabaceae	*Orbexilum stipulatum*	falls-of-the-Ohio scurfpea	KY	1881
Lamiaceae	*Monardella pringlei*	Pringle's monardella	CA	1921
Liliaceae	*Calochortus indecorus*	Sexton Mountain mariposa lily	OR	1948
Rosaceae	*Potentilla multijuga*	ballona cinquefoil	CA	1890
Scrophulariaceae	*Mimulus brandegeei*	Santa Cruz Island monkeyflower	CA	1932
	Mimulus traskiae	Santa Catalina Island monkeyflower	CA	pre-1904
	Mimulus whipplei	Whipple's monkeyflower	CA	1854
Solanaceae	*Lycium verrucosum*	San Nicolas Island boxthorn	CA	1901
Vertebrate animals				
Amphibians				
Ranidae	*Rana fisheri*	Las Vegas leopard frog	NV	1942

(continued)

Taxonomic group	Scientific name	Common name	U.S. distribution	Date last observed
Birds				
Alcidae	*Pinguinus impennis*	great auk	MA, ME, NH	1844
Anatidae	*Camptorhynchus labradorius*	Labrador duck	CT, MA, MD, ME, NH, NJ, NY, RI	1878
Columbidae	*Ectopistes migratorius*	passenger pigeon	AL, AR, CT, DC, DE, FL, GA, IA, ID, IL, IN, KS, KY, LA, MA, MD, ME, MI, MN, MO, MS, MT, NC, ND, NE, NH, NJ, NV, NY, OH, OK, PA, RI, SC, SD, TN, TX, UT, VA, VT, WI, WV, WY	1914
Fringillidae	*Chloridops kona*	Kona grosbeak	HI	about 1894
	Ciridops anna	ula-ai-hawane	HI	early 1890s
	Drepanis funerea	black mamo	HI	1907
	Drepanis pacifica	Hawaii mamo	HI	1898
	Dysmorodrepanis munroi	Lanai hookbill	HI	1918
	Hemignathus ellisianus	greater akialoa	HI	1894
	Hemignathus obscurus	lesser akialoa	HI	1903
	Hemignathus sagittirostris	greater 'amakihi	HI	1901
	Rhodacanthis flaviceps	lesser koa-finch	HI	1891
	Rhodacanthis palmeri	greater koa-finch	HI	1896
Meliphagidae	*Chaetoptila angustipluma*	kioea	HI	1859 or 1860s
	Moho apicalis	Oahu 'o'o	HI	1837
	Moho bishopi	Bishop's 'o'o	HI	1981?
	Moho braccatus	Kauai 'o'o	HI	1988
	Moho nobilis	Hawaii 'o'o	HI	1898
Psittacidae	*Conuropsis carolinensis*	Carolina parakeet	AL, AR, CO, FL, GA, IA, IL, IN, KS, KY, LA, MD, MO, MS, NC, NE, NJ, NY, OH, OK, PA, SC, SD, TN, TX, VA, WI, WV	1914
Rallidae	*Porzana palmeri*	Laysan rail	HI	1944
	Porzana sandwichensis	Hawaiian rail	HI	1884
Turdidae	*Myadestes woahensis*	amaui	HI	1825
Fishes				
Catostomidae	*Chasmistes muriei*	Snake River sucker	WY	1927
	Moxostoma lacerum	harelip sucker	AL, AR, GA, IN, KY, OH, TN, VA	1893
Cottidae	*Cottus echinatus*	Utah lake sculpin	UT	1928
Cyprinidae	*Gila crassicauda*	thicktail chub	CA	1957
	Lepidomeda altivelis	Pahranagat spinedace	NV	1938
	Notropis orca	phantom shiner	NM, TX	1975
	Pogonichthys ciscoides	Clear Lake splittail	CA	1970
	Rhinichthys deaconi	Las Vegas dace	NV	1940
Cyprinodontidae	*Fundulus albolineatus*	whiteline topminnow	AL	1889
Goodeidae	*Empetrichthys merriami*	Ash Meadows poolfish	NV	1948
Petromyzontidae	*Lampetra minima*	Miller lake lamprey	OR	1953
Poeciliidae	*Gambusia amistadensis*	Amistad gambusia	TX	1973
	Gambusia georgei	San Marcos gambusia	TX	1983

Taxonomic group	Scientific name	Common name	U.S. distribution	Date last observed
Salmonidae	*Coregonus johannae*	deepwater cisco	IL, IN, MI, MN, WI	1955
	Coregonus nigripinnis	blackfin cisco	IL, IN, MI	1969
	Salvelinus agassizi	silver trout	NH	1930
Mammals				
Phocidae	*Monachus tropicalis*	West Indian monk seal	FL	1952
Invertebrate animals				
Crustacea	*Branchinella lithaca*	Stone Mountain fairy shrimp	GA	
	Pacifastacus nigrescens	sooty crayfish	CA	1860s
Insecta	*Alloperla roberti*	Robert's alloperlan stonefly	IL	1860
	Ephemera compar	Colorado burrowing mayfly	CO	
	Glaucopsyche xerces	xerces blue	CA	early 1940s
	Pentagenia robusta	robust pentagenian burrowing mayfly	IN, KY, OH	
Mollusca				
Bivalvia	*Alasmidonta mccordi*	Coosa elktoe	AL, GA	
	Alasmidonta robusta	Carolina elktoe	NC, SC	pre-1979
	Alasmidonta wrightiana	Ochlockonee arcmussel	FL, GA	1931
	Epioblasma arcaeformis	sugarspoon	AL, KY, TN, VA	1940s
	Epioblasma biemarginata	angled riffleshell	AL, KY, TN	1960s
	Epioblasma cincinnatiensis		OH	
	Epioblasma flexuosa	leafshell	AL, IL, IN, KY, OH, TN	1940s
	Epioblasma haysiana	acornshell	AL, KY, TN, VA	1937
	Epioblasma lenior	narrow catspaw	AL, TN, VA	1965
	Epioblasma lewisii	forkshell	AL, KY, OH, TN, VA	early 1960s
	Epioblasma personata	round combshell	AL, IL, IN, KY, OH, TN	1925
	Epioblasma propinqua	Tennessee riffleshell	AL, IL, IN, KY, OH, TN	1930
	Epioblasma sampsonii	Wabash riffleshell	IL, IN, KY, OH, TN	1950s / 1960s
	Epioblasma stewardsonii	Cumberland leafshell	AL, KY, TN, VA	1930
	Medionidus mcglameriae	Tombigbee moccasinshell	AL, MS	
	Pleurobema bournianum	Scioto pigtoe	OH	
	Quadrula tuberosa	rough rockshell	KY	
Gastropoda	*Achatinella buddii*	Oahu treesnail, pupu kuahiwi	HI	early 1900s
	Achatinella caesia	Oahu treesnail, pupu kuahiwi	HI	early 1900s
	Achatinella casta	Oahu treesnail, pupu kuahiwi	HI	
	Achatinella decora	Oahu treesnail, pupu kuahiwi	HI	early 1900s
	Achatinella lehuiensis	Oahu treesnail, pupu kuahiwi	HI	1922
	Achatinella papyracea	Oahu treesnail, pupu kuahiwi	HI	1945
	Achatinella spaldingi	Oahu treesnail, pupu kuahiwi	HI	1938
	Achatinella thaanumi	Oahu treesnail, pupu kuahiwi	HI	1900s
	Amastra elongata	amastrid land snail	HI	
	Amastra forbesi	amastrid land snail	HI	
	Amastra umbilicata	amastrid land snail	HI	
	Gyrotoma excisa	excised slitshell	AL	
	Gyrotoma lewisii	striate slitshell	AL	1924
	Gyrotoma pagoda	pagoda slitshell	AL	1924
	Gyrotoma pumila	ribbed slitshell	AL	1924
	Gyrotoma pyramidata	pyramid slitshell	AL	1924

(continued)

Taxonomic group	Scientific name	Common name	U.S. distribution	Date last observed
	Gyrotoma walkeri	round slitshell	AL	1924
	Leptoxis formani	interrupted rocksnail	AL	
	Oreohelix florida	Florida mountainsnail	NM	pre-1939
	Physella microstriata	Fish Lake physa	UT	1929
	Pyrgulopsis carinata	carinate duckwater pyrg	NV	
	Pyrgulopsis ruinosa	Fish Lake pyrg	NV	
	Somatogyrus amnicoloides	Ouachita pebblesnail	AR, IA	
	Somatogyrus crassilabris	thick-lipped pebblesnail	AR	
	Somatogyrus wheeleri	channelled pebblesnail	AR	
	Stagnicola pilsbryi	Fish Springs marshsnail	UT	1971

List 2: Species missing or possibly extinct (status GH)

Vascular plants

Aizoaceae	*Sesuvium trianthemoides*	Texas sea-purslane	TX	1947
Amaranthaceae	*Achyranthes atollensis*		HI	1970s
Apiaceae	*Sanicula kauaiensis*	Kauai sanicle	HI	early 1900s
Apocynaceae	*Ochrosia kilaueaensis*	holei	HI	1927
Asclepiadaceae	*Matelea radiata*	Falfurrias anglepod (milkvine)	TX	1941
Aspleniaceae	*Asplenium leucostegioides*		HI	1800s
	Diellia mannii		HI	1800s
Asteraceae	*Argyroxiphium virescens*	greensword	HI	1945
	Brickellia chenopodina	chenopod brickell-bush	NM	1803
	Erigeron mariposanus		CA	1900
	Helianthus praetermissus	lost sunflower	NM	1851
	Isocoma humilis		UT	1971
	Lipochaeta bryanii	nehe	HI	1931
	Lipochaeta degeneri	nehe	HI	1928
	Lipochaeta perdita	nehe	HI	1949
	Solidago porteri	Porter's goldenrod	GA	1800s
	Tetramolopium conyzoides		HI	1919
	Tetramolopium tenerrimum		HI	1800s
Boraginaceae	*Cryptantha aperta*	Grand Junction cat's-eye	CO	1892
	Cryptantha insolita	unusual cat's-eye	NV	1942
	Plagiobothrys glaber	hairless allocarya	CA	1955
	Plagiobothrys hystriculus	bearded allocarya	CA	1892
	Plagiobothrys lithocaryus	Mayacamas popcorn-flower	CA	late 1800s
Brassicaceae	*Arabis fructicosa*	fruit rock cress	WY	1899
	Rorippa coloradensis	Colorado watercress	CO	1875
	Streptanthus lemmonii		AZ	pre-1890
	Thelypodium tenue	Fresno Creek thelypody	TX	1986
	Tropidocarpum capparideum	caper-fruited tropidocarpum	CA	1957
Burmanniaceae	*Thismia americana*	American thismia	IL	1913
Callitrichaceae	*Callitriche fassettii*	Fassett's water-starwort	OR	1898
Campanulaceae	*Clermontia multiflora*	'oha, 'oha wai	HI	1870
	Cyanea arborea	tree cyanea	HI	1928
	Cyanea comata		HI	late 1800s
	Cyanea cylindrocalyx		HI	1909
	Cyanea dolichopoda		HI	
	Cyanea eleeleensis	'oha, haha, 'ohawai	HI	1977
	Cyanea giffardii	Giffard's cyanea	HI	1917
	Cyanea linearifolia	linear-leaved cyanea	HI	early 1900s

Taxonomic group	Scientific name	Common name	U.S. distribution	Date last observed
	Cyanea longissima		HI	1927
	Cyanea mauiensis		HI	
	Cyanea parvifolia	small-leaved cyanea	HI	1909
	Cyanea pohaku		HI	1910
	Cyanea profuga		HI	1912
	Cyanea pycnocarpa		HI	1800s
	Cyanea quercifolia	oakleaf cyanea	HI	1870
	Cyanea truncata		HI	1983
	Delissea fallax		HI	1800s
	Delissea laciniata	cut-leaf delissea	HI	1800s
	Delissea lauliiana		HI	1800s
	Delissea parviflora	small-flowered delissea	HI	1800s
	Delissea sinuata	wavy-leaf delissea	HI	1937
	Lobelia remyi	Remy's lobelia	HI	1850s
Caprifoliaceae	*Symphoricarpos guadalupensis*	McKittrick snowberry	TX	1954
Caryophyllaceae	*Schiedea amplexicaulis*	ma'oli'oli	HI	early 1900s
	Schiedea implexa	Sherff's schiedea	HI	1910
	Silene cryptopetala		HI	1800s
	Silene degeneri	Degener's catchfly	HI	1927
Cucurbitaceae	*Sicyos hillebrandii*	Hillebrand's bur-cucumber	HI	1800s
Cyperaceae	*Cyperus kunthianus*		HI	early 1900s
	Cyperus rockii		HI	early 1900s
Dryopteridaceae	*Deparia kaalaana*		HI	early 1900s
Fabaceae	*Dalea sabinalis*	Sabinal prairie-clover	TX	1950s
	Orbexilum macrophyllum	bigleaf scurfpea	NC	1899
Gesneriaceae	*Cyrtandra crenata*	round-toothed cyrtandra	HI	1947
	Cyrtandra gracilis	slender cyrtandra	HI	1800s
	Cyrtandra kohalae		HI	1933
	Cyrtandra olona		HI	1909
	Cyrtandra pruinosa		HI	1933
	Cyrtandra waiolani	Waiolani cyrtandra	HI	1943
Goodeniaceae	*Scaevola hobdyi*		HI	1980
Hydrocharitaceae	*Elodea schweinitzii*	Schweinitz's elodea	NY, PA	1832
Iridaceae	*Sisyrinchium farwellii*	Farwell's blue-eyed-grass	MI	1898
Lamiaceae	*Haplostachys bryanii*	Bryan's haplostachys	HI	1918
	Haplostachys linearifolia	linear-leaved haplostachys	HI	1928
	Haplostachys munroi	Munro's haplostachys	HI	1935
	Haplostachys truncata	truncate haplostachys	HI	1850s
	Hedeoma pilosa	old blue pennyroyal	TX	1940
	Monardella leucocephala	Merced monardella	CA	1941
	Phyllostegia helleri	Heller phyllostegia	HI	1916
	Phyllostegia hillebrandii	Hillebrand's phyllostegia	HI	1800s
	Phyllostegia imminuta		HI	1979
	Phyllostegia rockii	Rock's phyllostegia	HI	1912
	Phyllostegia variabilis	variable phyllostegia	HI	1964
	Phyllostegia waimeae		HI	1969
	Stenogyne cinerea	Gray's stenogyne	HI	1865
	Stenogyne haliakalae	Haleakala stenogyne	HI	1984
	Stenogyne kanehoana		HI	1996
	Stenogyne oxygona		HI	1952
	Stenogyne viridis	green stenogyne	HI	1870

(continued)

Extinct and Missing Species of the United States 327

Taxonomic group	Scientific name	Common name	U.S. distribution	Date last observed
Liliaceae	*Calochortus monanthus*	single-flowered mariposa lily	CA	1876
Malvaceae	*Hibiscadelphus bombycinus*	Kawaihae hibiscadelphus	HI	prior to 1868
	Hibiscadelphus crucibracteatus		HI	1980s
	Hibiscadelphus wilderianus		HI	1912
	Kokia lanceolata	koki'o	HI	1870
	Sida inflexa	Virginia pine sida	VA	1946
	Sphaeralcea procera	Luna County globemallow	NM	1943
Ophioglossaceae	*Botrychium subbifoliatum*	makou	HI	1935
Orchidaceae	*Triphora latifolia*	broad-leaved nodding-caps	FL	1969
Piperaceae	*Peperomia degeneri*	Degener's peperomia	HI	1928
Poaceae	*Dissanthelium californicum*	California dissanthelium	CA	1912
	Eragrostis mauiensis	Maui love grass	HI	1841
	Muhlenbergia californica	California muhly	CA	1951
Polemoniaceae	*Phlox peckii*	spreading phlox	OR	1940
Polygalaceae	*Polygala piliophora*	Huachuca Mountain milkwort	AZ	1894
Polygonaceae	*Eriogonum truncatum*	Mt. Diablo buckwheat	CA	1940
	Rumex tomentellus	Mogollon dock	NM	pre 1954
Primulaceae	*Lysimachia forbesii*	Forbes' loosestrife	HI	1934
	Lysimachia haupuensis		HI	1927
	Lysimachia kahiliensis		HI	
Rosaceae	*Rubus aliceae*	Santa Fe raspberry	NM	1945
Rubiaceae	*Hedyotis foliosa*	leafy bluet	HI	1870s
Rutaceae	*Melicope macropus*		HI	1800s
	Melicope nealiae	Neal's melicope	HI	1960
	Melicope obovata	obovate melicope	HI	late 1800s
	Melicope wailauensis	Wailau melicope	HI	1933
Saxifragaceae	*Astilbe crenatiloba*	crenate-lobed false goat's-beard	NC, TN	1885
Scrophulariaceae	*Agalinis caddoensis*	Caddo parish false-foxglove	LA	1913
	Agalinis calycina	Leoncita false-foxglove	TX	1936
	Agalinis nuttallii	Nuttall's false-foxglove	AR, OK	1819
	Micranthemum micranthemoides	Nuttall's micranthemum	DC, DE, MD, NJ, NY, PA, VA	1941
	Penstemon campanulatus	bellflower beardtongue	NM	1890
	Penstemon leptanthus	Sevier Plateau beardtongue	UT	1875
	Penstemon parviflorus	Montezuma County beardtongue	CO, NM	1890
Thymelaeaceae	*Wikstroemia hanalei*		HI	1916
	Wikstroemia villosa	hairy wikstroemia	HI	1928

Nonvascular plants

	Brachymenium andersonii	Anderson's brachymenium	NC	1951
	Cephaloziella obtusilobula	roundleaf leafy liverwort	GA, NC	pre-1961
	Cylindrocolea andersonii		NC	pre-1949
	Erioderma pedicellatum			
	Fissidens clebschii		TN	1946
	Pyrenula micheneri		NC, ON, PA	1893

Vertebrate animals

Amphibians

Plethodontidae	*Plethodon ainsworthi*	a salamander	MS	1964

Taxonomic group	Scientific name	Common name	U.S. distribution	Date last observed
Birds				
Fringillidae	*Paroreomyza flammea*	kakawahie	HI	1962 or 1963
Parulidae	*Vermivora bachmanii*	Bachman's warbler	AL, AR, FL, GA, IL, KY, LA, MO, MS, OK, SC, TN, TX, VA	1962
Picidae	*Campephilus principalis*	ivory-billed woodpecker	AL, AR, FL, GA, IL, IN, KY, LA, MD, MO, MS, NC, OK, SC, TN, TX	1986
Fishes				
Ictaluridae	*Noturus trautmani*	Scioto madtom	OH	1957
Invertebrate animals				
Arachnida	*Thermacarus nevadensis*	a water mite	NV	1927
Crustacea	*Branchinella alachua*	Alachua fairy shrimp	FL	
	Dexteria floridana	Florida fairy shrimp	FL	
	Hemigrapsus oregonensis	yellow shore crab	TX	
	Procambarus angustatus	a crayfish	GA	1856
	Procambarus connus	Carrollton crayfish	MS	
	Stygobromus lucifugus	rubious cave amphipod	IL	
Insecta	*Acroneuria flinti*	Flint's common stonefly	VA	1962
	Agrotis cremata	cremata agrotis noctuid moth	HI	
	Agrotis crinigera	Poko noctuid moth	HI	1926
	Agrotis fasciata	Midway agrotis noctuid moth	HI	
	Agrotis kerri	Kerr's agrotis noctuid moth	HI	1923
	Agrotis laysanensis	Laysan agrotis noctuid moth	HI	1911
	Agrotis melanoneura	black-veined agrotis noctuid moth	III	
	Agrotis microreas	microreas agrotis noctuid moth	HI	
	Agrotis potophila	potophila agrotis noctuid moth	HI	
	Agrotis procellaris	procellaris agrotis noctuid moth	HI	pre-1900
	Anisota manitobensis			
	Anomala tibialis	tibial scarab	TX	
	Apamea smythi	Smyth's apamea moth	IL, VA	1966
	Appalachia hebardi	a grasshopper		pre-1970
	Argyresthia castaneella	chestnut ermine moth	NH, VT	1915
	Asaphomyia texanus	Texas asaphomyian tabanid fly	TX	
	Autoplusia olivacea			
	Belocephalus micanopy	Big Pine Key conehead katydid	FL	
	Belocephalus sleighti	Keys short-winged conehead katydid	FL	
	Brachycercus flavus	yellow brachycercus mayfly	LA	
	Calephelis dreisbachi	Dreisbach's metalmark	AZ	
	Calephelis freemani	Freeman's metalmark	TX	
	Campsicnemus mirabilis	Ko'olau spurwing long-legged fly	HI	
	Ceraclea floridana	Florida ceraclean caddisfly	FL	1903
	Chersodromia hawaiiensis	Hawaiian chersodromian dance fly	HI	
	Cheumatopsyche vannotei	Vannote's cheumatopsyche caddisfly	MN, PA	1968
	Cophura hurdi	Antioch cophuran robberfly	CA	1939
	Cyrtopeltis phyllostegiae	phyllostegian leaf bug	HI	
	Desmopachria cenchramis	fig seed diving beetle	FL	
	Drosophila lanaiensis	Lanai pomace fly	HI	

(continued)

Taxonomic group	Scientific name	Common name	U.S. distribution	Date last observed
	Ectoedemia castaneae	American chestnut nepticulid moth	MD	
	Ectoedemia phleophaga	phleophagan chestnut nepticulid moth	MD	
	Ephemera triplex	West Virginia burrowing mayfly	WV	
	Ethmia monachella	lost ethmiid moth	CO	
	Euchalcia borealis			1960
	Eximacris phenax	big cedar grasshopper	OK	1937
	Eximacris superbum	superb spharagemon grasshopper	OK, TX	1912
	Farula davisi	Green Springs Mountain farulan caddisfly	OR	1950
	Flexamia rebranura	red-veined prairie leafhopper	IL, WI	
	Haliplus nitens	disjunct crawling water beetle	TX	
	Hedylepta anastrepta	Molokai sedge hedyleptan moth	HI	
	Hedylepta asaphombra	'Ohe hedyleptan moth	HI	1970s
	Hedylepta epicentra	Oahu swamp hedyleptan moth	HI	early 1900s
	Hedylepta euryprora	Ola'a banana hedyleptan moth	HI	
	Hedylepta fullawayi	Fullaway's banana hedyleptan moth	HI	
	Hedylepta giffardi	Giffard's 'ohe hedyleptan moth	HI	
	Hedylepta iridias	Kilauea pa'iniu hedyleptan moth	HI	
	Hedylepta laysanensis	Laysan hedyleptan moth	HI	
	Hedylepta meyricki	Meyrick's banana hedyleptan moth	HI	
	Hedylepta monogona	Hawaiian bean leafroller moth	HI	
	Hedylepta musicola	Maui banana hedyleptan moth	HI	
	Hedylepta telegrapha	telegraphic hedyleptan moth	HI	
	Heliothis minuta	minute helicoverpan noctuid moth	HI	
	Horologion speokites	Arbuckle cave ground beetle	WV	1931
	Hydroporus elusivus	elusive hydroporus diving beetle	NH	
	Hydroporus spangleri	Spangler's hydroporus diving beetle	UT	1949
	Hydroporus utahensis	Utah hydroporus diving beetle	UT	1941
	Hydroptila wakulla	Wakulla Springs vari-colored microcaddisfly	FL	
	Hygrotus artus	Mono Lake hygrotus diving beetle	CA	
	Hypena laysanensis	Laysan dropseed noctuid moth	HI	1911
	Hypena plagiota	lovegrass noctuid moth	HI	
	Isonychia diversa	diverse isonychian mayfly	TN	
	Isoperla conspicua	a stonefly	IL	
	Isoperla emarginata	a stonefly	MN	1952
	Isoperla irregularis	a stonefly		
	Isoperla jewetti	a stonefly		
	Isoperla maxana	a stonefly	MN	1952
	Lambdina canitiaria	a looper moth	NY	
	Leuctra laura	a stonefly		
	Limnebius aridus	Animas limnebius minute moss beetle	NM	
	Limnebius texanus	Texas minute moss beetle	TX	
	Limnebius utahensis	Utah limnebius minute moss beetle	UT	
	Megalagrion jugorum	Maui upland damselfy	HI	
	Megalagrion molokaiense	Molokai damselfly	HI	
	Mesocapnia bakeri	a stonefly	CA	1918
	Mesocapnia ogotoruka	a stonefly	AK	1963
	Myrmosula pacifica	Antioch mutillid wasp	CA	1952
	Neduba extincta	Antioch Dunes shieldback katydid	CA	1937
	Nepytia pellucidaria	a moth		
	Nesopeplus serratus	souring beetle	HI	1954
	Nesoprosopis andrenoides	andrenoid yellow-faced bee	HI	
	Nesoprosopis angustula	Lanai yellow-faced bee	HI	

Taxonomic group	Scientific name	Common name	U.S. distribution	Date last observed
	Nesoprosopis anthricina	anthricinan yellow-faced bee	HI	
	Nesoprosopis assimulans	assimulans yellow-faced bee	HI	
	Nesoprosopis blackburni	Blackburn's yellow-faced bee	HI	
	Nesoprosopis caeruleipennis	bluewing yellow-faced bee	HI	
	Nesoprosopis chlorosticata	chlorostictan yellow-faced bee	HI	
	Nesoprosopis comes	Comes yellow-faced bee	HI	
	Nesoprosopis coniceps	conehead yellow-faced bee	HI	
	Nesoprosopis connectens	connected yellow-faced bee	HI	
	Nesoprosopis crabronoides	crabronoid yellow-faced bee	HI	
	Nesoprosopis difficilis	difficult yellow-faced bee	HI	
	Nesoprosopis dimidiata	dimidiatan yellow-faced bee	HI	
	Nesoprosopis erythrodemas	erythrodeme yellow-faced bee	HI	
	Nesoprosopis facilis	easy yellow-faced bee	HI	
	Nesoprosopis filicum	fern yellow-faced bee	HI	
	Nesoprosopis finitima	finitiman yellow-faced bee	HI	
	Nesoprosopis flavipes	yellow-foot yellow-faced bee	HI	
	Nesoprosopis haleakalae	Haleakala yellow-faced bee	HI	
	Nesoprosopis hilaris	hilaris yellow-faced bee	HI	
	Nesoprosopis hirsutula	hirsute yellow-faced bee	HI	
	Nesoprosopis homeochroma	monocolor yellow-faced bee	HI	
	Nesoprosopis hostilis	hostile yellow-faced bee	HI	
	Nesoprosopis hula	Hulan yellow-faced bee	HI	
	Nesoprosopis insignis	insignis yellow-faced bee	HI	
	Nesoprosopis kauaiensis	Kauai yellow-faced bee	HI	
	Nesoprosopis koae	Koa yellow-faced bee	HI	
	Nesoprosopis kona	Kona yellow-faced bee	HI	
	Nesoprosopis laeta	Laetan yellow-faced bee	HI	
	Nesoprosopis laticeps	broadhead yellow-faced bee	HI	
	Nesoprosopis longiceps	longhead yellow-faced bee	HI	
	Nesoprosopis mauiensis	Maui yellow-faced bee	HI	
	Nesoprosopis melanothrix	melanothrix yellow-faced bee	HI	
	Nesoprosopis mutata	mutatan yellow-faced bee	HI	
	Nesoprosopis neglecta	Molokai yellow-faced bee	HI	
	Nesoprosopis nivalis	snowy yellow-faced bee	HI	
	Nesoprosopis obscurata	obscuratan yellow-faced bee	HI	
	Nesoprosopis ombrias	ombrias yellow-faced bee	HI	
	Nesoprosopis pele	pele yellow-faced bee	HI	
	Nesoprosopis perspicua	perspicuan yellow-faced bee	HI	
	Nesoprosopis psammobia	psammobian yellow-faced bee	HI	
	Nesoprosopis pubescens	furry yellow-faced bee	HI	
	Nesoprosopis rubrocaudatus	redtail yellow-faced bee	HI	
	Nesoprosopis rugulosa	rugulose yellow-faced bee	HI	
	Nesoprosopis satellus	satellus yellow-faced bee	HI	
	Nesoprosopis setosifrons	bristlefront yellow-faced bee	HI	
	Nesoprosopis simplex	simple yellow-faced bee	HI	
	Nesoprosopis specularis	specular yellow-faced bee	HI	
	Nesoprosopis sphecodoides	sphecodoid yellow-faced bee	HI	
	Nesoprosopis unica	unique yellow-faced bee	HI	1935
	Nesoprosopis vicina	vicinan yellow-faced bee	HI	
	Nesotocus kauaiensis	Kauai nesotocus weevil	HI	
	Ochthebius putnamensis	Indiana ochthebius minute moss beetle	IN	
	Oecetis floridana	Florida long-horn sedge	FL	
	Oecetis parva	little oecetis longhorn caddisfly	AL, FL	before 1907

(continued)

Taxonomic group	Scientific name	Common name	U.S. distribution	Date last observed
	Paleoxenus dohrni	Dohrn's elegant eucnemid beetle	CA	
	Papaipema aerata		IL, NJ, PA	1963
	Papaipema aweme	aweme borer	MI, NY	1930s
	Paracapnia disala	a stonefly		
	Paracapnia ensicala	a stonefly		
	Parapsyche extensa	King's Creek parapsyche caddisfly	CA	1947
	Philanthus nasalis	Antioch sphecid wasp	CA	1959
	Philocasca oron	Clatsop philocascan caddisfly	OR	1949
	Photuris bethaniensis	a lampyrid firefly	DE	
	Pseudanophthalmus krekeleri	Rich Mountain cave beetle	WV	1957
	Rhaphiomidas trochilus	valley mydas fly	CA	
	Rhyacophila amabilis	Castle Lake rhyacophilan caddisfly	CA	
	Ruspolia remotus	remote conehead katydid	HI	
	Scotorythra megalophylla	Kona giant looper moth	HI	early 1900s
	Scotorythra nesiotes	Ko'olau giant looper moth	HI	early 1900s
	Scotorythra paratactis	Hawaiian hopseed looper moth	HI	early 1900s
	Serratella spiculosa	spiculose serratellan mayfly	NC, TN	
	Serratella frisoni	Frison's serratellan mayfly	AL, IL, MO	
	Stonemyia velutina	volutine stonemyian tabanid fly	CA	
	Swammerdamia castaneae		PA	1914
	Tischeria perplexa	chestnut leaf miner moth	VA	
	Triaenodes phalacris	Athens triaenodes caddisfly	OH	
	Triaenodes tridonta	three-tooth triaenodes caddisfly	AL, FL, OK	
	Trigonoscuta rossi	Fort Ross trigonoscuta weevil	CA	
	Trigonoscuta yorbalindae	Yorba Linda trigonoscuta weevil	CA	
	Tritocleis microphylla	'Ola'a peppered looper moth	HI	1890s
	Usingerina moapensis	a naucorid bug	NV	

Mollusca

Bivalvia

Taxonomic group	Scientific name	Common name	U.S. distribution	Date last observed
	Anodonta dejecta	Woebegone floater		
	Elliptio nigella	winged spike	AL, FL, GA	
	Epioblasma metastriata	upland combshell	AL, GA, TN	1968
	Epioblasma othcaloogensis	southern acornshell	AL, GA, TN	1974
	Epioblasma turgidula	turgid blossom	AL, AR, TN	1972
	Lampsilis binominata	lined pocketbook	AL, FL, GA	
	Lampsilis haddletoni	Haddleton lampmussel	AL, FL	
	Pleurobema altum	highnut	AL, GA	
	Pleurobema avellanum	hazel pigtoe	AL	
	Pleurobema hanleyianum	Georgia pigtoe	AL, GA, TN	
	Pleurobema johannis	Alabama pigtoe	AL, TN	
	Pleurobema marshalli	flat pigtoe	AL, MS	1978
	Pleurobema murrayense	Coosa pigtoe	AL	
	Pleurobema nucleopsis	longnut	AL	
	Pleurobema rubellum	warrior pigtoe	AL	
	Pleurobema verum	true pigtoe	AL	
	Quadrula couchiana	Rio Grande monkeyface	TX	1898
	Quadrula stapes	stirrupshell	AL, MS	1978
	Toxolasma corvunculus	southern purple lilliput	AL, GA, OK	1911
	Truncilla cognata	Mexican fawnsfoot	TX	1975

Gastropoda

Taxonomic group	Scientific name	Common name	U.S. distribution	Date last observed
	Achatinella abbreviata	Oahu treesnail, pupu kuahiwi	HI	1963
	Achatinella cestus	Oahu treesnail, pupu kuahiwi	HI	1966
	Achatinella dimorpha	Oahu treesnail, pupu kuahiwi	HI	1967

Taxonomic group	Scientific name	Common name	U.S. distribution	Date last observed
	Achatinella elegans	Oahu treesnail, pupu kuahiwi	HI	1952
	Achatinella juddii	Oahu treesnail, pupu kuahiwi	HI	1958
	Achatinella juncea	Oahu treesnail, pupu kuahiwi	HI	1951
	Achatinella lorata	Oahu treesnail, pupu kuahiwi	HI	1974
	Achatinella phaeozona	Oahu treesnail, pupu kuahiwi	HI	1965
	Achatinella rosea	Oahu treesnail, pupu kuahiwi	HI	1949
	Achatinella swiftii	Oahu treesnail, pupu kuahiwi	HI	1970s
	Achatinella taeniolata	Oahu treesnail, pupu kuahiwi	HI	1978
	Achatinella turgida	Oahu treesnail, pupu kuahiwi	HI	1974
	Achatinella valida	Oahu treesnail, pupu kuahiwi	HI	1951
	Achatinella vittata	Oahu treesnail, pupu kuahiwi	HI	1960
	Achatinella vulpina	Oahu treesnail, pupu kuahiwi	HI	1965
	Amastra albolabris	amastrid land snail	HI	
	Amastra cornea	amastrid land snail	HI	
	Amastra crassilabrum	amastrid land snail	HI	1951
	Amastra pellucida	amastrid land snail	HI	
	Amastra porcus	amastrid land snail	HI	
	Amastra reticulata	amastrid land snail	HI	
	Amastra subrostrata	amastrid land snail	HI	
	Amastra subsoror	amastrid land snail	HI	1946
	Amastra tenuispira	amastrid land snail	HI	
	Amphigyra alabamensis	shoal sprite	AL	
	Auriculella expansa	achatinellid land snail	HI	1960
	Auriculella uniplicata	achatinellid land snail	HI	1946
	Carelia bicolor	amastrid land snail	HI	1947
	Carelia cochlea	amastrid land snail	HI	1952
	Carelia dolei	amastrid land snail	HI	1952
	Carelia evelynae	amastrid land snail	HI	1952
	Carelia kalalauensis	amastrid land snail	HI	1951
	Carelia lirata	amastrid land snail	HI	pre-1945
	Carelia mirabilis	amastrid land snail	HI	pre-1945
	Carelia necra	amastrid land snail	HI	pre-1945
	Carelia olivacea	amastrid land snail	HI	1952
	Carelia paradoxa	amastrid land snail	HI	pre-1945
	Carelia pilsbryi	amastrid land snail	HI	pre-1945
	Carelia tenebrosa	amastrid land snail	HI	1948
	Carelia turricula	amastrid land snail	HI	1953
	Carelia waipouhiensis	amastrid land snail	HI	pre-1945
	Clappia cahabensis	Cahaba pebblesnail	AL	1976
	Clappia umbilicata	umbilicate pebblesnail	AL	
	Elimia brevis	short-spire elimia	AL	
	Elimia clausa	closed elimia	AL	
	Elimia cylindracea	cylinder elimia	AL, MS	
	Elimia fusiformis	fusiform elimia	AL	
	Elimia gibbera		AL	
	Elimia hartmaniana	high-spired elimia	AL	
	Elimia impressa	constricted elimia	AL	
	Elimia jonesi	hearty elimia	AL	
	Elimia lachryma	nodulose Coosa River snail	AL	
	Elimia laeta	ribbed elimia	AL	
	Elimia macglameriana	Macglamery's Coosa River snail	AL	
	Elimia olivula	caper elimia	AL	
	Elimia pilsbryi	rough-lined elimia	AL	

(continued)

Taxonomic group	Scientific name	Common name	U.S. distribution	Date last observed
	Elimia pupaeformis	pupa elimia	AL	
	Elimia pupoidea	bot elimia	AL	
	Elimia pygmaea	pygmy elimia	AL	
	Elimia vanuxemiana	cobble elimia	AL	
	Erinna aulacospira		HI	
	Leptoxis clipeata	agate rocksnail	AL	
	Leptoxis compacta	oblong rocksnail	AL	1935
	Leptoxis crassa	boulder snail	AL, GA, IA, TN	pre-1941
	Leptoxis formosa	maiden rocksnail	AL	
	Leptoxis ligata	rotund rocksnail	AL	
	Leptoxis lirata	lirate rocksnail	AL	
	Leptoxis occultata	bigmouth rocksnail	AL	
	Leptoxis picta	spotted rocksnail	AL	
	Leptoxis showalterii	Coosa rocksnail	AL	
	Leptoxis torrefacta		AL	
	Leptoxis vittata	striped rocksnail	AL	
	Lyropupa perlonga	pupillid land snail (mirapupa)	HI	1980
	Marstonia olivacea	olive marstonia	AL	
	Neoplanorbis carinatus		AL	
	Neoplanorbis smithi		AL	
	Neoplanorbis tantillus		AL	
	Neoplanorbis umbilicatus		AL	
	Newcombia philippiana	achatinellid land snail	HI	1964
	Oreohelix parawanensis		UT	
	Paravitrea aulacogyra	striate supercoil	AR	
	Perdicella fulgurans	achatinellid land snail	HI	pre-1945
	Perdicella mauiensis	achatinellid land snail	HI	pre-1945
	Perdicella zebra	achatinellid land snail	HI	pre-1945
	Perdicella zebrina	achatinellid land snail	HI	
	Planorbella multivolvis	acorn rams-horn	MI	1907
	Pyrgulopsis nevadensis	corded pyrg	NV	1883
	Somatogyrus biangulatus	angular pebblesnail	AL	
	Somatogyrus constrictus	knotty pebblesnail	AL	
	Somatogyrus coosaensis	Coosa pebblesnail	AL	
	Somatogyrus crassus	stocky pebblesnail	AL	
	Somatogyrus currierianus	Tennessee pebblesnail	AL	
	Somatogyrus decipiens	hidden pebblesnail	AL	
	Somatogyrus excavatus	ovate pebblesnail	AL	
	Somatogyrus georgianus	Cherokee pebblesnail	AL	
	Somatogyrus hendersoni	fluted pebblesnail	AL	
	Somatogyrus humerosus	atlas pebblesnail	AL	
	Somatogyrus nanus	dwarf pebblesnail	AL	
	Somatogyrus obtusus	moon pebblesnail	AL	
	Somatogyrus pygmaeus	pygmy pebblesnail	AL	
	Somatogyrus quadratus	quadrate pebblesnail	AL	
	Somatogyrus sargenti	mud pebblesnail	AL	
	Somatogyrus strengi	rolling pebblesnail	AL	
	Somatogyrus substriatus	Choctaw pebblesnail	AL	
	Somatogyrus tennesseensis	opaque pebblesnail	AL, TN	
	Stagnicola utahensis	thickshell pondsnail	UT	1933
Platyhelminthes	*Sphalloplana holsingeri*	Holsinger's groundwater planarian	IL, VA	1973
	Sphalloplana subtilis	Bigger's groundwater planarian	VA	1973

List 3: Species extinct or missing in the wild, but still extant in cultivation or captivity (status GXC or GHC)

Taxonomic group	Scientific name	Common name	U.S. distribution	Date last observed
Vascular plants				
Arecaceae	*Pritchardia affinis*	a palm	HI	
Malvaceae	*Hibiscadelphus giffardianus*	Kilauea hau kuahiwi	HI	1930
	Hibiscadelphus hualalaiensis	Hualalai hau kuahiwi	HI	1990s
	Kokia cookei	Cooke's koki'o	HI	early 1900s
Theaceae	*Franklinia alatamaha*	Franklinia	GA	1803
Crustacea				
	Thermosphaeroma thermophilum	Socorro isopod	NM	

Appendix B

STATE DIVERSITY, ENDEMISM, AND RARITY

These data tables form the basis for the state-level maps of diversity, endemism, and rarity presented in chapter 5. Figures in the "aggregated" columns include vascular plants, vertebrate animals, freshwater mussels, and crayfishes. Except where noted otherwise, data derive from the Natural Heritage Central Databases 1999. Figures include state-level distributions only for native species that regularly occur (or occurred) in a state—that is, species that are resident year-round, breed or overwinter, or regularly pass through on migration. State distributions for animals are based primarily on state-level status ranks developed by state natural heritage programs. Number of native plant species by state are adapted and revised from Kartesz 1994 and Kartesz unpublished data except for figures for California and Hawaii, which derive from Hickman 1993 and W. L. Wagner pers. comm. respectively. Plant endemism figures were revised and updated from Gentry 1986 based on a variety of sources, including Gawler et al. 1996 (ME), Hickman 1993 (CA), Stone 1998 (UT), Wunderlin 1998 (FL), and the following personal communications: J. Amoroso (NC), B. Heidel (MT), J. Ladyman (NM), R. Lipken (AK), J. Logan (AR), C. Ludwig (VA), M. Mancuso (ID), J. Morefield (NV), C. Nordman (TN), J. Poole (TX), A. Schotz (AL), S. Spackman (CO), W. L. Wagner (HI), D. White (KY), and G. Yatskievych (IN, MO).

	Vascular plants			Vertebrate animals			Mammals		
	Number of species	Number of endemics	Number at risk (GX to G3)	Number of species	Number of endemics	Number at risk (GX to G3)	Number of species	Number of endemics	Number at risk (GX to G3)
Alabama	2,851	11	272	848	16	92	62	0	6
Alaska	1,327	35	107	442	8	34	102	7	16
Arizona	3,480	164	588	725	2	45	136	0	3
Arkansas	2,179	6	83	688	7	52	69	0	6
California	4,839	1,416	1,699	804	62	111	185	18	27
Colorado	2,628	54	304	613	1	20	124	0	2
Connecticut	1,801	1	46	427	0	14	57	0	3
Delaware	1,669	0	52	474	0	13	50	0	4
District of Columbia	1,287	0	22	409	0	6	43	0	1
Florida	2,995	155	449	763	12	63	84	1	15
Georgia	2,986	25	350	847	7	93	91	0	14
Hawaii	1,207	1,048	737	141	57	74	14	1	9
Idaho	2,415	37	175	466	3	13	106	1	1
Illinois	2,135	3	50	664	0	34	65	0	5
Indiana	2,047	1	52	629	0	37	67	0	6
Iowa	1,556	0	25	564	0	17	68	0	2
Kansas	1,755	0	32	634	0	23	82	0	3
Kentucky	2,050	2	78	693	3	52	71	0	7
Louisiana	2,353	0	104	725	1	40	75	0	9
Maine	1,579	1	48	462	0	20	74	0	8
Maryland	2,226	0	81	585	1	27	78	0	9
Massachusetts	1,929	1	52	473	1	22	73	1	9
Michigan	2,078	1	57	556	3	21	67	0	3
Minnesota	1,782	2	28	572	0	14	79	0	0
Mississippi	2,314	0	119	714	7	42	53	0	3
Missouri	2,064	0	69	694	4	39	73	0	6
Montana	2,235	6	117	476	0	13	103	0	2
Nebraska	1,541	1	18	576	0	16	83	0	2
Nevada	2,857	94	464	548	16	43	127	1	3
New Hampshire	1,606	1	34	434	1	8	62	0	1
New Jersey	2,134	0	65	552	0	19	70	0	5
New Mexico	3,266	79	400	762	4	46	147	1	9
New York	2,193	1	84	654	0	34	92	0	10
North Carolina	2,743	8	258	829	6	79	105	0	14
North Dakota	1,183	0	11	522	0	15	87	0	3
Ohio	2,041	0	47	576	1	28	66	0	4
Oklahoma	2,326	3	74	743	0	42	102	0	9
Oregon	3,142	109	357	619	14	54	150	3	14
Pennsylvania	2,219	3	66	577	0	25	69	0	3
Rhode Island	1,374	0	29	412	0	15	53	0	5
South Carolina	2,543	1	220	670	1	45	96	0	13
South Dakota	1,487	0	12	565	0	13	90	0	2
Tennessee	2,376	15	158	789	12	92	79	0	6
Texas	4,458	251	424	1,038	36	102	161	1	18
Utah	2,964	157	514	529	4	28	125	1	3
Vermont	1,599	1	37	420	0	6	59	0	2
Virginia	2,546	6	154	737	4	69	82	0	13
Washington	2,443	36	190	604	4	40	128	1	15
West Virginia	1,876	0	65	541	2	27	67	0	5
Wisconsin	1,866	2	40	563	0	15	67	0	0
Wyoming	2,265	31	169	506	3	18	112	1	3

Birds			Reptiles			Amphibians		
Number of species	Number of endemics	Number at risk (GX to G3)	Number of species	Number of endemics	Number at risk (GX to G3)	Number of species	Number of endemics	Number at risk (GX to G3)
345	0	9	85	1	13	69	2	11
286	1	16	0	0	0	7	0	1
436	0	9	100	0	5	25	1	5
303	0	10	69	0	1	49	2	5
418	2	20	83	5	15	50	17	19
376	0	7	48	1	2	17	0	0
279	0	4	27	0	5	22	0	0
297	0	2	37	0	6	28	0	0
243	0	2	31	0	0	24	0	0
387	1	14	91	6	16	56	1	6
328	0	11	83	1	10	77	2	13
115	52	56	6	0	5	0	0	0
283	0	2	23	0	0	13	0	2
311	0	9	61	0	3	40	0	0
283	0	7	55	0	3	39	0	1
289	0	5	47	0	2	22	0	0
340	0	9	64	0	2	29	0	0
287	0	9	53	0	2	55	0	1
341	0	10	77	0	9	53	0	2
294	0	5	21	0	4	17	0	0
317	0	8	47	0	5	40	0	1
303	0	5	30	0	6	20	0	0
303	0	3	27	0	2	24	0	0
309	0	5	30	0	1	20	0	0
303	0	8	82	1	12	57	1	3
309	0	8	67	0	2	43	0	0
287	0	6	17	0	0	13	0	1
346	0	8	47	0	1	13	0	0
307	0	7	52	0	1	17	2	5
283	0	4	17	0	0	21	0	0
340	0	6	42	0	6	32	0	0
448	0	6	95	0	4	25	2	3
329	0	5	36	0	6	32	0	0
364	0	9	71	0	7	79	1	13
317	0	6	15	0	0	12	0	0
284	0	6	41	0	2	39	0	2
345	0	13	81	0	2	50	0	3
339	0	8	33	0	5	30	1	10
271	0	5	38	0	3	35	0	1
278	0	4	25	0	4	18	0	0
312	0	8	73	0	6	67	0	6
340	0	7	31	0	0	15	0	0
292	0	7	58	0	2	70	0	12
472	0	16	149	6	19	68	11	10
310	0	6	50	0	0	15	0	1
242	0	1	19	0	0	21	0	0
323	0	7	61	0	5	72	2	7
377	0	14	21	0	1	24	2	7
243	0	3	38	0	0	44	2	4
295	0	5	35	0	1	19	0	0
303	0	5	22	0	0	13	1	1

(continued)

	Freshwater Fishes			Aggregated Totals (Plants, Vertebrates, and Selected Invertebrates)		
State	Number of species	Number of endemics	Number at risk (GX to G3)	Number of species	Number of endemics	Number at risk (GX to G3)
Alabama	287	13	53	3,947	43	497
Alaska	47	0	1	1,772	43	141
Arizona	28	1	23	4,206	166	634
Arkansas	198	5	30	3,003	30	186
California	68	20	30	5,653	1,480	1,815
Colorado	48	0	9	3,248	55	324
Connecticut	42	0	2	2,244	1	63
Delaware	62	0	1	2,159	0	68
District of Columbia	68	0	3	1,698	0	28
Florida	145	3	12	3,870	203	570
Georgia	268	4	45	4,004	58	533
Hawaii	6	4	4	1,348	1,105	811
Idaho	41	2	8	2,889	40	191
Illinois	187	0	17	2,899	5	119
Indiana	185	0	20	2,769	1	121
Iowa	138	0	8	2,178	0	55
Kansas	119	0	9	2,442	0	61
Kentucky	227	3	33	2,894	11	191
Louisiana	179	1	10	3,179	6	172
Maine	56	0	3	2,058	1	70
Maryland	103	1	4	2,836	1	113
Massachusetts	47	0	2	2,420	2	77
Michigan	135	3	13	2,689	4	90
Minnesota	134	0	8	2,408	2	52
Mississippi	219	5	16	3,164	24	210
Missouri	202	4	23	2,856	11	136
Montana	56	0	4	2,718	6	130
Nebraska	87	0	5	2,159	1	43
Nevada	45	13	27	3,413	109	510
New Hampshire	51	1	3	2,055	2	45
New Jersey	68	0	2	2,701	0	88
New Mexico	47	1	24	4,037	84	448
New York	165	0	13	2,908	1	129
North Carolina	210	5	36	3,658	22	375
North Dakota	91	0	6	1,725	0	26
Ohio	146	1	14	2,714	1	107
Oklahoma	165	0	15	3,158	7	145
Oregon	67	10	17	3,773	122	415
Pennsylvania	164	0	13	2,873	3	112
Rhode Island	38	0	2	1,798	0	45
South Carolina	122	1	12	3,286	8	293
South Dakota	89	0	4	2,083	0	27
Tennessee	290	12	65	3,372	40	347
Texas	188	18	39	5,571	301	552
Utah	29	3	18	3,498	161	544
Vermont	79	0	3	2,038	1	45
Virginia	199	2	37	3,388	11	272
Washington	54	1	3	3,055	42	233
West Virginia	149	0	15	2,501	2	114
Wisconsin	147	0	9	2,485	2	64
Wyoming	56	1	9	2,779	34	188

Appendix C

KÜCHLER POTENTIAL NATURAL VEGETATION TYPES

This list summarizes the potential natural vegetation types in the conterminous United States recognized by Kuchler (1964, 1985).

Potential natural vegetation type	Area (km²)	Percent of U.S.
Oak-hickory pine forest (*Quercus-Carya-Pinus*)	629,935	8.14
Oak-hickory forest (*Quercus Carya*)	524,877	6.78
Sagebrush steppe (*Artemisia-Agropyron*)	391,377	5.06
Grama-buffalo grass (*Bouteloua-Buchloë*)	321,784	4.16
Juniper-pinyon woodland (*Juniperus-Pinus*)	282,923	3.66
Bluestem prairie (*Andropogon-Panicum-Sorghastrum*)	281,390	3.64
Wheatgrass-needlegrass (*Agropyron-Stipa*)	248,808	3.21
Southern mixed forest (*Fagus-Liquidambar-Magnolia-Pinus-Quercus*)	247,462	3.20
Appalachian oak forest (*Quercus*)	242,884	3.14
Northern hardwoods (*Acer-Betula-Fagus-Tsuga*)	223,571	2.89
Mosaic of bluestem prairie and oak-hickory forest	220,765	2.85
Grama-needlegrass-wheatgrass (*Bouteloua-Stipa-Agropyron*)	204,790	2.65
Southern floodplain forest (*Quercus-Nyssa-Taxodium*)	177,717	2.30
Great Basin sagebrush (*Artemisia*)	166,573	2.15
Saltbush-greasewood (*Atriplex-Sarcobatus*)	157,247	2.03
Douglas fir forest (*Pseudotsuga*)	140,444	1.81
Wheatgrass-bluestem-needlegrass (*Agropyron-Andropogon-Stipa*)	134,051	1.73
Bluestem-grama prairie (*Andropogon-Bouteloua*)	131,372	1.70
Beech-maple forest (*Fagus-Acer*)	119,223	1.54
Grama-tobosa shrubsteppe (*Bouteloua-Hilaria-Larrea*)	111,630	1.44
Oak savanna (*Quercus-Andropogon*)	111,371	1.44

(continued)

Potential natural vegetation type	Area (km^2)	Percent of U.S.
Western spruce-fir forest (*Picea-Abies*)	111,321	1.44
Creosote bush (*Larrea*)	101,530	1.31
Mixed mesophytic forest	100,867	1.30
(*Acer-Aesculus-Fagus-Liriodendron-Quercus-Tilia*)		
Western ponderosa forest (*Pinus*)	94,789	1.22
Mesquite-buffalo grass (*Bouteloua-Buchloë-Prosopis*)	92,918	1.20
Trans-Pecos shrub savanna (*Fourensia-Larrea*)	90,361	1.17
Creosote bush-bur sage (*Larrea-Ambrosia*)	85,809	1.11
Cross timbers (*Quercus-Andropogon*)	80,641	1.04
Grama-galleta steppe (*Bouteloua-Hilaria*)	78,045	1.01
Great Lakes pine forest (*Pinus*)	77,252	1.00
Pine-Douglas fir forest (*Pinus-Pseudotsuga*)	75,816	0.98
Sandhills prairie (*Andropogon-Calamovilfa*)	75,098	0.97
Northern hardwoods-spruce forest	74,547	0.96
(*Acer-Betuld-Fagus-Picea-Tsuga*)		
Northern floodplain forest (*Populus-Salix-Ulmus*)	71,808	0.93
Mesquite-acacia savanna	67,695	0.87
(*Andropogon-Setaria-Prosopis-Acacia*)		
Juniper-oak savanna (*Andropogon-Quercus-Juniperus*)	63,136	0.82
Maple-basswood forest (*Acer-Tilia*)	61,339	0.79
Mixed conifer forest (*Abies-Pinus-Pseudotsuga*)	58,841	0.76
Cedar-hemlock-Douglas fir forest	53,227	0.69
(*Thuja-Tsuga-Pseudotsuga*)		
California steppe (*Stipa*)	51,500	0.67
Blackland prairie (*Andropogon-Stipa*)	51,263	0.66
California oakwoods (*Quercus*)	49,672	0.64
Grand fir-Douglas fir forest (*Abies-Pseudotsuga*)	44,916	0.58
Foothills prairie (*Agropyron-Festuca-Stipa*)	44,775	0.58
Bluestem-sacahuista prairie (*Andropogon-Spartina*)	40,764	0.53
Great Lakes spruce-fir forest (*Picea-Abies*)	38,465	0.50
Northern hardwoods-fir forest (*Acer-Betula-Abies-Tsuga*)	36,966	0.48
Wheatgrass-bluegrass (*Agropyron-Poa*)	36,662	0.47
Chaparral (*Adenostoma-Arctostaphylos-Ceanothus*)	32,761	0.42
Sandsage-bluestem prairie (*Artemisia-Andropogon*)	29,562	0.38
California mixed evergreen forest	29,202	0.38
(*Quercus-Arbutus-Pseudotsuga*)		
Alpine meadows and barren	28,721	0.37
(*Agrostis, Carex, Festuca, Poa*)		
Conifer bog (*Picea-Larix-Thuja*)	28,355	0.37
Palo verde-cactus shrub (*Cercidium-Opuntia*)	28,204	0.36
Silver fir-Douglas fir forest (*Abies-Pseudotsuga*)	28,064	0.36
Wheatgrass-needlegrass shrubsteppe	26,786	0.35
(*Agropyron-Stipa-Artemisia*)		
Eastern ponderosa forest (*Pinus*)	26,254	0.34
Shinnery (*Quercus-Andropogon*)	24,029	0.31
Mountain mahogany–oak scrub (*Cercocarpus-Quercus*)	22,688	0.29
Southern cordgrass prairie (*Spartina*)	22,434	0.29
Desert: vegetation largely absent	22,131	0.29
Elm-ash forest (*Ulmus-Fraxinus*)	21,798	0.28
Northeastern spruce-fir forest (*Picea-Abies*)	20,981	0.27
Fescue-wheatgrass (*Festuca-Agropyron*)	20,898	0.27
Transition between oak-juniper woodland and mountain mahogany scrub	20,541	0.27
Cedar-hemlock-pine forest (*Thuja-Tsuga-Pinus*)	19,619	0.25
Fir-hemlock forest (*Abies-Pinus-Pseudotsuga*)	18,804	0.24

Potential natural vegetation type	Area (km^2)	Percent of U.S.
Oak-juniper woodland (*Quercus-Juniperus*)	18,135	0.23
Blackbelt (*Liquidambar-Quercus-Juniperus*)	16,041	0.21
Arizona pine forest (*Pinus*)	15,900	0.21
Spruce-cedar-hemlock forest (*Picea-Thuja-Tsuga*)	15,090	0.19
Grama-tobosa prairie (*Bouteloua-Hilaria*)	14,761	0.19
Everglades (*Mariscus* and *Magnolia-Persea*)	12,686	0.16
Blackbrush (*Coleogyne*)	12,043	0.16
Black Hills pine forest (*Pinus*)	11,918	0.15
Palmetto prairie (*Serenoa-Aristida*)	11,449	0.15
Mosaic of cedar-hemlock-Douglas fir forest and Oregon oakwoods	11,091	0.14
Southwestern spruce-fir forest (*Picea-Abies*)	10,664	0.14
Cedar glades (*Quercus-Juniperus-Sporobolus*)	10,531	0.14
Fescue-oatgrass (*Festuca-Danthonia*)	9,682	0.13
Tule marshes (*Scirpus-Typha*)	9,463	0.12
Lodgepole pine subalpine forest (*Pinus-Tsuga*)	9,291	0.12
Coastal sagebrush (*Salvia-Eriogonum*)	9,070	0.12
Pocosin (*Pinus-Ilex*)	8,864	0.11
Mesquite-oak savanna (*Andropogon-Prosopis-Quercus*)	8,742	0.11
Northeastern oak-pine forest (*Quercus-Pinus*)	8,406	0.11
Ceniza shrub (*Leucophyllum-Larrea-Prosopis*)	7,691	0.10
Fayette prairie (*Andropogon-Buchloë*)	7,486	0.10
Red fir forest (*Abies*)	7,151	0.09
Mesquite-live oak savanna (*Andropogon-Prosopis-Quercus*)	6,571	0.08
Fescue-mountain muhly prairie (*Festuca-Muhlenbergia*)	6,367	0.08
Spruce-fir-Douglas fir forest (*Picea-Abies-Pseudotsuga*)	4,286	0.06
Live oak-sea oats (*Quercus-Uniola*)	3,860	0.05
Oregon oakwoods (*Quercus*)	3,800	0.05
Mangrove (*Avicennia-Rhizophora*)	3,187	0.04
Cypress savanna (*Taxodium-Mariscus*)	2,688	0.03
Wheatgrass-grama buffalo grass (*Agropyron-Bouteloua-Buchloë*)	2,431	0.03
Sub-tropical pine forest (*Pinus*)	1,930	0.02
Sand pine scrub (*Pinus-Quercus*)	1,858	0.02
Galleta-three awn shrubsteppe (*Hilaria-Aristida*)	1,715	0.02
Northen cordgrass prairie (*Distichlis-Spartina*)	1,439	0.02
Redwood forest (*Sequoia-Pseudotsuga*)	1,033	0.01
Mesquite bosques (*Prosopis*)	665	0.01
Southeastern spruce-fir forest (*Picea-Abies*)	282	<0.01
Pine-cypress forest (*Pinus-Cupressus*)	191	<0.01
Total	7,740,507	100.00

Appendix D

PRINCIPAL SOURCES FOR U.S. SPECIES NAMES IN THE NATURAL HERITAGE CENTRAL DATABASES

Sources for Vertebrates

Mammals: Wilson and Reeder 1993; Jones et al. 1997. Birds: American Ornithologists' Union (AOU) 1998. Reptiles: King and Burke 1989; Collins 1997; Ernst et al. 1994. Amphibians: Frost 1985; Duellman 1993; Collins 1997; Petranka 1998. Fishes: Robins et al. 1991.

Sources for Invertebrates

General: Pennak 1989; Thorp and Covich 1991. Mollusks: Turgeon et al. 1998; Cowie et al. 1995. Crustaceans: A. B. Williams et al. 1989. Lepidoptera: Opler et al. 1999; Emmel 1998; Peigler and Opler 1993; Smith 1993; Tuskes et al. 1996; Quinter 1983. Tiger beetles: Boyd et al. 1982; Pearson et al. 1997. Other insects and allies: Poole and Gentili 1996–1997; Nishida 1994.

Sources for Plants

Kartesz 1994; Wagner et al. 1990.

LITERATURE CITED

Abrams, M. D., and C. M. Ruffner. 1995. Physiographic analysis of witness-tree distribution (1766–1798) and present forest cover through north central Pennsylvania. Canadian Journal of Forest Research 25: 659–668.

Agee, J. K. 1990. The historical role of fire in Pacific Northwest forests. In *Natural and Prescribed Fire in Pacific Northwest Forests*, ed. J. D. Walstad, S. R. Radosevich, and D. V. Sandberg, pp. 25–38. Corvallis: Oregon State University Press.

Airola, D. A. 1988. *Guide to the California Wildlife Habitat Relationships System*. Sacramento: California Department of Fish and Game.

American Ornithologists' Union (AOU). 1998. *Check-List of North American Birds*, 7th ed. (as modified by any supplements and corrections). Washington: American Ornithologists' Union.

Anderson, L. E., H. A. Crum, and W. R. Buck. 1990. List of the mosses of North America and Mexico. The Bryologist 93: 448–499.

Anderson, M., P. Bourgeron, M. T. Bryer, R. Crawford, D. Faber-Langendoen, K. Goodin, D. H. Grossman, S. Landaal, K. Metzler, K. D. Patterson, M. Pyne, M. Reid, L. Sneddon, and A. W. Weakley. 1998. *International Classification of Ecological Communities: Terrestrial Vegetation of the United States. Volume II: List of Vegetation Units*. Arlington, Va.: The Nature Conservancy.

Anderson, M., D. Grossman, C. Groves, K. Poiani, M. Reid, R. Schneider, B. Vickery, and A. Weakley. 1999. *Guidelines for Representing Ecological Communities in Ecoregional Conservation Plans*. Arlington, VA.: The Nature Conservancy.

Arnett, R. H., Jr. 1985. *American Insects*. Gainesville, Fla.: Flora and Fauna Publications.

Aselmann, I., and P. J. Crutzen. 1989. Global distribution of natural freshwater wetlands, rice paddies, their net primary productivity, seasonality, and possible methane emissions. Journal of Atmospheric Chemistry 8: 307–358.

Austin, M. P., and T. M. Smith. 1989. A new model for the continuum concept. Vegetatio 83: 35–47.

Austin, W. C. 1985. *An Annotated Checklist of Marine Invertebrates in the Cold Temperate Northeast Pacific*. 3 vols. Vorino, British Columbia, Canada: Khoyatan Marine Laboratory.

Bailey, R. G. 1989. *Ecoregions of the Continents*. Washington: U.S. Department of Agriculture, Forest Service. Map 1:30,000,000.

———. 1994. *Ecoregions of the United States*, rev. ed. Washington: U.S. Department of Agriculture, Forest Service. Map 1:7,500,000.

———. 1995. *Description of Ecoregions of the United States*. Miscellaneous Publication 1391. Washington: U.S. Department of Agriculture, Forest Service.

———. 1998a. *Ecoregions: The Ecosystem Geography of the Oceans and Continents*. New York: Springer-Verlag.

———. 1998b. *Ecoregions Map of North America*. Miscellaneous Publication 1548. Washington: U.S. Department of Agriculture, Forest Service. Map 1:15,000,000.

Baldwin, R. G., and M. J. Sanderson. 1998. Age and rate of diversification of the Hawaiian silversword alliance (Compositae). Proceedings of the National Academy of Sciences 95: 9402–9406.

Barbour, M. G. 1997. Ecological fragmentation in the fifties. In *Uncommon Ground: Toward Reinventing Nature*, ed. W. Cronon, pp. 233–255. New York: W. W. Norton and Co.

Barbour, M. G., and W. D. Billings, eds. 1988. *North American Terrestrial Vegetation*. Cambridge: Cambridge University Press.

Barbour, M. G., and N. L. Christensen. 1993. Vegetation. In *Flora of North America North of Mexico*, vol. 1, ed. Flora of North America Committee, pp. 97–131. New York: Oxford University Press.

Baskin, J. M., and C. C. Baskin. 1988. Endemism in rock outcrop plant communities of unglaciated eastern United States: An evaluation of the roles of edaphic, genetic, and light factors. Journal of Biogeography 15: 829–840.

Bean, M. J., S. J. Fitzgerald, and M. A. O'Connell. 1991. *Reconciling Conflicts under the Endangered Species Act: The Habitat Conservation Planning Experience*. Washington: World Wildlife Fund.

Bean, M. J., and M. J. Rowland. 1998. *The Evolution of National Wildlife Law*, 3d ed. Westport, Conn.: Praeger.

Bean, M. J., and D. S. Wilcove. 1997. The private-land problem. Conservation Biology 11: 1–2.

Berger, A. J. 1981. *Hawaiian Birdlife*. Honolulu: University Press of Hawaii.

Berger, L., R. Speare, P. Daszak, D. E. Green, A. A. Cunningham, C. L. Goggin, R. Slocombe, M. A. Ragan, A. D. Hyatt, K. R. McDonald, H. B. Hines, K. R. Lips, G. Marantelli, and H. Parkes. 1998. Chytridiomycosis causes amphibian mortality associated with population declines in the rain forests of Australia and Central America. Proceedings of the National Academy of Science 95: 9031–9036.

Berkeley, E., and D. S. Berkeley. 1982. *The Life and Travels of John Bartram*. Tallahassee: University Presses of Florida.

Betancourt, J. L., T. R. Van Devender, and P. S. Martin. 1990. *Packrat Middens: The Last 40,000 Years of Biotic Exchange*. Tucson: University of Arizona Press.

Blair, W. F. 1958. Distributional patterns of vertebrates in the southern United States in relation to past and present environments. In *Zoogeography*, ed. C. L. Hubbs, pp. 433–468. Washington: American Association for the Advancement of Science.

Blaustein, A. R., P. D. Hoffman, D. G. Hokit, J. M. Kiesecker, S. C. Walls, and J. B. Hays. 1994a. UV repair and resistance to solar UV-B in amphibian eggs: A link to population declines? Proceedings of the National Academy of Science 91: 1791–1795.

Blaustein, A. R., D. B. Wake, and W. P. Sousa. 1994b. Amphibian decline: Judging stability, persistence, and susceptibility of populations to local and global extinctions. Conservation Biology 8: 60–71.

Bogan, A. E. 1993. Freshwater bivalve extinctions (Mollusca: Unionidae): A search for causes. American Zoologist 33: 599–609.

Boufford, D. E., and S. A. Spongberg. 1983. Eastern Asian–North American phytogeographical relationships: A history from the time of Linneaus to the twentieth century. Annals of the Missouri Botanical Garden 70: 423–439.

Boyd, H. P., and Associates. 1982. *Checklist of Cicindelidae, the Tiger Beetles*. Marlton, N.J.: Plexus Publishing.

Brewer, R., G. A. McPeek, and R. J. Adams Jr. 1991. *The Atlas of Breeding Birds of Michigan*. East Lansing: Michigan State University Press.

Briggs, J. C. 1986. Introduction to the zoogeography of North American fishes. In *The Zoogeography of North American Fishes*, ed. C. H. Hocutt and E. O. Wiley, pp. 1–16. New York: John Wiley and Sons.

———. 1994. The genesis of Central America: Biology versus geophysics. Global Ecology and Biogeography Letters 4: 169–172.

Britten, H. B., P. F. Brussard, and D. D. Murphy. 1994. The pending extinction of the Uncompaghre fritillary butterfly. Conservation Biology 8: 86–94.

Brooks, D. R., and D. A. McLennan. 1991. *Phylogeny, Ecology, and Behavior*. Chicago: University of Chicago Press.

Brouillet, L., and R. D. Whetstone. 1993. Climate and physiography. In *Flora of North America North of Mexico*, vol. 1, ed. Flora of North America Editorial Committee, pp. 15–46. New York: Oxford University Press.

Brown, D. E., F. Reichenbacher, and S. E. Franson. 1998. *A Classification of North American Biotic Communities*. Salt Lake City: University of Utah Press.

Brown, J. H., and M. V. Lomolino. 1998. *Biogeography*, 2d ed. Sunderland, Mass.: Sinauer Associates.

Brown, P. M., and T. W. Swetnam. 1994. A cross-dated fire history from coast redwood near Redwood National Park, California. Canadian Journal of Forest Research 24: 21–31.

Buchmann, S. L., and G. P. Nabhan. 1996. *The Forgotten Pollinators*. Washington: Island Press.

Bury, R. B., P. S. Corn, C. K. Dodd Jr., R. W. McDiarmid, and N. J. Scott. 1995. Amphibians. In *Our Living Resources*, ed. E. T. LaRoe et al., pp. 124–126. Washington: U.S. Department of the Interior, National Biological Service.

Byers, J. A. 1997. *American Pronghorn: Social Adaptations and the Ghosts of Predators Past*. Chicago: University of Chicago Press.

Caicco, S. L., J. M. Scott, B. Butterfield, and B. Csuti. 1995. A gap analysis of the management status of the vegetation of Idaho, U.S.A. Conservation Biology 9: 498–511.

Cairns, S. D., D. R. Calder, A. Brinckman-Voss, C. B. Castro, P. R. Pugh, C. E. Cutress, W. C. Jaap, D. G. Fautin, R. J. Larson, G. R. Harbison, M. N. Arai, and D. M. Opresko. 1991. *Common and Scientific Names of Aquatic Invertebrates from the United States and Canada: Cnidaria and Ctenophora*. Special Publication No. 22. Bethesda, Md.: American Fisheries Society.

California Department of Fish and Game (CDFG). 1993. Natural community conservation planning: Conservation guidelines. Unpublished document. Sacramento: California Department of Fish and Game.

California Natural Diversity Database (CNDDB). 1999. *RareFind 2/GIS*. March 1999 edition. Sacramento: California Department of Fish and Game.

Carlquist, S. 1974. *Island Biology*. New York: Columbia University Press.

———. 1980. *Hawaii: A Natural History*. Lanai, Hawaii: Pacific Tropical Botanical Garden.

Carson, H. L., and D. A. Clague. 1995. Geology and biogeography of the Hawaiian Islands. In *Hawaiian Biogeography: Evolution on a Hot Spot Archipelago*, ed. W. L. Wagner and V. A. Funk, pp. 14–29. Washington: Smithsonian Institution Press.

Chapman, A. D., and J. R. Busby. 1994. Linking plant species information to continental biodiversity, inventory, climate modeling, and environmental monitoring. In *Mapping the Diversity of Nature*, ed. R. I. Miller, pp. 180–195. London: Chapman and Hall.

Church, R. L., and C. ReVelle. 1974. The maximal covering location problem. Papers of the Regional Science Association 32: 101–118.

Clague, D. A., and G. B. Dalrymple. 1987. The Hawaiian-Emperor volcanic chain. In *Volcanism in Hawaii*, ed. R. W. Decker, T. L. Wright, and P. H. Stauffer, pp. 1–54. U.S. Geological Survey Professional Paper 1350. Washington: U.S. Government Printing Office.

Clements, F. E. 1916. *Plant Succession: An Analysis of the Development of Vegetation*. Carnegie Institute Publication no. 242. Washington: Carnegie Institute.

Cohen, A. N., and J. T. Carlton. 1995. *Nonindigenous Aquatic Species in a United States Estuary: A Case Study of the Biological Invasions of the San Francisco Bay and Delta*. Washington and Groton, Conn.: U.S. Fish and Wildlife Service and the National Sea Grant College Program.

Collar, N. J., M. J. Crosby, and A. J. Stattersfield. 1994. *Birds to Watch 2: The World List of Threatened Birds*. Cambridge, Eng.: BirdLife International.

Collins, J. T. 1997. Standard common and current scientific names for North American amphibians and reptiles, 4th ed. Society for the Study of Amphibians and Reptiles. Herpetological Circular no. 25.

Comer, P. J., D. A. Albert, H. A. Wells, B. L. Hart, J. B. Rabb, D. L. Price, D. M. Kashian, R. A. Corner, D. W. Schuen (map interpretation); M. B. Austin, T. R. Leibfreid, K. M. Korroch, L. Prange-Gregory, J. G. Spitzley, C. J. DeLain, L. J. Scrimger (digital map production). 1995. Michigan's presettlement vegetation, as interpreted from the General Land Office surveys 1816–1856. Lansing, Michigan: Michigan Natural Features Inventory. Digital Map.

Comer, P. J., D. A. Albert, H. A. Wells, B. L. Hart, J. B. Rabb, D. L. Price, D. M. Kashian, R. A. Corner, and D. W. Schuen (map interpretation); T. R. Leibfreid, M. B. Austin, C. J. DeLain, K. M. Korroch, L. Prange-Gregory, L. J. Scrimger, and J. G. Spitzley (digital map production). 1998. Mapping the vegetation of Michigan, circa 1880: Map development and selected applications. Proceedings of the 1998 Gap Analysis Conference, Santa Barbara, Calif.

Conant, R., and J. T. Collins. 1998. *A Field Guide to Reptiles and Amphibians: Eastern and Central North America*, 3d ed. Boston: Houghton Mifflin.

Constantz, G. 1994. *Hollows, Peepers, and Highlanders*. Missoula, Mt.: Mountain Press.

Core, E. L. 1968. The botany of Ice Mountain, West Virginia. Castanea 33: 345–348.

Cort, C. A. 1996. A survey of the use of natural heritage data in local land-use planning. Conservation Biology 10: 632–637.

Costanza, R., R. d'Agre, R. de Groot, S. Farber, M. Grasso, B. Hannon, K. Limburg, S. Naeem, R. V. O'Neill, J. Paruelo, R. G. Raskin, P. Sutton, and M. van den Belt. 1997. The value of the world's ecosystem services and natural capital. Nature 387: 253–260.

Cowardin, L. M., V. Carter, F. C. Golet, and E. T. LaRoe. 1979. *Classification of the Wetlands and Deepwater Habitats of the United States*. Washington: U.S. Fish and Wildlife Service.

Cowie, R. H., N. L. Evenhuis, and C. C. Christensen. 1995. *Catalog of the Native Land and Freshwater Molluscs of the Hawaiian Islands*. Leiden, The Netherlands: Backhuys.

Cox, G. W. 1986. Mima mounds as an indicator of the presettlement grassland-chaparral boundary in San Diego County, California. American Midland Naturalist 116: 64–77.

Cox, J., R. Kautz, M. MacLaughlin, and T. Gilbert. 1994. *Closing the Gaps in Florida's Wildlife Habitat Conservation System*. Tallahassee: Florida Game and Freshwater Fish Commission.

Croker, R. A. 1991. *Pioneer Ecologist: The Life and Work of Victor Ernest Shelford*. Washington: Smithsonian Institution Press.

Cronon, W. 1983. *Changes in the Land: Indians, Colonists, and the Ecology of New England*. New York: Hill and Wang.

Crozier, R. H. 1997. Preserving the information content of species: Genetic diversity, phylogeny, and conservation worth. Annual Review of Ecology and Systematics 28: 243–268.

Crumpacker, D. W., S. W. Hodge, D. Friedly, and W. P. Gregg. 1988. A preliminary assessment of the status of major terrestrial and wetland ecosystems on federal and Indian lands in the United States. Conservation Biology 2: 103–115.

Csuti, B., and A. R. Kiester. 1996. Hierarchical gap analysis for identifying priority areas for biodiversity. In *Gap Analysis: A Landscape Approach to Biodiversity Planning*, ed. J. M. Scott, T. H. Tear, and F. W. Davis, pp. 25–37. Bethesda, Md.: American Society of Photogrammetry and Remote Sensing.

Csuti, B., A. J. Kimerling, T. A. O'Neil, M. Shaughnessy, E. P. Gaines, and M. M. P. Huso. 1997a. *Atlas of Oregon Wildlife*. Corvallis: Oregon State University Press.

Csuti, B., S. Polasky, P. H. Williams, R. L. Pressey, J. D. Camm, M. Kershaw, A. R. Kiester, B. Downs, R. Hamilton, M. Huso, and K. Sahr. 1997b. A comparison of reserve selection algorithms using data on terrestrial vertebrates in Oregon. Biological Conservation 80: 83–97.

Culliney, J. L. 1988. *Islands in a Far Sea: Nature and Man in Hawaii*. San Francisco: Sierra Club Books.

Culver, D. C., and J. R. Holsinger. 1992. How many species of troglobites are there? National Speleological Society Bulletin 54: 79–80.

Currie, D. J. 1991. Energy and large-scale patterns of animal- and plant-species richness. American Naturalist 137: 27–49.

Curtis, J. T. 1959. *The Vegetation of Wisconsin: An Ordination of Plant Communities*. Madison: University of Wisconsin Press.

Cutright, P. R. 1969. *Lewis and Clark, Pioneering Naturalists*. Urbana: University of Illinois Press.

Dahl, T. E. 1990. *Wetlands Losses in the United States, 1780s to 1980s*. Washington: U.S. Fish and Wildlife Service.

Daily, G. C., S. Alexander, P. R. Ehrlich, L. Goulder, J. Lubchenco, P. A. Matson, H. A. Mooney, S. Postel, S. H. Schneider, D. Tilman, and G. M. Woodwell. 1997. Ecosystem services: Benefits supplied to human societies by natural ecosystems. Issues in Ecology no. 2.

Danko, D. M. 1992. The digital chart of the world. GeoInfo Systems 2: 29–36.

Daubenmire, R. 1966. Vegetation: Identification of typal communities. Science 151: 291–298.

Davis, F. W., P. A. Stine, D. M. Stoms, M. I. Borchert, and A. D. Hollander. 1995. Gap analysis of the actual vegetation of California 1: The southwestern region. Madroño 42: 40–78.

Davis, F. W., D. M. Stoms, R. L. Church, B. J. Okin, and N. L. Johnson. 1996. Selecting biodiversity management areas. In *Sierra Nevada Ecosystem Project: Assessments and Scientific Basis for Management Options, Final Report to Congress*, vol. 2, pp. 1503–1528. Davis: Centers for Water and Wildlands Resources, University of California, Davis.

Davis, F. W., D. Stoms, J. Scepan, J. Estes, and J. M. Scott. 1990. An information systems approach to the preservation of biological diversity. International Journal of Geographic Information Systems 4: 55–78.

Davis, M. B. 1981. Quaternary history and the stability of plant communities. In *Forest Succession: Concepts and Application*, ed. D. C. West, H. H. Shugart, and D. B. Botkin, pp. 132–153. New York: Springer-Verlag.

——— . 1983. Quaternary history of deciduous forest of eastern North America and Europe. Annals of the Missouri Botanical Garden 70: 550–563.

———, ed. 1996. *Eastern Old-Growth Forests: Prospects for Rediscovery and Recovery*. Washington: Island Press.

Davis, S. D., V. H. Heywood, O. Herrera-MacBryde, J. Villa-Lobos, and A. C. Hamilton. 1997. *Centres of Plant Diversity: A Guide and Strategy for Their Conservation*. Vol. 3: *The Americas*. Cambridge, Eng.: IUCN Publications Unit.

Defries, R., M. Hansen, and J. Townshend. 1995. Global discrimination of land cover types from metrics derived from AVHRR Pathfinder data. Remote Sensing of Environment 54: 209–222.

Dietrich, W. 1995. *Northwest Passage: The Great Columbia River*. New York: Simon and Schuster.

Dobson, A. P., J. P. Rodriguez, W. M. Roberts, and D. S. Wilcove. 1997. Geographic distribution of endangered species in the United States. Science 275: 550–553.

Dorney, J. R. 1981. The impact of Native Americans on presettlement vegetation in southeastern Wisconsin American Indians. Transactions of the Wisconsin Academy of Sciences, Arts, and Letters 69: 26–36.

Dott, R. H., and D. R. Prothero. 1994. *Evolution of the Earth*, 5th ed. New York: McGraw Hill.

Duckworth, W. D., H. H. Genoways, and C. L. Rose. 1993. *Preserving Natural Science Collections: Chronicles of Our Environmental Heritage*. Washington: National Institute for the Conservation of Cultural Property.

Duellman, W. E. 1993. Amphibian species of the world: additions and corrections. University of Kansas Museum of Natural History, Special Publication 21: 1–372.

Duffy, D. C., and A. J. Meier. 1992. Do Appalachian herbaceous understories ever recover from clearcutting? Conservation Biology 6: 196–201.

Easter-Pilcher, A. 1996. Implementing the Endangered Species Act: Assessing the listing of species as endangered or threatened. BioScience 46: 355–363.

Ehrenfeld, D., R. F. Noss, and G. K. Meffee. 1997. Letter to the editor. Science 276: 515–516.

Ehrlich, P. R. 1988. The loss of diversity: Causes and consequences. In *Biodiversity*, ed. E. O. Wilson, pp. 21–27. Washington: National Academy Press.

Ehrlich, P. R., D. S. Dobkin, and D. Wheye. 1992. *Birds in Jeopardy*. Stanford: Stanford University Press.

Ehrlich, P. R., and P. H. Raven. 1965. Butterflies and plants: A study in coevolution. Evolution 18: 586–608.

Eisner, T., K. D. McCormick, M. Sakaino, M. Eisner, S. R. Smedley, D. J. Aneshansley, M. Deyrup, R. L. Myers, and J. Meinwald. 1990. Chemical defenses of a rare mint plant. Chemoecology 1: 30–37.

Eldredge, L. G., and S. E. Miller. 1995. How many species are there in Hawai'i? Bishop Museum Occasional Papers 41: 1–18.

———. 1996. Number of Hawaiian species: Supplement 1. Bishop Museum Occasional Papers 45: 8–17.

———. 1998. Numbers of Hawaiian species: Supplement 3, with notes on fossil species. Bishop Museum Occasional Papers 55: 3–15.

Elman, R. 1977. *First in the Field*. New York: Mason/Charter.

Elphick, J. 1995. *The Atlas of Bird Migration*. New York: Random House.

Emmel, T. C., ed. 1998. *Systematics of Western Butterflies*. Gainesville, Fla.: Mariposa Press.

Ernst, C. H., R. W. Barbour, and J. E. Lovich. 1994. *Turtles of the United States and Canada*. Washington: Smithsonian Institution Press.

Erwin, T. L. 1991. How many species are there? Revisited. Conservation Biology 5: 330–333.

Esslinger, T. L., and R. S. Egan. 1995. A sixth checklist of the lichen-forming, lichenicolous, and allied fungi of the continental United States and Canada. The Bryologist 98: 467–549.

Eyre, F. H., ed. 1980. *Forest Cover Types of the United States and Canada*. Washington: Society of American Foresters.

Farr, D. F., G. F. Bills, G. P. Chamuris, and A. Y. Rossman. 1989. *Fungi on Plants and Plant Products in the United States*. St. Paul: APS Press.

Federal Geographic Data Committee (FGDC). 1997. *Vegetation Classification Standard*. Washington: FGDC.

Fischer, H. 1994. *Building Economic Incentives into the Endangered Species Act*. Washington: Defenders of Wildlife.

Fitzpatrick, J. W., G. E. Woolfenden, and M. T. Kopeny. 1991. Ecology and development-related habitat requirements of the Florida scrub jay (*Aphelocoma coerulescens coerulescens*). Final Report to the Florida Game and Fresh Water Fish Commission, Tallahassee, Contract no. GFC-84-101.

Flather, C. H., L. A. Joyce, and C. A. Bloomgarden. 1994. *Species Endangerment Patterns in the United States*. USDA Forest Service General Technical Report RM-241. Fort Collins, Colo.: U.S. Department of Agriculture, Forest Service, Rocky Mountain Forest and Range Experiment Station.

Flather, C. H., M. S. Knowles, and I. A. Kendall. 1998. Threatened and endangered species geography: Characteristics of hot spots in the conterminous United States. BioScience 48: 365–376.

Flather, C. H., K. R. Wilson, D. J. Dean, and W. C. McComb. 1997. Identifying gaps in conservation networks: Of indicators and uncertainty in geographic-based analyses. Ecological Applications 7: 531–542.

Flora of North America Editorial Committee (FNA). 1993. *Flora of North America North of Mexico*. Vol. 2: *Pteridophytes and Gymnosperms*. New York: Oxford University Press.

Franklin, J. F. 1988. Pacific Northwest forests. In *North American Terrestrial Vegetation*, ed. M. G. Barbour and W. D. Billings, pp. 103–130. Cambridge: Cambridge University Press.

Franklin, J. F., and R. H. Waring. 1980. Distinctive features of the northwestern coniferous forest. In *Forests: Fresh Perspectives from Ecosystem Analysis*, ed. R. H. Waring, pp. 59–86. Proceedings of the Annual Biological Colloquium. Corvallis: Oregon State University.

Frost, D. R., ed. 1985. *Amphibian Species of the World: A Taxonomic and Geographical Reference*. Lawrence, Kans.: Allen Press and the Association of Systematics Collections.

Gawler, S. C., J. J. Albright, P. D. Vickery, and F. C. Smith. 1996. Biological diversity in Maine: An assessment of status and trends in the terrestrial and freshwater landscape. Report prepared for the Maine Forest Biodiversity Project, Maine Natural Areas Program, Department of Conservation, Augusta.

Gehlbach, F. R. 1984. Introduction. In *The Snakes of Texas*, ed. A. Tenant, pp. 17–18. Austin: Texas Monthly Press.

Gentry, A. H. 1982. Neotropical floristic diversity: Phytogeographical con-nections between Central and South America, Pleistocene climatic fluctu-ations, or an accident of the Andean orogeny? Annals of the Missouri Botanical Garden 69: 557–593.

———. 1986. Endemism in tropical versus temperate plant communities. In *Conservation Biology: The Science of Scarcity and Diversity*, ed. M. Soulé, pp. 153–181. Sunderland, Mass.: Sinauer.

Gerrard, R. A., R. L. Church, D. M. Stoms, and F. W. Davis. 1997. Selecting conservation reserves using species-covering models: Adapting the Arc/Info GIS. Transactions in GIS 2: 45–60.

Gleason, H. A. 1917. The structure and development of the plant association. Bulletin of the Torrey Botanical Club 53: 7–26.

———. 1926. The individualistic concept of the plant association. Bulletin of the Torrey Botanical Club 53: 7–26.

Golvan, Y. 1994. Nomenclature of the Acanthocephala. Research and Reviews in Parasitology 54: 35–205.

Gottlieb, L. D. 1973. Genetic differen-tiation, sympatric speciation and the origin of a diploid species of *Stephanomeria*. American Journal of Botany 60: 545–553.

Graham, A. 1993. History of the vegetation: Cretaceous Maastrich-tian)— Tertiary. In *Flora of North America North of Mexico*, vol. 1, ed. Flora of North America Editorial Committee, pp. 57–70. New York: Oxford University Press.

———. 1999. *Late Cretaceous and Cenozoic History of North American Vegetation North of Mexico*. New York: Oxford University Press.

Grande, L., and W. E. Bemis. 1998. *A Comparative Phylogenetic Study of Amiid Fishes (Amiidae) Based in Comparative Skeletal Anatomy*. Chicago: Society of Vertebrate Paleontology.

Grant, M. C., J. B. Mitton, Y. B. Linhart. 1992. Even larger organ-isms. Nature 360: 216.

Greller, A. M. 1988. Deciduous forest. In *North American Terrestrial Vegetation*, ed. M. D. Barbour and W. D. Billings, pp. 287–316. Cambridge: Cambridge University Press.

Grossman, D. H., D. Faber-Langendoen, A. W. Weakley, M. Anderson, P. Bourgeron, R. Crawford, K. Goodin, S. Landaal, K. Metzler, K. D. Patterson, M. Pyne, M. Reid, and T. Sneddon. 1998. *International Classification of Ecological Communi-ties: Terrestrial Vegetation of the United States*, vol. 1. Arlington, Va.: The Nature Conservancy.

Grossman, D. H., K. L. Goodin, and C. L. Reuss. 1994. *Rare Plant Communities of the Conterminous United States: An Initial Survey*. Arlington, Va.: The Nature Conservancy.

Grove, N. 1992. *Preserving Eden: The Nature Conservancy*. New York: Harry N. Abrams.

Groves, C. R., M. L. Klein, and T. F. Breden. 1995. Natural heritage programs: Public-private partner-ships for biodiversity conservation. Wildlife Society Bulletin 23: 784–790.

Hale, S. G., C. R. Schwalbe, H. L. Jarchow, C. J. Lowe, and T. B. Johnson. 1995. Disappearance of the Tarahumara frog. In *Our Living Resources*, ed. E. T. LaRoe et al., pp. 138–140. Washington: U.S. Department of the Interior, National Biological Service.

Hammond, P. M. 1995. The current magnitude of biodiversity. In *Global Biodiversity Assessment*, ed. V. Heywood, pp. 113–138. Cambridge: Cambridge University Press.

Hannah, L., J. L. Carr, and A. Lankerani. 1995. Human disturbance and natural habitat: A biome level analysis of a global set. Biodiversity and Conservation 4: 128–155.

Hannah, L., D. Lohse, C. Hutchinson, J. L. Carr, and A. Lankerani. 1994. A preliminary inventory of human disturbance of world ecosystems. Ambio 23: 246–250.

Hanski, I., J. Clobert, and W. Reid. 1995. Ecology of extinctions. In *Global Biodiversity Assessment*, ed. V. Heywood, pp. 232–245. Cambridge: Cambridge University Press.

Hanski, I., and M. Gyllenberg. 1997. Uniting two general patterns in the distribution of species. Science 275: 397–400.

Hartfield, P., and R. Butler. 1995. Observations on the release of superconglutinates by *Lampsilis perovalis* (Conrad 1834). In *Conservation and Management of Freshwater Mussels II: Initiatives for the Future*, ed. K. S. Cummings, A. C. Buchanan, C. A. Mayer, and T. J. Naimo, pp. 11–13. Proceedings of a UMRCC symposium. Rock Island, Ill.: Upper Mississippi River Conservation Committee.

Hartman, R. L., and B. E. Nelson. 1998. Taxonomic novelties from North America north of Mexico. Monographs in Systematic Botany from the Missouri Botanical Garden 67: 1–59.

Hawksworth, D. L. 1995. The resource base for biodiversity assessment. In *Global Biodiversity Assessment*, ed. V. H. Heywood, pp. 545–606. Cambridge: Cambridge University Press.

Hawksworth, D. L., and M. T. Kalin-Arroyo. 1995. Magnitude and distribution of biodiversity. In *Global Biodiversity Assessment*, ed. V. H. Heywood, pp. 107–191. Cambridge: Cambridge University Press.

Hayes, T. B., and N. Noriega. 1997. Endocrine disruptors: A role in amphibian declines? Abstract from Third World Congress in Herpetology, Prague, Czech Republic.

Hickman, J. C., ed. 1993. *The Jepson Manual: Higher Plants of California*. Berkeley: University of California Press.

Higgins, J., M. Lammert, M. Bryer, M. DePhilip, and D. Grossman. 1998. *Freshwater Conservation in the Great Lakes Basin: Development and Application of an Aquatic Community Classification Framework*. Report to the George Gund Foundation and U.S. Environmental Protection Agency. Chicago: The Nature Conservancy, Great Lakes Program.

Hogan, K., and C. ReVelle. 1986. Concepts and applications of backup coverage. Management Science 32: 1434–1444.

Holdridge, L. R., W. C. Grenke, W. H. Hatheway, T. Liang, and J. A. Tosi. 1971. *Forest Environments in Tropical Life Zones*. Oxford: Pergamon Press.

Hollander, A. D., F. W. Davis, and D. M. Stoms. 1994. Hierarchical representations of species distributions using maps, images, and sighting data. In *Mapping the Diversity of Nature*, ed. R. I. Miller, pp. 71–87. London: Chapman and Hall.

Hood, L. C. 1998. *Frayed Safety Nets: Conservation Planning under the Endangered Species Act*. Washington: Defenders of Wildlife.

Houghton, J. T., L. G. Meira Filho, B. A. Callander, N. Harris, A. Kattenberg, and K. Maskell, eds. 1995. *Climate Change 1995*. Cambridge: Cambridge University Press.

Howarth, F. G., and W. P. Mull. 1992. *Hawaiian Insects and Their Kin*. Honolulu: University of Hawaii Press.

Hsü, J. 1983. Late Cretaceous and Cenozoic vegetation in China, emphasizing their connections with North America. Annals of the Missouri Botanical Gardens 70: 490–508.

Hultén, E. 1937. *Outline of the History of Arctic and Boreal Biota during the Quaternary Period*. Stockholm: Bokforlags Aktiebolaget Thule.

Hunter, M. L., G. L. Jacobson Jr., and T. Webb III. 1988. Paleoecology and the coarse-filter approach to maintaining biological diversity. Conservation Biology 2: 375–385.

Hunziker, J. H., R. A. Palacios, L. Poggio, C. A. Naranjo, and T. W. Yang. 1977. Geographic distribution, morphology, hybridization, cytogenetics, and evolution. In *Creosote Bush: Biology and Chemistry* of Larrea *in New World Deserts*, ed. T. J. Mabry, J. H Hunziker, and D. R. DiFeo Jr., pp. 10–47. Stroudsburg, Pa.: Dowden, Hutchinson, and Ross.

Hylton, R. E. 1998. Setback hinders endangered mussel recovery. Triannual Unionid Report 16: 24–25.

IUCN. 1994. *IUCN Red List Categories*. Gland, Switzerland: IUCN.

———. 1996. *1996 IUCN Red List of Threatened Animals*. Gland, Switzerland: IUCN.

Jacobi, J. D., and C. T. Atkinson. 1995. Hawaii's endemic birds. In *Our Living Resources*, ed. E. T. LaRoe et al., pp. 376–381. Washington: U.S. Department of the Interior, National Biological Service.

Jenkins, R. E. 1985. Information methods: Why the Heritage programs work. Nature Conservancy News 35: 21–23.

———. 1988. Information management for the conservation of biodiversity. In *Biodiversity*, ed. E. O. Wilson, pp. 231–239. Washington: National Academy Press.

———. 1996. Natural Heritage Data Center Network: Managing information for managing biodiversity. In *Biodiversity in Managed Landscapes: Theory and Practice*, ed. R. C. Szaro and D. W. Johnston, pp. 176–192. New York: Oxford University Press.

Jenkins, R. E., E. A. Lachner, and F. J. Schwartz. 1972. Fishes of the central Appalachians drainage: Their distribution and dispersal. In *The Distributional History of the Biota of the Southern Appalachians, Part III: The Vertebrates*, ed. P. C. Holt, pp. 43–117. Monograph 4. Blacksburg: Virginia Polytechnic University Research Division.

Jones, C., R. S. Hoffman, D. W. Rice, M. D. Engstrom, R. D. Bradley, D. J. Schmidly, C. A. Jones, and R. J. Baker. 1997. Revised checklist of North American mammals north of Mexico, 1997. Occasional Papers, Museum of Texas Tech University 173: 1–19.

Kaiser, J. 1997. When a habitat is not a home. Science 276: 1636–1638.

Kaneshiro, K. Y., R. G. Gillespie, and H. L. Carson. 1995. Chromosomes and male genitalia of Hawaiian Drosophila: Tools for interpreting phylogeny and geography. In

Hawaiian Biogeography: Evolution on a Hot Spot Archipelago, ed. W. L. Wagner and V. A. Funk, pp. 57–71. Washington: Smithsonian Institution Press.

Kartesz, J. T. 1994. *A Synonymized Checklist of the Vascular Flora of the U.S., Canada, and Greenland*, 2d ed. 2 vols. Portland: Timber Press.

Kartesz, J. T., and A. Farstad. 1999. Multi-scale analysis of endemism in vascular plant species. In *A Conservation Assessment of the Terrestrial Ecosystems of North America. Vol. 1: The United States and Canada*, ed. T. Ricketts et al., pp. 51–54. Washington: Island Press.

Keystone Center. 1995. *The Keystone Dialogue on Incentives for Private Landowners to Protect Endangered Species*. Keystone, Colo.: The Keystone Center.

Kiester, A. R. 1971. Species density of North American amphibians and reptiles. Systematic Zoology 20: 127–137.

Kiester, A. R., J. M. Scott, B. Csuti, R. F. Noss, B. Butterfield, K. Sahr, and D. White. 1996. Conservation prioritization using GAP data. Conservation Biology 10: 1332–1342.

Kimmins, J. P. 1997. *Forest Ecology: A Foundation for Sustainable Management*, 2d ed. Upper Saddle River, N J.: Prentice Hall.

King, W. F., and R. L. Burke. 1989. *Crocodilian, tuatara, and turtle species of the world*. Washington: Association of Systematics Collections.

Kirch, P. V. 1982. The impact of the prehistoric Polynesians on the Hawaiian ecosystem. Pacific Science 36: 1–14.

Kirkpatrick, J. B. 1983. An iterative method for establishing priorities for the selection of nature reserves: An example from Tasmania. Biological Conservation 25: 127–134.

Klopatek, J. M., R. J. Olson, C. J. Emerson, and J. L. Jones. 1979. Land-use conflicts with natural vegetation in the United States. Environmental Conservation 6: 191–199.

Kosztarab, M., and C. W. Schaefer. 1990. Systematics of the North American insects and arachnids: Status and needs. Information Series 90–1, Virginia Agricultural Experiment Station, Blacksburg, Va.

Kruckeberg, A. R. 1984. *California Serpentines: Flora, Vegetation,*

Geology, Soils, and Management Problems. Berkeley: University of California Press.

Küchler, A. W. 1964. Potential natural vegetation of the conterminous United States. Special Publication 36. New York: American Geographical Society (with separate map at 1:3,168,000).

———. 1975. Potential natural vegetation of the conterminous United States (map at 1:3,168,000), 2d ed. New York: American Geographical Society.

———. 1985. Potential natural vegetation (map). Revised. Reston, Va.: National Atlas of the United States, U.S. Geological Survey (scale 1:7,500,000).

Kuehne, R. A., and R. W. Barbour. 1983. *The American Darters*. Lexington: University Press of Kentucky.

Lambshead, P. J. D. 1993. Recent developments in marine benthic biodiversity research. Oceanis 19: 5–24.

Lammert, M., J. Higgins, D. Grossman, and M. Bryer. 1996. *A Classification Framework for Freshwater Communities*. Proceedings of The Nature Conservancy's Aquatic Classification Workshop, New Haven, Mo., April 9–11, 1996. Arlington, Va.: The Nature Conservancy.

Lammertink, M. 1995. No more hope for the ivory-billed woodpecker *Campephilus principalis*. Cotinga 3: 45–47.

Land Trust Alliance. 1998. *1998 National Land Trust Census*. Washington: Land Trust Alliance.

Langner, L. L., and C. H. Flather. 1994. *Biological Diversity: Status and Trends in the United States*. Technical Report RM-244. Washington: U.S. Department of Agriculture, Forest Service.

LaRoe, E. T., G. S. Farris, C. E. Puckett, P. D. Doreen, and M. J. Mac, eds. 1995. *Our Living Resources: A Report to the Nation on the Distribution, Abundance, and Health of U.S. Plants, Animals, and Ecosystems*. Washington: U.S. Department of the Interior, National Biological Service.

Latham, R. E., and Ricklefs, R. E. 1993. Continental comparisons of temperate-zone tree species diversity. In *Species Diversity: Historical and Geographical Perspec-*
tives, ed. R. E. Ricklefs and D. Schulter, pp. 294–314. Chicago: University of Chicago Press.

Lawton, J. H., and R. M. May. 1995. *Extinction Rates*. Oxford: Oxford University Press.

LeBlond, R. J., A. S. Weakley, A. A. Reznicek, and W. J. Crins. 1994. *Carex lutea* (Cyperaceae), a rare new coastal plain endemic from North Carolina. Sida 16: 153–161.

Leslie, M., G. K. Meffe, J. L. Hardesty, and D. L. Adams. 1996. *Conserving Biodiversity on Military Lands: A Handbook for Natural Resources Managers*. Arlington, Va.: The Nature Conservancy.

Lewis, R. E., and J. H. Lewis. 1994. The Siphonaptera of North America north of Mexico: Hystrichopsyllidae. Journal of Medical Entomology 31: 795–812.

Lindenmayer, D. B., H. A. Nix, J. P. McMahon, M. F. Hutchinson, and M. T. Tanton. 1991. Bioclimatic modelling and wildlife conservation—a case study on Leadbetter's possum, *Gymnobelideus leadbeateri*. Journal of Biogeography 18: 371–383.

Loveland, T. R, and A. S. Belward. 1997. The IGBP-DIS global 1 km. land cover data set, DISCover first results. International Journal of Remote Sensing 18: 3289–3295.

Loveland, T. R., and H. L. Hutcheson. 1995. Monitoring changes in landscapes from satellite imagery. In *Our Living Resources*, ed. E. T. LaRoe et al., pp. 468–473. Washington: U.S. Department of the Interior, National Biological Service.

Loveland, T. R., J. W. Merchant, D. O. Ohlen, and J. F. Brown. 1991. Development of a land-cover characteristics database for the conterminous United States. Photogrammetric Engineering and Remote Sensing 5: 1453–1463.

Lydeard, C., and R. L. Mayden. 1995. A diverse and endangered aquatic ecosystem of the southeastern United States. Conservation Biology 9: 800–805.

MacArthur, R. H. 1972. *Geographical Ecology: Patterns in the Distribution of Species*. New York: Harper and Row.

MacArthur, R. H., and E. O. Wilson. 1967. *The Theory of Island Biogeography*. Monographs in Population Biology no. 1. Princeton: Princeton University Press.

Mace, G. M., and R. Lande. 1991. Assessing extinction threats: Towards a reevaluation of IUCN threatened species categories. Conservation Biology 5: 148–157.

Mann, C., and M. Plummer. 1997. Qualified thumbs up for habitat plan science. Science 278: 2052–2053.

Margulis, L., and K. V. Schwartz. 1998. *Five Kingdoms: An Illustrated Guide to the Phyla of Life on Earth*, 3d ed. New York: W. H. Freeman and Co.

Martin, W. H., S. G. Boyce, and A. C. Echternacht, eds. 1993. *Biodiversity of the Southeastern United States: Lowland Terrestrial Communities (Volume 1) and Upland Terrestrial Communities (Volume 2)*. New York: John Wiley.

Master, L. L. 1991. Assessing threats and setting priorities for conservation. Conservation Biology 5: 559–563.

Master, L. L., S. R. Flack, and B. A. Stein. 1998. *Rivers of Life: Critical Watersheds for Protecting Freshwater Biodiversity*. Arlington, Va.: The Nature Conservancy.

Matthews, E. 1983. Global vegetation and land use: New high resolution databases for climate studies. Journal of Climate and Applied Meteorology 22: 474–487.

Maxwell, J. R., C. J. Edwards, M. E. Jensen, S. J. Paustian, H. Parrott, and D. M. Hill. 1995. *A Hierarchical Framework of Aquatic Ecological Units in North America*. General Technical Report NC-176. St. Paul: U.S. Department of Agriculture, Forest Service, North Central Forest Experiment Station.

May, R. M. 1994. Conceptual aspects of the quantification of the extent of biodiversity. Philosophical Transactions of the Royal Society of London B-345: 13–20.

Maybank, B. 1998. The 1997 big day report and the 1997 list report. Birding 30, no. 4 (supplement): 1–96.

Mayr, E. 1982. *The Growth of Biological Thought: Diversity, Evolution, and Inheritance*. Cambridge: Belknap Press of Harvard University Press.

McAllister, D. E., S. P. Platania, F. W. Schueler, M. E. Baldwin, and D. S. Lee. 1986. Ichthyofaunal patterns on a geographic grid. In *The Zoogeography of North American Freshwater Fishes*, ed. C. H. Hocutt and E. O. Wiley, pp. 17–52. New York: John Wiley and Sons.

McClintock, E. 1985. Escaped exotic weeds in California. Fremontia 12: 3–6.

McCullough, D. R. 1996. *Metapopulations and Wildlife Conservation*. Washington: Island Press.

McGhie, R. G., J. Scepan, and J. E. Estes. 1996. A comprehensive managed areas spatial database for the conterminous United States. Photogrammetric Engineering and Remote Sensing 62: 1303–1306.

McKenna, M. C. 1983. Holarctic landmass rearrangement, cosmic events, and Cenozoic terrestrial organisms. Annals of the Missouri Botanical Garden 70: 459–489.

McNab, W. H., and P. E. Avers. 1994. *Ecological Subregions of the United States: Section Descriptions*. WO-WSA-5. Washington: U.S. Department of Agriculture, Forest Service, ECOMAP Team.

McPeek, M. A., and T. E. Miller. 1996. Evolutionary biology and community ecology. Ecology 77: 1319–1320.

Meffe, G. K., and C. R. Carroll. 1997. *Principles of Conservation Biology*. Sunderland, Mass.: Sinauer Associates.

Menges, E. 1990. Population viability analysis for an endangered plant. Conservation Biology 4: 52–62.

———. 1997. Ecology and conservation of Florida scrub. In *The Savanna, Barren, and Rock Outcrop Communities of North America*, ed. R. C. Anderson, J. S. Fralish, and J. Baskin. New York: Cambridge University Press.

Merriam, C. H. 1894. The geographic distribution of animals and plants in North America. Yearbook of the United States Department of Agriculture 1894: 203–214.

Mershon, W. G. 1907. *The Passenger Pigeon*. New York: Outing Publishing Co.

Metrick, A., and M. L. Weitzman. 1996. Patterns of behavior in endangered species preservation. Land Economics 72: 1–16.

Millar, C. I., and W. J. Libby. 1991. Strategies for conserving clinal, ecotypic, and disjunct population diversity in widespread species. In *Genetics and Conservation of Rare Plants*, ed. D. A. Falk and K. E. Holsinger, pp. 149–170. Oxford: Oxford University Press.

Miller, R. I. 1994. *Mapping the Diversity of Nature*. London: Chapman and Hall.

Miller, R. R., and E. P. Pister. 1971. Management of the Owens pupfish, *Cyprinodon radiosus*, in Mono County, California. Transactions of the American Fisheries Society 100: 502–509.

Miller, R. R., J. D. Williams, and J. E. Willams. 1989. Extinctions of North American fishes during the past century. Fisheries 14: 22–38.

Mooney, H. A., J. Lubchenco, R. Dirzo, and O. E. Sala. 1995. Biodiversity and ecosystem functioning: Basic principles. In *Global Biodiversity Assessment*, ed. V. H. Heywood, pp. 275–325. Cambridge: Cambridge University Press.

Morain, S. A. 1984. *Systematic and Regional Biogeography*. New York: Van Nostrand Reinhold.

Morse, L. E. 1993. Standard and alternative taxonomic data in the multi-institutional Natural Heritage Data Center Network. In *Designs for a Global Plant Species Information System*, ed. F. A. Bisby, G. F. Russell, and R. J. Pankhurst. Oxford: Oxford University Press.

Morse, L. E., L. S. Kutner, G. D. Maddox, J. T. Kartesz, L. L. Honey, C. M. Thurman, and S. J. Chaplin. 1993. The potential effects of climate change on the native vascular flora of North America: A preliminary climate envelopes analysis. Report no. EPRI TR-103330. Palo Alto, Calif.: Electric Power Research Institute.

Moyle, P. B., and R. A. Leidy. 1992. Loss of biodiversity in aquatic ecosystems: Evidence from fish faunas. In *Conservation Biology: The Theory and Practice of Nature Conservation*, ed. P. L. Fiedler and S. K. Jain, pp. 127–169. New York: Chapman and Hall.

Mueller, G. M. 1995. Macrofungi. In *Our Living Resources*, ed. E. T. LaRoe et al., pp. 124–126. Washington: U.S. Department of the Interior, National Biological Service.

Mueller-Dombois, D., and H. Ellenberg. 1974. *Aims and Methods of Vegetation Ecology*. New York: John Wiley and Sons.

Murphy, D. D. 1992. Scientists and Endangered Species Act reauthorization. Endangered Species Update 9: 10.

Murphy, D. D., K. E. Freas, and S. B. Weiss. 1990. An environment-metapopulation approach to population viability analysis for a threatened invertebrate. Conservation Biology 4: 41–51.

National Research Council (NRC). 1993. *Setting Priorities for Land Conservation*. Washington: National Academy of Sciences.

———. 1994. *Rangeland Health: New Methods to Classify, Inventory, and Monitor Rangelands*. Washington: National Academy Press.

———. 1995. *Wetlands: Characteristics and Boundaries*. Washington: National Academy Press.

Natural Heritage Data Center Network. 1993. *Perspectives on Species Imperilment*. Arlington, Va.: The Nature Conservancy.

Natural Resources Conservation Service. 1996. *America's Private Land: A Geography of Hope*. Washington: U.S. Department of Agriculture, Natural Resources Conservation Service.

Nehlsen, W., J. E. Williams, and J. A. Lichatowich. 1991. Pacific salmon at the crossroads: Stocks at risk from California, Oregon, Idaho, and Washington. Fisheries 16: 4–21.

Nei, M. 1972. Genetic distance between populations. American Naturalist 106: 283–292.

Newmark, W. D. 1995. Extinction of mammal populations in western North American national parks. Conservation Biology 9: 512–526.

Nishida, G. M., ed. 1994. Hawaiian terrestrial arthropod checklist, 2d ed. Bishop Museum Technical Reports 4: 1–287.

Noss, R. F. 1988. The longleaf pine landscape of the Southeast: Almost gone and almost forgotten. Endangered Species Update 5: 1–8.

———. 1992. The Wildlands Project: Land conservation strategy. Wild Earth 1: 10–25.

Noss, R. F., and A. Y. Cooperrider. 1994. *Saving Nature's Legacy: Protecting and Restoring Biodiversity*. Washington: Island Press.

Noss, R. F., E. T. LaRoe III, and J. M. Scott. 1995. *Endangered Ecosystems of the United States: A Preliminary Assessment of Loss and Degradation*. Biological Report 28. Washington: U.S. Department of Interior, National Biological Service.

Noss, R. F., M. A. O'Connell, and D. D. Murphy. 1997. *The Science of Conservation Planning: Habitat Conservation under the Endangered Species Act*. Washington: Island Press.

Noss, R. F., and R. L. Peters. 1995. *Endangered Ecosystems: A Status Report on America's Vanishing Habitat and Wildlife*. Washington: Defenders of Wildlife.

Nowak, R. M. 1991. *Walker's Mammals of the World*. Baltimore: Johns Hopkins University Press.

Office of Technology Assessment (OTA). 1993. *Harmful Non-Indigenous Species in the United States*. Washington: U.S. Government Printing Office.

Olson, D. M., and E. Dinerstein. 1998. The global 200: A representation approach to conserving the earth's most biologically valuable ecoregions. Conservation Biology 12: 502–515.

Olson, J. S., J. A. Watts, and L. J. Allison. 1985. *Major World Ecosystems Complexes Ranked by Carbon in Live Vegetation: A Database*. Oak Ridge, Tenn.: Oak Ridge National Laboratory.

Olson, S. L., and H. F. James. 1982. Fossil birds from the Hawaiian Islands: Evidence for wholesale extinctions by man before Western contact. Science 217: 633–635.

Omernik, J. M. 1987. Ecoregions of the conterminous United States. Annals of the Association of American Geographers 77: 118–125.

———. 1995a. Ecoregions: A framework for environmental management. In *Biological Assessment and Criteria: Tools for Water Resource Planning and Decision Making*, ed. W. Davis and T. Simon. Chelsea, Mich.: Lewis Publishers.

———. 1995b. Level III ecoregions of the continent. National Health and Environment Effects Research Laboratory. Washington: U.S. Environmental Protection Agency. Maps at 1:1,7,500,000.

Omernik, J. M., and R. G. Bailey. 1997. Distinguishing between watersheds and ecoregions. Journal of the American Water Resources Association 33: 935–949.

O'Neill, R. V., C. T. Hunsaker, K. B. Jones, K. H. Riitters, J. D. Wickham, P. M. Schwartz, I. A. Goodman, B. L. Jackson, and W. S. Baillargeon. 1997. Monitoring environmental quality at the landscape level: Using landscape indicators to assess biotic diversity, watershed integrity, and landscape stability. BioScience 47: 513–519.

Opler, P. A., J. M. Burns, J. D. LaFontaine, R. K. Robbins, and F. Sperling. 1999. Scientific names of North American butterflies. Unpublished review draft. Fort Collins, Colo.

Osborn, C. T., F. Llacuna, and M. Linsenbigler. 1995. The conservation reserve program: Enrollment statistics for signup periods 1–12 and fiscal years 1986–93. Statistical Bulletin no. 925. Washington: U.S. Department of Agriculture, Economic Research Service.

Parmesan, C. 1996. Climate and species' range. Nature 382: 765–766.

Pavelis, G. A. 1987. Economic survey of farm acreage. In *Farm Drainage in the United States—History, Status, and Prospects*, pp. 110–136. MP-1455. Washington: U.S. Department of Agriculture, Economic Research Service.

Pearson, D. L., T. G. Barraclough, and A. P. Vogler. 1997. Distributional maps for North American species of tiger beetles (Coleoptera: Cicindelidae). Cicindela 29: 33–40.

Peigler, R. S., and P. A. Opler. 1993. *Moths of Western North America: 1. Distribution of Saturniidae of Western North America*. Fort Collins: C. P. Gillette Insect Biodiversity Museum, Department of Entomology, Colorado State University.

Pennak, R. W. 1989. *Fresh-Water Invertebrates of the United States*, 3d ed. New York: John Wiley and Sons.

Peterjohn, B. J., J. R. Sauer, and S. Orsillo. 1995. Breeding bird survey: Population trends 1966–92. In *Our Living Resources*, ed. E. T. LaRoe et al., pp. 17–21. Washington: U.S. Department of the Interior, National Biological Service.

Petranka, J. W. 1998. *Salamanders of the United States and Canada*. Washington: Smithsonian Institution Press.

Péwé, T. L. 1983. The periglacial environment in North America during Wisconsin time. In *Late-Quaternary Environments of the United States: The Late Pleistocene*, ed. S. C. Porter, pp. 157–189. Minneapolis: University of Minnesota Press.

Pianka, E. R. 1966. Latitudinal gradients in species diversity: A review of concepts. American Naturalist 100: 33–46.

Pickett, S. T. A., R. S. Ostfeld, M. Shachak, and G. E. Likens. 1997. *The Ecological Basis of Conservation: Heterogeneity, Ecosystems, and Biodiversity*. New York: Chapman and Hall.

Pielou, E. C. 1991. *After the Ice: The Return of Life to Glaciated North America*. Chicago: University of Chicago Press.

Pimm, S. L., M. P. Moulton, and L. J. Justice. 1995a. Bird extinctions in the Central Pacific. In *Extinction Rates*, ed. J. H. Lawton and R. M. May, pp. 75–87. Oxford: Oxford University Press.

Pimm, S. L., G. J. Russell, J. L. Gittleman, and T. M. Brooks. 1995b. The future of biodiversity. Science 269: 347–350.

Pister, E. P. 1993. Species in a bucket. Natural History 102: 14–19.

Poff, N. L. 1997. Landscape filters and species traits: Towards mechanistic understanding and prediction in ecology. Journal of the North American Benthological Society 16: 391–409.

Poole, R. W., and P. Gentili, eds. 1996–1997. Nomina Insecta Nearctica: A Check List of the Insects of North America. 4 vols. Rockville, Md.: Entomological Information Services.

Pounds, J. A., M. P. L. Fogden, and J. H. Campbell. 1999. Biological response to climate change on a tropical mountain. Nature 398: 611–615.

Pounds, J. A., M. P. Fogden, J. M. Savage, and G. C. Gorman. 1997. Test of null models for amphibian declines on a tropical mountain. Conservation Biology 11: 1307–1322.

Prendergast, J. R., R. M. Quinn, J. H. Lawton, B. C. Eversham, and D. W. Gibbons. 1993. Rare species, the coincidence of diversity hotspots and conservation strategies. Nature 365: 335–337.

Pressey, R. L., H. P. Possingham, and C. R. Margules. 1996. Optimality in reserve selection algorithms—when does it matter and how much? Biological Conservation 76: 259–267.

Quammen, D. 1996. *The Song of the Dodo: Island Biogeography in an Age of Extinctions*. New York: Scribner.

Quinter, E. L. 1983. Papaipema. In *Check List of the Lepidoptera of America North of Mexico*, ed. R. W. Hodges et al., pp. 138–139. London: E. W. Classey Lmtd. and The Wedge Entomological Research Foundation.

Raven, P. H. 1963. Amphitropical relationships in the floras of North and South America. Quarterly Review of Biology 29: 151–177.

Raven, P. H., and D. I. Axelrod. 1974. Angiosperm biogeography and past continental movements. Annals of the Missouri Botanical Garden 61: 539–673.

———. 1978. Origin and relationships of the California flora. University of California Publications in Botany 72: 1–134.

Raven, P. H., R. F. Evert, and S. E. Eichhorn. 1999. *Biology of Plants*. New York: W. H. Freeman and Co.

Raven, P. H., and E. O. Wilson. 1992. A fifty-year plan for biodiversity surveys. Science 258: 1099–1100.

Reid, W. V. 1992. How many species will there be? In *Tropical Deforestation and Species Extinction*, ed. T. C. Whitmore and J. A. Sayer, pp. 55–74. London: Chapman and Hall.

Reid, W. V., S. A. Laird, C. A. Meyer, R. Gamez, A. Sittenfeld, D. H. Janzen, M. A. Gollin, and C. Juma. 1993. *Biodiversity Prospecting: Using Genetic Resources for Sustainable Development*. Washington: World Resources Institute.

Reveal, J. L., and J. S. Pringle. 1993. Taxonomic botany and floristics. In *Flora of North America North of Mexico*, vol. 1, ed. Flora of North America Editorial Committee, pp. 157–192. New York: Oxford University Press.

Richter, B. D., D. P. Braun, M. A. Mendelson, and L. L. Master. 1997. Threats to imperiled freshwater fauna. Conservation Biology 11: 1081–1093.

Ricketts, T., W. Dinerstein, D. Olson, C. Loucks, W. Eichbaum, K. Kavanagh, P. Hedao, P. Hurley, K. Carney, R. Abell, and S. Walters. 1999. *A Conservation Assessment of the Terrestrial Ecosystems of North America*. Vol. 1: *The United States and Canada*. Washington: Island Press.

Robbins, C. S., D. Bystrak, and P. H. Geissler. 1986. The breeding bird

survey: Its first fifteen years, 1965–
1979. Resource Publication 157.
Washington: U.S. Fish and Wildlife
Service.

Robbins, C. S., J. R. Sauer, R. S.
Greenberg, and S. Droege. 1989.
Population declines in North
American birds that migrate to the
Neotropics. Proceedings of the
National Academy of Science 86:
7658–7662.

Robins, C. R., R. M. Bailey, C. E.
Bond, J. R. Brooker, E. A. Lachner,
R. N. Lea, and W. B. Scott. 1991.
*Common and Scientific Names of
Fishes from the United States and
Canada*, 5th ed. Special Publication
no. 20. Bethesda, Md.: American
Fisheries Society.

Robinson, S. K. 1997. The case of the
missing songbirds. Consequences
3: 3–15.

Rohlf, D. J. 1991. Six biological reasons
why the Endangered Species Act
doesn't work—and what to do
about it. Conservation Biology
5: 273–282.

Rosenzweig, M. L. 1995. *Species
Diversity in Space and Time*.
Cambridge: Cambridge University
Press.

Rossman, A. Y. 1995. Microfungi:
Molds, mildews, rusts, and smuts. In
Our Living Resources, ed. E. T.
LaRoe et al., pp. 124–126. Washing-
ton: U.S. Department of the
Interior, National Biological Service.

Roth, V. D. 1993. *Spider Genera of
North America*, 3d ed. Gainesville,
Fla.: American Arachnological
Society.

Rowe, J. S., and J. W. Sheard. 1981.
Ecological land classification: A
survey approach. Environmental
Management 5: 451–464.

Ruppert, E. E., and R. D. Barnes. 1994.
Invertebrate Zoology, 6th ed. New
York: Saunders College Publishing.

Sailer, R. I. 1978. Our immigrant insect
fauna. Entomological Society of
America Bulletin 24: 3–11.

Sakai, A. K., W. L. Wagner, D. M.
Ferguson, and D. R. Herbst. 1995a.
Origins of dioecy in the Hawaiian
flora. Ecology 76: 2517–2529.

———. 1995b. Biogeographical and
ecological correlates of dioecy in the
Hawaiian flora. Ecology 76: 2530–
2543.

Sampson, F. B., and F. L. Knopf. 1994.
Prairie conservation in North
America. BioScience 44: 418–421.

Schaefer, C. W., and M. Kosztarab.
1991. Systematics of insects and
arachnids: Status, problems, and
needs in North America. American
Entomologist 37: 211–216.

Schafale, M. P., and A. S. Weakley.
1990. *Classification of the Natural
Communities of North Carolina:
Third Approximation*. Raleigh: North
Carolina Natural Heritage Program, Division of Parks and
Recreation, Department of Environ
ment, Health, and Natural Resources.

Schemske, D. W., B. C. Husband,
M. H. Ruckelshaus, C. Goodwillie,
I. M. Parker, and J. G. Bishop. 1994.
Evaluating approaches to the
conservation of rare and endangered
plants. Ecology 75: 584–606.

Schorger, A. W. 1955. *The Passenger
Pigeon: Its Natural History and
Extinction*. Madison: University of
Wisconsin Press.

Schulman, E. 1958. Bristlecone pine,
oldest known living thing. National
Geographic 113: 354–372.

Schultz, J. 1995. *The Ecozones of the
World: The Ecological Divisions of the
Geosphere*. Berlin: Springer-Verlag.

Scotese, C. R. 1997. PALEOMAP
Paleogeographic Atlas.
PALEOMAP Progress Report no.
90. Arlington: Department of
Geology, University of Texas.

Scott, J. M., B. Csuti, J. D. Jacobi, and
J. E. Estes. 1987. Species richness: A
geographic approach to protecting
future biological diversity.
BioScience 37: 782–788.

Scott, J. M., F. W. Davis, B. Csuti,
R. Noss, B. Butterfield, C. Groves,
H. Anderson, S. Caicco, F. D'Erchia,
T. C. Edwards, J. Ulliman, and R. G.
Wright. 1993. Gap analysis: A geo-
graphic approach to protection of
biological diversity. Wildlife Mono-
graphs 123: 1–41.

Scott, J. M., T. H. Tear, and F. W.
Davis, eds. 1996. *Gap Analysis: A
Landscape Approach to Biodiversity
Planning*. Bethesda, Md.: American
Society for Photogrammetry and
Remote Sensing.

Scott, J. M., and D. S. Wilcove. 1998.
Improving the future for endangered
species. BioScience 48: 579–580.

Shaffer, H. B., R. N. Fisher, and C.
Davidson. 1998. The role of natural
history collections in documenting
declines. Trends in Ecology and
Evolution 13: 27–30.

Shaffer, M. L. 1981. Minimum population sizes for species conservation. BioScience 31: 131–134.

———. 1987. Minimum viable populations: Coping with uncertainty. In *Viable Populations for Conservation*, ed. M. E. Soulé, pp. 69–86. Cambridge: Cambridge University Press.

Shelford, V. E., ed. 1926. *Naturalist's Guide to the Americas*. Baltimore: The Williams and Wilkins Company.

Shimwell, D. W. 1971. *The Description and Classification of Vegetation*. London: Sidgwick and Jackson.

Simberloff, D. 1986. Are we on the verge of a mass extinction in tropical rain forests? In *Dynamics of Extinction*, ed. D. K. Elliot, pp. 165–180. New York: John Wiley.

———. 1995. Why do introduced species appear to devastate islands more than mainland areas? Pacific Science 49: 87–97.

Simpson, G. G. 1980. *Splendid Isolation: The Curious History of Mammals in South America*. New Haven: Yale University Press.

Sims, R. A., W. D. Towill, K. A. Baldwin, and G. M. Wickware. 1989. *Field Guide to the Forest Ecosystem Classification for Northwestern Ontario*. Thunder Bay, Ontario: Forestry Canada, Ontario Ministry of Natural Resources.

Singer, F. J., W. T. Swank, and E. E. C. Clebsch. 1984. Effects of wild pig rooting in a deciduous forest. Journal of Wildland Management 48: 464–473.

Smith, M. J. 1993. *Moths of Western North America: 2. Distribution of Sphingidae of Western North America*. Fort Collins: C. P. Gillette Insect Biodiversity Museum, Department of Entomology, Colorado State University.

Snyder, D. 1993. Extinct, extant, extirpated, or historical? or In defense of historical species. Bartonia 57 (supplement): 50–57.

Soulé, M. E. 1987. *Viable Populations for Conservation*. New York: Cambridge University Press.

Soulé, M. E., and M. A. Sanjayan. 1998. Conservation targets: Do they help? Science 279: 2060–2061.

Stattersfield, A. J., M. J. Crosby, A. J. Long, and D. C. Wege. 1998. *Endemic Bird Areas of the World: Priorities for Biodiversity Conservation*. Cambridge, England: Birdlife International.

Steadman, D. W. 1995. Prehistoric extinctions of Pacific island birds: Biodiversity meets zooarchaeology. Science 267: 1123–1131.

Stebbins, G. L., and J. Major. 1965. Endemism and speciation in the California flora. Ecological Monographs 35: 1–35.

Stehli, F. C., and S. D. Webb. 1985. *The Great American Biotic Interchange*. New York: Plenum Press.

Stein, B. A. 1993. Toward common goals: Collections information in conservation databases. Association for Systematics Collections Newsletter 21: 1–6.

———. 1997. Designing information systems to support biodiversity conservation. In *Biodiversity Information: Needs and Options*, ed. D. L. Hawksworth, P. M. Kirk, and S. Dextre Clarke. London: CAB International.

Stein, B. A., T. Breden, and R. Warner. 1995a. Significance of federal lands for endangered species. In *Our Living Resources*, ed. E. T. LaRoe et al., pp. 398–401. Washington: U.S. Department of Interior, National Biological Service.

Stein, B. A., and S. R. Flack. 1996. *America's Least Wanted: Alien Species Invasions of U.S. Ecosystems*. Arlington, Va.: The Nature Conservancy.

———. 1997. *1997 Species Report Card: The State of U.S. Plants and Animals*. Arlington, Va.: The Nature Conservancy.

Stein, B. A., L. L. Master, L. E. Morse, L. S. Kutner, and M. Morrison. 1995b. Status of U.S. species: Setting priorities for conservation. In *Our Living Resources*, ed. E. T. LaRoe et al., pp. 399–400. Washington: U.S. Department of Interior, National Biological Service.

Stoms, D. M., F. W. Davis, K. L. Driese, K. M. Cassidy, and M. P. Murray. 1998. Gap analysis of the vegetation of the Intermountain Semi-Desert Ecoregion. Great Basin Naturalist 58: 199–216.

Stone, R. D. 1998. *Endemic and Rare Plants of Utah: An Overview of Their Distribution and Status*. Salt Lake City: Utah Division of Wildlife Resources.

Storey, K. B. 1986. Freeze tolerance in vertebrates: Biochemical adaptation of terrestrially hibernating frogs. In *Living in the Cold: Physiological and Biochemical Adaptations*, ed. X. J. Musacchia and L. C. H. Wang, pp. 131–138. New York: Elsevier.

Stork, N. E., and M. J. Samways. 1995. Inventory and monitoring of biodiversity. In *Global Biodiversity Assessment*, ed. V. H. Heywood, pp. 453–544. Cambridge: Cambridge University Press.

Stotler, R., and B. Crandall-Stotler. 1977. A checklist of the liverworts and hornworts of North America. The Bryologist 80: 405–428.

Sun, G., D. L. Dilcher, S. Zheng, and Z. Zhou. 1998. In search of the first flower: A Jurassic angiosperm, Archaefructus, from northeast China. Science 282: 1692–1695.

Sutherland, W. J., ed. 1996. *Ecological Census Techniques: A Handbook*. Cambridge: Cambridge University Press.

Sykes, M. T., I. C. Prentice, and W. Cramer. 1996. A bioclimatic model for the potential distributions of north European tree species under present and future climates. Journal of Biogeography 23: 203–233.

Szaro, R. C., and D. W. Johnston. 1996. *Biodiversity in Managed Landscapes: Theory and Practice*. New York: Oxford University Press.

Takhtajan, A. L. 1986. *Floristic Regions of the World*. Berkeley: University of California Press.

Tarr, C. L., and R. C. Fleischer. 1995. Evolutionary relationships of the Hawaiian honeycreepers (Aves, Drepanidinae). In *Hawaiian Biogeography: Evolution on a Hot Spot Archipelago*, ed. W. L. Wagner and V. A. Funk, pp. 147–159. Washington: Smithsonian Institution Press.

Taulman, J. F., and L. W. Robbins. 1996. Recent range expansion and distributional limits of the nine-banded armadillo (*Dasypus novemcinctus*) in the United States. Journal of Biogeography 23: 635–648.

Taylor, A. H. 1993. Fire history and structure of red fir (*Abies magnifica*) forests, Swain Mountain Experimental Forest, Cascade Range, northeastern California. Canadian Journal of Forest Research 23: 1672–1678.

Taylor, C. A., M. L. Warren Jr., J. F. Fitzpatrick Jr., H. H. Hobbs III, R. F. Jezerinac, W. L. Pflieger, and H. W. Robison. 1996. Conservation status of crayfishes of the United States and Canada. Fisheries 21: 25–38.

The Nature Conservancy (TNC). 1977. *Preserving Our Natural Heritage*. Vol. 1: *Federal Activities*. Washington: U.S. Government Printing Office.

———. 1982. *Natural Heritage Operations Manual*. Arlington, Va.: The Nature Conservancy.

———. 1996. *Conservation by Design*. Arlington, Va.: The Nature Conservancy.

———. 1997. *Designing a Geography of Hope: Guidelines for Ecoregion-Based Conservation in The Nature Conservancy*. Arlington, Va.: The Nature Conservancy.

———. 1998a. Ecoregion-based conservation in the central short-grass prairie. Unpublished report.

———. 1998b. Northern Appalachian/Boreal Ecoregion plan. Unpublished report.

———. 1999. Ecoregional Map of the United States. May 1999 edition. Arlington, Va.: The Nature Conservancy.

The Nature Conservancy (TNC) and Association for Biodiversity Information (ABI). 1999. Element occurrence data standard: Working draft, part 1. Unpublished document.

The Nature Conservancy (TNC) and Environmental Systems Research Institute (ESRI). 1994. *Field Methods for Vegetation Mapping: NBS/NPS Vegetation Mapping Program*. Arlington, Va.: The Nature Conservancy.

Thompson, F. C. 1997. Names: The keys to biodiversity. In *Biodiversity II: Understanding and Protecting Our Biological Resources*, ed. M. L. Kreaka-Kudla, D. E. Wilson, and E. O. Wilson, pp. 199–216. Washington: Joseph Henry Press.

Thorne, R. R. 1993. Phytogeography. In *Flora of North America North of Mexico*, vol. 1, ed. Flora of North America Editorial Committee, pp. 132–153. New York: Oxford University Press.

Thorp, J. H., and A. P. Covich, eds. 1991. *Ecology and Classification of*

North American Freshwater Inverte-brates. New York: Academic Press.

Tiffney, B. H. 1985. The Eocene North Atlantic land bridge: Its importance in the Tertiary and modern phytogeography. Journal of the Arnold Arboretum 66: 243–273.

Toregas, C. 1971. Location under maximal travel time constraints. Ph.D. diss., Cornell University.

Toregas, C., R. Swain, C. ReVelle, and L. Bergman. 1971. The location of emergency service facilities. Operations Research 19: 1363–1373.

Turgeon, D. D., J. F. Quinn, A. E. Bogan, E. V. Coan, F. G. Hochberg, W. G. Lyons, P. M. Mikkelsen, R. J. Neves, C. F. E. Roper, G. Rosenberg, B. Roth, A. Scheltema, F. G. Thompson, M. Vecchione, and J. D. Williams. 1998. *Common and Scientific Names of Aquatic Inverte-brates from the United States and Canada: Mollusks*, 2d ed. Special Publication no. 26. Bethesda, Md.: American Fisheries Society.

Tuskes, P. M., J. P. Tuttle, and M. M. Collins. 1996. *The Wild Silk Moths of North America*. Ithaca: Cornell University Press.

Udvardy, M. D. F. 1975. A classifica-tion of the biogeographical prov-inces of the world. IUCN Occa-sional Paper no. 18.

UNESCO. 1973. *International Classification and Mapping of Vegetation*. Series 6, *Ecology and Conservation*. Paris: UNESCO.

U.S. Bureau of the Census. 1995. *Statistical Abstract of the United States: 1995*. Washington: U.S. Government Printing Office.

U.S. Department of Agriculture (USDA). 1997. *Agricultural Resources and Environmental Indicators, 1996–1997*. Agricultural Handbook no. 712. Washington: U.S. Department of Agriculture, Economic Research Service.

U.S. Department of the Interior (USDOI). 1999. Land and Water Conservation Fund appropriations history. Unpublished briefing document. Washington: U.S. Department of the Interior.

U.S. Fish and Wildlife Service (USFWS). 1988. *Endangered Species Act of 1973, as Amended through the 100th Congress*. Washington: U.S. Department of the Interior, U.S. Fish and Wildlife Service.

———. 1995. *Report to Congress: Endangered and Threatened Species Recovery Program*. Washington: U.S. Department of the Interior, Fish and Wildlife Service.

U.S. Forest Service. 1997. Landowner assistance programs. Unpublished briefing document. Washington: U.S. Department of Agriculture.

———. 1999. Forest legacy program. Unpublished briefing document. Washington: U.S. Department of Agriculture.

U.S. Government Accounting Office (USGAO). 1995. *Endangered Species Act: Information on Species Protection on Nonfederal Lands*. GAO/RCED-95–16. Washington: U.S. Govern-ment Accounting Office.

Vankat, J. L. 1979. *The Natural Vegetation of North America*. New York: John Wiley.

Vasek, F. C. 1980. Creosote bush: Long-lived clones in the Mojave desert. American Journal of Botany 67: 246–255.

Vuilleumier, F. 1985. Fossil and recent avifaunas and the interamerican interchange. In *The Great American Biotic Interchange*, ed. F. C. Stehli and S. D. Webb. New York: Plenum Press.

Wagner, W. L., D. R. Herbst, and S. H. Sohmer. 1990. *Manual of Flowering Plants of Hawai'i*. Honolulu: University of Hawaii Press and Bishop Museum Press.

———. 1999. *Manual of the Flowering Plants of Hawai'i*, rev. ed. with supplement by W. L. Wagner and D. R. Herbst. Honolulu: University of Hawaii Press.

Wake, D. B. 1996. A new species of Batrachoseps (Amphibia: Plethodontidae) from the San Gabriel Mountains, Southern California. Los Angeles County Museum Contributions in Science 463: 1–12.

Walter, H. 1985. *Vegetation of the Earth, and Ecological Systems of the Geobiosphere*, 3d ed. New York: Springer-Verlag.

Walter, K. S., and H. J. Gillett, eds. 1998. *1997 IUCN Red List of Threatened Plants*. Gland, Switzer-land, and Cambridge, England: IUCN—The World Conservation Union.

Warren, M. L. Jr., and B. M. Burr. 1994. Status of freshwater fishes of the United States: Overview of an imperiled fauna. Fisheries 19: 6–18.

Webb, S. D. 1985. Main pathways of mammalian diversification in North America. In *The Great American Biotic Interchange*, ed. F. C. Stehli and S. D. Webb. New York: Plenum Press.

———. 1990. Historical biogeography. In *Ecosystems of Florida*, ed. R. L. Myers and J. J. Ewel, pp. 70–100. Orlando: University of Central Florida Press.

Webb, S. D., and L. G. Marshall. 1982. Historical biogeography of recent South American land mammals. In *Mammalian Biology in South America*, ed. M. A. Mares and H. H. Genoways, pp. 39–52. Special Publication 6. Pittsburgh: Pymatuning Laboratory of Ecology, University of Pittsburgh.

Weeks, W. W. 1997. *Beyond the Ark: Tools for an Ecosystem Approach to Conservation*. Washington: Island Press.

White, D. A., J. Kimerling, and W. S. Overton. 1992. Cartographic and geometric components of a global sampling design for environmental monitoring. Cartography and Geographic Information Systems 19: 5–22.

Whitney, G. G. 1994. *From Coastal Wilderness to Fruited Plain: A History of Environmental Change in North America 1500 to Present*. Cambridge: Cambridge University Press.

Whittaker, R. H. 1956. Vegetation of the Great Smoky Mountains. Ecological Monographs 26: 1–80.

———. 1962. Classification of natural communities. Botanical Review 28: 1–239.

———. 1975. *Communities and Ecosystems*, 2d ed. New York: Macmillan.

Wiebe, K., A. Tegene, and B. Kuhn. 1996. *Partial Interests in Land: Policy Tools for Resource Use and Conservation*. Agriculture Economic Report no. 744. Washington: U.S. Department of Agriculture, Economic Research Service.

Wilcove, D. S., and M. J. Bean. 1994. *The Big Kill: Declining Biodiversity in America's Lakes and Rivers*. Washington: Environmental Defense Fund.

Wilcove, D. S., M. J. Bean, R. Bonnie, and M. McMillan. 1996. *Rebuilding the Ark: Toward a More Effective Endangered Species Act for Private Land*. Washington: Environmental Defense Fund.

Wilcove, D. S., and L. Y. Chen. 1998. Management costs for endangered species. Conservation Biology 12: 1405–1407.

Wilcove, D. S., M. McMillan, and K. C. Winston. 1993. What exactly is an endangered species?: An analysis of the U.S. endangered species list, 1985–1991. Conservation Biology 7: 87–93.

Wilcove, D. S., D. Rothstein, J. Dubow, A. Phillips, and E. Losos. 1998. Quantifying threats to imperiled species in the United States. BioScience 48: 607–615.

Williams, A. B., L. G. Abele, D. L. Felder, H. H. Hobbs, R. B. Manning, P. A. McLaughlin, and I. P. Farfante. 1989. *A List of Common and Scientific Names of Decapod Crustaceans from America North of Mexico*. Special Publication no. 17. Bethesda, Md.: American Fisheries Society.

Williams, J. D., M. L. Warren Jr., K. S. Cummings, J. L. Harris, and R. J. Neves. 1993. Conservation status of freshwater mussels of the United States and Canada. Fisheries 18: 6–22.

Williams, J. E., J. E. Johnson, D. A. Hendrickson, S. Contreras-Balderas, J. D. Williams, M. Navarro-Mendoza, D. E. McAllister, and J. E. Deacon. 1989. Fishes of North America endangered, threatened, or of special concern. Fisheries 14: 2–20.

Williams, P., D. Gibbons, C. Margules, A. Rebelo, C. Humphries, and R. Pressey. 1996. A comparison of richness hotspots, rarity hotspots, and complementary areas for conserving diversity of British birds. Conservation Biology 10: 155–174.

Wilson, D. E., and D. M. Reeder, eds. 1993. *Mammal Species of the World: A Taxonomic and Geographic Reference*, 2d ed. Washington: Smithsonian Institution Press.

Wilson, E. O. 1988. *Biodiversity*. Washington: National Academy Press.

———. 1992. *The Diversity of Life*. Cambridge: Belknap Press of Harvard University Press.

Wilson, J. B. 1991. Does vegetation science exist? Journal of Vegetation Science 2: 289–290.

———. 1994. Who makes the assembly rules? Journal of Vegetation Science 5: 75–278.

Woolfenden, G. E., and J. W. Fitzpatrick. 1984. *The Florida Scrub Jay: Demography of a Cooperative-Breeding Bird*. Monographs in Population Biology no. 20. Princeton: Princeton University Press.

World Resources Institute, World Conservation Union, and United Nations Environment Programme (WRI, IUCN, and UNEP). 1992. *Global Biodiversity Strategy: Guidelines for Action to Save, Study, and Use Earth's Biotic Wealth Sustainably and Equitably*. Washington: WRI, IUCN, and UNEP.

Wright, S. 1978. *Evolution and the Genetics of Populations*. Vol. 4: *Variability within and among Natural Populations*. Chicago: University of Chicago Press.

Wunderlin, R. P. 1998. *A Guide to Vascular Plants of Florida*. Tallahassee: University Presses of Florida.

Young, T. F., and C. H. Congdon. 1994. *Plowing New Ground: Using Economic Incentives to Control Water Pollution from Agriculture*. Oakland, Calif.: Environmental Defense Fund.

Zeiner, D. C., W. F. Laudenslayer Jr., K. E. Mayer, and M. White, eds. 1990. *California's Wildlife*. 3 vols. Sacramento: California Department of Fish and Game.

Zhong, C. 1983. A comparative summary of the vegetation of Hubei province, China, and the Carolinas of the United States. Annals of the Missouri Botanical Garden 70: 571–575.

INDEX

alliance, in vegetation classifications, 51, 218, 293

alligator, American (*Alligator mississippiensis*), 73

Alligator mississippiensis, 73

Alloperla roberti, 116

alpaca, 88

alpha (α) diversity, 65

Alps, 86

Altamaha River, 19

altitude
    as diversity gradient, 7–8, 47, 252
    in ecoregion classifications, 205, 208–209
    in rangewide ecological assessment, 295–298

Amargosa Desert, 5

Amargosa River, 74

Amastra, 79

Amazilia beryllina, 125

Amazon River, 155

ambush predation, 77–78

America
    biological discovery of, 10, 14, 19–20
    shared biota in, 14, 20
    See also specific continent

American Fisheries Society (AFS), 110–111

Amerindians, 225

Amia calva, 75

amphibians
    breeding requirements, 152–153
    conservation status, 101–104
    continental exchange of, 88
    diversity in U.S., 61, 67, 73–74, 136–138
    diversity by state, 152–153, 196
    diversity worldwide, 58, 67
    endemism, 73–74, 153–154
    extinct U.S. species, 115, 154
    federal status, 108
    imperiled species of, 167, 243
    rarity by state, 153–154
    threats to, 243, 246

amphitropical distribution, 89

Anax junius, 78

Andes Mountains, 89, 204

anemones, 62

angiosperms. *See* flowering plants

animals
    diversity in U.S., 61–63
    diversity worldwide, 62–63
    invertebrate. *See* invertebrate animals
    non-native, 64. *See also* alien species
    as state property, 276
    trade regulations, 271–273
    vertebrate. *See* vertebrate animals

annelid worms, 63, 79

Anoplophora glabripennis, 64

Antarctica, 144

anteaters, 88

antelopes, 71

pronghorn (*Antilocapra americana*), 70–71, 202

Antilocapra americana, 70–71, 202

ants, 76
    fire (*Solenopsis invicta*), 250

Apachian/Madrean region, 134

Apalachicola River, 123, 151, 197

Aphelocoma californica, 145

Aphelocoma coerulescens, 145, 159, 161

Aphelocoma insularis, 145

Aphredoderus sayanus, 75

Apis mellifera, 76

Aplodontia rufa, 71

Appalachian Mountains (region)
    conservation strategies, 237–238, 314
    diversity in, 56, 74, 87, 98, 148, 152, 156–157, 190, 204, 225
    as ecoregion, 167–168, 209
    endemic species in, 133–134, 154, 191
    Pleistocene effects on, 127–128
    as hot spot, 165–169, 172–175, 187, 190–192, 301
    imperiled species in, 165, 167–169, 172–173, 175, 187, 190–192, 278
    Southern, 165, 167–169, 172–173, 187, 190–192

Appalachian Piedmont, 120

aquaculture, 243, 272

aquatic species
    biodiversity in, 8, 178–184, 195
    classification systems, 217
    hot spots of, 176, 178–184, 301
    land ownership issues, 278, 318
    threats to, 241–242, 247, 253, 304

Arabis, 134

arachnids, 63, 79, 246

Ararat, Mount, 81

archipelagos. *See* specific islands

Arctic Circle, 9, 55–56, 76

arctic communities, disturbance to, 223–224

Arctic Ocean, 83

Arctomecon humilis, 76

Arctomecon merriamii, 198

Arctostaphylos uva-ursi, 217

Arenaria ursina, 195

Argentina, 89, 144

Argyroxiphium sandwicense, 91

Arisaema, 86

Aristotle, 34

bunting, McKay's (*Plectrophenax hyperboreus*), 145
Bureau of Biological Survey, 61
Bureau of Land Management, U.S.
    land managed by, 50, 257, 294
    species on lands owned by, 281–283, 288
butterflies
    conservation status, 102–104
    diversity in U.S., 67, 76–77
    diversity worldwide, 67
    Edith's checkerspot (*Euphydryas editha*), 252, 310
    endemism, 76–77
    federal status, 108
    giant swallowtail (*Papilio cresphontes*), 77
    mission blue (*Icaricia icarioides missionensis*), 266
    monarch (*Danaus plexippus*), 77
    threats to, 243, 252
    uncompaghre fritillary (*Boloria acrocnema*), 252

caddisflies (Trichoptera), 78
Cahaba River, 184
Calidris canutus, 144
California
    amphibian diversity, 21–23, 73–74, 98
    animal diversity in, 70, 73–74, 77, 136–137, 143–144
    biodiversity in, 123–124
    climate, 3–7, 70, 73, 76
    ecological status, 219–220, 223, 228–229, 231–232
    endangered species in, 3–5, 162
    endemic species in, 124, 132–134, 137, 140–141, 145, 150–151, 153, 156
    extinct species from, 117–118
    geographical diversity of, 119, 126, 130, 275
    habitat conservation plans, 265–266, 316–317
    as hot spot, 165–169, 172–176, 184, 187, 192–195, 198–199, 301–302
    human population growth, 194, 251–252
    imperiled species in, 165, 169, 172–176, 184, 187, 192–195, 278, 301–302
    land ownership issues, 278, 282, 316–317
    plant diversity in, 14, 61, 68, 91–92, 131–134, 296
    rare species in, 124, 129, 134–135, 137, 146–147, 154, 156

California coast
    as ecoregion, 167–168
    imperiled species in, 167–168, 173, 187, 194–195, 301–302
    See also Pacific coast
California Floristic Province, 133
California Natural Diversity Database, 22
Callinectes sapidus, 120
Calochortus tiburonensis, 275–276, 285
Cambarus pristinus, 110
Cambrian Period, 57
Campephilus principalis, 148
Camp Pendelton Marine Base, 23, 280
Camptorhynchus labradorius, 114, 148
Canada
    animal diversity in, 71–72, 75, 88, 143, 308
    diversity in, 55, 102, 125, 207, 252
    heritage programs in, 25, 271
    plant diversity in, 68–69, 217
candidate species, federal
    defined, 105, 107
    land ownership and, 278–279
    national distribution mapping, 42–45
    federal listings, 106–107
Candolle, Augustin de, 47
caracara, crested (*Caracara plancus*), 145
Caracara plancus, 145
Carboniferous Period, 78, 152
Carduelis lawrencei, 145
Carex lutea, 46, 69
Caribbean region, 25, 102, 125, 144
caribou, 119–120, 125
carnivorous plants, 131, 134
Cascade Mountains, 126, 209, 212
    leeward forests, 231
Castanea dentata, 128, 225, 234
catastrophes, 95, 185, 214
Castilleja affinia ssp. *neglecta*, 275
Castilleja cinerea, 195
caterpillars, 76–78
catfish, yellow-fin madtoms (*Noturus flavipinnis*), 156
Catharus fuscescens, 144
catocala moths, 77
cavefishes, 75
caves
    conservation status, 230
    invertebrates found in, 78–79, 131, 191, 302
    as habitat, 190–191, 196
    vertebrates found in, 131, 153, 171
ceanothus, Jepson's (*Ceanothus jepsonii*), 130
Ceanothus jepsonii, 130
cedars, 68
centipedes, 63

endemism, 69, 191
extinct U.S. species, 115
federal status, 108
Connecticut, 12, 128
conservation
    biodiversity focus, 8–9, 12, 15–18, 255–
        258, 316
    data for, 10–11, 13–15, 23, 27–28, 53,
        320
    ecological community-based, 299–300
    ecoregion-based, 16–18, 185–186, 209–
        211, 235–238, 302–303, 314–316
    ecosystem-based, 47, 49, 186, 203
    effectiveness, 160, 302, 306–310, 320
    efficiency, 160–161, 173, 185
    evolution of U.S. efforts, 10–18
    federal appropriations for, 258–259
    goals of, 160–161, 168, 174, 209, 288,
        310–311, 314
    habitat based, 23–24, 265–267, 311–319
    national blueprint for, 302–303, 305–
        307, 314–316, 319–321
    population focus, 280–282
    scale of U.S. challenge, 184–186, 302–
        303
    species-based, 203, 280, 310–311
    wildlife focus, 253–254, 257–258, 268,
        270
conservation biology, 17–18, 177
Conservation Data Centers, 25
conservation easements, 260–263
conservation lands
    ecological communities on, 288–300
    ecoregional portfolio approach, 314–
        316
    rangewide representation of forests
        on, 296–298, 300
    See also reserve networks
conservation leases, 260–261
conservation planning
    ecological focus, 47, 49, 186, 209–211,
        235–238, 299–300, 314–316
    goals of, 160, 185–186
    habitat focus, 23–24, 265–267, 311–319
    hot spots, 159–160, 171–173
    minimum set identification, 174–176,
        185, 311–312
    multiple occurrence protection, 177–
        179
    National Vegetation Classification in,
        232–233
    priority setting, 167, 173–174, 177, 182
    redundancy principle in, 177–179,
        307–312, 314
    representation principle in, 307–308,
        311, 314

resiliency principle in, 307–311, 314–
    315
species focus, 162, 203, 280, 310–311
targets of, 160–161, 168, 174, 209, 265,
    288, 310–311, 314
Conservation Reserve Program, 270–271
conservation reserve systems. See reserve
    networks
conservation status assessment, 95–96,
    99, 104–105, 110–112, 232–234
conservation status ranks, global
    American Fisheries Society
        comparisons, 110–111
    confidence assessments, 99–100
    defined, 29–30, 95, 97–98
    for ecological communities, 49, 232–
        235
    Endangered Species Act comparisons,
        108–111
    heritage standards for, 97–100
    IUCN comparisons, 112–113
    of U.S. species, 100–104
conservation strategies
    alien species control, 265–266
    coarse filter/fine filter, 12–13, 16, 29–
        30, 47, 203
    for endangered species, 11–13, 105,
        311
    financial incentives, 254, 270, 301–302,
        318–319
    habitat-focused, 23–24, 253–254, 265–
        268, 284, 311
    for imperiled communities, 235–238,
        276
    for imperiled species, 311–318
    land acquisition, 15, 160, 256–263, 275
    land management, 257–258, 260, 266–
        267, 275, 281–287, 317–319
    land ownership, 255–262, 271, 275–
        276, 284, 317
    land use regulations, 256, 258, 263–
        265, 276
    nonregulatory, 256, 276, 312–317
    population focus, 160–161, 173–178,
        182–186
    regulatory, 253, 256–258, 263–268,
        271–273
    tax incentives, 261, 269–270, 284
    for watersheds, 182–185
    water use regulations, 256, 260, 263–
        265
    wildlife-focused, 253–254, 257, 268,
        270, 276
Contia tenuis, 151
continental drift. See plate tectonics
continuum, ecological, 48, 205

Death Valley National Park, 6, 199
deciduous forests
    changes over time, 229–230
    diversity in U.S., 9, 56, 85–86, 204, 215
    Pleistocene effects, 127–128
deep-sea environments, microbes in, 59–60
deer, 87, 208
    mule (*Odocoileus hemionus*), 202, 308
    white-tailed (*Odocoileus virginianus*), 97
DeGeer land bridge, 84
degradation. *See* ecological degradation; habitat destruction
Delaware Bay, 144
Democratic Republic of Congo, 74
Dendroica cerulea, 144
Dendroica chrysoparia, 103, 105, 146
Dendroica kirtlandii, 129, 144, 146
Department of Agriculture, U.S., 270, 283
Department of Defense, U.S., 279, 281–283
Department of Energy, U.S., 294
Department of Interior, U.S., 38, 258
Desert Fishes Council, 5
deserts
    diversity in U.S., 5–9, 56, 69–70, 73, 76, 198, 206–207, 215
    worldwide, 76, 207
development rights, 262–263, 269–270
Devils Hole, 5–6, 156, 198
Devonian Age, 57
Dicamptodon ensatus, 74
Dicerandra christmanii, 159–160
Dicerandra frutescens, 159–160
dicyemids, 62
Didelphis virginiana, 71, 88
Dionaea muscipula, 134
Dipodomys, 138–140
Dipodomys ingens, 70
Dipodomys spectabilis, 139
Dipodomys stephensi, 195
dippers, American (*Cinclus mexicanus*), 72
Discus brunsoni, 116
diseases
    avian, 189, 239
    threats from, 189, 239–241, 243, 248–249
disharmonic biota, 90
disjunct species, 81–82, 85–86, 103
Disney Wilderness Preserve, 268
dispersal, modes of, 89–90, 188
District of Columbia. *See* Washington, D.C.

division, ecoregion, 208
dogwoods, 191
    dwarf (*Cornus canadensis*), 128
dolphins, 139
domain, ecoregion, 208
dragonflies
    conservation status, 101–104
    diversity of, 67
    federal status, 108
    green darner (*Anax junius*), 78
    imperiled species, 184, 241
drainage projects, 243, 301
Dreissena polymorpha, 251, 273
Drosophila, 77–78, 91
Drosophila digressa, 91
Drosophila heteroneura, 78
dry ballast, 250–251, 272–273
Duck River, 155
duck, Labrador (*Camptorhynchus labradorius*), 114, 148
duck stamps, 259

Eagle Lake, 184
easements, 260–263
echinoderms, 63
Ecological Classification and Mapping Task Team (ECOMAP), 210
ecological communities
    classification approaches, 47–53, 204–207, 216–217
    as conservation planning tool, 288–300
    conservation status, 29–30, 49, 232–235
    conservation strategies, 16–18, 47, 49, 185–186, 203, 265, 276–277
    data for, 13, 47, 289
    distribution across U.S., 219–220, 276–277
    diversity in U.S., 7–10, 17–18, 39, 206–211, 215–220, 235, 303
    emergent properties of, 47–48
    imperiled, 233–236
    inventory strategies, 49–50
    land ownership patterns and, 288–300
    mapping techniques, 49–53
    vegetation classifications, 48–53, 204–207, 209–211, 216, 289
    viability assessment, 39–41
ecological degradation
    assessment strategies, 225–231
    in forests, 97, 223–229
    in U.S., 202–203, 229–231, 303–306
    in temperate zones, 223–225
    in wetlands, 231–232
    See also specific threat or region

endemic species
  ecoregion endemics, 167–168
  state endemics, 121–125, 131–134,
    137–138, 140–141, 145–147, 150–
    151, 153–154, 156
  U.S. national endemics, 67–79, 102–
    105
endemism
  defined, 66, 103, 122
  See also endemic species
Endothia parasitica, 225
Enhydra lutris, 139
entoprocts, 63
environmental gradients, 8
  See also altitude; latitude; longitude
environmental impact reports, 22–24
Environmental Monitoring and
    Assessment Program (EMAP),
    164
Environmental Protection Agency, U.S.,
    37, 164, 209
environmental uncertainty, as extinction
    factor, 95, 99
EO. *See* element occurrences
Eocene Epoch, 83–84, 86, 89
EOR. *See* element occurrence record
EO rank. *See* element occurrence rank
epeiric sea, 83
Ephemera compar, 114
Epioblasma florentina walkeri, 309
Epioblasma sampsonii, 114
equal-area grids
  for imperiled species analyses, 164,
    166, 168–178
  imperiled species distribution by, 169–
    173
  limitations of, 168–169, 171–172
  range size calculations, 37, 170–171
  See also hexagons
equilibrium theory, 80
Erethizon dorsatum, 88
Eriogonum, 134
erosion, 9, 64, 126, 182, 190
Erwin, Terry, 59
ESA. *See* Endangered Species Act
ESU. *See* evolutionarily significant unit
Etheostoma caeruleum, 87
Eubalaena glacialis, 140
Eumeces, 149
Euphydryas editha, 252, 310
Eupithecia, 77
Eupithecia staurophragma, 78
Eureka Dunes grass (*Swallenia
    alexandrae*), 199
Europe
  diversity in, 47, 74–76, 78, 86
  tectonic history of, 82–84, 87

Eurycea, 153
Eurycea rathbuni, 130–131, 153
Eurycea robusta, 153
Eurycea sosorum, 153–154
evening primrose (*Oenothera deltoides*),
    6
  Antioch Dunes (*Oenothera deltoides*
    ssp. *howellii*), 196
Everglades, Florida, 159, 218, 232, 255–
    256, 263
Everglades National Park, 263
evergreen forests, 218–219, 223–224
evolution, 7, 46, 81–82, 89–92, 112–113,
    136, 185, 319–320
evolutionary distinctiveness, 66
evolutionary radiation, 83, 86–87, 91
evolutionarily significant unit (ESU),
    106
excise taxes, on hunting, 259
exotic species. *See* alien species
extinction
  area effect, 80–81
  current rate and magnitude, 113, 320
  as evolutionary process, 319–320
  as global crisis, 15–16, 64
  nature of, 93–95, 112–113
  species' risk of. *See* conservation status
    ranks
extinct species
  documentation challenges, 113–114
  extinction status ranks defined, 30, 97
  rediscovery of, 46, 116
  state distributions, 116–118, 140, 148,
    154, 157, 304
  from U.S., 93–94, 108, 111, 114–118,
    239–240
  See also missing species

falcon, peregrine (*Falco peregrinus*), 249–
    250
Falco peregrinus, 249–250
Farm Bill of 1996, 262
farming. *See* agriculture
farmland programs, 262, 269–271
Farmland Protection Program, 262
Federal Geographic Data Committee,
    52, 216
federal government
  land acquisition appropriations, 258–
    259
  land ownership of, 255, 257–259, 279–
    282, 285–288
  regulatory role, 271. *See also* specific
    act or issue
  endangered species listings, 105–110
federal land management agencies, 279

federally listed species
   comparison with heritage status
      assessments, 108–110
   on federal land, 279–283, 285–288
   land ownership issues, 277–279
   listing, 105–110
   on nature reserves, 287–288
   on private land, 283–286
Felis concolor, 98, 308
Felis concolor coryi, 98–99, 255
fens, 207
fern allies, 69, 102–104, 115
ferns
   conservation status, 102–104
   diversity in U.S., 62, 67
   diversity worldwide, 58, 62, 67
   endemism, 69
   extinct U.S. species, 115
   federal status, 108
   whisk, 62
ferret, black-footed (*Mustela nigripes*), 70
field surveys, 21–23, 36, 40, 290
Fifth Amendment, 268
figworts (Scrophulariaceae), 69
finches, 72, 145
   Hawaiian. *See* honeycreepers
fine filter strategy. *See* coarse filter/fine
      filter strategy
fires
   effect of, 8, 46, 95, 214, 222
   for habitat restoration, 225, 253
   suppression of, as threat, 194, 196–197,
      203, 243, 246–248, 304
firs
   balsam (*Abies balsamea*), 128, 217–218
   Douglas (*Pseudotsuga menziesii*), 222
   Fraser (*Abies fraseri*), 128, 191
   white (*Abies concolor*), 289, 295–296,
      298
Fish and Wildlife Service, U.S.
   conservation role, 105–107, 161, 216,
      257, 270
   endangered species listings, 105–110,
      241, 244, 247–248, 253, 265
   species on lands owned by, 280–284, 294
fishes
   alien, 64
   American Fisheries Society status
      assessments, 110–111
   ancient, 75
   diversity in U.S., 6, 9, 50, 61, 67–68,
      136–138
   diversity by state, 155–157
   diversity worldwide, 58, 67, 75
   evolution of, 86–87
   extinct species, 115, 157

federal status, 106
imperiled species, 167, 179–184, 183n
minimum-set analyses, 177
threats to, 182–184, 242–243, 245–248,
   251
viability assessment, 182–184
See also freshwater fishes and
   individual species
fishing, 256–257, 259, 263–264, 271–273, 310
Fish Slough, 3–5, 7, 18
flatwoods, 196–197
flatworms, 62, 79
flies, 67, 76–78
   See also specific type
flood control, 229, 243, 304
flooding, 46, 66, 83, 95, 123, 214, 252
floodplains, 196, 207, 215
Florida
   conservation programs, 279, 312–314
   diversity in, 25, 123, 132
   ecological status, 228–229, 231–232
   endangered species in, 162
   endemic species in, 132–133, 137, 141,
      145, 150–151, 197
   geographical diversity of, 119, 196–
      197, 211
   conservation planning in, 312–314
   as hot spot, 159–160, 165, 169, 172–
      173, 187, 196–197, 318
   human population growth, 251–252
   imperiled species in, 159–160, 165,
      169, 172–173, 278–279
   public land ownership, 278–279
   rare species in, 129, 134–136
   restoration projects, 255–256
   Strategic Habitat Conservation Areas,
      313
Florida Game and Freshwater Fish
   Commission, 312
Florida Keys, 125, 136, 140
Florida Natural Areas Inventory, 313
Florida Panhandle, 133, 165, 172–173,
   187, 196–197
floristics, 51
flowering plants
   conservation status, 101–104
   diversity in U.S., 61–62, 67–68, 91
   diversity by state, 131–132, 135
   diversity worldwide, 58, 62, 67
   endemism, 68–69, 91, 133–134
   extinct U.S. species, 115–116
   federal status, 108
flycatchers, monarch, 72, 91
forest bank, 318
Forest Legacy Program, 262–263
forest reservations, 257

forestry, 11, 24, 189, 203, 223, 262, 264, 270, 318
    See also logging
forests
    boreal, 9, 56, 223–224, 231, 237
    broadleaf, 9, 56, 85–86, 128–127, 204, 213, 223
    changes over time, 94, 225–230
    coniferous. *See* conifers
    cove, 190
    deciduous. *See* deciduous forests
    diversity in U.S., 9–10, 55–56, 66, 196–197, 212–213, 218–219, 227
    in eastern Asia, 55
    evergreen, 218–219, 223–224
    Florida's hardwood, 196–197
    Hawaiian dry, 210, 230
    imperiled associations, 236
    mixed mesophytic, 204, 212–213
    needleleaf, 213, 218
    in Pacific Northwest, 218–220, 222–223
    rain forests, 9, 56, 67, 189, 206–207, 218, 222–223
    second-growth, 224–225
    temperate, 9, 56, 197, 206–207, 215, 222–225
    tropical, 9, 56, 67, 188, 215, 218, 223
Forest Service, U.S.
    Classification involvement, 208, 210, 216, 235
    conservation role, 50, 167, 181n, 257, 280, 290
    species on lands owned by, 280–283
Forest Stewardship Incentives Program, 270
Forster, Johann Reinhold, 80
fossils, 57, 66–67, 82, 86, 88, 115, 209
Fouquieria splendens, 69
fox, island gray (*Urocyon littoralis*), 140
Franklin, Benjamin, 19
Franklinia alatamaha, 19–20, 134
freshwater fish
    American Fisheries Society status assessments, 110–111
    conservation status, 101–104, 180
    distribution by watersheds, 180–182
    diversity in U.S., 9, 61–63, 67–68, 74–75, 137
    diversity by state, 155–156, 196
    diversity worldwide, 62–63
    endemism, 75, 156
    extinct U.S. species, 115, 157
    federal status, 108
    imperiled species, 179–182, 183n
    rarity by state, 155–157
    threats to, 182–184, 242–243, 246

freshwater mussels
    conservation status, 101
    distribution by watersheds, 180–182
    diversity in U.S., 67–68, 78–79, 196
    diversity worldwide, 67–68, 78–79
    endemism, 67–68, 78
    extinct U.S. species, 115–116, 180
    federal status, 108, 309
    imperiled species, 179–182, 183n, 309
    tan riffleshell (*Epioblasma florentina walkeri*), 309
    threats to, 183–184, 242–243, 246
freshwater biodiversity, 101–104, 179–184, 190–191, 242–243, 246, 251
fringe-toed lizards (*Uma*), 130
    Coachella Valley (*Uma inornata*), 130, 150, 266
frogs
    bull (*Rana catesbeiana*), 94
    California red-legged (*Rana aurora draytoni*), 154
    chorus (*Pseudacris ornata*), 137
    Florida bog (*Rana okaloosae*), 197
    Las Vegas leopard (*Rana fisheri*), 154
    spring peeper (*Pseudacris crucifer*), 154
    state distributions, 152–154
    tailed (*Ascaphus truei*), 74
    Tarahumara (*Rana tarahumarae*), 154
    wood (*Rana sylvatica*), 153
fruit flies (*Drosophila*), 77–78, 91
    picture wings (*Drosophila digressa*), 91; (*D. heteroneura*), 78
fungi
    Asian (*Endothia parasitica*), 225
    diversity in U.S., 62, 67
    diversity worldwide, 58–60, 62, 191
    extinct U.S. species, 115

Gambelia sila, 98
gamma (γ) diversity, 65
GAO. *See* Government Accounting Office, U.S.
Gap Analysis Program
    applications of, 37, 52, 258
    land management categories, 286–287, 299
    limitations of, 293n
    rangewide vegetation assessment, 296–298
gar (*Lepisoteus*), 75, 136
garter snakes
    Butler's (*Thamnophis butleri*), 151
    shorthead (*Thamnophis brachystoma*), 151

in temperate zones, 223–225, 229–231
threats from, 240–242, 247–249, 252
in U.S., 229–231, 303–305
habitat restoration
for imperiled species, 310–318
mitigation banking, 267–268
for prairie ecoregions, 314–316
See also ecological restoration
habitats
as conservation focus, 23–24, 265–267,
310–319
diversity in U.S., 51, 80–81, 92, 127,
196–197
in ecoregion classifications, 210
maintenance issues, 253–254
relationship to population size, 80–81,
307, 310
See also specific type
Haeckel, Ernst, 47
Haldane, J. B. S., 59
Haliaeetus leucocephalus, 108, 165, 250,
282
Hall Island, 145
Harvard Museum of Comparative
Zoology, 136
harvesting, as threat, *See*
overexploitation
Hawaiian Islands
bird endemism, 71–72, 91, 188–189
colonization of, 90–92, 115, 135, 144,
146, 189
diversity in, 9, 55, 90–92, 123–125, 149,
152, 188
ecoregions in, 210–211
extinct species from, 114–117, 148, 189
as hot spot, 162, 169, 172–175, 187–189
human population growth, 251–252
imperiled species in, 162, 169, 172–
173, 175, 187–189
insect endemism, 76–77, 91–92
invertebrate endemism, 79, 91–92
plant endemism, 69, 91, 131–133
rare species in, 124, 129, 134–135, 137,
140, 146, 151, 156
tectonic history of, 89–90
threat analysis, 235, 242–244, 247–248,
253
vertebrate endemism, 103–104, 137,
141, 145–147
Hawaii-Emperor volcanic chain, 90
hawks, Hawaiian, 91, 147
hazardous chemicals, 256, 308–309
heavy metals, 130, 301
Heliamphora, 134
Heloderma horridum, 73
Heloderma suspectum, 73

Helonias bullata, 30
Hemignathus wilsoni, 189
Hemizonia conjugens, 302
hemlock
Carolina (*Tsuga caroliniana*), 55–56
eastern (*Tsuga canadensis*), 128, 218
in eastern Asia, 55
heritage programs. *See* natural heritage
programs
herptiles, minimum-set analyses, 177
Hesperolinon, 130
Hesperomannia arbuscula, 189
hexagons
in hot spot identification, 169, 171–173
of imperiled species, 168–173, 185,
311–312
limitations of, 312
minimum set calculations, 173–177,
185, 311–312
multiple occurrence protection, 177–179
range size calculations, 170–171
Himalayan Mountains, 89
Holocene Epoch, 85
honeybee (*Apis mellifera*), 76
honeycreepers, Hawaiian, 56–57, 72, 91,
146, 147
akiapolaau (*Hemignathus wilsoni*), 189
Maui (*Paroreomyza montana*) 91
honeyeaters, 72, 91, 147
Hooker, Joseph Dalton, 64
hornworts, 62
horsetails, 61
hot spots
Appalachians as, 165–169, 172–175,
187, 190–192, 301
aquatic, 176, 178–184, 301–302
assessment techniques, 161–174, 176,
187, 307
California as, 165–169, 172–176, 184,
187, 192–301–302, 195
Clinch Valley as, 301–302
conservation planning and, 159–160,
171–173
Death Valley as, 172–173, 187, 198–199
Florida Panhandle as, 159–160, 165,
169, 172–173, 187, 196–197, 318
geological, 89–92, 185
Hawaii as, 162, 169, 172–175, 187–189
of imperiled species, 14, 159–173, 187–
199, 301–302, 306
Nevada as, 198–199
San Francisco Bay Area as, 175, 187,
192–194
humans
threats to biodiversity, 223–231, 239–
241, 251–252, 319–320

Humboldt, Alexander von, 47, 204
hummingbirds, 56
  Allen's (*Selasphorus sasin*), 145
  berylline (*Amazilia beryllina*), 125
  broad-billed (*Cynanthus latirostris*), 7
  white-eared (*Hylocharis leucotis*), 125
hunting
  regulatory controls, 256–257, 263–264,
    271–273, 280, 310
  threats from, 93, 249
Huron, Lake, 25
hurricanes, 95, 197
Hyalophora cecropia, 77
hybridization,
  threats from, 248
hydras, 62
hydrologic processes, 48, 130–131, 180,
  248
  regional distributions. *See* watersheds
Hydromantes brunus, 153
hydropower, 212
Hylocharis leucotis, 125
Hylocichla mustelina, 148
Hyposmocoma, 77
Hystrichopsylla schefferi, 71

Icaricia icarioides missionensis, 266
Ice Age
  effects on diversity, 79, 85, 136, 182, 316
  Pleistocene Epoch, 127–129, 155, 182,
    190
  Wisconsin glaciation, 127–128
Ice Mountain, 128
Idaho, 141, 262, 296
iguanas, 149
Iliamna corei, 12
Illicium, 85, 134
Illinois, 49, 64, 127, 129, 171
imperiled communities, 233–235
imperiled species
  detailed distribution mapping, 42–45,
    165–166, 306
  distribution by ecoregion, 166–168,
    305–306
  equal-area grid analyses, 164, 166,
    168–178
  on federal land, 279–283, 285–288
  global status ranks defined, 30, 97, 168
  hot spot distributions, 14, 159–173,
    187–199, 301–302, 306
  land ownership issues, 276–278, 280–
    283
  on nature reserves, 286–288
  on private land, 283–286
  protection requirements, 173–178, 185

range sizes by hexagon, 170–171
  threat analysis. *See* threats
federal listings of, 21–23, 42, 108–111,
  159, 165
impoundments, water, 243, 245
inbreeding depression, 95
incentives
  for habitat maintenance, 254, 270,
    301–302, 318–319
  tax, 261, 269–270, 284
inchworms, 77
India, 78, 89
Indiana, 140, 157, 171, 228
Indian Ocean, 188
Indo-Malaysia, 91
Indonesia, 65, 74, 188
infraspecific taxa, 97–98
infrastructure development,
  threats from, 243, 246–247, 251
insectivorous plants, 131, 134
insects
  alien, 64
  conservation status, 102
  diversity in U.S., 6, 63, 68, 75–79, 91
  diversity worldwide, 59, 63
  endemism, 76–78, 91
  extinct U.S. species, 115–116
  freshwater, 68, 78, 92, 184
  threats to, 246
  See also individual species
insular biotas, 135
intensive-use lands, 286, 288, 294
Intergovernmental Panel on Climate
  Change, 252
Interior Highlands region, 181
introduced species. *See* alien species
invasive species. *See* alien species
inventories. *See* biological inventories
invertebrate animals
  conservation status, 101–104
  diversity in U.S., 62–63, 78–79
  diversity by state, 123–124
  diversity worldwide, 58–59
  endemism, 78–79
  extinct U.S. species, 115
  federal status, 106–111
  threat analysis, 242–243, 246
  See also individual species
Iowa, 127, 129, 316
irrigation, 192, 199
island biogeography, 80
islands
  diversity impact, 80, 89–92, 185
  See also specific islands
isolation, of populations, 80, 82, 87, 90,
  128–129, 182

Israel, 76
IUCN. *See* World Conservation Union

jack-in-the-pulpit (*Arisaema*), 86
Jackrabbit Spring, 197
Japan, 209
jays, 89
　See also scrub jays
Jefferson, Thomas, 201
jellyfish, 62
Jenkins, Robert, Jr., 12, 24
Jepson Prairie, 193
jewelflower, Tiburon (*Streptanthus niger*),
　275
jojoba bean (*Simmondsia chinensis*), 69
Jordan, David Starr, 61, 136, 155
Joshua tree (*Yucca brevifolia*), 6
Jurassic Period, 75, 82–83

Kalm, Peter, 35, 201
Kalmia, 35
kangaroo rats (*Dipodomys*), 138–140
　banner-tailed (*Dipodomys spectabilis*),
　　139
　giant (*Dipodomys ingens*), 70
　Stephen's (*Dipodomys stephensi*), 195
kangaroos, Australian, 71
Kansas, 129, 315
karst topography, 63, 130–131, 190–191,
　230
Kauai, 90, 169–170, 239
Kauai o'o (*Moho braccatus*), 239–240
Kentucky, 93, 157, 171, 191
Kilauea volcano, 90
kingfishers
　green (*Chloroceryle americana*), 142
　ringed (*Ceryle torquata*), 142
kinorhynchs, 63
kittiwake, red-legged (*Rissa brevirostris*),
　146
Klamath-Siskiyou region, 134, 173, 176,
　210
Kokia kauaiensis, 133
Küchler, A. W., 212–214
kudzu (*Pueraria montana*), 64

lady's slipper orchid (*Cypripedium
　reginae*), 272
Laguna Beach, 195
lakes, 80, 178, 195, 198
　See also specific lake
Lake Wales Ridge, 18, 133, 159–161
Lama guanicoe, 88, 308

Lampetra minima, 157
lamprey, Miller Lake (*Lampetra minima*),
　157
lampshells, 63
Lampsilis perovalis, 179
lancelets, 63
land acquisition
　as conservation strategy, 15, 160, 256–
　　263, 275–276, 312–317
　costs of, 258–262
　in government conservation efforts,
　　255–259, 312–314, 316–317
　by local land trusts, 261
　by The Nature Conservancy, 12, 15,
　　260, 285
　See also land ownership
Land and Water Conservation Fund,
　258–259
land bridges, 84–88
land conversion, threats from, 243, 245–
　248, 251–252
land cover, 226–229
　See also vegetation
land donations, 261, 270
land easements, 260–263
landforms. *See* topography
land leases, 260–261
land management
　as conservation strategy, 257–267, 275–
　　276, 278, 317–319
　federal agencies role, 279, 281–283
　GAP categories, 286–287, 299
　multiple-use, 285–287
land ownership
　as conservation strategy, 255–262, 271,
　　275–277
　ecological communities by, 288–300
　endangered species by, 253–254, 277–
　　286
　heritage data management of, 29
　imperiled species by, 276–278, 280–286
　by The Nature Conservancy, 12, 15,
　　260, 275, 277, 284
　private, 255, 258, 268–269, 276–277,
　　281–286, 318–319
　public, 255, 257, 259, 260, 276–282,
　　285–286, 318
　rights conveyed by, 275–276
　by state government, 258–259, 279
　See also land acquisition
Landsat Thematic Mapper satellite
　imagery, 22
landscape context, 40–41, 48–49, 96, 205,
　217, 263
landscape diversity, 7–9, 119–121, 126–
　131, 316–319

Malaysia, 65, 91
Malesian floristic affinities, 91
mammals
    conservation status, 101–104, 141
    continental exchange of, 71, 87–91
    diversity in U.S., 6, 9, 66–67, 70–71,
        136–138
    diversity by state, 138–140
    diversity worldwide, 58, 67, 308
    endemism, 70–71, 139–141
    extinct U.S. species, 115, 140, 310
    federal status, 108–109
    imperiled species of, 167, 171
    marine, 70, 139–140, 271
    minimum-set analyses, 177
    rarity by state, 139–140
    threats to, 241, 243, 246
Mammoth Cave, 191
managed areas
    in heritage data management, 29
manatees, West Indian. *See Trichechus
        manatus*
Manitoba, 316
maples, 128
    big-leaf (*Acer macrophyllum*), 194
    sugar (*Acer saccharum*), 204, 212
mapping, 21–23, 31–32, 36–45, 49–53
    See also species mapping
map turtles
    Cagle's (*Graptemys caglei*), 150
    ringed (*Graptemys oculifera*), 151
    southeastern radiation of, 150–151
    Texas (*Graptemys versa*), 150
    yellow-blotched (*Graptemys
        flavimaculata*), 150–151
Marine Mammal Protection Act, 271
marine mammals
    diversity of, 70, 139–140
    in Hawaii, 79, 91–92, 188
marsupials, 71, 83
Martha (passenger pigeon), 93–94
Maryland, 119–120, 144
Mashomack Preserve, 13, 144
Massachusetts, 141, 151
maximal covering location problem
        (MCLP), 175–176
mayapple (*Podophyllum*), 86
mayflies (Ephemeroptera), 78
    Colorado burrowing (*Ephemera
        compar*), 114
McKinley, Mount, 9
MCLP. *See* maximal covering location
        problem
MCP. *See* multicovering problem model
meadowfoam (Limnanthaceae), 69
Mediterranean, 86, 223

Mediterranean climate, 14, 76, 194, 223
Mediterranean shrublands, 14, 194
Megachasma pelagios, 58
Meganeuropsis permiana, 78
Merced River, 153
Merriam, C. Hart, 61, 204–205
mesquite vegetation, 199, 213, 228
metapopulations, 39
Mexico
    animal diversity in, 71, 73, 76, 139,
        143–144, 149
    diversity in, 6, 65–66, 125, 148, 154,
        252
    endemic species in, 68–69, 89, 132, 198
    shared biota with, 60, 69, 102, 137
Miami Ridge rocklands, 133
Mianus Gorge, 12
mice, 70
    desert pocket (*Chaetodipus
        penicillatus*), 70
    salt-marsh (*Reithrodontomys
        raviventris*), 193
Michigan, 25, 144, 146, 226, 228
microbes. *See* microorganisms
microlepidopterans, 77
microorganisms
    biotechnology applications, 8
    deep-sea, 59–60
    diversity in U.S., 61–63
    diversity worldwide, 58–60
    freshwater, 60, 62–63
Mid-Atlantic Coastal Plain, 289–292
Migration, avian, 6, 137, 143–144, 148,
        197, 231, 259, 271
Migratory Bird Conservation Fund,
        258–259
Migratory Waterfowl Program, 38
military activities, threats from, 243,
        246–247
military bases, conservation role, 23, 280,
        283, 318
milk vetch (*Astragalus*), 134
    Ash Meadows (*Astragalus phoenix*), 5
    funeral (*Astragalus funereus*), 130
    See also locoweed
milkweed, Mead's (*Asclepias meadii*), 129
millipedes, 63
Mimulus traskiae, 114
minimum set analyses for imperiled
        species, 173–176, 185
mining, 11, 24, 190, 203, 243, 246–248, 258
Minnesota, 49–50, 154, 165, 217, 316
minnows, 75
    Colorado pikeminnow (*Ptychocheilus
        lucius*), 75, 182
    See also Colorado Squawfish

mints (Lamiaceae), 69
    Lake Placid scrub (*Dicerandra frutescens*), 159–160
    Otay Mesa (*Pogogyne nudiuscula*), 302
Miocene Epoch, 83–85
Mirounga angustirostris, 7
missing species, 97, 114, 116, 154
    See also extinct species
Mississippi, 150–151, 154
Mississippi River (Basin)
    discovery efforts, 204, 208, 211
    fish diversity in, 155–156
    Pleistocene effects, 127–128
Mississippi Valley, 144, 150
Missouri, 129, 171
Missouri River, 205, 207, 215
Missouri Valley, 208
mites, 57
mitigation banking, 267–268
mixed mesophytic forests, 204, 212–213
Mobile Bay, 151
Mobile River (Basin), 179, 181
Moho braccatus, 239–240
Mojave Desert
    geological features, 6–7, 195, 198
    species diversity in, 6–7, 73, 89, 139, 198
mollusks
    diversity in U.S., 6, 63, 78–79
    diversity worldwide, 63
    imperiled species of, 167, 246
    minimum-set analyses, 177
Monachus tropicalis, 114, 140
mongoose, Indian, 189
monitoring, of species, 36–38
monkeyflower, Santa Catalina (*Mimulus traskiae*), 114
Montana
    diversity in, 70, 119, 125, 207, 296
    extinct species in, 116, 118
monuments, 52
mormon tea (*Ephedra*), 62, 68
mosquitoes, as disease vector, 189, 239–240
mosses, 62
moths
    cecropia (*Hyalophora cecropia*), 77
    diversity in U.S., 76–77
    endemism, 77, 92
    Hawaiian, 78
    showy underwings (*Catocala*), 77
mountain laurel (*Kalmia*), 35
mountain lion (Felis concolor), 70, 98–99, 138, 255, 308
mountain mallow, Peter's (Iliamna corei), 12

mountains
    diversity in U.S., 7, 9–10, 126, 138, 198, 206–207
    in ecoregion classifications, 208–210
    plant endemism, 133–134
    See also specific mountains
Moxostoma lacerum, 157
mucket, orange-nacre (*Lampsilis perovalis*), 179
multicovering problem model (MCP), 178n
multiple-use lands, 285–287, 294
museum collections, 22–23, 30, 35–36, 40
mussels
    American Fisheries Society status assessments, 111
    conservation status, 101–104
    diversity in U.S., 9, 67–68, 78–79
    diversity by state, 123–124
    diversity worldwide, 67, 78–79
    freshwater. *See* freshwater mussels
    threats to, 183–184, 242–243, 245–246
    white wartyback (*Plethobasus cicatricosus*), 96
    zebra (*Dreissena polymorpha*), 251, 273
mustards (Brassicaceae), 69, 130
Mustela nigripes, 70
Mycteria americana, 72, 255–256
Myotis grisescens, 140
Myotis leibii, 140
Myotis sodalis, 140, 171

National Audubon Society, 142
National Environmental Policy Act, 256
National Forest System, 257–258
National Marine Fisheries Service, 105, 161
National Park Service
    conservation role, 50, 52, 216, 221, 257, 310
    species on lands owned by, 281, 283–284
    See also specific park
National Resource Land System, 257–258
National Vegetation Classification, U.S. (USNVC)
    association concept, 216–217
    conservation applications, 232–233
    distribution of communities, 219–220
    diversity levels, 49–53, 217–218, 220
    Scotts Bluff example, 220–222
National Wildlife Refuge System, 6, 257–259

North Carolina
   diversity in, 46, 66, 136, 139, 152, 219
   imperiled species in, 173, 190, 288
   restoration projects, 255–257, 260, 267
North Carolina Natural Heritage
   Program, 290–291
North Cascades National Park, 17
North Dakota
   diversity in, 123, 125, 143, 211, 316
   extinct species in, 118, 229
Northern Great Plains Steppe, 168
Northern Tallgrass Prairie, 316
North Korea, 209
Noturus flavipinnis, 156
Numenius tahitiensis, 72, 145–146
nutmeg
   California (*Torreya californica*), 123
   Florida (*Torreya taxifolia*), 123, 133, 197

oak savanna, 229–231
oaks, 191, 193, 195–196, 204, 212
occurrences. *See* element occurrences
ocotillo (*Fouquieria splendens*), 69
Odobenus rosmarus, 139–140
Odocoileus hemionus, 202, 308
Odocoileus virginianus, 97
Oenothera deltoides, 6
Oenothera deltoides ssp. *howellii*, 196
Office of Technology Assessment
   (OTA), 250
off-road vehicles (ORVs), 198, 243, 245
Ohio, 157, 204, 228
Ohio River (Basin), 96, 157, 181, 207, 211
oil extraction, threats from 243, 246, 248
Okeechobee, Lake, 159
Oklahoma, 139, 154
Oligocene Epoch, 83
Olympic Mountains, 134
Omernik, James, 209
Oncorhynchus clarki, 184
Oncorhynchus mykiss, 184
opossum (*Didelphis virginiana*), 71, 88
Orange County (California), 194, 317
Orbexilum stipulatum, 114
orchids, 20
   lady's slipper (*Cypripedium reginae*), 272
Oregon
   diversity in, 74, 122, 130, 143
   endemic species in, 134, 137, 140–141, 156
   imperiled species in, 173, 176, 235
   land ownership issues, 282, 296
   rare species in, 146, 154

Ornithorhynchus anatinus, 87
Ortalis vetula, 72
Ortelius, Abraham, 82
orthonectids, 62
ORVs. *See* off-road vehicles
osprey (*Pandion haliaetus*), 144
OTA. *See* Office of Technology
   Assessment
Otay Mountains, 302
Ouachita Mountains, 156
outdoor recreation,198, 243, 245–246, 248, 258
Outer Coastal Plain Mixed Forest, 211
ouzel, water (*Cinclus mexicanus*), 72
overexploitation, threats from, 240–241, 248–250
Owens River, 3–4, 6
Owens Valley, 3–4, 7–9, 126
owls, 89
   burrowing (*Athene cunicularia*), 145
   northern spotted (*Strix occidentalis caurina*), 165, 282, 316
Ozark Mountains, 74, 87, 127, 156
ozone layer, 154

Pacifastacus fortis, 304
Pacific Coast, 61, 71, 74, 116, 148
   See also California Coast
Pacific Flyway, 193
Pacific Islands, 68, 72, 114, 116, 145, 188, 195
Pacific Northwest
   diversity in, 74, 151–152, 156–157
   endangered species in, 162, 165, 178
   forests in, 218–220, 222–223
   land ownership issues, 282
Pacific Ocean, 126, 132, 139, 193
paddlefish (*Polyodon spathula*), 75, 191
paedomorphosis, 153
paintbrush, 133
   ash gray Indian (*Castilleja cinerea*), 195
   Tiburon (*Castilleja affinis* ssp. *neglecta*), 275
Paleocene Epoch, 83
paleoendemic species, 122–123
paleotropics, 144
Paleozoic Era, 82, 149
palmetto, Texas (*Sabal mexicana*), 98–99
palm, Mexican sabal (*Sabal mexicana*), 98–99
Palouse grasslands, 212, 225, 229–230
Panax ginseng, 86
Panax quinquefolius, 86
Pandion haliaetus, 144
Pangea, 82–84

reptiles (*continued*)
  diversity worldwide, 58, 67
  endemism, 73, 150–151
  extinct U.S. species, 115
  federal status, 108–109
  imperiled species of, 167, 243
  rarity per state, 150–151
  threats to, 243, 246
  See also individual species
reserve networks
  adequacy assessment, 286–288
  continental-scale, 36, 138
  extent in U.S., 276, 299–300
  land management categories, 286–287
  minimum areas needed, 173–176, 185
  optimization models, 160–161, 173, 185, 300
  species populations on, 287–288, 299
resiliency principle, in conservation, 307–310, 314–315
restoration. *See* ecological restoration and habitat restoration
Rhineura floridana, 73, 150
Rhinichthys deaconi, 157
Rhode Island, 120, 123, 125, 140, 184
Rhododendron maximum, 218
Rhyacotriton kezeri, 122
Rhynchopsitta pachyrhyncha, 72–73
riffle-shell, Wabash (*Epioblasma sampsonii*), 114
Ring Mountain, 275–276
Rio Grande River, 156
Rio Grande Valley, 137
Rio Pecos River, 156
riparian communities, 214, 293, 318
Rissa brevirostris, 146
rivers
  basin regions, 180–181, 196
  diversity in, 178, 180–182, 184, 190, 196
  See also specific river
Riverside County (California), 194
roads
  threats from, 243, 246–247, 250
  See also urbanization
Roanoke River, 260
rockcress (*Arabis*), 134
Rocky Mountains
  diversity in, 119, 126, 152, 218, 220
  as ecoregion, 208–209
rodents, 70–71, 138–139
Roosevelt, Franklin D., 259
Roosevelt, Theodore, 257
roses (Rosaceae), 69
Rostrhamus sociabilis, 255

rotifers, 63
roundworms. *See* nematodes
Russia, 55, 86
RWRI. *See* rarity-weighted richness index

Sabal mexicana, 98–99
Sacramento River, 192
safe harbor agreements, 267
sagebrush
  big (*Artemisia tridentata*), 292
  low (*Artemisia arbuscula*), 292
sagebrush steppe, 212–213, 292–295
sage scrub, 21, 195, 212–213, 302
St. John River, 66
St. Louis, 201–202, 204
St. Matthew Island, 145
salamanders
  Barton Springs (*Eurycea sosorum*), 153–154
  black warrior waterdog (*Necturus alabamensis*), 74
  Blanco Blind (*Eurycea robusta*), 153
  brook (*Eurycea*), 153
  Columbia torrent (*Rhyacotriton kezeri*), 122
  diversity in U.S., 9, 67–68, 136–137, 152–153, 204
  endemism, 73–74, 153
  Fourche Mountain (*Plethodon fourchensis*), 42
  greater siren (*Siren lacertina*), 74
  hellbender (*Cryptobranchus alleganiensis*), 14, 74, 191
  Jordan's (*Plethodon jordani*), 190
  limestone (*Hydromantes brunus*), 153
  lungless (*Plethodon*), 73–74
  Mississippi (*Plethodon ainsworthi*), 154
  Pacific giant (*Dicamptodon ensatus*), 174
  Peaks of Otter (*Plethodon hubrichti*), 285
  San Gabriel (*Batrachoseps gabrieli*), 153
  Shenandoah (*Plethodon shenandoah*), 74
  Texas blind cave (*Eurycea rathbuni*), 130–131, 153
  torrent, 74, 122, 154
salmon
  Chinook (*Oncorhynchus tshawytscha*), 192
  diversity of, 40, 136–137, 156–157
  population decline, 178, 182, 184
  runs, on Columbia River, 212
salt marshes, 192–193

silverswords, 92
    Haleakala (*Argyroxiphium sandwicense*), 91–92
Simmondsia chinensis, 69
Simpson, G. Gaylord, 87
Siren lacertina, 74
Siskiyou region. *See* Klamath-Siskiyou region
Sisturus, 149
site information
    in heritage data management, 29
skinks
    sand (*Neoseps reynoldsi*), 150
    See also Eumeces, 149
skippers
    conservation status, 102–104
    diversity in U.S., 67, 76–77
    endemism, 76–77
    federal status, 108
    threats to, 243
sky islands, 138, 173, 205
sloths, giant ground, 88
Smithsonian Institution, 36, 60–61
snail kite (*Rostrhamus sociabilis*), 255
snails
    diversity in U.S., 9, 67–68, 79, 184
    diversity worldwide, 67
    extinct U.S. species, 114–116
    freshwater, 67–68, 198
    Hawaiian tree (*Achatinella apexfulva*), 189; (*A. sowerbyana*), 79
    See also Discus brunsoni, 116
snakes, 73, 83, 149, 151
    copperhead (*Agkistrodon contortrix*), 191
    garter (*Thamnophis*), 151
    Kirtland's (*Clonophis kirtlandii*), 151
    rattlesnakes, 149
    sharp-tailed (*Contia tenuis*), 151
    water (*Nerodia*), 149
snow-wreath, Shasta (*Neviusia cliftonii*), 61
software, for biological and conservation data, 27–34
soils
    influence on distributions 8, 130–131, 193, 209, 219
    microbe diversity in, 59–60
    serpentine, 130, 192–193, 275–276
    ultramafic, 130
    volcanic, 90–91, 95, 130
Solenopsis invicta, 250
Somateria fischeri, 146
songbirds, 197, 204, 231
Sonoran Desert, 6–7, 73, 89, 139
Sorex cinereus, 138
Sorex lyelli, 70
Sorex palustris, 128

sources of information
    in heritage data management, 29
South Africa, 194, 223
South America
    diversity in, 81, 132, 144
    tectonic history of, 82, 84, 87–89
South Carolina Department of Wildlife and Marine Resources, 24
South Carolina Heritage Program, 11
South Dakota, 316
Southeastern Coastal Plain, 209
Southeastern U.S., 219–220, 278
Southern Blue Ridge, conservation analysis, 289–292
Southern Ridge and Valley, 167–168
sparrows, Bachman's (*Aimophila aestivalis*), 72
Spea intermontana, 152
speciation, 319–320
species
    classifications of. *See* taxonomy
    as conservation focus, 203, 280, 310–311
    defined, 35, 106
    global status ranks defined, 29–30, 97
    inventories of. *See* biological inventories
    nonindigenous, 64, 189, 239–249, 272–273
    number in U.S., 9–10, 57–63, 303–304
    number worldwide, 58–60
    preservation of. *See* conservation
    status assessment, 95–96, 99, 104–105, 110–112
species accumulation curve, for minimum set analyses, 175–176, 185
species-area relationship
    conservation applications, 29, 173–177, 185, 286–288, 294, 313, 317
    diversity influences, 79–81, 124–125, 197, 307, 310
species at risk
    defined, 97, 99
    detailed distribution, 161–178
    state distribution, 124, 131, 137–138
    in U.S., 101–103, 184–186
    See also rare species
species distributions
    candidate species, 42–45
    endangered species, 42–45, 162–165, 176
    endemic species, 122–124, 130–134, 167–168
    extinct species, 116–118, 140, 148, 154, 157, 304

Torreya californica, 123
Torreya taxifolia, 123, 133, 197
Torrey Pine State Reserve, 195
tortoises,
    desert (*Gopherus agassizii*), 6
    gopher (*Gopherus polyphemus*), 313
    See also turtles
Toxostoma redivivum, 145
tracts
    in heritage data management, 29
trade regulations, 271–273
transportation technology
    threats from, 243, 246–247, 250
    regulatory controls on, 256, 265–265,
        309
trees. *See* forests; *individual species*
trend information, 29–30, 33, 37–38, 40,
    95–96, 112–113
Trichechus manatus, 71, 139
trichoplaxes, 62
Trifolium stoloniferum, 32–33
trillium, 191
troglobites, 79
Trogon elegans, 125
trogon, elegant, 125
tropical birds, 119 120, 251
tropical fish, 251
tropical forests
    diversity in, 9, 56, 67, 188
    ecological status, 215, 218, 223
tropical zones, 58–59, 66–67, 144
tropic of Cancer, 9, 55, 65
trout, 129, 156
    cutthroat (*Oncorhynchus clarki*),
        184
    rainbow (*Oncorhynchus mykiss*), 184
Tsuga canadensis, 128, 218
Tsuga caroliniana, 55–56
tube noses, 146
tulip poplar (*Liriodendron*), 85–86, 191,
    212
tundra, 56, 80, 215, 231, 295
tunicates, 63
turtles, 9, 68, 83, 150–151
    bog (*Clemmys muhlenbergii*), 40, 151
    map (*Graptemys*), 150–151
    sea, 151, 188
    snapping (*Macroclemys temminckii*),
        149
    See also tortoises
twinflower (*Linnaea borealis*), 35, 128
twinpod, Bell's (*Physaria bellii*), 286
Tympanuchus cupido, 78
Tympanuchus cupido attwateri, 267
Tympanuchus pallidicinctus, 71–72
type specimen, 35

Udvardy, Miklos, 206–208
Uma, 130
Uma inornata, 130, 150, 266
United Nations Environment
    Programme, 59–60
United States
    biological discovery of, 10, 14, 19–20,
        201–215
    conservation status ranks, 100–104
    ecological diversity in, 9–10, 15, 202,
        206–207, 303–306
    ecoregions of, 10–11, 17, 119–121,
        126–131
    endemism. *See* endemic species
    geographical diversity, 7, 9–10, 55–56,
        119–121, 138, 303
    government. *See* federal government;
        specific department or agency
    habitat diversity in, 80–81, 92, 127
    settlement patterns, 120, 202, 223–225
    species diversity in. *See* species
        diversity
    vegetation diversity in, 201–238, 303
    See also America; states
universities, 25, 34, 287
urbanization
    environmental impact of, 8, 11, 21,
        117, 135, 159, 185, 195, 203,
        223
    threats from, 240, 243–246, 251, 302–
        303, 316–317
    regulatory controls on, 256
Urocyon littoralis, 140
Ursus arctos, 70, 136
Ursus arctos horribilis, 106, 108, 138,
    202
USNVC. *See* National Vegetation
    Classification, U.S.
Utah
    endemic species in, 141, 156
    geographical features, 6, 60
    imperiled species in, 173, 176
    rare species in, 134, 156
    trees in, 56–57, 228, 296

Vaccinium macrocarpon, 128
vascular plants
    conservation status, 101–104
    diversity in U.S., 9, 61
    diversity by state, 123–124, 131–132
    diversity worldwide, 58–59
    endemism, 91, 132
    extinct U.S. species, 115
    See also individual species
veery (*Catharus fuscescens*), 144

vegetation
associations, 217
changes over time, 212–215, 225–229
climax, 48, 212
on conservation lands, 289, 293
assessment, 229–231
diversity in U.S., 212–215, 217–220
ecological community classifications
by, 48–53, 204–206, 216, 289, 293
ecoregion classifications by, 207, 209–
211
herbaceous, 130, 218–219, 225, 236
historical reconstructions, 226–229
imperiled communities, 235–238
late seral, 212–215
major North American formations,
215
mapping levels, 50–53, 212–215
Mediterranean-type, 14, 194
Nature Conservancy classifications,
216–220
potential natural, 212–216, 227–229
scrub, 159, 193–195, 228
structure and composition, 51
rangewide conservation assessment of,
295–298, 300
See also forests; plants; *individual
species*
Venezuela, 74, 134
Venus-flytrap (*Dionaea muscipula*), 134
Verde River, 185
Vermivora bachmanii, 72, 97, 148
Vermont, 130, 237
vernal pools, 192–195, 232
vertebrate animals
conservation status, 101–104
diversity in U.S., 60–61, 63, 135–138
diversity by state, 123–124, 135–138
diversity worldwide, 58–59, 63
endemism, 91, 137–138
extinct U.S. species, 115
federal status, 106–111
non-native, 64
range of species, 137
rarity by state, 137–138
red list of, 112
threat analysis, 242–243, 246
See also individual species
viability
as conservation concept, 309–310
Florida assessment in, 312–313
population assessment, 40–41, 96, 112,
310
vicariance, 89
vicuña, 88
Vireo olivaceus, 144

vireos, 88
red-eyed (*Vireo olivaceus*), 144
Virginia
diversity in, 74, 120, 144, 152
imperiled species in, 169–170, 286,
301–302
rare species in, 16, 157
Virgin Islands, U.S., 25, 106
viruses, 59
volcanos, 90–91, 95, 130
volunteers, 111
voucher specimens, 35, 40
vulnerable communities, 233–234
vulnerable species
available data, 42, 105
global status ranks defined, 30, 97

Wallace, Alfred Russell, 64–65, 82
Wallace's line, 65
walrus (*Odobenus rosmarus*), 139–140
warblers, 88, 136
Bachman's (*Vermivora bachmanii*), 72,
97, 148
cerulean (*Dendroica cerulea*), 144
golden-cheeked (*Dendroica
chrysoparia*), 103, 105, 146
Kirtland's (*Dendroica kirtlandii*), 129,
144, 146
Old World, 91
prothonotary (*Protonotaria citrea*), 142
Wasatch Mountains, 60
Washington, D.C., 42, 120, 125
Washington (state)
diversity in, 74, 122
endemic species in, 134, 141
extinct species in, 118
land ownership issues, 282, 296
rare species in, 140, 146, 154
wasps, 67, 76, 92
water
diversions, 192, 199, 243
impoundments, 243, 245
ownership, 256–260
pollution, 190, 231, 251, 272–273, 301–
302, 309
regulation, 9, 243, 248
sources in U.S., 3–6, 190, 192, 198
use, controls on, 256, 263–265, 269–271
water bears (Tardigrada), 63
water development projects
environmental impact of, 3, 117–118
threats from, 243, 245–246, 248, 251
waterfowl
conservation programs, 6, 36, 257,
259